Management Science / Operations Research

The Wiley/Hamilton Series in Management and Administration
Elwood S. Buffa, Advisory Editor University of California, Los Angeles

PRINCIPLES OF MANAGEMENT: A Modern Approach Fourth Edition Henry H. Albers

OPERATIONS MANAGEMENT: Problems and Models, Third Edition Elwood S. Buffa

PROBABILITY FOR MANAGEMENT DECISIONS William R. King

MODERN PRODUCTION MANAGEMENT: Managing the Operations Function Fifth Edition Elwood S. Buffa

CASES IN OPERATIONS MANAGEMENT: A Systems Approach James L. McKenney and Richard S. Rosenbloom

ORGANIZATIONS: Structure and Behavior, Volume I, Second Edition Joseph A. Litterer

ORGANIZATIONS: Systems, Control and Adaptation, Volume II Joseph A. Litterer

MANAGEMENT AND ORGANIZATIONAL BEHAVIOR: A Multidimensional Approach Billy J. Hodge and Herbert J. Johnson

MATHEMATICAL PROGRAMMING Claude McMillan

DECISION MAKING THROUGH OPERATIONS RESEARCH. Second Edition Robert J. Thierauf and Robert C. Klekamp

QUALITY CONTROL FOR MANAGERS & ENGINEERS Elwood G. Kilpatrick

PRODUCTION SYSTEMS: Planning, Analysis and Control, Second Edition James L. Riggs

SIMULATION MODELING: A Guide to Using Simscript Forrest P. Wyman

BASIC STATISTICS FOR BUSINESS AND ECONOMICS, Second Edition Paul G. Hoel and Raymond J. Jessen

COMPUTER SIMULATION OF HUMAN BEHAVIOR John M. Dutton and William H. Starbuck

INTRODUCTION TO GAMING: Management Decision Simulations John G. H. Carlson and Michael J. Misshauk

PRINCIPLES OF MANAGEMENT AND ORGANIZATIONAL BEHAVIOR Burt K. Scanlan

COMMUNICATION IN MODERN ORGANIZATIONS George T. and Patricia B. Vardaman

THE ANALYSIS OF ORGANIZATIONS, Second Edition Joseph A. Litterer

COMPLEX MANAGERIAL DECISIONS INVOLVING MULTIPLE OBJECTIVES Allan Easton

MANAGEMENT SYSTEMS, Second Edition Peter P. Schoderbek

ADMINISTRATIVE POLICY: Text and Cases in the Policy Sciences Richard M. Hodgetts and Max S. Wortman, Jr.

THE ECONOMICS OF INTERNATIONAL BUSINESS R. Hal Mason, Robert R. Miller and Dale R. Weigel

BASIC PRODUCTION MANAGEMENT, Second Edition Elwood S. Buffa

FUNDAMENTALS OF MANAGEMENT COORDINATION: Supervisor, Middlemanagers and Executives Thomas A. Petit

QUANTITATIVE BUSINESS ANALYSIS David E. Smith

OPERATIONS MANAGEMENT: The Management of Production Systems Elwood S. Buffa

PERSONNEL ADMINISTRATION AND HUMAN RESOURCES MANAGEMENT Andrew F. Sikula

MANAGEMENT SCIENCE/OPERATIONS RESEARCH: Model Formulation and Solution Methods Elwood S. Buffa and James S. Dyer

MANAGEMENT PRINCIPLES AND PRACTICES Robert J. Thierauf, Robert Klekamp and Daniel Geeding

Management Science/ Operations Research

Model Formulation and Solution Methods

Elwood S. Buffa
University of California, Los Angeles

James S. Dyer
University of California, Los Angeles

A Wiley/Hamilton Publication

John Wiley & Sons, Inc.   Santa Barbara   New York   London   Sydney   Toronto

This book was designed by Michael Rogondino,
copyedited by Carolyn Geiger and set in
10 point Electra by Allservice Phototypesetting.
Illustrations were prepared by Pat Rogondino
and Graphics Two, cover design by Tri-Arts and
printing and binding was done by Vail-Ballou
Press. Chuck Pendergast and Jean Varven
supervised production.

Library of Congress Cataloging in Publication Data
Buffa, Elwood Spencer, 1923–
     Management science/operations research.
     (The Wiley/Hamilton series in management and
administration)
     "A Wiley/Hamilton publication."
     1. Operations research.   I. Dyer, James S.,
joint author.   II. Title.
HD20.5.B768   658.4'034   76-25058
ISBN 0-471-11915-6

Printed in the United States of America.
10 9 8 7 6 5 4 3 2 1

Preface

Management Science/Operations Research is intended for use in introductory, undergraduate survey courses in Management Science/Operations Research (MS/OR). It may also be appropriate for similar courses required during the first year of many MBA programs. We presume that the user of the book *does not* intend to specialize in MS/OR; thus, he will never be involved in the details of formulating sophisticated mathematical models and obtaining solutions through the use of special-purpose algorithms. At one extreme, he may be a user of the results of large-scale MS/OR studies. Operating in this role, he must have the following skills:

1. The ability to recognize situations in which MS/OR might be used effectively.

2. The ability to conduct two-way communication with a technical specialist; that is, he must be able to
    a. explain the nature of his problem to a specialist in a meaningful way, and
    b. understand the specialist's product sufficiently well to verify its appropriateness and potential usefulness.

3. The ability to understand the results of MS/OR studies so that he can obtain full value from the information available to him from such studies.

At the other extreme, we have the student who plans to work in a small business, where the size of the operations would make it unlikely that a formal MS/OR analysis would ever be performed. For this student, we can provide a way of thinking and organizing information that should aid his "intuitive" decisions. The general concept of model building as an integral part of problem solving is stressed throughout the book. We are convinced that the process of problem definition associated with MS/OR (bound the problem and identify the decision variables, the objective function, and the constraints) can provide a useful conceptual framework for any manager if it is presented properly. We devote considerable attention to this point.

Somewhere between these two extremes is the individual who occasionally encounters relatively small straightforward problems amenable to analysis using MS/OR techniques. Examples are simple inventory problems, project scheduling problems, and even simple resource allocation problems. We would expect the user of this book to be able to formulate models appropriate for analyzing these problems, utilize canned computer programs (perhaps in time-share) to obtain solutions, and evaluate results.

The recognition of the needs of the users of this book is important, since these needs should determine both the content and the level of presentation of materials. For example, these needs seem to stress the importance of model building and formulation skills among all users of the book. At the same time, there is little justification for devoting much space to technical details of algorithms or computer codes. The only apparent justification for introducing such materials would be to remove some of the mystery from the solution strategies and to provide a basis for understanding the limitations of the various approaches.

Thus, we emphasize model building and formulation, and interpretation and use of the results from an analysis. In order to implement these objectives, transfer to reality is emphasized by giving examples of the use of quantitative methodology in real organizations. Relatively less emphasis is placed on algorithms. When they are presented, an effort is made to provide an intuitively appealing description of the solution process. The mathematical treatment has been kept very light, and no mention is made of theorems or mathematical derivations without a significant pedagogical justification.

These same considerations have also been the basis for omitting some topics found in many other introductory textbooks in MS/OR. For example, we can find little justification for requiring a future manager to learn about duality theory in linear programming, even though the MS/OR specialist would rightfully consider this to be an extremely important topic. On the other hand, the related concepts of sensitivity analysis do have important managerial implications, so this material is covered. Similarly, the details of the relatively complex algorithms for solving nonlinear programming problems are not covered, although they would provide important tools for the specialist. Another topic, game theory, was omitted because of our inability to find a significant number of real-world applications of the methodology. We have restricted our coverage to the MS/OR models and methods that have proven useful in practice.

Other topics have been omitted because of our assumptions regarding the background of the reader. We do presume that he has been exposed to the fundamentals of probability and statistics, although a brief summary of the basic concepts are included in Appendixes B and C for convenient reference and review. We do not cover the fundamentals of statistical decision making. The only other required mathematical background is an understanding of basic algebra. Again, a review of the rudiments of some concepts of mathematics is provided in Appendix A.

Another unique feature of this book is an attempt to provide numerous examples from the public and not-for-profit sectors of the economy. There are several arguments for including these types of examples. The student can be impressed with the generality of both the techniques and mathematical models by avoiding a series of "maximize profit" or "minimize costs" objective functions. In addition, more and more students entering schools of business administration or management plan to work in the public and not-for-profit sectors. Finally, it is conceivable that the book might be appropriate for use in similar introductory courses that are now evolving in schools of education, public administration, and public health.

The organization of a book as well as the content should depend on the needs of its users. When a specialist learns about the models and methods of MS/OR, he must be concerned with the basic mathematical structure that is involved. Therefore, it seems natural to organize the materials according to the mathematical structure, with an obvious dichotomy being deterministic versus stochastic models and methods. Many introductory textbooks intended for managers rather than specialists maintain this same organization of the materials and simply "water down" the mathematics. Other textbooks are organized on the basis of the relative importance of the topics and generally begin with linear programming.

In our opinion, neither of these approaches is appropriate for the presentation of these materials to the nonspecialist. The manager is not really concerned with the mathematical structure of the models and methods, but rather with how and when they should be used. Similarly, he needs some assistance in relating what may seem like a confusing list of models and solution techniques. An organization of materials based on relative importance cannot offer this assistance.

We have attempted to organize the materials in a manner that will assist the manager in relating the various models and methods by defining a relationship among evaluative, predictive, and optimizing models. We are aware that many instructors will not use the full range of topics provided by our book because of time limitations, the desire for a special focus, or simple personal preference and emphasis of favorite topics. Nevertheless, several scenarios for the use of this book benefit from our organization of the materials. We have isolated four scenarios that we think might be commonly used: a basic coverage of MS/OR, a focus on optimizing models, a model-building focus, and a public sector and not-for-profit focus.

For a *basic coverage*, we recommend Chapter 1, which sets the basic rationale for the whole book; Part Two (Evaluative Models), Chapters 2 and 3; Part Three (Predictive Models), Chapters 5 through 11 with Chapters 5 and 9 being optional; and Part Four (Optimizing Models), Chapters 12, 13, and 15 (omitting the Appendix to Chapter 15).

For a focus on *optimizing models*, we recommend Chapter 1 plus the entire Part Four section, which deals with optimizing models.

For a *model-building focus* that minimizes the exposure to the mathematical details of the techniques of MS/OR, we recommend Chapter 1; Part Three (Predictive Models), Chapters 6 through 11 with Chapter 9 being optional; and Part Four, Chapters 12, 13, 15 (omitting the Appendix to Chapter 15), 16, 17 (omitting the discussion of the branch and bound solution algorithm), and 18 (optional).

Finally, for a *public and not-for-profit focus*, the issue of the evaluative model becomes critical, and the optimizing models may be relatively less useful. Therefore, we recommend Chapter 1, Part Two (Evaluative Models), Part Three (Predictive Models), and Part Four, Chapters 12, 13, and 16.

Naturally, other combinations and orderings of the chapters are possible. However, we do recommend that Chapter 1 always be read first, as it presents the organizational and conceptual framework for the book. We also recommend that the brief introduction to each part of the book be read before assigning any chapters within that part.

The book draws heavily on the literature of Management Science and Operations Research and where specific materials have been used, they are cited. We have benefited greatly from reviews and comments by well-known professors such as Linus Schrage, University of Chicago; Steven C. Wheelwright, Harvard University; Robert Winkler, Indiana University; Edwin Shapiro, University of San Francisco; Norman R. Baker, University of Cincinnati; David Goodman, Southern Methodist University and Ross E. Lanser, San Jose State University.

Elwood S. Buffa
James S. Dyer

January 1977

Contents

About the Authors

Elwood S. Buffa is Professor of Management Science and Operations Management at the Graduate School of Management of the University of California, Los Angeles. He received his B.S. and M.B.A. degrees from the University of Wisconsin, and his Ph.D. from the University of California, Los Angeles. He worked as an Operations Analyst at the Eastman Kodak Company before entering the teaching profession, and has engaged in consulting activities in a wide variety of settings during the past twenty years. He has served as Assistant Dean and Associate Dean at the Graduate School of Management, and has held visiting appointments at IPSOA in Turin, Italy and at the Harvard Business School. Professor Buffa has published many research papers and books in Management Science and Operations Management and is Advisory Editor for the Wiley/Hamilton series in Management and Administration. Currently he serves on the Board of Directors of On-Line Decisions Incorporated.

James S. Dyer is Associate Professor of Management Science at the Graduate School of Management, University of California, Los Angeles. He received his B.A. degree in physics and his Ph.D. degree in business administration from the University of Texas at Austin. At UCLA, he teaches courses in the areas of systems analysis and operations research. These courses emphasize materials on mathematical programming and utility theory.

Dr. Dyer has consulted for such organizations as the RAND Corporation, the Jet Propulsion Laboratory, the Western Interstate Commission on Higher Education (WICHE), and the County of Los Angeles. His experience with the Jet Propulsion Laboratory included the use of utility and game theoretic concepts to structure a group decision-making process for the Mariner Jupiter/Saturn 1977 Project. His articles have appeared in various professional journals, including *Management Science* and *Operations Research*.

Dr. Dyer is a member of The Institute of Management Science and of the Operations Research Society of America.

x

Part One

INTRODUCTION

1

An Introduction to Management Science

The Beginnings. The old adage that "necessity is the mother of invention" was proven correct in the field of management science. Although examples of the use of the basic concepts of management science can be found in the eighteenth and nineteenth centuries, and especially in the early 1900s, the field as we know it today really had its beginnings during World War II. The simultaneous participation of the United States and its allies in military action in both the Pacific and European theaters created unprecedented problems of resource allocation, production scheduling, quality control, and logistics.

The enormous complexity of these problems, and their uniqueness, made their solution through a combination of intuition and experience very risky. No one had the experience of dealing with problems such as these, and their complexity made the application of intuition no better than a guess. The stakes were too high to justify such haphazard approaches. Therefore, teams of natural scientists, mathematicians, and engineers were formed to study these problems and to recommend solutions.

In order to understand these enormous problems better, these scientists began to think of them in the language of mathematics. A natural language of their respective disciplines, mathematics had the advantage of clarifying intuitively understood relations, as well as identifying areas of ignorance.

At approximately the same time that these teams were constructing large-scale mathematical models of operational problems, a technological development, the computer, was underway that would revolutionize the field of mathematical analysis. Thus, while large-scale mathematical models of significant problems were being formulated and the *need* for their analysis was being recognized, the *means* for performing this analysis was becoming available. This fortuitous set of circumstances provided the necessary environment for the beginning of a new field of study.

After World War II, many of those who participated in the analysis of military problems realized that the same approaches and techniques could be applied to the problems of an industry operating in a peacetime economy. However, it was not until computers had been further developed and made available commercially in the 1950s that these ideas really began to find their way into industry. At first, the problems that were studied were parallels of military problems. Inventory policies, production scheduling, and transportation systems were subjected to analysis. Most of the individuals engaged in these studies had no related formal training; rather, they relied on their experiences during the war. Their backgrounds were in engineering, mathematics, or the natural sciences (e.g., physics).

In the first issue of a new journal entitled *Management Science* published in October of 1954, A. Vazsonyi made the following prophetic statement:

> It is becoming increasingly apparent that some new scientific and mathematical theories are now being developed in this country, which in combination with the remarkable performance of electronic data processing machines, will bring about significant changes in current managerial techniques. [Vazsonyi, 1954]*

The Growth. Although applications of management science were becoming commonplace during the 1950s, academic programs emphasizing this new field were not well established until the 1960s. Thus, the first graduates from schools of business administration and management who had significant formal exposure to the concepts and techniques of management science did not begin to appear until the middle 1960s. As these individuals move into positions of leadership within organizations over the next decade, the use of these ideas is certain to proliferate. The notion of using computerized mathematical models to analyze significant managerial problems, that seemed so revolutionary only a generation ago, is now generally accepted throughout the management profession.

One result of the growth of the academic program in management science during the 1960s was a focus of interest and research on the techniques and tools of management science, rather than an emphasis on further application and strategies for implementing these ideas. Perhaps this focus is natural, since a new field, much like an adolescent, seems concerned with developing an awareness of its limitations and expanding its potentials. On the positive side, many new advances were made in the state of the art in various areas associated with solution techniques or certain mathematical models.

---

* References enclosed in brakets are listed alphabetically at the ends of chapters. When the author's names are used in a sentence only the publication date is enclosed in brackets.

An unfortunate aspect of this concentration on tools and techniques was that some individuals lost sight of the original motivation for the development of this field—to aid decision making and problem solving. Some graduates of academic programs in management science were accused by their employers of being more interested in finding a problem that fit their favorite technique than in starting with a problem of genuine managerial concern and deciding how best to analyze it. Thus, the initial experience of some organizations with management science was less than successful.

The Maturation. However, the 1970s have witnessed the maturation of the field of management science. Now that the growing pains have passed, management science is again concentrating on providing an aid to decision making, and fitting into the total mainstream of the organization. As the novelty and mystique of management science have worn away, we are in a much better position to assess its true capabilities and potential contributions.

The field of management science has grown significantly over the past two decades, both in terms of techniques and areas of application. New techniques of mathematical analysis have been developed that, coupled with the availability of the modern computer, have greatly expanded the range and size of problems that can now be analyzed. The development of time-sharing computer systems has made it possible to allow the decision maker to interact directly with management science models, thus lessening the need for a management science "expert" to interface between the decision maker and the computer. These same time-sharing systems have made the power of large-scale computers available to small businesses at a reasonable price.

The original applications of management science were primarily to operational problems of relatively small scope in private industry, such as inventory control. However, recently the breadth of the problems that are routinely considered has grown. The techniques of management science have proven valuable in strategic planning, marketing, and finance, as well as in many public and not-for-profit organizations. Management science models have been used to analyze problems of political redistricting [Garfinkel and Nemhauser, 1970], to staff hospital wards and emergency rooms [Warner and Prawda, 1972], to control inventories of human blood [Frankfurter et al., 1974], to analyze the costs of air pollution [Cohen and Hurter, 1974], and to deploy fire-fighting equipment [Kolesar and Walker, 1974].

One rash prophecy of the early 1950s has *not* come to pass. The models of management science have not replaced the need for competent managers. People no longer talk about organizations being run by a "black box." The methods of management science have proven to be exceedingly valuable in improving a manager's decision-making abilities, but they have not relieved him of the responsibility for decisions. Nevertheless, in order to maximize the potential benefit to be gained, the modern manager must have an understanding of and an appreciation for the field of management science.

To focus briefly on terminology, we have used the term "management science" in our discussion of the use of mathematical models as an aid in the decision-making process. Other terms that are often used interchangeably with management science are operations research, operations management, decision analysis, policy analysis, systems engineering, and systems analysis. If we wished to delve into details, we could probably identify some distinguishing characteristics generally associated with each of these terms. However, we will attempt to be concerned with substantive issues and to avoid debate over terminology.

The basic approach in applying management science to any problem is generally based on mathematical model building. The purpose of this activity is to aid the problem-solving process. We shall provide some perspective for understanding the importance of model building by first considering the problem-solving process.

THE PROBLEM-SOLVING PROCESS

Whether he is in a private, not-for-profit, or public organization, the most important and the distinguishing function of a manager is problem solving (or, if you prefer, decision making). Much has been written about problem solving, and various authors have provided their own descriptions of the problem-solving process. These descriptions tend to be influenced by the experiences and concerns of the individual authors, but they do exhibit a significant degree of commonality.

Problem Solving Defined   Just what is problem solving? Certainly it is an activity in which you are successful, or you would not be in a position to read this book. You have solved the basic problems of survival and of education in the modern world, but perhaps you have never explicitly considered what problem solving is all about. Jackson [1974] defines problem solving very simply as " . . . the business of *purposefully* inventing and choosing among ways to get you where you want to go." Perhaps the simplest description of the problem-solving process was provided by John Dewey [1910]:

1. define the problem
2. identify the alternatives
3. select the best alternative

This description seems straightforward enough. The key, of course, is to go through this process in such a manner that the "best" alternative is actually identified and selected. In a similar spirit, Jackson [1974] suggests that the most crucial tasks of a problem solver are identifying "things that might be done," determining "ways to anticipate results," and developing "ways to evaluate results." While other authors have elaborated on certain aspects of the problem-solving process and provided suggestions regarding how these tasks might be accomplished, these basic statements are common to most descriptions of the problem-solving process.

Is the problem-solving process the same as the scientific method? The scientific method is generally considered to be composed of the following steps:

1. observation
2. generalization
3. experimentation
4. validation

The scientist examines a part of nature and generates hypotheses, which hopefully explain what he has observed. In much the same way, a problem solver defines a problem by studying a system and creating hypotheses to explain how his decision might influence that system. The scientist performs experiments to test whether his hypotheses actually explain the phenomena of interest, and he either accepts or rejects the hypotheses on this basis. However, the problem solver goes beyond this interest in being able to explain or predict the behavior of a system. He is also concerned with discovering how, based on his understanding, to best modify this system in order to achieve some desirable outcome.

Thus, there is a similarity between the approaches of a scientist and of a problem solver. Both seek an understanding of a system that will allow them to predict its behavior. However, the needs of the problem solver extended beyond this passive desire to understand "how things work." He is also concerned with modifying the system according to some notion of the way it should behave. For the sake of simplicity, we might say that the natural scientist is concerned with the way things are, while the problem solver is concerned with the way things ought to be.

On the basis of this subtle but important distinction, Simon [1969] has described the management problem solver as the scientist of the artificial. That is, he is concerned with understanding how things work in an artificial world of man-made institutions, rules, and roles of behavior. He may use his knowledge of how things work to modify his world in terms of how things ought to be.

Somewhat cynically, another author [Little, 1970] provided a waggish summary of the difference between the traditional manager and the scientist. A paraphrase of his comments suggests that traditional managers tend to act before they think, if they ever think; whereas the scientists think before they act, if they ever act. Naturally this statement should not be taken literally, but it does point out the potential dangers of extreme approaches. Precipitous actions not preceded by careful thought and analysis can lead to disastrous results. At the other extreme, a delay in actions based on the need for more time for thought, for better data, and for more analysis, can be tantamount to the decision not to act at all. Hopefully, the modern manager will possess the ability both to think clearly and to analyze problems carefully, and yet have the judgment to act decisively at the appropriate time.

Elements of the Process   At this point, it may be helpful to provide some additional detail regarding the problem-solving process. One extended view of this process is provided in Figure 1. First, the existence of a problem must be recognized. That is, someone must observe reality and note that his perception is not consistent with his conception of how things ought to be. This occurrence may be caused by changes in reality (we elect to ignore the philosophical issues related to the notion of "reality"), changes in the individual's perception, or changes in his notion of what ought to be. The reason for this recognition of a problem need not concern us here, although we do suggest that the management problem solver take an active role in identifying problems before they become so serious as to create a crisis. Rather, we are more concerned with what he should do once a problem has been identified.

A problem solver's first task is bounding the problem. In essence, he must think about what to think about. The event that created his awareness of a problem may be only a symptom of the actual problem. For example, the event that caused his concern may have been an unusually large number of items out-of-stock in inventory. If he decides to "solve" the problem

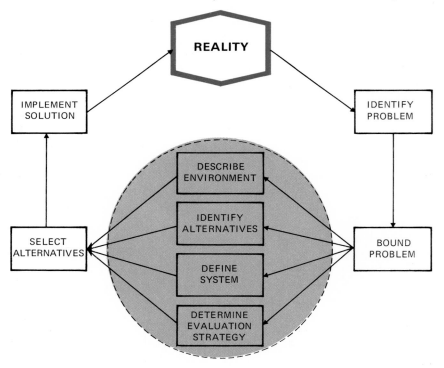

Figure 1. The problem-solving process

by focusing his attention on inventory policies, he may overlook the "real problem," which may lie in the production scheduling operations.

As a second example, a problem solver may consider the de facto racial segregation of public schools to be undesirable. While busing or redistricting may provide some racial balance in the schools, the real problem may lie in the housing patterns of individuals and in the concept of the neighborhood school. The long-term solution of this difficult problem may require a strategy focused on issues quite different from the transportation of students.

Certainly the task of bounding a problem is not a trivial one. It may be the most important step in the problem-solving process, since asking the right questions may be the most significant determinant of a successful solution. One way of getting started is the use of an exploratory scenario as suggested by Jackson [1974]. The problem solver begins by letting his mind "run loose," and talking about or writing down ideas concerning possible alternatives, their potential effects, obstacles that might be encountered, etc. In essence, this is simply an active way of "mulling things over," and clearly requires insight and judgment on the part of the problem solver.

After the problem has been recognized and bounded, the problem solver can begin the other required tasks. He must devise alternative means of dealing with the problem. He must have an understanding, or definition, of the system he is dealing with and its environment, so that he can predict the effects of implementing his alternative solutions. Finally, he must determine the criteria by which he will evaluate these different effects.

In some instances, the search for alternative solutions may require a great deal of creativity. New ways of dealing with problems may be sought. In other cases, it may be relatively easy to identify the alternatives because conditions that we call constraints eliminate many courses of action.

The system definition is an attempt to specify how the implementation of an alternative will actually affect the system. That is, if you take a particular action, your system definition should provide the means of predicting the results. In some cases, this system definition may remain implicit and never be verbalized by the problem solver. He may indicate that he can not describe how a particular system behaves, and yet, using his intuition, he comfortably predicts the effects of different alternatives. Unless his intuition is equivalent to a wild guess, he must at least have some gross hypothesis about how things work in the system of concern.

Finally, the problem solver must determine a strategy for evaluating the effects of the alternatives. In some cases, this strategy will be obvious. If the only effect of the selection of an alternative is on the profits of an organization, his evaluation strategy may be to rank one alternative higher than another if it generates more profit. In other cases involving uncertain or risky effects from the alternatives, or involving multiple effects that must be considered, the determination of the evaluation strategy may not be so straightforward. For example, how would you evaluate alternative plans for deploying ambulances, even if the results from the different alternatives could be forecasted with complete certainty? How would you trade off the cost of the alternative vs. the number of lives saved? What is it worth to save another human life? Is your answer different if you know that the person whose life you save will be a rich man or a poor man? a young man or an old woman? a member of your family or a stranger? you? These are difficult questions that have no simple answers acceptable to everyone.

After forecasting the effects of implementing each alternative and determining his evaluation strategy, the problem solver should be in a position to select an alternative. This alternative becomes the solution to the problem he has identified. One final step remains: he must implement this solution in the real world. Otherwise, he is guilty of the behavior of the scientist characterized as "one who thinks before he acts, if he acts at all."

By now it should be clear why organizations are not being run by the models of management science. Time and again we saw the need for human judgment during our discussion of the problem-solving process. It seems unlikely that machines will ever be created that are sufficiently sensitive to detect all the problems of an organization. Mechanical sensors might very well detect changes in the real world or even improve our perception of it. However, the concept of the way the world ought to be is purely artificial and dependent on human judgment. Once a problem has been identified, judgment is required in thinking about what to think about. Obviously, creating alternatives, defining the system, and determining an evaluation strategy all require judgmental inputs. Finally, after an alternative has been selected, only a trivial technological change can be implemented in an organization without involving the manager in the role of change agent.

Where then do the models of management science fit into the problem-solving process? The use of these models generally falls into the area within the dashed circle in Figure 1. That is, management science models can be used to help forecast what the environment will be like, identify alternatives, provide a system definition that predicts outcomes, and implement an evaluation strategy. The intent of these models is to aid the problem solver in performing these vital tasks in the problem-solving process. Seldom, if ever, can it be said that these models actually solve his problem.

MANAGEMENT SCIENCE MODELS

Models and Problem Solving   As we have seen, the natural scientist and the management problem solver have a common interest in being able to predict "how things work." One important role of the model is to increase an individual's understanding of how things work. This potential for increased understanding should motivate a manager to learn more about model building as an aid to problem solving.

Broadly defined, a model is a device for aiding rational thinking. More specifically, the models we are interested in provide a simplified representation of a complex system or phenomenon. To be helpful in problem solving, a model must include the essential, relevant features of the system being studied.

In order to deal with the complexity of the world, all individuals use models to aid their understanding of the surrounding environment. For example, we have models of certain shapes within our heads that help us to recognize important traffic signs, such as stop signs, from among the multitude of other shapes we perceive in our environment. A model is an economizing device that reduces the infinite number of possibilities to a much smaller, finite number of categories. It ignores much information potentially available to the problem solver and uses categories to collect together many other bits of information that may be considered similar for the process of problem solving. While all stop signs differ at some level of detail, they may all be placed in the same category when determining a driver's behavior.

If a model simplifies a problem solver's view of a problem by leaving out much information and by creating categories, what features must it retain in order to be useful? Ideally, a model used for problem solving will include the important features, or elements, of the system under study, as well as the interrelationships among these elements that determine causes and effects. If such a model exists, the problem solver may actually manipulate the elements of the system within the model and observe their effects. Either by trial and error or by using more sophisticated approaches, he will determine how to adjust these elements so that the resulting impact on the system is consistent with his objectives.

Thus, the managerial problem solver can use such a model, if it exists, to perform experiments and test hypotheses much as a natural scientist uses his laboratory. Because of this similarity, the area of management concerned with model building is often referred to as management science.

Examples of Models   Let us now consider three examples of models that have been used in problem solving. Figure 2 shows a model of an aircraft in a wind tunnel. The problem that is being studied is the determination of the appropriate external shape of the aircraft. This model captures the central features of shape very well. However, it does not include important elements of the aircraft, such as the internal workings, that are largely irrelevant to this problem.

Figure 3 illustrates a dummy under observation during a staged automobile accident. This model captures the essential features of the behavior of a human body involved in an accident, but detailed physical appearance, skin coloring, and internal workings are omitted because they are irrelevant to the problem being studied.

A third example of a model is provided by the diagram of the problem-solving process shown in Figure 1, as you may have recognized. The problem-solving process is exceedingly complex and may vary from individual to individual according to his own unique style. Nevertheless, in Figure 1, we have attempted to capture the essential elements of this process in order to

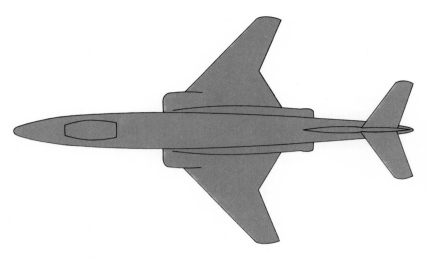

Figure 2. Aircraft shape in a wind tunnel

solve the problem of organizing our discussion. In doing so we have omitted certain details. For example, the steps in the process are all interdependent. The task of defining the system may affect the range of alternatives that are considered, and vice versa. Similarly, there may be interactions between the evaluation strategies and the alternatives that are considered. Thus, this model would be more realistic if arrows were drawn in both directions between all pairs of blocks. However, such arrows would make the drawing extremely messy and would perhaps defeat our purpose of presenting a simplified view of a complex process. In addition, it is important to note that this is not the only model of the problem-solving process that could be drawn. (Try to construct your own.) Nevertheless, this model will have been useful if it aided your understanding of the important aspects of the process.

This same feature of nonuniqueness is common to almost any model of a complex process. Other models, perhaps very different ones, may also be useful in enhancing a problem solver's understanding of a complex process. The danger of model building is that the problem solver will come to regard the model as the problem and forget that it is only one way (generally very limited) of looking at the problem.

Mathematical Models   We have been describing models in general. While any form of a model may be useful to the problem solver, and thus should be encouraged, the field of management science is generally concerned with mathematical models. Why, you may ask, is this so? You may feel that the world is complex enough without hiding it behind a screen of mathematical symbols and notation. However, those who have mastered the language of mathematics (even to a very limited extent) find that they can benefit significantly from the use of mathematical models. A mathematical model forces

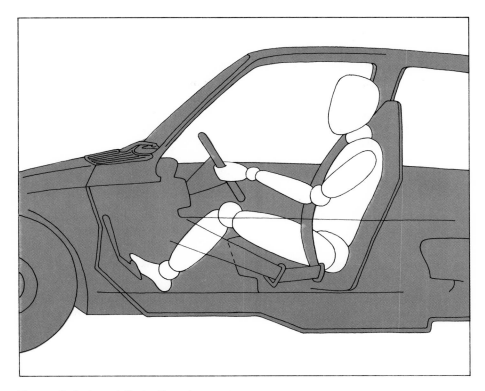

Figure 3. Automobile testing dummy

the model builder to make explicit his assumptions about the important elements of the problem and the cause-effect relationships that exist within the system of interest. Using the logical rules of mathematical analysis, he can check these assumptions and relationships to ensure their internal consistency. The logic of mathematics also provides a means of exploring the consequences of these assumptions. Further, the results of these analyses can be independently verified by others.

THE MODERN MANAGER AND MANAGEMENT SCIENCE

We have argued that problem solving is the most important function of a manager, that model building is an aid to problem solving, and that the mathematical models of management science are an important special class of models. Hopefully, you are persuaded that you should learn something about the field of management science. We do not feel that you should be subjected to a detailed discussion of mathematical techniques and theories. However, you should learn enough about the field so that you will be in a position to use effectively the models and techniques that are available in real-world situations. The question is, how much should you really know about management science?

We shall presume that the typical reader of this book does not intend to specialize in management science and become a professional in this field. Thus, it seems unlikely that he will ever be involved in the details of formulating sophisticated mathematical models and obtaining solutions through the use of special-purpose computer programs. At one extreme, he may be the user of the results of large-scale management science studies. Operating in this role, he should have the following skills:

1. The ability to recognize situations in which management science might be used effectively.

2. The ability to conduct two-way communication with a technical specialist; that is, he must be able to
   a. explain the nature of his problem to a specialist in a meaningful way, and
   b. understand the specialist's product sufficiently well to verify its appropriateness and potential usefulness.

3. The ability to understand the results of management science studies so that he can obtain full value from the information available to him.

At the other extreme, he may find himself working in a small business. The size of the operations would make it unlikely that a formal management science analysis would ever be performed. Nevertheless, the models of management science provide a way of thinking and of organizing information that should aid his "intuitive" decision making. One of the most powerful aids in problem solving is the use of analogies. A justification for the "case method" in management education is the expectation that the graduate, when faced with a real-world problem, will be able to say, "Aha, this problem is similar to the problem faced by the company in the XYZ case. With only a few modifications, the analysis and solution for that case may apply here." Similarly, by gaining an exposure to the models of management science, the manager may be able to recognize a problem as being similar to those analyzed using a particular management science technique. This recognition should be helpful to him in identifying the data he needs and in exploring possible alternative solutions.

Somewhere between these two extremes, the manager may be in an organizational position in which he occasionally encounters relatively small, straightforward problems amenable to analysis by management science techniques. He should be able to formulate models appropriate for analyzing these problems, utilize standard computer programs written by others to obtain solutions, and interpret the results.

In each of these contexts, the manager should have the ability to recognize problems amenable to analysis using management science models and should have some model formulation skills. Therefore, we will present numerous examples of models throughout this text and attempt to illuminate the process of thought that developed these formulations. In order to avoid extraneous details, the initial presentations of these example formulations will be in the context of "toy" problems that we have created to illustrate certain points. We then will discuss examples of real-world implementations of management science models and techniques and attempt to examine their significance critically. At the same time, we will emphasize the interpretation of the results obtained from these models and attempt to point out where managerial discretion and judgment must be used to provide a meaningful interpretation in the real world.

We shall avoid devoting a great deal of time to the technical details of the mathematical analyses associated with the different management science models. Nevertheless, the manager should have some idea how these analyses are performed. This knowledge is important to his understanding of both the power and the potential limitations of these techniques. Further, such understanding will help remove the mystique often associated with the "black box" known as the computer, and should increase his self-confidence in challenging and analyzing the results that pour from it. In order to obtain this understanding, it will be necessary for you to work through some small examples by hand. Please keep in mind while you are pushing the pencil that these exercises are not suggested because they are "good for you" per se, or because we expect that you will actually be performing similar analyses by hand in your position as a manager. Rather, you should concentrate on understanding what each technique is doing in a substantive sense. What kinds of results are being generated, and how do these results follow from your formulations of the problem? Although we will attempt to help you in gaining this insight, it will require careful reflection on your part.

THE PLAN OF THE BOOK

We have seen that management science is primarily concerned with those aspects of problem solving related to identifying alternatives, understanding "how things work," and evaluating the predicted effects of implementing alternatives. Each different mathematical model of management science may focus on one or more of these aspects. Therefore, it is helpful to categorize these models according to their primary functions.

Figure 4 provides more detail regarding the items within the circle in Figure 1. One important category of management science models is represented by the *evaluative model* ((1) in Figure 4). While a natural scientist would be satisfied with a predictive model that describes "how things are," a manager also needs an evaluative model to determine "how things ought to be." Such models may be implicit in simple cases involving decisions that produce only a single, certain effect on the system. However, in cases involving risk so that different effects may occur with different probabilities,

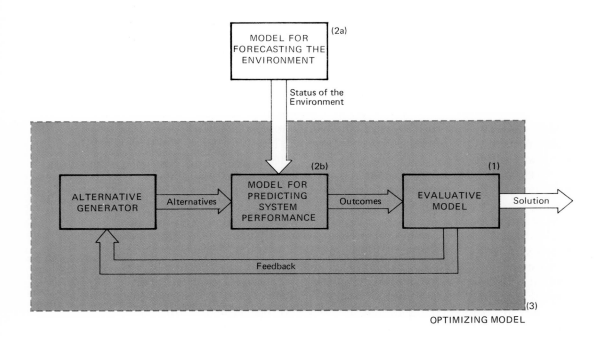

Figure 4. Models of management science

or in cases involving multiple effects that must be evaluated according to multiple criteria, a manager may require an explicit evaluative model in order to select the alternative most consistent with his view of the way things ought to be.

In Part Two of this book, we shall assume that we know how things work. That is, given an alternative, we can predict the result of choosing it, subject, perhaps, to factors in the environment beyond our control. For example, our alternatives might be 1) to take an umbrella to work or 2) not to take an umbrella to work. We can easily predict the result of selecting either alternative if we know whether or not it will rain. Unfortunately, we cannot control whether or not it will rain. How do we go about making decisions in cases like this? As we shall see, we can construct an evaluative model to help us analyze this problem. These evaluative models are based on a field of management science known as decision theory. An understanding of decision theory can be a very practical aid to a manager, even when the required mathematical calculations are made on the back of an envelope rather than on a computer.

The model for forecasting the environment and the model for predicting system performance [2(a) and 2(b) respectively in Figure 4] represent two important categories of models concerned with understanding "how things work" and with predicting the effects of alternative decisions. Part Three will be concerned with these *predictive models*. First, we shall see how models may be used to predict, or forecast, the status of the environment. For example, our decision regarding whether or not to take an umbrella to work might be greatly simplified if we could forecast the weather more accurately. Similarly, a decision regarding what price to charge for a new product might be much simpler if we could accurately forecast demand. Again, we could easily determine the appropriate staffing for a hospital emergency room if we knew how many patients to expect.

Next, we shall make more precise the notion of a "system" and a "system definition," and see how a mathematical model may be used to provide this system definition, thus becoming a predictive model of system performance. We shall illustrate how the familiar break-even model may be viewed as a predictive model, then provide several real-world examples of the actual use of predictive models in the form of large-scale corporate planning models in private, public, and not-for-profit organizations. Other examples will be given of applications of predictive models to urban planning and environmental control problems. Finally, we shall study predictive models that explicitly include risk and uncertainty. These models are generally required when we are unable to control the effects of the environment on our system of interest or to forecast them with certainty. Even the most experienced weatherman occasionally offers rainfall predictions in terms of probability statements rather than simply stating that it will or will not rain. Many of the predictive models incorporating risk are based on the fields of queuing (waiting line) theory and Monte Carlo simulation.

There is a third category of models (3) indicated by the dashed line in Figure 4, which combines predictive and evaluative models with a feedback mechanism to an alternative generator. These models actually allow the rules of mathematical analysis (usually implemented on a computer) to generate and search through the set of all alternative solutions and to select the one with the best predicted outcome according to an evaluative model. These models are termed *optimizing* (or prescriptive) models, since the result of their use is actually a proposed solution to the problem that is optimal (or "best") in terms of the evaluative model.

In Part Four, we shall see how evaluative and predictive models can be combined in certain special cases to create an optimizing model. These models include the important class of mathematical programming models. It will be important for you to understand the characteristics of problems that can be analyzed using these methods, the manner in which these models are formulated, and the way the associated mathematical analysis produces a solution.

You should study Figure 4 carefully to ensure that you understand this categorization of models. This figure will be repeated at the beginning of each subsequent chapter with one or more aspects highlighted in order to emphasize how the particular topic under discussion fits into this overall framework. By referring to this figure, you should avoid becoming so absorbed in technical details that you lose sight of the basic purpose of the management science model or solution technique. As a manager, this conceptual understanding may be of much more potential value than any mathematical details.

Appendixes A, B, and C present the rudiments of mathematics, probability theory, and statistics that are necessary to understand the materials included in this text. These appendixes provide a convenient review and reference. Readers who seek a "refresher" in these topics should study them carefully before proceeding. Others may prefer to consult some basic programmed texts such as those offered by Martin [1969a, 1969b] and Mason [1970, 1971]. Before doing so, look over the material in the appendixes to identify which topics should be covered.

Check Your Understanding

1. Consider each of the following hypothetical situations:
   a. Suppose you are an urban planner who has been involved in the study of a large-scale, sociotechnical system, such as a rapid transit system. What would you consider to be the most important phase of the problem-solving process (refer to Figure 1)?
   b. Suppose you are an architect who must design a new building. Again referring to Figure 1, what do you consider to be the most important phase of the design process?

2. Are there fundamental differences in the problem-solving processes followed by an urban planner and an architect, or are there only different emphases on phases of the process? Discuss.

3. What are the important implications of the notion that a management problem solver is a "scientist of the artificial"?

4. Select a problem of personal interest to you, such as the choice of a career, the purchase of a new car, or the travel plans for your vacation. Create an "exploratory scenario" by listing possible alternatives, potential effects of alternatives, obstacles that might be encountered, etc. Intermix these items while letting your mind "run loose." Did you gain any additional insights into the problem?

5. Although you will be able to sharpen the definition of the following terms

as you proceed through the book, on the basis of the discussion in this chapter, define:

a. predictive model

b. evaluative model

c. optimizing model

What are the relationships among them?

6. Suppose you must purchase a new car. List the criteria or factors that you would consider in selecting a particular model. Explain how these criteria relate to the concept of an *evaluative* model.

7. Are the models of the aircraft in Figure 2 and of the dummy in Figure 3 examples of evaluative, predictive, or optimizing models? Explain.

8. List three examples of problems you may be required to solve in following your own career plans. For each example, discuss how a model might be a potential aid. What do you need to know about the models of management science?

References

Cohen, A. S., and A. P. Hurter, Jr., "An Input-Output Analysis of the Costs of Air Pollution Control," *Management Science,* Vol. 21, No. 4, December 1974.

Dewey, J., *How We Think,* D. C. Heath, 1910.

Frankfurter, G. M., K. E. Kendall, and C. C. Pegals, "Management Control of Blood Through a Short Term Supply-Demand Forecast System," *Management Science,* Vol. 21, No. 4, December 1974.

Garfinkel, R. S., and G. L. Nemhauser, "Optimal Political Districting by Implicit Enumeration Techniques," *Management Science,* Vol. 16, No. 8, April 1970.

Jackson, J. R., "Coping with Complexity," mimeographed, Graduate School of Management, University of California, Los Angeles, 1974.

Kolesar, P., and W. E. Walker, "An Algorithm for the Dynamic Relocation of Fire Companies," *Operations Research,* Vol. 22, No. 2, March–April 1974.

Little, J. D. C., "Models and Managers: The Concept of a Decision Calculus," *Management Science,* Vol. 16, No. 8, April 1970.

Martin, E. W., *Mathematics for Decision Making: A Programmed Basic Text,* Vols. 1 and 2, Richard D. Irwin, Inc., Homewood, Ill., 1969a.

———, *Programmed Learning Aid for Basic Algebra,* Learning Systems Company, Homewood, Ill., 1969b.

Mason, R. D., *Programmed Learning Aid for Business and Economic Statistics,* Learning Systems Company, Homewood, Ill., 1970.

———, *Programmed Learning Aid for College Mathematics,* Learning Systems Company, Homewood, Ill., 1971.

Mathes, R. C., "'D' People and 'S' People" (letter), *Science,* Vol. 164, No. 9, May 1969.

Simon, H., *The Sciences of the Artificial,* MIT Press, Cambridge, Mass., 1969.

Vazsonyi, A., "The Use of Mathematics in Production and Inventory Control," *Management Science*, Vol. 1, No. 1, October 1954.

Warner, D. M., and J. Prawda, "A Mathematical Programming Model for Scheduling Nursing Personnel in a Hospital," *Management Science*, Vol. 19, No. 4, December 1972.

Part Two

EVALUATIVE MODELS

Introduction to Evaluative Models

In Part Two we shall assume that we know how things work, subject perhaps to factors in the environment beyond our control. However, even in those situations where the environment is not known with certainty, we shall assume that we can list each of the possible states of the environment and provide probability estimates of their occurrence. To illustrate this point, consider again the decision of whether or not to take an umbrella to work. If we take the umbrella to work and it actually rains, having the umbrella to avoid getting wet is a desirable outcome. On the other hand, if we take the umbrella and it does not rain, we have unnecessarily burdened ourselves with the trouble of carrying it. We may not know with complete certainty whether or not it will rain. However, in Part Two we shall assume that we can estimate the probability of rain. Given this information, we can use the concepts of decision theory to develop an *evaluative model* that aids in making decisions.

Thus, in Part Two we shall be concerned primarily with the evaluative models of management science as shown in Figure 1. Later, we shall turn our attention to the issues of how we obtain these predictions regarding the state of the environment (for example, rain or no rain) and how we predict the outcome of choosing an alternative given a particular state of the environment.

The choice of the appropriate evaluative model will depend on the circumstances under which the decision is actually being made. One of the important considerations is whether the outcome is known with certainty or only in terms of probability statements. For example, suppose we have $100 to invest. If we place it in a federally insured savings account paying 7 percent interest, we will receive $107 in return at the end of one year. We know this result with certainty. Naturally, we are ignoring such events as a political revolution, a world war, or other such catastrophes that might prevent the bank from meeting its obligations. (In most real-world situations, we also ignore these "surprise" events that could happen but are sufficiently unlikely.) For practical purposes, we can say that the outcome of the decision to place $100 in a federally insured savings account is known with certainty.

The second important consideration in defining the appropriate evaluative model is the number of different criteria that are relevant for evaluating the desirability of an action. For example, if we are trying to invest $100, the only important criterion may be the amount of money we receive in return. Thus, we would say that there is only a single criterion to be considered. In other cases, there may be multiple goals involved, and therefore multiple criteria must be considered. In purchasing an automobile, we consider not only cost but also such criteria as appearance and performance.

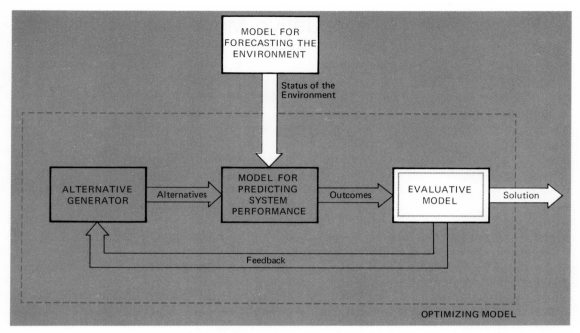

Figure 1. The evaluative model in relation to the environment forecasting model, the alternative generator, and the predictive system model

The simplest decisions from the viewpoint of the evaluative model involve only a single criterion, and the outcome associated with each alternative is known with complete certainty. An appropriate evaluative model in such cases can easily be identified. However, even with a single criterion, the introduction of risk creates the need for an explicit evaluative model to aid in the decision making. The introduction of risk recognizes that there are several possible outcomes, each of which may occur with a known probability. Similarly, multiple criteria complicate the evaluation process even when the outcomes are known with certainty. Finally, the most difficult situations involve both risk and multiple criteria. Figure 2 illustrates two dimensions of a decision problem: certainty versus risk and single versus multiple criteria. These are independent dimensions of complexity, and the most complex cases involve some combination of risk and multiple criteria.

An Example

Let us pause for a moment to fit these ideas into the framework of an example. Assume that you are president of a company that manufactures electrical relays. The position in which you find yourself requires some interrelated decisions involving a labor dispute and bids on two government contracts.

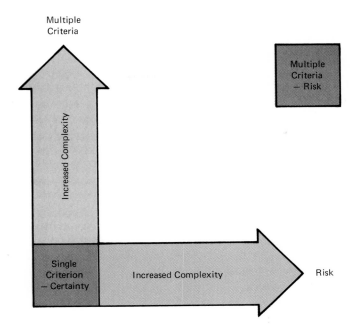

Figure 2. Problem characteristics in relation to model complexity affecting the choice of evaluative models

Labor Dispute

The union has set a strike deadline of midnight tonight if you do not accept their demand for a 10 percent wage increase. You are certain that the union will carry out its threat and the resulting strike will cost you about $300,000. If you give in to the demand, the total cost per relay unit will increase to $4.05, compared to the present cost of $3.80 per unit. On the other hand, you feel certain that the union will be defeated if it strikes, and therefore your present costs would remain fixed for the coming year. You must decide between the following alternatives:

UNION DISPUTE—TACTICAL DECISION

A. Give the employees the wage increase and absorb the higher cost of production.
B. Hold to the present wage scale and suffer the resulting strike loss.

Bids on Government Contracts

The labor dispute is complicated by the fact that the government is letting a large contract for 10 million relay units within the next month and *you will not be in a position to bid on this contract if your employees go on strike.* However, even if you give in to the union demands and avert a strike, you still are not assured of getting the contract unless you can underbid your competitors. Possible bids and resulting probabilities of winning the contract are estimated as follows:

GOVERNMENT CONTRACT — TACTICAL DECISION

X. Not eligible to bid, company on strike (see preceding *B* decision).

Eligible to bid (see preceding *A* decision):

	Price per Unit	Probability of Getting Contract
C.	$4.15	0.3
D.	4.12	0.5
E.	4.10	0.6
F.	4.07	0.8

Test Equipment Investment   Fortunately a second major government contract is anticipated in the latter part of the year if you do not receive the lucrative contract mentioned previously. (Because of production limitations it will not be possible for you to assume both contracts should you receive the first contract.) To be in a position to bid on the second contract, it is necessary at this time for you to secure adequate financial backing to guarantee the government that you can provide certain expensive testing equipment.

The larger the test facilities you can provide, the more likely it is that you will be awarded the contract. The anticipated net profit for this second project is $3 million if your unit cost is $4.05 and $4 million if your unit cost is $3.80. These figures do not include the large investment in special test equipment, which must be written off over the life of the contract. This investment is actually made only if you receive the contract.

TEST EQUIPMENT INVESTMENT — TACTICAL DECISION

	Investment	Probability of Getting Contract
G.	$2,000,000	0.2
H.	2,400,000	0.4
I.	2,600,000	0.5
J.	2,900,000	0.6

We will not attempt the full solution of this problem at this time; however, let us fit it into the structure of Figure 1. First, predicting the outcomes of the labor dispute involves the essence of a forecasting model. We have also provided data that make it possible to construct a model for predicting system performance, which involves the bid prices and the probabilities of success in obtaining the government contracts.

Driving the predictive model, however, is the system for generating alternatives. It may be a surprise to see that there are twenty alternatives available. Sixteen alternatives result if the basic strategy A (no strike) is adopted and four more are possible with the basic strategy B (strike).

We recognize that if B is followed, we may bid only on the second contract, so that we have only the alternatives BXG, BXH, BXI, and BXJ. Recall that X denotes that we cannot bid on the first contract because of the strike. On the other hand, if we follow the basic strategy A, both contracts are open to us even though we can only accept one of them because of production limitations. Therefore, the strategy can combine both contracts according to the structure of Figure 3. If we are awarded the first contract we cannot accept the second. If we lose the first, we still have a chance for the second. Therefore, since there are four basic alternatives of bidding for the first contract and four for bidding on the second contract, there are sixteen combinations (4 × 4).

Our example contains all of the elements with which we will deal in Part Two. We have stopped short of developing the evaluative model; however, we have a verbal model for forecasting the state of the environment and a system for generating alternatives to drive a model that predicts system performance for given inputs. Certainty is involved in one part of our model in terms of the strike costs: the certainty that the strike threat will be carried out and the certainty that the strike will be defeated if carried out. On the other hand, risk is involved in getting the government contracts. The risk is based on the bid price for the first contract and the equipment investment for the second contract. Of course, we will be interested in how we assess the risks and determine the probabilities used in the bidding example.

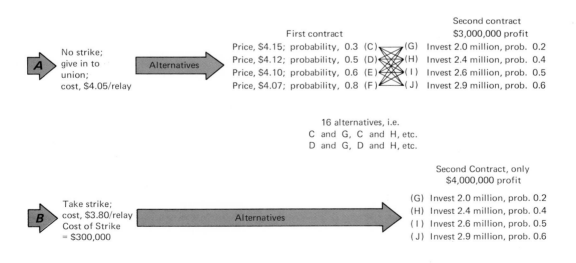

Multiple goals and criteria are also involved, though we have not stated them explicitly. The obvious criterion is future net profit. Yet, at some point we must also take into consideration the longer run effects that the strike will have on employee relationships and possibly future costs. What are the social obligations of a manager in this situation? How would you as the decision maker trade off short-run profits against the longer term considerations?

Are the techniques of management science really useful in dealing with problems such as this one, or can the experienced manager determine the correct decision based on his "intuition" alone? To test this question, this problem was presented to fifty-two members of the University of California, Los Angeles, (UCLA) Executive Program. The fifty-two members were all successful executives at the level of president, vice-president, head of a major division, etc. The executives were instructed to choose the alternative that maximizes the expected future net profit to the firm.

The choices of the executives are shown in Figure 4, where the alternatives are coded as *ADH*, *ACH*, etc. The desirability of each strategy is indicated by the left scale; the percentage of the executives who selected the various alternatives is shown to the right. Only 10 percent of the executives made the best possible decision, and, significantly, all of these individuals worked out the solution mathematically using the approaches we shall describe in Chapter 2. Intuition, judgment, and emotion all proved poor seconds. What does this result mean? This problem, although complex, did not approach the complexity of many real-world problems. It suggests that business judgment is falling short of ideal results in many real-world situations.

An Overview of Part Two

The need for evaluative models distinguishes the manager from the natural scientist. In order to be useful, the evaluative model must reflect the manager's concept of what ought to be. This latter concept requires a subjective judgment on the part of the manager. Thus, the evaluative model can only be considered right or wrong on the basis of how well it reflects these subjective judgments. In this sense, the evaluative model is also subjective. Some individuals make the mistake of interpreting this subjectivity to mean that the evaluative model is arbitrary, since it is not "objective." However, there is a significant difference between a subjective model and an arbitrary model. An evaluative model is a good one if it reflects the subjective judgments of the manager. It cannot be arbitrary, since otherwise it might not reflect these judgments properly. This is an important point that we shall return to throughout Part Two.

In Chapter 2, we shall presume only a single criterion and briefly discuss the notion of an evaluative model in cases of certainty. We shall then see how the introduction of risk may be analyzed through the use of decision trees and simple probability concepts. In Chapter 3, we consider which eval-

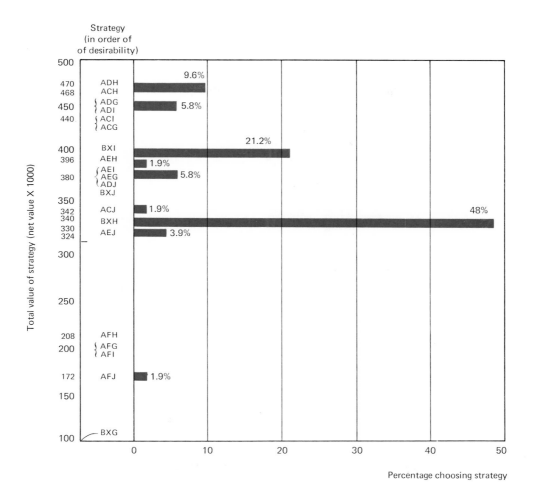

Figure 4. Distribution of decisions made by fifty-two members of the UCLA Executive Program on a bidding problem containing twenty alternatives

Source: J. B. Boulden and E. S. Buffa, "The Strategy of Interdependent Decisions," *California Management Review,* Vol. I, No. 4, 1959, pp. 94–98.

uative models are appropriate for dealing with risky situations involving only a single criterion. Finally, in Chapter 4, we study how to deal with multiple criteria in both certain and risky decisions.

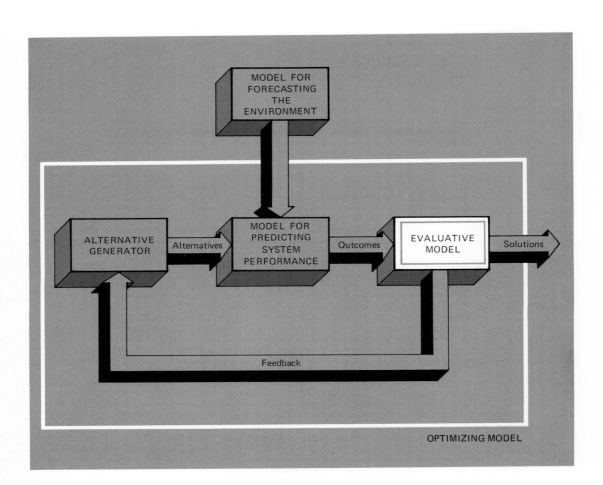

2

An Introduction to Evaluative Models and Decision Trees

The purpose of an evaluative model is to reflect the subjective judgments of the decision maker regarding the desirability of an outcome resulting from a decision. The choice of such a model is easy in situations involving a single criterion and certainty but becomes more difficult as risk and multiple criteria are introduced.

Since the purpose of such a model is merely to reflect subjective judgments, it would be natural to question the model's practical usefulness. After all, the decision maker should simply be able to look at the different outcomes and state which one he prefers. However, in truly complicated situations involving risk and multiple criteria, determining perference may be a difficult task. The development of an evaluative model can proceed on a step-by-step basis, so that the decision maker is not overwhelmed with the complexity of the total problem. In addition, for certain problems having very specific characteristics, the explicit identification of an evaluative model may allow the use of the powerful optimizing models of management science, which identify the best, or optimal, solution to a problem on the basis of the evaluative model.

Suppose we have only two alternatives for consideration, A_1 and A_2. We have assumed that we can predict the outcomes of choosing these alternatives, and have labeled these O_1 and O_2 respectively. Now, suppose we construct an evaluative model to aid us in choosing between these alternatives. What properties should such a model have? First, it would seem reasonable to require this model to be a function of information regarding the outcomes O_1 and O_2 alone. That is, the choice of the alternative should not be influenced by extraneous information unrelated to the effects of selecting either alternative. While this may appear to be a trivial point, in complex situations it will be a difficult task to identify correctly all of the potential impacts from adopting an alternative.

Therefore, let us define our evaluative model U as a function of the outcomes O_1 and O_2. Since U is a function, $U(O_1)$ and $U(O_2)$ are simply numbers. For example, we may obtain $U(O_1) = 0.6$ and $U(O_2) = 0.4$. (It may be helpful at this point to review the notion of a function presented in Appendix A.) Now let us consider the second desirable property of an evaluative model. It should have the property that $U(O_1)$ is greater than $U(O_2)$ if and only if the decision maker prefers O_1 to O_2. Thus, it follows that $U(O_1) = U(O_2)$ if and only if the decision maker is indifferent between receiving either outcome O_1 or O_2. Clearly, if O_1 is preferred to O_2, then alternative A_1 is the correct decision, and vice versa. In our previous example, if $U(O_1) = 0.6$ and $U(O_2) = 0.4$, then we should choose alternative A_1 over alternative A_2.

These are the two essential properties of an evaluative model. First, that it be a function solely of information regarding the outcomes of the decision and, second, that $U(O_1)$ is greater than $U(O_2)$ if and only if O_1 is preferred to O_2. We shall now turn our attention to the problem of constructing such models in practical situations. The choice of U depends on the preferences of the decision maker. We shall investigate what kind of information the decision maker must provide in order to allow the construction of U.

A SINGLE CRITERION UNDER CERTAINTY

The simplest case from the standpoint of evaluative models involves a single criterion under conditions of certainty. To illustrate this case, let us return to our bank example. Suppose we have $100 to invest. For simplicity, assume that there are only two alternative investments available to us. The first, A_1, is a bank deposit paying 7 percent per year, while the second alternative, A_2, is another bank deposit paying 5 percent per year. Both accounts are fully insured and alike in every respect except for the interest rate.

Certainly this seems like a trivial example. No doubt you have already noted that the outcome O_1 from the first alternative A_1 is $107, while O_2 is only $105. Thus, we have identified the alternatives A_1 and A_2 and predicted their outcomes with certainty. According to our diagram of the models of management science, we still need an evaluative model in order to make the decision. However in this case, the correct decision A_1 seems obvious. Why is this so?

The reason is deceptively simple. There is a single criterion, money. Further, at least in our culture, most persons would agree that more money is preferred to less. That is, most persons would prefer having $107 to having $105. Therefore, we have actually used an evaluative model in making our decision, but since we agree that more money is preferred to less, and since there is no risk involved to complicate matters, the choice of the evaluative model is not a critical issue. An obvious evaluative model can be constructed by defining $U(O_i) = O_i$ for $i = 1$ or 2. That is, we simply define the evaluative function so that it assigns the number 107 to the outcome $107, and the number 105 to the outcome $105. Notice that this definition satisfies both desirable properties of an evaluative model. It is a function of the outcome, and $U(O_1) > U(O_2)$ if and only if O_1 is preferred to O_2. Further, this accurately reflects the feelings of *most* persons in our culture. When we are dealing with a single criterion such as money, we can often let $U(O_i)$ equal O_i. Therefore, we can speak of maximizing profit (or minimizing cost) without making explicit our evaluative model. Nevertheless, the choice of such a model is implied.

The function $U(O_i) = O_i$ is not the only function that satisfies these properties. For example, $V(O_i) = 2 \, O_i$ would also be acceptable as would $V(O_i) = O_i^2$ so long as $O_i \geqslant 0$. Both of these functions preserve the same ordering of the outcomes as $U(O_i) = O_i$.

Since any order preserving transformation of the simple evaluative function $U(O_i) = O_i$ is appropriate for our problem, it is clear that we have a wide choice of evaluative models that will lead to the same decision. We could easily agree on the correct decision for our problem, A_1, without much concern regarding the appropriate form of U. As we shall see, this will not always be the case when risk or multiple criteria are introduced.*

One should not conclude, however, that decision making under certainty is always simple. In many problems of interest to managers, the models required to generate the alternatives may be very complex, involving possibly thousands of alternatives. Given the explicit identification of an evaluative model as a basis for ranking alternatives, it may be possible to use certain optimizing models of management science, such as linear programming, as aids in these more complex situations.

A SINGLE CRITERION UNDER RISK

The simplest examples of decisions involving a single criterion and some risk regarding the outcome are provided by several gambles. Suppose you are offered the possibility of playing one of two games. In either game, you will flip a "fair" coin. By a "fair" coin, we mean one with an equal probability of landing heads or tails. In the first game (A_1) you win $10 if the coin lands on heads, but lose $2 if it lands on tails. In the second game (A_2), you win $2 if heads occurs, but lose $1 if the coin falls on tails.

What are the outcomes O_1 and O_2 for the two games? In this case, the outcomes depend on an external event, heads or tails on the coin flip, as well as on our decision. Thus, we may call the payoffs for the gambles "conditional outcomes." That is, they are conditional on the result of the coin flip.

---

* There is one situation involving a single criterion and certainty in which some information regarding the decision maker's preferences may be required: the situation in which the decision maker has a "target-value" or "goal" in mind for the criterion. An approach for constructing the appropriate evaluative model is described in Chapter 3 as a special case of the evaluative model for a single criterion under risk.

We also know the probability of receiving each conditional outcome given the choice of either alternative. This information may be summarized in tabular form as shown in Table 1.

TABLE 1. Outcomes of Alternatives Involving Risk

	Events	
Alternatives	Heads $(p_1 = 0.5)$	Tails $(p_2 = 0.5)$
Game 1 (A_1)	$10 ($O_{11}$)	−$2 ($O_{12}$)
Game 2 (A_2)	$ 2 (O_{21})	−$1 ($O_{22}$)

Now let us consider an evaluative model that might be appropriate for decision making in situations such as this one. Recall that an evaluative model should be a function of the outcomes of the alternatives. In this case, alternative A_1 has two *conditional* outcomes, each of which may occur with probability 0.5. Let us denote these conditional outcomes as O_{11} and O_{12} where the first subscript identifies these conditional outcomes as resulting from alternative one, while the second subscript distinguishes between the two possible results of selecting A_1. We have $O_{11} = \$10$, and $O_{12} = -\$2$. Similarly, we can define $O_{21} = \$2$ and $O_{22} = -\$1$ for A_2. In addition, these results can occur with probability $p_1 = 0.5$ for O_{11} and O_{21}, and of $p_2 = 0.5$ for O_{12} and O_{22}. Thus, we may define the *outcome* O_1 associated with A_1 as the gamble summarized by $(p_1, O_{11}; p_2, O_{12})$, and the *outcome* O_2 associated with A_2 as $(p_1, O_{21}; p_2, O_{22})$. Filling in the appropriate numbers for our hypothetical situation, we obtain $O_1 = (0.5, \$10; 0.5, -\$2)$, and $O_2 = (0.5, \$2; 0.5, -\$1)$.

Let us now consider an evaluative model for the first alternative A_1. Since an evaluative model U is a function of the outcome O_1, we must have $U(p_1, O_{11}; p_2, O_{12})$.

Expected Value

A widely used evaluative model calculates the *expected value* of each outcome. The expected value of an outcome is simply the sum of the possible conditional values that can result for the outcome, weighted by their respective probabilities of occurrence. For example, the expected value of the first gamble A_1 is

$$(0.5) (\$10) + (0.5) (-\$2) = \$5 - \$1 = \$4 .$$

Similarly, for A_2 we have

$$(0.5)\ (\$2.00) + (0.5)\ (-\$1.00) = \$1.00 - \$0.50 = \$0.50.$$

The expected value of an outcome has an intuitively appealing interpretation. If we were to accept the first gamble A_1 many times, we would expect to win $10 half of the time and to lose $2 the other half of the time. The net result would be equivalent to winning the expected value of the gamble, $4, on each coin flip; thus, $4 is what we would expect to gain per flip if the coin were flipped many times. However, it is important to emphasize that this expected value is not one of the actual outcomes of the coin flip, which will be either "win $10" or "lose $2."

Because of this interpretation, the expected value of an outcome has desirable properties for use as an evaluative model by managers. Throughout his career, the manager may be faced with many decisions involving risky outcomes. If he selects only those alternatives with positive expected values, there is a high probability that his decisions will result in a positive increment to his company's profits. This statement does not mean that every decision will result in a desirable outcome, but we *can* say that the odds are in favor of the manager who abides by this evaluative model.

An Example   The Pacific Oil Company (POCO) is concerned with determining the appropriate strategy for developing its oil shale leases in Colorado and Canada. Oil shales are actually mined, much like coal, but liquid petroleum products can be extracted from the oil shales through a heating process. At the current state of the art, it is not economical to obtain oil in this manner, even with the recent increases in the price of crude oil. However, as the world's reserves of crude are depleted, it is likely that this price will eventually rise even further. In addition, improvements in techniques for extracting the petroleum from oil shales would reduce the costs of obtaining this resource. Thus, it appears that oil shales may eventually be an economical source of petroleum.

POCO has identified three basic strategies for developing their oil shale leases over the near term (the next 10 to 15 years). The choice of a near-term strategy will have little effect on long-run profits after this 10- to 15-year time horizon. The *first strategy* would concentrate exclusively on research work related to oil shale processing. Such a strategy would place POCO in a position to exploit these resources eventually, but they would be unable to respond significantly to any opportunities for actually selling petroleum products from oil shales over the near term. These opportunities might occur because of higher crude prices or as a result of an oil embargo from the major oil-producing nations. An embargo would ensure higher crude prices coupled with a high demand for domestically produced oil.

The *second strategy* would be to combine a research program with some actual development of production capabilities. At the current world prices of crude, the output from this process would not quite break even, but the loss would not be great. However, the company would be in a position to actually profit from increases in crude oil prices or from the excess demand for domestic oil created by an embargo.

The *third strategy* would be a crash program aimed at developing the capability to produce petroleum products from oil shales in quantity as quickly as possible. Such a venture would lose money at the current crude oil prices and only break even at higher prices. However, POCO would be in a position to make considerable profits if another embargo occurred.

If crude oil prices were to fall in the near term due to significant new discoveries of additional reserves, all three of these strategies would result in losses. However, such an event is considered unlikely by POCO.

How can POCO go about making a decision in this case? First, the manager may recognize that he can gain some insights into this problem by viewing it as a decision involving a single criterion (money) under risk. There are three alternatives, and each has a different conditional outcome depending on the future price of oil or the occurrence of an oil embargo. Thus, the manager may construct a table to display the relevant alternatives and the events that affect the outcomes from selecting each alternative. Such a display is shown in Table 2.

The construction of this table is an important exercise, since the manager now has identified the primary alternatives for consideration as well as the events that will determine the outcomes from these alternatives. It will generally be advantageous for the manager to discuss his assumptions with others at this point using this table as the basis for this discussion. In such a discussion, additional alternatives or other important events might be identified. For the sake of simplicity, we have used the events of lower prices, current prices, higher prices, and embargo. In an actual study, a manager might consider many more events. For example, he might consider all possible crude oil prices from $5 to $20 per barrel in increments of $1. This would lead to sixteen possible events regarding prices plus the additional event of an embargo. Even the latter could be stated in more detail by specifying embargos of various lengths of time.

TABLE 2 Identification of Alternatives and Events

	Events			
Alternatives	Lower Prices	Current Prices	Higher Prices	Embargo
Research only				
Combined research and development				
Crash				

The next task would be to predict the conditional outcome associated with each alternative and event. Such a task will be simplified if the manager has access to explicit predictive models such as those we shall describe in Part Three of this book. Finally, he must provide an estimate of the probability of the occurrence of each event. For our example, we suppose that the manager has performed these tasks and now has the information available in Table 3.

TABLE 3 Identification of Conditional Outcomes and Probabilities

| | Events | | | |
Alternatives	Lower Prices ($p = 0.1$)	Current Prices ($p = 0.3$)	Higher Prices ($p = 0.4$)	Embargo ($p = 0.2$)
Research only	− 50*	0	50	55
Combined research and development	−150	− 50	100	150
Crash	−500	−200	0	500

*Conditional outcomes given in millions of dollars.

Finally, the manager must identify some evaluative model in order to choose an alternative. In many practical situations, once the analysis has come this far, the solution will be obvious. However, in other cases the use of an explicit evaluative model may be helpful in making the final decision. The manager of POCO may apply the expected value evaluative model to this data and obtain the following results:

research only: $(0.1)\ (−50) + (0.3)\ (0) + (0.4)\ (50) + (0.2)\ (55) = 26$

research and
development: $(0.1)\ (−150) + (0.3)\ (−50) + (0.4)\ (100) + (0.2)\ (150) = 40$

crash development:
$(0.1)\ (−500) + (0.3)\ (−200) + (0.4)\ (0) + (0.2)\ (500) = −10$.

Thus, on the basis of the expected value model, the choice of a combined research and development strategy would be preferable.

However, it would be naive to think that a manager facing a decision with such important consequences would stop his analysis at this point. For example, the conditional outcomes and the probabilities of the events are only estimates and may contain some errors. Thus, the manager would want to test the sensitivity of his decision to small changes in these estimates. For example, if the probability of current prices had been 0.5, and of higher prices 0.2, then alternative 1 (research only) would have been preferred. (Check this yourself.) Therefore, the manager may decide to invest some additional time and effort obtaining better information regarding the probability of higher prices. How much should he be willing to spend for this information? The answer to this question will be our next topic.

The Value of Information

To examine the value of information, let us return to our coin flipping example. Suppose someone tells you he is clairvoyant; that is, he can predict the future, including the result of flipping a coin. How much should you offer to pay him for his services? In other words, what is the value of resolving the risk in the gambling situation?

To compute this, we need to identify the best alternative, given that each possible event has occurred (see Table 1). For example, if we know that the coin will land on heads, we would choose alternative A_1 and win $10. However, if we know it will land on tails, we would choose alternative A_2 to minimize our losses. Thus, we would have the following strategies and outcomes:

Event	Strategy	Outcome
Heads	A_1	+$10
Tails	A_2	— 1

Now, suppose the clairvoyant tells us whether the coin will land on heads or tails just prior to its being flipped. Since the coin is fair, the probability that it will fall on heads is 0.5, and the probability that it will fall on tails is 0.5. Therefore, the probability that the clairvoyant will predict "heads" prior to a flip is also 0.5, as is the probability that he will predict "tails." He *cannot* control the future by changing the probability of each event, but his prediction is always correct.

If he predicts "heads," we will choose A_1 and win $10, and if he predicts "tails" we will choose A_2 (assuming we must play) so that we only lose $1. Thus, given the predictions of the clairvoyant just prior to each flip of the coin, we have a 0.5 chance of winning $10 and a 0.5 chance of losing $1.

We can compute the *expected value* of playing the game with perfect information. It is simply the probability of being told each event will occur multiplied by the outcome we would receive if we knew that event were going to occur. In this case, it would be

$$(0.5) (\$10.00) + (0.5) (-\$1.00) = \$4.50 .$$

However, the expected value of choosing alternative A_1 *without* perfect information was $4. Thus, the expected value of playing the game with the clairvoyant (with perfect information) is $4.50, while the expected value of playing the game without the clairvoyant, but choosing alternative A_1, is $4. So the value of having a clairvoyant (perfect information) in this case is only $4.50 − $4.00 = $0.50. The value of perfect information is obtained by determining the expected value of the decision made with perfect information, and subtracting the expected value of the best alternative without this information. This amount is an important upper limit or bound on what we should be willing to pay for the information.

An Example Given the data in Table 3, the choice of the appropriate oil shale strategy for POCO would be trivial *if* the occurrence of future events were known with certainty. For example, if prices drift lower, POCO would be well advised to delay work in oil shales entirely, but if prices stay constant a research-only strategy would just break even. For higher prices, a combined research and development program would provide the greatest returns, while the crash program would be most desirable, given the occurrence of an oil embargo in the near future. Clearly, it would be worth something to POCO to obtain a certain forecast of the future, but how much?

The computation of this value of information is straightforward. First, we note what the outcome would be for each event if we knew it were going to occur. For example, if we knew that current prices were going to continue over the near term, we would choose a research-only strategy with a break-even outcome. For simplicity, let us assume that even if prices in the near term were to fall, we would still continue the research strategy at a cost of $50 million in anticipation of long-run payoffs. Thus, we would have the following decisions summarized from Table 3:

Event	Probability	Strategy	Outcome
lower prices	0.1	research only	−50
current prices	0.3	research only	0
higher prices	0.4	research and development	100
embargo	0.2	crash development	500

Our current expectations are that there is a 0.1 chance of lower prices, a 0.3 chance of current prices continuing, a 0.4 chance of higher prices, and a 0.2 chance of an embargo in the near term. If we resolve this uncertainty and obtain perfect information, we will determine which event will actually occur. However, the probability of finding that each event will occur is simply the same as our current expectation. For example, the probability that we will find that prices will be lower when we resolve the risk in this problem is simply 0.1. Likewise, the probability that perfect information will reveal that prices will move higher is 0.4. Thus, we calculate

$$(0.1)\ (-50) + (0.3)\ (0) + (0.4)\ (100) + (0.2)\ (500) = 135$$

as the expected return from a decision, *given* that we do obtain perfect information.

What is this information worth? To find the value of the perfect information, we subtract from the expected return determined above ($135 million) the expected value of the best decision under risk, which was $40 million for the research and development strategy. Thus the value of perfect information would be $135 − $40 = $95 million. Clearly, this is a substantial sum.

Again, the practicing manager would recognize that he will be unable to obtain perfect information regarding the future in most realistic situations. Nevertheless, this analysis does suggest that additional marketing research to obtain better estimates would be a worthwhile investment. In addition, this result provides an upper bound on such expenditures.

Conditional and Joint Probabilities

In order to use the expected value evaluative models in more complicated situations, it is necessary to use the concepts of conditional and joint probabilities. For example, we have created a table for POCO with all of the possible future events, or states of the environment, that will affect their decisions. In complicated situations, it may be very difficult to identify these events and their associated probabilities of occurrence, especially since some events may be dependent on others.

As an example of dependent outcomes, let us introduce a third alternative gamble, A_3, for a comparison against our original two. Suppose this gamble has the rules that follow. If the fair coin lands on heads, you flip it again. On the second flip if it lands on heads, you win $20; but if it lands on tails, you lose $5. If the fair coin lands on tails on the first flip, you flip a second coin which is "unfair." This coin is weighted and has only a 0.4 chance of landing on heads and a 0.6 chance of landing on tails. Nevertheless, if it falls on heads, you will win $5; but if it lands on tails, you lose $10. Which alternative is preferred using the expected value evaluative model?

Alternative A_3 has four conditional outcomes. That is, you either win $20, win $5, lose $5, or lose $10. However, the probability of receiving each of these outcomes is not immediately clear, so we must do some additional calculations.

In order to deal with the dependence of one outcome on several events, we need to be able to compute both conditional and joint probabilities. (See Appendix B for a review of these concepts.) At this point, it will be helpful to introduce some new notation: let H_1 denote the event of heads on the first toss of the coin and let H_2 denote heads on the second toss. Similarly, T_1 and T_2 denote tails on the first and second tosses of the coin, respectively.

Since the first coin is fair, the probability of heads on the first toss, written $P(H_1)$, equals 0.5. In addition, the probability of heads on the second toss, *given* that heads appeared on the first toss, written $P(H_2|H_1)$, also equals 0.5. Note the $P(H_2|H_1)$ is a *conditional probability*. That is, the probability of the event H_2 is dependent on the occurrence of the event H_1. However, if T_1 occurs, then $P(H_2|T_1) = 0.4$, since we would be using the unfair coin for the second toss. We say that $P(H_1)$ and $P(T_1)$ are *unconditional* (or *marginal*) *probabilities*, since they are not dependent on any other event.

Thus, we have $P(H_1) = P(T_1) = P(H_2|H_1) = P(T_2|H_1) = 0.5$, $P(H_2|T_1) = 0.4$, and $P(T_2|T_1) = 0.6$. However, what we really need to know is the probability of receiving each outcome. The outcome of a \$20 win will occur if we obtain both H_1 and H_2. We may write $P(H_1H_2)$ as the probability that *both* H_1 and H_2 occur. This is called the *joint probability* of H_1 and H_2.

An important relationship exists among the unconditional probabilities, the conditional probabilities, and the joint probabilities. Using even more general notation, if A and B are two independent events, the joint probability that both A and B will occur, $P(AB)$, is equal to $P(A) \cdot P(B)$. However, if the probability that event B will occur is affected by whether or not event A occurs, then we must replace $P(B)$ by the conditional probability $P(B|A)$. Then the joint probability

$$P(AB) = P(B|A) \cdot P(A) .$$

If the probability of event A depends on event B, we would write

$$P(AB) = P(A|B) \cdot P(B) .$$

One of these two relationships may be used to calculate joint probabilities.

In some cases, we may know the joint probability $P(AB)$ of two events, A and B, and the unconditional probability of one of the events, $P(A)$. We can rearrange the relationship for determining joint probabilities, and obtain

$$P(B|A) = \frac{P(AB)}{P(A)} ; P(A) \neq 0 .$$

In words, this relationship says that the conditional probability of some event B, given that event A has occurred, is equal to the joint probability that both A and B occur divided by the probability that A occurs, assuming that $P(A)$ is not zero. (See Appendix B for a further review of these concepts.)

We may now apply the relationship for calculating joint probabilities to our problem and obtain the following results:

$$P(H_1H_2) = P(H_2|H_1) \cdot P(H_1) = (0.5)\,(0.5) = 0.25$$
$$P(H_1T_2) = P(T_2|H_1) \cdot P(H_1) = (0.5)\,(0.5) = 0.25$$
$$P(T_1H_2) = P(H_2|T_1) \cdot P(T_1) = (0.4)\,(0.5) = 0.20$$
$$P(T_1T_2) = P(T_2|T_1) \cdot P(T_1) = (0.6)\,(0.5) = 0.30 .$$

Now we can use these probabilities to compute the expected value of this third alternative A_3. We have the following data:

Events	H_1H_2	H_1T_2	T_1H_2	T_1T_2
Probabilities	0.25	0.25	0.2	0.3
Outcomes	\$20	−\$5	\$5	−\$10

which gives the expected value

$$(0.25) (\$20.00) + (0.25) (-\$5.00) + (0.2) (\$5.00) + (0.3) (-\$10.00) = \$1.75 \, .$$

Thus, on the basis of the expected value evaluative model, A_3 is preferred to gamble A_2, which had an expected value of $0.50, but not to A_1 with an expected value of $4 (see Table 4).

Thus it seems that we can use the concept of expected value even in rather complex situations and even though we must be very careful to keep track of the relationships among events and to perform our probability calculations correctly. What we really need is a tool to aid us in structuring or visualizing these complex relationships more easily, and a means of simplifying the probability calculations. The decision tree, which is one of the most practical and useful quantitative managerial aids, is such a tool.

TABLE 4. Summary of Outcomes of Three Alternatives

	Events					
Alternatives	H_1 ($p = 0.5$)	T_1 ($p = 0.5$)	H_1H_2 ($p = 0.25$)	H_1T_2 ($p = 0.25$)	T_1H_2 ($p = 0.2$)	T_1T_2 ($p = 0.3$)
Game 1 (A_1)	\$10 (O_{11})	-\$2 (O_{12})	---	---	---	---
Game 2 (A_2)	\$ 2 (O_{21})	-\$1 (O_{22})	---	---	---	---
Game 3 (A_3)	---	---	\$20 (O_{31})	-\$5 (O_{32})	\$5 (O_{33})	-\$10 (O_{34})

DECISION TREES

The idea of the decision tree is delightfully simple. Instead of compressing all of the information regarding a complex decision into a table such as those we have used previously, one draws a schematic representation of the problem that displays the information in a more easily understood fashion. In addition, the complex probability computations can be simplified through the use of this tree.

An Example   To illustrate how a decision tree can be used, let us refer again to our problem of selecting from three gambles. How can we schematically represent the problem of choosing among three alternatives? We can do it simply by showing each alternative as one of three possible branches on a tree, as illustrated in Figure 1.

The next step is to show the events that could occur in a similar fashion as branch points on the tree, with each branch representing the occurrence of a particular event. In the case of alternative A_3, the second toss of each coin can be represented with additional branches of the tree. Finally, the

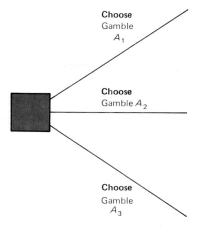

Figure 1. The beginnings of a decision tree

outcomes can be written on the branches where they are realized. A careful study of Figure 2 should clarify these concepts.

In the decision tree in Figure 2, we have indicated a decision point by a box, and a chance point where events are realized by a circle. There is no hard and fast rule requiring drawing the tree in this way. However, in more complex trees it may be helpful to distinguish decision points from chance points in some manner such as this. Further, we have shown the decisions, then the events, and finally the outcomes, in that order. In some practical situations, we will make an initial decision, and then have the opportunity to wait until some events have actually occurred before making another decision. This situation can also be represented in the decision tree format as we shall see in a later example.

One important advantage of the decision tree is that a manager can quickly visualize the alternatives, the possible future events, and their outcomes. The logic and the assumptions that are the basis for a decision are laid out for easy scrutiny. Such trees can be useful in promoting a healthy discussion regarding the alternatives, the possible events, their probabilities, and the outcomes. In practical situations, a decision tree may be modified many times before general agreement can be reached that it accurately portrays the real problem. However, each revision of the tree will represent some additional learning about the nature of the problem.

Thus, merely drawing a decision tree can have a significant benefit for the manager. In addition, the calculation of the expected values associated with the alternative decisions can be simplified by studying each branch point, beginning at the tips of the branches. For example, let us begin by considering the one branch point for alternative A_1. We compute the expected value of this branch point by multiplying the probability on each branch by the outcome associated with the branch, and summing these results. For the

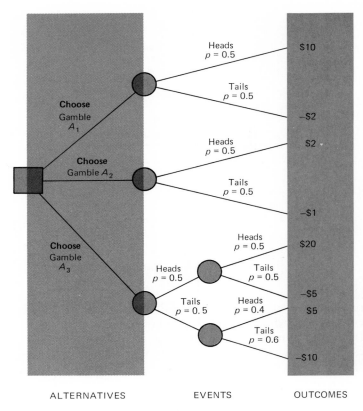

Figure 2. A decision tree for the
gamble selection problem

branch point of A_1 we obtain (0.5) ($10) = $5 on the first branch, and (0.5)
(−$2) = −$1 on the second branch. Summing these, we get $4, and we re-
place the branch point on the tree by its expected value, as shown in Figure 3.

Since there was only one branch point for alternative A_1, the result is
that the expected value of the branch point is also equal to the expected value
of alternative A_1. A similar analysis would determine an expected value of
$0.50 for alternative A_2.

Now consider alternative A_3, which includes a series of branches. Again,
let us begin at the far right, and compute the expected value of each chance
branch. The first branch of alternative A_3 corresponds to the toss of the fair
coin on the second trial, and has an expected value of (0.5) ($20) + (0.5)
(−$5) = $7.50. The other branch corresponds to the toss of the unfair coin
and has an expected value of (0.4) ($5) + (0.6) (−$10) = −$4. Now, and this
is important, we replace each of these two branches by their respective expected values. We now have the tree shown in Figure 4.

We now have only one chance branch point in the tree for alternative
A_3, corresponding to the toss of the first coin. The two chance branch points
corresponding to the toss of the second coin have been replaced by their re-

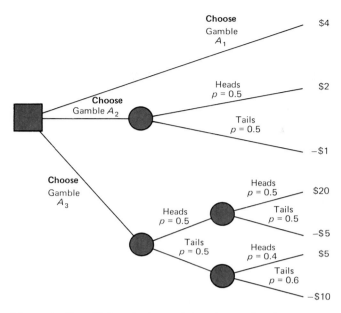

Figure 3. Simplifying the branch for alternative A_1

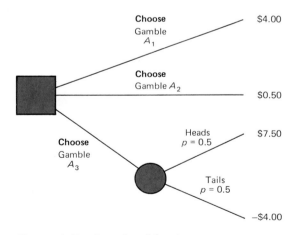

Figure 4. Further simplifications

spective expected values. Finally, we compute the expected value of this remaining chance branch point in exactly the same manner as before, and obtain $(0.5) (\$7.50) + (0.5) (-\$4) = \$1.75$, the expected value of alternative A_3. Notice that this number was computed *without* using the concepts of joint or conditional probabilities. It is important to realize, however, that the probabilities on the second branch of the tree actually are *conditional* probabilities (conditional on the first [leftmost] chance outcome). Thus, the use of the decision tree also simplifies the probability calculations that are required to obtain expected values.

This process of starting at the right and successively replacing each branch by its associated expected value is referred to as "rolling back" the tree. Even when the tree gets very large and many different calculations are involved, they always remain simple in the sense that only expected values are calculated for each branch point. As a final result, the tree of Figure 2 has been reduced to Figure 5, and the desirability of alternative A_1 based on the expected value evaluative model is apparent. This strategy of "rolling back" is based on the more general concept of *dynamic programming*, which is discussed in Chapter 18.

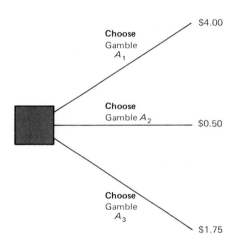

Figure 5. The results of the analysis; expected values for three alternatives

The Value of Perfect Information   The value of perfect information can be computed directly from the decision tree. Further, this concept can be illustrated on the decision tree. Suppose our clairvoyant friend says that he can predict the outcome of the flip of the fair coin. We would still have to leave the result of flipping the second coin in alternative A_3 to chance.

Let us construct a decision tree to represent the problem, given the assistance of our friend. He can predict the outcome of flipping the fair coin before it occurs. Therefore, we will *know* whether heads or tails will occur before we must choose A_1, A_2, or A_3. However, since the first coin flip is fair, there is still a 0.5 chance that he will tell us it will be heads and a 0.5 chance he will tell us tails. The first branch in our revised decision tree must, therefore, be a chance branch which represents the 0.5 probability that our friend predicts heads and the 0.5 probability he predicts tails.

The concept of perfect information does not mean that the chance branch point regarding the flip of the fair coin can be removed from the tree. Rather, it means that the result of the event will be known *prior* to our decision, so the chance branch point appears *before* the decision branch points, as shown in Figure 6, rather than after the decision branch points, as shown in Figure 2. In order to understand this important concept, carefully compare Figures 2 and 6.

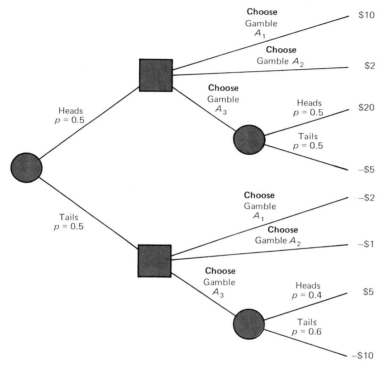

Figure 6. A decision tree for calculating the value of perfect information regarding the flip of the first coin

If our clairvoyant friend predicts heads, we have the option of choosing alternative A_1 with outcome "win \$10," A_2 with outcome "win \$2," or A_3 with an expected value of $(0.5)(\$20) + (0.5)(-\$5) = \$7.50$. Using our expected value model, we would choose A_1. Similarly, if our clairvoyant says tails on the first flip, we would choose A_2 with a loss of \$1. Thus, we would have a 0.5 chance of winning \$10 and a 0.5 chance of losing \$1 prior to the flip of the coin when the clairvoyant is on our side. The expected value of our decision using this perfect information regarding the first flip of the coin is $(0.5)(\$10) + (0.5)(-\$1) = \$4.50$. Comparing this value with the expected value of $4 without this information, we find that again our friend's advice is worth only $0.50.

What would be the value of his advice if he could successfully predict the results of *both* coin flips (if we choose A_3) before we select an alternative? We shall leave this question for an exercise.

A POCO Example   Suppose we complicate the problem of POCO by recognizing the possibility of a breakthrough in oil shale processing technology resulting from the research efforts carried out either under the research-only strategy or under the combined research and development strategy. This breakthrough would significantly reduce the costs of extracting petroleum products from oil shales. POCO estimates the probability of such a breakthrough from following the research-only strategy at 0.4 and from following the combined research and development strategy at 0.3. Under the alternative of a crash development of production capabilities, the current state-of-the-art technology would be used.

If such a breakthrough occurred, POCO would have the option of changing strategies. If they had initially selected a research-only posture and a breakthrough occurred, they would begin either a combined research and development effort immediately or shift into the crash development program. If they were already in a combined research and development operating mode and the breakthrough occurred, they could continue in this mode or begin crash development. The conditional outcomes would depend on both the strategy selected after the breakthrough and the strategy the company selected initially. For example, the costs of shifting from a combined research and development strategy to a crash development program would be less than shifting from a research-only strategy to a crash development program. In addition, the news of the breakthrough in oil shale technology would reduce the probability of higher oil prices or an embargo, because the oil shales would provide additional supplies of petroleum products. The conditional outcomes for the different strategies and the probabilities of each event, *given* the occurrence of a breakthrough, are shown in Table 5.

It would be difficult to organize all of this information regarding POCO's options in tabular form. However, the decision tree can be used to advantage here. The first branch in a decision tree used to analyze this problem would be the choice of an initial strategy — research only, a combined research and development activity, or a crash development program. At the end of the research-only and the combined research and development branches there would be a chance branch point representing the possibility of a breakthrough in technology. If a breakthrough occurs, another decision point would follow allowing POCO to modify its initial strategy. The decision tree for this problem is shown in Figure 7. Notice that there are 28 different paths through the tree, and each leads to a distinct outcome. Also notice that there are several decision branch points in the tree, as well as the chance branch points.

TABLE 5. Conditional Outcomes and Probabilities,
Given the Occurrence of a Breakthrough

	Events			
Alternatives	Lower Prices ($p = 0.1$)	Current Prices ($p = 0.5$)	Higher Prices ($p = 0.3$)	Embargo ($p = 0.1$)
Change to research and development from research only	−100*	0	100	120
Change to crash from research only	−150	− 50	200	300
Continue research and development	− 50	50	150	200
Change to crash from research and development	−125	100	300	500

*Conditional outcomes given in millions of dollars.

Now let us analyze this situation by rolling back the tree. First we re-place the chance branch points at the far end of the tree by their respective expected values and obtain the tree shown in Figure 8. Notice that the re-sults at the end of the no-breakthrough branches are the same expected val-ues that we computed previously for each strategy. At the end of the break-through branches, we have the decision branches with an expected value for each strategy. On the basis of the expected value model, the best strat-egy in each case would be to begin a crash development program if a break-through occurs.

Branches broken by vertical parallel lines (see Figure 8) would be ignored if this decision point were reached. Thus, we can represent the decision point by the expected value of the best decision at that point, and continue to "roll back" the tree. That is, we would replace the decision point follow-ing the breakthrough from the research only strategy by 50, the expected value of the crash development strategy at that point. Similarly, the decision point following a breakthrough resulting from an initial combined research and development effort would be replaced by the expected value of the crash development effort, 177.5.

Thus, the expected value of the initial research strategy and of the ini-tial combined research and development strategy would be computed as

research only: $(0.6) (26) + (0.4) (50) = 35.6$

combined research
and development: $(0.7) (40) + (0.3) (177.5) = 81.25$.

Even allowing for the possibility of a breakthrough, the combined research and development strategy still remains the best alternative according to the

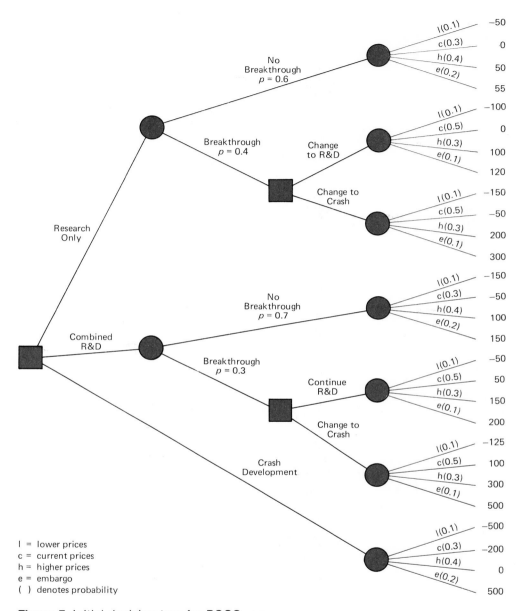

Figure 7. Initial decision tree for POCO

l = lower prices
c = current prices
h = higher prices
e = embargo
( ) denotes probability

expected value evaluative model. The tree reflecting these final calculations is shown in Figure 9.

At this point, there are several important observations to be made:

1. POCO does not expect to make $81.25 million from following an initial

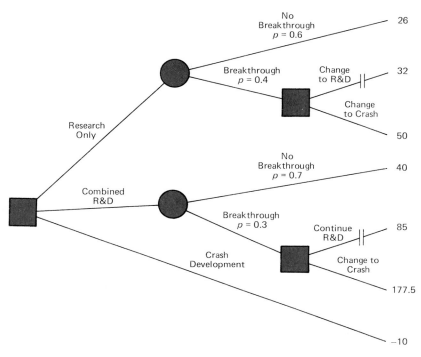

Figure 8. Rolling back the tree

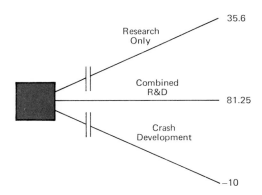

Figure 9. The results of the analysis for POCO

research and development strategy. They will actually receive one of eight different outcomes, which range from losing $150 million to making $500 million. *The expected value evaluative model provides a means of ranking alternatives under risky choice situations, but it does not give the actual result that will occur.*

2. Even though the problem was becoming complex because of the different strategies and events, the decision tree provided a useful means of organizing the relationships and the data.

3. The probability calculations at each step were straightforward and consisted of simple expected values.

As can be seen, even when the problem becomes rather "messy" in terms of several alternative strategies, some of which may depend on future events, and when many different future events are possible, the decision tree can provide a practical, useful means of analyzing a problem.

The Value of Perfect Information   What if POCO could spend additional research funds immediately and determine whether or not a breakthrough in the processing technology could be made? How much would this information be worth? In order to answer this question, we must revise the decision tree using an approach like the one employed in determining the value of perfect information from our clairvoyant friend regarding the toss of the coin. If we could resolve the uncertainty of the breakthrough, we would decide on an initial strategy after having this knowledge. When we obtain perfect information, the probability of discovering that a breakthrough will occur from an initial research-only strategy is 0.4, while there is a 0.6 chance we will be told that no breakthrough will occur from this strategy. Therefore, the first branch point in our revised tree (Figure 10) represents the resolution of the uncertainty regarding whether or not a breakthrough will occur, given that we follow a research-only strategy.

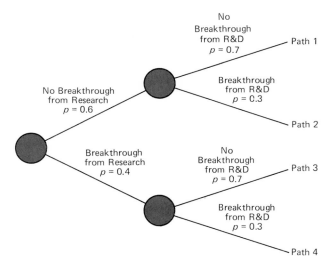

No
Breakthrough
from R&D
$p = 0.7$
— Path 1

Breakthrough
from R&D
$p = 0.3$
— Path 2

No Breakthrough
from Research
$p = 0.6$

Breakthrough
from Research
$p = 0.4$

No
Breakthrough
from R&D
$p = 0.7$
— Path 3

Breakthrough
from R&D
$p = 0.3$
— Path 4

Figure 10. Partial tree

Next, we need chance branches to represent the resolution of the uncertainty regarding the probability of a breakthrough, given that we follow initially a combined research and development strategy. There is a 0.3 probability that such a breakthrough will occur and a 0.7 probability that it will not. The chance node representing this event should be placed at the tips of both branches from the chance node representing the research-only strategy, as illustrated in Figure 10.

There are four paths through the partial decision tree in Figure 10. Path 1 corresponds to discovering from our source of perfect information that no breakthrough would occur from a research-only strategy, *and* no breakthrough would occur from a combined research and development effort. Path 2 corresponds to discovering that no breakthrough would occur from a research-only strategy, but that a breakthrough *would occur* if we choose a combined research and development strategy initially. Similar interpretations hold for paths 3 and 4, with path 4 indicating that a breakthrough would occur given either of these initial strategies.

Notice that the partial tree in Figure 10 could have begun with a single chance point representing the resolution of the uncertainty regarding the combined research and development strategy. Then two chance points corresponding to the research-only strategy would have been placed at the tips of these branches. Verify that the same four paths can be identified in such a partial tree.

At the end points of the four resulting paths through the partial tree, the uncertainty regarding the possibility of a breakthrough has been resolved, and the decisions that can be made in each case are shown in Figure 11. Notice that the final chance branch points, labeled A through G, occur two or more times in the tree. For example, the chance branch point A appears following the research-only decision after the two decision points at the top of the tree. By labeling these redundant chance branch points as shown, we simplify the presentation of the tree.

On the uppermost path in Figure 11, corresponding to no breakthrough from a research-only strategy and no breakthrough from a combined research and development strategy, the decisions are simply to choose the research-only strategy, the combined research and development strategy, or a crash program initially, without hope of a breakthrough. The outcomes are still conditional on the price of oil or the possibility of an embargo, as before. The expected value of each decision would be the same as the expected value that we computed using the tabular display of information in the previous discussion of the POCO problem (Table 3).

However, the lower path in the tree corresponds to knowing that a breakthrough will occur if we initially choose the research-only strategy *and* also if we choose the combined research and development strategy. Therefore, our alternatives are as follows:

1. to begin the research-only strategy, then change to either a combined

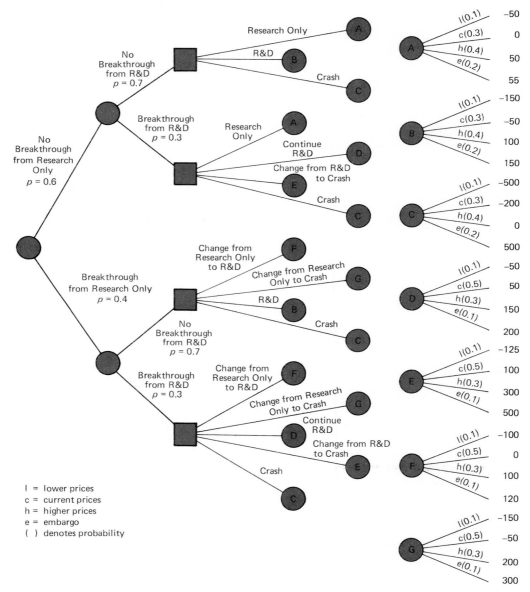

Figure 11. The decision tree for computing the value of perfect information regarding a breakthrough for POCO

2. to begin with and continue the combined research and development strategy when a breakthrough occurs

3. to begin with a research and development effort and switch to a crash development program when the breakthrough occurs

4. to start the crash development program using the state-of-the-art technology immediately

The expected value of resolving these uncertainties is computed by rolling back this tree as before, and the result is $84.05 million. This result compares with the expected value of $81.25 million for choosing the combined research and development strategy without resolving the uncertainty regarding the breakthrough. Therefore, POCO should be willing to spend *up to* $84.05 − $81.25 = $2.8 million immediately to determine if a breakthrough will actually occur given an initial research-only or a combined research and development strategy.

WHAT SHOULD THE MANAGER KNOW?

Up to this point, we have been involved in the technical details of decision making with a single criterion under the cases of certainty and of risk. In order to ensure that we have an overall grasp of this subject matter, it will be worth our time to step back and view this material from the perspective of a practicing manager and ask the question, "What does the manager really need to know?"

The decision-making process with a single criterion under certainty is relatively straightforward. As long as all persons agree that more (or less) of the criterion is always better, the simple decision rule of finding the alternative that maximizes (or minimizes) this criterion obviously holds. Thus, the real task is in predicting the outcomes associated with each alternative.

However, when risk is involved in the problem, there is no longer a single outcome associated with each alternative. Rather, the "outcome" consists of several conditional outcomes, each with an associated probability of occurrence. In order to rank alternatives some means of transforming these conditional outcomes and probabilities into a single number may be helpful. One evaluative model that performs this task is the expected value model, which weights each conditional outcome by its associated probability of occurrence.

The interpretation of the expected value has an intuitive appeal. Basically, this value represents what the manager would receive, *on the average*, if the decision were made many times. However, given a decision that is made only once, the outcome will actually be one of the conditional outcomes and not the expected value.

As problems under risk become more complicated, it becomes difficult to organize the information and to maintain an understanding of the logical relationships among the possible decision alternatives and the chance events. One important aid in dealing with these problems is the decision tree.

The central issues related to the use of quantitative aids such as the decision tree are the following:

1. What are the characteristics of problems that should be analyzed with decision trees?
2. How should the decision tree be formulated?
3. What are the information requirements of the procedure?
4. How are the computations performed?
5. How should the results of the analysis be interpreted?

And, finally,

6. What are the advantages of using decision trees?
7. What are the possible problems and pitfalls that must be overcome in practice?

Let us briefly consider each of these issues in turn.

Problem Characteristics   Decision trees are especially helpful in analyzing nonrepetitive decisions that involve risk and substantial costs or potential rewards. In problems of this type, simply identifying the alternative strategies and the possible events that may influence the outcomes, and gaining some appreciation of the probabilities of the occurrence of these events may be the most important part of the analysis. Certainly, these are steps that successful managers must perform in any case, even if they have never heard of decision trees. However, the manager who has a knowledge of this technology has a means of organizing his thoughts and improving his understanding of a complex problem.

Several examples of the actual use of decision trees have been reported. Notable examples are the following:

> Pillsbury switched from a box to a bag for one of its grocery products — and even scrapped plans to undertake an extensive market test — when the analysis indicated high expected profitability from this strategy. The switch was successful.
>
> General Electric decided to raise prices, rather than increase manufacturing capacity, for a mature industrial product. As part of the strategy, research and development expenditures were increased twenty-fold, and the decision resulted in a highly profitable sales of some $20 million a year.
>
> Ford Tractor chose to introduce a new model into a regional market suffering from competitive inroads, rather than reduce prices. The strategy worked. [Raiffa, 1974]

Notice that these applications tend to be in the area of determining a marketing strategy for products. This fact is not surprising, since such situations often involve nonrepetitive decisions, risk, and the potential for significant costs or profits.

Other areas which offer potential applications are decisions to expand production or service capacities, the determination of competitive bidding strategies, and the analysis of major governmental policies such as the decision to seed hurricanes (for an example see Howard et al. [1972]). Thus, the manager should be sensitive to problems with these characteristics in order to take advantage of this useful decision-making aid.

Formulation   The issue of who should actually formulate the decision tree is an important one. In extremely complicated problems involving perhaps millions of dollars, the manager may wish to call on his analytic staff or on outside consultants for assistance. However, the *manager* should be involved in the formulation of the decision tree in order to ensure that he understands the assumptions made by the analysts and to ensure that the analysts actually understand the "real" problem. It is important that the manager have confidence in the analysis, which is unlikely to happen without his personal involvement.

One approach would be for the manager to actually sketch out the first decision tree in gross terms. The major alternatives and events would be shown, perhaps with rough estimates of probabilities, in order to obtain some idea of the important aspects of the problem. Using only a crude analysis of this sort, that would be carried out "on the back of an envelope" in only an hour or so, the manager might be able to eliminate some alternatives as being undesirable, thus reducing the complexity of the problem. The rough tree consisting of the remaining alternatives could then be presented to the professional analysts as a takeoff point for a more detailed analysis.

Information Requirements   The information requirements for a decision tree are basically the same as those for the manager who does not use the decision tree. That is, he must obtain the following:

1.   the alternative decisions and their relationships to possible future events
2.   the outcomes of selecting each alternative, given the occurrence of each future event
3.   the probabilities of the occurrence of each event

In a complex, real-world problem, the decision tree could grow to enormous proportions and require many bits of information. However, a preliminary analysis can be used to eliminate some alternatives from a detailed consideration and to determine the sensitivity of the results to certain future events, so that the number of chance branches can be held down. This process requires judgment on the part of the analyst, and it is another reason for encouraging the active participation of the manager in the initial formulation and analysis of the problem. The eventual information requirements can be significantly reduced by this process. In the following chapters we will be concerned with how the estimates of the outcomes and probabilities can actually be obtained.

Computations Since the computation of expected values is a straightforward task, there is no reason why managers cannot perform their own analysis of decision trees that are of "reasonable" size. It would be especially desirable to do so in the initial phase of the analysis of a large, complex problem, or perhaps might be sufficient in the case of a problem where the potential losses or rewards do not justify a more elaborate analysis. Thus, the decision tree is one practical analytical aid for which the modern manager should actually be able to perform the required simple computations.

However, in larger, complex problems, the information regarding the decision tree can be input into specially programmed computer routines. Use of a computer would be especially helpful in checking the sensitivity of the solution to various estimates, since the results from changes in the information can be obtained instantly. In addition, the calculations necessary to compute the value of perfect information could also be accomplished quite easily.

Interpretation of Results We continually emphasize that the expected value does not represent the actual profit or loss that the company will obtain as a result of its decision. Rather, one of the conditional outcomes will actually occur (if all the predictions are accurate). This is an important point that should not be overlooked by the manager. An alternative with a high expected value may have some small probability of leading to a disastrous result, and *such a result could actually happen*. If it does, it does not mean that the original decision was bad, but merely that an unfortunate conditional outcome occurred. All that the manager can hope for in situations involving risk is to keep the odds in his favor. However, if the manager is really averse to making a decision involving even a small probability of an undesirable outcome, he can compensate with another evaluative model, as we shall see in the following chapter.

As a second point, the results from the use of the decision tree should always be subjected to an analysis of their sensitivity to the predictions of the conditional outcomes and the probabilities of the chance events. One approach is to deliberately bias the outcomes and probabilities against the best alternative from the initial analysis and to recompute the expected values. If this alternative remains the most desirable even when this deliberate bias is introduced, the manager's confidence that he has identified the best alternative should be improved. However, if the rankings of the alternatives are changed drastically by this second analysis, he may be well advised to spend more time and effort in obtaining better predictions. The value of perfect information can be used as a guide in these efforts.

Advantages of Decision Trees The crucial question for the practicing manager is whether the use of a decision-making aid is really worth the effort. Will the actual decision be improved over what he would decide based on his intuition? This question is difficult to answer, since the manager seldom has the opportunity to make the same decision both with and without a decision making aid.

Certainly, we can point to numerous advantages of using decision trees. They force the manager to organize his thoughts and to specify his alternative decisions and the important events that will affect the outcomes from choosing each of these. Further, the decision tree can be scrutinized by others, and used as the basis for a discussion regarding the alternatives and the assumptions that have been made by the manager. This discussion can be carried on by a manager and his advisers or by a committee. Without being overly dramatic, we can say that the decision tree structure provides a useful *language* for discussing complex problems among those who understand the technology. Even when the actual computation of expected values is not carried out, the construction of the decision tree with outcomes described in qualitative terms can be an extremely useful exercise.

Disadvantages of Decision Trees The only objection to the use of decision trees is that problems in the real world are so complex that the tree expands beyond the limits of human comprehension. There are so many uncertain events and so many alternatives that the decision tree can quickly become a "bushy mess." However, at this point the involvement of the manager in the preliminary analysis of the problem is required to quickly eliminate certain alternatives and to aid in identifying the uncertain events that will have a major impact on the decision. There are no hard and fast rules for this pruning of the decision tree; it requires the judgment and, yes, perhaps the intuition of the manager. The final result of this combination of analysis and intuition would seem to provide the basis for improved decisions that the responsible manager is seeking.

Check Your Understanding

1. When a decision is made on the basis of a single criterion under certainty, why is it often easy to identify an acceptable evaluative model?

2. Explain what is meant by the phrase "order preserving transformation." Give two examples of such transformations.

3. Give an example of a decision involving a single criterion under certainty for which it is *not* appropriate to simply maximize or minimize the criterion.

4. Explain why the expected value evaluative model may be appropriate

for repetitive decisions but perhaps not appropriate for very significant decisions which are made rarely. Give an example of each type of decision.

5. Explain the difference between a good decision and a good outcome. Should managers be evaluated on the basis of their decisions or on the basis of the outcomes that result from their decisions? Discuss.

6. What is meant by the term "perfect information"?

7. What are the limitations of a tabular presentation of alternatives and events?

8. What are the advantages of a decision tree presentation of alternatives and events?

9. What is the role of the manager in a decision tree analysis of a substantive, real-world problem?

10. Suppose we have five alternatives under consideration, which result in the following monetary returns with certainty:

Alternative	Outcome
A_1	$ 20
A_2	100
A_3	10
A_4	50
A_5	70

a. Using the obvious evaluative model of maximizing returns $[U(O_i) = O_i]$, rank these alternatives.
b. Rank these same alternatives using the following evaluative models:

1) $U(O_i) = (2) (O_i) - 300$
2) $U(O_i) = (3) (O_i^2)$
3) $U(O_i) = O_i - (0.1) (O_i^2)$
4) $U(O_i) = \$1000/O_i$

c. Which of these alternative models are "order preserving transformations" of $U(O_i) = O_i$?
d. Would your answer to c) change if a sixth alternative A_6 with a certain outcome of $-\$20$ (a loss) were introduced?

11. Which of the three oil shale development strategies would be preferred for POCO if the probabilities in Table 3 were revised as follows:

	Lower Prices	Current Prices	Higher Prices	Embargo
a.	0.1	0.4	0.3	0.2
b.	0.0	0.3	0.4	0.3
c.	0.0	0.2	0.5	0.3

Use the expected value evaluative model and the data in Table 3 to determine your answers. What are the implications of this analysis? How does it relate to the value of perfect information for POCO?

12. Consider the three gambles A_1, A_2, and A_3 illustrated in Figure 2.
   a. Suppose your clairvoyant friend will predict the outcome of flipping the second coin in A_3, but not the first coin. He charges $0.50 for this service. Should you pay him?
   b. Now suppose he offers to predict the outcome of flipping the first coin *and* the outcome of the second coin in A_3 (if you select A_3) for only $1. Should you accept this offer?

13. Referring to Figure 7, what if POCO could spend additional funds immediately and determine if a breakthrough in the processing technology could be made *from the initial research-only strategy?* The probability of a breakthrough from the initial strategy of a combined research and development effort would remain at 0.3. How much would this information be worth? Draw a decision tree appropriate for analyzing this question and perform the necessary "roll back" calculations.

Problems

1. POCO owns a lease that will allow it to explore for oil on the Aleutian Islands just west of Alaska. They have been offered $80 million for this lease by the Essex Oil Company. The three possible results of the exploration are shown below, along with their associated probabilities and monetary returns. The latter are based on the most recent estimates by the POCO engineers.

Result	Probability	Monetary Outcome (millions of $)
Dry well	0.4	−100
Discovery of oil reserves of moderate size	0.4	200
Discovery of oil reserves of major proportions	0.2	300

   a. Draw a decision tree and compute the expected value of the decision to explore the islands. Should POCO sell the lease to Essex?

b. Do you think that the expected value evaluative model is appropriate for a decision such as this one? Would you use the results of this analysis if you were a manager at POCO? Discuss.

2. The objective of the U.S. Hurricane Modification Program is to determine whether any hurricane threatening the U.S. coast should be seeded with silver iodide crystals in an attempt to mitigate its destructive effects. In order to analyze this question, probability estimates were obtained on the likely impacts of seeding a hurricane on the maximum sustained surface wind speed. A predictive model was then developed to estimate the property damage that results from hurricanes with various wind speeds. As a result of the analysis, the following estimates were obtained for seeding and not seeding a hurricane:

Probability (Hurricane Seeded)	Probability (Hurricane not Seeded)	Change in Max. Sustained Wind (%)	Property Damage Loss (millions of $)
0.038	0.054	+32	335.8
0.143	0.206	+16	191.1
0.392	0.480	0	100.0
0.255	0.206	−16	46.7
0.172	0.054	−34	16.3

The cost of seeding a hurricane is relatively cheap, only $0.25 million dollars.
a. Compute the expected monetary values of the decisions to seed a hurricane and not to seed a hurricane.
b. Draw a decision tree to summarize the decisions and the outcomes.
c. As stated by Howard, Matheson, and North [1972]: " . . . the results of extensive sensitivity analysis may be summarized as follows: The expected loss in terms of property damage appears to be about 20 percent less if the hurricane is seeded. Varying the assumptions of the analysis causes this reduction to vary between 10 and 30 percent but does not change the preferred alternative." Place yourself in the position of a government administrator responsible for making the hurricane seeding decision. Why might you recommend against seeding, despite the results of this analysis? In other words, what considerations may have been left out of the analysis? Discuss.

3. Solve the example problem described in the Introduction to Part Two that was presented to the members of the UCLA Executive Program. Use the expected value evaluative model.

4. Consider the question of whether to take an umbrella to work. The best result would be not to take an umbrella on a pretty day. Suppose you consider this to be the nominal case and assign it a value of $0. You might carry an umbrella on a pretty day, which would be an unnecessary bother. Suppose you decide that you would pay $2 to avoid this. If it rains and you have an umbrella, you will stay dry. However, you would pay $4 to avoid the hassle of using the umbrella on a rainy day. If it rains and you do not have an um-

brella, you get soaking wet. You would pay $10 to avoid this inconvenience.

a. Set up a table like Table 1 which shows the alternative decisions, the possible events, and the outcomes. Give both a verbal description of the outcomes and the associated payments you would be willing to make to avoid them.

b. Using the expected value evaluative model with the payments, determine the best decision where the forecasts of the probability of rain are the following:
1) 0.0
2) 0.25
3) 0.5
4) 0.75
5) 1.0

c. What is the value of perfect information regarding rain, given each of the above forecasts?

5. Mid-Valley Manufacturers has the opportunity to bid on a government contract for 100,000 high pressure valves to be used in the hydraulic systems of aircraft. They estimate that these valves could be manufactured by their existing equipment at a cost of $12.50 per unit. However, one of their engineers has suggested a new process for manufacturing the valves.

The unit cost estimates for the new process are only $7.50 if all goes exceptionally well. If there are minor complications, the cost estimate is $9.50 per unit; but if major complications arise, the costs would be prohibitive, so they would have to return to the old process. The engineers estimate the probability of minor complications at 0.5, the probability of major complications at 0.2, and the probability of no complications at 0.3. The investment required for the new process is $100,000, which would not be recoverable even if the process is a failure.

The company must make its bid on the contract before the new process can be tested. The various bids under consideration and the estimated probability of obtaining the contract associated with each bid are shown below:

Bid	Probability of Receiving Contract
$17	0.2
14	0.6
12	0.9

a. Construct a decision tree to analyze this problem using the expected value evaluative model. What should Mid-Valley bid? Which process should they use if they get the contract? Does the choice of the process depend on the bid price?

b. What would be the value to Mid-Valley of resolving the risk regarding the new process?

c. For an investment of $20,000, the company can conduct a pilot test on the new process. Unfortunately, the results of the pilot test would not be conclusive. However, if the results are positive, the engineers would revise their probability estimates to 0.6 for no complications, 0.3 for minor complications, and only 0.1 for major complications. If the results of the test are negative, the probabilities would remain as before. The probability is 0.5 that the results will be positive. If they receive the contract, should Mid-Valley conduct this pilot test? Does your answer depend on the bid price? Why or why not?

6. A chemical company must decide whether to build a small plant or a large one to manufacture a new product with an expected market life of 10 years.* If the company decides to build a small plant now, then finds demand high during the initial period, it can choose to expand its plant after two years.

Marketing estimates indicate a probability of 0.6 of a large market in the long run, and a 0.4 probability of a long-term low demand, developing initially as follows:

Demand Pattern	Probability
Initially high demand, sustained high	0.60
Initially high demand (yrs. 1–2), long-term low (yrs. 3–10).	0.10
Initially low demand, long-term low	0.30
Initially low demand, long-term high	0.0

Estimates of annual income are made under the assumptions of each alternative demand pattern:

1) A large plant with high volume would yield $1,000,000 annually in cash flow.
2) A large plant with low volume would yield only $100,000 because of high fixed costs and inefficiencies.
3) A small plant with low demand would be economical and would yield annual cash income of $400,000.
4) A small plant, during an initial period of high demand, would yield $450,000 per year, but this yield would drop to $300,000 yearly in the long run because of competition. (The market would be larger than under alternative 3, but would be divided up among more competitors.)
5) If the small plant were expanded to meet sustained high demand, it would yield $700,000 cash flow annually (less efficient than a large plant built initially).
6) If the small plant were expanded but high demand were not sustained, estimated annual cash flow would be $50,000.

It is estimated further that a large plant would cost $3 million to put into operation, a small plant would cost $1.3 million, and the expansion of the small plant would cost an additional $2.2 million.

* From J. F. Magee, "Decision Trees for Decision Making," *Harvard Business Review*, July–August 1964.

a. Draw a decision tree to structure the problem.

b. What should the initial decision of the company be on the basis of the expected value evaluative model?

c. Repeat the above analysis using a discount factor of 0.10 to adjust for the time value of money. Assume that the first year cash flow is not discounted, the second year cash flow is discounted one year, etc.

d. If you were the manager of this company, what additional information would you wish to obtain before making your decision? Discuss.

7. A large manufacturer of heavy capital equipment operates on a multinational basis.* The firm's treasurer was concerned about a large, recently completed sale of equipment to a French firm. The balance on the terms of this sale was 25 million francs (about $5 million at the current exchange rate), which was receivable in a little less than 30 days. Recent events in France had shaken people's confidence in the franc. The current exchange rate for the franc was 0.2011 U.S. dollars, just above the lower rate of $0.2010 guaranteed by the French government. In addition, the franc could be bought or sold "forward" 30 days at only $0.2000, which reflected the possibility that it would be devalued.

If a devaluation did occur, the firm would lose a great deal of money. For example, a 20 percent devaluation would result in a loss of about $1 million.

The treasurer has two basic alternatives. He can "hedge" against devaluation by selling "forward" the 25 million francs for a sure return of $5 million. If he does *not* hedge, he estimates that there is only one chance in twenty that a new government will be formed within 30 days. If the old government remains in power, he is certain that the franc will *not* be devalued, and the return will be $5,025,000. However, if a new government is formed, he estimates that there is a 0.5 chance of an immediate devaluation.

Given a devaluation, the treasurer estimates that the possible range is from 5 to 20 percent, so he assigns returns of $4,750,000; $4,500,000; $4,250,000; and $4,000,000 equal probabilities of 0.25.

a. Construct a decision tree and analyze this problem. What is the better decision on the basis of the expected value evaluative model?

b. The argument has been made that a large company should *never* hedge against exchange devaluations because the market for currency futures is "perfect." Thus, it represents the expectations of persons involved in the market who obviously know more than a corporate treasurer (see Wheelwright [1975]). Would you support this argument or prefer the use of the decision tree? Discuss.

References

Brown, R., "Do Managers Find Decision Theory Useful?" *Harvard Business Review,* Vol. 48, 1970.

Howard, R. A., "Social Decision Analysis," *Proceedings of the IEEE,* Vol. 63, No. 3, March 1975.

* From S. C. Wheelwright, "Applying Decision Theory to Improve Corporate Management of Currency-Exchange Risks," *California Management Review,* Summer 1975.

Howard, R. A. (ed.), "Special Issue on Decision Analysis," *IEEE Transactions on Systems Science and Cybernetics*, Vol. SSC-4, No. 3, September 1968.

———, J. E. Matheson, and D. W. North, "The Decision to Seed Hurricanes," *Science*, Vol. 176, June 17, 1972.

Jones, J. M., *Statistical Decision Making*, Richard D. Irwin, Inc., Homewood, Ill., 1977.

Magee, J. F., "Decision Trees for Decision Making," *Harvard Business Review*, July–August 1964.

———, "How to Use Decision Trees in Capital Investment," *Harvard Business Review*, September–October 1964.

Raiffa, H., *Decision Analysis*, Addison-Wesley, Reading, Mass., 1968.

———, *Analysis for Decision Making* (an audiographic, self-instructional course), Encyclopedia Britannica Educational Corporation, Chicago, 1974.

Schlaifer, R., *Analysis of Decisions Under Uncertainty*, McGraw-Hill, New York, 1969.

Wheelwright, S. C., "Applying Decision Theory to Improve Corporate Management of Currency-Exchange Risks," *California Management Review*, Vol. 17, No. 4, Summer 1975.

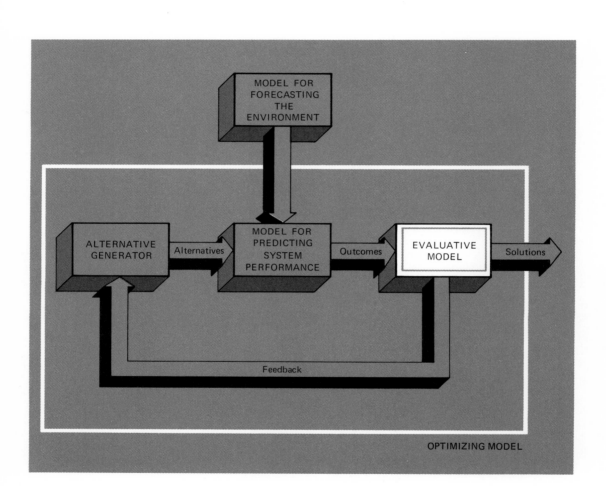

3

Utility Theory and Subjective Probability

We have seen that the expected value evaluative model can be a useful guide to decisions involving risk, especially when the decisions are to be made over and over again, as in many low- to middle-level company decisions. The expected value represents the "average" return a manager expects to receive given that the same (or similar) decision is made many times. Thus, a manager who makes many capital budgeting decisions under conditions of risk might be well advised to adopt the expected value evaluative model as a useful aid.

However, suppose you face a decision involving risk, and you make the decision only once. For example, suppose you are offered the following choice, and you have only one opportunity to accept it. You may receive $25 with certainty, or you may accept the results of a gamble in which a fair coin will be tossed. If the coin falls on heads, you will win $150; but if the coin lands on tails, you will lose $50. Which do you prefer? Think hard about this. Many people, including perhaps yourself, would prefer taking the $25 even though the expected value of the gamble is $50, *twice as much* [(0.5) ($150) + (0.5)(−$50) = $50]. Does this mean they are irrational? No, they are simply expressing their feelings,and they would prefer to accept the $25 rather than run the risk of losing $50 even though there is an equal chance of winning $150.

If the people who prefer the certain value of $25 are not irrational, then something must be wrong with the expected value evaluative model. This conclusion would also be incorrect. Expected value is a useful evaluative model only so long as it adequately reflects the preferences of the decision maker. In situations involving similar choices that are repeated many times or that have relatively low stakes, the decision maker may feel that his preferences are consistent with the simple expected value of the outcomes. However, in decisions made only once involving relatively high stakes, he may wish to avoid the possibility of an unfortunate outcome, even though the "odds" are actually in his favor. If so, we would say he is risk averse.

Most persons are risk averse in their decision making, at least in some decision situations, although the degree of risk aversion varies greatly and is a personal matter. A few individuals, including some oil wildcatters, have actually expressed preferences that indicate they prefer to accept high risk situations. For example, they might prefer accepting the gamble we have posed to accepting $60 with certainty, because there is a "good chance" they can win $150. Numerous experiments with subjects have shown that such individuals are in the minority.

The really important decisions that a manager makes generally represent unique opportunities and involve high stakes. Since the expected value evaluative model may not be appropriate for such decisions, the manager should be aware of alternative evaluative models. As we shall see, these evaluative models have the disadvantage of requiring the decision maker to explicitly reveal information about his preferences. Therefore, the information requirements are much more demanding than those of the simple expected value evaluative models. Nevertheless, these evaluative models do aid the decision maker in dealing with perhaps the most important class of problems that he must solve — one-time, high-stake problems.

The requirement that the decision maker provide information about his preferences is related to another issue — the probabilities that are used in assessing risky situations. In some situations, we may be able to obtain "objective" probabilities from predictive models. In other circumstances, we may not have access to predictive models. Therefore, these probabilities will also be based on the subjective judgment of the decision maker. Again, we shall be concerned with how to acquire the necessary information from the decision maker.

UTILITY THEORY: SUBJECTIVE EXPRESSIONS OF WORTH

Utility theory provides a means of capturing subjective expressions of worth. The expected value of several conditional outcomes does not consider what each conditional outcome is actually worth to the decision-maker. Thus, we need some means of transforming conditional outcomes into measures of worth or utility. Let us think about how this might be done.

Consider again the three gambles introduced in Chapter 2 and displayed in the decision tree in Figure 2 of Chapter 2. The conditional outcomes are expressed in dollars. How can we transform them into measures of utility? The best and worst conditional outcomes are "win $20" and "lose $10" respectively. To get started, we might assign the conditional outcome "win $20" a utility of 1.00, and the conditional outcome "lose $10" a utility of 0.0. Then we would assign each of the other conditional outcomes some utility between 1.00 and 0.0, depending on how it compares with "win $20" and "lose $10." Thus, the utility number we assign to "win $10" will be larger than the one we assign to "win $2," since we would prefer the former to the latter.

We might assign these numbers on the basis of our personal reactions regarding what seems right. For example, you might think that winning $14 would make you almost as happy as winning $20, so you would assign the conditional outcome "win $14" a utility of perhaps 0.9. Similarly, you might think that you would be really happy if you won $20, but really sad if you lost $10. If you broke even, that would be about halfway between these two extremes *in terms of your feelings*, so you would give "win/lose $0" a utility of 0.5. You might continue assigning utility values and search your own mind until you felt comfortable with the responses. However, such a process is *ad hoc*, and you may feel uncomfortable with it no matter how long or how hard you think about the problem.

Constructing the Utility Function

What we really want to do is generate values for these outcomes that can be used in risky situations. Therefore, we should introduce risk into a procedure for obtaining these values. Consider a simple gamble where you win $20 if a fair coin lands on heads but lose $10 if it lands on tails. The coin will be flipped only once, and you either win or pay off immediately. As an alternative, you can take a fixed sum rather than play the game. Suppose you are offered the choice of taking the expected value of the game or having the coin flipped. The expected value of this game is (0.5) $($20) + (0.5)$ $(-$10) =$ $5. Which would you prefer? Think seriously about this.

To continue the example, suppose you responded after considerable thought that you would take $5. Instead of being paid, you are asked a similar question, except this time the payoff is only $2 for sure, or the result of the coin flip. Again, suppose you prefer the certain payoff of $2 because you really do not like the 0.5 chance of losing $10. The next question, then, is would you *pay* $1 rather than have the coin flipped? Suppose you respond that you would accept the result from the gamble rather than pay to avoid it. After a few more questions of this sort, suppose you finally agree that if you are offered *any* certain winning, you would accept this certain payoff, but you would not *pay* to avoid the coin flip. Thus, at $0 for certain, you are indifferent about having the coin flipped. That is to say, you would just as soon walk away without winning or losing anything as play the game, or you would accept the result of the coin flip. You just do not care at that point.

Thus, you are indifferent between receiving $0 for sure and the gamble shown in Figure 1. We would like to use this information to assign a utility number to the outcome of winning or losing $0 (breaking even), relative to the utility number 1.0 assigned earlier to winning $20, and of 0.0 assigned to losing $10. These utility numbers are also shown in parentheses in Figure 1.

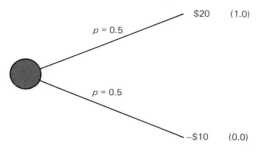

Figure 1. The gamble

In our previous analysis, we have used the expected value of the conditional outcomes of a chance point to replace the chance point in a decision tree. This time, let us compute the expected value of the *utility numbers* associated with the conditional outcomes of the chance point, obtaining $(0.5) (1.0) + (0.5) (0.0) = 0.5$. Much as before, we can let 0.5 be the utility number that we assign to this chance point. Since we were indifferent between breaking even ($0) and this risky situation, we will assign $0 a utility value of 0.5 also. This procedure is summarized in Table 1.

We can continue this procedure by creating 50–50 gambles between $0 and win $20, and between lose $10 and $0. For example, suppose you are asked to indicate the least amount you would take for certain, rather than have a fair coin flipped with a $20 payoff on heads and a break-even payoff on tails. If you think hard about this question, you might say to yourself:

> Well, I would certainly rather have $15, and also I would prefer $10. However, I would rather flip the coin than accept only $5 for sure, so it's somewhere between $5 and $10. Let's see, I would prefer flipping the coin if I were offered only $6, $7, or even $8. However, if I could get $9 for sure . . . well, I think I would take it. So, the least I would take is somewhere between $8 and $9, probably closer to $8, say $8.25.

Thus, we assign $8.25 a utility number equal to the expected value of the utility numbers of the new gamble, which is $(0.5) (1.0) + (0.5) (0.5) = 0.75$.

Now suppose we ask a similar question regarding a coin flip between losing $10 and breaking even. This time you say you would pay up to $5.85 to avoid facing this coin toss. Notice that you are willing to *pay more* than the expected monetary value of the coin flip in order to avoid the possibility of losing $10. The expected value of the utility number for this gamble is 0.25, which we assign to "lose $5.85."

What we are obtaining are values for some function that assigns utility numbers to conditional outcomes. We call such a function a utility function and denote it as $u(O_i)$. For example, we have $u(+\$20) = 1.0$, $u(-\$10) = 0.0$, $u(\$0) = 0.5$, $u(\$8.25) = 0.75$, and $u(-\$5.85) = 0.25$. We could continue this process to obtain more utility numbers by creating hypothetical gambles

TABLE 1. Summary of the Estimation of $u(\$0) = 0.5$

Question	Response	Implication
Do you prefer $5 for sure or the coin toss in Figure 1?	$5	utility of $5 is greater than 0.5
Do you prefer $2 for sure or the coin toss in Figure 1?	$2	utility of $2 is greater than 0.5
Do you prefer to pay $1 or to have the coin toss in Figure 1?	coin toss	utility of −$1 is less than 0.5
Do you prefer to neither gain nor lose any money for sure ($0), or to have the coin toss in Figure 1?	indifferent	utility of $0 is equal to 0.5

between $20 and $8.25, between $8.25 and $0, between $0 and −$5.85, and between −$5.85 and −$10.

As an alternative, we could ask the same type of question in another way. Suppose you are offered the choice of either $5 for sure or a gamble with payoffs of "win $20" or "lose $10." If the probability of winning $20 is 0.5 (and of losing $10 is $1.0 - 0.5 = 0.5$), you say you would prefer taking the $5. Now suppose there is a 0.9 chance of winning $20, but only a 0.1 chance of losing $10. Then, you might prefer the gamble. What we are looking for is the *probability* of winning the $20 that would make you indifferent between the $5 for certain and the gamble. To help you find this probability, questions such as those above might be asked explicitly. Alternatively, you might find it easier to ask such questions of yourself.

After much thought, suppose you say that if the odds favor the outcome of "win $20" by at least 2 to 1, then you would take the gamble. Thus, the probability of winning $20 must be about 0.67 for you to be indifferent between the $5 for sure and the gamble, so we have $u(\$5) = 0.67$.

We can now plot these utility function values as shown in Figure 2, and sketch a smooth curve (the upper white line) that goes through these points. Notice that the curve is "bowed" slightly. This bow is a characteristic of utility functions that reflect risk averse preferences. Relatively more "bow" in the curve reflects relatively more risk aversion. A person who is risk neutral would make choices based directly on the expected values of the conditional outcomes of a gamble, and his utility function would be a straight line (also shown in Figure 2 for comparison). The utility curve of a risk taker, a person who prefers high risk situations, would have an "inverted bow" as illustrated by the dashed curve in Figure 2. It is also possible that a person might be a risk taker for certain values of money and a risk avoider for others, so he would have an S-shaped utility curve.

To summarize, we have described two methods of determining a utility function. The steps of the first method are as follows:

1. Select the best conditional outcome O_i^* and the worst conditional outcome O_{i*}. Let $u(O_i^*) = 1.0$ and $u(O_{i*}) = 0.0$.

2. Ask the decision maker to identify some other outcome, $\overline{O}_i$, such that he would be indifferent between receiving $\overline{O}_i$ with certainty or accepting the results of a 50–50 gamble between the best and worst conditional outcomes, O_i^* and O_{i*}. Then, $u(\overline{O}_i) = (0.5)\,(u(O_i^*)) + (0.5)\,(u(O_{i*}))$, the expected value of the utility function values assigned to the conditional outcomes appearing in the gamble.

3. Continue by constructing 50–50 gambles between O_i^* and $\overline{O}_i$, and between O_{i*} and $\overline{O}_i$. Repeat the procedure until enough points have been obtained to determine a curve as shown in Figure 2.

The second method is very similar to the first, except this time we specify O_i^*, O_{i*}, *and* $\overline{O}_i$ in advance. We ask the decision maker to specify the probability of getting O_i^* in the gamble that will make him indifferent between receiving $\overline{O}_i$ with certainty or accepting the results of the gamble.

These two approaches for estimating utility functions are the most commonly used ones and have a sound theoretical basis. Other approaches have been suggested; these are reviewed by Fishburn [1967]. (For a more detailed discussion, see Keeney and Raiffa [1976, Chapter 4.]

The utility function through the points can be drawn by hand in many cases. As an alternative, statistical curve fitting techniques can be used. For

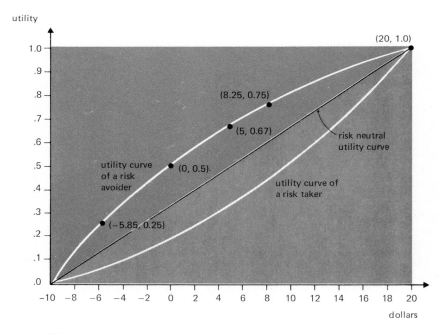

Figure 2. A utility function

theoretical reasons that are beyond the scope of this discussion, a utility function for a risk averse individual can often be approximated by a function of the form $u(O_i) = a + b \ln (O_i + c)$, where c is chosen to ensure $O_i + c > 0$. By introducing a new variable $z = \ln (O_i + c)$, this function becomes linear in z, and the curve can be fit using simple linear regression (see Appendix C) with alternative values of c until the best fit is determined. The curve shown in Figure 2 corresponds to the utility function $u(O_i) = -1.66 + 0.721 \ln (O_i + 20)$.

The Utility Function As an Evaluative Model

The purpose of constructing a utility function for a decision maker is to use it in an evaluative model. In the decision tree, we replaced a chance point with conditional outcomes by the expected value of the conditional outcomes. Thus we implicitly assumed that the decision maker was indifferent between the chance point and the expected value of the conditional outcomes. As we have discussed, this assumption is only appropriate if the decision maker is risk neutral, but many persons are risk averse.

The assignment of the utility numbers was based on the following procedure. Consider a chance point or a gamble where the utility numbers of the conditional outcomes are known. Find a certain outcome such that the decision maker is indifferent between receiving that outcome and the chance point. Then assign that certain outcome a utility number equal to the expected value of the *utility numbers* associated with the conditional outcomes. The certain outcome may not be the expected value of the conditional outcomes, but by our rules for constructing the utility function, the utility number associated with the certain outcome will be the expected value of the utility numbers of the conditional outcomes.

This result suggests that rather than using the expected value of the conditional outcomes to evaluate alternatives, we can use the expected value of the utility numbers associated with these outcomes. This evaluative model is identical to the simple expected value model except for the introduction of the utility function u, which is unique to a particular decision maker. The practical disadvantage of the model is that it requires more information, since we must interact with the decision maker to obtain an estimate of u. Further, the result will be different for different decision makers, so there is no single answer.

Some persons would object to the use of this model on the grounds that it is not objective, as is the simple expected value model, because it incorporates subjective judgments. However, as we have stressed, the proper criterion for choosing an evaluative model is how well it captures the true preferences of the decision maker. Since the expected utility model explicitly incorporates these preferences, it is superior on this criterion. Notice that if the decision maker is actually risk neutral and is willing to act on the basis of the expected values of conditional outcomes, this attitude will also

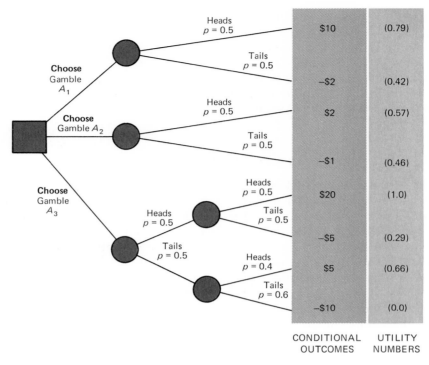

Heads
$p = 0.5$ $10   (0.79)

Tails
$p = 0.5$ −$2   (0.42)

Choose
Gamble
A_1

Choose
Gamble A_2

Heads
$p = 0.5$ $2   (0.57)

Tails
$p = 0.5$ −$1   (0.46)

Choose
Gamble
A_3

Heads
$p = 0.5$ $20   (1.0)

Tails
$p = 0.5$ −$5   (0.29)

Heads
$p = 0.5$

Tails
$p = 0.5$

Heads
$p = 0.4$ $5   (0.66)

Tails
$p = 0.6$ −$10   (0.0)

CONDITIONAL   UTILITY
OUTCOMES   NUMBERS

Figure 3. Utility numbers for the gamble selection decision tree

be reflected as a special case of the utility function, which is the straight line shown in Figure 2.

An Example with Gambles Consider again the problem of choosing among three alternative gambles. The decision tree for analyzing the problem is shown again in Figure 3. However, this time, the utility function values associated with the outcomes are shown in parentheses to the right of the outcomes. These values were obtained from the utility function we constructed earlier, as illustrated in Figure 4. Now let us roll back this decision tree by taking expected values at the chance points. However, rather than taking the expected values of the conditional outcomes, we take the expected values of the utility numbers associated with those outcomes. Performing these calculations, we have the results shown in Figure 5, with A_1 receiving an expected utility number of 0.608, A_2 of 0.516, and A_3 of 0.455. According to the expected utility evaluative model, the decision maker for whom we constructed this utility function should prefer A_1 to A_2 or A_3, and A_2 to A_3.

This result is the same for A_1, which was also preferred according to the expected value of the conditional outcomes model. However, using the ex-

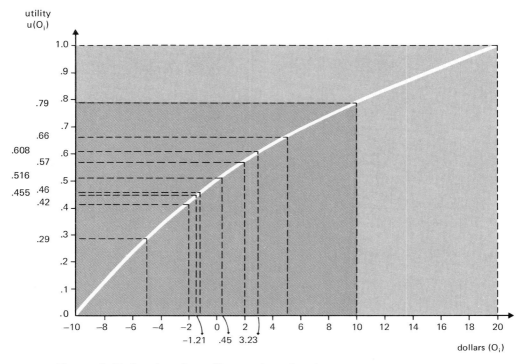

Figure 4. Estimating the utility numbers for the gamble selection problem

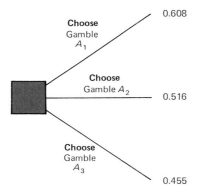

Figure 5. The results of the analysis with utility numbers

pected value of the conditional outcomes, A_3 with a value of $1.75 was preferred to A_2 with a value of $0.50. By the expected utility model, A_2 is preferred to A_3. Looking at the decision tree (Figure 3), we see that very little risk is involved in A_2. Although you can win only $2, you can lose only $1, at worst. However, A_3 includes the possibilities of losing either $5 or $10. These negative outcomes are penalized heavily by the utility function, so the "safer" alternative, A_2, is now preferred to A_3.

We can also transform these utility numbers associated with the alternatives back into dollars. These results represent the least amount the decision maker would accept for certain in each case, rather than choose the gamble. For A_1, the monetary value corresponding to a utility number of 0.608 can also be read from the curve in Figure 4, and is $3.23. Similarly, the dollar value corresponding to 0.516 or A_2 is $0.45, and for A_3 it is $-1.21. Notice that each of these numbers is less than the expected value of the conditional outcomes for the gambles, as we would expect since the decision maker is risk averse. Note also that this decision maker would actually be willing to *pay* up to $1.21 to avoid the third gamble, A_3, even though the expected value of the conditional outcomes is $1.75.

An Example with POCO   Now let us reconsider the oil shale problem of POCO. Suppose we can find the decision maker in POCO who is responsible for this decision (perhaps not an easy task). He may say that for relatively small investment decisions, POCO is willing to make decisions based on the expected value of the conditional outcomes. Since many such decisions are made, they expect to actually realize total returns roughly equivalent to the total of these expected values. However, for a major decision, such as the oil shale development strategy, the possibility of losing up to $500 million is a serious outcome. Therefore, he agrees to answer several questions involving 50–50 gambles, and we eventually construct the utility curve for him displayed in Figure 6.

You may question why we should use this decision maker's utility function. What we really want is a utility function for POCO, if such a thing exists. Perhaps so, however, we may assume that the decision maker is not reflecting his *personal* risk aversion in his responses. Rather he is reflecting his view of how POCO should respond in risky situations. If so, his responses may provide the basis for the best approximation to a utility function for POCO that we can hope to obtain. After all, POCO does not actually make decisions; this person makes the decisions. For an example of an attempt to determine such a utility function for a real company, see the account by Spetzler [1968].

Now, let us substitute the corresponding utility function values for the conditional outcomes in the decision tree for POCO, as shown in Figure 7. Rolling back the tree, we obtain expected utility function values of 0.722 for the initial research-only strategy, 0.752 for the research and development strategy, and 0.633 for the crash development strategy. These results and the expected utility function values at the other chance branch points and decision points are shown in Figure 7. Notice that the relative ranking of these three strategies is the same when the utility function values are used as when

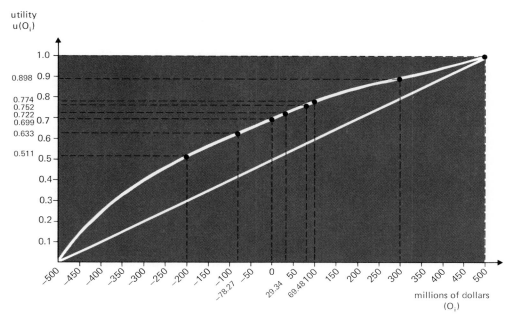

Figure 6. A utility function for POCO

the expected values of the conditional outcomes were computed. The certain returns corresponding to these utility values, which can be obtained from Figure 6, are $29.34 million for the initial research-only strategy, $69.48 million for the initial research and development strategy, and a loss of $78.27 million for the crash development strategy. Again, each of these certain equivalents is less than the corresponding expected value of the associated conditional outcomes.

An Example with Nonmonetary Outcomes   It is important to realize that utility functions can be constructed over outcomes other than money. For example, suppose an elementary school principal is trying to decide whether to continue his or her current reading program for third graders or to adopt a new reading program based on a new approach to teaching reading.

The performance of students in a subject area such as reading can be measured by a standard test in terms of percentile scores. The principal feels certain that if the current program is continued, the third graders would score at the 50 percentile level on such a test. The new program has had a mixed record. Where it has truly been successful, the reading score of a class generally increases relative to conventional programs (such as the current one) by about 10 percentile points. However, in some cases it has little effect. Moreover, in a few situations, the results have been disastrous. The teachers have not been able to modify their methods to the new materials, and scores have actually fallen by as much as 15 percentile points.

Based on a knowledge of the students and teachers, this principal estimates the probabilities of the possible effects of the new program as follows:

Effect of Reading Program	Probability
Performance increased to 60th percentile	0.4
Performance unchanged (50th percentile)	0.4
Performance decreased to 35th percentile	0.2

Should the principal adopt this new program?

The answer to this question depends on how one values the different outcomes expressed in percentiles. If we calculate the expected value of the conditional outcomes of the decision to adopt the new program, we obtain $(0.4)(60) + (0.4)(50) + (0.2)(35) = 51$. Since this result is slightly higher than the outcome received with the current program, the new program should be introduced on the basis of the expected value evaluative model. However, this does not explicitly consider preferences regarding the relative value of these percentile scores, especially in risky choice situations such as this one.

Therefore, suppose we ask the principal a series of questions and obtain an estimate of his/her utility function for the performance of a class of students as measured in percentile scores. The results are shown in Figure 8. Calculating the expected utility of the conditional outcomes, we obtain $(0.4)(0.83) + (0.4)(0.78) + (0.2)(0.63) = 0.77$. The utility number 0.77 corresponds to a percentile score of 49, which the principal should be willing to accept for certain rather than choose this alternative involving risk. This is 1 percentile point lower than the score of 50 which pupils will score with the current program. Therefore, the principal should feel virtually indifferent between the alternative of adopting the new program and the alternative of continuing this existing program. Notice that this result differs slightly from the one based on the expected value evaluative model.

The utility curve in Figure 8 was actually obtained by interviewing 72 different elementary school principals and eliciting their preferences for percentile scores. Notice that this utility curve can be closely approximated by three linear segments over the following ranges of test performance: 0 to 15, 15 to 50, and 50 to 100. The difference in utility values between 0 and 15 is about equal to the difference in utility values between 15 and 50. This result indicates that elementary school principals associate great value with improving student performance from the worst possible score to the 15th percentile. Of nearly equal value, but involving a larger difference in student achievement, is improving student performance from the 15th to the 50th percentile. It is not surprising that the slope of the utility function changes abruptly at the 50th percentile, since the 50th percentile is the "na-

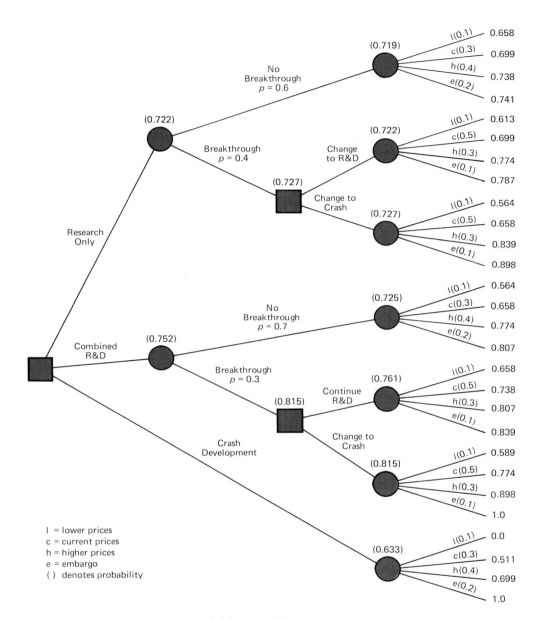

Figure 7. The decision tree for POCO with utility numbers

tional average" and becomes a "target" or aspiration level for the principals. A principal would probably experience less criticism if the school's performance is at least average than if the school's performance is below average. It is interesting to note that this utility curve exhibits the "bowed" appearance

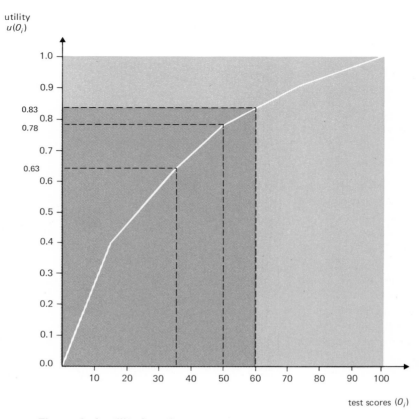

utility
$u(O_i)$

test scores (O_i)

Figure 8. A utility function on test scores

of a risk averse utility function that is commonly found when the criterion is money.

The information regarding elementary school principals' utility functions has been incorporated into a procedure for selecting educational subject areas for new programs. This procedure has been packaged in a "do-it-yourself" kit, and has been made available to all elementary school principals (see Hoepfner et al. [1973]). The details of this study are described by Dyer, Farrell, and Bradley [1973].

The Assumptions Underlying Utility Functions

We have attempted to provide an intuitively appealing introduction to the subject of utility theory. However, there exists a formal body of knowledge that supports these ideas. The concept of a utility function is dependent on a set of assumptions regarding rational behavior. These assumptions are, loosely speaking, the following:

1. The decision maker can compare any two alternatives and consistently state his preference for one or state that he is indifferent between the two alternatives.

2. Suppose the decision maker prefers A_1 to A_2, and he prefers A_2 to A_3. Then he must prefer A_1 to A_3. That is, his preferences are transitive.

3. Suppose the decision maker prefers A_1 to A_2, and he prefers A_2 to A_3. There must exist then some probability p such that the decision maker is indifferent between A_2 and a gamble with a p chance of obtaining A_1 and a $(1 - p)$ chance of obtaining A_3.

4. Suppose the decision maker is indifferent between A_1 and A_2. Then for any alternative A_3 and the probability p, the decision maker is indifferent between a gamble with a p chance of obtaining A_1 and a $(1 - p)$ chance of obtaining A_3, and a gamble with a p chance of obtaining A_2 and a $(1 - p)$ chance of obtaining A_3.

Most people are not perfectly consistent in their decisions at all times and may violate one or more of the above assumptions in some situations. However, these assumptions seem to provide a definition of behavior that agrees with the notion of rational decision making. Further, if one accepts these assumptions, it follows that maximizing expected utility function values is the appropriate evaluative model for use in risky choice situations.

In problems involving a single criterion under certainty, it may also be necessary to construct a utility function for use as an evaluative model where the decision maker has a "goal" in mind for the criterion. For example, an individual purchasing an automobile might consider 300 horsepower to be superior to any smaller value because of performance considerations *and* superior to any larger value because of safety considerations. In such a case, it is not true that either more or less of the criterion is always preferred. These same techniques can be used to construct a utility function for use as an evaluative model in these instances.

The utility functions we constructed were all chosen so that $u(O_i^*) = 1.0$ and $u(O_{i*}) = 0.0$. This selection for the upper and lower bounds for the utility function values is often used since it provides certain computational conveniences. However, any other values could have been selected, so long as $u(O_i^*) > u(O_{i*})$. Thus, the utility function u is not unique. Suppose v is another utility function that faithfully represents the preferences of the same decision maker in risky choice situations. Then it will be possible to write $u(O_i) = av(O_i) + b$, for $a > 0$ and b any arbitrary constant. That is, any *positive linear transformation* of u is also a valid utility function for a decision maker. However, nonlinear transformations of u are *not* equivalent to u, as they were in decisions involving a single criterion under certainty. Thus, we say that a utility function u that satisfies the four assumptions of rational decision making is unique to a *positive linear* transformation.

SUBJECTIVE PROBABILITIES

In the examples for POCO, we used probabilities of low, current, and high prices, an embargo, and a technological breakthrough. We now consider how these probabilities might be obtained from subjective estimates. In order to construct a utility function, it is necessary for the decision maker to explicitly reveal information about his preferences. In some real-world situations, it may also be necessary for the decision maker to reveal information about his subjective estimates for the probabilities of the occurrences of future events.

We have assumed in Part Two that predictive models are available to the decision maker, and his task is simply to evaluate the outcomes of various alternatives. In many situations, such predictive models are unavailable, especially for the purpose of forecasting those future events that may affect the outcomes for an alternative. Therefore, we shall consider how similar approaches to those used in constructing a utility function might be applied to the problem of estimating the probability of the occurrence of an event. In such circumstances, the decision maker or some other individual will actually be playing the role of the predictive model of the environment.

Subjective Versus Objective Probabilities

The concept of probability is often introduced in terms of the notion of a *relative frequency of occurrence*. Most of us would agree that a fair coin has a 0.5 probability of landing on heads and a 0.5 probability of landing on tails when it is tossed. Thus, if we flip the coin many times, we would expect the coin to land on heads on roughly *half* of the tosses. The more times we toss the coin, the closer we would expect the *relative frequency* of heads to approach 0.5, the probability of the coin landing on heads on a single toss. The definition of the probability of an event as the relative frequency of the occurrence of that event in a long series of trials is *objective*, since it relates to a phenomenon we can observe in the real world.

Suppose you are shown a coin and asked to state the probability that it will land on heads if it is tossed. You might assume that it is a fair coin and state that this probability is 0.5. In doing so, you would say that this is an objective probability. Now suppose you are shown a thumb tack, and asked to state the probability that it will land "point up" if it is tossed. More than likely, you have never conducted a long series of experiments of tossing thumb tacks and observing the relative frequency of a "point up." Moreover, you may have neither any information regarding such experiments by others nor the information and skills necessary to develop a predictive model based on the laws of physics. Nevertheless, you are forced to respond. After some reflection, suppose you say: "Well, I feel that the thumb tack is more likely to fall point up than point down. In fact, based on my understanding of how physical bodies behave when they hit the ground, I would say it is about twice as likely to land point up. Therefore, I would estimate the probability of a 'point up,' given the toss of a thumb tack, at about 0.67."

Since this estimate is not based on any historical experience or rigorous analysis, we would call 0.67 a *subjective probability*. In decisions faced by managers, subjective probabilities generally play a much more important role than objective probabilities. Organizations and their environments are in a constant state of flux, making the development of actual data on the relative frequency of important events a difficult task. In some cases, predictive models can be used to provide "objective" probability estimates. However, in most cases, the assignment of a probability to an event will be based on some individual's personal experience and understanding of the event, and it will thus be *subjective*. Further, it is only natural that two persons might make different probability assignments to the same event, since their experience and understanding of the event may differ.

The decision maker is the person who has the responsibility for the decision to be made. It follows that the decision should be based on *his* preferences and expectations regarding future events. But he may choose to designate other persons as his experts when it comes to estimating the probability of occurrence of a particular event, since the expert might have a better information base.

In a practical application, experts will be drawn from different fields. Estimates of market variables, such as sales volume, are likely to come from the marketing department; production variables, such as manufacturing costs, will be provided by engineers. Some variables may even require experts from outside the organization.

In much the same manner as in the construction of utility functions, we could ask these experts to "think hard" and give us these probability assessments. However, the fact that a person is an expert in a particular area does not mean that it will be easy for him to express his judgments in probabalistic terms. Most people have difficulty in translating their feelings about risk into a probability number. For this reason, they can not directly express their knowledge about an event in terms of a probability distribution. Techniques should be used that employ simple, understandable concepts to aid them in expressing these probabilities.

Assessing Subjective Probabilities

Reconsidering the problem of POCO offers a good context for discussing assessment of subjective probabilities. An important factor in determining POCO's final profit (or loss) for its oil shale development strategy is the near-term price of crude oil. Suppose the manager wishes to obtain an estimate of this price. Further, we shall assume that POCO has no formal predictive models to provide these estimates (although many oil companies actually do have such models). Therefore, the manager identifies the person in the organization with the most knowledge in this area, perhaps the chief purchasing agent. Rather than simply asking for the probability of crude selling at different prices, the manager tries to assist the purchasing agent in determining these estimates. First the manager ensures that there is no ambiguity in his questions. He might tell the purchasing agent that he is looking for the agent's estimate of the probability of the various prices of crude oil five years hence, for example, under the assumption that *there is no oil embargo*. Further, the purchasing agent is to assume that no breakthrough in oil shale processing technology will occur. Then the manager begins a dialogue.

The manager may wish to simply describe an event to the purchasing agent and ask for the estimate of a probability. He may ask, "What is the probability that crude oil prices will be $10 per barrel or lower five years from now, given that the current price is $11 per barrel?" The purchasing agent may find it difficult to respond to that question. He might say, for example, that the "chances are slim," but that he can not be more precise.

The Probability Wheel As an aid to the purchasing agent, the manager might use a probability wheel—a disk with two sectors, one light and the other dark. A pointer is spun in the center of the disk and lands on either the light or the dark zone (see Figure 9). The dark zone can be adjusted to any size.

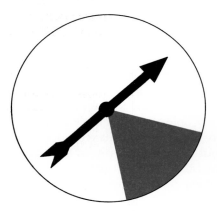

Figure 9. A probability wheel

The manager can begin with approximately one-half of the disk dark. He can ask the purchasing agent whether he would prefer to bet on the price of oil being $10 per barrel or below in five years, or on the spinner falling on the dark portion of the disk. Suppose the purchasing agent says he thinks the spinner is more likely to fall on the dark portion; the manager then reduces the dark portion to one-fourth of the disk. Again the purchasing agent would prefer to bet on the spinner hitting the dark sector, so the manager reduces it to one-eighth (0.125) of the disk. This time, suppose the pur-

TABLE 2. Summary of Elicitation of
Subjective Probabilities with the Probability Wheel

Situation: You may bet that the price of oil will be $10 or less in five years **or** that the spinner will fall on the dark portion of the probability wheel.		
Appearance of Wheel	Response	Implication
	Prefer Spinner	$P(\text{price} \leq \$10) < 0.5$
	Prefer Spinner	$P(\text{price} \leq \$10) < 0.25$
	Indifferent	$P(\text{price} \leq \$10) = 0.125$

chasing agent wavers, and says, "Well, I would not really prefer betting on the spinner now. On the other hand, I would not really like to bet that prices will be $10 per barrel or lower. I guess I would be roughly indifferent between the two bets." Thus, the manager would assign the probability of prices falling below $10 per barrel a value of 0.125. This dialogue is summarized in Table 2.

Next, suppose the manager asks the purchasing agent about the probability that prices will be higher than $12, and finds that he is indifferent between bets immediately when one-half of the disk is dark. Thus, since the probability of prices falling below $10 is 0.125, and the probability of their rising above $12 is 0.5, the probability that they will be between $10 and $12 is $1.0 - (0.125 + 0.5) = 0.375$. As a check, the manager should cover 0.375 of the disk with the dark sector and ask the purchasing agent if he would be indifferent between betting that prices are actually between $10 and $12 or that the spinner will fall on the dark sector. If the purchasing agent is not indifferent to this bet, the manager should return to the first series of questions to discover the source of this inconsistency.

Now, in order to obtain additional detail the manager might continue this dialogue using the probability wheel as an aid and find the following estimates:

Price Range	Probability
$ 6.00– 7.99	.010
8.00– 9.99	.110
10.00–11.99	.375
12.00–13.99	.360
14.00–15.99	.135
6.00–18.99	.010
	1.000

If the initial set of probability estimates do not sum to 1.00, but they are "close" (say within ±0.05), the manager may wish to normalize them by simply dividing each estimate by the initial sum. Otherwise, he will have to interact further with the purchasing agent. Based on this information the manager could construct the histogram shown in Figure 10.

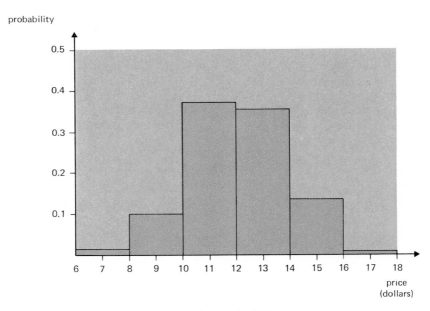

Figure 10. A histogram of subjective probability estimates

Successive Subdivisions As an alternative to the use of a probability wheel, the manager may use the method of successive subdivisions to aid the purchasing agent in reaching his conclusion. He would say to the purchasing agent, "State the price of crude oil such that you would be indifferent between betting that the actual price will be higher than your stated price and betting that it will be lower." If the purchasing agent still finds it hard to respond, the manager may suggest a price. He might ask if the purchasing agent would bet that prices will be higher than the current price of $11 per barrel. If so, he might increase the price to $12 per barrel and ask again. Suppose this time the purchasing agent is indifferent between betting that the actual price will be less than $12 or greater than $12. Then the probability of each is 0.5.

Now the manager chooses a higher price, say $14, and asks if the purchasing agent would be willing to bet that the actual price will be between $12 and $14 or greater than $14. Suppose the purchasing agent says he would bet on the actual price being between $12 and $14. Next, the manager asks a similar question regarding a price between $12 and $13 or one greater than $13. This time, the purchasing agent would prefer betting on "greater than $13." This dialogue continues until the purchasing agent is indifferent between a bet on the actual price falling between $12 and $13.25 and the actual price being greater than $13.25. Since the probability that the price will be greater than $12 is 0.5, and since this indifference implies that the probability the price will be between $12 and $13.25 is equal to the probability that the price will be greater than $13.25, the manager estimates the probability of each of these latter two events at 0.5 divided by 2, which is 0.25.

Similarly, the manager might find the probability that the price will be between $10.75 and $12 is 0.25, and the probability that it will be lower than $10.75 is also 0.25. Now, the manager could use the same approach to subdivide each of these four intervals, if he desires.

When the probability wheel is used, the interval is specified and the objective is to determine the probability that the actual price will fall within this interval. The probability wheel helps the respondent to conceptualize the meaning of probabilities other than 0.0, 0.5, and 1.0. When such a device is unavailable, the respondent may find it very difficult to relate to probability statements. The method of successive subdivisions has the advantage of using only the probability 0.5, which most persons can conceptualize by relating it to the flip of a fair coin.

Use of Probability Estimates The amount of detail required by the manager will depend on how the results are to be used. In this example, suppose the manager realizes that the results are to be used in a decision tree. He may choose to use only three price estimates in order to reduce the number of chance branches.

The first estimate might correspond roughly to the current price, $11 per barrel. The purchasing agent estimates that the probability of the actual price being between $10 and $12 in five years is 0.375. Thus, the manager might take the current price of $11 as *representative* of this price range and calculate the profit (or loss) from each alternative oil shale development strategy at that price of crude oil. The probability of these outcomes, *given no embargo*, would be roughly 0.375.

Next, the manager has the estimate that the probability that prices will be lower than $10 per barrel (lower prices) is 0.125. Again, he may choose a representative price, say $9 per barrel, and compute the outcome from each alternative. Finally, the probability of a price higher than $12 (higher prices) is 0.5, so he might compute the outcomes of the alternatives at a representative price such as $13.25.

These probabilities are based on the assumption that no oil embargo will occur. Now suppose the manager consults with another "expert," perhaps an outside consultant, and obtains the estimate that the probability of an embargo is 0.2. He can then use the formula for a joint probability to modify his probability estimates for his prices as follows:

P(lower prices and no embargo) = P(lower prices|no embargo) $\times$
    P(no embargo) = (0.125) (0.8) = 0.1

P(current prices and no embargo) = P(current prices|no embargo) $\times$
    P(no embargo) = (0.375) (0.8) = 0.3

P(higher prices and no embargo) = P(higher prices|no embargo) $\times$
    P(no embargo) = (0.5) (0.8) = 0.4

These are the probabilities used in the POCO example (see Table 3 in Chapter 2).

WHAT SHOULD THE MANAGER KNOW?

Utility functions and subjective probabilities are useful decision aids for the modern manager. At a conceptual level, the manager should recognize that the expected value of conditional outcomes is not the only available evaluative model for use in decision making when risk is involved. The simple expected value model does not take into consideration the decision maker's feelings regarding risk. He may be extremely risk averse, and thus wish to avoid even small chances at realizing unfortunate outcomes.

A utility function can be constructed for a decision maker that reflects this risk aversion. The utility function values can be substituted for the corresponding conditional outcome values. The expected values of the utility numbers, which can be organized in tabular form or in a decision tree, can be computed and used to rank the alternatives. Most persons are risk averse, so the outcome value associated with the expected utility function value of an alternative is generally smaller than the expected value of the conditional outcomes.

Similarly, subjective probabilities are also based on the judgments of the decision maker. These probabilities can be used as a basis for decision making even when no "objective" probabilities are available from historical data or predictive models.

The approaches for eliciting utility functions and subjective probabilities from an individual are similar. In the case of the utility function, one may use either of the following approaches:

1. Specify the conditional outcomes of a 50–50 gamble and ask the deci-

sion maker to state a certain outcome such that he would be indifferent between receiving that outcome or accepting the results of the gamble.

2. Specify a certain outcome and the conditional outcomes of a gamble and ask the decision maker to identify the probabilities of the conditional outcomes such that he is indifferent between the certain outcome and accepting the result of the gamble.

In order to elicit subjective probabilities, either of the following approaches may be used:

1. Specify an event and ask the subject to identify the area of a disk such that he is indifferent between betting that the event will occur or that a spinner will stop in that area of the disk.

2. Ask the decision maker to subdivide an interval of outcome values into smaller intervals, each with an equal probability of occurring.

The utility function will generally be obtained directly from the decision maker, while the subjective probabilities may be elicited from experts and perhaps modified by the decision maker.

Now let us consider each of the central issues related to the use of quantitative aids by managers.

Problem Characteristics   Utility functions and subjective probabilities are useful in analyzing nonrepetitive decisions involving risk and substantial costs and potential rewards. The nonrepetitive nature of the decision is especially important to the use of the utility function, since for repetitive decisions simple expected value would be an appropriate evaluative model. In addition, the potential rewards and costs must be substantial in order to justify the time and effort required to obtain the subjective estimates. It is important to note that utility functions can be used with nonmonetary conditional outcomes, such as scores on standardized tests.

Obtaining Subjective Estimates   The modern manager may find himself in the role of the decision maker from whom information is required to estimate a utility function or of the expert from whom subjective probabilities are sought. It seems unlikely that he will ever be interviewing others and trying to obtain subjective estimates from them. Why, then, did we present the methodology for eliciting this information in some detail?

If the manager is questioned by an analyst, he should recognize what the analyst is doing and cooperate with him. Perhaps more important, the manager may be drawing a decision tree and performing the necessary calculations himself. If so, he may find it helpful to carry on a structured dialogue *with himself* to elicit the necessary information; that is, he may pose these questions involving gambles to himself in order to crystallize his own thinking. Therefore, it is important that he be aware of the basic approaches for eliciting judgmental responses.

Information Requirements The information required for using utility functions and subjective probabilities in analyzing problems is essentially the same as that required for using decision trees. Thus, the manager must obtain the following:

1. the alternative solutions and their relationships to possible future events
2. the outcomes of selecting each alternative, given the occurrence of each future event
3. the probabilities of the occurrence of each event and, in addition,
4. the approximation of the decision maker's utility function.

Since the process of eliciting subjective probabilities is time consuming, it is especially important to reduce the size of a decision tree as much as possible through a preliminary analysis. In addition, the manager may prefer to perform a preliminary analysis with simple expected values. In many practical problems, the best alternative will be obvious from these analyses. Recall that the decision for POCO was not changed by the introduction of utility function values. However, if two or more alternatives are "close" on the basis of an expected value model, an analysis using utility functions might then be performed.

No quantitative aid should be applied blindly. Why use a procedure requiring the gathering of expensive information when a simpler approach will work just as well? The manager should always trade off the benefit of using a quantitative aid against the cost of the required information.

Computations The computations with the utility function values and the subjective probabilities are straightforward. Subjective probabilities are simply used in the analysis in the place of objective probabilities. The utility function values are substituted for the corresponding conditional outcomes, and expected values are computed in the usual fashion. These numbers may be used in the existing computer codes developed for the analysis of decision trees.

Interpretation of Results The expected utility function values resulting from the analysis may be used to rank the alternatives. In addition, the outcome value corresponding to the expected utility value associated with an alternative can be estimated from the utility function. This value is the least amount that the decision maker should actually be willing to accept for certain, rather than choosing the alternative. Again, we must emphasize that this certain value of the alternative will not actually occur; instead any one of the conditional outcomes associated with the alternative will be the result of the decision.

A sensitivity analysis should be performed to ensure that small errors in estimating the utility function and in eliciting the subjective probabilities will not affect the decision. For example, a slightly more risk averse utility function (more bowed) might be used in a second analysis. Similarly, subjective probability estimates might be varied to study their impacts on the ranking of the alternatives.

Check Your Understanding

1. In the following situations, would the expected value of the outcomes or expected utility be a more appropriate evaluative model? Explain your reasoning.
   a. the determination of daily inventory policies
   b. the expansion of capacity by building a large plant
   c. the selection of a new product to market when approximately 20 new products are introduced by the firm each year
   d. the selection of a new product to market when a commitment of a high proportion of the firm's capital will be required
   e. the purchase of personal life insurance
   f. the decision to seed hurricanes

2. Distinguish between an outcome and the *worth* of the outcome to the decision maker.

3. Distinguish between a person who is "risk averse" and a "risk taker." What professions might appeal to a "risk taker"?

4. Estimate the utility function values associated with each of the outcomes in the gamble selection decision tree of Figure 3 from the utility curve of a *risk taker* shown in Figure 2.
   a. Which gamble would the risk taker prefer?
   b. What is the least amount he would accept for certain in each case rather than choose a gamble?

5. Obtain the cooperation of a friend, a roommate, or your spouse. Using questions involving gambles, find at least five points on his or her utility function over the range of monetary values from −$10 (lose $10) to +$20 (win $20).
   a. Is the individual risk averse, risk neutral, or a risk taker?
   b. Plot these five points and draw in the corresponding utility curve. Using these results, analyze the gamble selection decision tree in Figure 3. Which gamble should he or she prefer?
   c. Describe the three alternative gambles to your friend. Ask him/her to choose one. Did this choice agree with your prediction in (b)?

6. By posing questions involving gambles to yourself, develop and plot your own utility curve over the range from −$10 to +$20.
   a. Are you risk averse, risk neutral, or a risk taker?

b. Using your own personal utility function values, analyze the gamble selection decision tree in Figure 3. Which gamble should you prefer according to this analysis?

c. Study the three alternative gambles carefully. Does your "gut reaction" agree with the analysis in (b)?

7. Review the assumptions of utility functions.

a. Give an example of two alternatives where it would be difficult to "consistently state your preference for one or indicate that you are indifferent between them." What seems to cause the difficulty?

b. Try to think of an example of a problem where your preferences may not be transitive.

8. Apply the positive linear transformation $U(O_i) = 2v(O_i) + 3$ to the utility function numbers in parentheses in Figure 3. For example, $U(\$10) = (2)\ (0.79) + 3 = 4.58$. Repeat the analysis of the decision tree using these revised utility numbers. Do you still obtain the same ordering of the alternatives?

9. Construct "pies" of different sizes from stiff paper that can be pinned to the center of a disk also made from stiff paper. By interchanging the pies, the disk can be used as a probability wheel. Obtain the cooperation of a friend. Using this crude probability wheel, develop a histogram like Figure 10 of his or her subjective probability estimates of the retail price of one gallon of gasoline two years from now. Repeat the experiment using the approach of successive subdivisions. Which approach did your friend prefer?

10. Through self-interrogation, develop a histogram like Figure 10 of your own subjective probability estimates of the retail price of one gallon of gasoline in two years. Use a crude probability wheel, which may be constructed as described in (9) above. Repeat the experiment using the method of successive subdivisions. Which approach do you prefer?

Problems

1. Suppose an individual is interested in purchasing an automobile and is concerned with the acceleration and performance of the automobile as determined by its horsepower. Without even considering other criteria such as cost and mileage, he may feel that 300 horsepower is the "ideal" figure. Suggest two different evaluative models that could be used to select an automobile for this individual based on the single, certain criterion of horsepower. Graph each one as a function of horsepower over the interval from 0 horsepower to 600 horsepower.

2. Consider POCO's problem of determining whether to drill in the Aleutian Islands as described in problem 1 of Chapter 2.

a. Find the utility function values of POCO for $80 million, −$100 million, $200 million, and $300 million from Figure 6.

b. Repeat the analysis of problem 1 in Chapter 2 substituting the utility function values for the monetary outcomes. Does the decision change?

c. If you were a manager of POCO, would you feel more comfortable with the analysis based on expected monetary value or the one based on expected utility? Explain.

3. Consider the problem of a government decision maker who must decide if a particular hurricane is to be seeded. He finds the analysis of the hurricane seeding issue as described in problem 2 of Chapter 2 most interesting, but it omits an important consideration. Once a hurricane has been seeded, it is no longer an "act of God," but it becomes an "act of man."

The result is that once a hurricane has been seeded, the government will be blamed for damages, even if they are smaller than they would have been otherwise. Hurricanes are unpredictable. If the surface wind speed should actually *increase* after it is seeded or if its direction of travel should shift into a heavily populated area, the public outcry would be tremendous.

Thus, the value of the outcome to him as a decision maker depends both on the property damage *and* on whether the hurricane was seeded. The best outcome would be the least damage, estimated at $16.3 million in problem 2 of Chapter 2, and no seeding. The worst outcome would be the highest property damage of $335.8 million after the hurricane was seeded. Suppose he assigns the best outcome a utility function value of 1.0 and the worst outcome a utility function value of 0.0, and uses the 50–50 gambles to assign utility function values to the remaining outcomes. The results and the probability estimates are shown below:

Property Damage Loss (millions of $)	Hurricane Seeded		Hurricane Not Seeded	
	Probability	Utility	Probability	Utility
335.8	0.038	0.0	0.054	0.30
191.1	0.143	0.61	0.206	0.68
100.0	0.392	0.82	0.480	0.89
46.7	0.255	0.89	0.206	0.98
16.3	0.172	0.90	0.054	1.0

Notice that the decision maker is indifferent between a property damage loss of $46.7 million from a seeded hurricane and a loss of $100 million from an unseeded hurricane because of the difference in government responsibility in each case.

The utility function value assigned to the cost of seeding, only $0.25 million, is negligible and can be ignored.

a. Compute the expected utility associated with each of the two decisions. Which one should be preferred?

b. Does the result differ from the one that would be obtained using the expected monetary value model? Is this surprising?

c. As a practical matter, if you were a government decision maker, would you like for these utility function values to be publicized? How would you defend the use of this procedure before a congressional committee?

utility

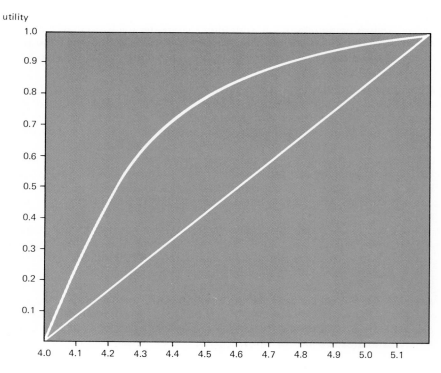

net outcome on project (millions of dollars)

Figure 11. A preference curve for the treasurer

Adapted from S. C. Wheelwright, "Applying Decision Theory to Improve Corporate Management of Currency-Exchange Rates," *California Management Review*, Vol. 17, No. 4, Summer 1975.

4. Consider the problem of whether to take an umbrella to work as described in problem 4 of Chapter 2.
   a. Use the plot of the utility function in Figure 4 to assign utility numbers to the outcomes of $0, −$2, −$4, and −$10.
   b. Using the expected utility evaluative model, determine the best decision when the forecasts of the probability of rain are the following:
      1) 0.0
      2) 0.25
      3) 0.5
      4) 0.75
      5) 1.0

      How do these decisions compare with those that result from using the expected value evaluative model?
   c. What are the certain returns (payments in this case) corresponding to the decisions for each of the five forecast probabilities?

5. Consider the problem of managing currency-exchange risks as described in problem 7 of Chapter 2. Suppose we ask the treasurer a series of questions involving 50–50 gambles and estimate the utility function for the firm as shown in Figure 11.

   a. Using the utility function in Figure 11, we obtain the following values: $u(\$5.025) = 0.98$, $u(\$5.0) = 0.974$, $u(\$4.75) = 0.88$, $u(\$4.5) = 0.75$, $u(\$4.25) = 0.49$, and $u(\$4.0) = 0.0$. Perform the decision tree analysis using the expected utility evaluative model. Do the results change?

   b. It has been argued that we should *not* obtain the utility function from the treasurer. Since he will be "blamed" if an unfortunate outcome is realized, he will be too risk averse. Thus, his views are not in the best interests of the firm. Do you agree? If so, suggest a remedy for this problem.

References

Brown, R., "Do Managers find Decision Theory Useful?" *Harvard Business Review*, Vol. 48, 1970.

Dyer, J., W. Farrell, and P. Bradley, "Utility Functions for Test Performance," *Management Science,* Vol. 20, No. 4, 1973.

Fishburn, P. C., "Methods of Estimating Additive Utilities," *Management Science,* Vol. 13, No. 7, March 1967.

———, "Utility Theory," *Management Science,* Vol. 14, No. 5, January 1968.

Grayson, C. J., "Decisions Under Uncertainty: Drilling Decisions by Oil and Gas Operators," Division of Research, Harvard Business School, Boston, Mass., 1960.

Hammond, J. S., "Better Decisions with Preference Theory," *Harvard Business Review,* November–December 1967.

Hoepfner, R., P. A. Bradley, S. P. Klein, and M. C. Alkin, *CSE Elementary School Evaluation Kit: Needs Assessment,* Allyn and Bacon, Boston, 1973.

Jones, J. M., *Statistical Decision Making*, Richard D. Irwin, Inc., Homewood, Ill., 1977.

Keeney, R. L., and H. Raiffa, *Decision Analysis with Multiple Objectives*, John Wiley & Sons, New York, 1976.

North, D. W., "A Tutorial Introduction to Decision Theory," *IEEE Transactions on Systems Science and Cybernetics,* Vol. SSC-4, No. 3, September 1968.

Raiffa, H., *Decision Analysis,* Addison-Wesley, Reading, Mass., 1968.

———, *Analysis for Decision Making* (an audiographic, self-instructional course), Encyclopaedia Britannica Educational Corporation, Chicago, Ill., 1974.

Schlaifer, R., *Analysis of Decisions Under Uncertainty*, McGraw-Hill, New York, 1969.

Shapley, L. S., and M. Shubik, "Game Theory in Economics, Chapter 4: Preferences and Utility," R-904/4-NSF, The Rand Corporation, Santa Monica, California, 90406.

Spetzler, C. S., "The Development of a Corporate Risk Policy for Capital Investment Decisions," *IEEE Transactions on Systems Science and Cybernetics,* Vol. SSC-4, No. 3, September 1968.

Wheelwright, S. C., "Applying Decision Theory to Improve Corporate Management of Currency-Exchange Risks," *California Management Review,* Vol. 17, No. 4, Summer 1975.

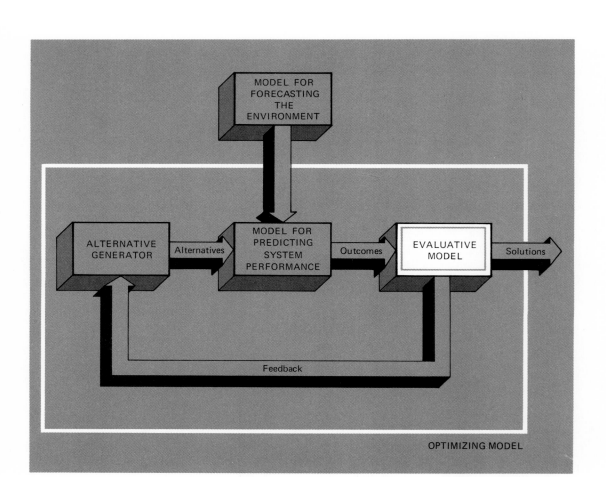

4

Evaluative Models for Multiple Criteria

In many real-world situations, there are significant problems that involve several criteria of approximately equal importance. The strategy of using an evaluative model with a single criterion may not be particularly helpful in these instances. For example, the effects of an alternative on the share of the market, prestige, and labor relations might be considered roughly as important as the effect on profit or loss in some business decisions. In the context of educational decision making, the number of students actually enrolled at the undergraduate, master's, and doctoral levels might be important criteria for some decisions [Geoffrion et al., 1972]. Similarly, the design of a rapid transit system must be evaluated on such criteria as noise pollution, air pollution, appearance, safety, and the number of persons using the system, as well as costs [Pardee et al., 1969].

Evaluative models may be used as an aid to decision making when there are multiple criteria. In Chapters 2 and 3, we assumed that there was only one outcome, or criterion, relevant for evaluating the alternatives. A more realistic interpretation would be that there was only one criterion of over-riding importance, such as profit or loss. Other considerations (which could be thought of as secondary criteria) could be brought into play to choose among alternatives that were "close" on the primary criterion. Thus, the approaches we have described could be used to identify a smaller subset of alternatives that are roughly equivalent based on a criterion of overriding importance such as profit (loss), but they are inappropriate for explicitly dealing with multiple criteria.

Multiple criteria of approximately equal importance generally arise because the problem is complex. This complexity is often associated with a major decision involving a significant allocation of resources. The initial issue in the case of a complex problem is the identification of the criteria, and this issue will be considered first. Next, the alternative evaluative models for problems involving multiple criteria will be reviewed. Finally, we will summarize the evaluative models for multiple criteria with an emphasis on what the practicing manager should know.

IDENTIFYING THE CRITERIA

An important issue that should be considered early in the problem-solving effort is the actual identification of the criteria that are relevant for comparing alternatives. These criteria (also called attributes, objectives, outcomes, or goals) are simply the outcomes that are both affected by the choice of an alternative and affect the decision maker's preference for the alternative. The task of recognizing the aspects of the system that will be affected by the choice of an alternative may be the most difficult and the most important task in the analysis. The development of an evaluative and a predictive model may have to be accomplished simultaneously or iteratively, since the criteria may change as the decision maker learns more about the problem.

As an example, consider the imposition of a 55-mile-per-hour speed limit during the oil embargo in 1974. The stated objective of this law was to conserve fuel by forcing automobiles to travel slower. It also had the effect of communicating the seriousness of the situation to the general public. In addition, deaths and injuries from traffic accidents fell drastically during this period. On the negative side, this law also touched off a nationwide strike by truckers and curtailed the demand at businesses depending on motorists and tourists. It is not clear that Congress or the president were aware of all of these outcomes prior to the passage of the legislation.

Thus, the criteria may include outcomes, such as the probability of a strike by truckers, not directly related to the primary purpose of the alternative—conserving gasoline, in this case. Nevertheless, these criteria must be included in the evaluative model if they affect the preference of the decision maker.

In order to get started in identifying criteria, one may use the "exploratory scenario" suggested by Jackson [1974] and discussed in Chapter 1. By merely mulling things over in an active fashion, one can identify many outcomes of choosing various alternatives. The manager can make a list of such outcomes, which may provide the basis for the determination of the final set of criteria.

As an alternative, the manager may begin with a general statement of his purpose, an over-all objective, and refine this statement into more and more specific items. The result is a hierarchical representation of criteria that eventually ends at the lowest level with criteria whose associated values can be determined. This approach has been described by Manheim and Hall [1968] and by Miller [1969]. This important problem of identifying criteria is discussed in depth in Chapter 2 of Keeney and Raiffa [1976].

A Transportation System Design Example The example used by Manheim and Hall dealt with the establishment of an urban transportation system. They began with a "super goal" of "the good life," which seems particularly noncontroversial. They then suggested that any transportation system would be a *means* to that *end* if it were convenient, safe, aesthetically appealing, and economically attractive. These four rather vague subgoals were each decomposed further into more specific criteria. For example, safety was specified more sharply by the three criteria of a decrease in fatalities, a decrease in injuries, and a decrease in property damage. The complete hierarchy of criteria is shown in Figure 1.

A Site Location Example Consider the problem of locating a pumped storage station site by a public utility. During periods of low demand for electricity, the excess capacity is used to pump water uphill from a low reservoir to a higher one where it is stored. When the demand for power reaches its peak, the water is allowed to run back downhill, passing through a turbine and generating additional electricity to meet the peak-period demand.

The super goal for this problem might be "choose a good site," which would be accomplished by considering economic impacts, environmental effects, and public acceptance. Becoming more specific, public acceptance could be decomposed into considerations regarding the recreational value of the project, aesthetic values, and the proximity of any sites of historical value that might be threatened. A completed hierarchy of criteria for this problem is shown in Figure 2.

The construction of such a chart may seem difficult and time consuming. However, it can provide an important learning experience for the manager as he attempts to complete the task. Additional learning takes place each time a new outcome of importance is recognized and added to the heirarchy.

MAKING TRADE-OFFS

Perhaps the primary role of the manager is to make trade-offs. That is, he must trade off the risk inherent in a new investment against the potential profits, or trade off the efficiency of a new automated production line against its effects on the work force. The intuitive notion of trade-offs can be formalized as an aid in evaluating alternatives with multiple outcomes or criteria (see Chapter 3 of Keeney and Raiffa [1976]).

Trade-Offs with Certain Outcomes

Under conditions of certainty, the outcome O_i associated with the choice of a particular alternative A_i is known. However, O_i is multivalued; that is, $O_i = (O_i^1, O_i^2, \ldots, O_i^k, \ldots, O_i^m)$, where the superscript refers to the outcome as measured on the kth criterion ($k = 1, \ldots, m$). This expression of

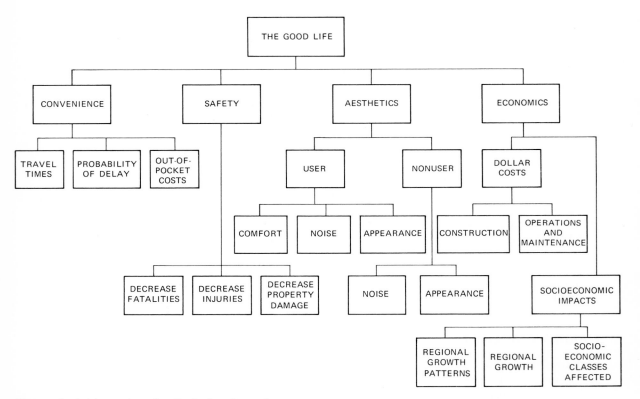

Figure 1. A hierarchy of criteria for the urban transportation system problem

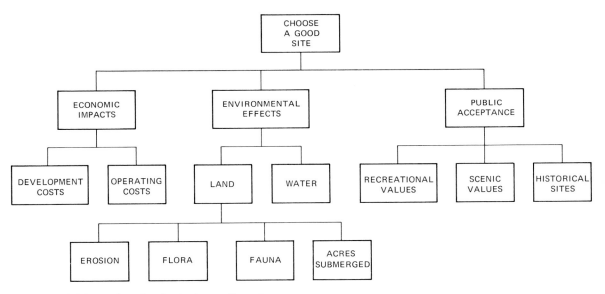

Figure 2. A hierarchy of criteria for a site selection problem

the multivalued outcome can be better understood if we use a concrete example.

Suppose we are trying to decide which automobile to purchase, and we have narrowed our choices to two alternatives, a Starburst (A_1) or a Palomino (A_2). We shall assume that there is no uncertainty in this situation, so that we do not have to worry about getting a "lemon."

The Starburst and the Palomino are approximately the same in size and weight, so we have decided to base our decision on only four criteria: cost measured in dollars, economy measured in miles per gallon, performance measured in horsepower, and appearance based on our subjective judgments. After some thought, we decide to categorize the appearance of the automobiles as either "ugly," "so-so," or "beautiful." Table 1 shows how each car compares on each of these criteria. In this case $O_1 = (\$3500, 140 \text{ hp},$ 20 mpg, ugly). Notice that the Starburst costs less and gets better mileage (a more "practical" alternative), but the Palomino has more horsepower and is better looking (more "sex appeal"). How can we go about making a decision in this case?

For the purpose of this discussion, we have assumed that—everything else being equal—lower costs, more horsepower, more miles per gallon, and a more appealing appearance are always preferable. It is important to realize that this does not have to be true in order to use the approaches we shall describe.

TABLE 1. Certain Outcomes with Multiple Criteria

Criterion	Starburst (A_1) O_1	Palomino (A_2) O_2
Cost	3500	3600
Horsepower	140	170
Miles per gallon	20	13
Appearance	ugly	beautiful

The Trade-Off Process   In order to use trade-offs, we must interact directly with the decision maker. Unfortunately, this interaction complicates the information requirements, as in the case of an evaluative model for a single criterion under risky choice situations, but it cannot be avoided. When multiple criteria are involved, an individual must make explicit his values in order to create an evaluative model. In addition, the forced interaction between a technical analyst and a manager may lead to a deeper understanding of the problem, and thus actually be a positive experience.

One approach to interacting with the decision maker would be to ask him to make trade-offs until he is indifferent between O_1 and a new outcome O_1', and until he is indifferent between O_2 and O_2'. We would structure this trade-off process so that O_1' and O_2' would have the same value for all criteria except one. Since O_1' and O_2' would be equal for all criteria but one, it would be easy to select one of them. If O_1' were chosen, this would indicate that the decision maker should choose A_1 since he is indifferent between O_1 and O_1', and between O_2 and O_2', but O_1' was preferred to O_2'. A trade-off is simply a statement of how much of one criterion you would be willing to give up in order to obtain a specific increase in some other criterion. Conversely, it could be the increase in one criterion that would be required to offset a loss in another criterion. The idea of using trade-offs is not particularly new, and was summarized in a letter written by Benjamin Franklin to Joseph Priestly in 1772.

Dear Sir,

In the affair of so much importance to you, wherein you ask my advice, I cannot, for want of sufficient premises, advise you what to determine, but if you please I will tell you how. When those difficult cases occur, they are difficult, chiefly because while we have them under consideration, all the reasons pro and con are not present to the mind at the same time; but sometimes one set present themselves, and at other times another, the first being out of sight. Hence the various purposes or informations that alternatively prevail, and the uncertainty that perplexes us. To get over this, my way is to divide half a sheet of paper by a line into two columns; writing over the one Pro, and over the other Con. Then, during three or four days consideration, I put down under the different heads short hints of the different motives, that at different times occur to me, for or against the measure. When I have thus got them all together in one view, I endeavor to estimate their respective weights; and where I find two, one on each side, that seem equal, I strike them both out. If I find a reason pro equal to some two reasons con, I strike out the three. If I judge some two reasons con, equal to three reasons pro, I strike out the five; and thus proceeding I find at length where the balance lies; and if, after a day or two of further consideration, nothing new that is of importance occurs on either side, I come to a determination accordingly. And, though the weight of the reasons cannot be taken with the precision of algebraic quantities, yet when each is thus considered, separately and comparatively, and the whole lies before me, I think I can judge better, and am less liable to make a rash step, and in fact I have found great advantage from this kind of equation, and what may be called moral or prudential algebra.

Wishing sincerely that you may determine for the best, I am ever, my dear friend, yours most affectionately.

B. Franklin (signed) [Franklin, 1956]

To illustrate, suppose we ask the decision maker how much cheaper O_1 would have to be before he would be indifferent between it and an otherwise identical automobile that gets only 15 miles per gallon. We might say, "Let us take ($3500, 140 hp, 20 mpg, ugly) as one alternative, but for the second we will reduce the miles per gallon to 15. Now if we do that to you, if we cut down the miles per gallon from 20 to 15 for the first alternative, how much cheaper does that automobile have to be before you would be indifferent between the first alternative and an automobile that is partially described by (140 hp, 15 mpg, ugly)?"

The decision maker should take a considerable amount of time before responding, especially if it is an important decision. He might decide that miles per gallon is only of interest in terms of its effect on operating expenses. He might estimate that he would drive the car approximately 10,000 miles per year and trade it in after five years. At a price of $0.60 per gallon (the estimated average price of gasoline), a mileage figure of 15 will cost him an extra $100 per year, as compared with a mileage figure of 20. If we assume a discount rate of 10 percent per year and round to the nearest dollar, the present value of additional costs over the next five years from 15 miles per gallon as compared to 20 miles per gallon is $379. Thus, the car would have to be $379 cheaper (cost $3121). Therefore, the decision maker would be indifferent between a car described by ($3500, 140 hp, 20 mpg, ugly) and ($3121, 140 hp, 15 mpg, ugly).

Next we say, "Now that you have handled that question, let us ask you one more. Let us take this alternative we have just identified ($3121, 140 hp, 15 mpg, ugly), and let us increase the horsepower to 150. We are giving you more horsepower. What does the cost have to be now to make you indifferent?" This time, there is no clear rationale for converting this change into money. Therefore the decision must be simply based on preferences. Suppose the decision maker replies, "I like a more powerful car, assuming the miles per gallon stays the same, so I would be willing to pay more for that extra 10 horsepower, but not a whole lot more. I would be willing to pay about $100 more, then I would be indifferent between the two cars described by ($3121, 140 hp, 15 mpg, ugly) and ($3221, 150 hp, 15 mpg, ugly)."

Finally, suppose we ask how much extra the decision maker would be willing to pay to improve the appearance from "ugly" to "so-so." Again there is no rationale for such a decision other than personal preference. Suppose he says, "Well, appearance is important to me, but the improvement from an ugly car to a so-so one would only be worth about $170 to me." Therefore, he would be indifferent between ($3221, 150 hp, 15 mpg, ugly) and ($3391, 150 hp, 15 mpg, so-so).

The trade-offs made by the decision maker are summarized in Table 2. We assume that expressions of indifference are transitive. That is, if the decision maker is indifferent between O_1 and O_2, and between O_2 and O_3, then he is indifferent between O_1 and O_3. Therefore, this decision maker should be indifferent between O_1 ($3500, 140 hp, 20 mpg, ugly) and the new alternative ($3391, 150 hp, 15 mpg, so-so), which we designate as O_1'.

Now let us repeat this process of interaction with the decision maker for the Palomino (A_2). Again, we will change the mileage figure to 15, and ask for the *additional* price he would be willing to pay for the car. Then we would reduce the horsepower to 150 and modify the beautiful appearance to so-so, asking at each step for the trade-off in monetary terms. The responses of the decision maker for A_2 are summarized in Table 3. Thus, the

TABLE 2. Summary of Trade-Offs for the Starburst (A_1)

The Decision Maker Is Indifferent:	Trade-Off
Between ($3500, 140 hp, 20 mpg, ugly) and ($3121, 140 hp, 15 mpg, ugly)	Give up 5 mpg for a price reduction of $379
Between ($3121, 140 hp, 15 mpg, ugly) and ($3221, 150 hp, 15 mpg, ugly)	Pay $100 for an additional 10 hp
Between ($3221, 150 hp, 15 mpg, ugly) and ($3391, 150 hp, 15 mpg, so-so)	Pay $170 to improve the appearance to "so-so"

TABLE 3. Summary of Trade-Offs for the Palomino (A_2)

The Decision Maker Is Indifferent:	Trade-Off
Between ($3600, 170 hp, 13 mpg, beautiful) and ($3833, 170 hp, 15 mpg, beautiful)	Pay $233 for a 2 mpg increase
Between ($3833, 170 hp, 15 mpg, beautiful) and ($3673, 150 hp, 15 mpg, beautiful)	Give up 20 hp for $160
Between ($3673, 150 hp, 15 mpg, beautiful) and ($3417, 150 hp, 15 mpg, so-so)	Change appearance to "so-so" for $256

decision maker should be indifferent between O_2 ($3600, 170 hp, 13 mpg, beautiful) and O_2' ($3417, 150 hp, 15 mpg, so-so).

Finally, we see that O_1' and O_2' are the same on the basis of horsepower, miles per gallon, and appearance, but O_1' is cheaper. Therefore the decision maker prefers O_1' to O_2', and thus he should prefer A_1, the Starburst, to A_2, the Palomino.

Trade-Offs with Risky Outcomes

Since the most complex and important managerial decisions generally involve both multiple criteria and risk, the modern manager should understand evaluative models for dealing with these situations. Under conditions of risk, an alternative A_1 has n conditional outcomes O_{1j}, $j = 1, \ldots, n$. In this case, each conditional outcome is represented by multiple criteria; that is, $O_{1j} = (O_{1j}^1, O_{1j}^2, \ldots, O_{1j}^m)$ for each conditional outcome $j = 1, \ldots, n$. For example, suppose there is a possibility that a smog device will be required for the automobile that we expect to purchase. If the smog device is required, the cost, horsepower, and miles per gallon will change as shown in Table 4. Thus, for the Starburst (A_1), we have two conditional outcomes, $O_{11} = $ ($3500, 140 hp, 20 mpg, ugly) and $O_{12} = $ ($3700, 120 hp, 18 mpg, ugly).

Suppose we estimate the probability that the smog device will be required at 0.6. Now which automobile should we purchase?

One approach is to proceed exactly as before and determine four new conditional outcomes O_{11}', O_{12}', O_{21}', and O_{22}' such that the decision maker

TABLE 4. Conditional Outcomes with Multiple Criteria

Criterion	Starburst (A_1)		Palomino (A_2)	
	Smog Device Not Required (O_{11})	Smog Device Required (O_{12})	Smog Device Not Required (O_{21})	Smog Device Required (O_{22})
Cost	3500	3700	3600	3800
Horsepower	140	120	170	140
Miles per gallon	20	18	13	12
Appearance	ugly	ugly	beautiful	beautiful

is indifferent between O_{11} and O'_{11}, between O_{12} and O'_{12}, between O_{21} and O'_{21}, and between O_{22} and O'_{22}. These new conditional outcomes would have identical values for all criteria except one. We would then construct a utility function for a single criterion under risk over this one criterion that varies, with the other criteria held constant, using the same approach described in Chapter 3. Thus, utility numbers could be assigned to the conditional outcomes, and the expected utility evaluative model could be used as in Chapter 3.

Example We have already determined O'_{11} and O'_{21} using trade-offs as described previously. Now, we follow the same procedure to determine O'_{12} and O'_{22} as illustrated in Table 5. Notice in Table 5 that when the cost of the automobile is $3800, the decision maker is willing to pay $160 to improve the appearance from "ugly" to "so-so". In Table 2, when the cost is $3221, he is willing to pay an extra $10, or a total of $170, for this same change. Is he being inconsistent? Not necessarily. His trade-offs depend on the levels of the criteria as well as the change in them. When the cost is cheaper, he may be willing to pay a bit more for the same change in other criteria.

As a result of this trade-off process, we obtain the following conditional outcomes:

	Original Conditional Outcome	Equivalent Conditional Outcome
Starburst with no smog device	(O_{11}): ($3500, 140 hp, 20 mpg, ugly)	(O'_{11}): ($3391, 150 hp, 15 mpg, so-so)
Starburst with smog device	(O_{12}): ($3700, 120 hp, 18 mpg, ugly)	(O'_{12}): ($3960, 150 hp, 15 mpg, so-so)
Palomino with no smog device	(O_{21}): ($3600, 170 hp, 13 mpg, beautiful)	(O'_{21}): ($3417, 150 hp, 15 mpg, so-so)
Palomino with smog device	(O_{22}): ($3800, 140 hp, 12 mpg, beautiful)	(O'_{22}): ($4025, 150 hp, 15 mpg, so-so)

Look closely at these results. If a smog device is *not* required, O'_{11} is preferred to O'_{21}, so the Starburst (A_1) should be purchased as we noted earlier.

TABLE 5. Summary of Trade-Offs with
the Smog Device Required

The Decision Maker Is Indifferent:	Trade-Off
Between ($3700, 120 hp, 18 mpg, ugly) and ($3447, 120 hp, 15 mpg, ugly)	Give up 3 mpg for $253 price reduction
Between ($3447, 120 hp, 15 mpg, ugly) and ($3800, 150 hp, 15 mpg, ugly)	Pay $353 for an additional 30 hp
Between ($3800, 150 hp, 15 mpg, ugly) and ($3960, 150 hp, 15 mpg, so-so)	Pay $160 to improve the appearance to "so-so"
Between ($3800, 140 hp, 12 mpg, beautiful) and ($4179, 140 hp, 15 mpg, beautiful)	Pay $379 for a 3 mpg increase
Between ($4179, 140 hp, 15 mpg, beautiful) and ($4260, 150 hp, 15 mpg, beautiful)	Pay $81 for an additional 10 hp
Between ($4260, 150 hp, 15 mpg, beautiful) and ($4025, 150 hp, 15 mpg, so-so)	Change appearance to "so-so" for $235

If the smog device is required, O'_{12} is preferred to O'_{22}, so again the Starburst should be chosen.

At this point, we could stop the analysis since the Starburst is preferred for each of the two possible states of the environment. In general, if one alternative is preferred to another for every possible state of the environment, we say it probabilistically dominates the other, and the latter alternative can be omitted from further consideration. This concept is important, since it can save needless effort in estimating a utility function.

Nevertheless, let us continue the example to illustrate alternative approaches. Since the criterion values are all identical in the equivalent conditional outcomes except for the cost, we could ignore them and compute the expected monetary value of the costs associated with the equivalent conditional outcomes for each alternative. Thus, the problem has been reduced to one with a single criterion under risk, and the approach of Chapter 2 can be applied. However, it is not always the case that the expected monetary value evaluative model will accurately reflect the preferences of the decision maker, especially in the analysis of complex problems in which multiple criteria often arise. As described in Chapter 3, we can develop utility functions over a single criterion under risk to account for the decision maker's preferences. To develop such utility functions for our example, we would assign a utility number of 1.0 to the best equivalent conditional outcome, O'_{11}, and a utility number of 0.0 to the worst equivalent conditional outcome, O'_{22}. We now require only two utility numbers, for O'_{12} and O'_{21}.

To obtain the utility number for O'_{12}, we ask the decision maker to specify the probability p such that he would be indifferent between receiving ($3960, 150 hp, 15 mpg, so-so) for certain, or facing the gamble shown in Figure 3. Since the alternatives in the gamble differ only in the first criterion, this task should be only slightly more difficult than specifying the probability for a simple gamble with a single criterion. Suppose the decision maker re-

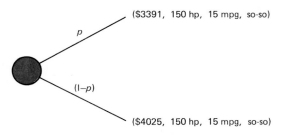

($3391, 150 hp, 15 mpg, so-so)

p

$(1-p)$

($4025, 150 hp, 15 mpg, so-so)

Figure 3. The gamble used to determine the utility number for O'_{12}

sponds that he would be indifferent if $p = 0.10$; then, the utility number assigned to O'_{12} is 0.10. By a similar question, suppose we assign O'_{21} a utility number of 0.95.

Now, since the decision maker is indifferent between O_{11} and O'_{11}, we can assign the same utility numbers to both, and so forth, until we obtain the following:

Outcomes	Utility Numbers
O_{11}, O'_{11}	1.0
O_{12}, O'_{12}	0.10
O_{21}, O'_{21}	0.95
O_{22}, O'_{22}	0.0

We can now use the expected utility evaluative model to analyze each alternative. Since there is a 0.6 chance that the smog device will be required, for the starburst (A_1) we have

$$(0.4)\,(1.0) + (0.6)\,(0.10) = 0.46\,,$$

and for A_2,

$$(0.4)\,(0.95) + (0.6)\,(0.0) = 0.38\,.$$

Thus, as we anticipated because of the probabilistic dominance, the Starburst (A_1) is still the preferred alternative.

Other examples of the use of trade-offs to simplify multiple criteria, as well as of the use of the utility function defined on multiple criteria where all values are equal except for one criterion, are provided by Raiffa [1969] and Howard [1973].

This process of making trade-offs is straightforward and conceptually simple. It provides an effective means of analyzing several distinct alternatives which must be evaluated on the basis of multiple criteria. Further it does not require any particular assumptions about the preferences of the decision maker. All that is required is that at least one criterion must be measurable on a continuous scale, such as in terms of monetary value. Often cost will play this role. However, the process can be time consuming for the decision maker, particularly if there are many criteria or a large number of alternatives. Therefore, other approaches may be preferable in these cases.

AN ADDITIVE EVALUATIVE MODEL FOR MULTIPLE CRITERIA

The trade-off approach does not provide an explicit evaluative model as a function of the outcomes. If there are a large number of alternatives to be evaluated, or if an evaluative model is required for use in an optimizing model that combines evaluative and predictive models with an alternative generator, then such a function would be desirable. What we would like to obtain would be a utility function $U(O_i^1, O_i^2, \ldots, O_i^m)$ of the multiple criteria, or outcomes. However, it would be difficult to interact with a decision maker to approximate such a function without some simplifying assumptions.

The simplest assumption is that $U(O_i^1, O_i^2, \ldots, O_i^m)$ is additive. This means that it can be written

$$U(O_i^1, O_i^2, \ldots, O_i^m) = w_1 u_1(O_i^1) + w_2 u_2(O_i^2) + \cdots + w_m u_m(O_i^m) ,$$

where the u_k are utility functions scaled from zero to one, and the w_k are scaling constants or "weights." The practical implication of this assumption is that we can now consider each criterion independently of the others and apply the methods of Chapter 3 to estimate the single criterion functions u_k.

Unfortunately, it is not always true that the evaluative model for multiple criteria for a particular decision maker can be written in this additive form. That is, it may not be possible to determine the functions u_k and the scaling constants w_k so that the additive model accurately reflects the preferences of the decision maker. This additive form is appropriate only if the criteria are *independent*.

Independent Criteria

The additive utility function can be used if the decision maker's preferences (or "feelings") regarding the values of one criterion are not influenced in any way by the *values* of the other criteria. This notion can best be understood by considering several examples.

An Automobile Selection Example Suppose that the only two criteria in the selection of an automobile are cost (in dollars) and power (in horsepower). In general, one would not expect that a decision maker's feelings about the cost of a car would be affected by changes in horsepower. Think about this for a moment. We are *not* saying that the decision maker would not be willing to pay more for a car with more horsepower (i.e., trade off cost against horsepower). Rather, a cost of $2800, for example, is just as "bad" when a car has 50 hp as when it has 150 hp, despite the fact that one might be willing to pay it only in the latter case. Thus, we can say that the two criteria are "independent."

Notice that we have defined independence only in terms of the decision maker's preferences, or feelings. It may be true that a more powerful car generally costs more money due to the increased cost of a larger or a more efficient engine. However, this relationship is in terms of the *technology* of the system, rather than in terms of the decision maker's preferences. The issue of technological independence is irrelevant to the notion of independent criteria in terms of preferences.

A Weapon Selection Example   Now consider a weapon selection problem where the criteria are accuracy, warhead payload, and costs. The two alternatives are shown in Table 6. Would an additive utility function be appropriate for this decision; that is, are the criteria "independent"?

TABLE 6. Outcomes of the Alternatives for a Weapon Selection Problem

Criterion	Weapon $X(A_1)$ O_1	Weapon $Y(A_2)$ O_2
Cost (millions of dollars)	3.5	3.0
Accuracy (mean distance from target in miles)	0.5	1.0
Payload (tons of TNT)	100	250

First of all, cost would probably be independent of accuracy and payload in this case for the same reason that we discussed in the automobile selection problem with two criteria. One would not expect that the decision maker's feelings about the cost of the weapon would be affected by changes in accuracy or in payload. A cost of $3.5 million dollars "feels" the same whether accuracy is 0.5 miles or 1.0 miles.

However, accuracy is not likely to be considered independent of the payload. For most decision makers, the value of high accuracy is simply worth less if the payload is high, 250 tons for example, than if it is low. Thus the two criteria, payload and accuracy, are *not* independent. Why is this so?

Both payload and accuracy relate to a specific objective of the weapon, target destruction. Neither one has an intrinsic value of its own. That is, accuracy is not really important for its own sake, and neither is payload. It is the *relationship* between these two criteria that is important. Therefore, we cannot justify using an additive evaluative model in this case.

How do we proceed? There are two alternatives. We could use the notion of trade-offs to choose between the two alternatives as before, since independent criteria are *not* required for the trade-off approach. Otherwise, we could redefine the criteria so that the dependent criteria of accuracy and payload are replaced by a new criterion, probability of target destruction, that is determined on the basis of their interaction.

For example, suppose that studies indicate that a weapon with a mean accuracy of 0.5 miles and a payload of 100 tons of TNT has a probability of 0.75 of destroying its target, while a weapon with a mean accuracy of 1.0 miles and a payload of 250 tons has a probability of 0.60 for target destruction. Thus, our description of the two alternatives is modified as shown in Table 7. The criteria of cost and probability of target destruction are most likely independent for a decision maker, so an additive evaluative model could be used.

TABLE 7. Outcomes for Redefined Criteria

Criterion	Weapon $X(A_1)$ O_1	Weapon $Y(A_2)$ O_2
Cost (millions of dollars)	3.5	3.0
Probability of target destruction	0.75	0.60

Verifying Independence with a Lottery   A decision maker may have a difficult time relating to the question of whether his "feelings" about one criterion are independent of the values of the others. If so, a lottery question can be used to help him much as a probability wheel helps in relating to questions regarding probabilities. If the decision involves multiple criteria and *risk*, the lottery question should be used to ensure that the criteria are independent even when risk must be considered.

To use the lottery, choose arbitrary values for the criteria in a 50–50 lottery, and switch around some of the values in a second 50–50 lottery. If the criteria are independent, the decision maker should be indifferent between any two such lotteries since the expected value of each criterion is the same in each lottery.

To illustrate, suppose we consider the automobile selection problem with only two criteria, cost and horsepower. In one lottery, we consider the two arbitrarily chosen alternatives of ($3500, 250 hp) and ($4500, 100 hp). In the second lottery, we "switch" the values of horsepower and ask the decision maker to compare the lotteries in Figure 4.

If the decision maker feels that the criteria are *independent*, he should be indifferent between lottery (a) and lottery (b). In lottery (a), there is a 0.5 probability that he will have to pay $4500 and a 0.5 probability that he will have to pay $3500. Similarly, there is a 0.5 probability that his car will have 100 hp and a 0.5 probability that it will have 250 hp. The same is true for lottery (b). If the criteria are independent, the way that they are paired in these lotteries should be irrelevant. Several such lotteries should be used to verify independence.

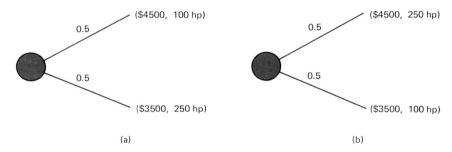

(a)   (b)

Figure 4. Lotteries to test independence for the
automobile selection problem with two criteria

Example Let us return to the problem of choosing the Starburst or the
Palomino under the risky situation involving a smog device (Table 4). To
test independence, suppose we use the lottery approach and arbitrarily
choose the values ($3500, 140 hp, 20 mpg, ugly) and ($4500, 120 hp, 12 mpg,
so-so) for the first lottery. In the second lottery, we switch the values of horsepower and miles per gallon and ask the decision maker to compare the two
lotteries shown in Figure 5.

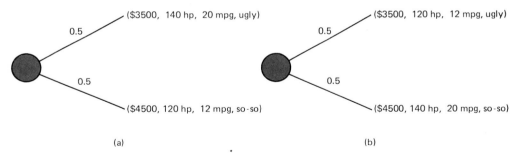

(a)   (b)

Figure 5. Lotteries to test independence for the
automobile selection problem with four criteria

Would we expect the typical decision-maker to be indifferent between
lottery (a) and lottery (b) in Figure 5? This is a personal matter, but in this
case there is some reason to believe that he would not be indifferent. The
decision maker might say, "Well, in lottery (b) I either get a relatively inexpensive car ($3500) with poor gas mileage (12 mpg), or a relatively expensive
car ($4500) with good gas mileage (20 mpg). At least these values tend to off-
set each other. In lottery (a) I have a 0.5 probability of obtaining a car that is
expensive and also has poor gas mileage, which would really be an economic
disaster for me. I would prefer lottery (b)." Thus, the criteria are not independent because of the relationship between cost and mileage in this decision
maker's mind.

In order to use the additive evaluative model, we must redefine the criteria. Let us *combine* the purchase price and miles per gallon into a total cost criterion by converting miles per gallon into gasoline required and adding the cost of the gasoline to the purchase price. For example, consider an automobile with a base price of $3500 that gets 12 miles per gallon. Suppose the decision maker expects to drive the car an average of 10,000 miles per year for five years. Therefore, he will require $(10,000/12) = 833.33$ gallons of gasoline per year. At $0.60 per gallon, the cost is $500 per year. Using a 10 percent discount rate over five years, the present value of this cost is $1895, which can be added to the purchase price of $3500 to obtain a total cost of $5395. As a result, the alternatives in Table 4 would be redefined as shown in Table 8.

TABLE 8. Redefining the Criteria to Obtain Independence

	Starburst (A_1)		Palomino (A_2)	
Criterion	Smog Device Not Required (O_{11})	Smog Device Required (O_{12})	Smog Device Not Required (O_{21})	Smog Device Required (O_{22})
Total costs	$4637	$4964	$5350	$5695
Horsepower	140	120	170	140
Appearance	ugly	ugly	beautiful	beautiful

Rather than adding the total cost of the gasoline, we could have added or subtracted the cost differential from what would be incurred if each automobile obtained the same miles per gallon—a figure of 15, for example. In effect, we would be obtaining the same results as in our first trade-off calculations when miles per gallon was set at 15 for all alternatives.

Now, suppose we construct several lottery pairs involving the criteria total cost, horsepower, and appearance where some of the values are "switched." This time, suppose the decision maker is indifferent between the lotteries in each pair. We can assume that the additive model can be used.

For additional details regarding the concept of independence in multiattribute utility theory, see Keeney [1973a], Raiffa [1969], and Keeney and Raiffa [1976].

Assessing the Additive Utility Function

There are two tasks in assessing the additive utility function. First, we must determine the single criterion utility function u_k for each criterion, and, second, we must estimate the scaling constants w_k.

Assessing the Single Criterion Utility Functions   If the independence assumptions are satisfied, we need to assess the utility functions u_k defined on the $k = 1, \ldots, m$ criteria. In this automobile selection example, $m = 3$ after the criteria have been redefined. We can do this by considering each criterion independently and assessing the utility function using one of the approaches described in Chapter 3.

We may begin by constructing the single criterion utility function u_1 for total cost. We must identify a "best" total cost that is as low or lower than any total cost of any alternative we shall consider, and a "worst" total cost that is as high or higher than any total cost we shall consider. Suppose we use $4500 as the best cost and $6000 as the worst. We then ask the decision maker to answer either 50–50 gambles or to identify probabilities as described in Chapter 3 in order to obtain a utility function for total cost. For example, we could ask the decision maker to identify the maximum total cost that he would accept for certain, rather than face the gamble shown in Figure 6. Suppose he says $5300. Then we assign $5300 the utility number 0.5. Continuing in this manner we eventually obtain the utility function shown in Figure 7.

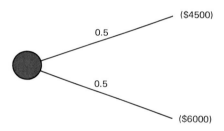

Figure 6. A gamble used to determine the utility function u_1 for total costs

Similarly, suppose we ask the decision maker a series of questions involving gambles and obtain the utility function u_2 shown in Figure 8. Finally, we have only three values for appearance, so the utility function u_3 illustrated in Figure 9 consists of only three points and can be obtained from one question to the decision maker, since u_3 (beautiful) $= 1.0$ and u_3 (ugly) $= 0.0$ by convention.

Assessing the Weights   The assessment of the scaling factor or weight w_k for the kth criterion seems simple, but there is a subtle point that must be emphasized. This weight is *not*, in general, a measure of the "relative importance" of each criterion. This point is especially important because it is often erroneously ignored in applications of additive evaluative models for multiple criteria.

The weight does reflect the relative importance of each criterion going from its *worst to its best value*, where the "worst" and the "best" values are the ones used in determining the single dimensional utility functions. For

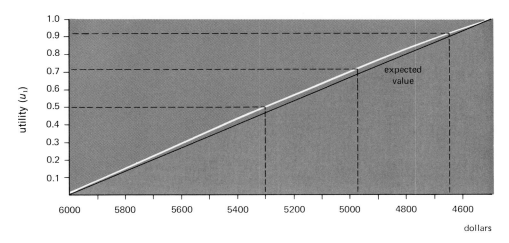

Figure 7. The utility function u_1 for total costs

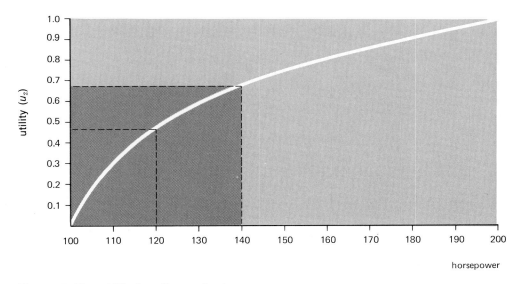

Figure 8. The utility function u_2 for horsepower

example, we would ask the decision maker if it is most important for cost to go from $6000 to $4500, horsepower to go from 100 hp to 200 hp, or appearance to go from ugly to beautiful. Suppose he says that the change in cost is most important, the change in horsepower is next, and the change in appearance is least important. Thus, we obtain a ranking of the relative importance of these *changes* in the criterion values, not of the criteria themselves.

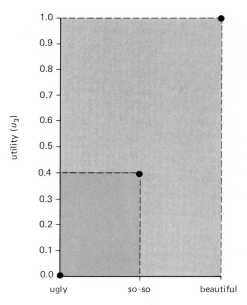

Figure 9. Utility function u_3 for appearance

We assign the criterion with the most important change a weight of 1.0. In this case, $w_1 = 1.0$. Next, we take the second most important change, which occurs in horsepower. We would say to the decision maker: "Relative to the change in cost from \$6000 to \$4500, how important is the change in horsepower from 100 to 200? Express this as a proportion." Suppose after some thought, the decision maker says that the change in horsepower is about one-half as important as the change in costs, so $w_2 = w_1/2 = 0.5$. Using a similar question, we determine that $w_3 = 0.167$.

As an alternative that is especially appropriate in risky situations, we can use gambles to estimate each w_k. Suppose we want w_k. We ask the decision maker to identify the probability p such that he is indifferent between 1) an alternative with the *best possible* value for criterion k and the *worst possible* value for all of the other criteria for certain or 2) facing a gamble with probability p of obtaining an alternative with the best possible values for all of the criteria (including k) and a probability of $1 - p$ of obtaining an alternative with the lowest possible values for all of the criteria.

To illustrate, suppose we want w_1. We ask the decision maker to specify p such that he is indifferent between receiving (\$4500, 100 hp, ugly) for certain, or taking the result of the gamble shown in Figure 10. Suppose, after some reflection, he says p is approximately 0.6, so we have $w_1 = 0.6$. (Think about this question and determine your own value for w_1).

For w_2 the decision maker would specify p such that he is indifferent between (\$6000, 200 hp, ugly) and the same gamble in Figure 10. This time, he might say $p = 0.3$, which gives $w_2 = 0.3$. In a similar fashion, suppose we

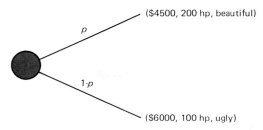

($4500, 200 hp, beautiful)

p

1-p

($6000, 100 hp, ugly)

Figure 10. Gamble used to determine the weights w_1, w_2, and w_3

obtain $w_3 = 0.1$. Thus, we need only ask as many questions as we have criteria in order to obtain the weights.

When the lottery approach is used, the sum of the weights should equal 1.0. If this is not the case, then the questions should be asked again. Otherwise, the fact that the weights do not sum to 1.0 is an indication that the additive model is inappropriate (for an example see Keeney [1974]).

Utilizing the Utility Function   Once the utility function has been estimated, any set of alternatives can be compared conveniently. For example, we have estimated the additive utility function

$$U(O_i^1, O_i^2, O_i^3) = 0.6 \, u_1(O_i^1) + 0.3 \, u_2(O_i^2) + 0.1 \, u_3(O_i^3) \, ,$$

where u_1, u_2, and u_3 are shown in Figures 7, 8, and 9 respectively, and the weights are those estimated from the gambles.

These results may be used for evaluating alternatives in risky choice situations or under conditions of certainty. For example consider the automobile selection problem in Table 8. From Figure 7, u_1 (4637) = 0.92; from Figure 8, u_2 (140) = 0.67; and from Figure 9, u_3 (ugly) = 0.0. Therefore, the utility number assigned to O_{11}, the Starburst when the smog device is not required, is given by

$$(0.6) \, (0.92) + (0.3) \, (0.67) + (0.1) \, (0.0) = 0.753 \, .$$

Similarly, since u_1 (4964) = 0.72, u_2 (120) = 0.46, and u_3 (ugly) = 0.0, the utility number assigned to the Starburst when the smog device is required is

$$(0.6) \, (0.72) + (0.3) \, (0.46) + (0.1) \, (0.0) = 0.57 \, .$$

Thus, the expected utility number to be associated with alternative A_1, choose the Starburst, is

$$(0.4) \, (0.753) + (0.6) \, (0.57) = 0.643 \, ,$$

since there is a 0.6 chance that the smog device will be required. Using the same approach, we can compute the expected utility number to be associated with alternative A_2, the Palomino, which is 0.518. Thus, again the Starburst appears to be the preferred alternative.

These calculations may be summarized in tabular form as illustrated in Table 9. Such a table is particularly useful in discussions among decision makers.

Using The Additive Model Under Certainty As we have just seen, the additive utility function assigns a value of 0.753 to the Starburst if no smog device is required. Similarly, this evaluative model assigns a utility function value of 0.637 to the Palomino when no smog device is required. If the probability of requiring a smog device is 0.0 rather than 0.6, then these will be the values assigned to the two alternatives, and again the Starburst is preferred.

Notice that the case of having the probability of the smog device being required equal to 0.0 is equivalent to the original problem of choosing between the two automobiles under conditions of complete certainty. Thus, this evaluative model, which is appropriate for use in situations involving risk, is also appropriate for use in situations involving certainty, which may be viewed as a special case of the more general risky choice decision.

A Site Selection Example In Figure 2, a hierarchy of criteria was presented for the problem of locating a pumped storage station for a public utility company. After the criteria have been identified, the next step in analyzing a problem such as this one is the identification of the alternatives, and the assessment of each one on each criterion. An example of a data sheet that might result is shown in Table 10. The columns correspond to the alternatives, while the rows represent the criteria.*

Next, an evaluative model must be selected. In this problem it was determined that the criteria are independent. For example, a change in the impacts of an alternative on the flora in the area would not affect the decision maker's "feelings" about its impacts on the fauna, because each criterion does have an intrinsic value of its own. Therefore, an additive evaluative model was used.

The first task is the determination of the single criterion utility function values, the u_k's, using the methods of Chapter 3. The "best" outcome on each criterion can be assigned a single dimensional utility function value of 1.0, and the "worst" can be given a 0.0. The remaining values are determined by "thinking hard" and assigning values directly, or by lotteries.

For example, the number of acres submerged by a pumped storage station site at Jose Basin is only 230, so its outcome is assigned a value of 1.0 on this criterion as shown in Table 11. In contrast, the Ruby Canyon site requires the submerging of 725 acres, which is given a value of 0.0. The value for Hookers Cove, where 300 acres are submerged, could be deter-

---

* Adapted from T. Mock, "Mock's Matrix Method," mimeographed, Graduate School of Management, University of California, Los Angeles, Spring 1973; used by permission. The example is based on actual data supplied by Southern California Edison. However, the data have been modified and the preferences are only illustrative.

TABLE 9. Summary of Calculations Using the Additive Evaluative Model

		Starburst (A_1)						Palomino (A_2)					
		Smog device not required ($p = 0.4$)			Smog device required ($p = 0.6$)			Smog device not required ($p = 0.4$)			Smog device required ($p = 0.6$)		
Criterion k	Weight w_k	Actual Value	u_k	$w_k \cdot u_k$	Actual Value	u_k	$w_k \cdot u_k$	Actual Value	u_k	$w_k \cdot u_k$	Actual Value	u_k	$w_k \cdot u_k$
Total Costs	0.6	4637	0.92	0.552	4964	0.72	0.432	5350	0.46	0.276	5695	0.23	0.138
Horsepower	0.3	140	0.67	0.201	120	0.46	0.138	170	0.87	0.261	140	0.67	0.201
Appearance	0.1	ugly	0.0	0.0	ugly	0.0	0.0	beautiful	1.0	0.1	beautiful	1.0	0.1
Sum				0.753			0.57			0.637			0.439
Expected Utility		$(0.4)(0.753) + (0.6)(0.57) = 0.643$						$(0.4)(0.637) + (0.6)(0.439) = 0.518$					

TABLE 10. Alternatives and Criteria for the Site Selection Problem

Criterion	Alternatives				
	Hideaway Ranch	Jose Basin	Hookers Cove	Ruby Canyon	San Mateo
Economic—development costs ($/kw)	213	231	232	202	202
Erosion—roads to be built	General drainage —good to excessive; high erosion hazard	General drainage —good to excessive; high erosion hazard; relocation of ½ mi of Old Rivergrade Rd. on upper reservoir site required	General drainage —good to excessive; high erosion hazard	General drainage —fair to good; very high erosion hazard	General drainage —fair to good; high erosion hazard
Flora—plant clearing	Limited ground cover; small area for dams	Unusual variety of vegetation due to Transition Zone	Unusual variety of vegetation due to Transition Zone	Sparse, rugged; chaparral	Sparse, rugged; chaparral
Fauna—fish and game	Poor fishing in San Joaquin River; resident deer population small (10–20); cattle grazing land; small animal population	Poor fisheries at Redinger Lake; intermediate winter deer range; cattle grazing	Good winter deer range; high density of migratory deer; cattle grazing	Condor refuge near site	Few fish species; deer and other small game prevalent

Acres submerged	Small reservoirs: upper—180 a.; lower—180 a.	Only one dam required: lower reservoir is Redinger Lake; upper reservoir—230 a.	Upper reservoir—190 a.; lower reservoir—110 a.	Upper reservoir—125 a.; lower reservoir—600 a.	Upper reservoir—130 a.; lower reservoir—270 a.
Effect on water system	Fluctuation rate on San Joaquin River 7 ft/hr; natural flow will be allowed	Redinger Lake used as lower reservoir; causes fluctuation of 1.7 ft/hr; natural flow will be allowed	Reservoir and river fluctuations 10 ft/hr; natural flow will be allowed	Project will allow natural stream flow; possible downstream sedimentation and/or eutrophication	Project will allow natural stream flow; possible downstream sedimentation and/or eutrophication
Recreational values—reservoir fluctuations and recreation potential	Upper reservoir—7 ft/hr; lower reservoir—7 ft/hr; sightseeing, picnicking, hiking	Upper reservoir—4.5 ft/hr; lower reservoir—1.7 ft/hr; possibility for fishing and recreation on upper reservoir; water ski area	Upper reservoir—5.5 ft/hr; lower reservoir—10 ft/hr; sightseeing, picnicking, hiking	Upper reservoir—16 ft/hr; lower reservoir—4 ft/hr; hiking	Upper reservoir—20.1 ft/hr; lower reservoir—9.6 ft/hr; hiking, picnicking
Scenic values	Little scenic value	Has scenic value	Has scenic value	Little scenic value	Little scenic value
Historical sites	Possible sites—archaeological survey needed	Indian sites in immediate area of upper dam; archaeological survey needed	Possible Indian sites; archaeological survey needed	No sites known of at this date—archaeological survey needed	Possible sites; archaeological survey needed

mined by choosing p for the lottery in Figure 11 so that the decision maker is indifferent between 300 acres submerged for sure or accepting the lottery instead. In this hypothetical example, $p = 0.8$. The remainder of the numbers within Table 11 were obtained in a similar manner.

TABLE 11. Evaluation of the Alternative Sites

Criterion	Weight (w_k)	Utility Numbers for:				
		Hideaway Ranch	Jose Basin	Hookers Cove	Ruby Canyon	San Mateo
Economic	1.0	0.7	0.05	0.0	1.0	1.0
Erosion	0.2	0.7	0.0	0.7	0.6	1.0
Flora	0.4	1.0	0.0	0.0	0.8	0.8
Fauna	0.6	1.0	0.8	0.0	0.1	0.5
Acres submerged	0.8	0.6	1.0	0.8	0.0	0.5
Effect on water system	0.2	0.8	0.8	0.0	1.0	1.0
Recreational values	0.5	0.3	0.8	0.8	0.0	1.0
Scenic values	0.4	0.0	1.0	1.0	0.0	0.0
Historical sites	0.6	0.5	0.0	0.2	1.0	0.5
Weighted Total		2.93	2.29	1.70	2.30	3.22
Rank		2	4	5	3	1

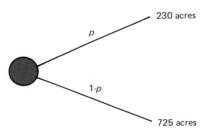

Figure 11. Lottery for use in assigning utility function values for the criterion "acres submerged"

The "weights" are assigned to each criterion by considering the relative importance of a change from the "worst" outcome associated with an alternative to the "best" outcome on that criterion. The weights, shown in Table 11, were assigned using the concept of "proportions" rather than lotteries.

Finally, the weights are multiplied by the entries in each column, and the results are added. On this basis, the sites are ranked from the most desirable to the least desirable. On the basis of the evaluative model, San Mateo is the superior site and Hideaway Ranch is a close second. Rather than choosing San Mateo at this point, the decision maker might wish to narrow his analysis to these two alternatives and gather additional data.

Estimating the Additive Model with Linear Regression

As an alternative to the procedures we have described for assessing the additive evaluative model, linear regression can be used. This approach assumes that the criteria are independent and that the u_k are linear (e.g., $u_k(O_i^1) = O_i^1$). The decision maker must consider a large number of alternatives described by multiple criteria and rate each one on a numerical scale, perhaps from 1 to 20. An alternative assigned a 20 would be perfect, while one receiving a 1 would be a relative disaster. Each criterion must also be represented by a numerical scale. Thus, in our automobile example, we would have to convert our verbal description of appearance into a numerical scale, from 1 to 5 perhaps (the upper and lower limits can be selected arbitrarily), where 1 corresponds to "ugly" and 5 to "beautiful." A car that appears so-so might be rated a 3 on this scale.

For example, the decision maker might consider ($3500, 150 hp, 15 mpg, 3 [so-so]), and assign it a 12, while ($3200, 170 hp, 25 mpg, 4 [between so-so and beautiful]) might rate an 18. These alternatives can be real, or they can be generated at random. The values of the criteria would then be treated as the independent variables in a linear regression model, and the rating would be the dependent variable (see Appendix C). The resulting linear equation can be used to predict the decision maker's choices among new alternatives. In fact, it has been found that because of the decision maker's inconsistencies, the evaluative model often does better than the decision maker (as measured by the actual performance of the alternatives selected by each, based on the criteria). Thus, the evaluative model may be used as a "check" on the decision maker in making repetitive choices.

Dawes [1971] has analyzed the judgments of a university committee admitting Ph.D. students. The criteria are test scores on a standard exam (GRE), the student's undergraduate grades (GPA), and the quality of the undergraduate school attended (QI). The evaluative model determined by the linear regression is .0032 GRE + 1.02 GPA + .0791 QI. When the predictions of the evaluative model and the committee's actual ratings were compared to later ratings of success in the Ph.D. program, the evaluative model did a much better job of predicting success. Kunreuther [1969] develops a similar model for describing and aiding a manager doing production scheduling.

The estimation of these evaluative models has been automated in a man-machine interactive program developed by K. R. Hammond and his associates [1971]. This program automatically generates alternatives for the decision maker to rate, and calculates his evaluative model. This approach has been used as an aid in community planning [Stewart and Gelberd, 1973] and in labor-management negotiations [Balke et al., 1973].

There is one serious disadvantage to the linear regression techniques. They assume that the decision maker can look at an alternative as described by multiple criteria and comfortably rate it on a numerical scale. In many important situations, the decision maker may be seeking aid from an evaluative model because he *cannot* accomplish this task. If he could rate the alternatives, he might not need the evaluative model at all. Nevertheless, this approach is useful in situations involving repetitive decisions, or for estimating an evaluative model for use with an optimizing model (for examples see McMillan and Stewart [1973] and Wilsted et al. [1973]). It is also useful as an aid in conflict resolution where it can be used to identify the differences in the evaluative models of individuals who disagree over the choice of alternatives. Such uses are described by Balke et al. [1973] and by Flack and Summers [1971].

WHAT SHOULD THE MANAGER KNOW?

If the result of all decisions could be measured in terms of a single criterion, if everyone agreed that more (or less) of the criterion was always desirable, and if reliable predictive models could be constructed, then there would be no need for managers to make decisions. It would be a mechanical process to search through alternatives until the one that maximizes (or minimizes) the criterion was discovered. However, multiple criteria must be considered, and the most important role of the manager is in determining the basis by which these multiple criteria can be reconciled. The evaluative models for multiple criteria can be useful aids in dealing with problems involving multiple criteria.

Problem Characteristics   The problems to which these evaluative models should be applied involve several criteria of approximately equal importance. In private industry, these problems often arise when the short-run profits from a decision are being compared against potential long-run effects of the decision. In theory, a manager in private industry might prefer to use the future net profit of all decisions as a guide to his decision making. He may be aware that certain decisions can have important effects on market share, customer service, labor relations, or the probability of government regulation. Eventually, he may feel that such effects will have long-run implications for profit or loss. However, he may have extreme difficulty in translating such effects into expected profit or loss figures, so that the future net profit can be computed. As an alternative, he may prefer to view the problem as involving multiple criteria where short-run profits must be balanced against the more easily predicted effects in these other areas.

In the public sector, the single criterion of profit or loss has little meaning. Public managers are continually dealing with problems involving multiple criteria. The example of selecting a transportation system was presented earlier. A similar hierarchy of criteria and objectives could be constructed in such fields as health or education. Examples of the application of evaluative models for multiple criteria in the public sector are given by Stimson [1969], Klee [1971], Dyer [1973], and Keeney [1973b], and several applications are reviewed by Keeney and Raiffa [1976].

Other problems common to both the private and the public sector can also be viewed as multiple criteria problems. Major equipment selection problems, such as the purchase of a new computer system, may involve multiple criteria. For example, the memory size, speed of execution, and cost of the alternative computers may be important criteria in such a decision. The selection of research and development projects for further investment is also an example of a common decision problem involving multiple criteria.

Formulation   The most important task in the formulation of a multiple criteria evaluative model is the identification of the criteria. It is crucial that the manager be involved in this task to ensure that the appropriate criteria are considered. In addition, the manager should recognize the importance of working with an analyst to obtain a set of "independent" criteria if the additive form of the evaluative model is to be used. This process may require combining several criteria, as in the case of the automobile example where the purchase price and mileage were combined into total cost in order to obtain independence.

Information Requirements   The information requirements for the multiple criteria evaluative models are relatively severe. The decision maker must cooperate in determining the rating necessary to use the regression approach, the trade-offs, or the utility function for each criterion, as well as the weights. Thus, these approaches should only be explicitly applied to problems in which the stakes are high, and the effort required to determine the evaluative model is thus justified. One area of current research (see Sarin [1975]) is directed towards the development of man-machine interactive computer programs to aid in the estimation of these utility functions.

The use of the additive model by the manager will probably require the assistance of an expert analyst. However, the trade-off approach to choosing among a relatively small number of alternatives can generally be accomplished through self-interrogation by the decision maker.

Interpretation of Results   Because of the possible errors in the estimation of the trade-offs and utility functions, the results of the analysis with the multiple criteria evaluative model should be interpreted with some caution. It would be inappropriate to blindly follow the rankings resulting from the models, especially if several outcomes are relatively "close." If the additive model is used, the manager should be careful to check the independence assumptions to ensure that the models are appropriate.

These approaches do not relieve the manager of the task of making trade-offs. They simply provide a systematic way of analyzing the alternatives. Often a manager may wish to revise his trade-offs or utility functions and weights as he learns more about the problem. This situation is especially true in the public sector where inputs from citizens and public reactions to initial proposals may provide a basis for these revisions.

Advantages and Disadvantages   The most important advantage of the multiple criteria evaluative models may arise from the *process* of their use. The explicit identification of the important criteria and an assessment of their relative worth can help the decision maker to clarify his own thinking on these issues. The only disadvantages are the information requirements of the models. Nevertheless, when the decisions to be made are significant, these evaluative models can provide an important aid to decision makers.

Check Your Understanding

1. List two or more criteria that might be considered of approximately equal importance for each of the following decision situations:
    a. the selection of a jet fighter from several alternative prototypes
    b. the design of an emergency medical system for a city
    c. the choice of a dam site on a river
    d. the creation of a new national park
    e. the purchase of a new computer system
    f. the selection of a particular product for further development and marketing
    g. the determination of the terms of a bargaining settlement in negotiating a labor contract
2. Use the approach of developing a hierarchical representation of criteria on (**1a**), (**1b**), (**1d**), and (**1f**). In each case, carry out the hierarchy until you reach the "fourth level" from the top, or further.
3. By actively mulling over the problems (**1a**), (**1b**), (**1d**), and (**1f**), can you identify other criteria of importance which may have been omitted in your hierarchy? List these, and revise the hierarchy accordingly.
4. How much would you be willing to pay for an extra 10 hp in an automobile (a small car) that currently has 30 hp? How much would you be willing to pay if it currently has 400 hp? Why are the amounts different? To what basic concept of economics does this phenomenon relate?
5. Develop your own trade-offs for the Starburst and the Palomino shown in Table 1. Use the "objective" analysis results that relate miles per gallon to cost that are shown in the example. Specify your trade-offs for horsepower versus cost and for appearance versus cost. Summarize the results in tables similar to Tables 2 and 3. Which alternative do you prefer?

6. Begin with the two automobiles described by ($3121, 140 hp, 15 mpg, ugly) and by ($3833, 170 hp, 15 mpg, beautiful). Obtain the cooperation of a friend.

   a. Using the trade-off approach, find the cost such that your friend would be indifferent between each car and another alternative with 150 hp, 15 mpg, and a so-so appearance. Which car should he prefer?

   b. Ask your friend to look at the two descriptions of the automobiles that you started with, then ask him which he prefers. Does his response agree with the result of your trade-off experiment?

7. Equivalent conditional outcomes with the same values for the criteria of horsepower, miles per gallon, and appearance were created for the Starburst and the Palomino if the smog device were required. Ignoring these identical values of the other criteria, we can create a table of costs similar to Table 1 in Chapter 2 as follows:

	Cost If:	
Alternatives	Smog Device Not Required ($p = 0.4$)	Smog Device Required ($p = 0.6$)
Starburst	$3391	$3960
Palomino	$3417	$4025

   a. Compute the expected monetary value associated with each alternative.

   b. For what kinds of problems might this approach be appropriate? For example, would the decisions most likely be repetitive or one-of-a-kind?

8. Suppose we introduce a third alternative, the Champion. The conditional outcomes associated with the Champion are shown below:

	Champion (A_3)	
Criterion	Smog Device Not Required (O_{31})	Smog Device Required (O_{32})
Cost	3800	4000
Horsepower	150	140
Miles per gallon	20	20
Appearance	so-so	so-so

Now, suppose we ask the decision maker to specify the necessary trade-offs, as before, and we find the following result:

	Original Conditional Outcome	Equivalent Conditional Outcome
Smog device not required	(O_{31}): ($3800, 150 hp, 20 mpg, so-so)	(O'_{31}): ($3420, 150 hp, 15 mpg, so-so)
Smog device required	(O_{32}): ($4000, 140 hp, 20 mpg, so-so)	(O'_{32}): ($3609, 150 hp, 15 mpg, so-so)

Finally, using lotteries, the decision maker assigns the utility function values of 0.95 to O'_{31} (O_{31}) and of 0.66 to O'_{32} (O_{32}).

Determine which of the three alternative automobiles should be preferred if the probability that the smog device will be required is as follows:

a. 0.6

b. 0.0

c. 0.3

d. 1.0

9. Distinguish between technological independence of criteria and criteria that are independent in terms of preferences.

10. In each of the following problems, state whether you would expect the criteria to be independent in terms of a decision maker's preferences and explain your reasoning:

a. in the design of an emergency medical system, the criteria of "lives saved" and "costs"

b. in the creation of a new national park, the criteria of "number of annual visitors" and "ecological damage"

c. in the selection of a new product for further development, the criteria of "price" and "expected cost of production"

11. In the additive utility model, why is the weight w_k for the kth criterion not simply a measure of the relative importance of each criterion?

12. Suppose the decision maker wishes to apply the additive utility function with u_1, u_2, and u_3 shown in Figures 7, 8 and 9 respectively, and with $w_1 = 0.6$, $w_2 = 0.3$, and $w_3 = 0.1$, to the Champion described in question (8). Since the purchase price and miles per gallon are not independent in terms of his preferences, he combines these two criteria into a total cost criterion as before. The results are shown below.

	Champion (A_3)	
Criterion	Smog Device Not Required (O_{31})	Smog Device Required (O_{32})
Total costs	$4937	$5137
Horsepower	150	140
Appearance	so-so	so-so

a. Estimating the appropriate values of u_1, u_2, and u_3 from Figures 7, 8 and 9 respectively, calculate the expected utility associated with the Champion from the additive utility function when the probability that a smog device will be required is 0.6.
b. Using the additive utility function, repeat this analysis for all three automobiles when the probability that the smog device will be required is as follows:
1) 0.0
2) 0.3
3) 1.0

Problems

1. Suppose you have just graduated, and you are trying to select your first job from several offers. You have decided to make your decision on the basis of the five criteria shown in the first column of Table 12. The criterion values associated with each alternative are also shown in Table 12.

TABLE 12. Alternative Jobs

Criterion	Job 1	Job 2	Job 3	Standard Values
Salary	$16,000	$18,000	$22,000	---
Population of City	250,000	1 million	10 million	1 million
Climate	Hot, dry summers; mild winters	Hot, humid summers; mild winters	Pleasant summers; cold snowy winters	Hot, humid summers; mild winters
Daily Commuting (one way)	0.25 hour	0.5 hour	1.0 hour	0.5 hour
Nature of Job	Much responsibility and opportunities for advancement	Routine work but opportunities for advancement	Routine work with few opportunities for advancement	Routine work but opportunities for advancement

a. Use the trade-off approach to choose between the alternatives. For each alternative, determine an alternative such that you are indifferent between the original alternative and one with the "standard" values for the last four criteria that are also shown in the last column of Table 12. For each alternative, develop a summary of trade-offs like that of Table 2.
b. Use the additive evaluative model to choose among the alternatives. Assess the single criterion utility function values for each alternative using the lottery approach. Also assess the weight for each criterion using the lottery approach. Develop a table to display your analysis similar to Table 11.
c. In terms of your individual preference, are the criteria independent? Try to verify independence with a lottery. If the criteria are not independent, how could they be redefined? If they are not independent, can you place any confidence in the results from the additive evaluative model?

2. Standard Oil of California proposes to construct a supertanker port and pipeline to supply its refinery at Richmond in the San Francisco Bay Area. The port would consist of a single-point mooring two or three miles from shore to unload supertankers. Submarine pipelines would take the oil into a shore-based pumping station where it would enter the pipeline to the Richmond refinery.

There are several alternative sites on the West Coast where a supertanker port could be located. On the basis of a preliminary screening, four sites were selected for a more detailed evaluation: Moss Landing, Estero Bay, Port Hueneme, and Oso Flaco Dunes. The major criteria to be used in evaluating these alternatives were economics, the local political environment, and the environmental impacts. The three major criteria were refined into the ten criteria listed in the left-hand column of Table 13. After some discussion, it was decided that the criteria were independent in terms of the preferences of decision makers at Standard Oil, so an additive evaluative model could be used.

In order to determine the utility function for each criterion, it is necessary to specify a "worst" and a "best" outcome. The second column in Table 13 specifies the worst outcomes, which are assigned the value of 0.0, and the third column contains the best values, which are assigned 1.0. Finally, the weights w_k for the criteria are in the fourth column. These were determined in a committee meeting using the concept of "proportions."

The characteristics of each alternative site for each criterion are shown in Table 14. On the basis of these characteristics, the committee assigned the utility function scores shown in Table 15. For example, the utility function score for Estero Bay on the criterion "facilities" is 0.3, while it is 0.0 for Moss Landing, Oso Flaco, and Port Hueneme.*

a. On the basis of these weights and utility function values, which of the four alternatives should be preferred? Construct a table similar to Table 11 to display your analysis.

b. What if the weights on the two environmental criteria are increased to 1.0 for each one? Would the preferred alternative be different?

3. Suppose you are an elementary school principal who is deciding which new educational program to introduce for third grade students. The major curriculum areas in your school are reading, mathematics, and spelling. The third graders currently achieve a mean percentile score of 50 in reading, 40 in mathematics, and 30 in spelling.

There are three alternative programs under consideration. Program 1 focuses on enhancing reading skills and has some spillover benefits in developing spelling abilities. If it is successful, you estimate that the mean reading score will increase by 15 percentile points, and the mean spelling score will increase by 5 percentile points. The score in mathematics will remain unchanged. However, if it is a failure because of the reactions of your teachers and students, you estimate that the mean scores in all three areas

---

* From G. Hill, A. Kokin, and S. Nukes, "Standard Oil Supertanker Port Evaluation: Where Should They Put It?" unpublished report, Graduate School of Management, University of California, Los Angeles, June 1975. The alternatives, criteria, weights, and utility function values are only illustrative and do not represent the views of Standard Oil of California.

TABLE 13. Criteria Value Ranges and Weights

Criterion	"Worst" Value for Each Criterion (lower limit—0.0)	"Best" Value for Each Criterion (upper limit—1.0)	Weights (w_k)
Facilities	No facilities to support supertanker operations	All facilities completed for supertanker port operations	0.25
Port characteristics	Very rough seas and more than four miles from shore	Calm seas and one mile from shore	0.50
Location (Estero Bay as base)	Near Los Angeles with poor access to the San Joaquin Valley and Richmond	Between the Elk Hills oil field and San Francisco, but closer to Elk Hills with easy pipeline access to the San Joaquin Valley	0.75
Initial cost (Estero Bay cost as base)	$60 million above base	$60 million below base	0.875
Annual cost (Estero Bay cost as base)	$5 million above base	$5 million below base	0.75
Possibilities for future development	No future development or expansion possible after initial part is completed	No limit on future growth or expansion of facilities	0.75
Attitude of local populace	Large, strong, vocal, and effective opposition	Small, weak, and ineffective opposition	0.50
Attitude of local politicians	Favorable vote unlikely	Favorable vote assured	1.0
Environmental impact from operation	Oil spill would seriously disrupt the community and harm wildlife; extreme danger due to proximity to military operations or other industry	Oil spill could be cleaned up relatively swiftly with no serious effect	0.50
Environmental impact from placement of facilities	Extreme blight on the area and interference with the natural environment	No major adverse effects from placement of facilities	0.25

TABLE 14. Characteristics of Alternatives

Criterion	Alternatives			
	Moss Landing	Estero Bay	Port Hueneme	Oso Flaco Dunes
Facilities	No	Yes	No	No
Port characteristics	Fair	Good	Excellent	Good
Location	Close to Richmond, farther from Elk Hills than base location	Central location	90 miles farther from Richmond than base location	Central location
Initial cost	$40 million less than Estero Bay	The cost-base location	$60 million more than Estero Bay	$5 million more than Estero Bay (estimate)
Annual cost	$2 million per year less than Estero Bay	Base location	$6 million more than Estero Bay	Near cost of base location
Possibilities for future development	Area already populated	Rolling terrain will hamper large expansion	Navy interference	Area available, subject to local politicians
Attitude of local populace	Possible opposition	Vocal opposition	Little effect on population	Little effect on population
Attitude of local politicians	Possibly opposed	Possibly favorable	Favorable	Possibly favorable
Environmental impact from operation	High impact—area is sandy to marshy, possibly difficult to clean up; possible long-term effects	High impact—tourism and fishing industry will be seriously affected; marshy area and rocky coastline extremely difficult to clean up; possible long-term damage to bird sanctuary and oyster beds	Minimal impact—area sandy; easy cleanup; area already industrialized	Minimal impact—area sandy; easy cleanup
Environmental impact from placement of facilities	Tank farm highly visible	Tank farm hidden; major restructure of existing creek	Tank farm visible (no nearby population)	Tank farm visible (no nearby population)

TABLE 15. Utility Function Values for Alternative Locations

Criterion	Location			
	Moss Landing	Estero Bay	Port Hueneme	Oso Flaco
Facilities	0.0	0.3	0.0	0.0
Port Characteristics	0.3	0.6	0.7	0.5
Location	0.7	0.5	0.3	0.5
Initial Cost	0.8	0.5	0.0	0.4
Annual Cost	0.7	0.5	0.3	0.4
Possibilities for Future Development	0.1	0.6	0.1	0.6
Attitude of Local Populace	0.1	0.1	0.5	0.7
Attitude of Local Politicians	0.1	0.5	0.7	0.5
Environmental Impact from Operation	0.1	0.1	0.1	0.3
Environmental Impact from Placement of Facilities	0.1	0.8	0.4	0.2

will remain unchanged. You estimate that the probability that Program 1 will be a success is 0.6, while the probability that it will be a failure is 0.4.

Program 2 is an intensive program for developing verbal skills. If it is successful, both reading and spelling scores will increase by 15 percentile points, while the mathematics score will be unchanged. However, if it is a failure, you estimate that the negative reactions will be so severe that reading and spelling scores will actually fall 10 points each, and the mathematics score will also fall by 5 points. On the other hand, the probability of success is estimated at 0.8, with only a 0.2 chance of failure.

Finally, Program 3 is almost a "sure thing" directed at developing mathematical skills. If successful, mathematical skills will rise by 20 percentile points, and they will rise by 10 percentile points even if it is a "failure." In either case, the reading and spelling scores will remain unchanged. The probabilities of success and "failure" are 0.5.

Suppose you decide to use the additive evaluative model to choose between the alternatives. You consider the criteria to be independent in terms of your preferences. For the single criterion utility functions, you decide to use the utility curve actually obtained from a survey of elementary school principals displayed in Figure 8 of Chapter 3. Thus, the same single criterion function can be used for each of the three criteria. After considering the opinions of the parents of your students and the teachers, you assign the criterion of reading percentile score a weight of 0.5, mathematics a weight of 0.3, and spelling a weight of 0.2. (A procedure very similar to this one has been incorporated into a series of do-it-yourself evaluation instructions for elementary school principals by Hoepfner, et al. [1973].)

a. Using the additive evaluative model, which program should the principal select? Set up a table similar to Table 9 to summarize your analysis.

b. Would the results be different if the current scores were 60 in reading, 20 in mathematics, and 50 in spelling?

References

Balke, W., K. Hammond, and G. Meyer, "An Alternative Approach to Labor-Management Negotiations," *Administrative Science Quarterly*, Vol. 13, 1973.

Dawes, R., "A Case Study of Graduate Admissions: Three Principles of Human Decision Making," *American Psychologist,* Vol. 26, 1971.

Dyer, J., "A Procedure for Selecting Educational Goal Areas for Emphasis," *Operations Research,* Vol. 21, No. 3, 1973.

Fishburn, P., "Methods of Estimating Additive Utilities," *Management Science,* Vol. 13, No. 7, March 1967.

Flack, J., and D. Summers, "Computer Aided Conflict Resolution in Water Resource Planning: An Illustration," *Water Resources Research*, Vol. 7, 1971.

Franklin, B., "Letter to Joseph Priestley," (1772), *The Benjamin Franklin Samples*, Fawcett, New York, 1956.

Geoffrion, A., J. Dyer, and A. Feinberg, "An Interactive Approach for Multi-Criterion Optimization with an Application to the Operation of an Academic Department," *Management Science,* Vol. 19, No. 4, 1972.

Hammond, K. R., "Computer Graphics as an Aid to Learning," *Science,* Vol. 172, May 28, 1971.

Hill, G., A. Kokin, and S. Nukes, "Standard Oil Supertanker Port Evaluation: Where Should They Put It?" unpublished report, Graduate School of Management, University of California, Los Angeles, June 1975.

Hoepfner, R., P. A. Bradley, S. P. Klein, and M. C. Alkin, *CSE Elementary School Evaluation Kit: Needs Assessment,* Allyn and Bacon, Boston, 1973.

Howard, R., "Decision Analysis in Systems Engineering," in *Systems Concepts,* edited by R. Miles, John Wiley & Sons, New York, 1973.

Jackson, J. R., "Coping with Complexity," mimeographed, Graduate School of Management, University of California, Los Angeles, 1974.

Keeney, R., "Utility Functions for Multiattributed Consequences," *Management Science,* Vol. 18, No. 5, Part I, January, 1972.

——, "Concepts of Independence in Multiattribute Utility Theory," in *Multiple Criteria Decision Making,* edited by J. Cochrane and M. Zeleny, University of South Carolina Press, Columbia, South Carolina, 1973a.

——, "A Decision Analysis with Multiple Objectives: The Mexico City Airport," *Bell Journal of Economics and Management,* Vol. 4, 1973b.

——, "Multiplicative Utility Functions," *Operations Research,* Vol. 22, No. 1, January–February 1974.

Keeney, R., and H. Raiffa, *Decision Analysis with Multiple Objectives,* John Wiley & Sons, New York, 1976.

Klee, A., "The Role of Decision Models in the Evaluation of Competing Environmental Health Alternatives," *Management Science,* Vol. 18, No. 2, October 1971.

Kunreuther, H., "Extensions of Bowman's Theory on Managerial Decision Making," *Management Science*, Vol. 15, 1969.

Manheim, M., and F. Hall, "Abstract Representation of Goals," P-67-24, Department of Civil Engineering, M.I.T., January 1968.

McMillan, C., and T. Stewart, "Goal Programming and Policy Capture in Education Planning," mimeographed, University of Colorado, 1973.

Miller, J., "Assessing Alternative Transportation Systems," RM-5865-DOT, The Rand Corporation, Santa Monica, California, April 1969.

Mock, T., "Mock's Matrix Method," mimeographed, Graduate School of Management, University of California, Los Angeles, Spring 1973.

Pardee, F., T. Kirkwood, K. Kraemer, K. MacCrimmon, J. Miller, C. Phillips, J. Ranftl, K. Smith, and D. Whitcomb, "Measurement and Evaluation of Transportation System Effectiveness," RM-5869-DOT, The Rand Corporation, Santa Monica, California, September 1969.

Raiffa, H., "Preferences for Multiattributed Alternatives," RM-5868-DOT/RC, The Rand Corporation, Santa Monica, California, April 1969.

Sarin, R., "Interactive Procedures for Evaluation of Multi-Attributed Alternatives," Working Paper No. 232, Western Management Science Institute, University of California, Los Angeles, June 1975.

Stewart, T., and L. Gelberd, "Capturing Judgment Policies: A New Approach for Citizen Participation in Planning," Report No. 151, Program of Research on Human Judgment and Social Interaction, Institute of Behavioral Science, University of Colorado, June 1973.

Stimson, D., "Utility Measurement in Public Health Decision Making," *Management Science,* Vol. 16, No. 2, October 1969.

Wilsted, W., T. Hendrick, and T. Stewart, "Judgment Policy for Capturing Bank Loan Decisions: An Approach to Developing Objective Functions for Goal Programming Models," paper presented to the Western Regional Meeting of AIDS, San Diego, California, 1973.

Part Three

PREDICTIVE MODELS

Introduction to Predictive Models

In Part Two, we assumed that we knew how our basic financial, productive, marketing, and behavioral systems would respond to forecasts of the environment and to alternatives that we might pose. Recall our basic diagram relating these models, which we reproduce here as Figure 1. Our emphasis in Part Two was to develop methodologies for deciding what the best strategies would be if we knew the outcomes from predictive models. Now, however, we shall focus our attention on the predictive models themselves.

Forecasting the Environment

In the context of predictive models, the means we use to forecast the behavior of the environment is also a predictive model with a special character. Forecasting models focus attention on the prediction of the exogenous (outside) factors that are normally not within our control, but that have a tremendously important influence on what happens. The most obvious of these outside factors in managerial systems is demand for the product or service with which we deal. Demand is a fundamental driving force for all of our systems in both private and public enterprises, as well as product and service systems. These exogenous factors drive the basic systems for which we wish to establish predictive models and have an extremely important influence on the behavior of these systems.

It is important that we think in broad terms about the kinds of systems, for there is an unfortunate currency for the idea that demand functions are related only to business enterprises, when in fact every organization is driven by some kind of demand function. Knowing more than naive information about the demand function may suggest some of the most important strate-

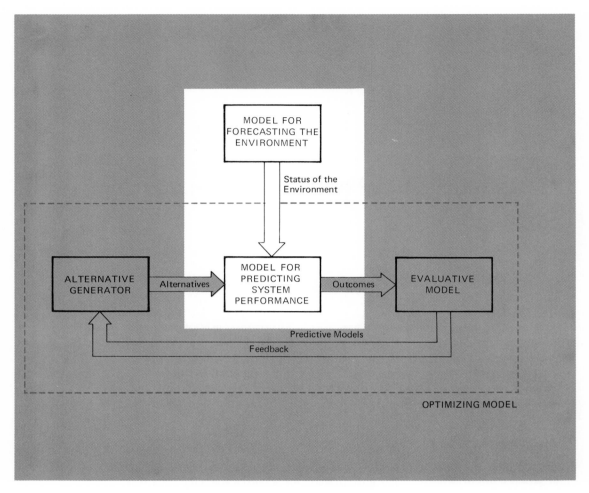

Figure 1. Predictive models in relation to alternatives and evaluation of outcomes

gies for managerial systems. For example, the delivery of mail to the post office peaks between 4:00 and 8:00 P.M. when 40 to 60 percent of the daily mail is delivered because of the day-end mailing practices of business. Given this fact, what are the best allocations of work force during the day and night shifts? With such a variable load pattern, how effective are proposals for mechanization likely to be?

Furthermore we all know that there is a very important seasonal pattern in mail volume. How do we forecast the mail volume pattern and also, the corollary question, what are the best strategies for allocating productive resources for a given forecast? Taking an even longer term viewpoint, what are the factors in our society that control the need for postal service in the future? How do we forecast the longer term needs for facilities and for systems appropriate to possibly much larger loads in the future?

The questions are similar for all kinds of systems. There are short-range, medium-range, and long-range variations in the demand for products and services of all kinds. In order to predict system performance we must forecast demand as an input.

Predicting System Performance

We can view our problem of predicting system performance (including the performance of the preceding forecasting models) in the context of any productive process as indicated in Figure 2. In Figure 2 we have input, process or transformation, and output in the general format of systems theory. Figure 2 simply says that given an input to a process, that input will be transformed in some way to produce an output.

Figure 2. Input-transformation-output module as a basis for predictive models.

First, let us take a physical process such as steel making with an electric furnace. As shown in Figure 3 (a), the inputs are basically iron ore, coke, limestone, and labor, and the output is steel. Between input and output there was a transformation process that we have simply called an electric furnace. We could replace "electric furnace" with a transformation function in order to compute output for given inputs. Suppose we are interested in output *quantity*. The transformation function would then be a simple mathematical statement of the tons of steel output for given quantities of the inputs. The mathematical transformation is a predictive model for output, given stated inputs. Now suppose you are a metallurgist. Your interest is in the transformation for certain qualities or steel alloys. In this case, the metallurgist's transformation function is in terms of the recipe and timing necessary to obtain the output of a specific alloy, rather than the quantity of output. His predictive model has a different purpose and is expressed in different units, but it is still a model that indicates how a system works.

Now let us expand our thinking to include a more highly aggregated system. The system is now an economic enterprise with inputs of consumer

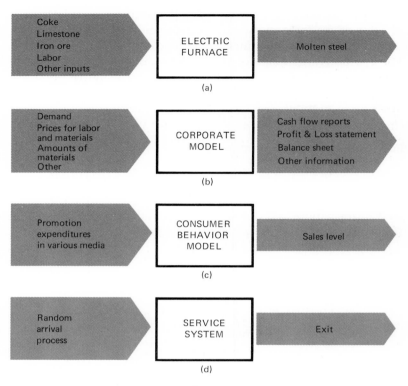

Figure 3. Input-transformation-output modules. In each case a predictive model can be substituted for the actual process or transformation to predict the outputs or outcomes

demand, labor, materials, and other costs, and the outputs are predictions of cash flow, profit and loss, balance sheet, and other information of interest. The transformation of input to output is accomplished by the enterprise itself, but we will substitute a model for the enterprise, which gives the equivalent transformations. We show the corporate model as a predictive model in Figure 3 (b). Such corporate models are now in common use in industry and some service and government operations as mechanisms for predicting performance, given stated inputs. Managers can use such models to test the effects of possible changes in demand, prices, wages, market structures, new equipment, and so on.

Obviously now, we can see that predictive models can be of any type. In Figure 3 (c), we show a model of consumer behavior, that might be developed to indicate the effect on sales of expenditures for promotion in various media. In Figure 3 (d), we show a service system model in which people arrive at the service window of a bank or post office, probably randomly. Since the time for service is itself variable, depending on many factors, there may be some interacting effects on the size of the waiting line and waiting time that will result.

The predictive models that we will discuss in Part Three are designed as the mechanisms for predicting the outcomes of alternative courses of action. These courses of action may be generated in some systematic way that attempts to exhaust a range of possibilities, or they may be hypotheses for what a manager thinks could be good strategies. In any case, the outcomes of the predictive model must still be evaluated according to the general methods of Part Two.

Plan for Part Three

We will begin in Chapter 5 with a survey of the models that can be used to forecast, or predict, the future status of the environment. These models play an important role as an input to other predictive models. Chapter 6 then discusses the general concepts of mathematical model building as applied to models for predicting system performance. Many of these concepts are illustrated by the corporate simulation models that are described in Chapter 7. These corporate simulation models are generally *static*; that is, they do not compute the effects of a change in the system during one time period on the outcomes in future time periods.

Chapters 8 through 11 all deal with *dynamic* predictive models, which do analyze the behavior of a system over time. The models of Chapter 8 emphasize the understanding of the relationships among the elements of extremely complex systems involving information feedback and other dynamic effects. It is assumed that these relationships can be specified with complete certainty. In other systems, the relationships among the important elements can only be described in terms of probabilistic statements. Models appropriate for the analysis of these systems are the topics of Chapters 9 through 11. The Markov chain models of Chapter 9 may be viewed as an extension of the dynamic structural models of Chapter 8 in which the dynamic relationships among the system elements can be described in simple, probabilistic terms. Finally, Chapters 10 and 11 deal with the analysis of systems characterized by the formation of waiting lines.

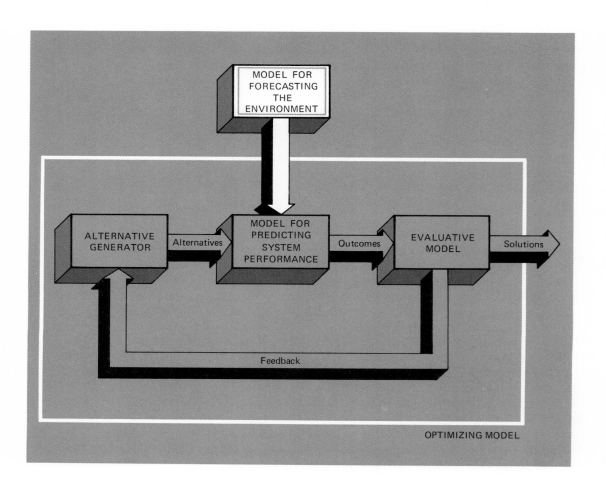

5

Forecasting the Environment

As we pointed out in the Part Three Introduction, forecasting models are predictive models that drive other predictive models. They fit into the input-transformation-output format. Normally historical data is the input which is transformed by a forecasting model to produce forecasts as the output. The models range from rather simple ones that process historical data through some averaging procedure, to sophisticated models that involve a rigorous framework of theory for the causes of changes in demand. Forecasting models can also be identified in terms of other dimensions such as qualitative versus quantitative, and in terms of the appropriate range or horizon for the forecast.

Uses of Forecasts

While we have already stated that forecasts are generally inputs to models that predict system performance, it may be of value to indicate the range of possible systems. We will not attempt to be exhaustive, rather we will relate uses to the dimension of range or horizon of the forecast.

Shortest Range   Suppose we are concerned with the scheduling of manpower (and possibly facilities) in service-oriented situations. We wish to provide the necessary short-term capacity in order to give good service. Capacity may be measured in practical terms such as the number of windows open for service in a post office or a bank, the number of nurses on duty in a hospital, the number of fire units ready to answer emergency calls, the number of ambulance units available to answer calls, or the number of police patrol units crusing. There is clear evidence in all of the kinds of systems just mentioned that the service load varies significantly over the day and that patterns are significant and sometimes stable, but sometimes depend on the day of the week and/or the season of the year. Since wide variation in load may exist from hour to hour and day to day, one of the opportunities available to managers of such systems is to forecast the shortest term demand and to key manpower schedules to the forecasts.

Short Range Forecasts in the range of one week to one month are common as inputs to guide current operations for the control of inventories and to set manpower and facility schedules. In industrial systems, managers need to make plans for production and employment levels for the upcoming period (commonly a month), and for the corollary plans to build or drain seasonal inventories. Such plans have an immediacy because there is often a minimum lead time to change plans and produce at a different level.

In service-oriented systems the one-week to one-month plans can be even more crucial because we cannot store the output of such systems, and therefore managers do not enjoy the slack provided by inventories. In such systems, if the capacity is not available when demanded, we may experience lost sales and grumbling over poor service, or possible disastrous effects in emergency situations requiring fire, police, or health services.

Medium Range In the medium term, managers need to be able to anticipate the impact of seasonal variations in demand. A manufacturer can reduce costs substantially by the adroit combination of the use of overtime, seasonal inventories, back ordering policies, and part-time workers, together with seasonal hiring and layoff.

In nonmanufacturing and service systems, forecasts in the medium term can provide managers with the bases for planning employment levels so that they can perhaps take advantage of natural turnover during seasonal lulls and use overtime, and part-time and new hires to meet peak seasonal demands.

Long Range In the longer term, managers need to make plans for new products and services, and for changes in product and service mix, locations, and facilities, as well as for financing to provide the needed future capacity. While looking far into the future is difficult and often unreliable, it must be done. Such forecasts, real or implied, must be made. Though the techniques are somewhat closer to "crystal ball gazing" than the more quantitative models we shall discuss, they are at a minimum conscious, systematic ways of scanning the future.

Forecasting Models and Uses The preceding survey of the managerial uses of forecasts indicates a rather wide range and implies that substantially different models may be involved. While we did not identify these uses as predictive models, this is exactly what they are. The manager is always using some rationale for the kinds of plans discussed. Our entire thrust will be to analyze and organize the rationale into as rigorous a model as is possible.

Figure 1 summarizes the uses in relation to the time spans, indicating the general kinds of forecasting methodologies that have been found useful and appropriate. In general, special studies to determine hourly and/or daily load distributions are appropriate for the shortest range, with continued sampling to be sure that the system is stable. Moving averages, exponential smoothing, and adaptive smoothing are appropriate in the short range and the causal methods for the short and medium range.

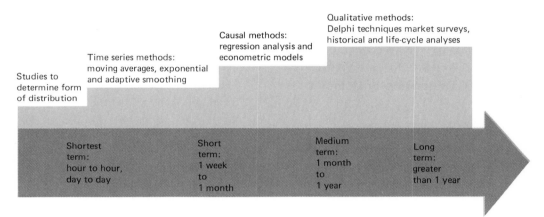

Figure 1. General applicability of forecasting methods to the intended range or horizon of the forecast

For the longer range, we are forced to use somewhat more qualitative methods such as the Delphi method, market surveys, and historical analogy and life-cycle analysis. "Technological forecasting" is a term used in connection with the longest term predictions, and the Delphi technique is the methodology often used as a vehicle. The objective of the Delphi technique is to probe into the future in the hope of anticipating new products and processes in the rapidly changing environment of today's culture and economy. Market surveys and the analysis of consumer behavior involve the use of questionnaries, consumer panels, and tests of new products and services in various kinds of surveys. Historical analogy and life-cycle analysis scan the performance of an ancestor of the product or service under consideration, applying an analysis of the S-curve. The S-curve traces demand for an ancestor product in the initial phases of development, accelerating in the middle-growth period, and culminating in market saturation. Comparisons are made, providing guidelines for future products.

Comparative Costs The various forecasting methodologies are not all equally expensive to install and maintain. In general, the shorter range time-series analyses such as moving averages and exponential forecasting models are relatively inexpensive to install and maintain. They are appropriate for item inventories, for example, and can be computerized to handle a large number of different items efficiently. On the other hand, the causal methods require a great deal of statistical analysis to establish relationships and these special studies can easily cost in the range of $5,000 to $10,000. The increased costs must be justified by the value of higher quality forecasts. In general, the shorter range time-series methods are most useful for lower valued items, while the causal methods may justify their costs when applied to higher valued items. The longer range qualitative methods are relatively expensive, costing in the range of $1,000 to $5,000 per item forecast [Chambers, et al., 1971].

Components of Demand

We can break down the components of demand changes into a few situations, and use them to characterize the combinations of components we may encounter. The components are average demand, random variation around the average, trends in the average, seasonal variations, and cyclic variations. Longer term cyclic variations dealing with the concept of the business cycle are beyond our scope.

We shall use a five-year record of demand for three hypothetical products or services as a basis for discussion. These three demand patterns typify the components of demand for a large number of actual products and services.

1. Figure 2 shows the record for product A, an item whose demand is affected by a large number of factors. The result is that there seems to be no dominant pattern other than considerable variation around the average of 102.33 units per month (standard deviation, 23.99 units). The maximum demand during the five-year period was 158 units in October of 1974, and the minimum was 42 units in January of 1975.

2. Figure 3 shows the five-year record for product B, and is typical of an item that is enjoying modest but steady growth throughout its five-year record. The average demand for the entire five years is 548 units and the average for 1977 was 654 units, but given the month-to-month variation, neither of these averages seems of much value for projecting into 1978.

3. Figure 4 shows product C. At first glance, product C may seem to be characterized by the random variation similar to product A; however, if one examines the timing of the peaks and valleys there appears to be seasonal variation with a summer peak, followed immediately by a seasonal low in the early fall. The average demand for the five years is 104 units; however, the seasonal cycle is the most intriguing component of demand for product C.

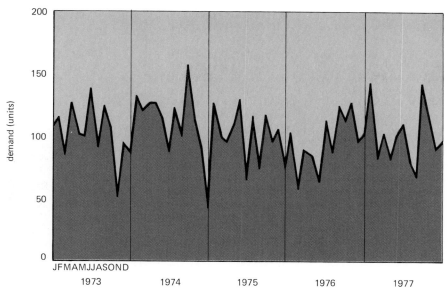

Figure 2. Monthly demand for product *A*

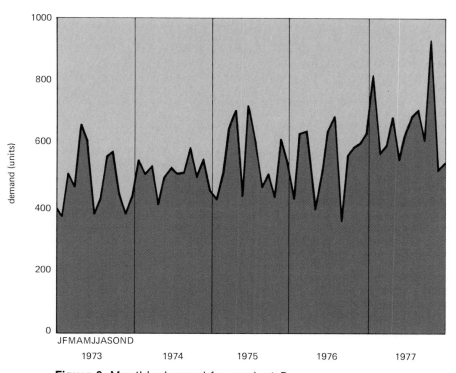

Figure 3. Monthly demand for product *B*

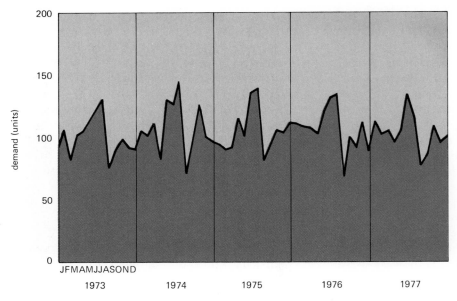

Figure 4. Monthly demand for product *C*

Through the time-series forecasting methods, we shall look more closely at the components of demand illustrated by products *A*, *B*, and *C*. In general, all three exhibit a certain amount of random variation, but products *B* and *C* exhibit trend and seasonality respectively.

TIME-SERIES FORECASTING METHODS

Recall from Figure 1 that time-series forecasting methods are applicable to the short-term (and shortest term) horizon. They are appropriate to the short term because they are in a sense "mindless" in that they deal with the historical data in an indiscriminant way, making no inquiry regarding why variations occur. Time-series methods simply record and process historical data in a consistent statistical fashion. The fundamental driving forces that cause demand changes are ignored. These methods are of considerable value, however, because they are relatively inexpensive to construct and maintain. In addition, they provide good forecasts if we are not attempting to look ahead too far.

We shall discuss moving averages, exponentially weighted moving averages, and adaptive methods. While the basic time-series models are applicable to the shortest term in Figure 1, we shall delay discussing the special problems of the shortest term until the end of this section.

Moving Averages

When we look at the actual demand for product A in Figure 2, we note wide variation from a possibly large number of chance causes. If in fact the variation from the mean is random, we wish to discount the effects of these causes. The common way of smoothing the effects of random variations in demand is to estimate average demand by some kind of moving average. Table 1 gives some sample demand data from Figure 2 (product A) for the first few months.

A moving average is simply the average of the n values centered on the month in question. For example, from Table 1, the first three months of actual demand are 106, 116, and 85, and the three-month average is $(106 + 116 + 85)/3 = 102.33$. Thus, an estimate of February demand that discounts random variations is 102.33. In moving to the March estimate, we drop the January figure of 106 and add the April figure of 127, and the new moving average centered on March is then $(116 + 85 + 127)/3 = 109.33$. In general, moving averages are centered on the month for which the average is quoted. For example, a five-month moving average for March would be the sum of the five demand figures from January through May divided by 5 or $(106 + 116 + 85 + 127 + 102)/5 = 107.20$.

Both Figure 2 and Table 1 show that actual demand is quite variable. The three-month moving average, however, is much more stable because the demand for any one month receives only one-third weight. Extreme values are discounted and if they are simply random variations in demand, we are not strongly influenced by them if we gauge demand by the three-month moving average.

Greater smoothing effect is obtained by averaging over a longer period, as is shown by the five-month moving average in Table 1. Extreme values are discounted even more since each period's demand carries only a one-fifth weight in the moving average. Figure 5 shows the three- and five-month moving averages plotted in comparison with actual demand for product A. Note the smoothing effects and the way in which the moving average lines reveal the most current average demand.

TABLE 1. Actual Demand for Product A and Three- and Five-Month Moving Averages

Date (1973)	Actual Demand	Three-Month Moving Average	Five-Month Moving Average
Jan.	106	---	---
Feb.	116	102.33	---
Mar.	85	109.33	107.20
Apr.	127	104.67	105.80
May	102	109.33	110.40
June	99	113.33	111.40
July	139	109.33	111.00
Aug.	90	118.00	---
Sept.	125	---	---

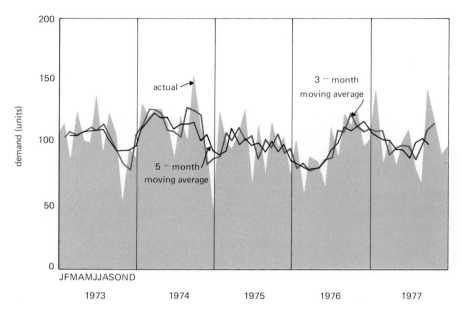

Figure 5. Actual demand and three- and five-month moving averages for product *A*

The five-month moving average discounts random variation more effectively; note that in the peaks and valleys of the two moving averages, the five-month line responds less to the extreme values. On the other hand, the three-month moving average gives more weight to the most recent data, and if demand were changing fundamentally it would track these changes more rapidly. In forecasting with moving averages, one extrapolates the last average into the future to obtain the forecast. Methodology is also available that can take account of trend and seasonal factors.

Exponentially Weighted Moving Averages

When demand is actually changing rather than reflecting only random variations, we have a keen interest in emphasizing the most current data in a moving average. One effective and convenient method for accomplishing differential weighting and smoothing is the use of exponentially weighted moving averages. The simplest exponential smoothing model estimates average smoothed demand for the upcoming period $\overline{F}_t$ by adding or subtracting a fraction α of the difference between actual current demand D_t and the last smoothed average $\overline{F}_{t-1}$. The new smoothed average $\overline{F}_t$ is then

$$\text{new smoothed average} = \text{old smoothed average} + \alpha \, (\text{new demand} - \text{old smoothed average}),$$

or stated symbolically,

$$\overline{F}_t = \overline{F}_{t-1} + \alpha(D_t - \overline{F}_{t-1}) \, . \tag{1}$$

The smoothing constant α is between 0 and 1 with commonly used values of 0.01 to 0.30. Equation (1) can be rearranged in a more convenient and possibly more understandable form as follows:

new smoothed average $= \alpha$ (new demand)
$+ (1 - \alpha)$ (old smoothed average),

or stated symbolically,

$$\overline{F}_t = \alpha D_t + (1 - \alpha) \overline{F}_{t-1} \, . \tag{2}$$

If $\alpha = 0.10$, then equation (2) says that the smoothed average in the upcoming period $\overline{F}_t$ will be determined by adding 10 percent of the new actual demand information D_t and 90 percent of the last smoothed average $\overline{F}_{t-1}$. For example, if $\alpha = 0.10$, $D_t = 106$, and $\overline{F}_{t-1} = 100$, then the new smoothed average is

$$\overline{F}_t = 0.1 \times 106 + 0.9 \times 100 = 10.6 + 90 = 100.6 \, .$$

Since the new demand figure D_t includes possible random variations, we are discounting 90 percent of those variations. Obviously then, small values of α will have a stronger smoothing effect than large values. Conversely, large values of α will react more quickly to real changes (as well as random variations) in actual demand. As an example, if $\alpha = 0.4$ and the previous data remain the same, the new smoothed average would be

$$\overline{F}_t = 0.4 \times 106 + 0.6 \times 100 = 42.4 + 60 = 102.4 \, .$$

Note that the components of current actual demand and the old average are now weighted quite differently, giving considerably more weight to current actual demand. The choice of α is normally guided by judgment, though studies could produce economically best or near best values.

Equation (2) actually gives weight to all past actual demand data, though this is not obvious. This weighting occurs through the chain of periodic calculations to produce smoothed averages for each period. In equation (2), for example, the term $\overline{F}_{t-1}$ was computed from

$$\overline{F}_{t-1} = \alpha D_{t-1} + (1 - \alpha) \overline{F}_{t-2} \, ,$$

which includes the previous actual demand D_{t-1}. The $\overline{F}_{t-2}$ term was calculated in a similar way, which included D_{t-2}, and so on back to the beginning of the series. Therefore, the smoothed averages are based on a sequential process representing all previous actual demands.

Figure 6 shows comparative weightings given data by three- and five-period moving averages and by exponentially weighted moving averages with $\alpha = 0.1$ and 0.3. Note the effectiveness of the exponentially weighted averages in placing heavier weight on the most recent data.

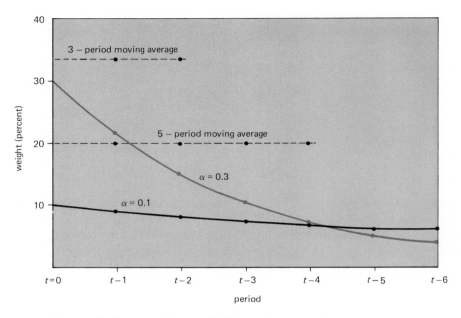

Figure 6. Comparative weightings given past data by three- and five-period moving averages and by exponentially weighted moving averages with $\alpha = 0.1$ and 0.3

Another factor implicit in Figure 6 is that exponentially weighted data give a weight to all prior data, though the effect of the old data will be small. Simple moving averages give weight only to the periods included in the average. It is also worth noting at this point that the exponential forecasting system is a direct application of feedback concepts. Equation (2) is a feedback equation in which a fraction of the output is fed back with lag to stabilize the output. It is by means of the feedback concept that the forecast produced by exponential smoothing is stabilized.

It is important to place the time periods for $\overline{F}_t$, D_t, and $\overline{F}_{t-1}$ in perspective and to recognize that the so-called new smoothed average $\overline{F}_t$ is not an extrapolation beyond known demand data. Rather, it is the most current smoothed average. It is not a forecast but a statement of current demand.

Extrapolation and Forecast Since no trend or seasonality is expected in the model of equation (2), direct extrapolation from $\overline{F}_t$ to infer a forecast is justified. Therefore, the forecast for the upcoming period D_{t+1}^* is taken directly as the computed value of $\overline{F}_t$. (Starred symbols $[D^*]$ represent extrapolated or forecasted values.) Table 2 shows the computations and forecasts for the first few months of the data for product A, when $\alpha = 0.10$.

TABLE 2. Sample Computations
for $\bar{F}_t$ and the Forecast D^*_{t+1} for the
Simple Exponential Smoothing
Model ($\alpha = 0.1$)

Date (1973)	Actuals†	Smoothed Average ($\bar{F}_t$)	Forecast (D^*_{t+1})
Initial	---	100	---
Jan.	106	100.600	---
Feb.	116	102.140	100.600
Mar.	85	100.426	102.140
Apr.	127	103.083	100.426
May	102	102.975	103.083
June	99	102.578	102.975
July	---	---	102.578

†Data from Table 1.

Frequently, a forecast is needed for more than one period in advance. Using equation (2) as a model one simply extrapolates further into the future. For example, in January $\bar{F}_t = 100.6$ and the forecast for February is also $D^*_{t+1} = 100.6$ from Table 2. If we were to forecast for July based only on the information available in January, $D^*_{t+6} = 100.6$, the same forecast as for February. We must point out, however, that the accuracy of such forecasts declines rapidly as the forecasting range increases.

Trend Effects

If there were a trend present in the data, equation (2) would respond to it but with a lag. But, the apparent trend each period is simply the difference between the last two smoothed averages $\bar{F}_t - \bar{F}_{t-1}$. This difference represents another series, that can be smoothed by exponentially weighted averages just as with average demand. Therefore, the new average trend adjustment $\bar{T}_t$ is

$$\bar{T}_t = \alpha(\bar{F}_t - \bar{F}_{t-1}) + (1 - \alpha)\,\bar{T}_{t-1}. \tag{3}$$

The expected demand $E(D_t)$ for the current period including trend adjustment is the smoothed average $\bar{F}_t$ computed in equation (2) plus a fraction of the new average trend adjustment T_t computed in equation (3):

$$E(D_t) = \bar{F}_t + \frac{(1 - \alpha)}{\alpha}\,\bar{T}_t. \tag{4}$$

The term $(1 - \alpha)/\alpha$ corrects for lag in the trend adjustment $\bar{T}_t$ [Brown, 1959, pp. 192–96]. Taking a specific example, if $\alpha = 0.1$, $D_t = 405$, $\bar{F}_{t-1} = 400$, $\bar{F}_t = 400.5$, and $\bar{T}_{t-1} = 0$, the average trend adjustment $\bar{T}_t$ is then

$$\bar{T}_t = 0.1\,(400.5 - 400) + 0.9 \times 0 = 0.05.$$

The expected demand for the current period including trend adjustment is then

$$E(D_t) = 400.5 + \frac{(1 - 0.1)}{0.1} \times 0.05$$

$$= 400.5 + 9 \times 0.05 = 400.95 \, .$$

Notice that the lag factor for $\alpha = 0.1$ is 9. This seems large, but actually indicates how sluggish the forecasting system is when small smoothing constants are used. When $\alpha = 0.4$, the lag factor is $(1 - 0.4)/0.4 = 1.5$. Note that the only facts and figures required to update a forecast are α, D_t, $\overline{F}_{t-1}$, and $\overline{T}_{t-1}$, yet all past actual demand data are weighted in the model, but with rapidly decreasing weights as we proceed backward in time. If a large number of items were to be forecast, as is commonly true in inventory control systems, the entire process could be computerized with minimum computer storage for each item. The only new data to be supplied the computing program each period would be the current actual demand D_t.

Extrapolation and Forecast   As with the no-trend model, equation (4) involves no extrapolation beyond known demand data. To extrapolate from equation (4) to forecast D_{t+1}^* requires that we add $\overline{T}_t$, the most recent average trend adjustment,

$$D_{t+1}^* = E(D_t) + \overline{T}_t = \overline{F}_t + \frac{1}{\alpha} \overline{T}_t \, . \tag{5}$$

To forecast k periods in the future, we simply add $k\overline{T}_t$ to $E(D_t)$, or

$$D_{t+k}^* = E(D_t) + k\overline{T}_t = \overline{F}_t + \left(\frac{1}{\alpha} + k - 1 \right) \overline{T}_t \, . \tag{6}$$

Both equations (5) and (6) result from an algebraic simplification of equation (4) plus the trend adjustment term. Again, however, we must note that forecasting accuracy decreases rapidly as the forecasting range increases. Table 3 shows sample computations of smoothed average, trend adjustment, and forecast for an exponential smoothing system with $\alpha = 0.10$. Note that if in January we attempt to forecast for July using equation (6), we have

$$D_{t+6}^* = 400.50 + \left(\frac{1}{0.1} + 6 - 1 \right) 0.05 = 401.25 \, .$$

Compare this figure with the forecast for July of 504.997 in Table 3, generated through the sequence of calculations where new actual demand data became available each period. The error of 103.7 is very large and demonstrates the danger of using this kind of model for anything but very short-range forecasts.

Figure 7 shows a graph of exponentially smoothed forecasts with and without trend adjustment for the product B data. Note that the two forecasts

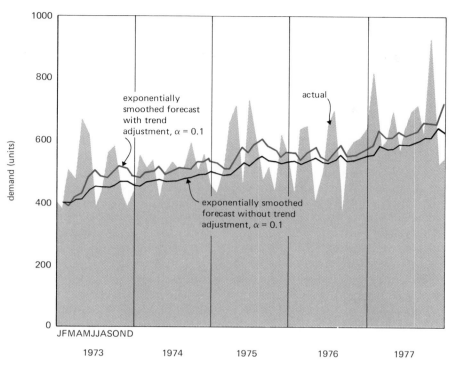

Figure 7. Forecasts for product *B* using exponential smoothing models with and without trend adjustments

TABLE 3. Sample Computations of Smoothed Averages **and** Trend Adjustments for an Exponential Smoothing Model ($\alpha = 0.1$)

Date (1973)	Actuals (D_t)	Smoothed Average†	Current Apparent Trend ($\bar{F}_t - \bar{F}_{t-1}$)	Average Trend Adjustment‡	Forecast for Period $t + 1$§
Initial	400	---	---	---	---
Jan.	405	400.500	0.500	0.050	---
Feb.	372	397.650	−2.850	−0.240	401.000
Mar.	504	408.285	10.635	0.848	395.250
Apr.	463	413.757	5.471	1.310	416.760
May	656	437.981	24.224	3.601	426.856
June	611	455.283	17.301	4.971	473.994
July	379	---	---	---	504.997

†$\bar{F}_t = \alpha D_t + (1 - \alpha)\,\bar{F}_{t-1}$.
‡$\bar{T}_t = \alpha(\bar{F}_t - \bar{F}_{t-1}) + (1 - \alpha)\,T_{t-1}$.
§$D^*_{t+1} = \bar{F}_t + (1/\alpha)\,\bar{T}_t$.

are similar in form; however, since the actual data have considerable trend in them, the forecast without trend adjustment lags behind and is lower than the forecast with trend adjustment. If the actual data were to stabilize, exhibiting no trend, the two forecasts would tend to converge.

Seasonal Adjustments

The basis for including a seasonal adjustment to an exponentially smoothed forecast model is to develop a *base series* that represents the seasonal cycle. The base series is usually constructed from last year's experience in some way. If the seasonal pattern is strong and relatively invariant, then the base series could simply be the period-by-period demand for last year, or an idealized cycle. If the peaks and valleys shift forward or backward slightly from year to year, then an averaging process may be used. For example, a three-month moving average could be used, centered on the month for which the average is being determined as in Table 1. The general methods used are similar to the trend model, though there is more complexity because of the seasonal component.

Figure 8 shows an exponentially smoothed forecast with trend and seasonal adjustments for product C. Two different base series were used in computing the forecasts in Figure 8. One used the ideal seasonal series from which the data were generated originally, and the other used the previous year's three-month moving average.

A common practical measure of the forecast accuracy is the Mean Absolute Deviation (MAD). MAD is simply the sum of the absolute deviations between actual demand and forecasts, divided by the number of observations. The MAD measure for the forecast using the ideal base series was 8.69 and for the three-month moving average base series it was 12.25.

Adaptive Methods

As we have noted, it is common to use fairly small values of α in exponential smoothing systems in order to filter out random variations in demand. When actual demand rates increase or decrease gradually, such forecasting systems can track the changes rather well. If demand changes suddenly, however, a forecasting system using a small value of α will lag behind the actual change substantially. For such situations, adaptive response systems have been proposed.

The basic idea of adaptive systems is indicated in Figure 9. Figure 9 shows the forecast error being monitored and, based on preset rules, the weights assigned to past data are adjusted by changing the parameter α. The forecast is then computed using the new weights. If, for example, a step change in demand were to occur because of a radical change in the market,

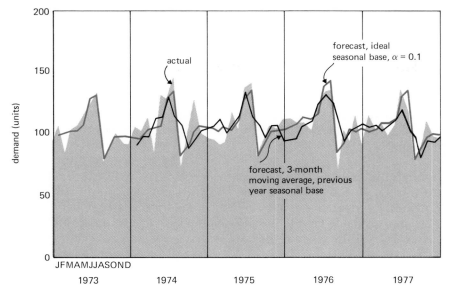

Figure 8. Forecasts for product *C* using exponential smoothing models with trend and seasonal adjustments

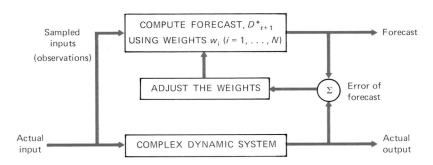

Figure 9. General structure of adaptive forecasting models in which the weights assigned past actual demand data are adjusted depending on the forecast error

From S. C. Wheelwright and S. Makridakis, *Forecasting Methods for Management;* John Wiley & Sons, New York, 1973 used by permission.

a large error would result. The large error signals that α should increase, giving greater weight to current demand. The forecast would then reflect the change in actual demand. When actual demand stabilizes at the new level, adaptive systems would reset the value of α to a lower level, that filters out random variations effectively.

A number of approaches to adaptive response systems have been proposed. Eilon and Elmaleh [1970] and Roberts and Reed [1969] have proposed systems in which the parameter α is reset periodically. Trigg and Leach [1967] and Whybark [1972] have proposed continuous tracking systems that can reset the parameter each period. Montgomery [1970] has proposed adaptive control of the smoothing parameters by evolutionary operation, and Rao and Shapiro [1970] have proposed a system using evolutionary spectra.

A Comparative Study Whybark [1972] tested six different forecasting models, four of which were adaptive, on the same demand function over 400 periods. Comparative results were recorded for the last 200 periods, the first 200 periods being used to initialize all models. The summary results are shown in Table 4. In general, the models that evaluate parameters continuously [Trigg and Leach, 1967, and Whybark, 1972] performed best.

Whybark also produces graphs that show the response of all systems to step changes in demand. The continuous evaluation systems both responded extremely well, as did the periodic model of Eilon and Elmaleh [1970]. The constant parameter model with $\alpha = 0.2$ had the poorest response in this respect.

TABLE 4. Comparative Results for 200 Periods for Six Forecasting Models

Model	Standard Deviation
Constant forecast	5.012
Constant α ($\alpha = 0.2$)	3.871
Eilon-Elmaleh (periodic)	4.477
Roberts-Reed (periodic)	3.632
Trigg-Leach (continuous)	3.204
Whybark (continuous)	3.070

Source: D. C. Whybark, "A Comparison of Adaptive Forecasting Techniques," *The Logistics and Transportation Review*, Vol. 8, No. 3, 1972, pp. 13–26; used by permission.

Modifications for the Shortest Term

In general, the time-series methods discussed also apply to the shortest term. The forecasting horizon can be as short as desired; however, the limitation is that we must have an information system that can react and provide a useful forecast within the shortest time frame defined. In most instances, the time and cost to gather the data for current actual demand, D_t, will place

TABLE 5. Numbers of Patients Arriving at the University Health Service to See Either a Physician or Nurse Concerning a Health Problem

	Average Number of Visits per Week	Average Number of Visits per Day	Average Number of Visits (percentages of average daily visits given in parentheses)					University Enrollment (approx.)
			Mon.	Tue.	Wed.	Thu.	Fri.	
Fall semester 1969	1487	297.4	351 (118%)	341 (114%)	264 (88%)	253 (84%)	288 (96%)	17,800
Fall semester 1970	1640	328.0	404 (123%)	342 (104%)	306 (93%)	290 (88%)	298 (91%)	19,125

Note: The data are selected to include only arrivals between 8 A.M. and 5 P.M. on Mondays through Fridays for weeks in which there are no holidays, and also exclude data for Fridays before holidays occurring on the following Monday.
Source: E. J. Rising, R. Baron, and B. Averill, "A Systems Analysis of a University-Health-Service Outpatient Clinic," *Operations Research*, Vol. 21, No. 5, Sept.–Oct. 1973, pp. 1030–1047; used by permission.

a lower limit on the forecasting period. If there is a need to have demand forecasts for an even shorter time period than can be justified for the basic forecasting system, then special studies can be made of the distribution of weekly demand by days of the week, or daily demand by hours of the day. The assumption is then made that for each forecast, the proportionate distribution applies in the shorter time frame. Periodic monitoring of the distribution to ensure that the system remains stable is then required.

Service systems are the typical situations in which the shortest term of the forecasts may be monthly, weekly, or daily, but distributions of that forecast on an even shorter term are needed. For example, in a study of a University Health Service Outpatient Clinic, Table 5 shows the daily variation of demand. These daily variations were important in developing predictive models involving the physician staffing and scheduling. But, in this kind of service system, forecasting demand for an ever shorter horizon was important in order to construct predictive models, since there was substantial hourly variation within the day as shown by Figure 10. We deal with predictive models for service type systems in Chapters 10 and 11 on queuing and waiting line systems.

When demand data can be summarized and forecasts made entirely automatically, the forecasting period can be extremely short. This was the case in a system installed in the business office of Bell, Canada [Church, 1973]. The office manager had to schedule enough service representatives to take calls throughout the day in order to give good service to calling customers. The office also was responsible for other activities such as arranging for telephone installations, investigating annoyance calls, and collecting accounts. The basic problem was to develop a predictive model for allocation and scheduling of effort between the two kinds of activities in such a way that good customer service was given and the other work was also accomplished.

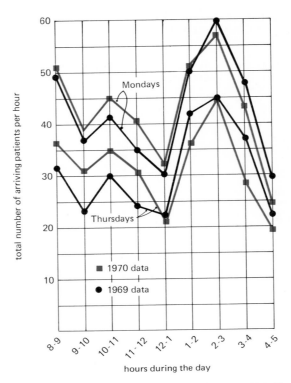

Figure 10. Hourly arrivals at the Student Health Service (Monday and Thursday averages for the fall semesters in 1969 and 1970)

From E. J. Rising, R. Baron, and B. Averill, "A Systems Analysis of a University-Health-Service Outpatient Clinic," *Operations Research*, Vol. 21, No. 5, Sept.–Oct. 1973, pp. 1030–1047 used by permission.

In order to forecast the call load, an exponential smoothing system was developed that forecasted daily load, treating daily variations through the week as the equivalent of seasonal variations. The base series was taken from the previous week and the general technique of exponential smoothing with trend and seasonal adjustments discussed previously was used. The forecast was then made for the following day, projecting call load for each half hour.

CAUSAL FORECASTING METHODS

When we have enough historical data and experience, it may be possible to relate forecasts to the factors in the environment that *cause* the trends, seasonals, and fluctuations. Thus, if we can *measure* the causal factors and have determined their *relationships* to the product or service of interest, we may be able to compute forecasts of considerable accuracy.

The factors that enter causal models are of every conceivable type: gross national product, disposable income, new marriages, housing starts, inventories, cost-of-living indexes, as well as predictions of dynamic factors and disturbances such as strikes, actions of competitors, sales promotion campaigns, and so on. The causal forecasting model expresses mathematical relationships between the causal factors and the demand for the item being forecast, and is indeed the most sophisticated of forecasting tools. As indicated in Figure 1, there are two general types of causal models and the costs range from medium to high for installation and operation.

Regression Analysis

Forecasting based on regression methods establishes a forecasting function called a regression equation. The regression equation expresses the series to be forecasted, such as dollar sales or quantities sold, in terms of other series that presumably control or cause the sales to increase or decrease. The rationale can be general or specific. For example, in furniture sales we might postulate that sales are in general related to disposable personal income — if disposable income is up, sales will increase, and if people have less money to spend, sales will be down. Establishing the empirical relationship is accomplished through the regression equation. To take more specific factors, we might postulate that furniture sales are controlled to some extent by the number of new marriages and/or the number of new housing starts. These are both specific indicators of possible demand for furniture. For a review of simple regression and correlation, see Appendix C.

Table 6 gives data on these three independent variables — housing starts, disposable income, and new marriages — and on sales of a hypothetical furniture company called the "Cherryoak Company." We propose to build a relationship between the observed variables and company sales, where the volume of sales is dependent on or caused by the observed variables. Therefore sales is termed the dependent variable and the observed variables are called the independent variables. The correlation coefficients between sales (S) and each of the independent variables are:

1. disposable personal income (I)   0.805
2. housing starts (H)   0.435
3. new marriages (M)   0.416

Since disposable income (I) correlates most strongly with company sales, let us start with it as an example. Using regression analysis, we can determine the straight line that best fits the data expressing the relationship between sales (S) and disposable income (I). From statistics, we know that the regression equation represents a straight line that minimizes the square of the

TABLE 6. Data for 24 Years (1947–70) Used in Performing Regression Analysis to Forecast 1971 Sales of Cherryoak Company

Year	Housing Starts (*H*) (thousands)	Disposable Personal Income (*I*) ($ billions)	New Marriages (*M*) (thousands)	Company Sales (*S*) ($ millions)	Time (*T*)
1947	744	158.9	2,291	92.920	1
1948	942	169.5	1,991	122.440	2
1949	1,033	188.3	1,811	125.570	3
1950	1,138	187.2	1,580	110.460	4
1951	1,549	205.8	1,667	139.400	5
1952	1,211	224.9	1,595	154.020	6
1953	1,251	235.0	1,539	157.590	7
1954	1,225	247.9	1,546	152.230	8
1955	1,354	254.4	1,490	139.130	9
1956	1,475	274.4	1,531	156.330	10
1957	1,240	292.9	1,585	140.470	11
1958	1,157	308.5	1,518	128.240	12
1959	1,341	318.8	1,451	117.450	13
1960	1,531	337.7	1,494	132.640	14
1961	1,274	350.0	1,527	126.160	15
1962	1,327	364.4	1,547	116.990	16
1963	1,469	385.3	1,580	123.900	17
1964	1,615	404.6	1,654	141.320	18
1965	1,538	436.6	1,719	156.710	19
1966	1,488	469.1	1,789	171.930	20
1967	1,173	505.3	1,844	184.790	21
1968	1,299	546.3	1,913	202.700	22
1969	1,524	590.0	2,059	237.340	23
1970	1,479	629.6	2,132	254.930	24

Source: Statistical Abstract of the United States (Washington, Bureau of the Census).
Source: G. G. C. Parker, and E. L. Segura, "How to Get a Better Forecast," *Harvard Business Review*, March–April, 1971; used by permission.

Note: Company sales and disposable per capita income have been adjusted for the effect of inflation and appear in constant 1959 dollars.

deviations from it and sets the sum of the simple deviations to zero. The regression equation for the data of company sales (*S*) versus disposable income (*I*) is

$$S = 72.5 + 0.23\,I,\qquad (7)$$

where the coefficient, 72.5, is the *y* axis intercept and the slope of the straight line is 0.23. Note that the form of the equation is in the standard format of the equation of a straight line, $y = a + bx$, where *y* is the dependent variable, *x* the independent variable, *a* the *y* intercept, and *b* the slope. In regression analysis, *a* and *b* are termed the regression coefficients and are the parameters that specify the equation.

The regression line is plotted in Figure 11, showing some specific points for selected years. These points illustrate the kinds of forecast errors that would have resulted if one had used this equation to forecast Cherryoak furniture sales. To use the regression equation to forecast sales, one simply inserts the value of *I* and computes sales *S*. For example, if $I = 700$, then the forecaster could compute the value of *S* as $S = 72.5 + 0.23 \times 700 = \$233.5$ (million).

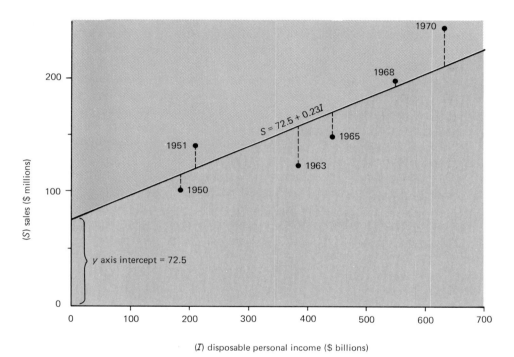

Figure 11. Simple regression line for sales dependent on disposable income (data from Table 6)

Reliability of Forecast   There are a number of statistical tests that can be performed to help determine how reliable the regression equation is as a forecasting device. Data resulting from these statistical tests are commonly generated automatically in standard regression analysis computer programs. Our interest is particularly in the coefficient of determination and the standard error of estimate. In addition, there are important statistical tests concerning the significance of the regression coefficients, but these tests are beyond our scope.

The coefficient of determination is simply r^2, the correlation coefficient squared. For our example, $r^2 = (0.805)^2 = 0.65$. The coefficient of determination states the proportion of the variation in the dependent variable of the regression equation that is explained by the independent variable. For our equation then, 65 percent of the variation in sales is controlled by variation in I, and 35 percent is unexplained. Thus, we can expect large forecast errors if we use equation (7). Apparently, other variables account for a substantial fraction of the changes in S that actually occur.

The standard error of estimate indicates the expected range of variation from the regression line of any forecast made. For example, the standard error of estimate for our data and equation (7) is 38.7. Since we assume a normal distribution of sales for each value of I, this means that we can expect with some confidence that two-thirds of the time our estimate of S will be in the range of $\pm\$38.7$ million. Therefore, if $I = 700$, then $S = 233.5$ as computed previously. However, with a standard error of estimate of 38.7, we are actually stating that two-thirds of the time we would expect the actual value of S to be in the range of 194.8 to 272.2, a rather broad range.

Obviously, we need to improve the forecasting ability of equation (7), and we can accomplish this by including other causal factors in the regression equation.

Multiple Regression   The general concepts of simple regression analysis can be extended to include the effects of several causal factors through multiple regression analysis. For the data of Table 6, Parker and Segura [1971] show that the regression equation would be

$$S = 49.85 - 0.068M + 0.036H + 1.22I - 19.54T \tag{8}$$

where

S = gross sales per year

49.85 = base sales, or starting point from which other factors have an influence

M = new marriages during the year

H = new housing starts during the year

I = disposable personal income during the year

T = time trend $(T = 1, 2, 3, \ldots, n)$,

and the coefficients that precede each of the causal factors represent the amount of influence on sales of each of the causal factors, M, H, I, and T.

The coefficient of determination for equation (8) is 0.92 and the standard error of estimate is 11.9, indicating that the value of the equation as a forecasting mechanism has been increased substantially over equation (7).

Parker and Segura [1971] then improve equation (8) as a forecasting mechanism by making additional changes. New marriages is dropped and last year's sales (S_{t-1}) is substituted in order to improve the overall forecasting accuracy. Also, last year's housing starts (H_{t-1}) is substituted for H, since this allows for the lag we would expect between construction time and the time home furnishing expenditures might be made. The revised equation is

$$S = -33.51 + 0.373S_{t-1} + 0.033H_{t-1} + 0.672I - 11.03T. \qquad (9)$$

Forecasting accuracy has improved again with $r^2 = 0.95$ and the standard error of estimate = 9.7. Table 7 summarizes the record of actual versus forecasted sales and of forecast errors for the entire 24-year period, and Figure 12 shows a comparative graph of actual versus forecasted sales.

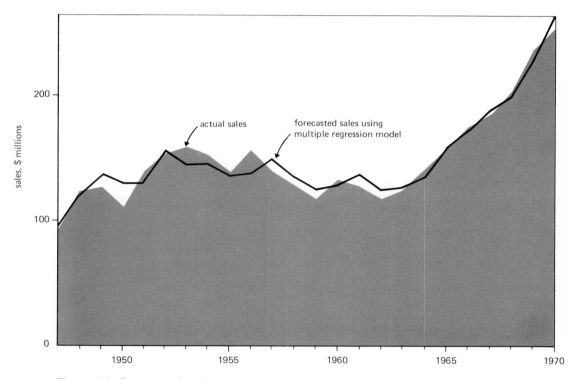

Figure 12. Forecasted sales versus actual sales (data plotted from Table 7)

We see then that multiple regression analysis can be a very powerful and accurate forecasting methodology. When forecasts must be made for longer terms, multiple regression is a logical forecasting method. Examples of applications might be when new products and services are contemplated or when new facility locations and capacities are being considered. It requires considerable time and cost since various hypotheses regarding the

TABLE 7. Differences in Actual Sales of Cherryoak Company, 1947–70, and Sales Forecasted by Multiple Regression (in millions of dollars)

	Actual Sales	Predicted Sales	Difference	Ratio of Actual Sales to Predicted Sales
1947	92.29	93.04	− 0.75	0.99
1948	122.44	117.72	4.72	1.04
1949	125.57	136.91	−11.34	0.92
1950	110.46	129.33	−18.87	0.85
1951	139.40	128.65	10.75	1.08
1952	154.02	154.90	− 0.88	0.99
1953	157.59	144.88	12.71	1.09
1954	152.23	145.17	7.06	1.05
1955	139.13	135.64	3.49	1.02
1956	156.33	137.44	18.89	1.13
1957	140.47	149.27	− 8.80	0.94
1958	128.24	134.99	− 6.75	0.95
1959	117.45	123.56	− 6.11	0.95
1960	132.64	127.31	5.33	1.04
1961	126.16	136.52	−10.36	0.92
1962	116.99	124.20	− 7.21	0.94
1963	123.90	125.56	− 1.66	0.99
1964	141.32	134.79	6.53	1.05
1965	156.71	156.61	0.10	1.00
1966	171.93	170.59	1.34	1.01
1967	184.79	187.90	− 3.11	0.98
1968	202.70	198.75	3.95	1.02
1969	237.34	227.95	9.39	1.04
1970	254.93	263.92	− 8.99	0.96

Source: G. G. C. Parker and E. L. Segura, "How to Get a Better Forecast," *Harvard Business Review*, March–April, 1971; used by permission.

effect of variables may need to be tested. However, standard computing programs for multiple regression that ease the burden and reduce the cost of application are now widely available.

A considerable historical record is necessary for regression analysis to have validity. As rules of thumb, a five-year record is needed for one independent variable, eight years for two independent variables, and a longer history for three or more independent variables [Parker and Segura, 1971]. These data requirements are often severe limitations to application.

Furthermore, there are four very important assumptions made in regression analysis that should be met. First, there is the assumption of linearity which states that the dependent variable is linearly related to the independent variables. Where the linear relationship does not hold, transformations can often be made that make it possible to meet the requirements of this assumption. The second basic assumption in regression analysis is that the variance of errors is constant. The third assumption is that errors from period to period are independent of each other, or not autocorrelated. Finally, regression analysis assumes that the errors are normally distributed. The nature and importance of these assumptions is covered in greater detail in Benton [1972], Huang [1970], and Wheelwright and Makridakis [1973]. Obviously, considerable knowledge of statistical methods is required for the appropriate application of regression analysis.

Beyond possibly ignoring one or more of the important assumptions, one of the great dangers in misapplying regression analysis is in assuming that a good fit to historical data guarantees that the regression equation will be a good forecasting device. The regression equation itself should be an expression of a good causal theory relating the factors in the regression model. In addition, we also need an understanding of the potential importance of factors that are not included in the model.

One of the differences then between time-series forecasting models and causal methods is that time series accept increases or decreases in demand in an unbiased way, not questioning the reasons for the increase or decrease. On the other hand, causal methods demand an explanation within the rationale of the forecasting system for demand changes that occur.

Econometric Forecasting Methods

In simplest terms, econometric forecasting methods are an extension of regression equations. If, for example, in equation (9) we attempted to include the effect of price and advertising, then we see the possibility of an interdependence, where our own sales can have an effect on these factors as well as vice versa.

For example, assume that sales is a function of GNP, price, and advertising. In regression terms, we would assume that all three independent variables are exogenous to the system and thus are not influenced by the level of sales itself or by one another. This is a fair assumption as far as GNP is concerned. If, however, we consider price and advertising, the same assumption may not be valid. For example, if the per unit cost is of some quadratic form, a different level of sales will result in a different level of cost. Furthermore, advertising expenditures will certainly influence the price of the product, since production and selling costs influence the per unit price. The price, in turn, is influenced by the magnitude of sales, which can also influence the level of advertising. As can be seen, all four of the variables in our equation are interdependent.

When this interdependence is at all strong, regression analysis cannot be used. If we want to be accurate, we must express this sales relationship by developing a system of four simultaneous equations that can deal with the interdependence directly.

Thus, in econometric form we have

sales = f (GNP, price, advertising),

cost = f (production and inventory levels),

selling expenses = f (advertising, and other selling expenses),

price = f (cost + selling expenses);

that is, instead of one relationship, we now have four. As in regression analysis, we must 1) determine the functional form of each of the equations, 2) estimate in a simultaneous manner the values of their parameters, and 3) test for the statistical significance of the results and the validity of the assumptions [Wheelwright and Makridakis, 1973].

Thus far, econometric models have been used largely in connection with relatively mature products where a considerable historical record is available and in industry and broad economic forecasts. For example, the Corning Glass Works developed econometric models to forecast TV tube sales [Chambers et al., 1971]. These models were used to forecast sales six months to two years in the future to help spot turning points far enough in advance to assist in making decisions for production and employment planning.

Industry econometric models have been developed to forecast activity in the forest products industry. Also, the economic forecasting models developed at the Wharton School are econometric models.

SELECTION OF AN APPROPRIATE FORECASTING MODEL

Autocorrelation is an important concept in determining the nature of the raw demand data and the kind of forecasting model that might be appropriate. Autocorrelation measures the degree to which demands in different time periods are correlated. For example, a strong trend in demand data would result in a high correlation between demands in different time periods. Also, a strong seasonal pattern would produce intercorrelation between demands in periods 1, 13, 25; 2, 14, 26; 3, 15, 27, and so on. Analyses of autocorrelation coefficients are therefore used to determine the best type of forecasting model to use.

Box and Jenkins [1970] have developed a highly sophisticated forecasting methodology in which a general class of forecasting methods is postulated for a particular situation. In stage 1, a specific model is tentatively identified as the forecasting method best suited to that situation. The forecasting models may range from moving averages through exponential and adaptive methods to regression analysis. In stage 2 the postulated model is fit to the available historical data and a check is run to determine whether or not the postulated model is adequate. Various statistical tests are involved, including the presence or absence of autocorrelation. If the postulated model is rejected, stage 2 is used to identify an alternative model, which is then tested. The process is repeated until a model that can be used to make forecasts for future time periods has been identified. Thus, the approach involves a philosophy that makes model selection dependent on a statistical analysis of data, so that the most appropriate specific model is selected. (See Nelson [1973] or Mabert [1975] for accessible discussions of the Box-Jenkins methods.)

An Interactive Forecasting System Makridakis, Hodgsdon, and Wheelwright [1974] have developed a generalized interactive forecasting system within the framework of the Box-Jenkins philosophy. A flow chart for the system is shown in Figure 13; the system is divided into two main segments: SIBYL and RUNNER. After data input, SIBYL allows the user to perform preliminary analyses in order to identify two or three forecasting models as the most likely candidates. The interactive system makes inquiries about the data and the characteristics of the situation, including the following:

1. the time horizon for decision making—immediate term, short term, medium term, and long term
2. the pattern of data—seasonal, horizontal, trend, cyclical, or random.
3. the type of model desired—time series, causal, statistical, or nonstatistical
4. the value of the forecast, and thus the costs that can be allocated to obtaining it
5. the accuracy that is required and justified
6. the complexity that can be tolerated
7. the availability of historical data

Autocorrelations for various time lags are computed and may be graphed. Through a series of queries, the program obtains information on the factors needed to select a forecasting model and supplys the user with a list of three or four that appear to be logical candidates, together with comparative statistics on those methods.

The user can then select any of the candidate methods and have that model used in the RUNNER portion of the system. The models listed in Figure 13 include those discussed in this chapter with some variations. Through a system of queries, the user can run additional candidate models with the same data and obtain comparison results.

LONG-TERM FORECASTING METHODS

Some of the most important managerial decisions are made in terms of longer term broader horizons and involve the commitment of resources to future products and services, locations of markets and facilities, and investment in physical facilities. Forecasts become the most crucial element in these kinds of predictive models. Unlike the short- and medium-term forecasting meth-

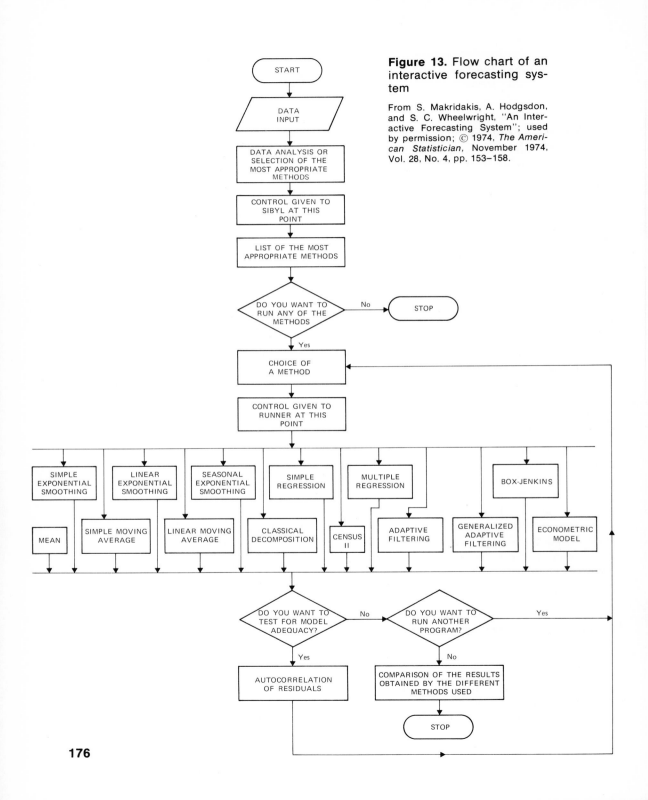

Figure 13. Flow chart of an interactive forecasting system

From S. Makridakis, A. Hodgsdon, and S. C. Wheelwright, "An Interactive Forecasting System"; used by permission; © 1974, *The American Statistician,* November 1974, Vol. 28, No. 4, pp. 153–158.

ods discussed previously, there is no historical record of a statistical nature on which to base long-term forecasts. Rather, what people think, samplings of how they react to market tests, knowledge of consumer behavior, and analogy with similar situations may be the best we can do.

Thus, longer term forecasting methods are more qualitative in nature and may be used in conjunction with the methods of Chapter 2 involving the subjective probabilities discussed in Chapter 3. Recall the POCO example discussed in Chapter 2 concerning the evaluation of alternative strategies for oil shale research and development. Implicit in that example were forecasts of longer term results for alternative strategies tempered by probabilities of the occurrence of events.

Delphi Method

"Technological forecasting" is a term used in connection with the longest term predictions and the Delphi technique is the methodology often used [Gerstenfeld, 1971]. The objective of the Delphi technique is to probe into the future in the hope of anticipating new products and processes in the rapidly changing environment of today's culture and economy. In the shortest range covered by this technique, it can also be used to estimate market sizes and timing.

The technique draws on a panel of experts in a way that eliminates the possible dominance of the most prestigious, the most verbal, the most persuasive, and so on. The attempt is to gain the benefit of expert opinion in the form of a consensus rather than a compromise. The result is pooled judgment showing the range of expert opinion and the reasons for differences of opinion. The Delphi technique was first developed by the RAND Corporation as a means of eliminating the undesirable effects of group interaction that may occur in conferences and panels where the individuals are in direct communication.

The panel of experts can be constructed in various ways and often includes individuals both inside and outside the organization. It may be true that each panel member is an expert in some aspect of the problem, but no one may be an expert on the entire problem. In general, the procedure involves the following:

1. Each expert in the group makes independent forecasts in the form of brief statements.

2. A coordinator edits and clarifies these statements.

3. The coordinator provides a series of written questions to the experts that combine the responses of the other experts.

One of the most extensive probes into the technological future was reported by TRW, Inc. [North and Pyke, 1969]. The project involved the coordination of 15 different panels corresponding to 15 categories of technologies and systems that were felt to have an effect on the company's future. Anonymity of panel members was maintained to stimulate unconventional thinking. The Delphi method was then used to question and requestion the experts. The result was a composite rating of each event on the basis of its desirability, its feasibility, the probability that the event would occur, and probability estimates of the timing of occurrence.

The extensive results of the project were then formed into logic networks. One such network shown by North and Pyke [1969] shows the milestone events that had to precede the technical achievement of holographic color movies. Holography is an optical projection technique that gives the viewer the illusion of the third dimension. The network also showed events that were likely to occur as "fallout" from the basic developments.

Market Surveys

Market surveys and the analysis of consumer behavior have become quite sophisticated and the resulting data become an extremely valuable input to forecasting market demand. In general, the methods involve the use of questionnaires, consumer panels, and tests of new products and services in various kinds of surveys. The entire field is a specialty in itself and beyond the scope of our discussion.

There is considerable literature dealing with the estimation of new product performance based on consumer panels [Ahl, 1970], analytical approaches [Bass, 1969; Claycamp and Liddy, 1969], and simulation and other techniques [Bass, et al., 1968]. Proposed products and services may be compared with the products and known plans of competitors, and new market segments may be exploited with variations of product designs and quality levels. In such instances, comparisons can be made with data on existing products. These kinds of data are often the best available to refine the designs of products and facilities for new ventures.

Historical Analogy and Life-Cycle Analysis

Market research studies can sometimes be supplemented by reference to the performance of an ancestor of the product or service under consideration, applying an analysis of the S-curve. A typical S-curve is shown in Figure 14 where demand in the initial phases of market development accelerates to the middle growth period, culminating in market saturation. Of course, following saturation there may be an actual decline.

For example, the assumption was made that color TV would follow the general sales pattern experienced with black and white TV, but that it would take twice as long to reach a steady state [Chambers et al., 1971]. Such comparisons provide guidelines during the initial planning phases and may be supplemented by other kinds of analyses and studies as initial actual demand becomes known.

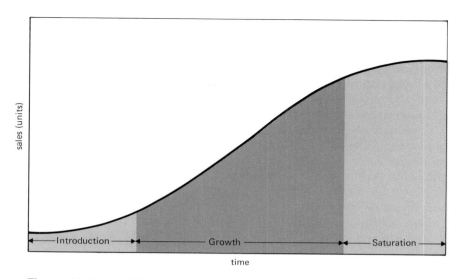

Figure 14. Typical S-curve of the introduction, growth, and market saturation in the life cycle of a product or service

WHAT SHOULD THE MANAGER KNOW?

The manager's interest in forecasting is significant because forecasts are invariably an input to decisions, and, as we have noted, forecasts drive the predictive models we shall discuss throughout Part Three.

The manager's use of forecasts and the required forecasting methodology can be related to the S-curve shown in Figure 14. During the product development phase, which actually precedes the introductory phase shown in Figure 14, the manager is concerned with decisions about the amount of development effort, product designs and their suitability for the market, and strategies for penetrating the proposed markets. He needs long-term forecasting methodologies in order to scan the future, and the only techniques available to him are the Delphi method, historical analysis of comparable products or services, and the various forms of market surveys. The decisions are risky and the manager will be interested in assessing these risks and employing the subjective probability concepts discussed in Chapter 3.

During the introduction phase of a new product or service, the nature of managerial decisions shifts somewhat because delivery systems must now be developed. Therefore, the decisions focus on marketing strategies, pricing, optimum facility size and location, and distribution systems. Again, however, the manager must rely mainly on nonquantitative forecasting methods involving consumer surveys and market tests, historical analogy and life-cycle analysis, and early warning tracking systems regarding the market. The decisions still involve considerable risk.

During the growth phase of the S-curve, the decisions become more operational and the manager is concerned with facilities expansion coupled with marketing strategy, and with mobilizing production and inventory planning decisions. The causal methods of forecasting can also provide excellent input regarding marketing and pricing decisions.

We have summarized the nature of applications, data needs, costs, and development time for the various forecasting methods in Table 8. In general, development time and cost are correlated with forecasting range. It is important for the manager to understand the limitations imposed by data needs for each of the methods. Usually, even the short-term methods require considerable historical data for statistical significance. For example, the moving average methods require a minimum of a one-year history and at least two years if seasonals are present. The causal methods require at least five years of historical data and considerably more if we are attempting to correlate demand with two or more variables. Obviously, the data requirements dictate that causal methods will be most useful in the saturation or steady state phase of the product life cycle.

Check Your Understanding

1. Thinking in terms of the horizon or range of forecast needed, state the requirement for each of the following as shortest, short-, medium-, or long-range:
   a. the decision concerning the size of a new manufacturing plant
   b. the market forecast for TV sales as a basis for 1) allocating promotion funds to alternative media, and 2) scheduling production
   c. the forecast as a basis for controlling component parts inventories for a lawn mower manufacturer
   d. the forecast of call load as a basis for shift scheduling of telephone operators
   e. the decision to make internally or purchase component parts
   f. the forecasts of demand for service at a "four window" post office

2. Following is a list of products and services. Based on general knowledge, what components of demand do you think are likely to be found if one were to make statistical analyses of data on actual demand:
   a. swim suits
   b. automobiles
   c. hula hoops
   d. X-ray service
   e. hospital inpatient census
   f. gross national product (annual)

3. If $\alpha = 0.2$, the last smoothed average is 102, and the current demand is 105, compute the current smoothed average, assuming no trend in the

TABLE 8. Summary of Forecasting Methods

Methods	Applications	Data Needs	Relative Cost	Development Time
Moving averages, and exponentially weighted moving averages	Short-range forecasts for operations, inventory control, scheduling, pricing, timing of special promotions	Minimum of a one-year history, two years if seasonals are present	Low	Very short
Regression analysis	Short- and medium-range forecasts for existing products and services; marketing strategies, production and facility planning	Several years history; rules of thumb: five years history for one variable, eight for two variables	Medium	Medium
Econometric models	Same as for regression analysis	Same as for regression analysis	High	Medium
Delphi, market surveys, historical analogy, and life-cycle analysis	Long-range predictions, new products and product development, market strategies, pricing, and facility planning	Variable for different methods; several years history for analogy and life cycle	Medium to high	Medium

model. How much weight is given the current demand? Based on this model, what forecast would be made for the next period?

4. If $\alpha = 0.25$, the last smoothed average is 99, the last average trend adjustment is 0.1, and current demand is 104, what is the estimate of current demand? What is the forecast for the next period? For two periods hence?

5. Explain the difference in equations (4) and (5).

6. Explain the rationale behind adaptive forecasting techniques. Why would one expect the continuous models to produce a smaller standard deviation of forecast errors than the periodic models?

7. When the forecasting need is for the very short term, perhaps demand for service on an hourly or half-hourly basis, more aggregate forecasts are often made on a daily or even weekly basis. The aggregate forecast is then distributed on the shorter term basis following known distributions resulting from special studies. Why not simply make the forecasts on an hourly or half-hourly basis, updating for each short time period?

8. If disposable income was $I = \$590$ billion in 1969, compute the forecasted sales for the Cherryoak Company using equation (7). Actual sales in 1969 were \$237.34 million. Is the forecast within the standard error of estimate? What is the significance of whether or not the forecast is within the standard error?

9. Given the data in Table 6 for the Cherryoak Company, compute the forecast for 1967 using both equations (8) and (9) and compare them

to actual sales of $184.79 million. Which forecasting equation would you choose? Why?

10. Explain the significance of the coefficient of determination and the standard error of estimate in judging the overall effectiveness of a regression equation as a forecasting device.

11. Examine Figure 11, the regression line for forecasting sales based on disposable income. Explain why it is not simply an extrapolation of existing trends.

12. What are the assumptions and limitations of regression analysis for forecasting?

13. If our regression equation included terms of GNP, new marriages, price, time trend and advertising expenditures, and we found a significant correlation between price and advertising, why would this relationship not actually improve our forecasting equation?

Problems

1. Table 9 gives monthly data on the sales of a product for two years.
   a. Compute a 3- and a 5-month moving average for the data.
   b. Compute an exponentially weighted moving average using equation (2) for $\alpha = 0.1$ and 0.3.
   c. Compute an exponentially weighted moving average using equation (4) for $\alpha = 0.1$.

TABLE 9. Monthly Sales for a Product

	Jan.	Feb.	Mar.	Apr.	May	June	July	Aug.	Sept.	Oct.	Nov.	Dec.
1976	47	42	16	47	38	34	45	50	47	54	40	43
1977	22	44	42	29	46	45	56	50	39	44	24	46

2. Based on the computations for problem 1, compute the forecasts that would be made for the months of 1976 using equations (2) and (4) for $\alpha = 0.1$ only, and compute the monthly forecast errors. Compute the mean absolute deviation of errors and compare them.

3. Based on the forecasts computed in problem 2 for the months of 1976, what forecasts for the months of 1977 do you think might be justified, assuming of course that the actuals for 1977 in Table 9 did not exist? How many months in advance do you feel justified in forecasting, using either equation (2) or (6)?

4. The Cherryoak Company discussed in the text was jolted by the economic downturn in 1974, as were many companies. The president of the company reacted badly to the fact that the forecast did not predict the downturn until sales had already disintegrated substantially. "Last year I didn't need the forecast. This year I needed it and it was off. What good is it?" Table 10 pro-

vides data for the years 1971, '72, '73, and midyear and year-end estimates for the annual rates for 1974. Based on the regression model of equation (9), what forecasts would have been made based on midyear and year-end estimates of the indicators? How bad is the forecast? Should the president drop the forecasting model?

TABLE 10. Data for Cherryoak Company

Year	Housing Starts	Disposable Income	Actual Sales
1971	1522	679.4	295.79
1972	1621	705.3	305.24
1973	1320	725.8	320.62
1974 (midyear)*	1024	726.5	291.32
1974 (year-end)	857	701.1	272.21

* Midyear values are annual rates.

References

Ahl, D. H., "New Product Forecasting Using Consumer Panels," *Journal of Marketing,* Vol. 7, No. 2, May 1970, pp. 159–67.

Bass, F. M., "A New Product Growth Model for Consumer Durables," *Management Science,* Vol. 16, No. 5, January 1969.

Bass, F. M., C. W. King, and E. A. Pessemeier, *Applications of the Sciences in Marketing Management,* John Wiley & Sons, 1968.

Benton, W. K., *Forecasting for Management,* Addison-Wesley, Reading, Mass., 1972.

Box, G. E. P., and G. M. Jenkins, *Time Series Analysis, Forecasting, and Control,* Holden-Day, San Francisco, 1970.

Chambers, J. C., S. K. Mullick, and D. D. Smith, "How to Choose the Right Forecasting Technique," *Harvard Business Review,* July–August 1971.

Church, J. G., "SURESTAF: A Computerized Staff Scheduling System for Telephone Business Offices," *Management Science,* Vol. 20, No. 4, December, Part II, 1973, pp. 708–20.

Claycamp, H. J., and L. E. Liddy, "Prediction of New Product Performance: An Analytical Approach," *Journal of Marketing Research,* Vol. 6, No. 4, November 1969, pp. 414–21.

Eilon, S., and J. Elmaleh, "Adaptive Limits in Inventory Control," *Management Science,* April 1970.

Gerstenfeld, A., "Technological Forecasting," *Journal of Business,* Vol. 44, No. 1, January 1971, pp. 10–18.

Huang, D. S., *Regression and Econometric Methods,* John Wiley & Sons, New York, 1970.

Mabert, V. A., "The Box-Jenkins Forecasting Technique," Paper No. 529, Institute for Research in the Behavioral, Economic, and Management Sciences, Purdue University, September 1975.

Makridakis, S., A. Hodgsdon, and S. C. Wheelwright, "An Interactive Forecasting System," *The American Statistician,* Vol. 28, No. 4, November 1974, pp. 153–58.

Montgomery, D. C., "Adaptive Control of Exponential Smoothing Parameters by Evolutionary Operations," *AIIE Transactions,* September 1970.

Nelson, C. R., *Applied Time Series Analysis for Managerial Forecasting,* Holden-Day, San Francisco, 1973.

North, H. Q., and D. L. Pyke, "Probes of the Technological Future," *Harvard Business Review,* May–June, 1969.

Parker, G. C., and E. L. Segura, "How to Get a Better Forecast," *Harvard Business Review,* March–April, 1971, pp. 99–109.

Raine, J. E., "Self-Adaptive Forecasting Reconsidered," *Decision Sciences,* Vol. 11, No. 2, April 1971.

Rao, A. G., and A. Shapiro, "Adaptive Smoothing Using Evolutionary Spectra," *Management Science,* Vol. 17, No. 3, November 1970, pp. 208–18.

Roberts, S. D., and R. Reed, "A Development of a Self-Adaptive Forecasting Technique," *AIIE Transactions,* December 1969.

Trigg, D. W., and A. G. Leach, "Exponential Smoothing with an Adaptive Response Rate," *Operational Research Quarterly,* Vol. 18, No. 1, March 1967, pp. 53–59.

Wheelwright, S. C., and S. Makridakis, *Forecasting Methods for Management,* John Wiley & Sons, New York, 1973.

Whybark, D. C., "A Comparison of Adaptive Forecasting Techniques," *The Logistics and Transportation Review,* Vol. 8, No. 3, 1972, pp. 13–26.

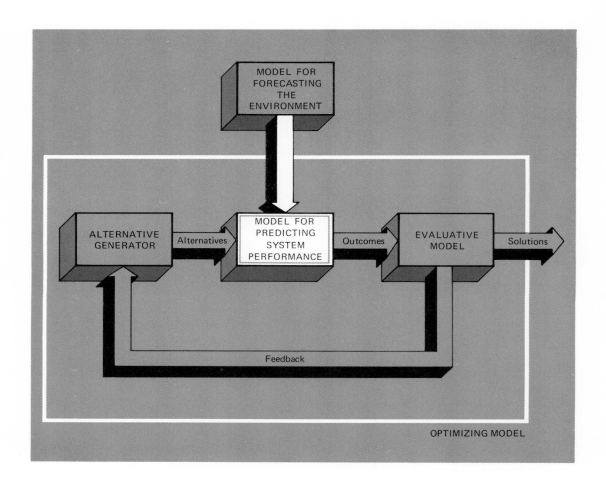

6

Building Mathematical Models
to Predict System Performance

Models for predicting system performance are probably the most familiar type of mathematical model. These models are designed to predict the outcomes of alternative courses of action. The alternatives may be generated in some systematic manner that attempts to exhaust the feasible alternatives, or they may be hypotheses for what a manager thinks could be a good strategy. The alternatives may be viewed as inputs being transformed by the predictive model into a set of outcomes. This transformation of alternatives into outcomes may be influenced by the nature of the environment.

The Components of a Model for Predicting System Performance

Variables   We often speak of the *variables* within a mathematical model. These are the elements of the model that can take on different values. An *alternative* is expressed as a particular set of values for these variables. For example, suppose we model a physical process such as steel making with an electric furnace as discussed in the Introduction to Part Three. The variables in this model would be the quantities of ore, coke, limestone, and labor that are used. An alternative would consist of specific values for these variables. That is, we would identify an alternative by specifying the exact quantities of ore, coke, limestone, and labor to be used. These variables are often called *decision variables* or *controllable* variables since their values can be determined by the decision maker.

Parameters   The *parameters* of a model are the known entities not directly controllable by the decision maker. Some parameters may be determined by the nature of the environment. For a specific set of assumptions regarding the environment, these parameters are constants. However, they may vary as the environment changes. These parameters are often called *uncontrollable variables* to indicate that they do vary with the environment but are not controlled by the decision maker. The values of some of these uncontrollable variables are determined from forecasting models as discussed in Chapter 5.

Other parameters are known and are not affected by the environment. They may be determined by physical laws and always maintain constant values in the model no matter how the environment may change.

The corporate model discussed in the Introduction to Part Three included costs of labor and materials as essential elements. These parameters would be considered uncontrollable variables, since the company cannot directly manipulate their values. For a given set of assumptions regarding the environment, these values will be determined within the model.

In the steel making example, the number of pounds of steel produced from quantities of iron ore and scrap is determined by physical laws. It does not change at the discretion of the decision maker, and it is not influenced by the environment. Thus, parameters reflecting these physical laws would be included in the model.

Logical Relationships   The logical relationships in a mathematical model are explicit statements regarding how the system actually functions. They are cause-effect relationships among the variables and parameters of the model. For example, we might write

$$I_t = I_{t-1} + P_t - D_t$$

to indicate that the inventory of a product at the end of time period t (I_t) equals the inventory at the end of period $t-1$ (I_{t-1}) plus the production of the product in period t (P_t) minus the demand for the product in period t (D_t). This is a mathematical statement of a simple accounting relationship.

Other logical relationships place upper and lower limits on the values of variables or on mathematical expressions involving several variables. For example, we might write

$$P_{t-1} + P_t \geqslant 100$$

to indicate that the production in time period $t-1$ plus the production in time period t must be greater than or equal to 100. The production levels are variables in this expression, while the number 100 is a particular value for the two-period production level parameter. Other logical relationships may involve probabilistic statements.

In some mathematical models, most notably the optimizing models to be discussed in Part Four, these logical relationships are called *constraints*.

The Purpose of a Model for Predicting System Performance

Commonly, the manager will play the role of alternative generator for a model for predicting system performance. In this role, he will specify values of the decision variables in the model. In addition, the manager will specify some scenario regarding the nature of the environment in which the system will be operating. The specification of this scenario must be sufficiently detailed to provide information to any forecasting models used to determine the parameters of the model for predicting system performance. In some cases, the manager may subjectively assign values to these parameters based on his implicit forecasting model for the environment.

Given this information, the model should predict the outputs of the system that would be created if the same alternative were actually chosen under identical environmental conditions in the real world. These outcomes would then be evaluated by the manager, perhaps using one of the evaluative models discussed in Part Two.

Notice that the manager has the option of analyzing many different alternatives under the same environmental assumptions or of analyzing the same alternative under many environmental assumptions. If the logical relationships are computerized, the process of making these analyses can be greatly simplified.

CREATING A MODEL FOR PREDICTING SYSTEM PERFORMANCE

Creating a useful mathematical model for predicting system performance is not a trivial task in a complex, real-world environment. Nevertheless, the investment of time and effort, especially by the manager who will eventually use the model, can lead to significant benefits. We shall now consider how such a model might be constructed. In order to provide a concrete reference for this discussion, we shall illustrate the concepts by developing a simple model for break-even analysis. It is important to emphasize that our interest here is on the model building procedure rather than on the break-even analysis per se.

Initial Formulation

Getting Started   Suppose a manager recognizes that he has a problem and believes that a model for predicting system performance might be useful to him. His first task is to *bound* the problem by identifying as specifically as possible those questions he would like to have answered by the model.

For example, suppose the manager of a small manufacturing firm that produces one item is having difficulty determining a proper pricing strategy and in forecasting profits or losses. He might feel that a predictive model could be useful to him in dealing with this task. He could bound his problem by identifying the following set of initial questions he would like to have assistance in answering:

1. For a given set of costs, production, and price figures, what will my profit or loss be?
2. What will be the effect on profits (or losses) if I change my price, given that costs and demand remain constant?
3. How will my profit or loss be affected if demand changes?
4. What if my variable costs of production increase? How will my profit or loss be affected?

Notice that a list of questions such as this should be provided by the manager who will actually be *using* the system. It should not be generated by a professional analyst on the basis of what he thinks the manager should want. The responsibility for such a list falls on the manager, and his developing the list is most important in ensuring that a mathematical model created for the manager will actually be used by him. Thus, he needs to have the proper expectations regarding the types of questions on which he can legitimately expect help from a mathematical model.

Identifying the Important Elements   The model builder must now abstract from the real world those essential elements of the system relevant to answering the questions posed by the manager. As illustrated in Figure 1, this process is one of *simplification* of the complexity of the real world.

The circles in Figure 1 indicate elements in the real world to be represented by variables and parameters in the model. The lines between the circles suggest that the connected elements are interdependent in some fashion, and this interdependence should be specified using logical relationships. Finally, the dotted line places bounds on the problem in the real world. It is the task of the model builder to observe this reality and to abstract a simplified model.

In our example, it is clear that the questions posed by the manager can be answered by considering the internal workings of one company, and then only its financial aspects. The linkage of this company to its environment will be through the demand for the product produced by the company. From studying the questions, it seems that the profit (or loss) is the most important element. Further, we know that the profit (or loss) of a company is determined by the relationship between revenues and costs, as illustrated in Figure 2.

Determining Logical Relationships   Next, the model builder must hypothesize the logical relationships among these elements to create the model. In some cases, these relationships may be based on empirical data, while in other cases we can only appeal to the criterion of "reasonableness." In our example, we know that

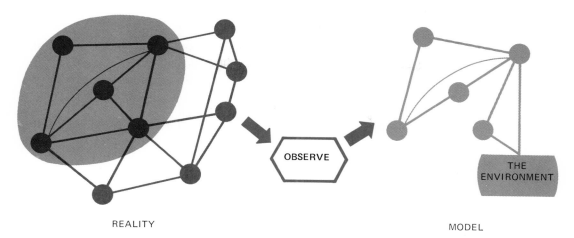

Figure 1. Modeling as a simplification of the real world

REALITY

OBSERVE

MODEL

THE ENVIRONMENT

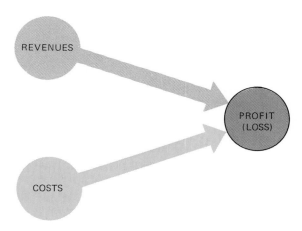

REVENUES

PROFIT (LOSS)

COSTS

Figure 2. Profit (loss) is determined by revenues and costs

$$\text{profit (loss)} = \text{revenues} - \text{costs} ,$$

which is a mathematical statement of the logical relationship among these elements.

This simple mathematical relation serves as our initial formulation of a model for predicting system performance. What have we learned from this model? It is clear from an analysis of this model that

1. if revenues increase, so do profits, or

2. if costs decrease, profits increase.

Further, this interpretation of the results seems reasonable in the real world. Although these statements may seem trivial and self-evident, the basic concepts employed in the more elaborate model building efforts in the real world are essentially the same.

Adding Additional Detail   We have begun with a simple model as our initial formulation. However, we do not have sufficient detail in this model to answer some of the questions posed by the manager. For example, we do not have logical relationships in the model that determine the effects of price, demand, and variable costs on revenues and total costs. Therefore, we must add additional detail to the model.

First let us consider the revenues in the model. Revenues are generated by selling items at a particular price. Therefore, the sales price and the number of items sold must be important elements in our model. The specific relationship among revenues, price, and items sold is

$$\text{revenues} = (\text{price}) (\text{items sold}) .$$

Let us use some simple mathematical notation to condense this model, defining p as the price per unit of our product and x as the number of units produced and sold. Now, we have the expression

$$\text{revenues} = px$$

to summarize this relationship. This expression is a logical relationship written in algebraic form.

The costs are a bit more complicated. First we have the costs of being in business, the fixed costs. These include rent or lease payments, license fees, and other costs that must be met even if we do not produce a single item. Next, there are the costs of doing business, the variable costs. These costs include expenditures for labor and raw materials and are influenced by the number of units we produce. Mathematically, the logical relationship dealing with costs is written

$$\text{total costs} = \text{fixed costs}$$
$$+ (\text{variable costs per unit}) (\text{number of units sold}) .$$

This logical relationship adds the fixed costs to the variable costs, which are determined by the product of the variable costs per unit produced times the number of units produced and sold. Now, let us simplify this expression by defining f as the fixed costs and c as the variable costs per unit sold. Then, the total costs equal $f + cx$.

We can now replace the elements of revenues and costs in our original model and obtain a new model with additional detail:

$$\text{profit (loss)} = px - (cx + f) .$$

Now, do we have sufficient detail in the model shown in Figure 3? Perhaps so. The manager may substitute values for the elements of this model and determine his profit or loss. Simultaneously, he may answer the other questions that he posed in his list.

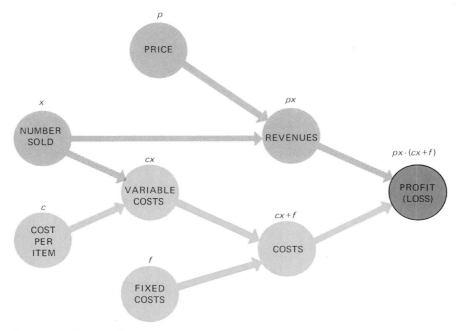

Figure 3. The simple break-even model

Bootstrapping   We shall use the term "bootstrapping" to refer to a strategy of model formulation based on beginning with a simple model and adding detail. We have illustrated this strategy with the simple break-even model, and it is a most important strategy in real-world applications.

Specialists in management science and operations research are often tempted to study a problem, then go off in isolation to develop an elaborate mathematical model for use by the manager. Unfortunately the manager may not understand this model and may either use it blindly or reject it entirely. The specialist may feel that the manager was too ignorant and unsophisticated to appreciate his model, while the manager may feel that the specialist lives in a dream world of unrealistic assumptions and irrelevant mathematics.

Such difficulty can be avoided if the manager works with the specialist to develop first a simple model that provides a crude but understandable analysis. After the manager has built up confidence in this model, additional detail and sophistication can be added, perhaps only a bit at a time. This process requires an investment of time on the part of the manager and sincere interest on the part of the specialist in solving the manager's real problem, rather than in playing with sophisticated models. However, a bootstrapping approach to model building seems to be one of the most important factors in determining the successful implementation of a mathematical model (for examples see Morris [1967], Little [1970], and Urban [1974]). This approach also simplifies the difficult task of validating the model.

The Appropriate Level of Detail   The creation of a mathematical model is still very much an "art" rather than a "science." Although there are a number of generally accepted rules of thumb, there is no simple list of steps that will lead automatically to a successful model. The objective of modeling is to obtain the benefits of a mathematical model at a relatively low cost. Naturally, the benefits from a model will increase, other things being equal, as the level of detail in the model increases to provide an improved representation of reality. Unfortunately, the costs of modeling also increase, since more detail requires more information and a heavier computation burden. The art of modeling requires trading off the benefits of an increased level of detail against their associated increases in the costs of information and computation. The criterion to be used in this trade-off is that of *user needs* (see Figure 4).

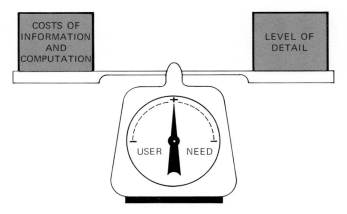

Figure 4. Trading off informational and computational requirements against level of detail

Figure 5, adapted from Geoffrion [1975], portrays the trade-offs to be made in selecting the appropriate level of detail. The gross benefits from additional detail increase at a decreasing rate, while the total costs increase at an increasing rate. Ideally, one would like to choose a level of detail at approximately point *B* on the net benefits curve corresponding to 1975 tech-

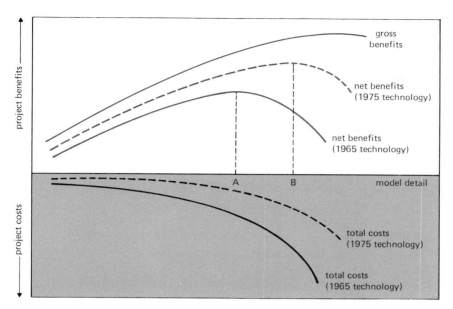

Figure 5. Influence of degree of model detail on project benefits and costs

From A. Geoffrion, "Progress in Computer Assisted Distribution System Planning," Working Paper No. 219a, Western Management Science Institute, University of California, Los Angeles, revised June 1975, used by permission.

nology (see Figure 5). Notice that similar curves are also corresponding to 1965 technology, and we can expect these curves to continue to move to the right as advances continue in computational techniques, management information systems, and computer hardware.

Since the technology will be available to construct and use more detailed models, the greatest bottleneck may be the ability of the manager to understand these more sophisticated models. On the one hand, this emphasizes the importance of a bootstrapping approach to model development. On the other, it emphasizes the need for managers to study and understand the basic concepts of management science so that they will be able to utilize the powerful decision-making aids that are available to them.

Validation of the Model

The next task is to validate the model. The objectives of this task are to ensure that the model accurately predicts the outcomes of alternatives and to simultaneously increase the manager's confidence in the model.

There are two potential dangers in not adequately validating a mathematical model. The first is that the manager will be so impressed by the elegance and sophistication of the mathematical model and its computer print-outs that he will never question whether the basic assumptions on which it depends are actually sound. As Churchman [1973] points out, a mathematical model may be precisely wrong. He suggests that we often mistakenly believe that he who thinks elaborately thinks well.

At the other extreme, the manager may not have sufficient confidence in the mathematical model to actually rely on it. Most individuals prefer a simple, crude analysis they can understand to a sophisticated analysis they cannot comprehend.

The validation should consider the internal logic of the model as determined by the logical relationships. All of the assumptions on which these relationships were based should be specified and made known to the manager. The logic of the model should reflect the manager's view of the real world and not the analyst's view. For example, analysts often assume that the variables in the model are related by linear rather than nonlinear relationships. While this assumption is valid in many real-world situations, in others it may seriously distort the model.

A second issue is the validity of the data used in the model. Forecasting models may be required to provide values for some of the parameters. These data sources should also be scrutinized.

Finally, the model must be run several times to ensure that the logical relationships and the mathematical analysis were correctly programmed in the computer. Geoffrion [1976] refers to these as probationary exercises. He suggests that the model be restricted by fixing many of the decision variables and logical relationships so that the appropriate answer will be obvious, or at least can be calculated by an experienced staff analyst. Then the results of the model can be compared against those obtained by hand. The source of any discrepancies should then be identified, whether it be errors in the basic assumptions, the logical relationships, the input data, or a bug in the computer program.

A second approach is to match the model against past history. The actual data used in prior time periods in the real-world system that the model is to represent can be put into the model, and the outcomes can be compared. Again, it should be possible to justify any discrepancies that occur.

Thus, validation requires that we manipulate the model and compare the results with what has happened (or what we would expect to happen) in the real world. This process may cause us to revise the model until we are satisfied with the results.

Figure 6 illustrates that the initial model formulation is compared against the real world. In this example, additional logical relationships are identified in the revised model in order to represent reality more closely.

The break-even analysis model should be validated by questioning whether the basic assumptions are appropriate. For example, we have assumed that costs consist of a fixed component and a variable component that remains constant no matter what the level of production actually is.

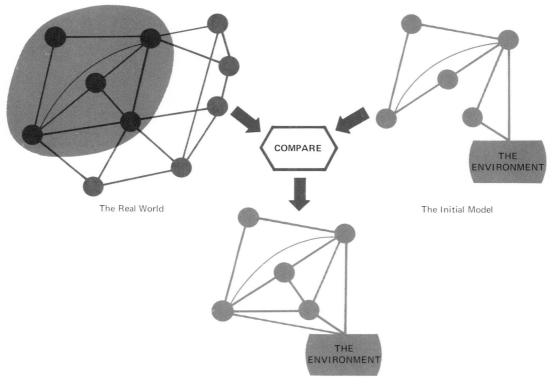

The Real World   COMPARE   THE ENVIRONMENT

The Initial Model

THE ENVIRONMENT

The Revised Model

Figure 6. Revision of a model

In a real-world situation, a more elaborate cost model would probably be required (for examples see Reisman and Buffa [1962]).

Analysis

A model for predicting system performance is analyzed by exploring the structure and behavior of the model as a consequence of the initial assumptions and the logical relationships. This analysis is "objective" in the sense that it can be verified or repudiated on the basis of logical arguments alone.

    Let us consider an example of analysis based on the break-even model. The manager may ask, "What if my fixed costs are $2000 per week, my price is $30 per unit, my variable costs are $15 per unit, and I sell 300 units per week? What will my profit or loss be?" We can use the break-even model to calculate the profit or loss using the logic of mathematical analysis. Substituting for the decision variables and parameters we have

$$f = 2000 \qquad c = 15$$
$$p = 30 \qquad x = 300 .$$

Using the logical relationship, we obtain

$$\text{profit (loss)} = (30)\,(300) - (15)\,(300) - 2000$$
$$= 9000 - 4500 - 2000 = 2500 .$$

Thus the profit in this situation would be $2500 per week.

The creation of a mathematical model requires a significant investment of time and money. However, once this capital investment has been made, the actual use of the model is generally very cheap. Therefore, it should be used often, even at the whim of the manager.

In addition to the probationary exercises to validate a model, Geoffrion [1976] suggests a series of computer runs. This series should include the runs described in the following paragraphs.

Base Case Runs   The model should be run with several future scenarios for the organization. These scenarios may correspond to different time horizons and to different forecasts of the organization's environment. Many different policy options should be used as alternatives. One important result of such a process is that the manager's intuition and understanding about the problem will be greatly increased as he views the results from different alternatives.

Sensitivity Analysis   Additional runs should be made to test the sensitivity of the model to any questionable assumptions made in the model. Such analyses will indicate whether these assumptions have significantly affected the results from the model.

Other runs can be made to test the sensitivity of the results to the values of key parameters. These runs may be useful in determining the *value of information* in much the same manner as illustrated in Chapter 2 in the context of decision trees.

"What If" Questions   In addition to the base case run under likely scenarios and the sensitivity analysis, the manager may wish to explore the results of even more unlikely events by asking a series of "what if" questions. Issues that might be explored include the following:

1. What if a new competitor enters the market for our product?
2. What if we suffer a strike that lasts for n weeks?
3. What if fuel shortages reduce our effective trucking capacity by 10 percent?

If the model is sufficiently flexible, the answers to such questions will be immediately available. The most important result of such exercises is the learning that takes place on the part of the manager.

Interpretation

Once the model has been analyzed and the results have been obtained, the manager must *interpret* their meaning back in the real world. In the few cases where the model captures or fits the problem in the real world perfectly, interpretation may be a straightforward task. More commonly, the model is not a perfect fit, so the results of the analysis may require careful scrutiny, since the best solution for the model may not be the best solution for the real-world problem.

Formulation is a process of simplification, of extraction from the real world. During interpretation, the manager must reconsider the results from the mathematical analysis in the context of the complexities omitted or ignored during formulation due to intangibility or to technical difficulties. The results may need to be modified to allow for other considerations. Returning to the break-even model, the manager finds from the analysis that a weekly profit of $2500 could be realized if he sells 300 units per week at a price of $30. He must still decide whether he can actually sell 300 units per week at this price, since the model only provides the profit calculation if he is successful. Could he sell more than 300 units at this price, or could he sell 300 units at an even higher price? These are issues that must be confronted before the results of the analysis are implemented in the real world.

WHAT SHOULD THE MANAGER KNOW?

The basic steps of model building are illustrated in Figure 7. Model formulation and the interpretation of the results of analysis require skill and insight on the part of the manager. Once the relatively straightforward tools of mathematical analysis are understood and available to a manager, *formulation and interpretation become the intellectually challenging activities.*

The manager must play an active role in the creation and use of mathematical models. This task cannot be successfully accomplished by a technical staff or an outside consultant working in isolation. The manager must be involved. He must bear the principal responsibility for recognizing problems that can be analyzed successfully by mathematical models. He must create the list of questions to be answered by the model as an aid in bounding the formulation. He must express his understanding of the system in a manner that can be captured by logical relationships. He must participate in the probationary exercises with the model in order to gain confidence in its validity. Finally, he must *use* the model in a creative way to attack and solve the problem of interest.

Models only reflect what has been structured; they cannot create a new structure. The model should serve to reduce the routine, pencil-pushing work of the manager, leaving him even more time for creative thought and innovation. The model can also assist by quickly computing the results of

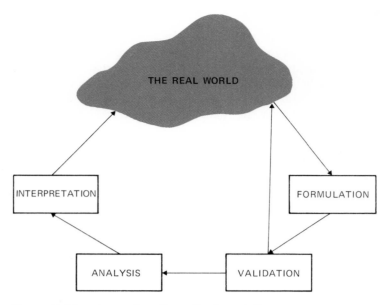

Figure 7. The steps of mathematical modeling

some of his innovative ideas and by helping him to develop his intuition regarding a particular problem area.

However, the most dramatic and creative new solutions will "break the model" in the sense that they cannot be represented with the existing structure of the model, even though a conscious effort has been made to provide sufficient flexibility to allow the manager to try a wide range of alternatives. These creative solutions are ideas that were not considered during model building because they are not a simple extension of the existing system or operations, but represent a significant innovation. Perhaps the highest compliment that could be paid to a model would be that it contributed to its own obsolescence by providing the insights to the manager that allowed him to leap beyond it. Certainly, the manager should be alert for such opportunities.

The important point to remember is that the manager will still be left with the responsibility of making the decision, and this responsibility cannot be delegated to the model. The model can aid the manager by sharpening his intuition and by predicting for him the outcomes from choosing alternative solutions. However, in the final analysis, the decision will be made by the manager. The degree to which this decision is improved as a result of the use of a mathematical model will generally be determined by the involvement of the manager in its creation.

Check Your Understanding

1. Consider each of the following problems:
   a. the development of a long-range plan for a large integrated forest products company
   b. the development of a production plan for a large steel manufacturing company
   c. the development of a plan for locating and dispatching ambulances
   For each problem, assume that a predictive model is to be developed to aid in its resolution and that you are the manager with the primary responsibility for the plan.
   (1) Bound the problem by listing the questions you would expect a predictive model to answer.
   (2) Identify the important elements in each problem. Indicate whether each element is a decision variable or a parameter.
   (3) Determine the important logical relationships among these elements using a diagram such as the one illustrated in Figure 3.

2. Explain the differences between a controllable variable, an uncontrollable variable, and a parameter determined by physical laws. Describe a problem in which you identify examples of each.

3. What is meant by the term "bootstrapping," and why is it so important?

4. For each of the problems in question 1, provide the following:
   a. At least two examples of "future scenarios" that you would expect to be used in base case runs of the predictive model. Be specific.
   b. At least two questionable assumptions or key parameters on which you would perform a sensitivity analysis.

5. For the break-even model developed in this chapter, develop the following:
   a. Base case analyses with forecasted sales of 200 and 400 units per week.
   b. Base case analyses with variable costs of $14 and $20 per unit.
   c. A sensitivity analysis of the assumption of linearity in the variable costs by supposing that the first 100 units produced per week have a variable cost of $25 per unit, the next 100 cost $15 per unit, and the remaining units cost $10 per unit. Is there a serious discrepancy with the linear model when the sales are 300 per week? 400 per week? 200 per week?
   d. A "What if" analysis of a new production system that would lower unit costs to $10 but would increase fixed costs to $3000. For what levels of weekly sales would the old production system be superior, and for what levels would the new system be superior?

6. Explain why model formulation and interpretation are the intellectually challenging activities in mathematical modeling for a manager.

References

Churchman, C. W., "Reliability of Models in the Social Sciences," *Interfaces,* Vol. 4, No. 1, November 1973.

Elmaghraby, S. E., "The Role of Modeling in IE Design," *The Journal of Industrial Engineering,* Vol. 19, No. 6, June 1968.

Geoffrion, A., "Progress in Computer Assisted Distribution System Planning," Working Paper No. 219a, Western Management Science Institute, University of California, Los Angeles, revised June 1975.

———, "Better Distribution Planning With Computer Models," *Harvard Business Review*, Vol. 54, No. 4, July–August 1976.

Little, J. D. C., "Models and Managers: The Concept of a Decision Calculus," *Management Science,* Vol. 16, No. 8, April 1970.

Morris, W. T., "On the Art of Modeling," *Management Science,* Vol. 13, No. 12, August 1967.

Reisman, A., and E. S. Buffa, "A General Model for Investment Policy," *Management Science,* Vol. 8, No. 3, April 1962.

Strauch, R. E., " 'Squishy' Problems and Quantitative Methods," The Rand Corporation, Santa Monica, California, P-5303, October 1974.

Urban, G. L., "Building Models for Decision Makers," *Interfaces,* Vol. 4, No. 3, May 1974.

Zeleny, M., "Managers Without Management Science," *Interfaces,* Vol. 5, No. 4, August 1975.

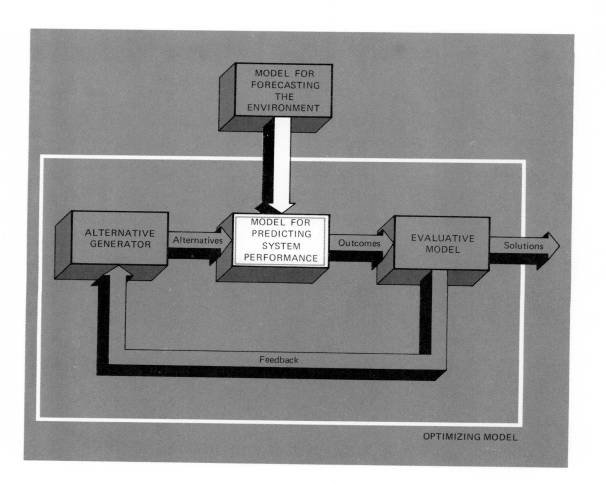

7

Computer-Based
Corporate Simulation Models

Computer-based predictive models are now quite commonly used by managers as vehicles for planning at various levels. The applications include steel making, forest products, various consumer products manufacturers, cigarette manufacturers, publishers, leasing companies, banking, aerospace companies, electric utilities, and governmental agencies.

These kinds of predictive models have been well received by practicing managers partly because they make no pretense at making managerial decisions. Rather, they are models that represent the financial or other flows in an enterprise and can therefore be queried with "what if" questions by managers. Since the models simulate the enterprise, a range of hypotheses concerning prices, volume, various costs, etc., can be tested to form a sound planning base. The models provide answers to questions asked, but the manager retains his traditional role as decision maker.

Computer-based corporate models have commonly been developed in a computer-based interactive mode to facilitate a "manager active" situation in which results from one query may stimulate new questions. We have then a powerful combination of decision maker and predictive model in a loop. Very complex computations reflecting assumptions about volume, price, costs, or the effects of a labor dispute, can be handled in a short turnaround time (as low as a few minutes), including data input, computing, and output.

Basically, the mathematical relationships are as simple as the accounting flows discussed in the previous chapter in connection with the break-even analysis example of model building. Figure 1 summarizes those relationships by showing eight elements that enter break-even models. In Chapter 6 we used the simple break-even model as a vehicle for developing the concepts of

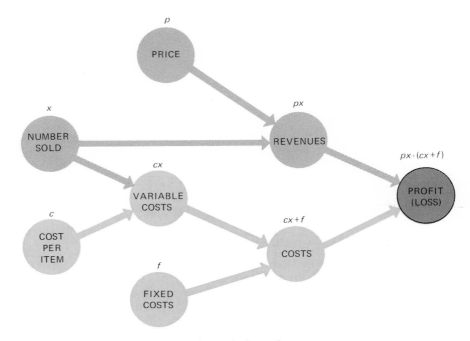

Figure 1. Elements entering the formulation of a profit (loss) function

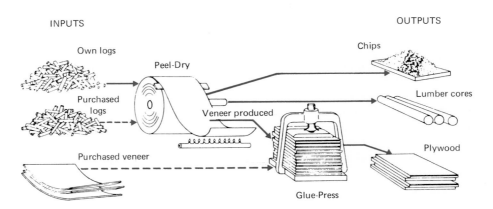

Figure 2. Overall flow of plywood operations

From J. B. Boulden and E. S. Buffa, "Corporate Models: On-Line Real-Time Systems," *Harvard Business Review*, July–August 1970; used by permission.

COMPUTER-BASED CORPORATE SIMULATION MODELS

model building. We shall now build on those ideas to develop a more sophisticated model. It will be more sophisticated because it will more closely represent the complexities of an enterprise and because we shall assume the power of a computing system. However, the relationships are no more sophisticated than those used to construct the simple break-even model.

PLYWOOD MANUFACTURING AS AN EXAMPLE

The physical flow of material for a plywood manufacturing operation is shown in Figure 2 where we see that the material inputs are company-owned logs together with purchased logs (if required). These materials are processed through the veneer manufacturing phase, that involves cutting a thin sheet of veneer from the surface of the log (peeling) and drying it to a specified moisture content. By-products of the peel-dry process are green lumber cores and chips, which are sold at transfer prices to other divisions of the enterprise. Plywood is then glued and pressed with veneer produced in the previous operation or (if required) purchased veneer.

While this description of the process is simplified, it serves as an adequate basis for our discussion. The capacity of the glue-press operation in relation to the available company-produced veneer determines the amount of purchased veneer required. Similarly, the capacity of the peel-dry operation in relation to desired veneer output determines the amount of purchased logs required.

Model Formulation

Let us begin with simple relationship diagrams that describe the profit or loss of the plywood company.

Revenue The three outputs that produce revenue are chips, lumber cores, and of course, plywood, as shown in Figure 3(a). For plywood, revenue is simply the quantity produced and sold multiplied by the price as indicated in Figure 3(b). The price is an estimate or an actual market price; however, the quantity is the lesser of two figures — the plant capacity or the desired production level determined by forecasts coupled with a planning process — as indicated by Figure 3(c). Now, if we enter into our model the specific numbers for plywood price, desired quantity, and capacity, we can obtain the total revenue generated by plywood sales through the simple mathematical relationship,

plywood revenue = price × minimum of (desired quantity, capacity) .

A similar analysis could be used to determine revenue from chips and lumber cores; we could then specify a model to estimate total revenues as the sum of the three components of revenue.

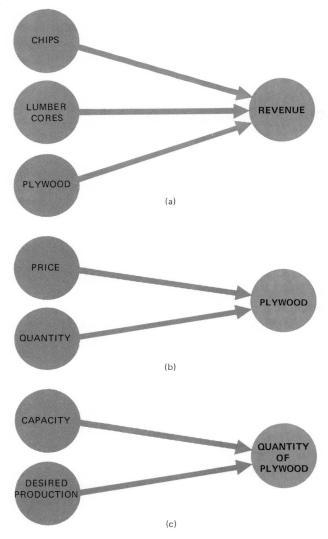

Figure 3. Plywood company revenue model formulation: (a) revenue components, (b) factors entering plywood revenue, and (c) factors determining quantity of plywood

Costs   Now let us consider the cost model. In an actual application we may wish to include very detailed cost breakdowns of the marketing costs, variable production costs, fixed costs, and miscellaneous costs shown as components in Figure 4(a). Each of these separate components of the total cost must be analyzed to develop the appropriate relationships. For example, the marketing costs might be generated from subcomponents of discounts and allowances, sales commissions, and freight charges, as shown in Figure 4(b).

Each of these costs might be estimated as a percentage of the total plywood sales revenues, for example. Therefore, our model would use the plywood sales revenue generated and apply specific percentages to de-

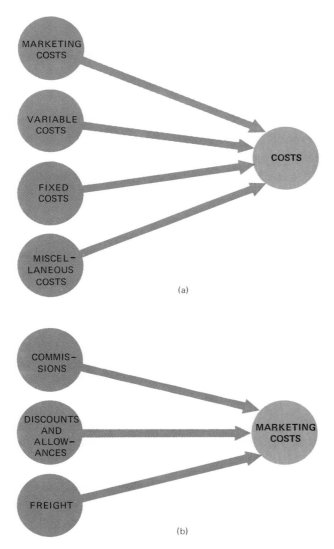

(a)

(b)

Figure 4. Plywood company cost model formulation: (a) cost components and (b) marketing cost components

termine marketing costs. Similar analyses would be required to develop models representing the behavior of the other costs.

We see now that the process of *formulating* a profit (loss) model is quite straightforward. The logic consists primarily of simple arithmetic operations, though the number of calculations will be large as we try to represent a real organization, since there will be various sizes, types, and grades of plywood. Because of the complexity, we program such models on a computer in order to retain the logic for repetitive use and to achieve rapid turnaround time for computing the effects of alternatives that reflect price and cost changes. To use such a profit (loss) model we must specify the inputs or values of the elements of the model. These values include the *parameters* that define specific conditions as we discussed in Chapter 6, and the *decision variables*, that may be changed at the discretion of the manager.

Use of Computer Version of the Plywood Model

Let us now assume the power of the computer and see how the plywood model can be of managerial use. We also assume now that the plywood operation is really only a division of a larger concern. The inputs and outputs of the plywood model are shown in Figure 5. We have added the product and overhead relationships to the forecasts of production volume and prices.

Depending on our needs, we can structure outputs in various ways, such as profit and loss statements, materials and sales analyses, manpower planning schedules, etc. The computer will not provide the necessary inputs for the model or the logical relationships—that is our function. The computer's function is to carry out the computations defined by the logic we provide.

Using a system of precoded commands we can call for model output in various forms. For example, in Figure 6 we have called for the profit and loss statement based on a set of parameters. Note that the model provides summary ratios such as gross and net profit to sales. Also, the output could have been called for by quarters or in some other format.

The problem-solving value of such a model lies in our ability to ask meaningful questions that may involve changing the values of the decision variables. Each set of values for the decision variables represents a different alternative. In addition, we may wish to determine the outcomes associated with each alternative, given several future scenarios. These scenarios are described by modifying the parameter values. For example, we can ask for a profit and loss report for a given profit objective and specific assumptions regarding the state of the environment. Also, using that concept we can perform a break-even analysis by specifying a profit objective of zero in response to the system's query as shown in Figure 7. The system responds by computing the sales and percentage of current forecasted sales necessary for break-even operation.

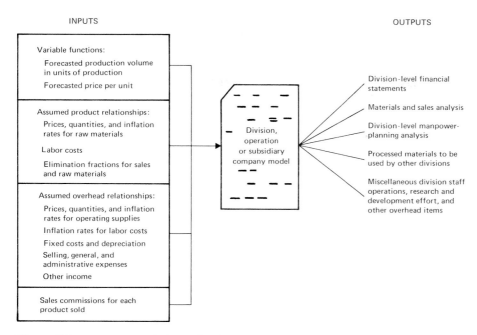

Figure 5. Input-output relationships for a division

From J. B. Boulden and E. S. Buffa, "Corporate Models: On-Line Real-Time Systems"; used by permission.

Now suppose we wish to assess the impact on profits of a labor cost increase. By reference to a parameter list, we know that labor cost is coded as P24. We call for "parameter sensitivity," and the system responds by asking which parameter we wish to test as well as the minimum-maximum limits of the test and the increments of variation. We respond by typing 24 for parameter 24, a minimum of $5, a maximum of $6, in increments of 0.25; that is, 24/5/6/.25, as shown in Figure 8. The system then computes net profit for each value of the labor cost parameter automatically generating outcomes, given four different scenarios (see Figure 8). Such a computation might be of great importance during a labor negotiation.

Larger Systems of Models Now, assuming that the plywood operation is a division of a much larger corporation, a straightforward extension of the concepts we have discussed can result in the consolidation of the outputs of the plywood division model with other divisions into a "group" consolidation model as shown in Figure 9. This process would require the specification of similar additional relationships.

Finally, the results of several group models can be consolidated at the corporate level, also shown in Figure 9. Top executives are likely to be most interested in the group and corporate consolidation models. Yet, by using the kind of structure illustrated by the plywood model as a basic building block, together with the successive layers of aggregation we have indicated, management can ask for effects of proposed changes in prices, costs, equipment, financing, and so on, at any level within the organization. Also, management can quickly estimate the net effects on the total enterprise.

```
YEAR 76

   LINE ITEMS       YRT
SALES PLY       138550.0
SALES CHIPS       7051.5
SALES LUMBER      4545.0
SALES ELIM
TOTAL SALES     150146.5
D&A PLYWOOD        2771.0
COM PLY           8313.0
FREIGHT PLY       1122.0
TOT COM          12206.0
NET SALES       137940.5
RAW MATERIAL     25570.0
VENEER PURCH     32356.5
OP SUPPLIES      14101.2
LABOR            33860.4
COST ELIMIN
COST OF SALE    105888.1
GROSS PROFIT     32052.4
FIXED COSTS       5000.0
SELLING EXP       3000.0
G&A EXPENSE       3000.0
OTHER EXPENSE      500.0
TOT IND EXP      11500.0
NET PROFIT       20552.4
GP/NS               .23
TIE/NS              .08
NP/NS               .15
```

Figure 6. Computation of profit and loss statement from predictive model. Output could have been called for by quarters or months and could have included actual experience plus projections based on forecasts, depending on input.

From J. B. Boulden and E. S. Buffa, "Corporate Models: On-Line Real-Time Systems"; used by permission.

```
DESIRED YEARLY PROFIT = 0/

    TOT SALES        PROFIT       FRAC 1
   150146.50       20552.36       1.0000
    53870.76            .00        .3588
```

Figure 7. Computation of break-even sales and fraction from predictive model

From J. B. Boulden and E. S. Buffa, "Corporate Models: On-Line Real-Time Systems"; used by permission.

```
P-L MODE =
PARAMETER SENSITIVITY
P#/MIN/MAX/INCREMENT/ = 24/5/6/.25/

    YEAR 76                    P/L

P24 = 5.000

LINE ITEMS                     YRT
NET PROFIT                  20552.4

P24 = 5.250

LINE ITEMS                     YRT
NET PROFIT                  18859.3

P24 = 5.500

LINE ITEMS                     YRT
NET PROFIT                  17166.3

P24 = 5.750

LINE ITEMS                     YRT
NET PROFIT                  15473.3

P24 = 6.000

LINE ITEMS                     YRT
NET PROFIT                  13781.0
```

Figure 8. Sensitivity of net profit to the parameter *P*24, labor cost per hour for the plywood case

From J. B. Boulden and E. S. Buffa, "Corporate Models: On-Line Real-Time Systems"; used by permission.

MANAGERIAL USE OF COMPUTER-BASED PREDICTIVE MODELS

Predictive models of enterprise operations of the type we have just discussed are in general use. Large-scale applications have been made at Van den Bergh & Jergens, a subsidiary of Unilever, [Buffa, 1972] and for a division of Imperial Chemical Industries [Stephenson, 1970] in England. Reports have been published of the use of corporate planning models at Xerox Corporation [Seaberg and Seaberg, 1973], financial institutions [Hamilton and Moses, 1973, 1974], and for aggregate production planning [Lee and McLaughlin, 1974]. In addition, we shall discuss applications at Potlatch Forests, the Inland Steel Company, the Food and Drug Administration, and in electric utilities.

INPUTS

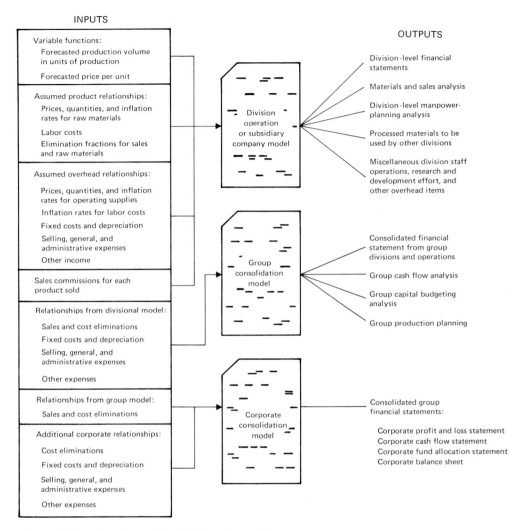

OUTPUTS

Variable functions:
  Forecasted production volume in units of production
  Forecasted price per unit

Assumed product relationships:
  Prices, quantities, and inflation rates for raw materials
  Labor costs
  Elimination fractions for sales and raw materials

Assumed overhead relationships:
  Prices, quantities, and inflation rates for operating supplies
  Inflation rates for labor costs
  Fixed costs and depreciation
  Selling, general, and administrative expenses
  Other income

Sales commissions for each product sold

Relationships from divisional model:
  Sales and cost eliminations
  Fixed costs and depreciation
  Selling, general, and administrative expenses
  Other expenses

Relationships from group model:
  Sales and cost eliminations

Additional corporate relationships:
  Cost eliminations
  Fixed costs and depreciation
  Selling, general, and administrative expenses
  Other expenses

Division operation or subsidiary company model

Group consolidation model

Corporate consolidation model

Division-level financial statements
Materials and sales analysis
Division-level manpower-planning analysis
Processed materials to be used by other divisions
Miscellaneous division staff operations, research and development effort, and other overhead items

Consolidated financial statement from group divisions and operations
Group cash flow analysis
Group capital budgeting analysis
Group production planning

Consolidated group financial statements:
  Corporate profit and loss statement
  Corporate cash flow statement
  Corporate fund allocation statement
  Corporate balance sheet

Figure 9. Input-output relationships for division or subsidiaries, group consolidation, and corporate consolidation

From J. B. Boulden and E. S. Buffa, "Corporate Models: On-Line Real-Time Systems"; used by permission.

Potlatch Forests

Potlatch Forests is a large integrated forest products company having annual sales in the range of about $35 million and employing over 12,000 individuals in 44 plants and 36 sales offices throughout the country [Boulden and Buffa, 1970].

The company developed 22 models to describe its various operations, groups, and subsidiaries. The plywood model previously discussed is an example of the types of models used by Potlatch, although the company's models are more complex and involve more relationships. By interrelating these models, management can obtain a model for the entire operation and see the end result of changes made at the operational or group level.

Before the existence of corporate models, management's assessment of the financial effects of interactions of interplant buying and selling and changing product mixes involved long time lags. The interactive system of models, however, greatly reduced the effort needed to evaluate alternative plans, because the logic of the 22 models takes into account the complex financial flows between divisions and groups.

Since the model development phase, the company has learned to use the models extensively and has developed a wide range of additional models. Potlatch's director of corporate planning states that the entire corporate planning process is highly interrelated with their on-line computer models. Major capital expenditure decisions are made only after testing a variety of alternative effects, using the models. The existence of the modeling system has made possible a much more thorough exploration of "what if" questions for two reasons. Answers can be computed in shorter turnaround times, and the known existence of the models and the system encourages the asking of "what if" questions throughout the organization.

Potlatch currently has 47 different models in use, 25 for primary corporate planning and 22 special-purpose project models. Potlatch is highly decentralized in a geographic sense, and corporate planners go directly into the field with portable computer terminals to develop and test alternative plans with field managers. In addition, field managers are now beginning to develop their own models.

Inland Steel Company

Inland Steel's use of predictive models focuses on the production process [Boulden and Buffa, 1970]. The models that have been developed and their relationships are shown in Figure 10. Using the models, corporate planners can quickly simulate the effects of a wide variety of planning assumptions. Each model deals with a basic process in the sequence from raw materials to finished products. The models simulate the various costs incurred in converting ores to molten iron, converting molten iron to steel ingots, processing ingots, and finishing the steel to various end products.

The types of questions asked by Inland Steel management using the models are typified by the following: How much raw material is required to meet production forecasts? What are the cost effects of various hot metal to scrap ratios and the resulting yield under various assumptions of raw material costs? What are the capacity requirements for proposed levels of operation?

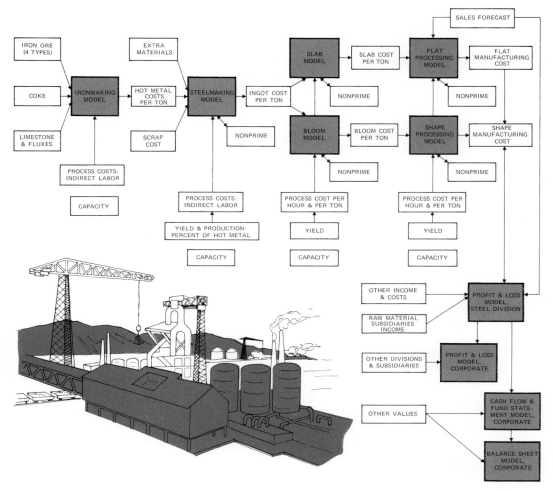

Figure 10. Relationships in Inland Steel model, courtesy *Inland Steel* and *Planmetrics, Inc.*

From J. B. Boulden and E. S. Buffa, "Corporate Models: On-Line Real-Time Systems"; used by permission.

The first actual test of the models was in the preparation for the 1971 profit plan and the related five-year profit and cash projection. For the first time, alternative strategies and assumptions were used during the planning process and during the executive review of the total corporate plan.

In approaching the profit-planning cycle for 1971, the company management was faced with unusual uncertainties. This situation led to the use of the models to simulate operations, given four significantly different scenarios. All four were based on a basic premise that a strike in the automotive industry was a near certainty during the fourth quarter of 1970, and that if this should occur there would be a significant impact on fourth-quarter shipments for the company. However, the sales forecast for 1971 indicated a very strong sales demand for the first seven months of that planning period, ending with the August 1 deadline date for negotiations with the Steel Workers Union, and a possible steel strike.

The *first scenario* of this basic premise was that the sales forecast for 1971 would follow a normal seasonal distribution of shipments, much like what would happen in any normal year, with no impact from the actions of customers through hedge buying of steel inventories in anticipation of a possible steel strike. This assumption gave a base condition for planning.

The *second scenario* was that the historic pattern of prestrike hedge buying would occur in the first seven months of 1971, as it had in all similar periods in the postwar period, and that there would be no steel strike, since agreement would be reached late on July 31. In this condition, sales demand would decline sharply in August, September, and October, with some recovery in the later months of the fourth quarter of 1971.

The *third scenario* involved a previous basic premise, but assumed a 30-day strike in the steel industry, with resumption of production and shipments after 30 days.

The *fourth scenario* assumed a 90-day steel strike, with the same prestrike hedge-buying sales pattern occurring.

The financial model was used to simulate operations, given these four basic scenarios, all with the basic premise that there would be an auto strike in the fourth quarter of 1970. Management determined a formal profit plan for 1971 consistent with scenario two, which included a prestrike build up of inventories, but no strike occurring in the steel industry. However, the other options were maintained in the profit-planning manual as alternative strategies in the event conditions should change as they approached the August 1 strike deadline.

In September 1970, top management made a major decision to build semifinished and finished inventories to the largest level in the company's history to capitalize on the strong demand forecast for the first half of 1971. The reason for this decision was that if the forecast were correct and inventories were not accumulated, the mills would not be able to produce steel fast enough to meet the customer delivery requirements, and there would be a loss of sales revenue. This plan was followed. The excess inventory was liquidated on schedule by June 1, 1971, and the company achieved an all-time record industry market share of 6.8 percent versus a normal rate of 4.8 to 5.2 percent.

In late June 1971, it became apparent that the sales demand would not hold up through July 31 as anticipated, and that the odds on a strike on August 1 were growing. Because the preliminary sales forecast from market research for 1972 indicated a very strong market, the company also evaluated similar inventory buildup strategies for both the poststrike period, should a steel strike occur, and for production over the last five months of 1971, should there be no strike.

In early July 1971, the management requested the five-year cash projection for the years 1972 through 1976 and an accelerated updating of the annual cash forecast for 1971. Management recognized that rigorous planning of capital expenditures and long-term financing was required to meet the heavy capital needs for normal expansion and replacement, pollution control equipment, long-term bond issues scheduled for retirement, and very large requirements and opportunities for investment in new projects.

The Inland Steel Company continues to develop the use of predictive models for production scheduling, developing raw materials and mines, and planning subsidiary operations.

The Food and Drug Administration

The Food and Drug Administration's development and use of predictive models for planning is an excellent example of the application of such models in an environment where the common profit measures are lacking as a basis for resource allocation [Rosenthal and Murphy, 1975]. The FDA operates through a network of 42 district and regional offices and national laboratories for sample analysis. In the general sense, the FDA's primary activities relate to the inspection of facilities, the collection of samples, and laboratory analysis at the various production and distribution points for consumer goods moving through the economy.

The goals and objectives set for the regional operations inspectors are established by the various bureaus of the FDA, and sometimes by congressional and executive action. These goals and objectives are then implemented in the field. A central planning group is responsible for the development and coordination of the specific compliance programs to be executed by the field staff, and they invariably exceed available manpower resources and budgets.

The planning process is similar to that found in any large organization. It is iterative in nature: a sequential process of testing various combinations of program plans to balance the requirements with the available resources. The testing is conducted by running through the enumerable calculations to convert inspection and sampling levels to manpower requirements, then assessing their feasibility. The results may cause modification of program plans and recomputation of manpower requirements. This process, designed to achieve a balanced, feasible plan, is critically affected by the computational cycle time, since several iterations may be necessary.

Before the installation of the Automated Planning Tool (the name given the predictive model), the cycle time to convert requirements to manpower and to test availability was approximately three months. This long cycle time frequently meant that the final plan might not balance with available staff and there might be distortions in setting goals for regional offices.

The occurrence of crises, such as the discovery of bacterial contaminants in the processed mushroom industry, further complicated the planning process. Such crises may mean a full-scale mobilization of a regional investigation to remove the products from distribution channels. Immediate decisions must be made on the number of investigators to be diverted and the areas from which they will come. These decisions have a significant impact on remaining programs. The trade-offs associated with the reduced availability of manpower mean, in effect, the revamping of the entire compliance program for all activities. In the past, the long cycle time impeded a thorough trade-off analysis.

The Automated Planning Tool reduces the cycle time to a few minutes. There are five levels of consolidation of activities built into the system. These include provision for 300 compliance programs, 65 project management system projects, 15 categories, 5 budget groups, and the consolidated total of operations. At each level of consolidation, forecasts can be displayed at the terminal by district, region, operations, and manpower class. Optionally, forecasts can also be displayed in terms of requirements for man-hours, man-years, number of personnel, costs (by applying average salary grade rates), and work space.

A macro flow chart of the interrelated models is shown in Figure 11. The system is composed of a set of separate modules that can be interrogated independently and at the option of the analyst. The forecasts can be injected throughout the system.

The system has two modes of operation, which might be characterized as top-down and bottom-up. It can work from the level of the official establishment of requirements and move up through the various consolidations. In the other mode, top level objectives can be set or broad questions can be asked, and actions simulated, such as a change in emphasis between inspections and sampling at a total bureau level. The results are displayed at a terminal in report formats consistent with those used before the development of the Automated Planning Tool.

Electric Utilities

Predictive models to simulate aspects of operations have been used extensively by electric power generation utilities [Dietz and Scavullo, 1974; Ogden, 1972; Ruhl, 1974]. Because electric utilities face a common set of problems, a large number of them have used the same basic set of models, that have been adapted to local conditions in each instance.

Figure 12 shows the corporate planning system model linkage, made up of five separate models. Four of the five models define separate problem areas: rate and revenue, operating costs, construction, and financing. Each of these models is linked to the others so that the effect of a change in plans in any one model will be reflected in the other models. The fifth model is a

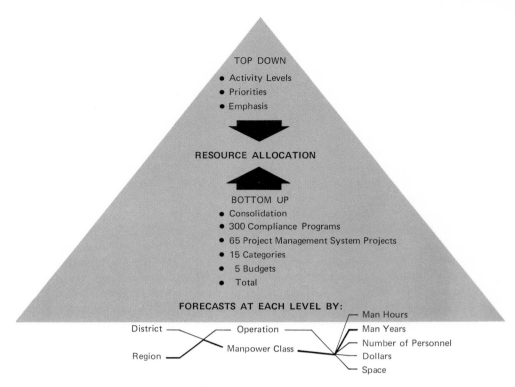

Figure 11. Hierarchy of planning process in the Food and Drug Administration, using predictive models

corporate consolidation model that allows the decision maker to examine the effects of strategies in each area on the total organization.

The rate and revenue model is designed to examine the effect on revenues of changes in demand or rate structure. Revenue is calculated by class of service within a specific area or division. Thus, revenues can be examined in detail from a particular segment of the organization with respect to the effect of a rate increase or change in demand.

The operating costs model deals mainly with fuel and payroll expenses. The model reflects load duration curves, maintenance schedules, curtailment, fuel prices, and other similar factors. Demand is taken from the rate and revenue model so that any forecasted change in usage will be reflected in a change in fuel costs. Payroll costs are a function of the current number of employees, average rate, a forecast of employees to be hired, etc.

The construction model is used to measure the effect of a change in the projected expenditure schedule on various construction projects. The effects are measured in terms of construction work in progress, cash flow, interest during construction, book depreciation, tax depreciation, and property

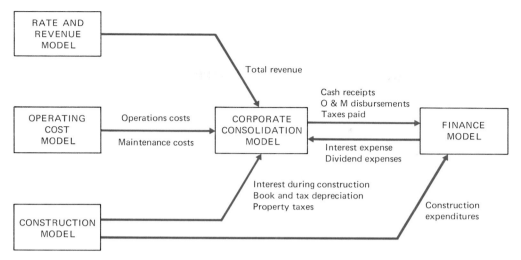

Figure 12. Model linkage of the corporate planning system for electric utilities

From J. Ogden, "'What Happens If' A Planning System for Utilities," *Public Utilities Fortnightly*, March 1972. Courtesy On-Line Decisions, Inc.

taxes. Details of individual projects of key significance can be broken out and looked at separately, the balance being consolidated.

The finance model allows one to examine the effects of different modes of financing on cash flow, capitalization structure, cost of capital, etc. The revenues, costs, and construction expenditures are fed in from the other models.

A summary of the experience of utilities using the modular predictive system indicates important applications [Dietz and Scavullo, 1974]. The applications fall under the general headings of financial planning, rate case preparation, long-range planning, budgeting and control, fuel contract allocation, facilities planning, fuel adjustment and purchased gas adjustment computations, and income tax planning.

WHAT SHOULD THE MANAGER KNOW?

Computer-based predictive models take a position in a manager's organizational environment similar to that of his staff. The manager calls on various members of his staff to perform special studies for him. In essence, the staff is providing him with answers to "what if" questions. Managers have always asked these kinds of questions in order to improve their own planning and decision making. By manual methods, however, the staff had to labor for many man-months to provide answers, as illustrated in the Potlatch, Inland Steel, and FDA examples. Computer-based predictive models perform the same question-answering function except that, since they are constructed to represent certain phases of operations, the models can answer the questions very quickly.

What the manager needs to know about predictive models is in general what he must know about his staff. He must have faith in his staff's competence to evaluate properly the alternatives he raises. Thus, for predictive models, the manager needs to be close enough to the original design of the models to be sure that they will have the capabilities he wants. He needs to know the kinds of questions he is likely to raise and to be sure that the models will have the flexibility required to deal with these kinds of questions.

Also, the manager must be interested in the model validation phase; he must be convinced that the models truly predict system performance in order for him to have the required faith. Given faith in the models, he is limited only by his imagination and the capability limits of the models.

Validation

The manager should (and does) insist on initial runs of these kinds of predictive models, using historical data input to test the validity of the models. The nature of the straightforward relationships within such models should produce a high level of conformance between model and known result. If the model builder approximates some functions by using averages, the manager should determine the sensitivity of the model to changes in the averages and the justifiability of using an approximation. For example, if product mix is fairly stable in sales, an average price could be used at higher levels of aggregation.

Formulating Scenarios

The manager's greatest interest will be in formulating alternative hypotheses or scenarios for what would happen if certain events were to occur. The specific questions may become quite detailed and quite dependent on the nature of the enterprise. However, the manager can take advantage of the sensitivity analysis capability of computer-based predictive models to "screen" variables to determine which ones are really important in his operations and which ones may be of only minor significance. A good manager will already have a feel for which are the important variables; however, using the model he can quantify the effects.

In general, in profit-oriented organizations the manager will be interested in what happens if prices, material costs, and labor costs change. In the Van den Bergh & Jurgens use of computer-based predictive models, a list of seventeen typical "what if" questions are reported [Buffa, 1972], including the testing of prices and costs, marketing plans for specific products and their effects, response to competitors' price actions, alternative forecasts, and the effect on resources and profits of the acquisition of a competitor.

In a banking application, management focused on the effects of changes in discount rate, reserve requirements, banking regulations, levels of earning assets, and the deposit base.

Interpretation of Results

The entire focus of computer-based predictive models seems to be on quantitative factors. On the surface, it appears that such models would be useful only for problems in which we accept a quantifiable criterion such as cost or profit. In fact, however, a modern manager is likely to use them as a part of a more complex decision process in which he considers the quantitative effects produced by the models as well as other factors that are not quantifiable. He then makes the trade-offs required in his decision process.

The predictive models actually facilitate this trade-off process, because the manager can ask for and obtain quickly and efficiently the quantitative effects of a scenario, which allows him to "price" the nonquantifiable advantages or disadvantages. In the case of Inland Steel's use of their computer-based models, management was undoubtedly using a complex set of criteria in deciding on their strategy. These criteria included the risk of inventory building in the face of market uncertainties, the impact on labor relations and the community, the reaction of stockholders, and so on. The models provided them with information regarding costs and profits for alternatives. This information could then be used in the judgmental trade-off process.

In essence then, the models provide input to the formal evaluative models discussed in Chapters 2, 3, and 4 where formal models, perhaps involving utility theory, provide mechanisms for trade-offs, using both single and multiple criteria. For example, subjective estimates of the probabilities of the occurrence of each of the scenarios could be made and this information could be used in a decision tree.

Check Your Understanding

1. A small fiberboard company is in the process of constructing a budget model and wishes to construct the model in the general format of computer-based corporate simulation. It is decided that the model will be set up for the first and second half plus the year summary. The fixed costs are simple, $1 million per six months. The company produces only one product, and sales forecasts in units by six-month periods are: 200,000 and 300,000, or 500,000 for the year. The price is $2 per unit and variable cost is $1.50 per unit.

   The output of the model will have six lines, as defined in Figure 13 under the heading "Output Description."

(1) Output Line	(2) Output Description	(3) Relationship	(4) Model Logic	(5) Definitions	(6) Input Data
1	Volume (units)	Volume	V1	V1 = Volume per quarter (units)	200,000/300,000
2	Sales ($)				
3	Variable cost				
4	Gross Margin				
5	Fixed cost				
6	Profits				

Figure 13. Work sheet for budget model

    a. Define the relationships required for each line of output in column (3). Output line 1 is simply listed as "volume" in column (3). Other lines of output might be the sum or product of items such as price, costs, etc.

    b. Following the relationships defined in column (3), define equivalent algebraic relationships in column (4), with the definitions of variables used in column (5). As symbols, use **V** for vectors of numbers (a vector is a series of numbers), P for parameters, and D for previously computed values in a line of output. For example, $D4$ would represent the result of the computation in line 4 and could be used in subsequent computations. As an example, we have shown **V1** for output on line 1 under column (4), and defined it as the vector of volume per six months.

    c. List the input data required to "drive" the budget model in column (6). For example, we have shown the volume vector previously given by six-month periods. Note that some lines will have no data input.

2. When Figure 13 is completed, the budget model is complete. If the variable costs increase by $0.10 per unit, what will be the impact on annual profits? What parameters, vectors, or other input data need to be changed to run the model with the new assumption?

3. Referring to the budget model, what is the sensitivity of profit in each of the two periods, and annually, to changes in variable cost? Compute the profit for variable costs of $1.50, $1.60, and $1.70 per unit. How would this be accomplished in the computer model?

4. Assuming that variable costs increase by $0.10 as in question 2, how

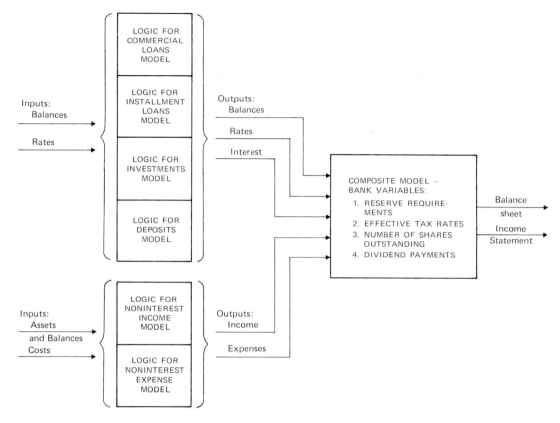

Figure 14. Inputs and outputs for six functional
models and a composite model for a bank

many units must be sold during the first six months to break even for
the first six months?

5. Why is it of value to maintain a modular concept in building large-scale
computer-based corporate models?

6. In a structural sense, how can a multitude of divisions, groups, and
subsidiary companies be related in large-scale corporate models?

Problems

1. The president of a large bank (assets of more than $2 billion) is consider-
ing the development of a computerized financial planning system to facilitate rapid analysis and comparison of short and longer term policies and
performance.

The present system requires largely manual computation of only a few alternatives that management feels are the most likely and promising. It is time consuming both in terms of man-hours and overall time to evaluate an alternative. In addition, the manual system does not consider all important interrelationships of financial flows and therefore does not reflect the full financial impact of alternatives. Specifically, the manual system is not able to evaluate rapidly and accurately the full impact of changes in the discount rate, reserve requirements, earning assets, and the deposit base.

In structuring the system of planning models, the bank decided on six functional modules plus a composite planning model to predict overall performance. The six functional models centered on commercial loans and installment loans in the fund-using category, investments and deposits in the funds-providing category, plus modules for noninterest income and expenses. The structure of basic inputs and outputs of the six functional models and the composite model is shown in Figure 14. The key bank variables are shown in the composite model in Figure 14.

List as many "what if" types of questions as you can, that the bank president should be able to pose and expect to be answered by the model. The detailed design of the models must take account of these kinds of questions.

2. Tax planning is an important reality for many individuals and most profit enterprises. Design the structure of a tax-planning model by developing a block diagram of the basic modules, indicating the inputs, transformations (what functions performed), and outputs for each module. The blocks in the diagram need not be thought of as separate models.

    Begin by listing the key factors, or "what if" questions, that might be important in determining the short- and long-term impact on taxes. Who would use such a tax model? Can it reflect tax laws as well as tax rulings? How can it be made flexible enough to allow for changes in tax laws and rulings?

3. The NEWSprint Company is a large supplier of paper to the newspaper industry. It operates through a system of four paper mills located in the U.S. and has an international division that operates two Canadian plants. Paper is supplied to the U.S. and international markets from both the domestic and Canadian plants; however, organizationally the international division is separate.

    NEWSprint is considering the development of computer-based corporate planning models. Discussions with management indicate that primary problems revolve around shifting patterns and changes in demand forecasts, demand at individual mills, distribution costs, and inventory levels. In addition, capital expenditures for the company as a whole are an important aspect of planning and affect mill output and productivity. Propose a structure of models and their linkage to meet company needs.

References

Ackoff, R. L., *A Concept of Corporate Planning*, Wiley-Interscience, New York, 1970.

Barkdoll, G., "Models—New Management Decision Aid," *Industrial Engineering,* December 1970, pp. 32–40.

Boulden, J. B., *Computer Based Planning Systems,* McGraw-Hill, New York, 1975.

Boulden, J. B., and E. S. Buffa, "Corporate Models: On-Line, Real-Time Systems," *Harvard Business Review,* July–August 1970.

Boulden, J. B., and E. R. McLean, "An Executive's Guide to Computer-Based Planning," *California Management Review,* Vol. 17, No. 1, Fall 1974, pp. 58–67.

Buffa, E. S., *Operations Management: Problems and Models,* Third edition, John Wiley & Sons, New York, 1972, Chapter 21.

Dietz, R. V., and R. V. Scavullo, "Industrial Progress: A System to Develop Utility Systems Planning," *Public Utilities Fortnightly,* May 9, 1974.

Gershefski, G. W., "Building a Corporate Financial Model," *Harvard Business Review,* January–February 1969, pp. 72–82.

———, "Corporate Models—The State of the Art," *Management Science,* Vol. 16, No. 6, February 1970.

Hamilton, W. F., and M. A. Moses, "An Optimization Model for Corporate Financial Planning," *Operations Research,* Vol. 21, No. 3, May–June 1973, pp. 677–92.

———, "A Computer-Based Corporate Planning System," *Management Science,* Vol. 21, No. 2, October 1974, pp. 148–159.

Lee, W. B., and C. P. McLaughlin, "Corporate Simulation Models for Aggregate Materials Management," *Production & Inventory Management,* 1st Quarter, 1974, pp. 56–67.

Naylor, T. H., and H. Schauland, "A Survey of Users of Corporate Planning Models," *Management Science,* Vol. 22, No. 9, May 1976, pp. 927–957.

Ogden, J., " 'What Happens If': A Planning System for Utilities," *Public Utilities Fortnightly,* March 1972.

Rivett, P., *Principles of Model Building,* John Wiley & Sons, New York, 1972.

Rosenthal, B., and R. C. Murphy, "Instant Manpower Replanning Is Here," *State Government Administration,* February 1975.

Ruhl, G. J., "Conservation: What Is It Worth? A Quantitative Approach Using a Rate and Revenue Model," *Public Utilities Fortnightly,* December 19, 1974, pp. 33–37.

Schrieber, A. N., editor, *Corporate Simulation Models,* Graduate School of Business Administration, University of Washington, 1970.

Seaberg, R. A., and C. Seaberg, "Computer Based Decision Systems in Xerox Corporate Planning," *Management Science,* Vol. 20, No. 4, December, Part II, 1973, pp. 575–84.

Stephenson, G. G., "A Hierarchy of Models for Planning in a Division of I.C.I.," *Operational Research Quarterly,* Vol. 20, 1970, pp. 221–45.

Wheelwright, S. C., and S. G. Makridakis, *Computer-Aided Modeling for Managers,* Addison-Wesley, 1972.

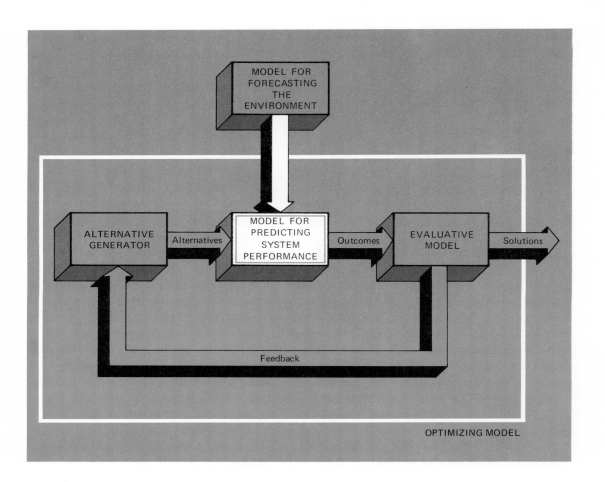

8

Dynamic Structural Models

Predicting the effects of an oil embargo, energy use and air pollution in transportation systems, of the population explosion, or of the effects of a finite pool of resources coupled with rapidly increasing use of resources, has become an important social issue. There are at least two things not said in the preceding sentence. First, predicting effects is important, yes, but effects on what? That is part of the issue — the effects in all of these types of problems are on many dimensions of our society and are interrelated in a complex way. To say that an oil embargo has the effect of producing a gasoline shortage is to say the obvious. To predict the quantitative effects and their timing on unemployment, inflation, home heating, the coal industry, and so on for an endless possible list, is something quite different. The central issue is *structurally* related to many other societal subsystems. Therefore, to develop some kind of predictive model requires first a way of unravelling the system structure.

Second, a characteristic of the kinds of problems suggested in the first sentence is that the effects over a period of time are of central interest. The immediate effects may not be dramatic, but the complex, interacting nature of the systems involved may be reinforcing, and the cumulative effects can be alarming. These are the *dynamic* effects.

In general, dynamic models establish relationships that describe the system at time t. The relationships then make it possible to compute the various dimensions of the system state at future time periods. The predictive models that we shall describe in this chapter derive from the internal system structure. There are a number of other dynamic models in management science. In fact, Chapters 8 through 11 all deal with dynamic effects. In addition, if the system structure is sufficiently simple and we can develop an appropriate evaluative model, we can use the concepts of dynamic programming discussed in Chapter 18.

While management science had developed dynamic structural models earlier, their existence was dramatized by the publication of the popularized *The Limits to Growth* [Meadows et al., 1972], a study using systems dynamics methods as predictive models for possible catastrophic results of current rates of use and increase of use of limited basic resources. The study triggered considerable controversy both in terms of its predictions and in terms of the assumptions and structure of the models themselves [Cole et al., 1973]. We shall have more to say about these studies near the end of the chapter, but now let us focus our attention on methods of developing structural models and on predicting dynamic effects.

FEEDBACK AND DYNAMIC EFFECTS

Implicit in the foregoing general description of the situations for which structural and dynamic models are of value is that the complex interrelationships of the variables act on one another, sometimes to reinforce or aggravate what is seen as the problem. On the other hand, we know that some complex systems are stable, even though there is also in their structure a complex interrelationship of variables. We need to understand the difference which results in a growth and compounding in one kind of situation and stability in the other. The nature of the feedback system provides insight into the reasons for the difference.

Negative Feedback We have been exposed to a negative feedback system earlier, in Chapter 5 where we discussed exponentially weighted moving averages. Equation (2) in that chapter was

$$\overline{F}_t = \alpha D_t + (1 - \alpha) \, \overline{F}_{t-1}, \tag{1}$$

where $\overline{F}_t$ is the smoothed average for period t, D_t is the actual demand, and α is the smoothing constant, which we will now call the feedback constant. The reason that the forecasting system tracks the actual demand and discounts random variations (is stable) has to do with the size of the feedback constant and the structure of the system. In Figure 1, we have shown the structure of the simple system. We feed back a portion of the output $\overline{F}_{t-1}$ (lagged one period) to the input of the forecasting system and merge it with the incoming data on current actual demand.

Recall that the degree to which the forecasting system discounts random errors depends on the value of α. If we feed back a large fraction of $\overline{F}_{t-1}$ (small value of α) it will dominate in determining the new forecast, and the random variations in D_t will be substantially discounted. Conversely, if we feed back only a small fraction of $\overline{F}_{t-1}$ (large α), the new forecast will be dominated by D_t. The feedback subtracts from the effect of actual de-

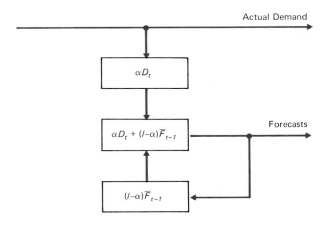

Figure 1. Negative feedback structure of a simple exponential forecasting system

mand, and its effect on D_t is negative. Note also that the sign of α is negative in the forecasting equation. What is the effect of changing the sign of α?

Positive Feedback   In our simple system we can change the feedback from negative to positive by simply changing the sign of α, resulting in

$$\bar{F}_t = \alpha D_t + (1 + \alpha)\,\bar{F}_{t-1}\,. \tag{2}$$

What is the effect on $\bar{F}_t$ of this simple change? Let us assume a constant value of $D_t = 100$ and $\alpha = 0.10$ and compute period-by-period values of $\bar{F}_t$ as in Table 1. Note that $\bar{F}_t$ grows rapidly in spite of the fact that D_t is constant. All of the growth comes from the feedback component as shown in Table 1 by the column for $1.1\,\bar{F}_{t-1}$. The general effect of the positive feedback loop has been to amplify the input.

TABLE 1.   Positive Feedback
Where $\alpha = 0.10$ and $\bar{F}_t = \alpha D_t + (1 + \alpha)\,\bar{F}_{t-1}$

Period	D_t	$0.1\,D_t$	$1.1\,\bar{F}_{t-1}$	$\bar{F}_t$
0	---	10	---	100
1	100	10	110	120
2	100	10	132	142
3	100	10	156	166
4	100	10	183	193
5	100	10	212	222
⋮				
10	100	10	409	419

Now, if we change the value of the feedback constant to $\alpha = 0.5$ and again assume a constant input of $D_t = 100$, the value of the output after ten periods is $\overline{F}_{10} = 11{,}433$. The result is clear: changing the feedback system from negative to positive causes amplification, and increasing the amount of positive feedback increases the amount of amplification dramatically. The dynamic effects are startling. In only ten periods the value of $\overline{F}_t$ grows by a factor of 4.19 even with the small value of $\alpha = 0.10$, and by a factor of 114 when $\alpha = 0.5$.

Now, let us cut the value of the positive feedback constant to $\alpha = 0.01$. In ten periods, $\overline{F}_{10} = 121$. The lesson is clear: the amount of positive feedback can be very small, yet the cumulative effect can be significant if that positive feedback continues over a long period of time. For complex systems involving energy use, population, pollution, etc., it is the dynamic effects over long periods that are of greatest concern. If the structure of such systems includes positive feedback loops that reinforce or aggravate the basic problems, we may need to predict the effects over periods of 50 to 100 years or more.

SIGNED DIGRAPHS AS STRUCTURAL MODELS

Let us take energy use as an example and develop the structure of cause and effect among the aggregate variables of energy use, quality of the environment, and population in a community. We will represent the variables as the nodes of a network as in Figure 2, which is called a signed digraph (directed graph). We ask the question, "What is the effect of an increase in the level of energy use (A) on the level of the quality of the environment (B), other factors being equal?" The answer is that the level of the quality of the environment decreases, so we mark the AB arc with a minus sign. Similarly, the BC arc is labeled with a plus sign as is the CA arc, since the effect of an increase in the level of the first variable for each pair is to increase the level of the second variable. Note that no functional relationships between the variables have been defined.

The three variables form a closed loop, that indeed is a feedback loop. Is the loop positive or negative? We can tell by simply observing whether or not there is an even or odd number of arcs marked with minus signs. An odd number results in a negative or stabilizing loop, and an even number in a positive or growth-producing loop.

Figure 2 is negative or stabilizing. If these variables were the only ones to consider, they would remain in balance. Deviations that occur in any of the variables are brought under control because the structure of the feedback loop is counteracting. There is no beginning or end to the loop. Each variable can cause and be affected by change in the loop.

Now let us add other variables of interest, taking energy use (A) as the focus. For example, we know that the cost of energy and the capacity for providing energy must be related variables, so we add them to the first net-

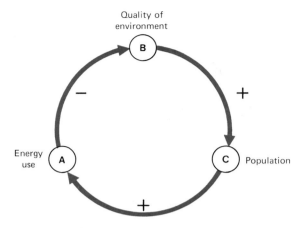

Figure 2. Signed digraph for three variables: energy use, quality of environment, and population. The signs on the arcs of the network indicate the direction of the effect of one variable on the other for each pair of nodes (variables). The arrowheads indicate which variable operates on the other

work to produce Figure 3. Taking energy cost (D) first, if energy cost were to increase, we assume that the impact on the level of energy use (A) is negative. Similarly, the impact of an independent increase in energy use on cost, AD, is taken as negative. The rationale could be in terms of efficiencies of scale. One could also take the opposite viewpoint and defend it, but the nature of the process will result in a scenario. However, this is not the whole story, for energy capacity must be taken into account, and the AE and ED arcs are added in Figure 3, AE being positive and ED being negative. The AED feedback loop is positive and results in amplification, since there is an even number of minus signs in the loop.

Now let us add two more variables, the number of factories (F) and the number of jobs (G), as shown in Figure 4. The arc FA is positive, meaning that an independent increase in the level of the first variable has the impact of increasing the level of the second variable. Also, the FG and GC arcs are marked positive, since an increase in the number of factories increases the number of jobs and in turn results in an influx of population. Similarly, a decrease in the number of factories causes a decrease in the respective levels of G and C. Note that there is no FC arc since that effect is through the variable G, the number of jobs.

We now have two more closed loops, AEF and AEFGC. Note that they are both positive feedback loops, which would have the effect of augmenting energy use.

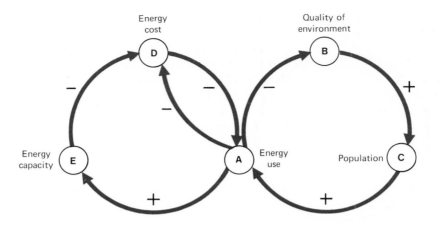

Figure 3. Signed digraph for energy use with the variables energy cost (D) and energy capacity (E) added. There are now two related feedback loops: *ABC* is negative and *AED* is positive

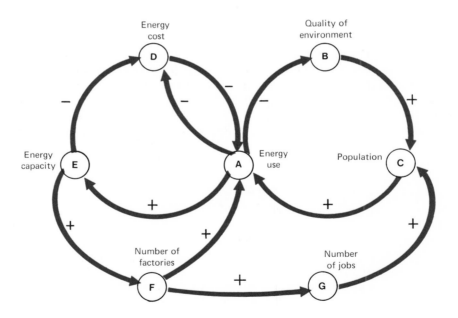

Figure 4. Completed signed digraph for energy use in a community

Adapted from F. S. Roberts, "Signed Digraphs and the Growing Demand for Energy, *Environment and Planning*, Vol. 3, 1971, pp. 395–410; used by permission.

Let us take Figure 4 as our completed digraph. Since our focus is on variable A, energy use, it is complete enough to illustrate the digraph methodology. This type of graph is called a signed digraph by Roberts [1971, 1973, 1974], digraph being short for "directed graph." Roberts has used digraphs extensively in the analysis of energy problems. The digraph is particularly useful in developing the broad structure of relationships, and its simplicity and visual character make it a tool that can be used with groups of people not acquainted with management science.

The Cross Impact Matrix

We can assign values to the signs on the arcs by the following convention:

$$\text{sign of arc } xy = \begin{cases} +1 \text{ if } xy \text{ is } + \\ -1 \text{ if } xy \text{ is } - \\ 0 \text{ if the graph contains no } xy \text{ arc,} \end{cases}$$

where xy connotes the arc from x to y. We can develop a matrix of the cross impacts based only on these values. However, by rating the relationships as mild $= \pm 1$, medium $= \pm 2$, and strong $= \pm 3$, we can differentially weight the impacts of one variable on another. Of course, there can be disagreement on the weighting, but it is commonly developed through a concensus procedure.

Table 2 represents a weighted cross impact matrix developed from the relationships in Figure 4. For example, the $+3$ in the row corresponding to A (energy use) and the column corresponding to C (population) indicates that increased population has a strong, positive impact on energy use. While the visual digraph has an important value in representing the structure graphically, the weighted cross impact matrix is more useful in computer programs designed to assess dynamic effects on the variables of the system.

TABLE 2. Weighted Cross Impact Matrix for the Energy Use Digraph of Figure 4

Impact on Variable	Impact of Variable:						
	A	B	C	D	E	F	G
A	0	0	+3	−1	0	+2	0
B	−1	0	0	0	0	0	0
C	0	+1	0	0	0	0	+2
D	−1	0	0	0	−1	0	0
E	+2	0	0	0	0	0	0
F	0	0	0	0	+1	0	0
G	0	0	0	0	0	+2	0

KSIM—A SIMULATOR FOR STRUCTURAL MODELS

Kane, Thomson, and Vertinsky [1972, 1973] have developed a simulator called KSIM, that is designed to produce the dynamic effects on variables in a structural system model such as the energy use digraph of Figure 4. They have applied it in analyses of health care delivery and water resource policy. The simulation system is used in combination with Delphi-like procedures for developing the basic structure of an initial model, with emphasis on participation in the entire process by policymakers. We will assume that the initial model has been formulated to produce a signed digraph and/or a cross impact matrix, and show how the graphs of variables versus time are developed.

Hawks, Rabbits, and Grassland Example

Kruzic [1974] uses a simplified ecosystem example involving the issue of hunting hawks in a ten-square-mile area where there is an interdependence of hawks (H), rabbits (R), and grassland (G).[*] These variables have been incorporated in the cross impact matrix shown in Figure 5(b) with justification for the matrix entries given in Figure 5(c). The values for the entries were guided by the ±3-point scale referred to earlier.[†] Note that the cross impact matrix provides a simple mechanism for allowing a variable to have an internal impact, that is, to operate on itself. For example, both hawks and rabbits breed, so the HH and RR entries are valid, as indicated in Figure 5(c).

Figure 5(a) shows the development of the initial values for each variable. The minimum values are all set at 0, and estimates are made of the maximum values as well as the present levels of each variable. For example, based on empirical studies, the maximum number of hawks possible is set at 500 per square mile, and the present density is estimated as 250 per square mile. The initial value is then set at $250/500 = 0.5$, or 50 percent of the maximum. *The scaling for all variables is then from 0 to 1.0.*

Computing Dynamic Effects   Given the cross impact matrix and the beginning levels of each variable specified in terms of decimal fractions of the maximum value of each variable, the next step is to compute the resultant levels for each variable as time rolls forward 1, 2, 3, . . . , n years hence. (The initial values are repeated as the numbers in parentheses at the heads of the columns in Figure 5(b), the cross impact matrix.) The mathematical model for these computations was developed by Professor J. Kane [1973] at the University of British Columbia and assumes the following:

---

[*]   This example was developed with Dr. G. P. Johnson, National Science Foundation.
[†]   In general, some scaling factor needs to be used. Otherwise, when computing dynamic effects, the values will quickly move to either 0 or 1. (see Kruzic [1973], Suta [1974]).

Variable	Label	Limits Min.	Limits Max.	Present	Initial Value
Hawks	H	0	500 / sq. mi.	250 / sq. mi.	0.5
Rabbits	R	0	2500 / sq. mi.	1000 / sq. mi.	0.4
Grassland	G	0	10 / sq. mi.	8 / sq. mi.	0.8

(a)

Impact on Variable	Impact of Variable $H(0.5)$	Impact of Variable $R(0.4)$	Impact of Variable $G(0.8)$
Hawks	+1	+1	−1
Rabbits	−2	+3	0
Grassland	0	−2	+1

(b)

Hawks: Hawks (+1)	The breeding cycle indicated a slight increase.
Rabbits: Hawks (+1)	Rabbits provide food for hawks.
Grassland: Hawks (−1)	After much discussion and in consideration of the high density of grasslands, the group concluded any increase in grasslands would hide the rabbits from the hawks and the hawk population would decline. The impact is very slight.
Hawks: Rabbits (−2)	Hawks are the main predator and feed primarily on the rabbits.
Rabbits: Rabbits (+3)	Rabbits were judged to breed about three times as fast as hawks.
Grassland: Rabbits (0)	Depending upon the state of the system, there might be some interaction. However, unless variables are close to maximum or minimum, there is no significant impact.
Rabbits: Grassland (−2)	The more rabbits there are, the less grassland.
Grassland: Grassland (+1)	Here is a regenerative effect, again, up to a point.

(c)

Figure 5. Data for the Hawks-Rabbits-Grassland example: a) Data for determining initial values, b) cross impact matrix with initial values for each variable; and c) justification for entries in the cross impact matrix

Adapted from P. G. Kruzic, "Cross-Impact Simulation in Water Resource Planning"; used by permission. U.S. Army Institute for Water Resources, Contract Report 74–12, *Stanford Research Institute*, Menlo Park, Ca., Nov. 1974.

1. All system variables are bounded, having a minimum value of 0 and a maximum value of 1.
2. Variables increase or decrease according to whether the net impact of the other variables on it is positive or negative, based on the cross impact matrix data.
3. If a variable approaches either bound, its response to impact goes to 0.
4. The impact of a given variable on the system depends on the level of that variable and its net impact derived from the cross impact matrix.

The change in the state of a variable x from one time period t to time period $t + \Delta t$ is then

$$x_{t + \Delta t} = x_t^{P_t} , \tag{3}$$

where

$x_{t + \Delta t}$ is the level of variable x at the end of time $t + \Delta t$,

x_t is the level of variable x at the present time t, and

P_t is the net impact on variable x computed by equation (4) from the coefficients in the cross impact matrix,

where

$$P_t = \frac{1 + \Delta t \ |\text{sum of negative impacts on } x|}{1 + \Delta t \ |\text{sum of positive impacts on } x|}$$

$$= \frac{1 + \Delta t \cdot \Sigma \ |a_- \cdot x_t|}{1 + \Delta t \cdot \Sigma \ |a_+ \cdot x_t|} , \tag{4}$$

and where a_- and a_+ are the negative and positive impact values from the cross impact matrix, and $|a \cdot x|$ denotes the absolute value of $(a \cdot x)$ ($|x| = x$ if $x \geq 0$; $|x| = -x$ if $x < 0$).
The net result is that when P_t is 1, computed by equation (4), then $x_{t + \Delta t}$ does not change during the time interval, as computed by equation (3); when P_t is less than 1, the positive impacts outweigh the negative impacts and the variable x increases during the time interval; and when P_t is greater than 1, the negative impacts are greater than the positive and the variable x decreases during the time interval. Note that if $P < 1.0$, x^P increases, and if $P > 1.0$, x^P decreases, since $0 \leq x^P \leq 1.0$.

An Example Kruzic [1974] develops the sequence of computations for the hawks-rabbits-grassland example as shown in Figure 6. Let us compute the net impact on hawks and the level of the variable H for one time period beyond the initial levels as an example. The net impact on hawks comes from the data in the cross impact matrix. The absolute value of the sum of the negative impacts on hawks from Figure 5 (b) is $1 \times 0.8 = 0.8$. The ab-

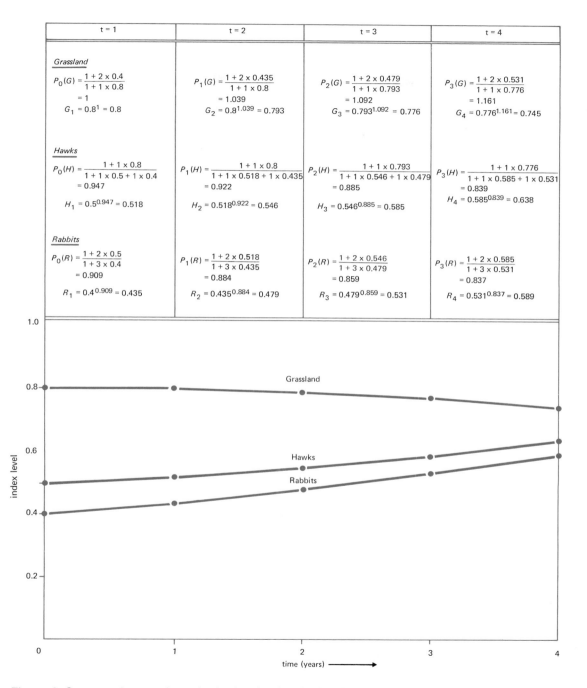

Figure 6. Computations and graphs for levels of variables *G*, *H*, and *R* for four time periods, based on cross impact matrix and initial values from Figure 5

solute value of the sum of positive impacts on hawks is $1 \times 0.5 + 1 \times 0.4 = 0.9$. Since the time interval is $\Delta t = 1$, the impact on hawks is

$$P_0\,(H) = \frac{1 + 0.8}{1 + 0.9} = \frac{1.8}{1.9} = 0.947\,.$$

The level of the hawks variable one period hence is then the present level, 0.5, raised to the power $P_0\,(H)$,

$$H_1 = 0.5^{0.947} = 0.518\,.$$

To compute for time period two, the new value of $H_1 = 0.518$ enters all computations involving equations (3) and (4), and is indicated by the sequence of computations in Figure 6. The graphs of the variables versus time shown in Figure 6 indicate growth for the level of hawks and rabbits, but a decline in grassland.

The value of KSIM is in the fact that the predictive model, represented by equations (3) and (4) and the cross impact matrix, is computerized and the longer time effects can be plotted easily as the four-year period shown in Figure 6. Furthermore, the effects of alternative policies can be tested by adding an additional column to the cross impact matrix in which ratings for the impact of the policy on each variable are inserted and the model is rerun. Sample policy questions for the hawks-rabbits-grassland example might deal with the effect of roads into the area, alternative hunting bag limits, hunting of rabbits as well as hawks, seasonal versus year-round hunting, and so on.

KSIM Applications

Applications of KSIM are reported for health care delivery [Kane et al., 1972], water resources in Canada (centered on the question of whether or not to sell water to the U.S. [Kane et al., 1973]), transportation planning [Kane, 1973], and water resource planning in the U.S. [Kruzic, 1974]. In all of these applications the investigators worked with policymakers to develop the cross impact data through a consensus process. The data for a base case and policy alternative were then processed by KSIM. The policymakers used KSIM as a predictive model to test alternatives and were active in the entire process, rather than giving the analysts the assignment of "solving the problem."

We shall describe briefly the results of the issue of whether or not Canada should sell water to the U.S. [Kane et al., 1973]. Water resources in northwest Canada occur in great surplus. The general procedure for analysis follows that which we have already described. The analysts worked with a panel of nontechnical experts (persons not expert in terms of KSIM). Through Delphi-like procedures, the cross impact data were developed. In addition to the cross impact matrix we described previously, a second matrix was developed describing *derivative* coupling between variables. The deriva-

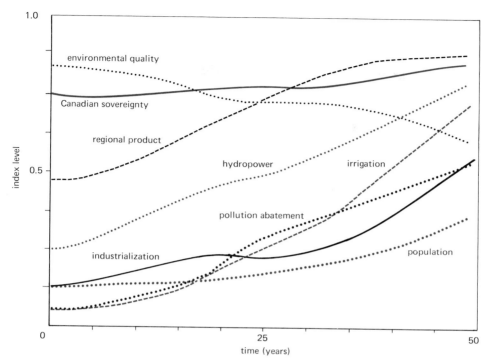

Figure 7. KSIM projected system behavior without water exports

From J. Kane, I. Vertinsky, and W. Thomson, "KSIM: A Methodology for Interactive Resource Policy Simulation," *Water Resources Research*, Vol. 9, 1973, pp. 65–79, used by permission; © by American Geophysical Union.

tive matrix describes the estimated *effect* of a change in variable A on B. The former matrix represents constant coupling describing the impact of A on B simply by virtue of the existence of A.

The issue of whether or not Canada should sell water to the U.S. is complex, involving many variables that interact through a system of feedback loops. The important variables are indicated by the labels on the curves for the basic case without water export, as shown in Figure 7. The model computed and plotted by KSIM shows a 50-year prediction of the indices of the variables shown. Two additional variables that entered the model are not plotted, roads and recreation.

Note the variable "Canadian sovereignty." This variable is particularly important to Canadians but would be difficult to take account of in many of the other types of predictive models we have discussed. It is not a measurable variable in the same sense as is population. Yet, *qualitatively*, one can define it and estimate whether or not it is being affected by other variables in a positive or negative direction. The structural model provides a mechanism for assessing something that cannot be counted.

As a contrast to Figure 7, Figure 8 shows a run involving the sale of 50 percent of the available supply of water. Note that there is a reversal in the direction of Canadian sovereignty, but regional product and hydropower are at higher levels. The population curve grows more slowly. Runs were also made for 25 percent water export, and for zero population growth with no water export and with 25 percent and 50 percent export.

One of the underlying effects is that storage capacity is needed to export substantial quantities of water. Kane and his coauthors [1973] state:

> A substantial storage capacity requires a significant flooding of valleys that are needed for the expansion of agriculture, industry, and population in the province. Thus the degree of freedom in land use and industrial development is considerably reduced. When 25 percent of the water supply is exported, this effect is reflected in the reduced population growth and the increased decline in environmental quality. However, the loss of potential industrial sites is not sufficient to retard severely industrial development over a 40-year period. In fact, the region receives an impetus from water sales, related activities, and injected revenues from sales to more than compensate for the negative impact of the sale of water on industry. However, when 50 percent of the water supply is exported, the water storage requirements are sufficiently high so that few sites remain for new industrial development. The severity of this constraint leads to a reduction in industrialization as compared with the case of no water exports, despite the economic impact of activities and revenues provided by the high level of water sales.

The intricately linked feedback systems indicate behavior that is perhaps counter-intuitive.

SYSTEMS DYNAMICS

J. W. Forrester [1961] developed industrial dynamics as a way of analyzing the structure of industrial firms. The industrial dynamics model developed for the Sprague Electric Company focused attention on the flow over time of orders, men, inventories, backlog, production rates, and other variables. The model paid particular attention to feedback loops and indicated that the system was unstable in many respects, resulting in wild oscillation of production rates, work force size, inventories, etc. Other studies of industrial situations have included the dynamic effects of resource acquisition in corporate growth [Packer, 1964], a management analysis of the salmon resource system [Paulik and Greenough, 1966], an analysis of the production and distribution systems of a carpet mill [Yurow, 1967], and an analysis of warehousing networks in the Ralston-Purina Company [Markland, 1973].

Forrester applied the industrial dynamics methodology to broader social systems such as urban dynamics [1969] and world dynamics [1973]. Also, his son, Nathan Forrester [1972], applied the methodology to the

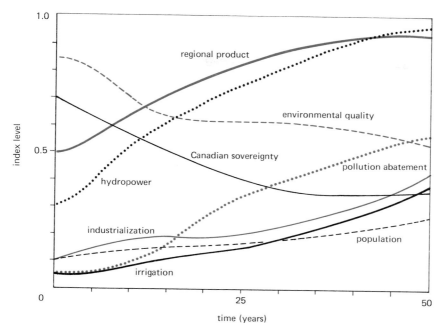

Figure 8. KSIM projected system behavior with water exports at 50 percent of supply

From J. Kane, I. Vertinsky, and W. Thomson, "KSIM: A Methodology for Interactive Resource Policy Simulation," *Water Resources Research,* Vol. 9, 1973, pp. 65–79, used by permission; © by the American Geophysical Union.

study of economic development, thereby completing another kind of feedback loop. These studies, that employ a specific structural modeling mode and use a computer simulation language called DYNAMO [Pugh, 1963], are now commonly called systems dynamics. *The Limits to Growth* [Meadows et al., 1972] was developed in a systems dynamics framework.

Nature of Systems Dynamics Modeling

Systems dynamics models are developed in the framework of the DYNAMO simulation language and include a flow charting format. An example of a flow chart for an industrial firm is shown in Figure 9. The flow chart symbols are keyed to the equations written to describe how elements of the system function.

Level equations represent reservoirs to accumulate flow rates that may increase or decrease the level. The new value of a level at time K is the old value at time J plus the net flow rate during the time interval. Figure 9 illustrates these reservoirs as the several rectangles labeled backlog, inventory,

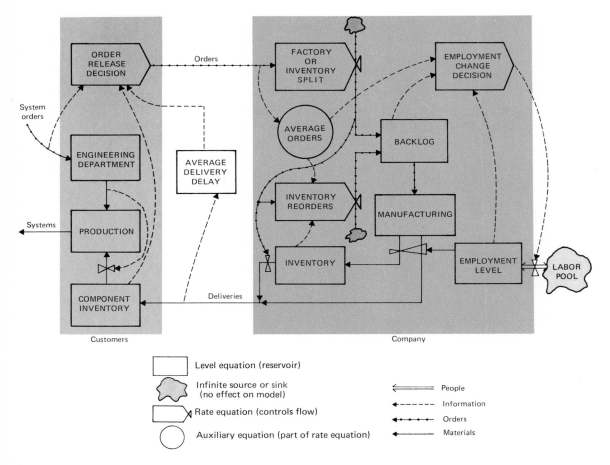

Figure 9. Systems Dynamics flow chart representing a manufacturer's organization structure and the associated customer system

From E. B. Roberts, "Industrial Dynamics and the Design of Management Control Systems," in C. P. Bonini, R. Jaedicke, and M. Wagner, *Management Controls,* McGraw-Hill, New York, 1964, pp. 102–126, used by permission of McGraw-Hill Book Company.

manufacturing, etc. *Infinite sources* and *sinks,* such as that for the labor pool in Figure 9, have no influence on the model of the system.

Rate equations are the means by which rates of flow are controlled. Examples in Figure 9 are the decisions to manufacture or supply from inventory, or to reorder items in inventory. A typical rate equation might state that the shipping rate over a specified time interval is the current level of unfilled orders divided by the delay in filling orders. The delay is expressed as a constant and is tagged on the rate symbol in the flow chart.

A third type of equation is the *auxiliary equation*, for example, "average orders" in Figure 9. Actually the auxiliary equations are a part of rate equations and could be incorporated in the rate equations; however, they have an independent meaning that may be useful in two or more rate equations. This is true for average orders in Figure 9. It is an input to both the inventory and employment decisions.

Finally, note in Figure 9 that several flow lines have been used to distinguish between classes of variables. There are several feedback loops involved in the system. For example, inventory, inventory reorders, backlog, and manufacturing form a closed loop. Another loop includes inventory, inventory reorders, backlog, employment change decision, and employment level.

A third feedback loop includes the customer system: changes in the company delivery delay will affect the customer release rate of new orders, which in turn will influence the company delivery delay. "This loop amplifies the system problems of the company, being able to transform slight variations in system orders into sustained oscillations in company order rate, producing related fluctuations in company inventories, backlog, employment, and profits" [Roberts, 1964]. An understanding of how and why the system reacts in this oscillatory way can lead to restructuring that can stabilize the desired variables, such as employment level. This stabilization was accomplished in the Sprague Electric Company Case [Forrester, 1961].

Differences between KSIM and systems dynamics are that in KSIM the variables are bounded between zero and one, but in systems dynamics methods, functional equations are written and variables take on values computed at each point in time. Rates of change are derived from the cross impact matrix in KSIM, while systems dynamics requires that expressions in the form of difference equations be written to describe each separate rate relationship. Thus, KSIM is easier to use, but systems dynamics allows more flexibility in modeling and choosing the appropriate relationships. Both produce dynamic computer output through plotter routines. In addition to the more detailed information on systems dynamics methods available in Forrester [1961, 1968] and Pugh [1963], an excellent summary is available in Meier, Newell, and Pazer [1969].

World Dynamics and the Limits to Growth

The largest scale structural model yet attempted is the world model [Forrester, 1973]. Forrester formulated the world model in terms of systems dynamics to represent the structural relationships of the major subsystems of nonrenewable resources, population, agriculture, capital and industrial output, services, and pollution. As an example of major relationships and feedback loops in the world model, Figure 10 shows the structure of the population, pollution, and natural resources subsystems. The important

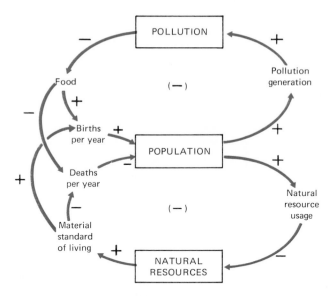

Figure 10. Feedback loops of population, pollution, and natural resources

feedback loops in Figure 10 are: negative loop—population, natural resource usage, natural resources, material standard of living, births per year; and negative loop—population, pollution generation, pollution level, food, births per year. These feedback loops and the other two associated loops in Figure 10 act to stabilize population.

Forrester then uses the world model to study the effects of exponential growth* in the use of resources, where the levels of resources are assigned finite limits. Figure 11 shows the computer plots for the standard run, which provides a picture of disaster for the human species. Note that the level of natural resources declines and the level of pollution increases to a maximum and then declines. Population reaches a peak in the year 2020 and then declines rapidly. A number of additional computer runs were made involving other assumptions, such as doubling the estimate of natural resource reserves; unlimited resources; unlimited resources and pollution controls; pollution controls and increased agricultural productivity; unlimited resources, pollution controls, and perfect birth control; and unlimited resources, pollution controls, increased agricultural productivity, and perfect birth control. All runs end with disaster, though the timing varies.

*   An exponential growth function follows the general form $y = me^{bt}$, where m and b are constants which fit the particular curve, and t is the time variable. The dependent variable y grows at an exponential rate with respect to time. For example, savings that grow at compound interest follow an exponential growth function.

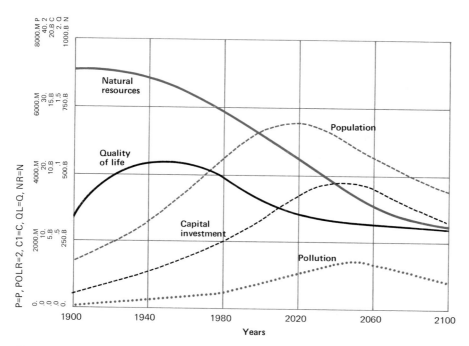

Figure 11. Basic behavior of the world model, showing the mode in which industrialization and population are suppressed by falling natural resources

From J. W. Forrester, *World Dynamics*; reprinted by permission; © 1973 by Wright-Allen Press.

The Limits to Growth [Meadows et al., 1972] is a popularized version of similar uses of Forrester's world model. The study triggered a great deal of controversy, including strong criticism by management scientists and other methodologists. One broadside critique, *Models of Doom*, uses Systems Dynamics methods to demonstrate rather different results [Cole et al., 1973]. This rebuttal takes issue with the structure of the model as well as virtually every important assumption. It will not be our purpose to decide which, if either, is correct, but rather to note the fact that both parties are actively using dynamic structural models.

WHAT SHOULD THE MANAGER KNOW?

Dynamic structural models have an important place in the world of models, for they can deal with problems on a broad aggregative basis and can provide the manager with a deeper understanding of the system with which he deals. He can gain insight into the effects of the interacting variables and into the dynamic aspects of how the system works. In short, he gains insight into how the system functions, *as a system*, rather than in a more disjointed way.

Problem Characteristics

The manager can recognize problems for which dynamic structural models may be of value in several ways. First and perhaps foremost, these problems tend to be embedded in large complex systems where informed people have different hypotheses concerning the nature of the problem. For example, informed observers might say: "We have smog because of the automobile"; "We have smog because of emissions from industry"; "We have smog because of population growth"; "We have smog because of the geographic and meteorologic nature of the area." The system-wise analyst might say: "We have smog because of a complex interaction of factors, some of which work in concert and build on each other to produce the hated result." Perhaps another way to characterize such problems is to say that they are ill defined, and problem definition in itself is an objective.

Another important characteristic of problems for structural models is suggested in the preceding paragraph. They are problems where feedback loops are important. The feedback loops, however, may not be as obvious as those that operate in home heating thermostats, the toilet float valve, or exponential growth of a bacterial colony. In large systems, the feedback loops may operate through an elusive sequence such as the two major population loops cited in connection with the world model. These loops are closed through a sequence of processes and may involve long time lags. Therefore, the net effects may be produced over long time periods and may not be readily seen in the short term.

A third characteristic is in dynamic effects. Suppose an industrial manager notes that, subject to random variations, demand for his product has been basically stable with a gently rising trend for the past several years. Yet factory employment and finished goods inventories have oscillated throughout the same period. Looking at the system as a whole, he might well ask, "If demand is basically stable, why shouldn't employment also be stable?" Yet the dynamic effects of the system produce costly hiring and layoff cycles. A structural model of the system might uncover the reasons. It is likely that system time lags have conspired with feedback loops to produce a result that is costly to the enterprise, to individual employees, and to society.

A fourth characteristic is that the relationships among the system elements can be described with certainty. If some of the relationships can only be described in terms of probabilistic (risky) statements, and *it is important to analyze the impacts of this probabilistic behavior* rather than simply work with estimates of expected values, then other models must be used. Possibilities include the Markov chain models of Chapter 9 in which the system structure is described in terms of the probability of transition from one state to another, and the queuing and Monte Carlo simulation models of Chapters 10 and 11, which analyze systems involving waiting lines of customers or objects to be serviced. In order to deal with the additional complexity of probabilistic relationships, the systems that are generally analyzed by these latter methods are otherwise much simpler than those analyzed by the dynamic structural models, involving fewer elements and fewer feedback loops.

Model Formulation

Many of the problems we have cited that have been approached by structural and dynamic model methods were public in nature, with diffused authority and responsibility. Defining variables and their general effects and system structure should reflect the collective expertise of many people, and not simply because it is a "political" problem. It may be political in nature, but the basic reasons for collective expertise are that the problem is ill defined, there are many legitimate points of view, and there are many interest groups. Each person or group may be an expert in some part of the system.

The process of formulating the model within the discipline of diagraphs and cross impact matrices can be effective with broadly based interest groups. The result is normally insight into the nature of relevant variables and their impacts on one another, an appreciation of the reinforcing and stabilizing effects of feedback, and understanding of the pluralistic nature of the system as a whole.

While much of the model formulation process is qualitative in nature, crucial quantitative information is abstracted, and, when coupled with a simulation system such as KSIM or DYNAMO, long-term projections can be made of the relevant variables.

The manager's role in the model formulation process is then crucial. Since model formulation and problem definition are interdependent, it is not normally as feasible for a manager to define a problem and delegate it to analysts, reentering the process for interpretation of results and decision. Involvement is necessary partly because many such problems may need the expertise of many people to generate a consensus, and partly because the manager's insight and experience with the system are so important to problem definition.

Interpretation of Results

The results of dynamic structural models provide managers and policymakers with predictions of the dynamic effects on relevant variables over time. The results are usually multidimensional, and deciding on actions or policies may involve new or altered structures, the results of which can be predicted through alterations in the model. The complex nature of the system involves multiple criteria for rational solution, and trade-offs between criteria are required. For example, in the Canadian water supply problem that we discussed, what trade-off is to be made between Canadian sovereignty, hydropower, and income from the sale of water? Here we have an area of application for the methods of Part Two dealing with the evaluation of outcomes. Chapter 4, which deals with evaluative models for multiple criteria, is particularly relevant.

Interpreting results and prescribing remedies will often come back to an analysis of structure and the impact of variables. For example, how can the polarity of a feedback loop be reversed from positive (resulting in growth) to negative (resulting in control and stability), or vice versa? We know from the signs on the arcs of digraphs that a loop containing an odd number of negative signs will be negative in the aggregate effect, and one containing an even number will be positive in effect. Therefore, if we can insert one additional variable (node) into a loop that has a negative effect, we can change the polarity of the loop. For example, in public systems, the addition of a new institution such as the Securities and Exchange Commission may provide such an effect. Or, if we can change the effect on one arc from positive to negative we can change loop polarity. Or, a third alternative may be to add an entirely new loop to the system—a loop designed to provide the necessary compensation.

The impact of paired variables is specified in the cross impact matrix. These coefficients represent the parameters that define the system. Therefore, another way of altering the system is to alter the parameters. Perhaps the structure provides the desired polarity of feedback loop, but the effects are too small or too large. Thus, we see policymakers attempting to change the values of the parameters in the energy field by increasing the import tax on crude oil, decontrolling domestic crude oil prices, etc.

There are pitfalls in the interpretation of effects of any model over long time spans. If we assume a change in a sensitive parameter, the effect for next year may seem plausible, but the fifty-year projection of the effect through an amplifying feedback system may be astonishing. With such sensitive parameters there is a "fulcrum effect" that multiplies the force of the effect when we project results for long periods.

Can we assume that any system's structure would remain stable over a fifty-year period? This was one of the basic criticisms of *The Limits to Growth* study. True, different assumptions were made and the model was rerun with the new assumptions, but those assumptions and the model structure were static in the new run. What would happen, for example, if an adaptive and flexible response to changing world circumstances were built into the model? Such adaptive behavior is indeed one of the prime characteristics of man and the actual behavior of the economy. To date, however, the term "dynamic model" has not meant that the model itself changed over time. Perhaps that is the next needed development in methodology.

Check Your Understanding

1. Why does negative feedback produce a deviation minimizing response? Why would negative feedback not produce a continuous degeneration of its input?

2. Why does positive feedback produce an amplification of the input?

3. Using equation (2) for a discrete positive feedback system with one period time lag, what is the value of $\overline{F}_2$ if $\alpha = 1.0$, D_t is constant at 100, and $\overline{F}_0 = 100$? What is the meaning of a 100 percent feedback rate? Are there any real processes represented by a 100 percent feedback rate?

4. Referring to the signed digraph of Figure 2, the sign of the AB arc is negative, meaning that if A decreases, B will increase. What is the important assumption in the statement?

5. In Figures 3 and 4, there is an additional closed feedback loop formed by AD. Is the loop positive or negative? Why? What is the meaning of your answer with respect to the two variables, energy use and energy cost?

6. Table 2 is a weighted cross impact matrix for the energy use digraph. Assume that the initial levels of the variables A through G are respectively 0.5, 0.6, 0.5, 0.3, 0.4, 0.8, and 0.7. What is the net impact on A for time = 0? Based on your computed value of $P_0(A)$, should A_1 be greater than, equal to, or less than A_0? Why?

7. Based on the data given in question 6, compute A_1 and A_2.

8. What is the practical meaning of the statement that in KSIM, variables are bounded between 0 and 1.0.

9. If the KSIM variables are in the range of 0 to 1.0, and we have computed the level of a variable to be 0.8 at some future time, how can we convert that prediction to the actual units of the variable? Use the hawks-rabbits-grassland example where H was originally measured in terms of numbers of hawks per square mile.

10. Suppose that after 50 years, the level of hawks in the text example has become 500 per square mile, and that the impact on hawks computed from the cross impact matrix and the levels of variables existing at that time is 0.85. How much will H respond to the impact of $P_n(H) = 0.85$?

11. How can something like "Canadian sovereignty" be seriously included as a measurable variable? What are its units?

12. Think in terms of the basic differences between KSIM and Systems Dynamics methods.
    a. Are variables bounded in both formulations?
    b. In Systems Dynamics, rate equations are written. What equivalent mechanism operates in KSIM to express rates of change?

c. In Systems Dynamics, level equations are written to represent reservoirs to accumulate flow rates that may increase or decrease the level. By what mechanism do levels of variables change in KSIM?

13. Suppose a manager or public policymaker is faced with a system that produces long-term growth in a variable. By existing criteria, the judgment is made to bring this variable under control. What are the structural options available?

Problems

1. Formulate signed digraphs for the variables listed in the items that follow. If they form closed feedback loops, indicate whether the loop is positive or negative. Also, write a short scenario that explains your rationale for the signs on arcs and on feedback loops.
   a. population and births per year
   b. population, births per year, and birth rate
   c. population, births per year, birth rate, and population density (Assume that there is some limit to population density.)
   d. population, births per year, birth rate, population density, and food per person

2. Suppose you are a manufacturer of a small appliance that you produce in substantial volume. A finished goods inventory is maintained in order to supply the market. One of the problems of considerable concern has been the seasonal hiring and layoff of employees caused by seasonal product demand.

   In your initial thinking about the problem, you have written down the following variables which seem important: demand (D), production rate (P), work force size (W), inventory level (I), labor productivity (L), and cost per unit of the product (C).

   Formulate an initial signed digraph that relates the variables. If there are feedback loops, indicate whether they are positive or negative.

3. As the manager of the manufacturing enterprise discussed in problem 2, you have now isolated some more specific cost items that you think can help in understanding the dynamics of the seasonal employment decisions.

   The costs are those of hiring and layoff, inventory holding costs, costs of reorganizing and rebalancing production lines when direct labor is added or deleted, and costs of lost sales or back ordering if inventory is not available to supply needs.

   You also recognize that you have the option of working labor overtime at a cost premium of 50 percent per hour. But since hiring and layoff are also costly, you are beginning to think that actual cost per unit might be lower in some instances if you were to take either the overtime option or an additional option of subcontracting some work in order to meet peak seasonal demand. The extra costs of subcontracting are significant, however.

   Reformulate the structure of the system by reflecting the relevant costs in the structure of the signed digraph.

4. Let us now take a small step toward solving the urban air pollution problem. The small step will be in attempting the formulation of a structural model of some of the main variables that might enter the problem. Formulate a structural model in the form of a signed digraph assuming the following list of variables:

P — population

F — number of factories

J — number of jobs available

V — number of services

W — number of power plants

R — quality of rapid transit system

C — number of cars on the road

S — smog level

Q — quality of the environment

5. Weight the signs on the arcs in the digraph developed for problem 4 according to your estimate of the severity of the effects, using a ±1, 2, or 3 scale. Place the results into the format of a cross impact matrix. Are there any effects of a variable operating on itself that you think should be represented in the cross impact matrix?

6. Examine the digraph developed for problem 4. Are there any feedback loops developed in the structure? If so, identify whether they are positive or negative. Now consider the possible effects of the following suggested remedies to air pollution in terms of a) where and how the intervention should be introduced into the structural model, and b) how should it affect the sign of arcs or of feedback loops:
a. increased tax on autos
b. increased gasoline tax
c. fines on industrial emissions
d. moratorium on building new factories or substantial expansion of existing factories

7. Energy use is an important issue in society today. Therefore, let us attempt to interrelate energy use and some associated variables. Formulate an energy use structural model for an urban community in the form of a signed digraph for the following variables:

P   — passenger miles

FE — fuel economy

POP — population size

Pr   — price of a commuter ticket

E   — emissions

A   — accidents

D   — delay probability

C   — fuel consumption

8. The manufacturer of a small appliance is trying to understand what happens in his system when demand changes at the retail level. There is a time lag of one week for a retailer order to be received from the wholesaler's warehouse. Also, when the wholesaler orders from the factory, it takes two weeks for the factory to adjust its production level to meet the wholesaler's order. Inventory levels are not changed to adjust to increases or decreases in sales.

The manufacturer writes down the following model to express the relationships of interest to him:

$$\text{retail receipts}_n = \text{retail orders}_{n-1}$$

$$\text{retail inventory}_n = \text{retail inventory}_{n-1} + \text{retail orders}_{n-1} - \text{retail sales}_n$$

$$\text{retail orders}_n = X - \text{retail inventory}_n$$
$$X = 200, \text{ for weeks 1–3 (old sales figure)}$$
$$X = 210, \text{ for weeks 4–11 (new sales figure)}$$

$$\text{warehouse receipts}_n = \text{warehouse orders}_{n-2}$$

$$\text{warehouse inventory}_n = \text{warehouse inventory}_{n-1} + \text{warehouse orders}_{n-2} - \text{retail receipts}_n$$

$$\text{warehouse orders}_n = Y - \text{warehouse inventory}_n$$
$$Y = 300, \text{ for weeks 1–6}$$
$$Y = 310, \text{ for weeks 7–11}$$

$$\text{factory production rate}_n = \text{warehouse orders}_{n-2}$$

Using the form shown in Figure 12, determine the effect of a ten percent increase in retail sales. Note that after three periods of increased sales the retailer will accept the new sales figure as constant. Also, after retail orders have stabilized, the wholesaler accepts the new order level as the new permanent level.

References

Cole, H. S. D., C. Freeman, M. Jahoda, and K. L. R. Pavitt, editors, *Models of Doom*, Universe Books, New York, 1973.

Forrester, J. W., *Industrial Dynamics*, MIT Press, Cambridge, Mass., 1961.

——, *Principles of Systems*, Wright-Allen Press, Cambridge, Mass., 1968.

——, *Urban Dynamics*, MIT Press, Cambridge, Mass., 1969.

——, *World Dynamics*, second edition, Wright-Allen Press, Cambridge, Mass., 1973.

Forrester, N. B., *The Life Cycle of Economic Development*, Wright-Allen Press, Cambridge, Mass., 1972.

Kane, J., "A Primer for a New Cross-Impact Language (with Examples Drawn from Transportation Planning)," *Technological Forecasting and Social Change*, Vol. 4, No. 1, 1973.

Period (weeks)	Retail sales	Retail receipts	Retail inventory	Retail orders	Warehouse receipts	Warehouse inventory	Warehouse orders	Factory rate
1	100	100	100	100	100	200	100	100
2	110							
3	110							
4	110							
5	110							
6	110							
7	110							
8	110							
9	110							
10	110							
11	110							
12	110							

Figure 12. Form for computing the effect of a ten percent sales increase

Kane, J., W. Thomson, and I. Vertinsky, "Health Care Delivery: A Policy Simulator," *Socio-Economic Planning Science*, Vol. 6, No. 3, 1972, pp. 283–93.

Kane, J., I. Vertinsky, and W. Thomson, "KSIM: A Methodology for Interactive Resource Policy Simulation," *Water Resources Research*, Vol. 9, 1973, pp. 65–79.

Kruzic, P. G., "KSIM Techniques for Evaluating Interactions Among Variables," SRI Technical Note OED TN-16, Stanford Research Institute, Menlo Park, Calif., June 1973.

———, "Cross-Impact Simulation in Water Resource Planning," U.S. Army Engineer Institute for Water Resources Contract, Report 74-12, Stanford Research Institute, Menlo Park, Calif., November 1974.

Markland, R. E., "Analyzing Geographically Discrete Warehousing Networks by Computer Simulation," *Decision Sciences*, Vol. 4, 1973, pp. 216–36.

Meadows, D. L., W. W. Behrens, D. H. Meadows, R. F. Naill, J. Randers, and E. K. O. Zahn, *Dynamics of Growth in a Finite World*, Wright-Allen Press, Cambridge, Mass., 1974.

Meadows, D. L., D. H. Meadows, J. Randers, and W. W. Behrens III, *The Limits to Growth*, Universe Books, New York, 1972.

Meier, R. C., W. T. Newell, and H. L. Pazer, *Simulation in Business and Economics*, McGraw-Hill, New York, 1969, Chapter 3.

Mesarovic, M., and E. Pestal, *Mankind at the Turning Point: The Second Report to the Club of Rome*, Dutton / Reader's Digest Press, New York, 1975.

Packer, D. W., *Resource Acquisition in Corporate Growth*, MIT Press, Cambridge, Mass., 1964.

Paulik, G. J., and J. W. Greenough, "Management Analysis for a Salmon Resource System," in *Systems Analysis in Ecology*, K. E. F. Watt, editor, Academic Press, New York, 1966, Chapter 9.

Pugh, A. L., *DYNAMO User's Manual*, second edition, MIT Press, Cambridge, Mass., 1963.

Roberts, E. B., "Industrial Dynamics and the Design of Management Control Systems," in *Management Controls*, C. P. Bonini, R. Jaedicke, and M. Wagner, editors, McGraw-Hill, New York, 1964, pp. 102–26. Also in *Organizations: Systems, Control and Adaptation*, Volume II, second edition, J. A. Litterer, editor, Wiley & Sons, New York, 1969, pp. 287–303.

Roberts, F. S., "Signed Digraphs and the Growing Demand for Energy," *Environment and Planning*, Vol. 3, 1971, pp. 395–410. Also in R-756, The Rand Corporation, May 1971.

———, "Building and Analyzing an Energy Signed Digraph," *Environment and Planning*, Vol. 5, 1973, pp. 199–221.

———, *Weighted Digraph Models for Energy Use and Air Pollution in Transportation Systems*, The Rand Corporation, R-1578-NSF, December 1974.

Suta, B. E., "KSIM Theoretical Formulation, A Parametric Analysis," SRI Technical Note TN-OED-25, Stanford Research Institute, Menlo Park, Calif., June 1974.

Yurow, J. A., "Analysis and Computer Simulation of the Production and Distribution Systems of a Tufted Carpet Mill," *Journal of Industrial Engineering*, Vol. 18, No. 1, January 1967.

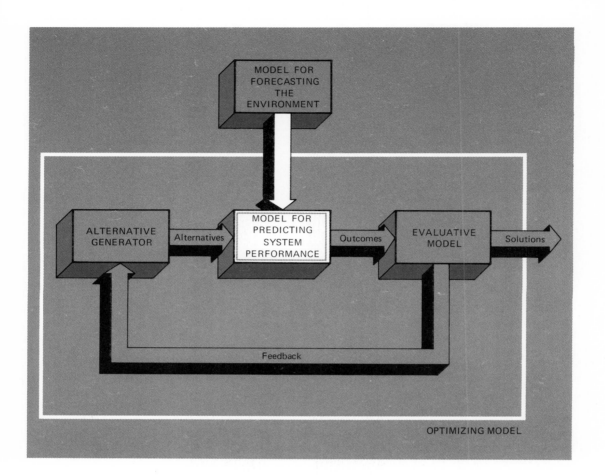

9

Predicting The Effects Of Risk:
Markov Chains

Suppose a person enrolls as a freshman in a four-year college. What is the probability that he will be enrolled as a sophomore the next year? What is the probability that he will actually graduate after four years? Suppose a person chooses Brand X from three competitive products X, Y, and Z. What is the probability that he will purchase Brand Y next time? Suppose a person is in a mental hospital in January. What is the probability that he will be in an outside home in May? Suppose a person has a job as a department head in a major corporation. What is the probability that he will be promoted to a corporate vice-president in five years?

In many real-world problems, it is convenient to classify individuals or items into distinct categories or *states*. We can then analyze the transitions of these individuals or items from one state to another over time. For example, if we are analyzing college enrollments, we may use the classifications of freshman, sophomore, junior, senior, graduated, and dropout as our "states." We can then investigate the probability that a freshman will become a sophomore after one year, or a senior after three years. If we are concerned with analyzing alternative marketing strategies, we may use the classification of a purchaser of Brand X, a purchaser of Brand Y, or a purchaser of Brand Z as our "states." What would be the appropriate states to use in the analysis of a mental hospital or of job advancement in a major corporation?

Generally, we speak in terms of the probability that a person or an item will move from one state to another during time period n. Suppose the probability that a person moves from state i to state j during time period n depends only on the previous state i, and is independent of the time period n.

Then the process can be analyzed using Markov chains. This approach will be illustrated through the use of several examples.

It may be helpful to view these Markov chain models as an important extension of the dynamic structural models of Chapter 8. The purpose of these latter models was to represent the structure of a complex system using deterministic, or *certain*, specifications of the relationships among the system elements, and to use these relationships to predict the dynamic behavior of the system. Again we are concerned with the dynamic behavior of a system, but this time the relationships among the system elements are probabilistic in nature. In order to use the concepts of Markov chains to analyze such a system, its structure must be much simpler than that of many of the complex systems analyzed in Chapter 8. Nevertheless, when the system can be described in terms of the probabilities of movement from one state to another, a Markov chain analysis may provide much useful information to a manager.

FORECASTING COLLEGE ENROLLMENTS

Accurate forecasts of college enrollments are extremely important for many decisions that relate to the management of higher education. The decision to expand the facilities at various campuses or to add a new campus may depend on enrollment forecasts. Questions that may be important include the following:

1.   If 100 new students enroll as freshmen each year in a four-year college, what will the total increase in the enrollment be after four years?
2.   If 100 new students enroll as freshmen each year, how many will actually graduate?

These questions can be answered by using the concepts of Markov chains.

Estimation of Transition Probabilities

The analysis of enrollments begins with the classification of students into mutually exclusive categories or states. The appropriate classification will depend on the particular problem that is being analyzed. For example, the states used to analyze enrollments in a major university might be lower division undergraduate, upper division undergraduate, master's level, and doctoral studies. For simplicity, we shall assume that we are analyzing enrollments in a four-year college with no graduate programs. The major student flows are illustrated in Figure 1.

Suppose we confine our interests to the states of dropout (*Do*), freshman (*Fr*), sophomore (*So*), junior (*Jr*), senior (*Sr*), and graduated (*Gr*). According to Figure 1, a freshman in one academic year either becomes a sophomore the next academic year or drops out. For simplicity in this example,

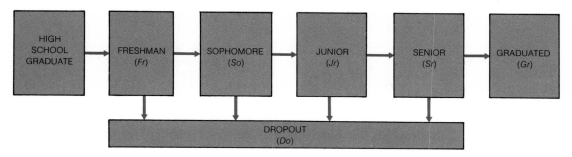

Figure 1. Major student flows in a four-year college

we are ignoring the relatively small proportion of individuals who may drop out of college for a year or more and then return, and the individuals who make less than "normal" progress and do not move from one state to another after each academic year. However, these complicating factors could be incorporated into a similar, more detailed analysis.

Now we need the probability that a freshman will become a sophomore, and the probability that he will become a dropout. Actual data on the progress of students in the public four-year colleges of Texas from 1960 through 1967 are shown in Table 1. The number of sophomores as a percentage of freshmen is relatively constant with a mean value of 54.0 and a range of from 51.3 to 55.4. Thus, it would seem reasonable to use 0.54 as an estimate of the probability that a freshman will become a sophomore, and to assume that this probability does not depend on the particular academic year, since the figures show no notable trend or other systematic variation. It follows that $1.0 - 0.54 = 0.46$ is the probability that a freshman will drop out after one academic year, since this is the only other state possible according to the student flow diagram of Figure 1.

Stated symbolically, we have the conditional probability that a freshman during academic year $n - 1$ will become a sophomore the next academic year n, $P(So_n | Fr_{n-1}) = 0.54$. Similarly, $P(Do_n | Fr_{n-1}) = 0.46$, and $P(Jr_n | So_{n-1}) = 0.87$ and $P(Do_n | So_{n-1}) = 0.13$ from Table 1.

Notice that the number of seniors as a percentage of the number of juniors has a mean value of 100.2, indicating perhaps that there are individuals who remain classified as seniors for two or more academic years. For simplicity, we assume that $P(Sr_n | Jr_{n-1}) = 1.0$ and $P(Do_n | Jr_{n-1}) = 0.0$ are reasonable estimates. We also assume that every individual who becomes a senior will actually graduate, so $P(Gr_n | Sr_{n-1}) = 1.0$ and $P(Do_n | Sr_{n-1}) = 0.0$.

These conditional probabilities can be conveniently summarized in tabular form as illustrated in Table 2. Each entry in Table 2 is the probability of moving from the state indicated by the corresponding row to the state indicated by the corresponding column. For example, the 0.87 entry indi-

TABLE 1. Progress of Entering Freshman Classes in the Public Four-Year Colleges of Texas

Fall Class Entered	No. of Freshmen	No. of Sophomores 1 Year Later	No. of Sophomores As Percentage of Freshmen	No. of Juniors 2 Years Later	No. of Juniors As Percentage of Sophomores	No. of Seniors 3 Years Later	No. of Seniors As Percentage of Juniors
1960	18,451	9,913	53.7	8,468	85.4	8,260	97.5
1961	20,687	11,473	55.4	9,235	80.5	9,350	101.2
1962	22,253	11,414	51.3	10,226	89.6	10,335	101.1
1963	23,611	12,695	53.8	11,446	90.2	11,373	99.4
1964	26,474	14,283	53.9	12,351	86.5	12,526	101.4
1965	30,484	16,652	54.6	14,685	88.2	---	---
1966	32,933	18,103	55.0	---	---	---	---
1967	33,411	---	---	---	---	---	---
Total	174,893	94,533	54.0	66,411	86.9	51,844	100.2

Source: Coordinating Board, Texas College and University System, unpublished reports of enrollment, Fall 1960–Fall 1967.

TABLE 2. Probabilities of Transition from One State to Another

From	To:					
	Do	Fr	So	Jr	Sr	Gr
Do	1.0	0.0	0.0	0.0	0.0	0.0
Fr	0.46	0.0	0.54	0.0	0.0	0.0
So	0.13	0.0	0.0	0.87	0.0	0.0
Jr	0.0	0.0	0.0	0.0	1.0	0.0
Sr	0.0	0.0	0.0	0.0	0.0	1.0
Gr	0.0	0.0	0.0	0.0	0.0	1.0

cates that the probability that a sophomore will become a junior after one academic year is 0.87.

Since the entries in Table 2 represent the probabilities of transition from one state to another, they are called *transition probabilities*. The table or matrix of probabilities is called the *transition matrix* for the problem.

Use of Transition Probabilities

The transition probabilities in the transition matrix can be used to answer the questions posed initially regarding the impact of 100 new students enrolling as freshmen. Since $P(So_n|Fr_{n-1}) = 0.54$, there would be $(100)(0.54) = 54$ additional sophomores the following year, and since $P(Jr_n|So_{n-1}) = 0.87$, there would be (54) (0.87) $\cong$ 47 new juniors two years hence.* Finally, since $P(Sr_n|Jr_{n-1}) = 1.0$, there would be 47 incremental seniors. The total increase in enrollment in the college after four years from an increase of 100 new students as freshmen each year would be 248, as calculated in Table 3. The number of additional persons who graduate each year would also be estimated as 47, since $P(Gr_n|Sr_{n-1}) = 1.0$.

TABLE 3. Total Increase in Enrollment After Four Years from an Additional 100 Freshmen Each Year

Increase in:	
Freshmen	100
Sophomores	54
Juniors	47
Seniors	47
Total	248

This example has illustrated how transition probabilities can be obtained and used to analyze a problem of enrollment forecasting. Additional insights can be obtained when the transition matrix is actually used in the analysis. This process will be illustrated through a second example.

BRAND SWITCHING

An important application of transition matrices is in the analysis of *brand switching* among consumers. For example, suppose there are three major automobile manufacturers who dominate the automobile market. During the previous month, manufacturer X sold a total of 120,000 automobiles, manufacturer Y sold 203,000, and manufacturer Z sold 377,000. However, the sales totals did not tell the full story regarding customer preferences.

Customers do not always purchase a new automobile from the same producer that manufactured their previous automobile. This phenomenon, called *brand switching*, has important implications for marketing analysis and for planning advertising strategies. In order to analyze this phenomenon, data are needed on the manufacturer of the car previously owned by each of these purchasers.

Table 4 shows how these data might be displayed. From Table 4, we see that the market share of manufacturer Z has declined from $400/700 = 0.571$ to $377/700 = 0.539$, with most of the gain going to manufacturer X.

*The symbol $\cong$ is read "is approximately equal to".

TABLE 4. Automobile Brand Switching

Previously Owned Automobile Made by:	Purchased New Automobile Made by:			Total	Previous Market Share
	X	Y	Z		
X	85	8	7	100	0.143
Y	20	160	20	200	0.286
Z	15	35	350	400	0.571
Total	120	203	377	700	
New Market Share	0.171	0.290	0.539		

Note: Data given in thousands.

Of the 120,000 new automobiles purchased from manufacturer X, 85,000 customers previously owned an automobile manufactured by X, 20,000 owned an automobile manufactured by Y, and 15,000 owned an automobile manufactured by Z. Of the 100,000 previous owners of automobiles manufactured by X, 8,000 purchased a new automobile from manufacturer Y, while only 7,000 purchased from Z. These data show not only the total sales and the market shares, but also indicate the relationship among the manufacturers in terms of customer brand loyalty and brand switching.

On the basis of these data, questions such as the following might be asked and analyzed:

1. Should the advertising campaign of manufacturer Z be directed toward attracting previous purchasers of automobiles manufactured by X or Y, or should it concentrate on retaining a larger proportion of the previous purchasers of automobiles manufactured by Z?

2. The purchaser of a new automobile keeps the car an average of three years. If this trend in brand switching continues, what will the market shares of the three companies be in three years? In six years?

3. If this trend in brand switching continues, will the market shares continue to fluctuate, or will an equilibrium eventually be reached?

These questions can be analyzed by developing and using transition probabilities and the transition matrix.

The Matrix of Transition Probabilities

Given the data in Table 4, it is a simple matter to compute the transition probabilities. The probability that a previous owner of an automobile manufactured by X will purchase a new automobile from Y is $8/100 = 0.08$, and from Z is $7/100 = 0.07$. The probability that X will retain a customer is $85/100 = 0.85$. Thus we simply divide each entry in Table 4 by the corresponding row total, as follows:

	X	Y	Z
X	$85/100 = 0.8500$	$8/100 = 0.0800$	$7/100 = 0.0700$
Y	$20/200 = 0.1000$	$160/200 = 0.8000$	$20/200 = 0.1000$
Z	$15/400 = 0.0375$	$35/400 = 0.0875$	$350/400 = 0.8750$

These calculations determine the transition matrix shown in Table 5.

TABLE 5. Transition Matrix for Brand Switching

From	To: (1) X	(2) Y	(3) Z
X	0.8500	0.0800	0.0700
Y	0.1000	0.8000	0.1000
Z	0.0375	0.0875	0.8750

Notice that the sum of the entries in each row in the transition matrix is 1.0. This is an important characteristic of a transition matrix. The columns of the transition matrix yield the following information:

(1) X retains 85 percent of its customers, gains 10 percent of Y's customers, and gains 3.75 percent of Z's customers.

(2) Y gains 8 percent of X's customers, retains 80 percent of its customers, and gains 8.75 percent of Z's customers.

(3) Z gains 7 percent of X's customers, gains 10 percent of Y's customers, and retains 87.5 percent of its customers.

We shall now consider how this matrix can be used to analyze marketing strategies.

An Example of a Markov Chain The matrix of transition probabilities can be used to study the dynamic behavior of consumer purchasing patterns if the following assumptions can be justified:

1. The probability that a customer will switch to another manufacturer or purchase again from the same manufacturer depends only on the brand of the automobile he now owns. The brands of the automobiles he has owned previously are irrelevant.

2. The probability that a customer will switch to another manufacturer or purchase again from the same manufacturer is independent of how many previous purchases he has made.

For example, suppose customer Jones owned an automobile manufactured by Z and then purchased an automobile from X, while customer Smith owned an automobile manufactured by X and purchased a new one from X. According to assumption (1), the probabilities that Jones and Smith will purchase their next cars from X, or switch to Y or Z, must be identical.

If these assumptions are reasonable, and in many real-world marketing analyses they are, then the series of purchases by consumers constitute a *Markov chain* of the first order. Under such conditions, the matrix of transition probabilities can be used to provide further insights into consumer purchasing patterns.

Prediction of Market Shares in Future Periods

The current market share for each of the manufacturers is 0.171 for manufacturer X, 0.290 for manufacturer Y, and 0.539 for manufacturer Z. These numbers appear in Table 4 and were obtained by dividing the number of automobiles sold by each manufacturer by the total number of automobiles sold by all three manufacturers.

Now, the average length of time that a new automobile purchaser keeps his automobile is three years. If the brand switching behavior of the customers continues in the same manner as described in the transition matrix of Table 5, what will the market shares be in three years, when the customers purchase new automobiles again? We can write the current market shares as the column of numbers shown below:

	Market Share
X	0.171
Y	0.290
Z	0.539

where the numbers represent the proportion of the total new automobile sales attributable to each manufacturer.

By using the following procedure we can estimate the market share of manufacturer X in three years. From column (1) of Table 5, we know that X retains 85 percent of its customers, or 85 percent of its market share. Thus, we expect X to retain $(0.171)(0.85) = 0.145$ of its current market share. X also gains 10 percent of the customers of Y, or 10 percent of Y's market share. Therefore, X would gain $(0.290)(0.10) = 0.029$ of the market from Y. Likewise, X would gain 3.75 percent of the market of Z, or (0.539)

$(0.0375) = 0.020$. Adding the proportion of the market share retained, 0.145, the proportion of the market gained from Y, 0.029, and the proportion of the market gained from Z, 0.020, gives

$$0.145 + 0.029 + 0.020 = 0.194$$

as the estimate of the market share of X in three years. This estimate represents a net gain of $0.194 - 0.171 = 0.023$, or 2.3 percent of the market.

Notice that these calculations are equivalent to simply multiplying the numbers in the market share column shown previously by the corresponding numbers in column (1) of the transition matrix (Table 5) and summing the results. That is, we have

Market Share Column		Column (1) of Transition Matrix		
0.171	×	0.8500	=	0.145
0.290	×	0.1000	=	0.029
0.539	×	0.0375	=	0.020
				0.194

To obtain the estimated market share for Y in three years, we can multiply the market share by the corresponding numbers in column (2) of the transition matrix as follows:

Market Share Column		Column (2) of Transition Matrix		
0.171	×	0.0800	=	0.014
0.290	×	0.8000	=	0.232
0.539	×	0.0875	=	0.047
				0.293

The net increase is 0.3 percent for the market share of Y. Verify that the estimate of the market share for Z in three years is 0.513.

Thus the estimated market share column in three years is

	Market Share
X	0.194
Y	0.293
Z	0.513

Now, to estimate the market shares of X, Y, and Z six years hence, when the typical customer will again purchase an automobile, we can multiply the

new values in the column of market shares times the corresponding numbers in the columns of the transition matrix in Table 5. Thus the estimated
market share of X in six years would be found as follows:

Market Share Column		Column (1) of Transition Matrix		
0.194	$\times$	0.8500	$=$	0.165
0.293	$\times$	0.1000	$=$	0.029
0.513	$\times$	0.0375	$=$	0.019
				0.213

Again the market share of X has increased. If the estimated total sales six
years hence is 900,000, then the estimated sales for manufacturer X would
be (0.213) $(900,000) = 191,700$.

By continuing this process, we can find the estimated market shares
for each manufacturer for any multiple of three years into the future. To
find the estimated market shares nine years hence, simply take the estimated
market shares in six years found as indicated above, and multiply them times
the columns in the transition matrix. Using these estimates and the transition matrix, we can find the estimated market shares twelve years hence,
etc. Naturally, this analysis assumes that the brand switching behavior of
the customers as indicated in Table 5 remains constant (assumption 2).

In our analysis, the market shares of X and Y increased, while that of
Z fell. If the brand switching behavior of the customers remains constant,
will this shift of customers from Z to X and Y continue indefinitely, or will
an equilibrium point be reached at which there are no more changes in the
market shares?

Equilibrium

Suppose we assume that at some future time, an equilibrium point will be
reached so that the market shares of X, Y, and Z do not change. At that
point, the same proportion of customers would switch *to* each brand as
switch *from* each brand over each purchase cycle of three years.

Let us assume that these equilibrium market shares are x for manufacturer X, y for manufacturer Y, and z for manufacturer Z. Thus the column
of market shares at equilibrium is

	Equilibrium Market Share
X	x
Y	y
Z	z

To estimate the market shares of each manufacturer in another three years, we would simply multiply the numbers in this column times the corresponding numbers in the transition matrix columns (Table 5), and sum the results. However, we know the results will remain unchanged at the equilibrium point, so the sum for X will be the market share for X, which is simply x.

That is, to calculate the market share for X in three years *after* equilibrium has been reached, we would simply perform the following calculations:

Equilibrium Market Share Column		Column (1) of Transition Matrix		
x	$\times$	0.8500	=	0.8500x
y	$\times$	0.1000	=	0.1000y
z	$\times$	0.0375	=	0.0375z
		Equilibrium market share for X =		x

But we know that the sum will simply be x, since the market share of X remains unchanged when equilibrium has been reached. We can rewrite this summation in the form of an equation,

$$0.8500x + 0.1000y + 0.0375z = x ,$$

which simplifies to

$$0.1500x - 0.1000y - 0.0375z = 0 . \tag{1}$$

Performing similar calculations for the market share of Y gives

$$0.0800x + 0.8000y + 0.0875z = y ,$$

which simplifies to

$$0.0800x - 0.2000y + 0.0875z = 0 . \tag{2}$$

Similarly, for Z we obtain

$$0.0700x + 0.1000y - 0.1250z = 0 . \tag{3}$$

Since the market shares are proportions, we also know that

$$x + y + z = 1 . \tag{4}$$

Thus, we have four equations and three unknowns. We may use equation (4) and any two of equations (1)–(3) and solve for the values of x, y, and z, using one of the methods reviewed in Appendix A. Substituting these values back into the fourth equation provides a check on our computations.

Suppose we choose equations (2), (3), and (4), and solve them by the method of substitution. We can eliminate y from (2) and (3) by multiplying (3) by 2 and adding it to (2) as follows:

$$0.1400x + 0.2000y - 0.2500z = 0 \quad \text{[(3) multiplied by 2]}$$
$$\underline{0.0800x - 0.2000y + 0.0875z = 0} \quad (2)$$
$$0.2200x \qquad\qquad - 0.1625z = 0 . \qquad\qquad\qquad (5)$$

We can eliminate y from (3) and (4) by multiplying (3) by -10 and adding it to (4) as follows:

$$-0.70x - 1.00y + 1.25z = 0 \quad \text{[(3) multiplied by } -10]$$
$$\underline{x + \quad y + \quad z = 1} \quad (4)$$
$$0.30x \qquad\qquad + 2.25z = 1 . \qquad\qquad\qquad (6)$$

Finally, we can eliminate x from (5) and (6) by multiplying (5) by -0.3, multiplying (6) by 0.22, and adding the resulting equations:

$$-0.066x + 0.04875z = 0 \qquad \text{[(5) multiplied by } -0.3]$$
$$\underline{0.066x + 0.49500z = 0.22} \quad \text{[(6) multiplied by 0.22]}$$
$$0.54375z = 0.22 .$$

Therefore, $z = 0.22/0.54375 = 0.4046$. Substituting this value back into (6), we have

$$0.3x + (2.25)(0.4046) = 1 ,$$

which simplifies to

$$0.3x = 0.0897 ,$$

so that $x = 0.0897/0.3 = 0.2990$. Finally, we substitute these values of x and z into (4) to obtain

$$y = 1.0 - 0.2990 - 0.4046$$

or $y = 0.2964$.

We can check these results by substituting them into equation (1), which gives

$$(0.1500)(0.2990) - (0.1000)(0.2964) - (0.0375)(0.4046) = 0.0 ,$$

as we expected. Note that these calculations are straightforward, but admittedly somewhat tedious, even for a problem with only three states. In real-world applications, there will generally be more than three states, but these calculations can be done efficiently on a computer in only a few seconds.

These results tell us that, at equilibrium, the market shares of manufacturers X, Y, and Z will be 0.30, 0.30, and 0.40, respectively (rounding to two decimal places). This result assumes that the brand switching behavior of the consumers continues according to the pattern in Table 5. Thus we would expect X's market share to continue to grow from its current value of 0.17, but to stabilize at 0.30. The market share of Y will remain virtually unchanged, since its current value is 0.29. Manufacturer Z will continue to lose customers from its current share of 0.539, but will fall only to 0.40, and will still be the dominant manufacturer in the industry.

Use of the Markov Chain Analysis

The Markov chain analysis can be used to analyze the effects of various marketing strategies. Recall that the equilibrium market shares of 0.30, 0.30, and 0.40 were derived on the basis of the assumption that the brand switching behavior of the consumers as described in Table 5 remains unchanged. What if Manufacturer X undertakes an aggressive marketing strategy designed to encourage more of the customers who previously purchased automobiles from Manufacturer Z to switch to automobiles manufactured by X? Recall advertisements that you have seen in which one manufacturer focuses its marketing campaign on one competitor while ignoring others.

Suppose the market analysts feel that such a campaign would increase the percentage of Z's customers who switch to automobiles manufactured by X from 3.75 to 7.5, so that the transition matrix for the automobile industry would become the one illustrated in Table 6. Verify that the new long-run (equilibrium) market shares of the three manufacturers based on this change would become 0.366 for X, 0.295 for Y, and 0.339 for Z. Thus, *a successful marketing campaign would make X the dominant force in the industry and relegate Z to second place.*

TABLE 6. New Transition Matrix
for Brand Switching

		To:		
		X	Y	Z
	X	0.8500	0.0800	0.0700
From	Y	0.1000	0.8000	0.1000
	Z	0.0750	0.0875	0.8375

AN ANALYSIS OF A GERIATRIC WARD

Meredith [1973] presents an example of an analysis of a real-world problem using Markov chains. At the California Napa State Hospital, a resocialization program was instituted in 1964 to deinstitutionalize geriatric (elderly) patients so that they could be placed in boarding homes or their equivalent outside the hospital. The analysis was performed to determine the costs and the benefits of the program.

For the purposes of the analysis, it was convenient to classify current or former patients into the following states:

1. in the Geriatric Resocialization Program (GRP)
2. in one of the hospital wards
3. in a home but placed from GRP
4. in a home but placed directly from a ward
5. dead

It seemed reasonable to assume that the movement of a patient from one state to another could be described by a Markov chain. This assumption implies that the probability of movement to the next state depends only on the patient's current state and not on the time period. The only concern was that for long-term projections, the probability of a patient's death would actually increase; however, since the probability of death is quite small, this effect was not considered significant, so the Markov chain assumption was made.

The probabilities of movement among the five states for a period of one month are given in Table 7. The cost of keeping a patient in each state for one month is shown in the right-hand column of Table 7. These probabilities were determined from actual hospital records in the same manner illustrated in the enrollment forecasting and in the brand switching examples.

TABLE 7. One-Month Transition Probabilities and Costs

From	To:					Cost per Month ($)
	GRP	Ward	Home (from GRP)	Home (from Ward)	Dead	
GRP	0.854	0.028	0.112	0.000	0.006	682
Ward	0.013	0.978	0.000	0.003	0.006	655
Home (from GRP)	0.025	0.000	0.969	0.000	0.006	226
Home (from Ward)	0.000	0.025	0.000	0.969	0.006	226
Dead	0.000	0.000	0.000	0.000	1.000	0

Source: J. Meredith, "A Markovian Analysis of a Geriatric Ward," *Management Science*, June 1972; used by permission.

Notice in Table 7 that the probability of moving to another state from "dead" is 0.0, and the probability of remaining "dead" is 1.0, as we would expect. What if we calculate the long-run, equilibrium probability of patients in each state? Once a patient reaches the state "dead," he can never leave it. In general terms, this is called an "absorbing state" in a transition matrix. In the enrollment forecasting example with the transition matrix shown in Table 2, the states "dropout" and "graduated" are absorbing states also. If an absorbing state exists in a transition matrix, all of the persons or items will eventually move into the absorbing state (unless the transition matrix has other unusual characteristics which need not concern us here).

For the transition matrix in Table 7, the long-run proportion of patients in each state is obviously 0.0 in GRP, ward, home (from GRP), and home (from ward), and 1.0 in dead. In other words, in the long run, all of the patients are dead. This analysis provides little useful information, so another type of long-run analysis is required when the transition matrix has absorbing states.

Using techniques slightly more involved than those presented here, Meredith computed the mean number of months a patient starting in each of the five nonabsorbing states would stay in each of these states before entering the absorbing state "dead." He multiplied these results times the costs of being in each of these states for one month, and obtained the results shown in Table 8. For example, these figures indicate that a patient starting in the GRP can be expected to be in the program for a total of 26 months, in a ward for 38 months, in a home after placement from the GRP for 95 months, and in a home after direct placement from a ward for 4 months before dying.

TABLE 8. Expected Stay Times (months) and Costs

Initial State	GRP	Ward	Home (from GRP)	Home (from Ward)	Cost ($)
GRP	26	38	95	4	64,950
Ward	17	77	63	7	77,800
Home (from GRP)	21	31	109	3	59,900
Home (from Ward)	14	62	51	38	70,250

Source: J. Meredith, "A Markovian Analysis of a Geriatric Ward," *Management Science*, June 1972; used by permission.

The total cost to the state of treating this patient will be $64,950. Notice that a patient starting in a ward expects to spend much more time in the hospital ward and much less time in a home, since all patients are not selected for the GRP. Also notice that the expected total cost of treating a patient in the GRP is about $13,000 less than for one in the ward.

What if there were no GRP? A transition matrix similar to Table 7 was developed with only three states—ward, home (from ward), and dead. The expected stay times for the average patient in each of the two states—ward and home (from ward)—before dying are shown in Table 9, along with the associated costs. The costs are significantly higher, about 30 percent. In addition, the average patient currently in the ward can now be expected to spend approximately 13 of his remaining 14 years in the ward (152 months in the ward and 15 months in a home after direct placement from a ward).

On the basis of this analysis Meredith was able to estimate that the GRP had resulted in a net savings to the state of some $15 million after only 5.5

TABLE 9. Expected Stay Times (months) and Costs Without GRP

Initial State	Ward	Home (from Ward)	Cost ($)
Ward	152	15	102,900
Home (from Ward)	123	44	90,400

Source: J. Meredith, "A Markovian Analysis of a Geratric Ward," *Management Science*, June 1972; used by permission.

years of operation. This amount corresponds to a savings of approximately $3 million per year.

WHAT SHOULD THE MANAGER KNOW?

Markov chains can be the basis for a predictive model for forecasting the future state of a person, a company, or an item. This predictive model is used when risk is involved in the form of probabilities of transition from one state to another. The approach is limited to problems with very special characteristics, but it does provide useful information to managers in those cases where it can be applied.

Problem Characteristics It must be possible to classify the items involved in the problem into unique "states." For example, students were classified by academic level or by dropout or graduated status: the customers were classified according to the brands of automobiles they purchased; and patients were classified according to whether they were in a program, a home, a hospital ward, or dead.

Next, it must be possible to determine the probability that a person or an item in each state will be in any other state in the next time period. This probability must

1. depend only on the current state, and
2. be independent of the particular time period.

These probabilities form a transition matrix.

Examples of real-world problems that often have these characteristics include enrollment forecasting, brand switching analysis, and health care system analysis. Trinkl [1974] presents an analysis of programs for the mentally retarded in Hawaii that is very similar to the analysis of Meredith [1973] in California. Pegels and Jelmert [1970] report the use of Markov chains to evaluate blood-inventory policies.

Several models for the evaluation of human resources and manpower planning also include Markov chains. For example, Flamholtz [1974] has used Markov chains to calculate the probabilities that individuals within an organization will occupy each of several jobs in the future. An example is shown in Table 10 for a hypothetical CPA firm. The probabilities that a staff accountant in 1974 will be a staff accountant, senior accountant, manager, partner, or will have left the firm in 1975, 1976, and so on, are shown. Charnes, Cooper, and Niehaus [1972] report that similar transition matrices have been developed for manpower planning in the U.S. Navy.

TABLE 10.   Transition Probabilities for a Staff Accountant in a C.P.A. Firm

State	Probability of Occurrence of Each State at Future Times			
	1975	1976	1977	1978
Staff accountant	0.57	0.25	0.06	0.01
Senior accountant	0.15	0.27	0.30	0.23
Manager	0.00	0.00	0.01	0.05
Partner	0.00	0.00	0.00	0.00
Transfer	0.03	0.05	0.06	0.07
Exit	0.25	0.43	0.57	0.65

Source: from *Human Resources Accounting*, 1st edition by Eric Flamholtz, Table 5-2; page 156. Copyright © 1974 by Dickenson Publishing Co., Inc., Encino, California. Reprinted by permission of the Publisher.

Formulation and Data   The transition matrices are not particularly difficult to formulate. The manager should be involved in the identification of the relevant states. An attempt should be made to keep the number of states to a minimum. For example, in a brand switching analysis, it may be possible to ignore a large number of minor competitors or to group them into the single state "other."

The required data are the transition probabilities. In cases such as the enrollment forecasting, mental retardation studies, and manpower planning studies, there may be sufficient historical data to determine proportions that can be converted into probabilities. However, the data must be carefully scrutinized. Adjustments may be required to compensate for recent trends or unusual patterns in the past that are not likely to repeat themselves. For example, data on college enrollments just before or just after a war should not be the basis for forecasts during peacetime. Similarly, brand switching data could be distorted by a strike in one of the companies during a particular year. The manager should be alert for such problems.

As a note of interest, the Market Research Corporation of America (MRCA) has established a sample of families who report their purchases of certain branded items to MRCA. These reports can be used as the basis for transition matrices in a brand switching analysis. Similar services are provided by other organizations.

When actual data are unavailable or of questionable validity for future projections, subjective probabilities can be used. The techniques of Chapter 3 can be applied to estimate them. Again, the manager should play an active role in the assessment of these subjective probabilities.

Computations   The computations are straightforward, but quickly become tedious. It is simple to develop or obtain computer programs that can rapidly perform the onerous arithmetic and present the results to the manager for interpretation.

Interpretation   There are three important results that can be obtained from the use of the transition matrices. First, forecasts of the proportion of individuals or items in each state can be attained for future time periods. These forecasts are obtained by multiplying a column of proportions (market shares in the brand switching example) times each column in the transition matrix, and summing the results. This information can be extremely useful for short-term forecasting of enrollments or sales.

Second, the long-run or equilibrium proportions can be developed for some transition matrices. The equilibrium state was illustrated for the brand switching problem. In the long run, these results indicate that the proportion of customers in each state will reach equilibrium values and remain unchanged. The sensitivity of these equilibrium values to changes in the probabilities in the transition matrices can be used as the basis for choosing among alternative marketing strategies.

Third, in some transition matrices, it is impossible to leave a state once it has been reached. Such a state is called an absorbing state. When absorbing states occur, the equilibrium analysis must take another form. The most relevant information is usually the expected number of time periods spent in each of the other states by an individual (or an item) before he (it) *is* absorbed. An example of this form of analysis was used in the study of the Geriatric Resocialization Program by Meredith. Although the mathematical details are straightforward, they are so tedious that they would be performed on a computer for any real-world application and have been omitted here. However, the manager should be aware of the use of this analysis. As illustrated, if the costs of being in each state are known, the results can be used in a cost analysis.

Check Your Understanding

1. List the appropriate *states* to use in the analysis of the following:
    a. consumer credit policies
    b. a blood-inventory system
    c. the long-run ratio of tenured to nontenured professors in a university

2. Identify the two absorbing states in Table 2. Is it reasonable to assume that each of these are absorbing states? Why or why not?

3. Suppose that forecasts indicate that 34,000 students will enter the four-year colleges of Texas next year, 36,000 in two years, and 40,000 in three years. There are 30,000 enrolled in the current freshman class.
   a. Using the transition probabilities in Table 2, compute the expected total enrollment in the four-year colleges in three years.
   b. Suppose the average variable cost per student in the four-year colleges of Texas is estimated to be $800 for a freshman, $900 for a sophomore, $1100 for a junior, and $1400 for a senior. What should the variable portion of the state budget for higher education in the four-year colleges be in three years time?

4. Suppose that the *proportions* of students in each of the states in the four-year colleges of Texas are as follows:

State	Proportion
Do	0.0
Fr	0.40
So	0.25
Jr	0.20
Sr	0.15
Gr	0.0

   a. Using the data in Table 2, what will the proportions in each state be next year if just enough freshmen are admitted to maintain the *same* total enrollment?
   b. If the total current enrollment is 100,000 students, how many freshmen should be admitted next year to allow the total enrollment to increase to 105,000?

5. Discuss the assumptions that must be justified in order to use a Markov chain analysis in the enrollment forecasting problem, the brand switching problem, and the analysis of the geriatric ward.
   a. Are the assumptions met in each case?
   b. If not, would you expect the potential error to be so large that the results would be in question?

6. Determine the following, using the transition matrix for brand switching (Table 5):
   a. the market share of Z in three years
   b. the estimated sales for manufacturers Y and Z in six years if the estimated total sales is 900,000 automobiles
   c. the equilibrium market shares for X, Y, and Z using equations (1), (3), and (4)

7. Verify that the long-run (equilibrium) market shares of the three manufacturers based on Table 6 are 0.366 for X, 0.295 for Y, and 0.339 for Z.

8. Suppose there are 100 geriatric patients in the Napa State Hospital in January. There are 20 in GRP, 60 in one of the hospital wards, 15 in a home but placed from GRP, and 5 in a home but placed directly from a ward. Using the information in Table 7, determine the following:
   a. the cost of caring for the patients in January
   b. the expected number of patients in each state in February
   c. the expected number of patients in each state in March
   d. the expected cost of caring for the patients in March

Problems

1. Suppose that new razor blades were introduced on the market by three companies at the same time. When they were introduced, each company had an equal share of the market, but during the first year the following changes took place:
   1) Company A retained 90 percent of its customers, lost 3 percent to B and 7 percent to C.
   2) Company B retained 70 percent of its customers, lost 10 percent to A, and 20 percent to C.
   3) Company C retained 80 percent of its customers, lost 10 percent to A, and 10 percent to B.
   Assume that no changes in the buying habits of the consumers occur.
   a. What were the market shares of the three companies at the end of the first year? The second year?
   b. What are the long-run (equilibrium) market shares of the three companies?

2. The University of Lufkin employs nontenured and tenured professors to teach its classes. By obtaining a promotion, a nontenured professor may receive tenure (security of employment). Currently there are 100 nontenured and 50 tenured professors. On the basis of past records, 20 percent of the nontenured professors are promoted each year, and another 20 percent leave the university because of resignation or retirement. Similarly, 10 percent of the tenured professors leave the university each year. For every two faculty members who leave the university, one nontenured faculty member and one tenured faculty member are hired to replace them.
   This situation may be summarized in the transition matrix shown in Table 11, where the state "outside" serves to indicate both resignations and new hires. (If the number of resignations did not equal the number of new hires, separate states would be required.) The mean salaries of tenured and nontenured faculty members are also shown. Assume that the number of faculty members initially classified as "outside" is 25.

a. Compute the current total annual cost of salaries at the University of Lufkin and the estimated total annual cost of salaries next year.

b. What are the long-run (equilibrium) proportions of nontenured and tenured faculty members? What total annual salary cost would be associated with these proportions, assuming that the total number of faculty members remains at 150?

c. Suppose a new policy is adopted so that every faculty member who leaves the university must be replaced by a nontenured faculty member (i.e., no one can be hired with tenure). What are the resulting long-run (equilibrium) proportions of tenured and nontenured faculty members? What total annual cost would be associated with these proportions assuming that the total number of faculty members remains at 150?

TABLE 11. Transition Probabilities and Mean Salaries for Faculty Members at the University of Lufkin

From	To: Nontenured	Tenured	Outside	Mean Salary
Nontenured	0.60	0.20	0.20	$14,000
Tenured	0.0	0.90	0.10	$20,000
Outside	0.50	0.50	0.0	---

3. Suppose we assume that approximately the same number of patients enter the geriatric program of the Napa State Hospital each month as the number who leave the system (die). Thus, we could ignore the absorbing state "dead" in Table 7. By combining the states of "home (from GRP)" and "home (from ward,)" we obtain the simplified data in Table 12.

a. In January, there are 20 persons in GRP, 70 persons in a ward, and 10 persons in a home. What is the cost of caring for these patients?

b. How many patients are expected to be in each state in February? In March? What are the expected costs in each month?

c. What are the long-run (equilibrium) proportions of patients in each state? What would be the cost of caring for 100 patients after equilibrium has been reached?

4. To compare the long-run costs of treating patients without GRP, we assume "that only those patients who would have been placed directly from the ward will now be placed at all, since the patients who actually *were* selected for GRP had been in the hospital for over five years already without being placed and no reason exists to assume things would change suddenly." [Meredith, 1973] The resulting transition matrix is shown in Table 13.

a. What are the long-run (equilibrium) proportions of patients in each state?

b. What would be the cost of caring for 100 patients after equilibrium has been reached?

TABLE 12. One-Month Transition Probabilities and Costs for the Simplified GRP Analysis

From	To: GRP	Ward	Home	Cost per Month ($)
GRP	0.859	0.028	0.113	682
Ward	0.013	0.984	0.003	655
Home	0.012	0.012	0.976	226

TABLE 13. Modified Transition Probabilities and Costs Without GRP

From	To: Ward	Home	Costs per Month ($)
Ward	0.997	0.003	655
Home	0.024	0.976	226

    c. Does this analysis provide sufficient justification for the GRP program? What weaknesses do you see in the analysis? What other considerations might influence a decision?

5.   Finally, suppose a program is being contemplated that would double the number of placements from GRP. Then the probability of going from GRP to home in Table 12 would increase to 0.226, and the probability of staying in GRP would fall to 0.746.

    a. What are the long-run (equilibrium) proportions of patients in each state?

    b. What would be the cost of caring for 100 patients after equilibrium has been reached?

    c. What other noncost issues might be influential in a final decision regarding this new program? If you were the decision maker, what other information would you want?

6.   A major travel and entertainment credit card company analyzed its credit history file to determine the transition probability matrix shown in Table 14.[*] For example, 6.4 percent of all current accounts (0 to 29 days past due) age to 30 to 59 days past due. The costs are based on estimates of the rate of return that the firm could obtain on investments if the money were not tied up in the accounts receivable.

    a. What are the long-run (equilibrium) proportions of accounts in each state?

    b. Suppose the company estimates that sending a letter to all account holders in the 30 to 59 days past due state would result in the modified

---

[*]   Adapted from L. H. Liebman, "A Markov Decision Model for Selecting Optimal Credit Control Policies," *Management Science*, Vol. 18, No. 10, June 1972.

TABLE 14. Transition Probability Matrix and Costs for Credit Card Receivables

Days Past Due at Month t	Days Past Due at Month $t + 1$			Costs ($)
	0–29	30–59	60+	
0–29	0.94	0.06	0.00	1
30–59	0.70	0.10	0.20	2
60+	0.65	0.10	0.25	4

TABLE 15. Modified Transition Matrix for Credit Card Receivables

Days Past Due at Month t	Days Past Due at Month $t + 1$			Costs ($)
	0–29	30–59	60+	
0–29	0.94	0.06	0.00	1
30–59	0.85	0.10	0.05	2
60+	0.60	0.10	0.30	4

transition matrix of Table 15. What would be the effect on the long-run (equilibrium) proportion of accounts in each state? Suppose that the incremental cost of sending 100 letters is $25. Would this strategy be justified on an economic basis?

References

Charnes, A., W. Cooper, and R. Niehaus, *Studies in Manpower Planning,* U.S. Navy Office of Civilian Manpower Management, Washington, D.C., 1972.

Dyer, J., "Cost-Effectiveness Analysis for a Public System of Higher Education," Ph.D. dissertation, The College of Business Administration, The University of Texas at Austin, May 1969.

Flamholtz, E., *Human Resource Accounting,* Dickenson Publishing Company, Inc., Encino, California, 1974.

Kemeny, J., and J. Snell, *Finite Markov Chains,* Van Nostrand, Princeton, New Jersey, 1960.

Liebman, L. H., "A Markov Decision Model for Selecting Optimal Credit Control Policies," *Management Science,* Vol. 18, No. 10, June 1972.

Meredith, J., "A Markovian Analysis of a Geriatric Ward," *Management Science,* Vol. 19, No. 6, February 1973.

Pegels, C., and A. Jelmert, "An Evaluation of Blood-Inventory Policies: A Markov Chain Application," *Operations Research,* Vol. 18, 1970, pp. 1087–98.

Trinkl, F., "A Stochastic Analysis of Programs for the Mentally Retarded," *Operations Research,* Vol. 22, No. 6, November–December 1974.

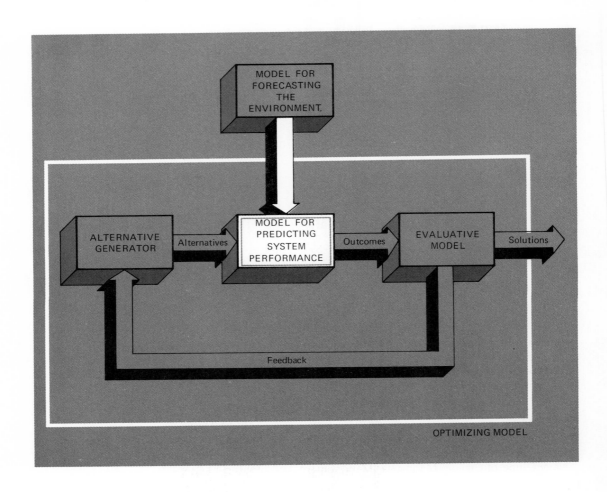

10

Predicting the Effects of Risk—
Queuing Models

Many systems and subsystems that occur throughout organized society can be conceptualized by the service facility module. The service facility module has the input-transformation-output structure we have used as a basis for all of the predictive models discussed in Part Three, but the input and the transformation have special characteristics.

The input is composed of "arrivals," and arrival times are controlled by some stochastic or probabilistic process. Similarly, the time required to process the input follows a probability distribution. The output of such a system will depend on the interplay between the random arrivals and the variable service times. Predicting the output depends on this complex interplay, and queuing or waiting line theory is the basis for these predictions.

We normally have or can obtain information about the probability distributions that control the arrivals and the service times, so we are dealing with decision problems involving risks.

In this chapter, we shall develop the concepts and methods of queuing theory and the mathematical solutions to relatively simple queuing problems. However, when the mathematical analysis becomes too complex, we must resort to simulation. That approach to formulating and using queuing models will be discussed in the next chapter.

NATURE OF SERVICE SYSTEMS

First, let us examine the characteristics of an emergency medical system. Such an example will help us to see how the concepts and methods described later in the chapter can be used. After we have discussed the assumptions and structure inherent in the models, the example will also help us to see the limitations of queuing theory. A study of the deployment of ambulance systems in Los Angeles [Fitzsimmons, 1970, 1973] forms the basis of the emergency medical system we shall discuss.

An Emergency Medical System

Figure 1 shows the essential activities of the ambulance and the patient in the emergency medical system. For the ambulance activities shown in Figure 1(a), Fitzsimmons indicates that ambulances are normally idle more than 70 percent of the time and that the dispatch delay is usually less than one minute. Travel to the scene and the return trip to the hospital will be highly variable, depending on the ambulance deployment, the size of the area served, population density, traffic conditions, and so on. Fitzsimmons states that the one-way trip in urban areas may be five to ten minutes, but it may be several times that figure for rural areas.

Figure 1(b) shows the service time as beginning with the trip to the scene and extending through the activities of on-scene care, transit to the hospital, and the transfer delay at the hospital. Waiting time is defined as

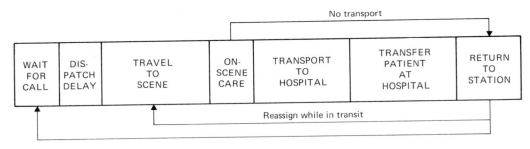

(a) AMBULANCE ACTIVITIES

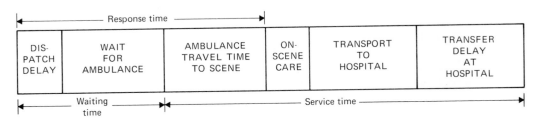

(b) PATIENT ACTIVITIES IN SYSTEM

Figure 1. Emergency medical system: (a) ambulance activities and (b) patient activities

From J. A. Fitzsimmons, "Emergency Medical Systems: A Simulation Study and Computerized Method for Deployment of Ambulances," Unpublished Ph.D. Dissertation, UCLA, 1970; used by permission.

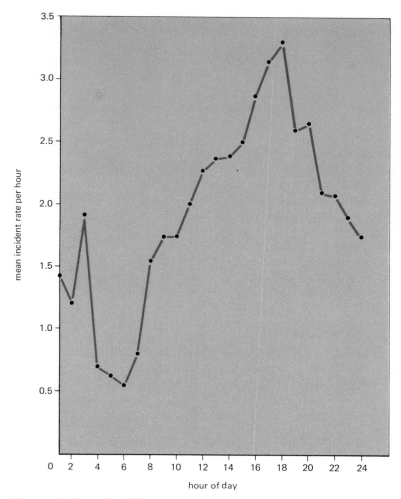

Figure 2. Mean ''call for service'' rate (incident rate) for the Los Angeles emergency medical system

From J. A. Fitzsimmons, ''Emergency Medical Systems: A Simulation Study and Computerized Method for Deployment of Ambulances,'' Unpublished Ph.D. Dissertation, UCLA, 1970; used by permission.

the period between receipt of a "call" and the beginning of the ambulance trip. Response time, however, includes the travel time, and is the sensitive political and psychological variable.

Demand for Service   Part of the difficulty in providing emergency medical service is indicated in Figure 2. The incident or "call for service" rate is highly variable throughout the day. The load varies from a low of just over 0.5 calls per hour at 6 A.M. to a high of almost 3.3 per hour at 6 P.M. The peak load is more than six times the minimum load. Not only that, the mean values do not reflect the expected variation in call rates. Previous research shows that call rates follow a Poisson distribution so that there is a 5 percent probability that the 6 P.M. call rate could be as high as approximately 7 per hour and a 5 percent probability that it could be as low as 1 per hour. (We shall discuss the Poisson distribution as a forecast of arrival or call rates later in this chapter.)

System Design and Decision Problems   Note the highly variable demand patterns through the day and for each mean call rate, and the highly variable service times depending on deployment, area served, population density, and traffic conditions. It is obvious that the way the system is designed and operates will have a significant effect on measures of performance. Given standards of response time, what should be the overall system capacity? How does the needed system capacity interact with the deployment plan? What should be the size of service areas for a given ambulance? Should the areas be fixed or variable? Should ambulances have fixed locations or should they be mobile? If an ambulance in one location has already been dispatched on a call, should the ambulances that remain in the "available" inventory be redeployed?

These are all important decisions for the design and operation of this kind of service system. Queuing theory will not answer all of these questions; however, it will provide insight into how such systems function and a methodology for predicting performance of simple systems. The general concepts of queuing theory carry over into more complex systems, which can be simulated to provide a basis for making many decisions such as the ones listed above.

WAITING LINE MODELS OF SERVICE SYSTEMS

As we have already pointed out, queuing or waiting line concepts provide insight into many problems in productive systems. The original work in waiting line theory was done by A. K. Erlang, a Danish telephone engineer. Erlang started his work in 1905 in an attempt to determine the effect of fluctuating demand (arrivals) on the utilization of automatic dial equipment. Since the end of World War II, Erlang's work has been extended and applied to a variety of situations that are now recognized as being described by the general waiting line model.

In all instances, the general input-output module is in operation, with the time between the arrival of individual inputs at the service facility commonly being random. Also, the time for service or processing is a random variable. Table 1 shows the waiting line model elements for a number of commonly known situations.

TABLE 1. Waiting Line Model Elements for Some Commonly Known Situations

Situation	Unit Arriving	Service or Processing Facility	Service or Process Being Performed
Ships entering a port	Ships	Docks	Unloading and loading
Maintenance and repair of machines	Machine breaks down	Repair crew	Repair machine
Assembly line, not mechanically paced	Parts to be assembled	Individual assembly operations or entire line	Assembly
Doctor's office	Patients	Doctor, his staff and facilities	Medical care
Purchase of groceries at a supermarket	Customers with loaded grocery carts	Checkout counter	Tabulation of bill, receipt of payment and bagging of groceries
Auto traffic at an intersection or bridge	Automobiles	Intersection or bridge with control points such as traffic lights or toll booths	Passage through intersection or bridge
Inventory of items in a warehouse	Order for withdrawal	Warehouse	Replenishment of inventory
Job shop	Job order	Work center	Processing

Structure of Waiting Line Models

There are four basic waiting line structures that describe the general conditions at the service facility. The simplest structure, shown in Figure 3(a), is our basic module. It is called the single-channel, single-phase case. There are many examples of the simple module: the cashier at a restaurant, any single-window operation in a post office or bank, a one-man barber shop. If the number of processing stations is increased but still draws on a single waiting line, we have the multiple-channel, single-phase case shown in Figure 3(b). A simple assembly line or a cafeteria line has, in effect, a number of service facilities in tandem and is called the single-channel, multiple-phase case shown in Figure 3(c). Finally, the multiple-channel, multiple-phase case can be illustrated by two or more parallel assembly lines as shown in Figure 3(d). Combinations of any or all of the basic four structures could also exist in networks of queues in very complex systems.

The analytical methods for waiting lines divide into two main categories for any of the basic structures in Figure 3, depending on the size of the source population of the inputs. When the source population is very large, and in theory at least the length of the waiting line could grow without fixed limits, the applicable models are termed "infinite." On the other hand, when the arriving unit comes from a source having a fixed upper limit, the applicable models are termed "finite." For example, if we are dealing with the maintenance of a bank of 20 machines and a machine breakdown represents an arrival, the maximum waiting line is 20 machines waiting for service, and

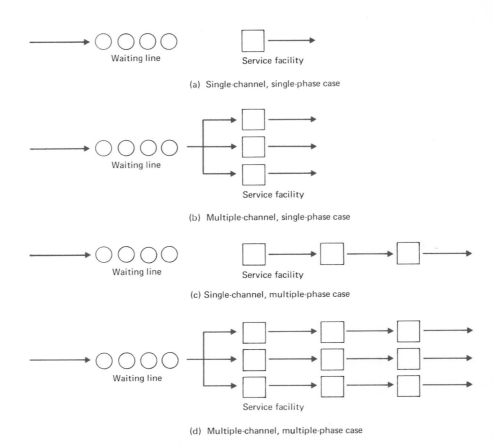

Figure 3. Four basic structures of waiting line situations

a finite model is needed. If, on the other hand, we operated an auto repair shop, the source population of breakdowns is very large and an infinite model would be appropriate. We shall discuss both infinite and finite models.

There are other variations in waiting line structures that are important in certain applications. The "queue discipline" implied in Figure 3 is first-come first-served. Obviously there are many other possibilities involving priority systems. For example, in a medical clinic, emergencies and patients with appointments are taken ahead of walk-in patients. In job shop scheduling systems there has been a great deal of experimentation with alternative priority systems. Because of mathematical complexity, simulation has been the common mode of analysis for systems involving queue disciplines other than first-come first-served.

Finally, the nature of the distribution of arrivals and service is an important structural characteristic of waiting line models. Some mathematical analysis is available for distributions that follow the Poisson or the Erlang process (with some variations), or that have constant arrivals or service. If distributions are different from those mentioned or are taken from actual records, simulation is likely to be the necessary mode of analysis.

INFINITE WAITING LINE MODELS

We shall not cover all possibilities of infinite models, but will restrict our discussion to situations involving the first-come first-served queue discipline and the Poisson distribution of arrivals. We will deal initially with the single-channel, single-phase case (our basic service facility module), but later we shall also discuss the multiple-channel case.

Poisson Arrivals

The Poisson distribution function has been shown to represent arrival rates in a large number of real-world situations. It is a discrete function dealing with whole units of arrivals, so that fractions of men, products, or machines do not have meaning, nor do negative values. The Poisson distribution function is given by

$$f(x) = \frac{\lambda^x e^{-\lambda}}{x!} \tag{1}$$

where

λ = the mean arrival rate,

x = the number arriving in one unit of time,

$x!$ = x factorial.

[Note: $x!$ is simply $(x)\,(x-1)\cdots(3)\,(2)\,(1)$. For example, $4! = 4 \cdot 3 \cdot 2 \cdot 1 = 24$. $0! = 1$.]

For example, if $\lambda = 4$, then the probability of an arrival rate of $x = 6$ per hour is

$$f(6) = \frac{4^6 e^{-4}}{6!} = \frac{4096 \times 0.0183}{720} = 0.104 \,.$$

The Poisson distribution for an average arrival rate of $\lambda = 4$ (as well as for other values of λ) is shown in Figure 4. The Poisson distribution is typically skewed to the right. The distribution is simple in that the standard deviation is expressed solely in terms of the mean, $\sigma_\lambda = \sqrt{\lambda}$. Also, tables for the cumulative Poisson distribution are given as Table 2 of Appendix E.

Evidence that the Poisson distribution in fact represents arrival rates in many applications is indeed great. Many empirical studies have validated the Poisson arrival rate in general industrial operations, traffic flow, and various service operations [Churchman et al., 1957; Larson, 1972; Morse, 1967; Prabhu, 1965; Theirauf and Klekamp, 1975].

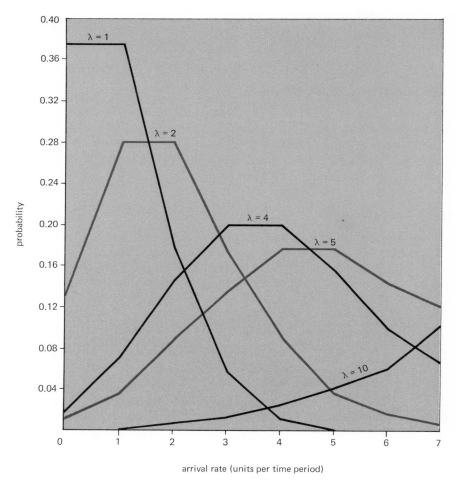

Figure 4. Poisson distributions for several mean arrival rates

Arrival distributions are sometimes given in terms of the time between arrivals, or interarrival times. Such distributions often follow the negative exponential distribution. However, if the *number* of arrivals in a given interval is Poisson distributed, then necessarily the times *between* arrivals are independent and exponentially distributed, and vice versa.

Although we cannot say that all distributions of arrivals per unit of time are adequately described by the Poisson distribution, we can say that it is usually worth checking to see if it is true, for then a fairly simple analysis may be possible. It is logical that arrivals may follow the Poisson distribution when many factors affect arrival time, since the Poisson distribution corresponds to completely random arrivals. This means that each arrival is independent of other arrivals as well as of any condition of the waiting line. The practical question, of course, is whether or not the Poisson distribution is a reasonable approximation to reality.

Poisson Arrivals—Service Time Distribution Not Specified

Since Poisson arrivals are common, a useful model is one that depends on Poisson arrivals but accepts any service time distribution. We assume also that the mean service rate is greater than the mean arrival rate, otherwise the system would be unstable and the waiting line would become infinitely large. The queue discipline is first-come first-served, and arrivals wait for service; that is, they neither fail to join the line nor leave it because it is too long. Under these conditions the expected length of the waiting line is

$$L_q = \frac{(\lambda\sigma)^2 + (\lambda/\mu)^2}{2(1 - \lambda/\mu)},$$ (2)

where

L_q is the expected length of the waiting line,

λ is the mean arrival rate from a Poisson distribution,

μ is the mean service rate,

σ is the standard deviation of the distribution of service times.

Because the ratio λ/μ is itself a useful concept, since it represents the average utilization of the service facility, we define $\rho = \lambda/\mu$. Substituting ρ in equation (2) leads to

$$L_q = \frac{(\lambda\sigma)^2 + \rho^2}{2(1 - \rho)}.$$ (3)

Since ρ represents the fraction of time that the service facility is in use, by analogy it also represents the expected number of individuals or units being served at any instant in time. For example, if $\rho = 0.4$ the service facility is in use 40 percent of the time. Also, $(1 - \rho)$ is the fraction of service facility idle time, or the fraction of time when no one is being served. Since ρ is the expected number being served, the total number in the waiting line plus the expected number being served is the total number in the system, L,

$$L = L_q + \rho.$$ (4)

Similar simple logic leads to the expected waiting time in line W_q, and time in the system including service W. The reciprocal of the mean arrival rate is the mean time between arrivals $(1/\lambda)$. The multiplication of the mean time between arrivals and the line length gives the waiting time or the time in the system

$$W_q = L_q/\lambda$$ (5)
$$W = L/\lambda.$$ (6)

Equations (3), (4), (5), and (6) are useful relationships. The general proce-dure would be to compute L_q from either (2) or (3), and compute the values of L, W_q, and W as needed, given the value of L_q. Note that equations (2) through (6) deal only with steady state or long-run equilibrium conditions.

An Example Trucks arrive at the truck dock of a wholesale grocer at the rate of 8 per hour and the distribution of arrivals is Poisson. The loading and/or unloading time averages 5 minutes, but the estimate s of the standard de-viation of service time is 6 minutes. Truckers are complaining that they must spend more time waiting than unloading and the following calculations ver-ify their claim:

$$\lambda = 8/\text{hour}; \ \mu = 60/5 = 12/\text{hour}; \ s = 6/60 = 1/10 \text{ hours}$$

$$L_q = \frac{(8/10)^2 + (8/12)^2}{2(1 - 8/12)} = 1.63 \text{ trucks in line}$$

$$L = 1.63 + 8/12 = 2.30 \text{ trucks in the system}$$

$$W_q = 1.63/8 = 0.204 \text{ hours, or } 12.24 \text{ minutes in line waiting for service}$$

$$W = 2.30/8 = 0.288 \text{ hours, or } 17.28 \text{ minutes in the system}$$

The calculations yield another verification of logic in that the average truck waits 12.24 minutes in line plus 5 minutes for service, or 17.28 minutes in the system. Thus, another logical relationship is $W = W_q + 1/\mu$.

Let us pause for a moment to reflect on the model. Which are the deci-sion variables and which are the uncontrollable parameters? The service-related variables can be altered by the manager if he is willing to invest capi-tal in new capacity or if he can devise new procedures that can reduce the variability of service time. On the other hand, the arrival rate of trucks is presumably not under managerial control, and thus is a parameter.

The grocer knows, of course, that he could probably solve the problem by expanding the truck dock so that two trucks could be handled simulta-neously. This solution, however, would require a large capital expenditure and disruption of operations during construction. Instead, he notes the very large standard deviation of service time, and on investigation he finds that some orders involve uncommon items that are not stored in a systematic manner. Locating these items takes a great deal of search time.

The grocer revamps the storage system so that all items can be easily located. As a result, the standard deviation is reduced to 3 minutes. Assum-ing that mean service time is not affected, we have an indication of the sensitivity of the system to changes in the variability of service time. The new values are $L_q = 0.91$, $L = 1.57$, $W_q = 6.8$ minutes, and $W = 11.8$ min-utes. Waiting time has been almost cut in half. The truckers are happier, and the grocer has improved his system without a large capital expenditure.

SERVICE TIME DISTRIBUTIONS

While there is considerable evidence that arrival processes tend to follow the Poisson distributions as has been indicated, service time distributions seem to be much more varied in their nature. It is, of course, for this reason that the previous model involving Poisson arrivals and an unspecified service time distribution is so valuable. With equation (2), one can compute the queuing statistics, knowing only the mean service rate and the standard deviation of service time.

The negative exponential distribution has been one of the prominent models for service time, and there is evidence that in some instances the assumption is valid. However, Nelson's study [1959] of distributions of arrivals and service times in a Los Angeles jobbing machine shop did *not* indicate that the exponential model fit the actual service time distributions adequately for all of the machine centers.

Figure 5 shows the service time distributions at a university outpatient clinic. The distributions for "walk-in" and "appointment" patients are definitely not exponential, while the "second-service" distribution is reasonably close to being represented by a negative exponential distribution. Second-service patients are those who have been seen by a physician, have been routed for tests or some other medical procedure, and are returning to complete the consultation with a physician.

Other evidence indicates that in some cases the negative exponential distribution fits. Figure 6, for example, shows that the service time at a tool crib was nearly exponentially distributed. The distribution of local telephone calls not made from a pay station has also been shown to be exponential.

Model for Poisson Input and Negative Exponential Service Times

Since the negative exponential distribution is completely described by its mean value, the standard deviation being equal to the mean, we can describe this model as a special case of equation (2). The mean of a negative exponential distribution is the reciprocal of the mean service rate, that is, $1/\mu$. Equation (7) can easily be derived from equation (2) (verify this derivation yourself):

$$L_q = \frac{\lambda^2}{\mu(\mu - \lambda)}. \tag{7}$$

Also, the probability of n units in the system is

$$P_n = \left(\frac{\lambda}{\mu}\right)^n \left(1 - \frac{\lambda}{\mu}\right). \tag{8}$$

The other relationships between L_q, L, W_q, and W, expressed by equations (4), (5), and (6), hold for the negative exponential service time distributions as well as for the case where no service time distribution is specified. For

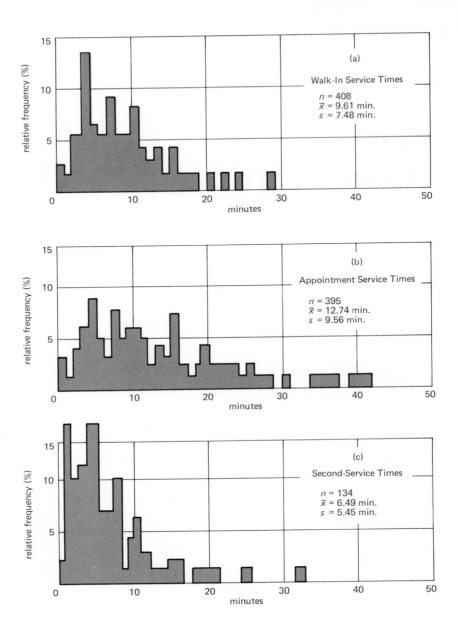

Figure 5. Histograms of service time for (a) walk-in, (b) appointment, and (c) second-service patients

From E. J. Rising, R. Baron, and B. Averill, "A Systems Analysis of a University-Health-Service Outpatient Clinic," *Operations Research*, Vol. 21, No. 5, Sept.–Oct. 1973, pp. 1030–1047; used by permission.

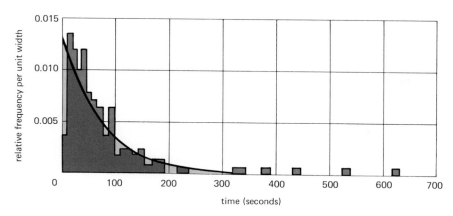

Figure 6. Service time at a tool crib

From G. Brigham, "On a Congestion Problem in an Aircraft Factory," *Operations Research*, Vol. 3, No. 4, 1955, pp. 412–28; used by permission.

the sake of simplicity, many individuals prefer to use equation (2) or (3), using the appropriate value of σ to reflect the special case.

We can now check to see the effect of exponential service times on queuing statistics for the truck dock problem. If we assume that the service time in that situation was represented by a negative exponential distribution, then $\sigma = 1/\mu = 1/12$, and the value of L_q from equation (2) is 1.33. The other queue statistics are $L = 2$, $W_q = 10$ minutes, and $W = 15$ minutes. The values are intermediate between the previous two calculations for the grocer's problem, since the value of σ is between the two previous values.

Model for Poisson Input and Constant Service Times

While constant service times are not common in actual practice, they may be reasonable in cases where a machine processes arriving items by a fixed-time cycle. Also, constant service times represent a boundary or lower limit on the value of σ in equation (2). As such, constant service time is also a special case of equation (2). The resulting equation for constant service times is

$$L_q = \frac{\lambda^2}{2\,\mu(\mu - \lambda)}.\tag{9}$$

You should derive equation (9) from equation (2) by substituting $\sigma = 0$ in equation (2).

Again, for comparison, and to gain insight into what happens in waiting lines, let us see what the result would have been if the grocer could have made service time constant at 5 minutes, that is, reduced the standard deviation to zero. Substituting in equation (9), we have $L_q = 0.67$, $L = 1.33$,

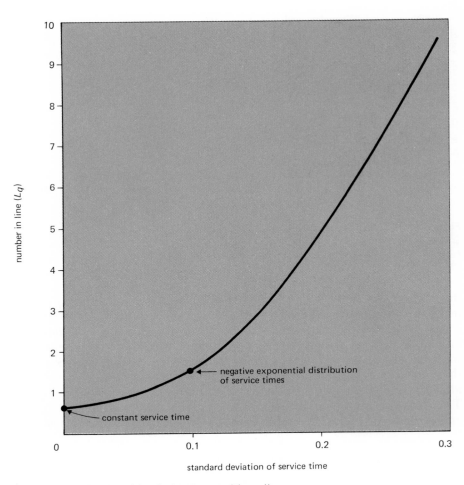

Figure 7. Relationship between waiting line length L_q and standard deviation of service time for the grocer's truck dock problem (Poisson input)

$W_q = 5$ minutes, and $W = 10$ minutes. Again, the other relationships between L_q, L, W_q, and W expressed by equations (4), (5), and (6) hold for the constant service time distribution as well as for the case where no service time distribution is specified.

We can consider then, equation (2) as a fairly general model with service time distributions described by the negative exponential, or constant service times as special cases. Figure 7 shows a graph of L_q for various values of the standard deviation, including the values for the negative exponential distribution and for constant service times. Values of the standard deviation greater than that for the negative exponential distribution occur and are

PREDICTING THE EFFECTS OF RISK — QUEUING MODELS

termed hyperexponential distributions. The extreme values of standard deviation are not representative of values found in practice; however, the tail of the curve in Figure 7 is shown to indicate how rapidly L_q increases with variability in the service time distribution.

Relationship of Queue Length to Utilization

Recall that the ratio of $\lambda/\mu = \rho$ represents the service facility utilization. If $\lambda = \mu$, then $\rho = 1$, and theoretically the service facility is used 100 percent of the time. But let us see what happens to the length of the queue as ρ varies from zero to one. Figure 8 summarizes the result for Poisson input and exponential service times. As ρ approaches unity, the number waiting in line increases rapidly and approaches infinity. Of course, we can see that this must be true by examining equations (2), (3), (7), and (9) for L_q. In all cases, the denominator goes to zero as ρ approaches unity and the value of L_q becomes infinitely large.

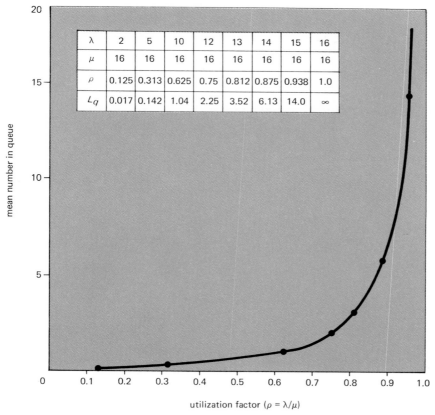

λ	2	5	10	12	13	14	15	16
μ	16	16	16	16	16	16	16	16
ρ	0.125	0.313	0.625	0.75	0.812	0.875	0.938	1.0
L_q	0.017	0.142	1.04	2.25	3.52	6.13	14.0	∞

Figure 8. Relationship of queue length to the utilization factor ρ

We see now that one of the requirements of any practical system is that $\mu > \lambda$; otherwise we cannot have a stable system. If units are arriving faster on the average than they can be processed, the waiting line and waiting time will increase continuously and no steady state can be achieved. This simple fact also indicates that there is a value to be placed on idle time in the service facility. We must trade off the value of rapid service against service facility costs, that may include substantial service facility idle time.

Multiple-Channel, Single-Phase Case

In the multiple-channel case we assume the same conditions of Poisson arrivals, exponential service times, and first-come first-served queue discipline. The effective service rate $M\mu$ must be greater than the arrival rate λ, where M is the number of channels. The facility utilization factor now becomes $\rho = \lambda/M\mu$, and we define $r = \lambda/\mu$. First, it is necessary to calculate P_0, the probability that there are zero units in the system (service facility idle), since the basic formulas all involve P_0 in their simplest forms*.

Then the formulas parallel to the single-channel case are:

mean number in waiting line

$$L_q = \frac{(r)^{M+1}}{(M-1)!(M-r)^2} \cdot P_0 , \tag{10}$$

mean number in system, including those being serviced,

$$L = L_q + r , \tag{11}$$

mean waiting time

$$W_q = \frac{L_q}{\lambda} , \tag{12}$$

---

*   Using $r = \lambda/\mu$,

$$P_0 = \frac{1}{\left[\sum_{n=0}^{M-1} \frac{r^n}{n!} \right] + \left[\frac{r^M}{M!\left(1 - \frac{r}{M}\right)} \right]} ,$$

where n is an index for the number of channels, the calculation of the term $\sum_{n=0}^{M-1} \frac{r^n}{n!}$ being the sum of $\frac{r^n}{n!}$ for all of the numbers of channels ranging from $n = 0$ to $n = M - 1$.

and mean time in system, including service,

$$W = W_q + \frac{1}{\mu}$$

$$= \frac{L}{\lambda}.$$

(13)

Wagner [1969] calculates the probability that all servers or channels are busy (the probability that there will be a delay), P(Busy). The value of L_q is then simple to compute from

$$L_q = P(\text{Busy}) \left(\frac{r}{M - r} \right).$$

(14)

If L_q is given, L, W_q, and W are easily computed from equations (11), (12), and (13). We have computed L_q for various values of M (the number of service channels) and $r = \lambda/\mu$ in Table 4 of Appendix E. The results are also plotted in Figure 9. Of course, P(Busy) can be computed from equation (14), using the values of L_q in Table 4 of Appendix E.

As an example, assume that the wholesale grocer decides to expand facilities and add a second truck dock. What is the effect on average truck waiting time? Recall the basic data: $\lambda = 8$ per hour, $\mu = 12$ per hour, but now $M = 2$. From Table 4 of Appendix E, for $M = 2$ and $r = \lambda/\mu = 8/12 = 0.67$, we find, by interpolating, that $L_q = 0.085$ trucks in line. Then $W_q = L_q/\lambda = 0.085/8 = 0.0106$ hours or 0.64 minutes. Compare these results with the single channel solution for exponential service time of $W_q = 10$ minutes. Obviously, adding the second dock eliminates the truck waiting problem. Note that overall utilization of the facilities declines from $\rho = \lambda/\mu = 0.67$ to $\rho = \lambda/M\mu = 0.34$.

The Effect of Pooling Facilities

To compare the effects of increasing or decreasing the number of channels, we can refer to the vertical distance between the curves in Figure 9. If for example, we were faced with a situation where $r = 0.9$ for the single channel case, then L_q is approximately 8 from Figure 9 or Table 4 of Appendix E. Adding a second channel reduces the average line length to $L_q = 0.23$. Adding a third channel reduces it to $L_q = 0.03$. The effects on L_q are surprisingly large; that is, we can obtain disproportionate gains in waiting time by increasing the number of channels. We can see intuitively that this might be true from Figure 8, since queue length (and waiting time) begins to increase very rapidly at about $\rho = 0.8$. A rather small increase in the capacity of the system (decrease in ρ) at these high loads can produce a large decrease in line length and waiting time.

We can examine pooling effects by comparing the doubling of capacity within the same service facility with doubling capacity through parallel

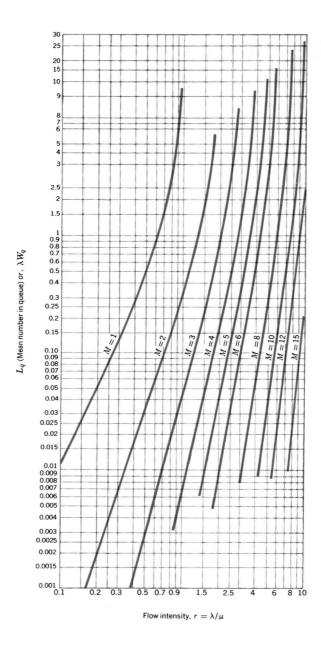

Figure 9. Flow intensity versus line length, plotted from Table 4 of Appendix E. (Poisson arrivals, negative exponential service times)

Source: E. S. Buffa, *Operations Management: The Management of Productive Systems*, Wiley/Hamilton, Santa Barbara, 1976, p. 319.

service facilities. Assume that $r = 0.8$ and $\lambda = 8$ for the base case with a single channel, as indicated in Table 2. From Table 4 of Appendix E and the interrelationships, the mean number in the system is $L = 4$ and the mean time in the system is $W = 0.5$ hours, or 30 minutes.

If we double capacity by increasing the service rate within the same channel, the mean number in the system falls to only $L = 0.67$, and the mean time in the system falls to $W = 5$ minutes, 16.7 percent of the former values (see Table 2).

TABLE 2. Effects of Doubling Capacity Within the Same Service Facility Versus Parallel Service Centers

	Base Case ($M = 1$, $r = 0.8$)	Capacity Doubled	
		Within Single Channel ($M = 1$, $r = 0.4$)	By Adding Second Channel ($M = 2$, $r = 0.8$)
L_q†	3.2000	0.2666	0.1533
$L = L_q + r$	4.0000	0.6666	0.9533
$W = L/8$	0.5000 hr.	0.0833 hr.	0.1192 hr.
	or	or	or
	30.0 min.	4.99 min.	7.15 min.

†Values from Table 4 of Appendix E.

If we double capacity by adding a second parallel channel, service improves, but not as dramatically. The mean number in the system falls to only $L = 0.95$ and the mean time to 7.15 minutes, 23.8 percent of the base values.

Looking at just the two alternatives of providing the same capacity with one large facility versus two equivalent smaller facilities (the two right hand columns of Table 2), it is clear that the single larger facility gives better service. While with the single large facility there is a larger queue ($L_q = 0.27$ versus 0.15) and waiting time is proportionately greater, this condition is compensated for by faster service, and the mean number in the system as well as the *total* time in the system are smaller for the system that pools resources.

An Example   A large manufacturing concern with a 100-acre plant had a well established medical facility, which was located at the plant offices at the eastern edge of the property. The plant had grown over the years from east to west and currently travel time to the medical facility was so great that management was considering dividing the facility. The second unit was to be established near the center of the west end of the plant. A study had been made of weighted travel times for the present single facility and for the proposed two-facility system. The result indicated that average travel time for the present large medical facility was 15 minutes. The volume averaged 1000 visits per week, or 250 man-hours for travel time. The two-facility plan would reduce the average travel time to 8 minutes, or 133 man-hours per week.

The question now was, what would happen to waiting time in the waiting rooms? For the one large facility, $\lambda = 25$ per hour, and average service time was 20 minutes, or $\mu = 3$ per hour. There were 10 physicians who handled the load. From Table 4 of Appendix E, $L_q = 2.45$, and $W_q = 2.45 \times 60/25 = 5.88$ minutes per person or 98 man-hours per week. Therefore, travel plus waiting time was $250 + 98 = 348$ man-hours per week.

The plan was to divide the medical staff for the two facilities, and it was assumed that the load would divide equally, so comparable data for the divided facilities are $\lambda = 12.5$ per hour per facility, $\mu = 3$ per hour, $M = 5$, and $r = 4.2$. From Table 4 of Appendix E, $L_q = 3.3269$ and $W_q = 16$ minutes per person or 267 man-hours per week. The travel plus waiting time for the dual facility plan was therefore $133 + 267 = 400$ man-hours per week, compared to 348 for the single large facility. Other alternatives could of course be computed, probably involving an increased medical staff.

The waiting time for the single large facility was 5.88 minutes per person compared to 16.0 minutes per person for the two-facility plan. Obviously one large facility can give better service than the two smaller facilities. If we visualize the two decentralized facilities functioning side by side, we can see intuitively why waiting time increases. If facility one were busy and had patients waiting while at the same time facility two happened to be idle, someone from the facility one waiting room could be serviced immediately by facility two, thereby reducing average waiting time. In this situation the two facilities are drawing from one waiting line. When they are physically decentralized, the facilities must draw on two independent waiting lines and the idle capacity of one cannot be used by the waiting patients of the other.

Costs and Capacity in Waiting Line Models

While many decisions concerning service systems may turn on physical factors of line length, waiting time, and the service facility utilization, very often system designs will depend on comparative costs for alternatives. The costs involved are commonly the costs of providing the service *versus* the waiting time costs. In some instances the waiting time costs are objective, as when the enterprise is employing both the servers and those waiting. The company medical facility just discussed is such a case. The company absorbed all of the travel time and waiting time costs, as well as the cost of providing the service. In such an instance, a direct cost-minimizing approach can be taken balancing the waiting costs, or the time-in-system costs, against the costs of providing the service.

When the arriving units are customers, clients, or patients, the cost of making them wait is less obvious. If they are customers, excessive waiting may cause irritation and loss of goodwill and eventually sales. Placing a value on goodwill, however, is not a straightforward exercise. In public service operations and other monopoly situations, the valuation of waiting cost may be even more tenuous because the individual cannot make alternative choices. In these situations where objective costs cannot be balanced, it may be necessary to set a standard for waiting time; for example, to adjust capacity to keep average waiting time at or below three minutes at supermarket checkout counters. Alternatively it is possible to use the multiple criteria methods of Chapter 4 and optimize over a two-criteria utility function involving time and cost. The following examples involve costs and waiting time standards.

Example One   Let us refer to the data for the company internal medical facility. Recall that there were 10 physicians, whom we will assume are paid $3000 per month, or about $6928 per week for the 10 physicians. Let us also assume that the average hourly wage of employees coming to the medical facility is $5. Computations for the single central facility yield a travel time cost of $250 \times 5 = 1250 per week, and a waiting time cost of $98 \times 5 = 490 per week. The total weekly cost is then $8668, including physicians' salaries. First, with the central facility only, how many physicians will minimize affected costs? Using Table 4 of Appendix E, we can easily determine average waiting time for 9, 10, and 11 physicians, and the resulting weekly costs. The results are shown in Table 3. So, the present policy of having 10 physicians is a little less costly than having either 9 or 11.

TABLE 3.   Utilization, Waiting Time, and Costs for Different Levels of Medical Service

	Number of Physicians		
	9	10	11
Utilization ($\rho = \lambda / M\mu$)	0.93	0.83	0.76
Mean waiting time (min.)	23.4	5.88	2.26
Weekly waiting time (hr.)	390	98	38
Cost of waiting time/week	$1950	$ 490	$ 190
Physicians' cost/week	6235	6928	7620
Total affected cost	$8185	$7418	$7810

Now, let us consider the dual facility concept, where travel cost is also affected. The travel, waiting, and physicians' cost for the central facility was $5(250 + 98) + $6928 = 8668 per week. The comparable figures for the dual facilities were $5(133 + 267) + $6928 = 8928. Would increased capacity in either or both of the dual facilities improve affected costs? The answer is no. The weekly travel and waiting costs and service costs for 5 physicians in each facility, 5 in one and 6 in the other, and 6 in each are respectively $8928, $9109, and $9292.

Now, of course, an important observation concerning the company medical facility is that the unit cost of providing the service is very large and tends to dominate, compared to unit waiting time costs. The physician is paid $3000 per month while the average employee waiting is paid only about $866 per month. If the unit costs change relative to each other, the best solution may be different.

Example Two   The manager of a large bank has the problem of providing teller service for customer demand, which varies somewhat during the business day from 10:00 A.M. to 4:00 P.M. He has a total capacity of six windows and can assign unneeded tellers to other useful work. He also wishes to give excellent service, however, which he defines in terms of customer waiting time as $W_q \leq 1$ minute. In order to give the best service for any situation, he has arranged the layout so that customers form one waiting line from which the customer at the head of the line goes to the first available teller.

TABLE 4.   Waiting Time for Different Numbers of Teller Windows Open at Different Times of Day

No. of Windows Open (M)	Length of Waiting Line (L_q)	Waiting Time in Minutes (W_q)
10:30–11:30 A.M.	$r = \lambda/\mu = 1.8$	
2	7.67	4.26
3	0.53	0.29
11:30 A.M. –1:30 P.M.	$r = \lambda/\mu = 4.8$	
5	21.64	4.5
6	2.07	0.43
1:30–3:00 P.M.	$r = \lambda/\mu = 3.8$	
4	16.94	4.45
5	1.52	0.40
3:00–4:00 P.M.	$r = \lambda/\mu = 4.6$	
5	9.29	2.01
6	1.49	0.32

The arrival pattern is as follows:

	Customers per Minute (λ)
10:00 A.M.–11:30 A.M.	1.8
11:30 A.M.– 1:30 P.M.	4.8
1:30 P.M.– 3:00 P.M.	3.8
3:00 P.M.– 4:00 P.M.	4.6

and each mean rate follows the Poisson distribution. The mean value of arrivals varies, but is always from a Poisson distribution. The mean service time is one minute and the distribution of service times is negative exponential. The service rate is $\mu = 1/1 = 1$ per minute.

The bank manager can make plans to adjust teller capacity to daily demand patterns very easily, maintaining the waiting time standard. The basic data comes from Table 4 of Appendix E and is tabulated here in Table 4. We see there that to maintain the one-minute standard for W_q, the number of windows open must be:

	No. of Windows Open
10:00 A.M.–11:30 A.M.	3
11:30 A.M.– 1:30 P.M.	6
1:30 P.M.– 3:00 P.M.	5
3:00 P.M.– 4:00 P.M.	6

FINITE WAITING LINE MODELS

Many practical waiting line problems that occur have the characteristics of finite waiting line models. This is true whenever the population of machines, men, or items that may arrive for service is limited to a relatively small finite number. The result is that we must express arrivals in terms of a unit of the population rather than as an average rate. In the infinite waiting line case the average length of the waiting line is effectively independent of the number in the arriving population, but in the finite case the number in the queue may represent a significant proportion of the arriving population, and therefore the probabilities associated with arrivals are affected.

The resulting mathematical formulations are somewhat more difficult computationally than those for the infinite queue case. Fortunately, however, finite queuing tables [Peck and Hazelwood, 1958] are available that make problem solution very simple. Although there is no definite number that we can point to as a dividing line between finite and infinite applications, the finite queuing tables have data for populations from 4 up to 250, and these data may be taken as a general guide. We have reproduced these tables for populations of 5, 10, 20, and 30 in Table 5 of Appendix E, to illustrate their use in the solution of finite queuing problems. The tables are based on a finite model for exponential times between arrivals and service times, and a first-come first-served queue discipline.

Use of the Finite Queuing Tables

The tables are indexed first by N, the size of the population. For each population size, data are classified by X, the service factor (comparable to the utilization factor in infinite queues), and by M, the number of parallel channels. For a given N, X, and M, three factors are listed in the tables: D (the probability of a delay; that is, if a unit calls for service, the probability that it will have to wait), F (an efficiency factor, used to calculate other important data), and L_q (the mean number in the waiting line). To summarize, we define the factors just expressed plus those that may be calculated as follows:

N = population (number of machines, customers, etc.)

μ = mean service rate

λ = mean arrival rate *per population unit*

X = service factor = $\dfrac{\lambda}{\lambda + \mu}$

M = number of service channels

D = probability of delay (probability that if a unit calls for service, it will have to wait)

F = efficiency factor

L_q = mean number in waiting line = $N(1 - F)$

W_q = mean waiting time = $\dfrac{1}{\mu X}\left(\dfrac{1 - F}{F}\right)$

H = mean number of units being serviced = $FNX = L - L_q$

J = mean number of units running = $NF(1 - X)$

$M - H$ = mean number of servers idle

The procedure for a given case is as follows:

1. Determine the mean service rate μ and the mean arrival rate λ, based on data or measurements of the system being analyzed.
2. Compute the service factor $X = \lambda/(\lambda + \mu)$.
3. Locate the section of the tables listing data for the population size N.

4. Locate the service factor calculated in (2) above, for the given population.
5. Read the values of D, F, and L_q for the number of channels M, interpolating between values of X when necessary.
6. Compute values for W_q, H, and J as required by the nature of the problem.

Example A hospital ward has thirty beds in one section, and the problem centers on the appropriate level of nursing care. The hospital management believes that patients should have immediate response to a call at least 80 percent of the time because of possible emergencies. Calls from patients follow a Poisson distribution, averaging almost 19 per hour for the thirty patients. The service time is approximated by a negative exponential distribution and mean service time is 5 minutes.

The hospital manager wishes to staff the ward to give service so that 80 percent of the time there will be no delay. Nurses are paid $5 per hour, and the cost of idle time at this level of service must be considered. Also, the manager wishes to know how much more patients will have to pay for the 80 percent criterion compared to a 50 percent service level for immediate response, which is the current policy.

The *solutions* to the problems posed by the hospital manager are developed through a finite queuing model. The situation requires a finite model because the maximum possible queue is 30 patients waiting for nursing care.

In terms of the finite queuing model for this situation, the mean service time is 5 minutes ($\mu = 0.2$/min., or 12/hr.), the mean time between calls is 95 minutes *per patient* ($\lambda = 0.0105$/min., or 0.632/hr.), and therefore the service factor is $X = \lambda/(\lambda + \mu) = 0.632/12.632 = 0.05$.

Scanning the finite queuing tables (Table 5 of Appendix E) under Population $N = 30$, and $X = 0.05$, we seek data for the probability of a delay of $D = 0.20$, since we wish to establish service such that there will be no delay 80 percent of the time. The closest we can come to providing this level of service is with $M = 3$ nurses and corresponding data (see Table 5 of Appendix E) of $D = 0.208$, $F = 0.994$, and $L_q = 0.18$. Note that we must select an integer number of service channels (nurses).

The cost of this level of service is the cost of employing 3 nurses or $5 \times 3 = \$15$ per hour, or $360 per day, assuming day and night care. The average number of calls waiting to be serviced will be $L_q = 0.18$ and the mean waiting time will be

$$W_q = \frac{1}{\mu X}\left(\frac{1-F}{F}\right) = \frac{1}{0.2 \times 0.05}\left(\frac{1-0.994}{0.994}\right) = 0.6 \text{ minutes}.$$

The waiting time due to queuing effects is of course negligible, as is intended.

The average number of patients being served will be $H = FNX = 0.994 \times 30 \times 0.05 = 1.49$, and the average number of nurses idle will be $3 - 1.49 = 1.51$. The equivalent value of this idleness is $1.51 \times 5 \times 24 = \$181.20$ per day.

Finally, the number of nurses needed to provide immediate service 50 percent of the time is $M = 2$ from Table 5 of Appendix E ($D = 0.571$, $F = 0.963$, and $L_q = 1.11$). The average waiting time under this policy is $W_q = 3.84$ minutes. The average cost to patients of having the one additional nurse to provide the higher level of service is, of course, $5 per hour or $120 per day. Divided among 30 patients, the cost is $4 per patient per day.

WHAT SHOULD THE MANAGER KNOW?

The waiting line models we have discussed have particular value in providing us with an insight into what happens in service systems. These models show why lines form and why waiting is probably necessary or at least costly to eliminate. They also indicate the effects of increased capacity, pooling of facilities, and variability in the service time distribution. Nevertheless, waiting line models themselves are useful only for fairly simple situations. For example, the emergency medical system discussed at the beginning of the chapter is too complicated for analysis, partly because we immediately wish to deal with multiple *mobile* service channels. In addition, the real focus of the emergency medical system problem is in location and deployment, and although queuing aspects are important, they are only part of the problem. In such situations we resort to simulation where both the probabilistic nature of the problem and its complexity can be handled effectively. We shall deal with the emergency medical system again in the next chapter.

Thus, for the manager, waiting line models can provide a better understanding of how service systems function. For example, with variable arrival rates and service times, it becomes immediately obvious that good facility utilization and good service are at odds. Indeed, there is a positive value to idle time for the service facility if we hope to provide rapid response in medical, fire protection, police protection, machine maintenance, and a variety of other services.

With a knowledge of waiting line models, a manager knows that adding parallel channels causes more than a proportional effect. Line length and waiting time drop dramatically with the addition of capacity through parallel channels. Also, the effect of pooling facilities is clear. If we wish to give good service, we can do it better with one large facility than with a number of smaller facilities offering equivalent capacity. Furthermore, the pooling effect is not one of economy of scale in the traditional sense, but results from the unique interplay between arrivals and service that allows the use of what would be idle time in decentralized smaller facilities.

Through an examination of waiting line models we noted that variation in the service time can have a very important effect on line length and waiting time. In the Poisson input, exponential holding time case, half of the queuing or congestion is in the service time variation. We see this by comparing equations (7) and (9). The other half of the congestion is due to the variable arrival process. Thus, managers who understand the source of the congestion can possibly make important improvements in service by *not* assuming that the arrival process is a given and out of their control. It may be possible to schedule arrivals or resort to other techniques to reduce variation in the arrival process. Indeed, a manager would wish to do everything possible to smooth demand, as has been commonly practiced in manufacturing systems.

In some instances we may be able to get the customer, patient, or client to do something productive while he is waiting. If we can transfer some of the service activity to the one being serviced, cost may be reduced, and this approach may be one of the few strategies available for managers in improving productivity in service activities. The acceptance of the idea of the customer doing part of the work himself has become quite widespread in self-service markets, gas stations, cafeterias, and other facilities.

Check Your Understanding

1. Discuss the nature of service systems. What characteristics of these systems make them candidates for study as queuing systems?

2. Classify the following in terms of the four basic waiting line structures:
   a. assembly line
   b. large bank—six tellers (one waiting line for each)
   c. cashier at a restaurant
   d. one-chair barbershop
   e. cafeteria line
   f. general hospital
   g. post office—four windows drawing from one waiting line

3. Define the following terms:
   a. arrival process
   b. queue discipline
   c. infinite waiting line model
   d. finite waiting line model
   e. single-phase model
   f. multiple-phase model
   g. single-channel model
   h. multiple-channel model

4. Identify the unit being processed, the server or service facility, and the waiting line structure for each of the following:
   a. car wash
   b. fire station

c. toll bridge
d. shipping dock
e. appliance repair shop
f. TV repairman
g. supermarket
h. large department store

5. Given a Poisson distribution of arrivals with mean of $\lambda = 5$ per hour, what is the probability of an arrival of $x = 4$ within an hour? What is the probability of the occurrence of 15 minutes between arrivals?

6. A community is served by a single ambulance based at the hospital. During peak periods the call rate averages 3 per hour (Poisson distribution) and the average service time is 15 minutes with a standard deviation of 5 minutes.
   a. Compute the average number of emergencies waiting during peak demand.
   b. Compute the average waiting time and the average system idle time. Which is most relevant as a criterion in this system?

7. A machine in a processing line is designed to perform its function automatically in a constant time of one minute. Items to be processed are fed from the operation upstream, which is manual. The arrival rate to the machine is Poisson distributed and averages 50 units per hour. In spite of the fact that the machine is faster than the preceding manual operation, the foreman is perturbed by the fact that there is an in-process inventory piled up in front of the machine and at the same time, the machine utilization is only 83 percent.
   Explain how the system functions. What is the average in-process inventory in front of the machine? Verify the machine utilization figure. How can the foreman improve the machine utilization?

8. A taxi cab company has four cabs that operate out of a given taxi stand. Customer arrival rates and service rates are described by the Poisson distribution. The average arrival rate is 12 per hour and the average service time is 17.5 minutes. The service time follows a negative exponential distribution.
   a. Calculate the utilization factor.
   b. From Table 4 of Appendix E, determine the mean number of customers waiting.
   c. Determine the mean number of customers in the system.
   d. Calculate the mean waiting time.
   e. Calculate the mean time in the system.
   f. What would be the utilization factor if the number of taxi cabs were increased from four to five?
   g. What would be the effect of the increase in the number of cabs from four to five on the mean number in the waiting line?

h. What would be the effect of reducing the number of taxi cabs from four to three on the mean number in the waiting line?

9. A secretary serves five faculty members, performing a variety of stenographic and other clerical duties. On the average, faculty members bring her three jobs per hour and the average job takes 10 minutes. Both arrival and service processes are adequately represented by the Poisson distribution.

   a. Compute the mean number of faculty members waiting to be served.
   b. Compute the mean waiting time.
   c. Compute the mean time a faculty member must wait from the time he gives his work to the secretary until receiving the work completed.
   d. What percent of the time is the secretary idle?
   e. What is the probability that a faculty member bringing work to the secretary will find her busy?

10. Explain the benefits that accrue from pooling facilities.

Problems

1. Present day universities have become complex systems of scholars where a value must be placed on communication, both within systems that are now multicampus giants and between systems throughout the nation. It is not surprising then that WATS (wide area telephone service) should be considered to allow faculty members and administrators to make unlimited toll-free long-distance calls.

   Data were gathered for one such system, that yielded the following information:

   1) The frequency of calls was estimated to be 10.4 per hour, based on present use of long-distance service plus an estimate of increased use if WATS were available (Poisson distribution).
   2) The length of calls was estimated to be 15 minutes (exponential distribution).
   3) The current long-distance telephone bill average was $10,000 per month.
   4) After much haggling, average faculty-administrator time was valued at $10 per hour.
   5) A WATS line costs $2000 per month.

   Assume an average of 173 hours per month. The central issue finally resolved into the number of WATS lines that would be justified.

   a. Formulate the problem as a decision to determine the number of WATS lines to install. What cost components are involved and how do the costs vary with the number of lines installed?
   b. Determine the number of WATS lines to install. What criteria have you used?

2. A supermarket chain has 30 stores in a large metropolitan area and supplies its stores from a central warehouse. The general routine is to supply each store every day on the basis of the store order list. Store managers compile these lists daily and transmit them to the warehouse.

At the warehouse, store orders are taken in sequence as they arrive and "order picker" crews assemble the order in designated staging areas using a hand truck system for smaller items and dispatching fork truck operators to fill skid load items. When a store order is complete, it awaits transportation.

A fleet of five large closed trucks transports the orders. Trucks are loaded at the truck dock, that can accommodate three trucks simultaneously. A special crew of loaders is used to load trucks from the staging areas. While the trucks are being loaded, the driver obtains the documents that indicate the list of items shipped and the store destination.

After loading, the trucks are driven to the store destination, and the contents are unloaded at the store truck dock by store personnel. The driver then returns the truck to the warehouse. At the end of the day, the truck is returned to the maintenance area at the warehouse where it is washed, refueled, and serviced for general maintenance and repair.

Formulate the system as a sequence of waiting line problems by first developing a flow chart that identifies the arrival, service, and exit processes. Identify each waiting line situation in terms of its structure and the type of waiting line model that might apply. In order to analyze the system as a queuing system, what information is needed?

3. The order picking crews for the warehouse described in problem 2 work an eight-hour day, and each of the 30 store orders must be filled during the shift. Studies indicate that the time to fill an order averages 47.9 minutes, and the distribution of times is approximated by the negative exponential distribution. Orders come in from store managers throughout the day, and the time between these orders is also approximated by the negative exponential distribution. The warehouse manager wants to be sure that orders are not delayed too long and wants an order backlog (unfinished orders) of no more than an average of one, in order to ensure that trucks do not wait.

How many crews does he need to maintain this standard? The aggregate wage of a crew is $10 per hour. What fraction of the time are the crews idle? What does the manager's policy on order backlog cost in terms of crew idleness?

4. After tires have been assembled, they go to curing presses where the various layers of rubber and fiber are vulcanized into one homogeneous piece and the final shape, including the tread, is molded. Different tires require somewhat different curing times, which may range up to 90 minutes or more. The press operator can unload and reload a press in 3 minutes, so that one operator would normally service a bank of curing presses. Each press may be molding tires of a different design, so that presses are "arriving" for service at nearly random times. The presses automatically open when the preset cure time is complete.

In servicing a bank of 30 presses, the operator is ranging over a wide area approximately 90 by 200 feet. Indicator lights flash on, signifying that the press is ready for service, and the operator walks to the open press, unloading and reloading it. Sometimes, of course, the position of the open press may be quite close to the operator so that his walk is fairly short. In rare instances the operator is at one end of the area and the press requiring service is at the other end, requiring a fairly long walk. Thus the operator's tasks in rendering service are made up of walking plus unloading and reloading the presses. The average time for these tasks is 3 minutes and is approximated by the negative exponential distribution.

When a press is idle, waiting to be serviced, the only costs that continue are the services to the press, mainly heat supply. The cost of supplying this heat is $4 per hour per press. Operators are paid $3.50 per hour, and contribution per tire is $5. If the average cure time of tires being produced is 80 minutes, determine the number of operators (number of channels) to be used when market demand is less than plant capacity. When market demand is above plant capacity.

5. In the manufacture of photographic film, there is a specialized process of perforating the edges of the 35-mm film used in movie and still cameras. A bank of 20 such machines are required to meet production requirements. The severe service requirements cause breakdowns that need to be repaired quickly because of high downtime costs. Because of breakdown rates and downtime costs, management is considering the installation of a preventive maintenance program, that they hope will improve the situation.

The present breakdown rate is 3 per hour per machine, or a time between breakdowns of 20 minutes. The average time for service is only 3 minutes. The breakdown rate follows a Poisson distribution, and the service times a negative exponential distribution. The crew simply repairs the machines in the sequence of breakdown. Machine downtime is estimated to cost $9 per hour, and present repair parts cost an average of $1 per breakdown. Maintenance repairmen are paid $6 per hour. The breakdown rates, service times, and repair parts costs are expected to change with different levels of preventive maintenance as indicated in Table 5.

What repair crew size and level of preventive maintenance should be adopted to minimize costs?

TABLE 5. Expected Changes in Breakdown Rates, Service Time, and Cost of Repair Parts for Three Levels of Preventive Maintenance

Level of Preventive Maintenance	Breakdown Rate (%)	Service Time (%)	Cost of Repair Parts (%)
L_1	−30	+20	+ 50
L_2	−40	+35	+ 80
L_3	−50	+75	+120

References

Brigham, F., "On a Congestion Problem in an Aircraft Factory," *Operations Research,* Vol. 3, No. 4, 1955, pp. 412–28.

Churchman, C. W., R. L. Ackoff, and E. L. Arnoff, *Introduction to Operations Research,* John Wiley & Sons, New York, 1957.

Cox, D. R., and W. L. Smith, *Queues,* John Wiley & Sons, New York, 1961.

Fitzsimmons, J. A., "Emergency Medical Systems: A Simulation Study and Computerized Method for Deployment of Ambulances," Ph.D. Dissertation, University of California, Los Angeles, 1970.

———, "A Methodology for Emergency Ambulance Deployment," *Management Science,* Vol. 19, No. 6, February 1973, pp. 627–36.

Larson, R. C., *Urban Police Patrol Analysis,* MIT Press, Cambridge, Mass., 1972.

Morse, P. M., *Queues, Inventories and Maintenance,* John Wiley & Sons, New York, 1958.

Nelson, R. T., "An Empirical Study of Arrival, Service Time, and Waiting Time Distributions of a Job Shop Production Process," Research Report No. 60, Management Sciences Research Project, University of California, Los Angeles, 1959.

Peck, L. G., and R. N. Hazelwood, *Finite Queuing Tables,* John Wiley & Sons, New York, 1958.

Prabhu, N. U., *Queues and Inventories,* John Wiley & Sons, New York, 1965.

Saaty, T. L., "Resumé of Useful Formulas in Queuing Theory," *Operations Research,* Vol. 5, No. 2, April 1957, pp. 161–200.

———, *Elements of Queuing Theory,* McGraw-Hill, New York, 1961.

Thierauf, R. J., and R. C. Klekamp, *Decision Making Through Operations Research,* second edition, John Wiley & Sons, New York, 1975.

Wagner, H. M., *Principles of Operations Research,* Prentice-Hall, Englewood Cliffs, N.J., 1969.

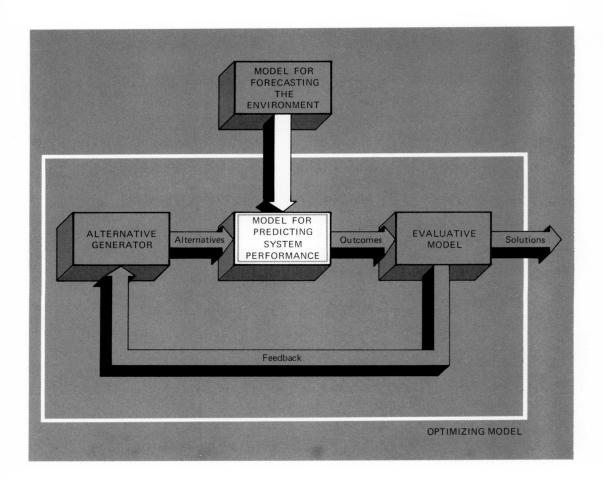

11

Predicting the Effects of Risk — Monte Carlo Simulation

The complexity of many managerial systems, as well as the need to include empirical data, often makes the prediction of performance by analytical models either impossible or impractical. In such situations, simulation is the common methodology for predicting performance.

Simulation is a general term that means "imitation." In fact, the rigorous technique of simulation that has developed in operations research and management science does imitate the essential characteristics of processes, usually with the aid of a computer. Most of the simulation models with which we deal in management science represent a problem by imitating what would happen in the real system, then keeping track of what happens in the model. By driving the system with a large sample of input data and recording results, we can build a representative record of what would probably happen if the policy, design, or system were actually installed. Simulation models are in a real sense management's laboratory.

Kinds of Simulation Models

Simulation models may be discrete or continuous, deterministic or stochastic. In continuous systems, the parameters that describe the system can take on any values within the ranges specified. Wind tunnel simulation of flight is an example of a continuous simulation system. Discrete systems take on only particular values within the possible ranges of parameters. These systems are characterized by the events that occur, and we keep track of the events, their timing, and other parameters that may describe them. In managerial systems we commonly deal with discrete simulation systems.

As noted, a system may also be deterministic or stochastic, depending on the nature of input, process, and output at various stages of the system. The output of a deterministic system, or the process within a system, is known exactly when the input is specified—there is no unaccounted for variation. In other words, the transformation function of the predictive model provides a completely determined output. The simple relationship in physics between force, mass, and acceleration is an example, $F = ma$. Given the mass m and the input state of the acceleration a, the force F is assumed to be determined exactly. Chapters 7 and 8 dealt with deterministic simulations.

Stochastic systems, however, respond to a given input with a range of possible outputs, following some distribution of values. For example, if in an emergency medical system there is a call for service, the time to perform the service is not a fixed time, as we noted in the discussion on queuing systems (Chapter 10). Service time will depend on many things that in themselves are not predictable, such as distance to the scene, traffic density, time of day, and availability of the ambulance. In addition, there may be random variation in service time that has no logical explanation.

Probably most processes in managerial systems are in fact stochastic; however, we often use deterministic relationships and average relationships when they reasonably represent what happens. They are simpler to handle and require less execution time in complex simulation models. On the other hand, many processes are only described adequately by probability distributions, such as those reflecting variable demand for services and products, and the queuing or waiting line models of Chapter 10. Special simulation techniques called Monte Carlo, or simulated sampling, are used to introduce statistical variations in simulation models. We shall concentrate our discussion on these methods at a later point in this chapter.

Simulation models in managerial systems, then, are usually of the discrete type and are often a combination of deterministic and stochastic processes, especially in models representing a complex system.

THE SIMULATION PROCESS

Conceptually, the simulation process is a simple one, once we have a carefully specified model. While many other variables may be involved in discrete event simulations, they are usually related in some way to the passage of time. There are in general two ways of organizing the simulation process: around the occurrence of discrete events and around updating events for discrete time periods.

Discrete Event Simulation

In the *discrete event* approach, the entire process follows the sequence of events or steps in the process, keeping track of what happens. Let us take a simple example, such as driving to the office each morning. Suppose the

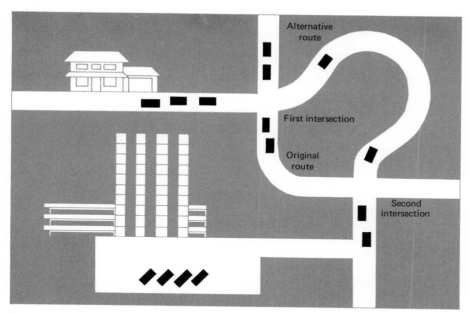

Figure 1. Pictorial representation of the drive to the office

From J. Reitman, *Computer Simulation Applications*, John Wiley & Sons, Inc., New York, 1971, Figure 2.3, p. 41; used by permission.

drive involves only two intersections as shown in Figure 1. A decision must be made at the first intersection: should the original or the alternative route be taken? The diagram of Figure 1 shows the alternative routes and gives a general description of how to get from home to office.

Suppose, however, that we are interested in choosing departure times for minimum driving time, or that we wish to predict driving time for different departure times. For these purposes, Figure 1 is inadequate. While some of the factors that bear on driving time are implied in Figure 1, they are not explicit. The flow chart of Figure 2 adds detail, indicating that competing traffic will be a factor. There is a traffic light at the first intersection, and the driver joins a queue and may have to wait. Also, at the traffic light, a decision between alternative routes must be made. Competing traffic is a factor with either route, though it may not have an equivalent effect for both routes. Finally, both routes lead to a second queue at the second intersection and a continuation to the office.

While the flow chart of Figure 2 is still incomplete, it comes closer to describing the probabilistic nature of the time required to make the drive. If we are to predict driving time, we obviously need more information regarding speed in relation to competing traffic, waiting time at intersec-

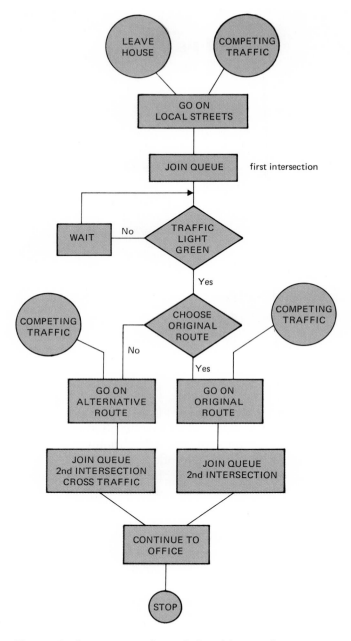

Figure 2. Coarse overview of the drive to the office

From J. Reitman, *Computer Simulation Applications*, John Wiley & Sons, Inc., New York, 1971, Figure 2.1, p. 32; used by permission.

tions, choice rules for the alternative routes, and the influence of abnormal events. We will not attempt prediction at this time, however.

If we were to attempt to simulate the drive to the office, we might logically follow the sequence of events shown in Figure 2 and record what happens at queues and intersections, and so on. Elapsed time between events would be recorded as the simulation progresses. Figure 3(a) is a simple flow chart describing the discrete event process.

Discrete Time Updating Simulation

If we were to attempt to simulate the drive to the office by the *discrete time updating* approach, we would select a smallest time unit for the study and examine the state of the system in all of its aspects at the end of each time interval, recording and updating the status of each element. The time interval might be 0.01 minute, 1 minute, 5 minutes, or 1 hour, as appropriate. When the total planned simulation time is equaled or exceeded, the process is stopped and the results printed out.

In the drive to the office example, perhaps the time interval would be set at 0.1 minute. At the end of the first 0.1 minute, we would determine where we were along the route, recording all relevant data at that time and reflecting all changes that might have occurred. These changes might be in the length of queues and traffic density. The time clock is then updated and the process repeated. Within some one of the time intervals, each of the events occurs, such as waiting for stop lights and the routing decisions. Figure 3(b) is a simple flow chart describing the discrete time updating simulation process.

In both the discrete event and the discrete time updating approaches, repetitions might be programmed to provide sample sizes large enough to average out stochastic effects.

In either the discrete event or discrete time updating simulation systems we could be dealing with stochastic processes or combinations of both deterministic and stochastic processes. Since dealing with stochastic processes as well as empirical data is so important in simulation, we now turn our attention to this subject.

MONTE CARLO — SIMULATED SAMPLING

Simulated sampling, generally known as Monte Carlo, makes it possible to introduce into a system data that have the statistical properties of some empirical distribution. If the model involves the flow of orders according to the actual demand distribution experienced, we can simulate the "arrival" of an order by Monte Carlo sampling from the actual distribution, so that the timing and flow of activities in the simulated system parallels the actual experience. If we are studying the breakdown of a certain machine (perhaps an office copying machine) caused by bearing failure, we can simulate

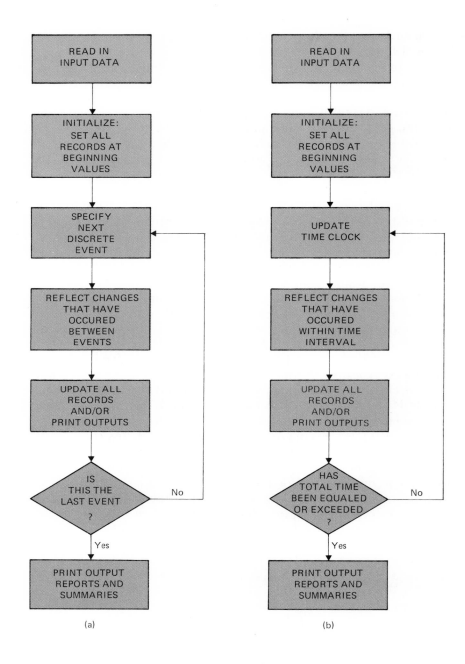

Figure 3. Overall simulation process organized around (a) discrete events and (b) discrete time updating

typical breakdown times through simulated sampling from the distribution of bearing lives.

An Example

Suppose we are dealing with an emergency medical system, and we wish to estimate the level of service that can be maintained by one ambulance. We have available, or must obtain, data concerning the frequency of calls for service and the service time. As we noted in Chapter 10, if these distributions followed certain mathematical functions, we could compute directly the results that we will determine here by simulation methods. However, the data summarized by Figures 4 and 5 are empirical data, and we shall assume that they are not adequately described by any known mathematical model that we can solve. Our procedure follows the steps described in the following paragraphs.

Step 1. Determine the distributions of the time between calls for service and service time. If they were not available directly, we would have to make a study to determine these distributions, or use records of calls for service and service time, if available, from which the distributions might be constructed. Figures 4 and 5 show the distributions of the time between calls for service and the service times for 161 emergencies. These distributions will be the basis for our simulation.

Step 2. Convert the frequency distributions to cumulative probability distributions (see Figures 6 and 7). This conversion is made by summing the frequencies that are less than or equal to each call or service time and plotting them. The cumulative frequencies are then converted to probabilities.

As an example, let us take Figure 4 and convert it to the cumulative distribution of Figure 6. Beginning at the lowest value for the time between calls, 5 minutes, there are 30 occurrences. For the call time 5 minutes, 30 is plotted on the cumulative chart. For the call time 10 minutes, there were 34 occurrences, but there were 64 occurrences of 10 minutes or less, so the value 64 is plotted for 10 minutes. For the call time 15 minutes, there were 27 occurrences recorded, but there were 91 occurrences of calls for 15 minute intervals or less.

Figure 6 was constructed from Figure 4 by proceeding in this way. When the cumulative frequency distribution was completed, a cumulative probability scale was constructed on the right of Figure 6 by assigning the number 1.0 to the maximum value, 161, and dividing the resulting scale into 10 equal parts. This process results in a cumulative empirical probability distribution. From Figure 6 we can say that 100 percent of the call time values were 50 minutes or less; 99 percent were 45 minutes or less, and so on. Figure 7 was constructed from Figure 5 in a comparable way.

Step 3. Sample at random from the cumulative distributions to determine specific times between calls for service and service times; use these data in simulating the emergency medical operation. This sampling is conducted

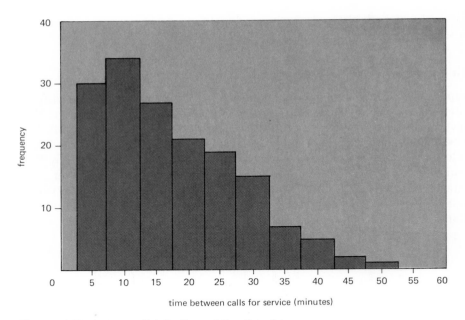

Figure 4. Frequency distribution of the time between calls for 161 emergencies ($n = 161$, $\bar{x} = 17.5$ minutes)

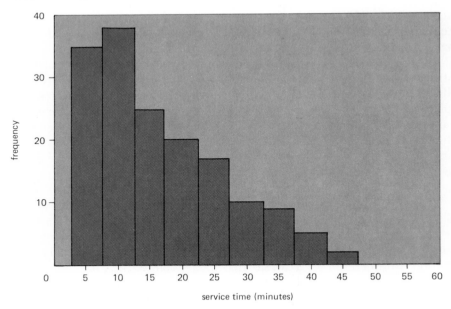

Figure 5. Frequency distribution for the service time of 161 emergency calls ($n = 161$, $\bar{x} = 16.5$ minutes)

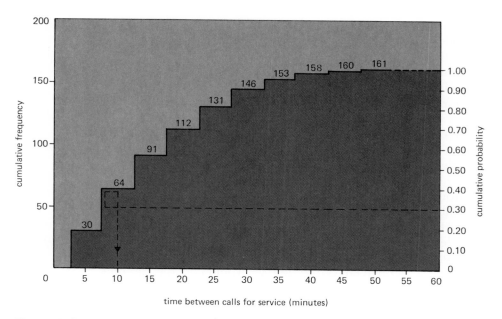

Figure 6. Cumulative distribution of the time between calls for service

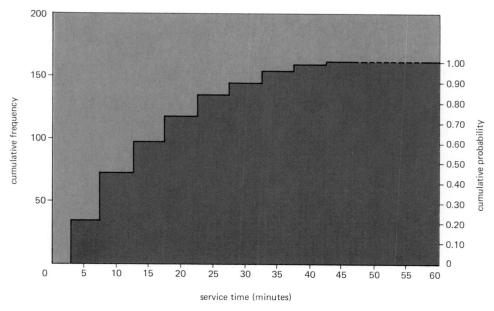

Figure 7. Cumulative distribution of service times

by selecting numbers between 0 and 100 at random (representing probabilities). The random numbers could be selected by any random process, such as drawing numbered chips from a box. The easiest way is to use a table of random numbers such as those included in Table 6 of Appendix E. (For example, select a starting point in the table at random and take two-digit numbers in sequence in that column.)

The random numbers were used to enter the cumulative distributions to obtain time values in proportion to their occurrence in the distributions. An example is shown in Figure 6 where the random number 30 is shown to select a call time of 10 minutes.

By using random numbers to obtain call time values in this fashion from Figure 6, we will obtain call time values in proportion to the probability of occurrence indicated by the original frequency distribution. As a matter of fact, at this point we can construct a table of random numbers that selects certain call and service times. For example, reading from Figure 6, the random numbers 1 through 19 give us a call time of 5 minutes, etc. That is to say, 19 percent of the time we would obtain a call time of 5 minutes, $40 - 19 = 21$ percent of the time we would obtain a call time of 10 minutes, and so on. Table 1 shows the random number equivalents for Figures 6 and 7.

Sampling from either the cumulative distributions of Figures 6 and 7 or from Table 1 will now give call times and service times in proportion to the original distributions, just as if actual calls and services were happening. Table 2 gives a sample of 20 times between calls for service and service times, determined in this way.

Step 4. *Simulate the actual operation of calls and services.* The structure of what we wish to do in simulating the emergency medical operation

TABLE 1. Random Numbers Used to Select Calls for Service and Service Times

Time Between Calls for Service			Service Times		
These Random Numbers	Select ⟶	These Call Times (min)	These Random Numbers	Select ⟶	These Service Times (min)
1–19		5	0–20		5
20–40		10	21–44		10
41–57		15	45–60		15
58–70		20	61–72		20
71–81		25	73–83		25
82–91		30	84–89		30
92–95		35	90–94		35
96–98		40	95–99		40
99		45	100		45
100		50			

Note: These data are in proportion to the occurrence probabilities of the original distribution.

TABLE 2. Simulated Sample of 20 Times Between Calls for Service and Service Times

Times Between Calls for Service		Service Times	
Random Number	Call Time* (min)	Random Number	Service Time† (min)
27	10	71	20
89	30	43	10
27	10	16	5
51	15	64	20
96	40	75	25
54	15	28	10
13	5	54	15
53	15	11	5
14	5	12	5
87	30	86	30
54	15	92	35
63	20	06	5
00	50	49	15
13	5	03	5
28	10	63	20
15	5	41	10
83	30	09	5
29	10	72	20
49	15	14	5
01	5	83	25

*Data from Figure 6.
†Data from Figure 7.

is shown by the flow chart of Figure 8. This operation involves selecting a call time, then determining whether or not the ambulance is available. If the ambulance is not available, the patient must wait until it is, and we can compute the wait time easily. If the ambulance is available, the question is, did the ambulance have to wait? If it did, we compute the ambulance idle time. If the ambulance did not have to wait, we select a service time and proceed according to the flow chart, repeating the overall process as many times as desired, providing a mechanism for stopping the procedure when the desired number of cycles has been completed.

The simulation of the emergency medical operation for 20 calls for service is shown in Table 3. Here we have used the call times and service times selected by random numbers in Table 2. We assume that time begins when the first call occurs, and we accumulate call time from that point. The service time required for the first call was 20 minutes, and since this occurrence is the first in our record, neither the patient nor the ambulance had to wait. The second call occurred at 30 minutes, but the ambulance was

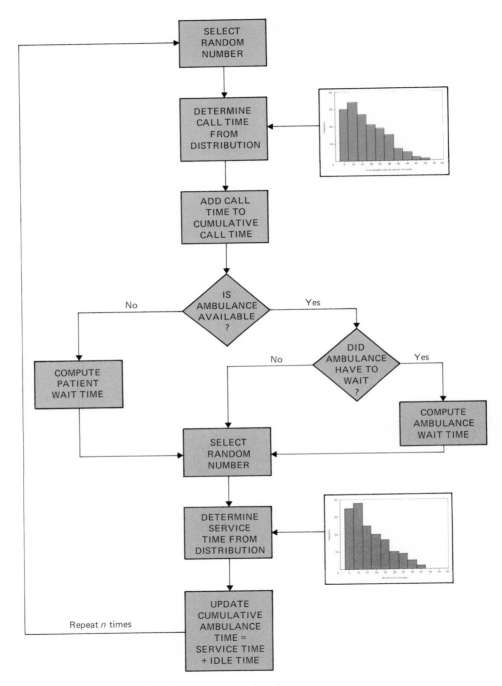

Figure 8. Flow chart showing structure of ambulance simulation

PREDICTING THE EFFECTS OF RISK—MONTE CARLO SIMULATION

TABLE 3. Simulated Ambulance Calls and Service

Time of Call for Service	Time Service Begins	Time Service Ends	Patient Waiting Time	Ambulance Idle Time
0	0	20	0	0
30	30	40	0	10
40	40	45	0	0
55	55	75	0	10
95	95	120	0	20
110	120	130	10	0
115	130	145	15	0
130	145	150	15	0
135	150	155	15	0
165	165	195	0	10
180	195	230	15	0
200	230	235	30	0
250	250	265	0	15
255	265	270	10	0
265	270	290	5	0
270	290	300	20	0
300	300	305	0	0
310	310	330	0	5
325	330	335	5	0
330	335	360	5	0
			145	70

available at the end of 20 minutes, so it waited 10 minutes for the next call to occur. Note that we are using the "discrete event" simulation process described by Figure 3(a).

We proceed in this fashion, making computations according to the requirements of the simulation model to obtain the record of Table 3. At the bottom of Table 3 we show that for the sample of 20 emergencies, total patient waiting time was 145 minutes, and total ambulance idle time was 70 minutes. Of course, to obtain a realistic picture we would have to use a much larger sample.

Interpretation of Results

Interpreting the results of the emergency medical system simulation is rather hazardous in view of the small sample; however, it would appear that the system is too heavily loaded for one ambulance to give really excellent service, since patient waiting time was required for 55 percent of the calls, while the ambulance was servicing another call. (Note, however, that response time for emergency medical systems, as defined in Figure 1 of Chapter 10, is somewhat longer, since response time includes waiting time plus ambulance travel time to the scene.)

The manager of such an emergency medical system would undoubtedly ask about the effect of doubling capacity by adding a second ambulance. We can, of course, predict the general effect from our knowledge of queuing systems—the patient waiting time will drop dramatically. In fact, using the same sample of call and service times from Table 2, but simulating for a system of two ambulances, a 5-minute patient waiting time is required in only one instance. The price paid for the improved service is the cost of a second ambulance and the added operating costs. The ambulance idle time increases from only about 20 percent to almost 60 percent for the small sample.

COMPUTER SIMULATION

If a computer were programmed to simulate the emergency medical system, we would place the two cumulative distributions in the memory unit of the computer. Through the random number generator program, the computer would generate a random number and thereby select a call time. By comparing cumulative call time with cumulative ambulance time, the computer program could determine whether or not the ambulance was available, and if it was available, whether or not it had to wait. The computations of patient waiting time, or ambulance idle time, would be routinely made and the program would direct the selection of another random number, thereby determining a service time. The necessary computations could then be made, with the resulting values being held in memory. The cycle would then repeat as many times as desired, so that a large run could be made easily and with no more effort than a small run. With the aid of a computer, a simulation model can become very realistic, reflecting all sorts of contingency situations that may be representative of the real problem.

The ambulance system example is a demonstration of a manual Monte Carlo simulation. Its value is in the close contact with the problem and the sequence of simulated sampling and resulting calculations. Often, however, the performance evaluation of systems through simulation is complex and large scale so that manual methods are entirely impractical. In addition, even for simple systems such as the emergency medical system example, the need for large samples to describe adequately the performance of stochastic elements of a system eliminates manual methods from consideration. Digital computer simulation is therefore almost synonymous with the term "simulation" so far as management science is concerned.

Simulation Languages

General purpose computer languages such as FORTRAN and PL/1 can be used to implement virtually any computing problem, and many simulation programs have been written in these languages. Because of some special common properties of simulation programs, however, simulation languages have been developed that have programming efficiency and are very powerful. We will not attempt a thorough coverage of these languages, but we will discuss the basic nature of two of them, GPSS and SIMSCRIPT. (See Reitman [1971, Chapter 5] for a discussion of criteria and comparative advantanges and disadvantages of various simulation languages.)

GPSS The fundamental structure of GPSS (General Purpose Simulation System) is conceptually different from the statement-oriented general purpose languages such as FORTRAN. GPSS defines four kinds of entities: dynamic, facility, statistical, and operational. Each of them has specific functions and calls forth automatically corollary functions commonly associated with simulation of systems. In so doing they provide a rational and efficient structure for simulation. We will discuss each briefly and then relate them to an example to illustrate their functions.

Dynamic entities are transactions of the system and they may be created and destroyed as required. The nature of each transaction is defined by stating values for parameters associated with the transaction. For example, in the drive to the office, the transactions represent vehicles that must be moved through blocks.

The *facilities* used by the system are specified as entities and they service the transactions. Examples of facilities might be a toll booth, a road, a check-out counter, a machine processing center, and so on. GPSS automatically keeps track of utilization and other statistics on facilities, and these data are a part of the output of the simulation.

Statistical entities may be called on for analysis of results. An example is a queue entity that can automatically handle the statistical properties of transactions that pile up for use by facilities.

Blocks determine the flow logic of the system as well as the logic for the flow of transactions. There are about 40 to 60 blocks in GPSS, depending on which version is used, and these blocks are the heart of the simulation structure, since they control the way transactions interact with facilities, the transaction parameters, output, flow direction, etc.

A GPSS Example.[*] The "drive to the office" example discussed earlier in the chapter and described by Figures 1 and 2 serves as an example that illustrates the use of the various entities as well as being a good example of simulation.

First, in order to simulate the drive to the office, there are many assumptions that must be made explicit.

1. The driver gets into his car every morning at the same time, 7:30 A.M.

2. The car leaves the driveway and merges into local street traffic without being delayed.

3. Average speed on local streets is considered to be 25 mph, unless subject to slowdown from traffic and abnormal conditions.

[*] Summarized from J. Reitman, *Computer Simulation Applications*, John Wiley & Sons, New York, 1971, pp. 40–77; used by permission.

4. At the first major intersection there is a control signal and interaction with other traffic.

5. Competing cars will interact to provide degrees of traffic density. These cars come from separate sources. Their arrival rate at the intersection is variable and externally controlled.

6. At the first intersection there is a choice of two routes to the next major intersection. The choice is determined by traffic density, intersection delays, and abnormal conditions.

7. Average speed to the next intersection depends on the selection of route, either 35 mph for the original route or 55 mph on the alternative route. Both are subject to slowdown from traffic and abnormal conditions.

8. The second intersection is considered in a similar manner except that there is no route selection.

9. Average speed to the office parking lot, 15 mph, is also subject to slowdown and abnormal conditions.

These nine assumptions provide a framework for the specific input data, logical relationships, and analytical equations required to simulate the drive to the office. The major items of these inputs are:

1. The average levels of competing traffic during the various parts of the trip in local traffic, over the original route and alternative route must be specified exactly. Over the local segment there is a maximum of 10 vehicles generated every three minutes for a rate of 200 vehicles per hour. The amount of traffic generated during each three-minute interval from 7:00 to 9:30 A.M. is used as a basis for each day's traffic. The actual traffic for each day is derived from the value for the three-minute interval as modified by a random number.

2. The equations for the time to traverse each part of the trip are in the following form: time = route distance/nominal speed × slowdown factor caused by traffic density × abnormal condition factor, where either the slowdown or abnormal factor is unity if there is no influence.

3. At each intersection, the rules are for the car to join the queue, if there is one. The queue discipline is first in, first out.

4. The rules for the route selection at the first intersection are either to continue on the original route or to take the alternative. The following factors control the choice:
   a. Signal condition at signal light—when the light is green or there is no queue, continue on the original route.
   b. Indication of traffic density—if there is light traffic, stay on original route.
   c. Abnormal conditions—when the weather is poor, rainy or snowy, or if there is an indication of an abnormal situation, take the alternative route.

We see that the simple problem of driving to the office becomes more complex if we hope to represent its crucial features in a simulation model.

As the oldest and most commonly used simulation language [Maisel and Gnugnuoli, 1972, p. 162], GPSS offers great power and a logical structure to evaluate system performance by means of simulation. Details for users are available in the *GPSS V Users' Manual* [IBM Corporation, 1970], and in works by Maisel and Gnugnuoli [1972] and Reitman [1971].

Results Based on a GPSS simulation involving a 100-day sample, the range of times to drive to the office was 14 to 17 minutes, with an average of 14.669 minutes. The standard output also gave a variety of other statistics for the original and alternative routes, and a full range of statistics on the queues at the three intersections. In addition, graphic output was called for as shown in Figures 9 and 10. Figure 9 shows a histogram for drive duration, indicating that the most likely trip time was 14 minutes. Figure 10 shows the maximum queue size at each of the three intersections with the queue statistics output shown above the histogram. The average transfer time through the intersections is given in seconds.

SIMSCRIPT Another very powerful computer language with special characteristics adapted to simulation is SIMSCRIPT. The conceptual framework is oriented around entities that can be assigned various attributes. For example, in the drive to the office problem, each intersection (an entity) has the attributes of a signal, a stated capacity, and a waiting line or queue.

The SIMSCRIPT user prepares his program following a prescribed format in which he names and numbers temporary and permanent variables and sets, assigning attributes to each. To this description he must add programs to perform the required operations. With the system described in standard format, the SIMSCRIPT compiler regards the system description and programs as input data, preparing computer instructions for performing the system simulation. While the foregoing statement is true, it is not meant to convey the idea that the process is simple.

SIMSCRIPT is the second most commonly used simulation language [Maisel and Gnugnuoli, 1972, p. 162] and also offers great power and a logical structure to evaluate system performance by simulation. Time and effort to develop a program in SIMSCRIPT would be greater than for GPSS; however, many users feel that it has more flexibility. Details for users are available in works by Kiviat et. al. [1969], Maisel and Gnugnuoli [1972], Reitman [1971], and Wyman [1970].

Validation of Simulation Models

Validation of all kinds of models is an important phase in their useful application. Given the model, how closely does it represent reality? Validation of complex simulation models has some extraordinary problems because their

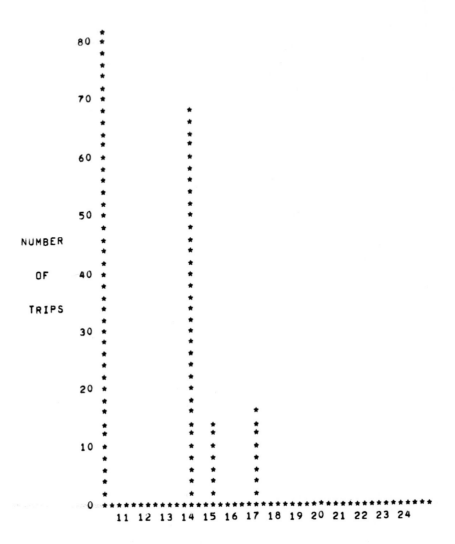

Figure 9. Graphic computer output of drive to the office duration

From J. Reitman, *Computer Simulation Applications*, John Wiley & Sons, New York, 1971, Figure 2.14, p. 72; used by permission.

complexity raises some issues of validation that may be more important with simulation than with other kinds of models. Complexity puts a greater burden on verifying internal logic, including program debugging. Thus in a first phase we must determine whether or not the simulation program actually represents what was intended in the program design by checking assump-

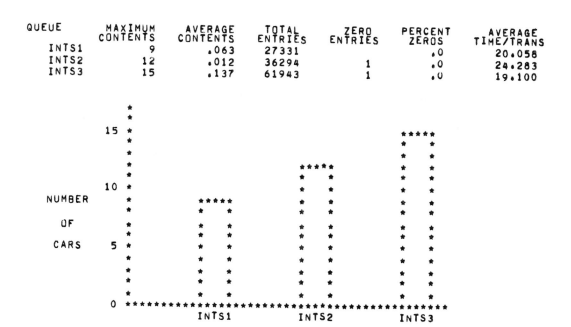

QUEUE	MAXIMUM CONTENTS	AVERAGE CONTENTS	TOTAL ENTRIES	ZERO ENTRIES	PERCENT ZEROS	AVERAGE TIME/TRANS
INTS1	9	.063	27331		.0	20.058
INTS2	12	.012	36294	1	.0	24.283
INTS3	15	.137	61943	1	.0	19.100

INTERSECTION NUMBER

Figure 10. Graphic computer output and queue statistics for the drive to the office simulation

Adapted from J. Reitman, *Computer Simulation Applications*, John Wiley & Sons, New York, 1971, Figures 2.16 and 2.17, pp. 74 and 75; used by permission.
[Note: Average transfer time is given in seconds.]

tions and reviewing the program with people familiar with the problem.

The second and crucial phase of validation requires us to determine in some satisfactory way whether the program represents the reality it was intended to simulate. If the simulation is meant to forecast the performance of a new system design, we are somewhat in the dark because there is no existing real system for comparative validation checks. In such situations, the nature of results can be reviewed by experts. Also, parts of a complex system may represent existing subsystems where direct validity checks can be made. Finally, statistical tests can be used to test hypotheses regarding general logic and validity.

Even though the final objective may be the design of a new system, we may develop simulation models to predict performance of an entire class of systems, a special case of which is an existing system. For example, in analyzing traffic flow, a simulator might be designed to take account of all of the main variables such as traffic density, traffic light settings, number of lanes, rules for left and right turns, special left turn lanes, etc. The simulator can be validated by predicting performance with the model for specified conditions, and comparing these results with actual field data.

Figure 11 represents just such a comparison in a traffic study. An intersection was selected within a network of five signalized intersections, and queue length predicted by the model (curved lines) was compared with measured queue length (vertical lines). The queue lengths are measured at 80-second intervals during the peak 15-minute period of the day. Eastbound traffic was 300 cars per 15 minutes over two through lanes and one left turn lane, and westbound traffic was 220 cars per 15 minutes. Average eastbound speed was measured as 7.3 mph compared to 6.3 mph predicted by the model, and westbound speed was measured as 10.2 mph versus 9.0 mph for the model. The comparison was judged to be satisfactory validation for the model.

Validation studies may result in model changes that could be as drastic as reformulating the problem.

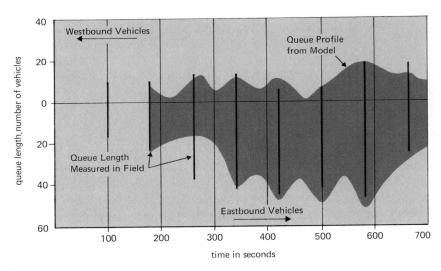

Figure 11. Queue length field data vs. model

From J. Reitman, *Computer Simulation Applications*, John Wiley & Sons, Inc., New York, 1971, Figure 12.13, p. 321; used by permission.

SIMULATION OF AN EMERGENCY MEDICAL SYSTEM

Earlier in this chapter, we developed the general Monte Carlo methodology around arrival and service distributions for an emergency medical system. Now, however, we wish to place these inputs in context with an actual simulation study of the emergency medical system of the City of Los Angeles.

The managerial objectives of the study were focused on the appropriate capacity and deployment of emergency medical facilities, and the results were an important input to the deployment decision.

The prediction of the performance of an emergency medical system is an ideal example of the need for a "systems" view because in such a system, performance cannot be inferred by examining the components separately. The demand for service, nature and location of medical need, ambulance availability, traffic problems, the location of hospitals, and so on, are all interacting parameters that define the system and have a bearing on the decision variables. The decision variables themselves are complex, involving deployment strategy, response time, system cost, and other factors.

The simulation methodology is an ideal vehicle for studying complex systems such as an emergency medical system, because it would not be feasible to perform the experiments on the real system in a controlled way. Since factors of known risk in the form of probability distributions enter the process, we can perform a large number of replications of the experiments to determine the expected values of measures of performance, and thus be able to make decisions based on the expected long-run conditions. In addition, with simulation we can assess the response of the system to peak loads. Indeed, in all kinds of emergency service systems such as police and fire protection, as well as medical systems, how the system performs when its capacity is stressed may be of the greatest importance.

The Computer Simulation Model

Fitzsimmons [1970, 1973] programmed the emergency medical system in SIMSCRIPT, driving the simulation process with an incident generator (call for service) that provided the forecasts of load.

The Incident Generator   Based on studies of past actual loads for each hour of the day, the hourly pattern shown in Figure 12 was developed. Therefore, a specific mean hourly rate could be determined from Figure 12 in proportion to load experience through the day. Furthermore, previous statistical studies had shown that the Poisson distribution was a good description of call rates for the mean values of Figure 12. For each hourly mean call rate, the generator could determine a specific call rate based on Monte Carlo methods. Recall that the shape of the Poisson distribution varies with the mean; three sample distributions at different load levels are shown in Figure 12. Note that at low loads the Poisson distribution has a fairly sharp peak with a relatively high probability of arrival rates near the mean. At high loads, however, the variability is rather great and there is a reasonably high probability of call rates substantially lower and higher than the mean rate. Finally, an exact time for an incident was determined by sampling over the hour from a uniform distribution.

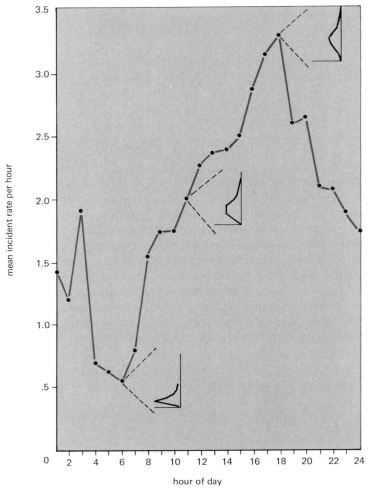

Figure 12. Mean call for service rate (incident rate) for the Los Angeles emergency medical system. Three sample miniature Poisson distributions are shown for widely differing mean incident rates

From J. A. Fitzsimmons, "Emergency Medical Systems: A Simulation Study and Computerized Method for Deployment of Ambulances." Unpublished Ph.D. Dissertation, UCLA, 1970; used by permission.

The Simulator The main program of the simulator begins with an incident at a specific time, and the incident is processed according to the general logic of the flow chart shown in Figure 13. Travel time is computed as the sum of x and y distances converted to travel time, to correspond to the usual

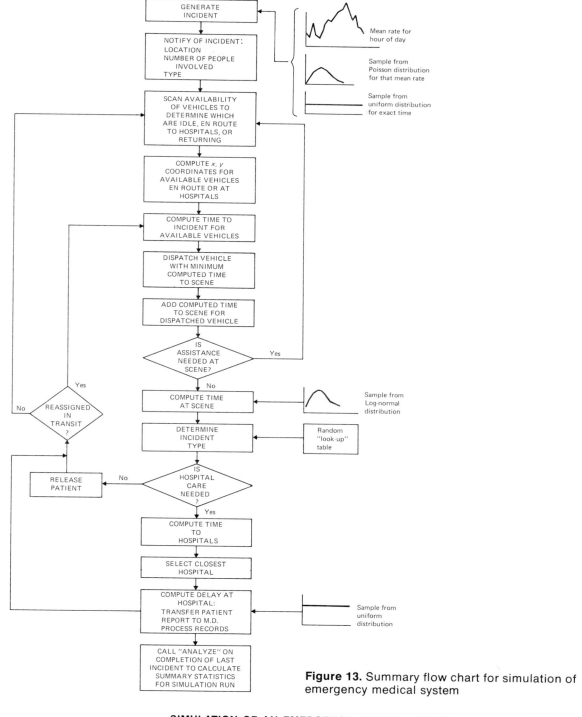

Figure 13. Summary flow chart for simulation of emergency medical system

urban layout plan. Additional Monte Carlo sampling is required to compute the time required at the scene, the type of incident, and the delay at the hospital. Thus, the simulation contains both deterministic and stochastic elements.

While each vehicle has a home base, the simulator is designed to accommodate a mobile system (which can be dispatched en route) since vehicles can be reassigned in transit. The simulator includes capability for both ambulances and helicopters.

Model Validation The model was validated both in terms of equivalent analytical models for simple cases and for a portion of the existing Los Angeles Ambulance System.

Fitzsimmons [1970] constructed single and multiple ambulance waiting line models using the basic definitions shown in Figure 1 of Chapter 10. The assumptions were first-come first-served queue discipline, Poisson input and exponential service time, and an infinite queuing system. On-scene care was assumed constant at seven minutes, all patients were transported to hospitals, and hospital transfer time was constant at three minutes in the validation studies. Simulation runs included 10,800 and 3,240 calls for the single and multiple ambulance cases respectively. Test of significance of various queue statistics were made comparing analytical and simulation results, and all results indicated high conformance between the simulation and analytical models.

In validating the computer simulation model against the real-world Los Angeles Ambulance System, Fitzsimmons tested its ability to predict the behavior of the San Fernando Valley portion of the Los Angeles system. Actual data for 1967 were used in developing the model and historical verification was performed by comparing records for 1967 with simulated results for the same period. A number of statistical tests were performed.

The Chi-square "Goodness of Fit" test was performed on the distribution of actual and simulated response times. Figure 14 shows the actual and simulated distributions of response times, and from a practical point of view it is clear that the simulated system closely duplicates reality. Furthermore, the Chi-square test result indicated that at the 5 percent significance level, one could not reject the hypothesis that the two distributions came from the same parent population.

Fitzsimmons used spectral analysis to test whether or not the hourly occurrence of calls for service in the simulated system corresponded with reality. In spectral analysis a frequency spectrum is derived that shows the magnitude of the contribution to total variance at each frequency. Thus, periodic behavior in the data can be identified and compared to actual observed data to see how well simulated and actual data compare. Again, statistical tests confirmed that the simulation system adequately duplicated reality.

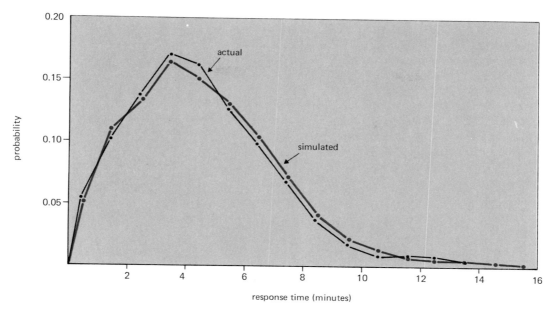

Figure 14. Distribution of response times for the San Fernando Valley Ambulance System

From J. A. Fitzsimmons, "Emergency Medical Systems: A Simulation Study and Computerized Method for Deployment of Ambulances." Unpublished Ph.D. Dissertation, UCLA, 1970; used by permission.

Use of the Emergency Medical Simulation Model

Given the validated simulation model, we have an effective vehicle for the managerial evaluation of practical alternatives in the form of sensitivity analysis and the evaluation of alternative control policies. The alternatives were evaluated mainly in terms of response time.

Number and Location of Ambulances   Fitzsimmons evaluated the effect on response time of having one to ten ambulances in the system for single and dispersed home stations. The single home stations were at a hospital. In general, the response time for a single station leveled off at about three ambulances in the system, as shown in Figure 15; however, response time for dispersed deployment continued to decline. Waiting time for the single station fell to near zero with three ambulances in the system.

A series of 20 experimental runs evaluated hypotheses concerning location deployment patterns, and dispersed deployment dominated the single station alternative for all system performance criteria. Furthermore, optimal locations improved mean travel time to the scene by about 12 percent, compared to existing locations. Finally, it was found that optimal deployment was a function of incident or call rate.

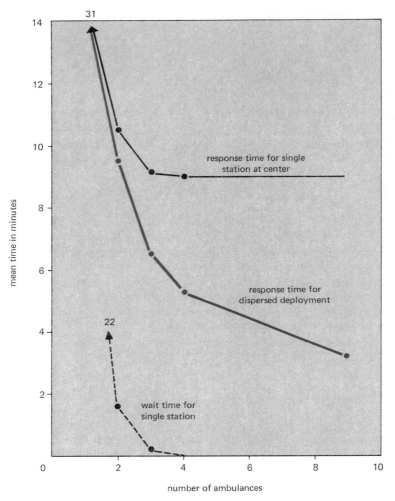

Figure 15. Response times for single ambulance station and dispersed locations for uniform distribution of calls within the geographic area

From J. A. Fitzsimmons, "Emergency Medical Systems: A Simulation Study and Computerized Method for Deployment of Ambulances." Unpublished Ph.D. Dissertation, UCLA, 1970; used by permission.

Number and Location of Hospitals   A series of runs was made in which the number of hospitals was varied from one to four, using a single ambulance located centrally. Mean time to the hospital was reduced considerably with the addition of hospitals to the system, but response time and waiting time were only slightly reduced, and ambulance utilization declined about 2 percent, as shown in Figure 16. Mean travel time to the scene actu-

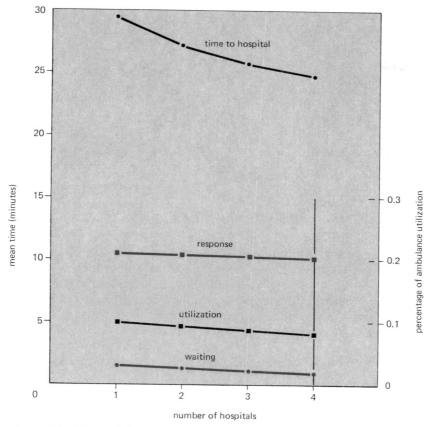

Figure 16. Effect of the number of hospitals in the system on response time

From J. A. Fitzsimmons, "Emergency Medical Systems: A Simulation and Computerized Method for Deployment of Ambulances." Unpublished Ph.D. Dissertation, UCLA, 1970; used by permission.

ally increased slightly. Locating hospitals optimally reduced mean waiting time only slightly, because of reduced ambulance utilization.

Control Policies   Alternate dispatch policies were evaluated for no radio communication, radio dispatch without mobile transmitters on board ambulances, and two-way radio communication. These alternative policies were evaluated under loads varying from call rates of 15 to 45 per day. Simulated response time was reduced by 7 to 8 percent with radio dispatch; however, the two-way radio dispatch system was very little better than the basic system. Nevertheless, the two-way system was recommended since it effected some improvement.

Even when ambulance stations were physically dispersed, simulation experiments showed a definite advantage of pooling ambulances into one central dispatch command, as would be predicted from queuing theory.

Alternative ambulance deployment policies were also evaluated, indicating an advantage for an adaptive system that allows repositioning of vehicles as load builds up, rather than having each vehicle return to its home base at the end of an incident. Fitzsimmons [1973] developed a computer program named Computerized Ambulance Location Logic (CALL) to determine optimum ambulance deployment. Based on evaluations for particular ambulance locations, a computer search routine directs changes in the ambulance locations to progressively decrease the system's mean response time.

WHAT SHOULD THE MANAGER KNOW?

Computer simulation is a powerful tool, and simulated sampling is an extremely important component that makes it possible to assess the risk factors entering complex problems. The manager should have an understanding of the kinds of problems for which simulation might be useful. These problems are in general those that must reflect the complexities of systems — problems in which there are important interactions between components of the system. The emergency medical simulation is such a problem. The effectiveness of the emergency medical system depends on the demand for service, the number of vehicles available and their locations, the number and locations of hospitals, population and traffic densities and patterns, and the control and deployment policies used. Most organizations have some problems that require a systems approach in order to represent the problem adequately, and simulation has been used effectively in industrial planning and control systems, hospital admissions systems, urban transportation systems, weapons systems, and other types of systems.

Model Formulation   In deciding whether or not to place faith in the results of a simulation model, a manager needs to be involved in the initial phases of model formulation to be sure that the model will have the capability to examine the kinds of questions in which he is interested. The manager's sense of the problems may be particularly important when risk factors need to be accounted for. While managers cannot be expected to know simulation languages and to program simulation problems, they need to be able to communicate effectively with the technical people who will implement the detailed formulation of the model. Thus, a manager should be able to make a flow chart of a problem, to indicate at least the major progressions involved and the decision points that he feels will be useful. In this process, the manager may also be defining basic data needs.

Problems for which simulation is particularly useful tend to be ones involving the evaluation of alternative policies and procedures. As such, they are commonly one-time studies. Thus, while a manager need not know programming languages in detail, he may nevertheless find it worthwhile to know the general characteristics of languages. For example, simulation languages are efficient in terms of programming effort, but not necessarily efficient in terms of computer run time. Languages such as FORTRAN and PL/1 have the opposite characteristics. For a large-scale simulation program, it may be worthwhile to obtain capability in specialized simulation languages.

Interpretation of Results   The validation process should be of great interest to managers in interpreting results. The manager will probably not use the results of a simulation model if he is not satisfied with the validation. With satisfactory validation, however, the sensitivity analysis should be of significant help to managers, for these studies can provide insight into how the real system functions, which variables are important and which are relatively unimportant, even though they may be under managerial control. Thus, the comments in Chapter 6 regarding validation and use of a model are especially significant for large-scale simulation models.

Check Your Understanding

1. What are the essential differences between discrete event and discrete time updating simulations? Illustrate by indicating how the simulation of the activities of a single ambulance might be handled in each of the two simulation modes.

2. Outline the procedure for simulated sampling (Monte Carlo). What is the purpose of each step?

3. How does Monte Carlo sampling ensure that data enter the simulation in proportion to their occurrence in the original distribution? Can you envision a situation where the data entering the simulation might not be representative of the original distribution?

4. The manager of a small post office is concerned that his growing township is overloading the one-window service being offered. He decides to obtain sample data concerning 100 individuals who arrive for service. The data obtained are summarized in Table 4.
    a. Convert the distributions to cumulative probability distributions.
    b. Using a simulated sample of 20, estimate the average percentage of customer waiting time and the average percentage of idle time of the postal clerk.

5. The manager of a bank is attempting to determine how many tellers he needs during his peak load period. He wishes to offer service so that the average waiting time of a customer does not exceed two minutes. How many tellers does he need if the arrival and service distributions are as

TABLE 4. Arrival and Service Time Data for a
One-Window Post Office

Time Between Arrivals (min.)	Frequency	Service Time (min.)	Frequency
0.5	2	0.5	12
1.0	6	1.0	21
1.5	10	1.5	36
2.0	25	2.0	19
2.5	20	2.5	7
3.0	14	3.0	5
3.5	10		100
4.0	7		
4.5	4		
5.0	2		
	100		

TABLE 5. Arrival and Service Time Data for a Bank

Time Between Arrivals (min.)	Frequency	Service Time (min.)	Frequency
0.0	10	0.0	0
1.0	35	1.0	5
2.0	25	2.0	20
3.0	15	3.0	40
4.0	10	4.0	35
5.0	5		100
	100		

shown in Table 5? Customers form a single waiting line and are serviced by the next available teller. Simulate for alternative numbers of tellers with a sample of 20 arrivals in each instance.

6. Discuss the basic differences between the two simulation languages, GPSS and SIMSCRIPT. How are they different from KSIM and DYNAMO discussed in connection with dynamic structural simulation models in Chapter 8?

7. You have carried through two simple simulations in connection with questions 4 and 5. How could you validate the results?

8. The discussion of the simulation of an emergency medical system is a report of how an extensive simulation was carried through, validated, and used. Place yourself in the position of the policy and decision maker responsible for the operation of the Los Angeles Emergency Medical System. Assume that a presentation has just been made to you similar

to the report of the study given in the text. What questions would you ask the researcher? How would you satisfy yourself concerning the value of the study? What criteria would you use in making such decisions as the number of ambulances to use, the number of hospitals to establish for the system, and the type of radio communication to use?

Problems

1. A manufacturing company has a large machine containing three identical electronic components that are the major cause of downtime. The current practice is to replace the components as they fail. However, a proposal has been made to replace all three components whenever any one of them fails in order to reduce the frequency with which the machine must be shut down.

   In the current situation, the machine must be shut down for one hour to replace one component or for two and one-fourth hours to replace all three.
   a. What are the data requirements to analyze and compare the alternatives using simulation?
   b. Formulate the problem in terms of a simulation system using the discrete event method. Prepare a flow chart of the simulation system similar to Figure 13 in the text.

2. Suppose we are dealing with the maintenance of a bank of 30 machines, and we wish to estimate the level of service that can be maintained by one mechanic. In order to make judgments about the effectiveness of the system, we need to have the simulation system generate data concerning the time that machines are down while waiting for service and being repaired. We also wish to know how well the mechanic is utilized in the system.
   a. What are the data requirements necessary to construct a simulation of the system?
   b. Formulate the problem in terms of a simulation system using the discrete time updating method. Prepare a flow chart of the simulation system similar to Figure 13 in the text.

3. A bank of 20 automatic machines is being maintained by a crew of six mechanics. Production forecasts indicate the need for two more machines to meet capacity needs. The question of whether or not the size of the repair crew should be enlarged has been raised.

   There are two basic kinds of repair situations: the "run" call and the "downtime" call. A run call is one in which the mechanic can service the machine while it is still operating. On the average, 67 percent of the calls for service are of the run type. A downtime call for service normally comes from a more serious problem resulting in machine breakdown. In such situations, the mechanic completes the repair and the machine is put back in service. However, the mechanic spends additional time with the machine after it has started again, to make final adjustments and ensure that it is ready for service. This period is the mechanic's "run-in time."
   a. What are the data requirements to develop a simulation of the repair system in order to analyze and compare the system for different numbers of machines in service and different numbers of mechanics?

b. Formulate the problem in terms of a simulation system using the discrete event method. Prepare a flow chart of the simulation system similar to Figure 13 in the text.

4. There are numerous full reports of simulations of complex systems, including those on the list that follows:

a. Simulation of a district office of the United States Social Security System [Maisel and Gnugnuoli, 1972, pp. 343–94].

b. Simulation in business [Meier, Newell, and Pazer, 1969, Chapter 2].

c. Simulation in economic analysis [Meier, Newell, and Pazer, 1969, Chapter 4].

d. Prediction of passenger railroad system performance [Reitman, 1971, Chapter 8].

e. Performance of a computer system [Reitman, 1971, Chapter 11].

f. Auto traffic flow through a series of intersections [Reitman, 1971, Chapter 12].

Read one of the simulation studies from the preceding list. Prepare a report giving a brief summary and reviewing data requirements, methodology, and interpretation of results. If the report were presented to you as decision maker, what questions would you raise? What criteria other than those specifically included in the simulation do you think are pertinent in judging and deciding on the issues raised by the simulation study?

5. A professional football coach has six running backs on his squad. He wants to evaluate how injuries might affect his stock of backs. A minor injury causes a player to be removed from the game and miss only the next game. A major injury puts the player out of action for the rest of the season. The probability of a major injury in a game is 0.05. There is at most one major injury per game. The probability distribution of minor injuries per game is:

Number of Injuries	Probability
0	0.2
1	0.5
2	0.22
3	0.05
4	0.025
5	0.005

Injuries seem to happen in a completely random manner, with no discernible pattern over the season. A season is ten games.

Using random numbers given in Table 6 of Appendix E, simulate the fluctuations in the coach's stock of running backs over the season. Assume that he hires no additional running backs during the season.

References

Emshoff, J. R., and R. L. Sisson, *Design and Use of Computer Simulation Models*, The Macmillan Company, New York, 1970.

Evans, G. W., G. F. Wallace, and G. L. Sutherland, *Simulation Using Digital Computers,* Prentice-Hall, Englewood Cliffs, N.J., 1967.

Fitzsimmons, J. A., "Emergency Medical Systems: A Simulation Study and Computerized Method for the Deployment of Ambulances," unpublished Ph.D. Dissertation, University of California, Los Angeles, 1970.

————, "A Methodology for Emergency Ambulance Deployment," *Management Science,* Vol. 19, No. 6, February 1973, pp. 627–36.

IBM Corporation, *GPSS V Users' Manual,* Form No. SH20-0851-0, 1970.

Kiviat, P. J., R. Villanueva, and H. M. Markowitz, *The Simscript II Programming Language*, Prentice-Hall, Englewood Cliffs, N.J., 1969.

Maisel, H., and G. Gnugnuoli, *Simulation of Discrete Stochastic Systems*, Science Research Associates, Chicago, 1972.

Meier, R. W., T. Newell, and H. L. Pazer, *Simulation in Business and Economics*, Prentice-Hall, Englewood Cliffs, N.J., 1969.

Naylor, T. H., J. L. Balintfy, D. S. Burdick, and K. Chu, *Computer Simulation Techniques*, John Wiley & Sons, New York, 1966.

Reitman, J., *Computer Simulation Applications*, John Wiley & Sons, New York, 1971.

Wyman, F. P., *Simulation Modeling: A Guide to Using SIMSCRIPT*, John Wiley & Sons, New York, 1970.

Part Four

OPTIMIZING MODELS

Introduction To Optimizing Models

The use of optimizing models is the most exciting and potentially valuable method of management science. This is true because, given a criterion, these models combine the elements of alternative generator, predictive, and evaluative models in such a way that the *best possible* solution can be determined. Best possible means that, given the criterion, there exists no superior combination of the decision variables for the model. These are the powerful optimizing methods of management science such as mathematical programming, network optimization, inventory models, and others.

Implicit in the preceding euphoric statement about best possible solutions are the assumptions that the submodel that predicts system performance is a valid representation of how the system works and that the evaluative model reflects the utility function of the decision maker. As we shall see these are important assumptions and it may be difficult to always meet them when we are combining the functions of alternative generator, system performance prediction, evaluation, and optimization in one grand system.

Let us begin by recalling the scheme of models in management science from Chapter 1, shown again in Figure 1. Parts Two and Three of this book have dealt with the processes of the models shown in Figure 1. Part Two focused on evaluative models. We assumed that we knew how the system worked and models that depended on utility theory, decision trees, expected values, and subjective probabilities were developed to evaluate outcomes for single and multiple criteria. In Part Three we removed the assumption that we knew how the system performed and developed models and methodologies for predicting system performance under conditions of certainty and risk.

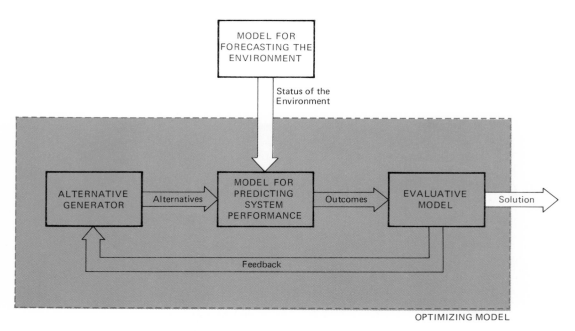

Figure 1. Elements of an optimizing model

In both Parts Two and Three we assumed that the decision maker played the role of alternative generator.

Optimizing models combine the alternative generator, predictive model, and the evaluative model, as indicated by the highlighted area in Figure 1. The output of the combined system is a combination of values for the decision variables that produces the best solution; we call this the optimum solution. In the optimizing models we shall study, the different elements of Figure 1 will not have a separate and distinct identity, yet their functions will be performed.

Let us see in general how the coupling can be made. In Figure 2 we have developed a flow chart that contains all of the elements of Figure 1. In addition, below the evaluative model we have inserted a test for optimality in which we determine whether or not the solution just produced can be improved. If it can be improved, we need some mechanism to determine the direction of change and the amount of change we should make in the decision variables for the next iteration. This information is sent back to the alternative generator to produce a new alternative. System performance is predicted and evaluated, and the cycle is repeated until the test for optimality indicates that no further improvement is possible. We have diagramed the process as an iterative one; however, some of the solution techniques combine these steps and go directly to the optimum solution, while others actually do iterate in the manner we have described.

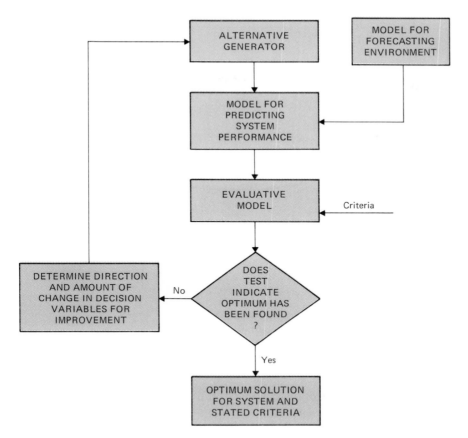

Figure 2. Flow chart showing test for optimality
and coupling to alternative generator

CONCEPT OF A TEST FOR OPTIMALITY

The simplest case of a test for optimality is one in which we have a single
decision criterion such as cost or profit, and the value of the criterion varies
as a function of a single decision variable. Suppose, for example, that we
wished to determine the least cost inventory to hold as a buffer to absorb
variations in demand. The larger the buffer inventory, the greater the inventory holding cost, but the lower the cost of lost sales and back ordering.
Since one component of cost is increasing and the other decreasing as buffer
inventory increases, the composite cost function plotted in relation to buffer
inventory size would be similar to Figure 3; that is, cost decreases to a minimum and then increases again as inventory holding costs become the dominant cost factor.

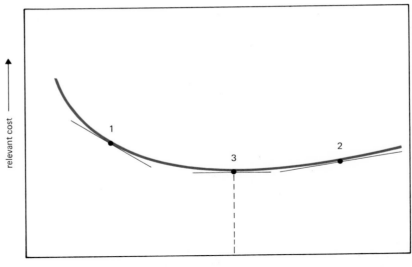

Figure 3. Typical curve of relevant cost versus the size of buffer stock indicating optimum at a point where the slope of the curve is zero

We can see by inspection that the optimum inventory size is at point 3 in Figure 3, the minimum point of the cost curve. Mathematically, the test for the minimum point is in terms of the slope of the curve. The minimum will be where the slope of the curve is zero. In this kind of situation the iterative process is not necessary since we can test for the minimum (or maximum) much more directly using appropriate mathematical techniques.

Complex Criterion Functions Now suppose that the criterion function is not so simple. In fact, suppose that it is highly complex being controlled by the influence of dozens of variables. In such an instance, there may be many "local" minima or maxima and possibly only one "global" optimum. Or, there may be more than one global optimum, given the criterion, resulting in management flexibility in decisions that are equally good from the point of view of the criterion.

Suppose, for example, that we wished to determine the most profitable employment and production rate decision for the coming months in an industrial situation. There are a large number of revenue and cost items that are affected by such decisions, including product price, payroll cost, hiring and layoff costs, inventory and shortage costs, overtime cost, and so on. Also, if the demands are seasonal we would have to include these revenues and costs for several months into the future so that the number of

INTRODUCTION TO OPTIMIZING MODELS

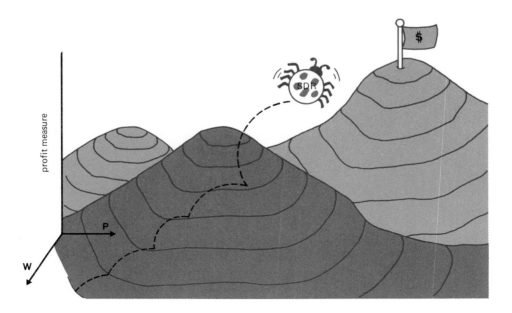

Figure 4. Computer search methods for finding optimum decisions in complex problems. A computer program searches the profit surface for the combination of variables (work force size *W* and production rate *P* in the example) that maximizes profit

Adapted from W. H. Taubert, "The Search Decision Rule: A New Approach to Operations Planning," paper presented at the 36th National Meeting, ORSA, Miami, Fla., November 1969.

variables could easily be above one hundred. How will we determine the optimum decision in such a situation?

In order to conceptualize an answer, let us reduce the problem to just two variables: the size of the work force and the production rate for the next month. Figure 4 is a representation of the three-dimensional profit surface for such a problem. It appears as a topographical map, and we wish to scan the surface to find the highest peak. We can use computer search methods to locate the peaks (or valleys for minimization).

Without attempting any detailed explanation at this point, all such computer programs operate by moving over a response surface, such as that shown in Figure 4, by a set of rules that determine movement from a particular point on the surface by two key questions: what is the next direction of movement? and how far should the movement be in the given direction? Each movement generates a new alternative and is followed by a test for optimality. The rules are designed to "climb the hills" and scan the horizon for higher peaks. With the power and speed of a computer, hundreds or thousands of alternative solutions can be generated and tested in a relatively small amount of computer time. While such methods do not find a guaranteed global optimum solution, they are nevertheless very effective in finding solutions that cannot be easily improved.

Analytical Solutions for Complex Problems   In some instances we can obtain analytical solutions to large complex problems of optimization. This result is achieved by restricting the mathematical form of the predictive and evaluative components of the system, as in linear programming where all of the relationships must be in linear form. Here again, we have a test for optimality that indicates whether or not improvement is possible. When the test indicates further possible improvement in the criterion, rules in the improvement strategy determine the direction of movement and the amount by which the decision variables are changed to generate the next alternative. The process converges on a provable optimum solution in a finite number of steps. The process is feasible as an analytical procedure because by the nature of the mathematical form of the model, only a relatively few alternatives need to be considered from among the thousands of possible solutions.

PLAN FOR PART FOUR

All of the models discussed in Part Four will be of the optimizing type. They combine the separate elements or functions in our framework of alternative generator, predictive model, and evaluative model in an optimizing system that has within it a criterion that functions to converge the system automatically on the best possible solution for the model. We will begin with elementary optimizing models used in inventory management in Chapter 12. We shall then discuss linear optimization models and linear programming methods in Chapters 13 and 14.

In Chapters 15 and 16 we consider mathematical models that have a visual interpretation in the form of a network. The models of Chapter 15 have important applications in the design of product distribution systems, while the network models of Chapter 16 provide aids to the management of large scale projects.

Chapter 17 contains a discussion of optimization models that include decision variables that can only assume integer values, such as 0, 1, 2, . . . , rather than fractional values. These models are often applied in the analysis of large-scale capital budgeting problems.

Finally, we discuss dynamic programming methods in Chapter 18. These methods are most commonly applied to problems involving a series of decisions to be made sequentially over time; hence the term "dynamic."

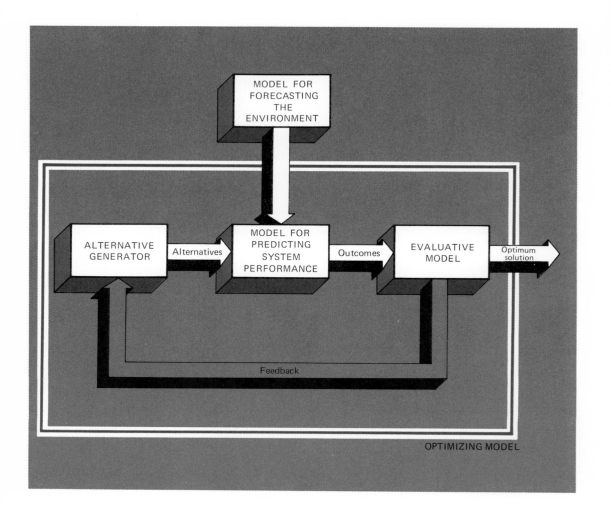

12

Elementary Optimizing Models
For Inventory Management

It is perhaps fitting that we should use an inventory problem as a vehicle to introduce optimizing models. The first optimizing model used by managers was an inventory model developed by F. W. Harris in 1915. Harris derived a formula for the Economic Order Quantity (EOQ), the optimum quantity of materials or items to purchase at one time.

Since World War II a great deal of research has been focused on inventory problems. We shall begin with a general discussion of inventories and their functions in managerial systems, and the relevant costs associated with inventories. We shall then formulate the alternative generator and the predictive and evaluative submodels, and show how these elements can be combined in a system that functions as an optimizing model to guide inventory reordering decisions and policy. Given the conceptual framework, we will then develop extensions that take account of some complicating factors, such as stock shortages and quantity discounts. Appendix D contains further extensions that consider risk.

Functions of Inventories

Inventories are necessary in many managerial systems in order to provide "off the shelf" service for stock items in retailing and wholesaling operations, and these needs are reflected back into the manufacturing and raw material supply functions as well. In systems that produce a service rather than a physical product, the proper functioning of that service is usually partially dependent on supply items — paper and forms in governmental and other offices, medical supplies in hospitals, repair parts in a maintenance operation, and so on.

Throughout the supply-manufacturing-distribution system, inventories are the "shock absorbers" that absorb the normal variations in demand and in supply lead time at each stock point. As such, they perform a *decoupling* function which makes it possible to carry on activities relatively independently and efficiently. Without inventories, such systems could not function effectively, and when inventories fall to dangerously low levels, we need virtually perfect coordination and scheduling to compensate. Unfortunately this perfection is not normally attainable. When such enterprises are forced into a hand-to-mouth supply situation by strikes or other choking of supply lines, the smoothly functioning machine breaks down. The vital nature of inventories is seen by examining the kinds of inventories that exist in a supply system.

Pipeline Inventories   To illustrate the function of pipeline inventories, assume a production-distribution system with one product for which there is an average demand of 200 units per week at the warehouse. Let us assume that normal warehousing procedures are to prepare a procurement order to the factory when the warehouse inventory falls to a critical level called the *reorder point*. It takes one week to prepare the order, get it approved, and have it received by the factory. Once the order is received at the factory, it takes two weeks for loading, trucking, and unloading at the warehouse.

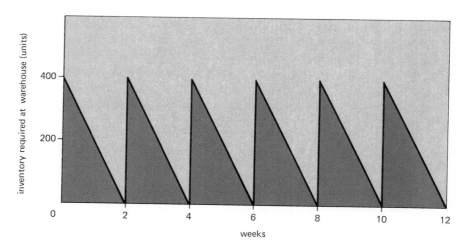

Figure 1. Idealized graph of inventories required at the warehouse to cover trucking time from the factory. The average transit inventory component of pipeline inventory is the product of truck time and demand rate, or $2 \times 200 = 400$ units. Average inventory for this component is $400/2 = 200$ units

The warehouse must carry enough stock on hand to meet demand during the transit time. Figure 1 shows an idealized graph of the inventories required at the warehouse just to cover trucking time from the factory. The average transit inventory is the product of the truck time and the demand rate, or $2 \times 200 = 400$ units. At all times, then, 400 units are in motion from the factory to the warehouse, or in an equivalent sense, the factory must maintain an inventory that takes account of this fact. The order time delay of one week has the same effect as a transit time, since the warehouse must also carry inventories to cover this delay. In general then, every lag in the system generates the need for inventory to fill the pipeline. These are the in-process inventories in production systems; however, the concept is completely general.

Lot Size or "Cycle" Inventories   To examine lot size inventories, let us continue with our simple example. Since the truck is to make the trip from the factory to the warehouse, how many items should be moved at one time? Most of the trucking costs are fixed regardless of lot size, so hand-to-mouth supply would be prohibitively expensive. Let us assume that orders are placed for a truck load of 800 units, equivalent to a four-week supply. Figure 2 shows an idealized graph of inventories required at the warehouse when orders are placed for a truckload. Warehouse inventories must therefore be increased to take account of the fact that materials are trucked 800 at a time to gain transportation cost advantages.

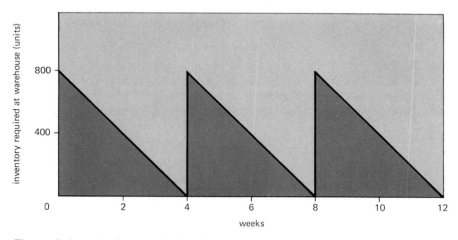

Figure 2. Inventories required at the warehouse when orders are placed for a truckload of 800 units. Average inventory for this component is $800/2 = 400$ units. Transit inventories are unchanged

Buffer Inventories At times, inventories must provide a buffer against variations. Figure 2 assumes that demand rate, truck time, and order time are all constant. We know, however, that these factors are not ordinarily constant, so we must have some way to protect against unpredictable variations in demand and in supply time. Figure 3 shows the contrast in inventory levels at the warehouse that might occur if the maximum demand* of 300 units per week occurred during the supply time of three weeks. In order to ensure that we do not run out of stock, a buffer inventory of 300 units is required [the difference in the maximum and average demand rates during the three-week supply time, $(300 - 200)\ 3 = 300$ units]. Techniques for taking account of these risk factors are of great importance in inventory models, and are discussed in Appendix D.

Seasonal Inventories Many products have a fairly predictable but seasonal pattern through the year. Where this is true, management has the choice of changing production rates over the year to absorb the fluctuation in demand or of absorbing some or all of the fluctuation in demand with in-

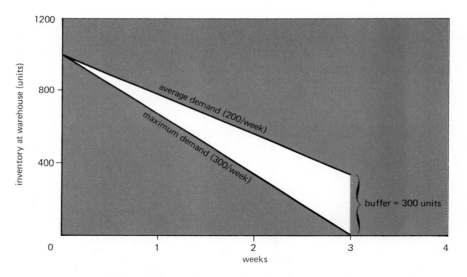

Figure 3. Buffer inventory required to avoid shortages. Difference between idealized average and maximum demand rates over the supply lead time represents a minimum or buffer stock required to protect against the occurrence of shortages resulting from random fluctuations in demand

---

*   The maximum demand is a point on the demand distribution curve that would not be exceeded more than a preset percentage of time. It is established in relation to a desire not to run out of stock.

ventories. If we attempt to follow the demand curve through the seasonal variations by changing production rates, the capital investment for the system must provide for the peak capacity, and we must absorb costs for overtime, hiring, training, and separating labor.

The discussion to this point has indicated the vital nature of inventories and the advantages gained by recognizing their functions. The question, however, is not one-sided. Inventories cost money and a knowledge of the behavior of inventory-related costs will be important to building inventory models and to the formulation of managerial objectives and an evaluative model.

Costs and Management Objectives

The following types of cost items are often relevant to inventory models: costs that depend on the number of orders, price or production costs, handling and storage costs, shortage costs, and capital costs.

Costs Depending on the Number of Orders   In deciding on purchase order quantities, there are certain clerical costs of preparing orders. These costs are the same regardless of the quantity ordered. They are important in the models with which we shall deal; however, our interest is in the true incremental cost of order preparation (or its equivalent). The average ordering cost derived by dividing the total cost of the purchasing operation by the average number of orders processed is not appropriate, since a large segment of the total costs are fixed. Our interest is in the variable cost component.

The parallel cost in production systems is the cost to prepare production orders, set up machines, and control the flow of orders through the plant.

Price or Production Costs   When quantity discounts must be taken into account, unit price becomes relevant in determining purchase order quantities. Comparably, production cost is relevant to determining the size of production lots.

Costs of Handling and Storing Inventory   There are certain costs associated with the level of inventories, represented by the costs of handling material in and out of inventory and the storage costs. The storage costs are made up of components such as insurance, taxes, rent, obsolescence, spoilage, and capital costs. These costs are commonly in proportion to inventory levels.

Capital Costs   As alluded to in the preceding paragraph, part of the storage cost is the opportunity cost of capital invested in inventory. The cost figure itself is the product of inventory value per unit, the time that the unit is in inventory, and the appropriate interest rate. In general, the appropriate interest rate should reflect the opportunities for the investment of comparable funds within the organization, and it should not be lower than the cost of borrowed money. Since the funds are tied up in inventories, they cannot be used for the purchase of other profit-producing investments, and an opportunity cost must be imputed.

Cost of Shortages   An extremely important cost that never appears on accounting records is the cost of running out of stock. Such costs appear in several ways. In profit-making concerns, sales may actually be lost as a result of stockouts. Or, there may be additional costs resulting from back ordering. In production systems, a part shortage may cause idle labor on a production line or subsequent incremental labor cost to perform operations out of sequence, usually at higher than normal cost. Alternately there may be costs of avoiding shortages. In nonprofit organizations, similar costs may be involved other than the cost of lost sales.

Management Objectives   The overall objective of management is to design policies and decision rules that view inventories in a "systems" context so that the broadly construed set of costs discussed are generally minimized. In addition, however, the existence of a cost of shortages raises a question concerning the appropriate service level. (Service level may be defined as the percentage of orders that can be filled from stock.) When shortage costs can be accurately estimated, the most economical service level can be determined by balancing buffer inventory costs against shortage costs. More commonly, however, shortage costs cannot be accurately determined, and the manager must reflect his trade-off for service versus buffer inventory cost in establishing service level policies.

FORMULATION OF A PURCHASE ORDER QUANTITY MODEL

Let us organize our knowledge about the functions of inventories, and inventory-related costs, with the objective of determining managerial policies concerning the number of units of an item to order at one time. We establish the following notation:

C = total incremental cost

C_0 = total incremental cost of an optimal solution

Q = order quantity

Q_0 = Economic Order Quantity (EOQ)

R = annual requirements in units

c_H = inventory holding costs per unit per year

c_P = preparation costs per order

c_S = shortage costs per unit per year

P = reorder point
L = supply lead time
B = buffer inventory level
t = time between orders

The decision variable under managerial control is the order quantity Q, and we assume that we have a forecasting model to provide an estimate of the annual requirements R. Our initial objective is to develop a model to determine the order quantity Q_0 that minimizes the relevant incremental costs.

Alternative Generator

In our discussion of predictive models, we generally assumed that the manager determined a specific alternative as input to the predictive model. When an optimizing model is used, rather than identifying a specific alternative, the manager defines the *set of all feasible alternatives*. That is, he must describe the characteristics of alternatives that will be acceptable solutions to his problem. In our inventory management problem the set of feasible alternatives consists of all of the possible order sizes, $Q = 1, 2, 3, \ldots, n$, where n may be an upper bound reflecting warehouse capacity, or some other constraint. The optimizing model must search through this entire set of alternatives to identify Q_0.

Model For Predicting System Performance

With the set of feasible alternatives defined, we must develop a model that relates system inputs. For the purchase order quantity system, given a specific order quantity, Q, the outcome of interest to the decision maker is the total incremental cost C with which it is associated. We must determine a logical relationship to relate the order quantity to these incremental costs.

Figure 4 describes the idealized functioning of the inventory system. When the inventory level of our item falls to the reorder point P, an order for Q units is placed. The reorder point P is set so that inventory is reduced to zero by normal usage at rate R precisely when the order for Q units is received. The inventory is then increased immediately by Q units and the cycle repeats as shown in Figure 4. The average inventory is simply $Q/2$.

The total incremental costs C for this simple system are the costs of holding inventory and the costs associated with the procurement of an order of size Q. (We are assuming no price discounts and no shortages, since deterministic usage rate and precise timing of order receipt are a part of the model.) Therefore, the logical relationship for the costs is

$$C = \text{inventory holding costs} + \text{preparation costs}.$$

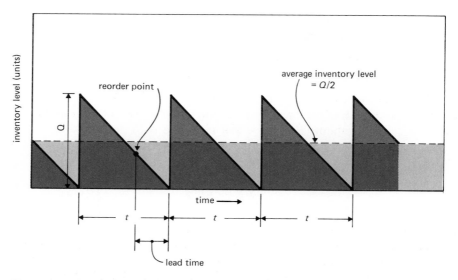

Figure 4. Graphic model of inventory levels when the number purchased at one time is Q units. The time between the receipt of orders is t

We can see from Figure 4 that if Q is increased, the average inventory level $Q/2$ will increase proportionately. If the inventory holding cost per unit per year is c_H, the annual incremental costs associated with holding inventories are

$$c_H\ (Q/2)\ .$$

If the cost to hold a unit of inventory for a specific product was $c_H = \$0.10$, we could express the inventory cost holding function as $0.10\ Q/2 = 0.05\ Q$, a simple linear function. The inventory holding cost function is plotted in Figure 5 as curve (a).

Similarly, the annual preparation costs depend on the number of times orders are placed per year and the cost to place an order. The number of orders required for an annual requirement of R will vary with the lot size Q of each order; that is, the number of orders equals R/Q. If it costs c_P to place an order, the annual preparation costs are

$$c_P\ (R/Q)\ .$$

If, for example, $R = 1600$ units per year, and $c_P = \$5$, we could express the annual preparation costs as $(5 \times 1600/Q) = 8000/Q$. This preparation cost function is plotted for different values of Q in Figure 5 curve (b).

The total incremental costs C are represented by the sum of the two cost components

$$C = c_H\ (Q/2) + c_P\ (R/Q). \tag{1}$$

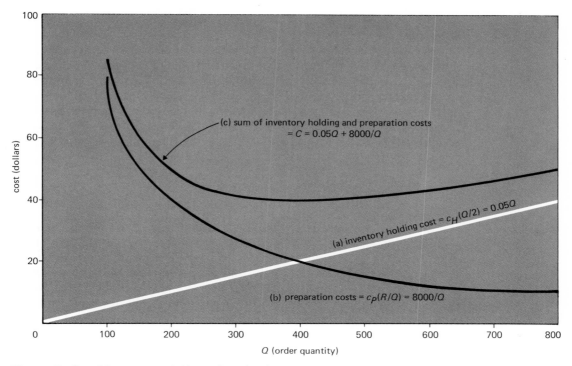

Figure 5. Graphic representation of evaluative model. $R = 1600$ units per year, $c_P = \$5.00$, $c_H = \$0.10$

Equation (1) is our predictive model. For the specific values of the parameters given, equation (1) becomes

$$C = 0.05\,Q + 8000/Q. \qquad (2)$$

Curve (c) in Figure 5 shows this total cost function plotted for different values of Q. Note that curve (c) declines to a minimum as order size increases and then increases again as inventory holding costs become dominant. We can now use equation (2) to evaluate different order quantity policies.

Evaluative Model

Given the predictive model, we must now evaluate the outcomes it produces. The simple inventory problem we have described involves a single criterion, total incremental costs, and complete certainty. That is, we have assumed that there is no uncertainty regarding demand, inventory holding costs, preparation costs, the supply lead time, or other elements of the problem. These assumptions may or may not be appropriate in a specific real-world application. Later, we shall see how additional detail can be added to this simple model, so that more realistic models may be obtained by "boot-strapping."

As we discussed in Chapter 2, in the case of a single criterion under certainty, we need only agree that more (or less) of the criterion is desirable. Since the criterion in this case is total incremental costs C, obviously we would like to minimize C. This could be accomplished by trial and error calculations using different alternative values of Q in equation (2), or by creating graphs such as Figure 5. However, an optimizing model exists that simplifies this search for Q_0, the economic order quantity.

Optimizing Model

We now have all but one of the basic elements necessary to construct the optimizing model. We have an alternative generator in that we can set the order quantity Q to some initial low value and with each iteration we can increase Q by small increments (as small as one unit). We have a forecasting model to estimate annual requirements R. We have a predictive model of the manner in which the system functions in the form of equation (1), or equation (2) for the specific parameter values of our example, and we have the simple evaluative model, minimize C. The missing element is, of course, the test for optimality.

By inspecting Figure 5, we can see that the form of the total incremental cost curve is such that the minimum cost occurs when the slope of the curve is zero. We have placed all of the elements of the optimizing model in the flow chart shown in Figure 6.

To use the iterative procedure we would start with a value of Q and evaluate it by equation (1) and determine the direction of the slope in order to get the next value of Q. In fact we will not actually use this iterative procedure, we will simply use a visual examination of the total cost curve of Figure 5 as our test. Let us start with $Q_1 = 100$ units and use increments of 100 units for sample calculations. Using equation (2) for the specific parameters of our example,

$$C = 0.05\,Q + 8000/Q$$
$$= 0.05 \times 100 + 8000/100 = \$85 \,.$$

Table 1 summarizes the successive calculations for $Q_2 = 200$, $Q_3 = 300$, $Q_4 = 400$, and $Q_5 = 500$ units, indicating the visual check for the direction of slope. In this instance we have actually gone past the zero slope point in calculating for Q_5 to indicate that the slope changes from negative to positive and that the value of C increases beyond the minimum at $Q_0 = 400$ units.

The power of the optimizing model is not in the iterative procedure we have just used to demonstrate conceptually what happens as we converge on the optimum solution, but in using mathematical methods to derive a

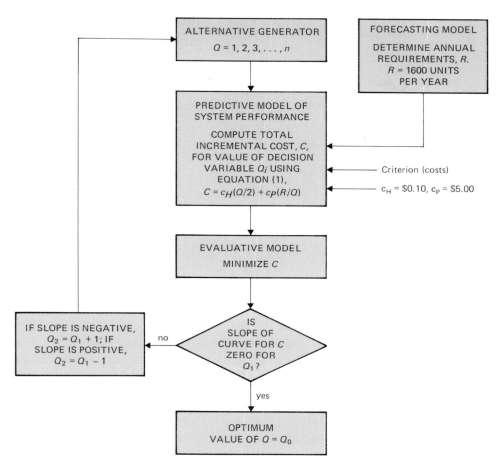

Figure 6. Flow chart for an optimizing inventory model that combines a forecasting model, an alternative generator, a predictive model, an evaluative model, a test for optimality, and a mechanism to direct changes in Q based on the test for optimality

general solution for the entire class of order quantity problems. Using appropriate mathematical methods we can determine the general form of the slope of equation (1):

$$\text{Slope} = c_H/2 - c_P(R/Q^2) \,. \tag{3}$$

The value of equation (3) is, in fact, the slope of the line tangent to the total incremental cost curve. We wish to know the value of Q when this slope is zero. Therefore, we set equation (3) equal to zero and solve for Q_0:

TABLE 1. Computation of Costs C for
Five Successive Values of Q_i

Order Quantity (Q_i)	Inventory Holding Costs $(0.05\ Q_i)$	Preparation Costs $(8000/Q_i)$	Total Incremental Costs* (C)	Visual Check of Slope of C for Value of Q_i
100	5.0	80.0	85.0	—
200	10.0	40.0	50.0	—
300	15.0	26.7	41.7	—
400 = Q_0	20.0	20.0	40.0	0
500	25.0	16.0	41.0	+

Note: $R = 1600$ units per year, $c_H = \$0.10$, and $c_P = \$5$.
*The sum of the second and third columns of the table.

$$0 = c_H/2 - c_P R/Q_0^2$$
$$Q_0^2 = 2\ c_P R/c_H$$

and

$$Q_0 = \sqrt{2\ c_P R/c_H}\ . \tag{4}$$

Equation (4) is a general solution for the optimum order quantity Q_0 and may be used for any values of requirements R and the cost parameters c_P and c_H. The cost of an optimal solution may be derived by substituting the value of Q_0 defined by (4) in equation (1),

$$C_0 = c_H Q_0/2 + c_P R/Q_0\ .$$

This reduces to

$$C_0 = \sqrt{2\ c_P c_H R}\ . \tag{5}$$

Now that we have equations (4) and (5), we may substitute the values for R, c_P, and c_H used in our example to obtain

$$Q_0 = \sqrt{2 \times 5 \times 1600/0.10} = \sqrt{160{,}000} = 400 \text{ units}\ ,$$

and

$$C_0 = \sqrt{2 \times 5 \times 0.10 \times 1600} = \sqrt{1600} = \$40\ .$$

The basic EOQ model involves quite restricted assumptions. For example, no shortages or back orders are allowed (the timing of the receipt of orders is assumed to be perfect), there are no price discounts, and all aspects of the model are deterministic (demand is assumed to be known and constant, as is supply lead time). Given the basic model, we can successively relax some of these assumptions and approach reality. In Chapter 6 we called this process of beginning with a simple model and then adding detail, "bootstrapping."

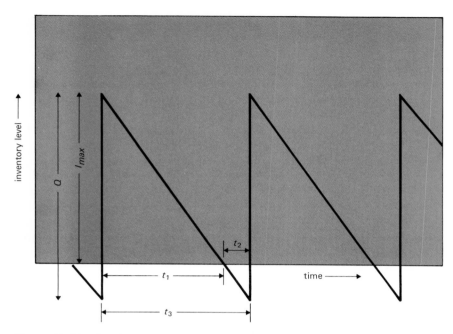

Figure 7. Idealized structure of inventory levels with back orders of $Q - I_{max}$ allowed; t_1 = time during which there are inventory balances on hand; t_2 = time during which there is an inventory shortage; t_3 = cycle time

Inventory Model That Allows Shortages

If the assumption that shortages and back orders are zero is relaxed, we have the graphical structure of Figure 7. The problem is now to determine the minimum cost order quantity when shortages are allowed at a cost of c_S. The inventory level rises to only I_{max} on the receipt of Q because the difference $(Q - I_{max})$ is assumed to meet back orders instantaneously.

When shortage costs are accounted for, the basic EOQ model becomes slightly more general and the optimizing model represented by equation (4) becomes a special case. The rationale for the derivation parallels the basic model, but it is somewhat more complex mathematically. Derivations may be found in Buffa and Taubert [1972], and the resulting formulas are

$$Q_0 = \sqrt{2c_P R / c_H} \cdot \sqrt{(c_H + c_S)/c_S} \tag{6}$$

$$C_0 = \sqrt{2c_P c_H R} \cdot \sqrt{c_S/(c_H + c_S)} \tag{7}$$

$$I_{max_0} = \sqrt{2c_P R / c_H} \cdot \sqrt{c_S/(c_H + c_S)} \tag{8}$$

Note that when comparing equations (6) and (7) with the comparable equations (4) and (5), Q_0 is increased by the factor $\sqrt{(c_H + c_S)/c_S}$, and C_0 is decreased by the factor $\sqrt{c_S/(c_H + c_S)}$. The influence of shortages, then, is dependent on the relative size of c_H and c_S. If c_H is large relative to c_S, the effect of shortages on Q_0 and C_0 is considerable; that is, Q_0 will be increased and C_0 decreased compared to equations (4) and (5). If, on the other hand, c_H is small relative to c_S, minor changes in Q_0 and C_0 will result.

The net effect of shortage costs on Q_0 and C_0 may at first seem to be strange. Recognize, however, that when the model permits shortages, average holding costs are reduced because of smaller average inventory balances. This reduction will result in a larger Q_0. For the shortage case, C_0 is smaller than when shortages are not included because both holding costs and annual preparation costs are somewhat lower. If we consider shortages in the previous example where $R = 1600$ per year, $c_P = \$5$ per order, $c_H = \$0.10$ per unit per year, and in addition, $c_S = \$0.50$ per unit per year, we have the following results:

$$Q_0 = \sqrt{(2 \times 5 \times 1600)/0.10} \cdot \sqrt{(0.10 + 0.50)/0.50}$$

$$= 400 \sqrt{1.2} = 400 \times 1.095 = 438 \text{ units},$$

$$C_0 = \sqrt{2 \times 5 \times 0.10 \times 1600} \cdot \sqrt{0.50/(0.10 + 0.50)}$$

$$= 40 \sqrt{0.833} = 40 \times 0.913 = \$36.51.$$

The limiting values of c_S provide valuable insight. As c_S becomes infinitely large the factor in equation (6), $\sqrt{(c_H + c_S)/c_S}$, becomes 1 in the limit and we have the basic inventory model of equation (4). This corresponds to a policy of no shortages permitted. On the other hand, if c_S is set at zero, then $\sqrt{(c_H + c_S)/c_S}$ and Q_0 become infinity. This corresponds to a policy of infinite back ordering, hand-to-mouth supply, or supply only on the basis of special order.

The Effect of Quantity Discounts

The basic EOQ model assumes a fixed price; therefore, the total cost equation (1) does not include the price of the item, since it is not a relevant cost in the basic model. Let us now consider a model that includes the value of the item as a factor in order to take account of price discounts. The total incremental cost associated with such a system is then:

$$
\begin{aligned}
C = &\text{(annual cost of placing orders)} \\
&+ \text{(annual purchase cost of R items)} \\
&+ \text{(annual holding cost for inventory)} \\
&= c_P(R/Q) + kR + kF_H(Q/2)
\end{aligned}
\tag{9}
$$

where k = cost or price per unit, and F_H = *fraction* of inventory value representing inventory holding cost on an annual basis ($kF_H = c_H$). For example, if k = \$1 and F_H = 0.25, then c_H = \$0.25 per unit per year.

Following the rationale developed previously, we seek the value of Q, Q_0, that minimizes this total incremental cost equation. This leads to

$$Q_0 = \sqrt{2c_P R / kF_H} \qquad (10)$$

$$C_0 = \sqrt{2c_P kF_H R} + kR . \qquad (11)$$

The derivations of equations (10) and (11) parallel the derivations for the previous EOQ formulas.

We may now use equations (10) and (11) in the analysis of inventory systems that involve a price break. For comparison let us assume the previous example data of R = 1600 units per year, c_P = \$5 per order, and F_H = 10 percent per year. Recall that Q_0 was 400 units. Now let us assume in addition that the purchase prices are quoted as \$1 per unit in quantities below 800 and \$0.98 per unit in quantities above 800. If we buy in lots of 800, we save \$32 per year on the purchase price plus \$10 on order costs, since only two orders need to be placed per year to satisfy annual needs. This saving of \$42 per year must be greater than the additional inventory costs that would be incurred if the price discount is to be attractive.

Referring to Figure 8, we see that there are two ranges of lot sizes where in fact two different total cost curves are effective. For the price k_1 = \$1, order sizes in the range of 0 to 799 are effective. For the discounted price of k_2 = \$0.98, order sizes greater than or equal to the price break order size of b = 800 are effective.

The logic of our analysis is to first note that the total incremental cost curve C_2 will fall below the curve C_1. This configuration is shown in Figure 8. The logical thing to do, then, is to calculate Q_{2_0} to see if it falls within the range where the price k_2 = \$0.98 applies. Performing this calculation using equation (10), we find that Q_{2_0} = 404 units, which is less than the break point b = 800 units (below the effective range for C_2). Since 404 units corresponds to the minimum point on the C_2 curve, we know that the lowest possible cost of C_2 within the range where the price k_2 applies is at the order size b = 800 units.

If it had happened that Q_{2_0} was in the range for price k_2, this would have determined immediately that the EOQ for the system was the value calculated as Q_{2_0}. Since this is not the case, however, we must continue our analysis to see if the minimum point on the curve C_1 is below C_2 (which we now know is at the order size b = 800 units). We may calculate the cost associated with Q_{1_0} (C_{1_0}) easily from equation (11), and its value is \$1640. Also, we may calculate the costs associated with the lot size b = 800 units (C_b) using equation (9), and we find this to be \$1617. The decision is now clear; $Q_0 = b$ = 800 units, since the total incremental costs at order size b are less than C_{1_0}.

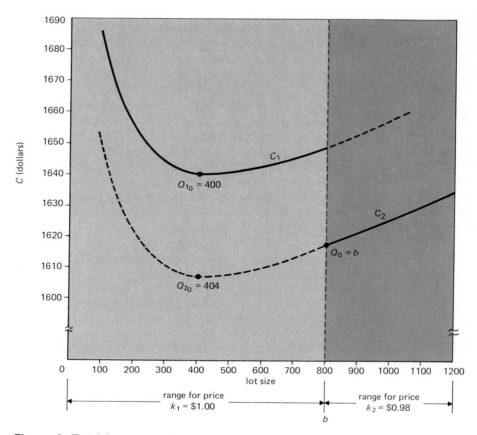

Figure 8. Total incremental cost curves for inventory model with one price break at $b = 800$ units. $R = 1600$ units per year; $c_P = \$5$; $F_H = 10$ percent of inventory value

The results can be easily seen from the graph of Figure 8, however, constructing the curves for each case would be laborious compared to the simple computations required to come to a decision. Figure 9 shows a decision flow chart for the inventory model with one price break, indicating the flow of computations and resulting decisions. In some instances, the final result is obtained with one calculation, as when Q_{2_0} falls in the order size range where the price k_2 is valid. Where this is not the case, simple calculations for comparitive total incremental cost yield a final result.

The flow chart in Figure 9 is a series of steps that must be followed in order to solve our optimizing inventory model. In general, the steps required to solve an optimizing model are called an *algorithm*. Often an algorithm can be programmed and implemented on a computer. Although the algorithm required to solve this simple inventory model consists of only a few

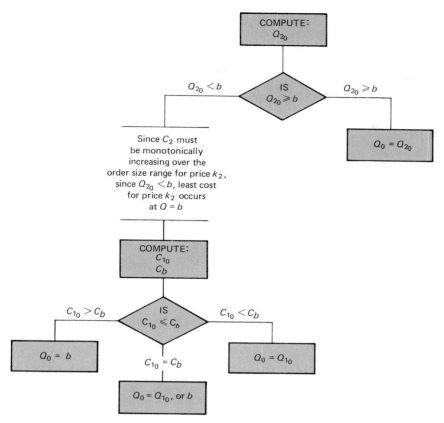

Figure 9. Decision flow chart for inventory model with one price break at the lot size b. Price k_1 applies in the order size range $0 < Q < b$, price k_2 applies in the order size range $Q \geqslant b$

steps, more complex optimizing models will require much more complex algorithms to determine a solution.

Using the same general rationale, we can develop decision processes for inventory models with two or more price breaks. Also, models can be constructed for quantity discount situations that also take account of other factors such as shortage costs.

We have used the purchase order quantity problem as a mechanism for introducing optimizing models. While simple, the conceptual framework for the EOQ involves all of the basic elements of optimizing models in which alternative generator, predictive model, and evaluative model are combined in an optimizing system. Of course, there is a great deal more to know about inventory models for managerial use. Some of the most important concepts in this category are those related to the assessment of risks that result from variability of both demand and of supply time. We have included a discussion of these concepts in Appendix D for those interested.

WHAT SHOULD THE MANAGER KNOW?

Depending on the nature of the enterprise, inventories can be of extreme importance. It is not uncommon for inventories to account for 15 to 40 percent of assets. Especially in high volume operations, a changing demand pattern can have an enormous effect on inventories. Recall the fantastic inventory buildup in the automobile industry during the latter part of 1974, where a decrease in demand resulted in an enormous inventory buildup which in turn caused a virtual shutdown of the production operations.

Interpretation of the Results of Inventory Models   In order to manage inventories effectively, managers need to know how they behave in relation to demand changes. The several components of system inventories behave differently in relation to average demand. First, the pipeline inventories vary directly with system volume. If the system is geared up for a higher volume, pipeline inventories must increase in direct proportion. Conversely, if volume declines, the pipeline inventory necessary to sustain the system declines and management must take action to ensure that inventories are reduced to reflect the change.

Note, however, that required cycle and buffer stocks may be a source of economy of scale in operations. If demand increases, the average cycle stock need increase only as the square root of demand [see equation (4)]. Thus, if demand doubles, cycle stock need increase by a factor of only $\sqrt{2} = 1.4$. There is a definite economy in larger scale operations. There may also be a similar economy of scale in relation to the size of buffer stocks needed to absorb the fluctuations in demand and supply time.

Another dimension in the interpretation of the results of inventory models has to do with the sensitivity of relevant costs to changes in order size from optimal levels. Note in equation (5) that relevant costs are proportional to the square root of demand, and the other relevant factors. Thus, near the optimum, costs do not change markedly as we deviate from optimality. We note this effect in Figure 5; that is, the total incremental cost curve is "shallow" near the optimum. This fact of relative insensitivity of costs provides managers with flexibility. They can take account of factors not included in the model that may call for deviations from optimal order sizes, realizing that costs will not be affected greatly unless the deviation is quite large. It is important to be operating in the optimal range, but strict adherence to the results of order size models is of little importance.

Information Requirements   Good inventory control systems are dependent on good forecasting and up-to-date inventory records. When this kind of information is available, inventory reordering decisions can be programmed in computing systems and become virtually automatic. In addition, however, the cost parameters need to be maintained up to date and the system parameters such as reorder points need to be examined periodically to ensure that the system remains appropriate to current conditions.

The Manager's Role and Optimizing Models   The manager's role in the predictive models discussed in Part Three was basically his traditional role. Those models in no way challenged the manager's traditional decision-making function. Optimizing models by their nature, however, suggest what the decision should be. This suggestive power is perhaps the great optimizing model trap. If the solution is optimum, what is left for the manager to decide? It is at this point that the need for managerial involvement in model formulation becomes crucial. If the manager understands what factors enter the model and the assumptions made, he can determine how to use the results intelligently. He should understand that the solution is optimal for the *model*. It is also optimal for the real-world counterpart of the model only insofar as the predictive component of the model duplicates actual system performance and the evaluative component reflects the criteria that bear on the decisions. If the evaluative component of the model cannot deal with all of the criteria, then the manager must do so by making trade-offs between model results and other criteria.

Check Your Understanding

1. Explain the decoupling function of inventories.
2. An auto manufacturer produces at the rate of 2000 cars per day, seven days per week. The autos are driven off the assembly line to a temporary storage lot where they await shipment for an average of two days. They are then loaded on trains or trucks and are moved to distribution points. The transit time averages five days. The cars remain in storage at distributors for an average of three days and are then shipped to dealers by truck, requiring an average of two days. They are unloaded at the dealers' lots and remain there until sold for an average of two days.
   a. Compute the transit inventory.
   b. Compute the finished goods pipeline inventory.
   c. What is the investment tied up in finished goods inventory if the average value of a car is $2500?
3. Define the following terms:
   a. cycle inventory
   b. buffer inventory
   c. seasonal inventory

4. List and define the cost components that are relevant to the control of inventories. Relate the costs to managerial objectives.

5. Define the following terms:
   a. order quantity
   b. Economic Order Quantity (EOQ)
   c. inventory holding costs
   d. preparation costs
   e. shortage costs
   f. reorder point
   g. lead time

6. If the cost of holding inventory is $c_H = \$0.25$ per unit per year, the cost of order writing is $c_P = \$10$ per order, and the annual requirements are $R = 10,000$ units,
   a. What is the alternative generator?
   b. What is the predictive model?
   c. What is the evaluative model?
   d. What is the test for optimality?
   e. What is the optimizing model?
   f. What is the EOQ?

7. What are the assumptions involved in equation (4)? Which assumptions are relaxed in the shortage model? In the model that allows price discounts?

8. If c_H is $100 \times c_S$, what is the effect on EOQ compared to the basic model of equation (4)? What is the effect on incremental costs compared to the basic model of equation (5)? Explain why this effect should be true in terms of the relative values placed on inventories and shortages.

9. In the text example concerning price discount models, the computed EOQ for the discounted price of $k_2 = \$0.98$ per unit was 404 units. The cost of a lot size of 404 units by equation (11) would be $1608, yet we chose the lot size of 800 units at a cost of $1617 as being more economical. Explain why.

10. If demand changes, perhaps an increase or decline of 50 percent, how do the following components of inventory change?
    a. buffer inventory
    b. cycle inventory
    c. transit inventory
    d. pipeline inventory
    e. decoupling inventory

11. If the EOQ for an item is 500 units, but there is a price advantage in ordering 550 units, how concerned should the manager be about deviating from the computed EOQ?

ELEMENTARY OPTIMIZING MODELS FOR INVENTORY MANAGEMENT

Problems

1. The pharmacy of a large hospital has established inventory-related costs to aid them in ordering and maintaining inventory levels of drugs for hospital use.

    In establishing inventory holding costs, there was some controversy over the appropriate interest charge. The hospital was nonprofit, so an internal rate of return would be zero. Interest on borrowed money was 10 percent. The cost of storage, insurance, obsolescence, and pilferage, averaged 15 percent of inventory value. The cost of storing some items such as narcotics, however, was 20 percent because of special precautions taken against theft. The cost of storing ordinary prescriptions was 15 percent, and of non-prescription items only 10 percent.

    The cost to place an order seemed to vary considerably because some items, for example narcotics, required special procedures to conform to control laws. At the other end of the spectrum were nonprescription items for which ordering was as simple as ordering any other common supply item. When aggregated, however, the average cost of preparing an order was $10, but the range seemed to be from $5 to $25.

    Another problem in controlling inventories was the wide range of item value. The value of aspirin was as low as $2 per thousand, but some exotic drugs could have a value as high as $1000 per ounce.

    Formulate an ordering policy for the pharmacy manager that takes account of his rather different supply items.

2. Suppose we are using an EOQ ordering policy on high valued items, and ordering costs have been established as $c_P = \$25$ per order, and inventory holding costs as $c_H = \$100$ per unit per year. Average annual requirements are $R = 1000$ per year and, therefore, $Q_0 = 22.36$.
    a. There is controversy over the appropriate ordering cost. Some think it too high and some too low. What difference in Q_0 results if c_P is $20? $30? What are the percentage differences? What are the incremental cost differences and their percentage differences?
    b. The inventory holding cost is also contested. What difference in Q_0 and C_0 results if c_H is $80? $120?

3. Suppose that the pharmacy manager in problem 1 has decided to adopt an EOQ policy that recognizes three general categories of items. One of the problems was the lead time of supply from vendors. Each vendor was fairly reliable in meeting his stated supply time; however, there were variations between vendors. Therefore, the manager had set order points for each item that depended on the vendor, the average usage rate, and a safety stock.

    Having installed the system, the manager now wishes to maintain it and adhere to the policy. Which parameters should he monitor most closely? Why?

4. A manufacturing company produces a line of small one-cylinder engines used in lawn mowers, portable compressors, portable pumps, etc. The parts for the engines are produced in lots and stored as manufactured parts for later use in assembly as needed. The costs of preparing manufacturing orders and controlling them through the shop are estimated as $50 per manu-

facturing order. The cost of holding in-process inventory is estimated as 25 percent of inventory value.

The cylinder block for one of the engines has a usage rate of 25,000 per year and the value of the completed block including all labor, materials, and overhead is $10 per unit.

How many manufacturing runs should be scheduled per year if incremental costs are to be minimized?

5. The Jensen Manufacturing Company has organized its inventory system into three main categories depending on urgency and the ordinary amount of follow-up required. It therefore wishes to simplify its use of equation (4) for use by ordering clerks. For class 1, 2, and 3 items ordering costs are respectively $5, $15, and $40.
   a. Derive formulas for the three classes of items.
   b. Further examination shows that inventory carrying cost is virtually constant at 18 percent of cost value for all items. Derive further simplified formulas for the three classes of items.

6. The Jensen Manufacturing Company converted its entire ordering procedure to the EOQ basis described by problem 5. On examining one of the class 3 items ($c_P = \$40$), however, they noted very high annual freight costs under the new policy. Freight costs have been $200 per order under the EOQ policy and would cost only $400 for a carload lot of 500 units. $R = 5000$ units per year, and the average value of the item is $222.22. Should Jensen order in carload lots?

7. The pharmacy discussed in problem 1 has some items for which a price discount is available. One such item is offered at $10 per unit in lots below 1000 and $9 per unit in lots above 1000. Annual requirements are 5000, $c_P = \$25$, and $F_H = 35$ percent of inventory value. Q_0 for the $10 price is 267 units and for the $9 price is 282 units. Is the price discount attractive?

References

Brown, R. G., *Decision Rules for Inventory Management,* Holt, Rinehart and Winston, New York, 1967.

Buchan, J., and E. Koenigsberg, *Scientific Inventory Management,* Prentice-Hall, Englewood Cliffs, N.J., 1963.

Buffa, E. S., and W. H. Taubert, *Production-Inventory Systems: Planning and Control,* revised edition, Richard D. Irwin, Inc., Homewood, Illinois, 1972.

Magee, J. F., and D. M. Boodman, *Production Planning and Inventory Control,* second edition, McGraw-Hill, New York, 1967.

Starr, N. K., and D. W. Miller, *Inventory Control: Theory and Practice,* Prentice-Hall, Englewood Cliffs, N.J., 1962.

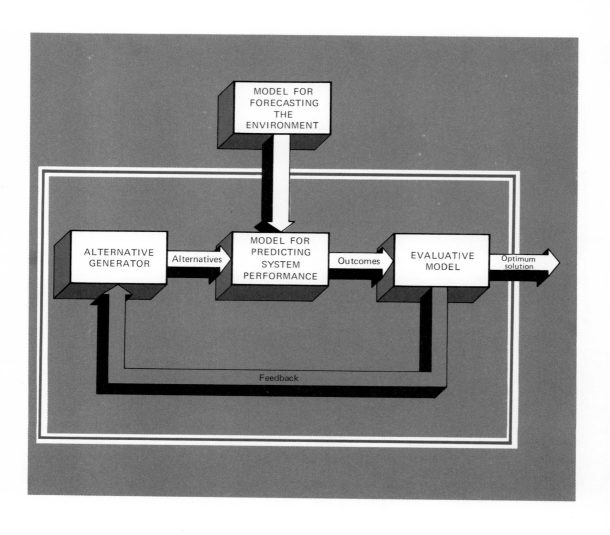

13

Linear Optimization Models

The optimizing models of the greatest significance to managers have been linear optimization models and their associated powerful solution technique known as linear programming. Linear optimization models have been applied in a wide variety of industries and nonprofit activities such as steel, oil refining, utilities, education, meat packing, health care, refuse collection, and many others.

The kinds of applications have included all sorts of resource allocation problems such as long-range financial planning, aggregate capacity planning, portfolio planning and selection, plant location, production planning and scheduling, political districting, corporate financial planning, warehousing and distribution, air pollution control, water pollution control, promotion and advertising decisions, and so on. (A special subsection of the reference list at the end of this chapter is devoted to reports of applications.) Obviously, linear optimization models are not simply theoretical concepts applicable to toy problems. They are powerful, useful managerial models.

In this chapter, we emphasize formulating linear optimization models and interpreting results. In fact, we assume a computer solution technique exists so that if we learn how to formulate linear optimizing problems, we can use a "black box" to provide solutions. Then we can take the manager's viewpoint and see how the results can be interpreted in the most useful way. In the next chapter, "The Simplex Method," we look inside the black box to see how the solution technique works.

NATURE OF LINEAR OPTIMIZATION MODELS

As with all optimizing models, linear optimization models combine the alternative generator, predictive model, and evaluative model with a test for optimality. The combination of these elements functions as a system to produce the best possible solution for the stated conditions and criteria. Just how these elements are combined in linear optimization models can be understood better at a later point. While we will maintain the general conceptual framework of the optimizing system, our first task will be to examine the special characteristics of linear models and their formulations.

Linear optimization models, then, are characterized by linear mathematical expressions. In addition, they are usually deterministic in nature; that is, they do not take account of risk and uncertainty. The parameters of the model are assumed to be known with certainty. Finally, as we shall see, linear programming is used most often when we are attempting to allocate some limited or scarce resource in order to make decisions that use the resource in question in such a way that a stated criterion is optimized (either minimized or maximized).

The Meaning of Linearity

In linear models, we *must* use only linear mathematical expressions. Recall our use of simple break-even analysis in Chapters 6 and 7. Figure 1 shows the elements of the profit (loss) function that we developed there. The relationships in the profit (loss) model are linear because the decision variable x (number sold) does not appear to any power other than 1. There are no squared or higher powers of the variable x, and there are no cross product terms where more than one variable is involved. Another way to say the same thing is to note that linear variables graph as straight lines.

In Figure 2 we show equations of both linear and nonlinear mathematical expressions, together with their graphs. In Figure 2, (a) and (b) are graphs of linear expressions and appear as straight lines. Figures 2(c) and (d) are graphs of nonlinear expressions, since (c) contains an x^2 term and (d) the cross product of $x_1 x_2$.

Figure 2 also illustrates the mathematical form of constraints. In Figure 2(b) in the shaded portion, we see the expression $x_1 - 2x_2 \geq 4$, which states that $(x_1 - 2x_2)$ must be greater than or equal to ($\geq$) 4. When it is equal to 4, we have the straight line. Otherwise, the inequality expression constrains all combinations of x_1 and x_2 to be in the shaded portion of the graph. Conversely, all combinations of x_1 and x_2 that fall above the straight line are not admissible, since they do not satisfy the constraint $x_1 - 2x_2 \geq 4$.

Figure 2(d) shows a nonlinear constraint expression in the shaded portion of the graph. That expression constrains combinations of x_1 and x_2 to be above the curve (in the shaded portion), since the expression states that

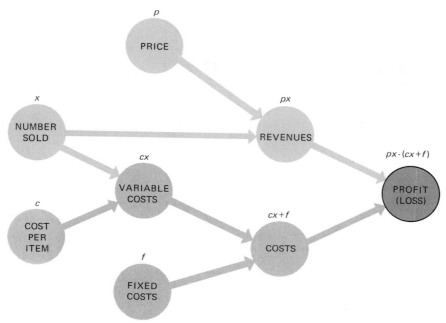

Figure 1. Elements entering the formulation of a profit (loss) function

$(x_1 - 2x_1x_2)$ must be less than or equal to ($\leq$) 4. Again, when the statement on the left-hand side of the expression is equal to 4, all points fall on the curve.

Mathematical statements of constraints may be less than or equal to ($\leq$), equal to ($=$), and greater than or equal to ($\geq$). *Linear* constraints, illustrated by the expression in the shaded portion of Figure 2(b), will be very important in linear optimization models.

Elements of the Model-Building Process

In order to develop a linear optimization model, we use the following process:

1. Define the decision variables.
2. Define the objective function, Z, a linear equation involving the decision variables that identifies our objective in the problem-solving effort. This equation predicts the effects on the objective of choosing different values for the decision variables.
3. Define the constraints—linear expressions involving the decision variables that specify the restrictions on the decisions that can be made. *Alternatives can be generated* by selecting values for the decision variables that satisfy these constraints.

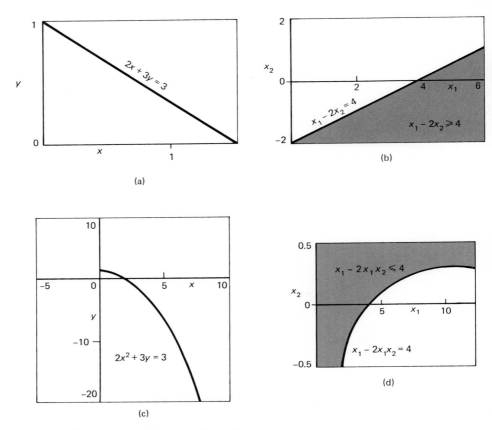

Figure 2. Examples of linear and nonlinear expressions; (a) and (b) are linear, and (c) and (d) are nonlinear, since (c) has an x^2 term, and (d) contains the cross product term $x_1 x_2$. The shaded portions of both (b) and (d) contain inequality expressions describing constraints; that is, values of x_1 and x_2 falling within the shaded areas are admissible but points beyond the curve are not

Let us illustrate the process using a simple break-even analysis model, including the structure and definitions that we developed previously and that are shown in Figure 1.

Define the Decision Variables   In the break-even analysis model we are interested in how profits vary as a function of the number of units sold. Since we are interested in determining a value for x, the number of units produced and sold, it is the decision variable in the model.

Define the Objective Function In the break-even analysis model, the manager wishes to make his profit as large as possible. Therefore the mathematical expressions for predicting the effect of the choice of a production level on profits is, from Figure 1,

$$\text{profit (loss)} = px - cx - f.$$

Now, since the manager wishes to maximize profits our objective function is

$$\text{maximize } Z = px - cx - f,$$

using the evaluative model "maximize profits."

The first two steps in the development of a linear break-even analysis model have been very simple. The decision variable is x, the number of units produced and sold, and the objective function is to maximize the simple mathematical statement of profit. Suppose we stop our model-building effort at this point and examine the break-even chart shown in Figure 3. If we attempt to implement the stated objective function to find a value of the decision variable x that maximizes profits, it is obvious that we should make x very large and produce as many units as we possibly can. We see immediately, however, that we do not yet have enough information. We know that we wish to make x large, but how large can we make it? We do not know, because we have not yet defined the constraints on our decision variable x.

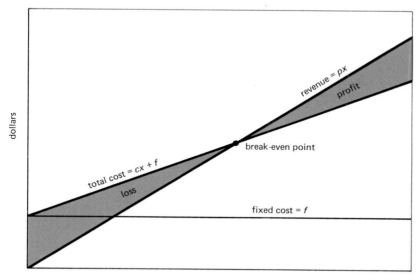

number of units produced (x)

Figure 3. Revenue and the relationship of costs with the number of units produced for a simple break-even chart

Define the Constraints Obviously we cannot ignore possible limitations on the size of x. We may have capacity limitations that restrict the number of units that can be produced within a given time period. If the monthly capacity of the production facility was C units—for example, 300 units per month—then we have a constraint on the decision variable x as follows:

$$x \leq C.$$

Of course, we can substitute the appropriate specific capacity limitation for C.

In addition, we may not be able to sell all units produced at capacity. Perhaps the forecast for monthly demand is D units, perhaps 200. We have, then, an additional constraint on the decision variable,

$$x \leq D.$$

To this point, the constraints define how large x can be. The linear model formulation process requires that we be very specific and also indicate how small x can be. Obviously, it cannot be negative, therefore,

$$x \geq 0.$$

Thus, we can generate alternatives for our analysis by selecting any value for x that satisfies these constraints.

In summary, the linear optimization model is developed as follows:

1. Define the decision variables: x = the number of units produced and sold.
2. Define the objective function: maximize $Z = px - cx - f$.
3. Define the constraints: $x \leq C$, $x \leq D$, $x \geq 0$.

Figure 4 shows the graphic relationships in the form of the well-known break-even chart to which we have added the constraints, the range of feasible solutions within the constraints, and the maximum possible profit for the model.

For the simple break-even model, it would not have been necessary for us to go through the process in order to identify the optimum solution. The solution is obvious. What is important, however, is that the more complex linear optimization models with which we shall deal are a straightforward extension of the process we have developed to this point.

Simplifications

While we can deal with the objective function for profit (loss) = $px - cx - f$ in break-even analysis, it can be simplified for linear models. First, let us factor out the decision variable x so that the profit function becomes

$$px - cx - f = x(p - c) - f.$$

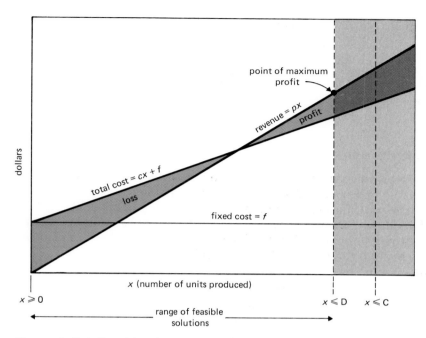

Figure 4. Relationship of revenues, costs, constraints, and range of feasible solutions for a simple break-even analysis

Now let us define the term $(p - c)$ as the contribution to profit and overhead, r, per unit sold. The objective function is then simplified to

$$\text{maximize } Z = rx - f.$$

Now let us examine the importance of the fixed cost element f in our decision problem. Note that f is not a function of the decision variable x. Therefore, our objective of making x as large as possible within the constraints is not affected by f. Thus, for decision-making purposes, we can eliminate the fixed costs, since they are irrelevant to the decision. This is an important notion in model building for managerial decision making and we have applied it previously, for example, in the inventory models of the previous chapter where we considered only the costs affected by the decision. The result of this step is that the objective function is further simplified to

$$\text{maximize } Z = rx,$$

that is, maximize the product of contribution per unit times the number of units produced and sold.

Our final linear optimization model written in the special form for linear programming is now

$$\text{maximize } Z = rx \,,$$
$$\text{subject to}$$
$$x \leqslant C \,,$$
$$x \leqslant D \,,$$
$$x \geqslant 0 \,.$$

A Specific Example

Let us now provide specific numbers for the variables and constraints. Suppose that the price per unit is $3.50, and the variable cost per unit is $2. Then r, the contribution to profit and overhead, is $p - c = 3.50 - 2.00 = $1.50. In addition, suppose that production capacity is 300 units per month and the market forecast of demand indicates that we could sell as many as 200 units per month. The specific linear optimization model is then

$$\text{maximize } Z = 1.5x \,,$$
$$\text{subject to}$$
$$x \leqslant 300 \,,$$
$$x \leqslant 200 \,,$$
$$x \geqslant 0 \,.$$

The simplified linear optimization model is shown graphically in Figure 5 where the objective function $Z = 1.5x$ is a straight line beginning at the origin. The constraints on capacity and demand are shown, but only the demand constraint is effective since it is more restrictive. The feasible range of solutions is between $x = 0$ and $x = 200$ units, and we have slack (unused) plant capacity of 100 units per month.

While it is true that the break-even analysis example is so simple that the answer was entirely obvious, it displays most of the elements of linear optimization model formulation and also introduces the important concept of a range of feasible solutions and the concept of slack in a resource.

FORMULATION OF A TWO-PRODUCT MODEL

Let us now consider a slightly more complex situation. A chemical manufacturer produces two products, which we shall call chemical x and chemical y. Each product is manufactured by a two-step process that involves blending and mixing in machine A and packaging on machine B. The two products complement each other since the same production facilities can be used for both products, thus achieving better utilization of these facilities.

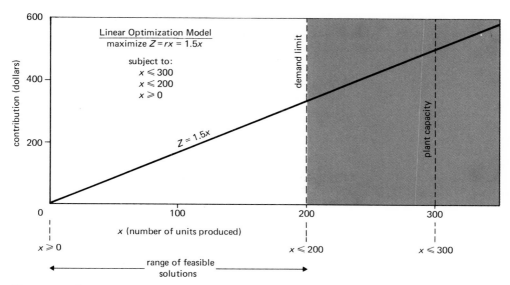

Figure 5. Graphic representation of a linear optimization model when $p = \$3.50$, $c = \$2.00$, and contribution per unit produced is $r = p - c = \$1.50$. Plant capacity is 300 units per month, and demand is forecast for a limit of 200 units per month

Definition of Decision Variables

Since these facilities are shared, and costs and profits from each product are different, there is the question of how to utilize the available machine time in the most profitable way. Chemical x is seemingly more profitable, but the manager once tried producing the maximum amount of chemical x within market limitations, using the balance of his capacity to produce chemical y. He found, however, that such an allocation of machine time resulted in poor profit performance. He feels now that some appropriate balance between the two products is best and he wishes to determine the production rates for each product per two-week period.

Thus, the decision variables are

> x, the number of units of chemical x to be produced,
> y, the number of units of chemical y to be produced.

Definition of the Objective Function

The physical plant and basic organization exists and represents the fixed costs of the organization. From the previous example, we know that these costs are irrelevant to the production scheduling decision, and they are ignored. The manager, however, has obtained price and variable cost information and has computed the contribution to profit and overhead per unit of each product sold as shown in Table 1. He wishes to maximize profit, and the contribution rates have a linear relationship to his objective. Therefore, the objective function that he wishes to maximize is the sum of the total contribution from chemical x ($60x$) plus the total contribution from chemical y ($50y$), or

$$\text{maximize } Z = 60x + 50y .$$

TABLE 1. Sales Prices, Variable Costs, and Contributions per Unit for Chemicals x and y

	Sales Price (p)	Variable Costs (c)	Contribution to Profit and Overhead $(r = p - c)$
Chemical x	$350	$290	$60
Chemical y	450	400	50

Definition of Constraints

The processing times for the two products on the mixing machine (A) and the packaging machine (B) are as follows:

Product	Machine A (hours)	Machine B (hours)
x	2	3
y	4	2

For the upcoming two-week period, machine A has available 80 hours and machine B has available 60 hours of processing time.

Machine A Constraint   Since we are limited by the 80 hours available on machine A, the total time spent in the manufacture of chemical x and chemical y cannot exceed the total time available. For machine A, since chemical x requires 2 hours per unit and y requires 4 hours per unit, the total time spent on the two products must be less than or equal to 80 hours, that is,

$$2x + 4y \leq 80 .$$

Machine B Constraint   Similarly, the available hours on the packaging machine are limited to 60, and since chemical x requires 3 hours per unit and *y* requires 2 hours per unit the total hours for the two products must be less than or equal to 60 hours, or

$$3x + 2y \leq 60 \,.$$

Marketing Constraints   Forecasts of the markets indicate that we can expect to sell a maximum of 16 units of chemical *x* and 18 units of chemical *y*. Therefore,

$$x \leq 16 \,,$$
$$y \leq 18 \,.$$

Minimum Production Constraints   The minimum production for each product is zero, therefore,

$$x \geq 0 \,,$$
$$y \geq 0 \,.$$

These constraints are shown graphically in Figure 6. Note that we have now bounded the possible solution by eliminating all of the production schedules in the shaded areas of Figure 6. The solution to our problem lies somewhere within the solution space *abcdef*, since any production schedule with a combination of amounts of *x* and *y* that falls outside the solution space is not feasible. This is important information for it limits our search for alternatives.

The Linear Optimization Model

We can now summarize a statement of the linear optimization model for the two-product chemical company in the standard linear programming format, as follows:

maximize $Z = 60x + 50y \,,$

subject to

$$2x + 4y \leq 80 \quad \text{(machine A)},$$
$$3x + 2y \leq 60 \quad \text{(machine B)},$$
$$x \leq 16 \qquad\quad \text{(demand for chemical } x),$$
$$y \leq 18 \qquad\quad \text{(demand for chemical } y),$$
$$x \geq 0 \qquad\quad\ \text{(minimum production for chemical } x),$$
$$y \geq 0 \qquad\quad\ \text{(minimum production for chemical } y).$$

Solution and Interpretation of the Two-Product Model

As we mentioned earlier, we will assume that we have a mechanism for solving linear optimization models when they are formulated in the preceding

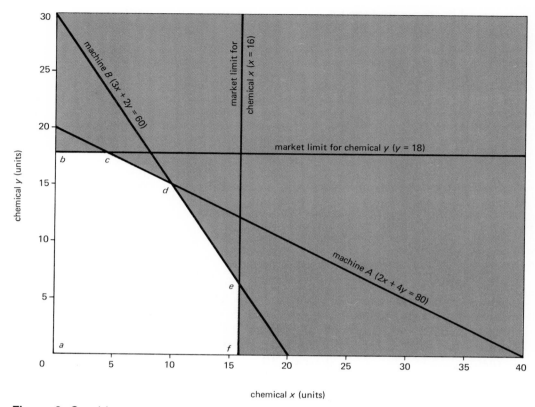

Figure 6. Graphic representation of the limitations imposed by machine capacity, marketing, and minimum production constraints. The area enclosed by *abcdef* includes all feasible solutions to the model

standard format. Indeed, linear programming computing codes are commonly available both in interactive mode (available from a time-share terminal) and in batch mode for large-scale linear programming problem solutions. In order to use either of these computing programs for the solution of linear optimization models, the problem must be presented to the "black box" in the precise form required. This input format is usually more user oriented in interactive time-share systems, and we shall use one of these programs to illustrate solutions to problems in this chapter [see Buckley et al., 1974].

Now, let us return to the chemical production problem for which we just formulated the linear optimization model in standard form. Figure 7 shows a portion of the computer output for the problem. Let us follow through the input steps as well as the solution output.

Computer Input   In Figure 7(a) we see the input steps following the "sign on" and "call up" of the linear programming subroutine. At this point, the user types "LPENTER," and the terminal prints "ENTER THE NAME OF THIS PROJECT." The user responds by typing "CHEMICAL PRODUC- TION."

The terminal then asks whether this problem will have an objective of maximizing or minimizing the objective function by typing "MAXIMIZE OR MINIMIZE." Since our problem is to maximize contribution, the user responds by typing "MAXIMIZE."

The terminal then asks for the statement of the objective function by typing, "OBJECTIVE FUNCTION." The user simply responds by typing in the objective function, "Z = 60 CHEMX + 50 CHEMY." In so doing, the user has named the variables and these names will be used for the balance of the problem. He could have used a purely symbolic notation, but varia- ble names that convey meaning within the context of the problem are com- mon.

Given the objective function, the terminal then requests the constraint equations and tells us how to indicate that all of the constraint equations have been entered, that is, "(STRIKE JUST A CARRIAGE RETURN TO STOP INPUT)." The user responds by typing each constraint on a separate line, using the variable names previously defined. We need not enter the

```
        LPENTER
ENTER THE NAME OF THIS PROJECT CHEMICAL PRODUCTION
MAXIMIZE OR MINIMIZE:  MAXIMIZE
OBJECTIVE FUNCTION:  Z=60CHEMX+50CHEMY
ENTER CONSTRAINT EQUATIONS,  (STRIKE JUST A CARRAGE RETURN TO STOP INPUT)
[001]  2CHEMX+4CHEMY≤80
[002]  3CHEMX+2CHEMY≤60
[003]  CHEMX≤16
[004]  CHEMY≤18
```

(A)

```
     LPRUN

                CHEMICAL PRODUCTION

THE OPTIMAL VALUE OF THE OBJECTIVE FUNCTION IS:     1350.000

               THE VARIABLES IN THE SOLUTION ARE

VARIABLE    CHEMX   AT LEVEL     1.0000E1
            CHEMY                1.5000E1
            SLK3                 6.0000E0
            SLK4                 3.0000E0
```

(B)

Figure 7. The chemical production problem: (a) computer input and (b) computer solution

last two constraints of $x \geq 0$ and $y \geq 0$, since the computer program assumes that none of the variables can take on negative values. Therefore, when the constraints have been entered, the user strikes the carriage return key as directed and the program is executed, computing the solution.

We have discussed the computer input in detail to show how simple it is to use such programs. Many computer programs for linear programming are available; the instructions for each individual program will be unique to that program and the documentation indicates exactly how to provide input. The form of the computer output may also vary from program to program, but will be similar in content.

Computer Output   Figure 7(b) shows the solution output. First, the terminal prints the optimum value of the objective function, $1350. In other words, it states that $Z = 1350$ in the objective function for an optimal solution.

Next, the terminal prints the values of the variables in the optimum solution. Note that scientific notation is used; that is, the value of each variable is followed by "E" and some number. This notation means that the number preceding the E is to be multiplied by that number of 10s. For example, E1 means multiply by 10, E2 by 100, etc. E0 indicates that the multiplier is "1", or simply that the value of the variable needs no modification.

Now let us consider only the first two variables listed in the solution, that we have named *CHEMX* and *CHEMY*. The solution states that their optimal values are 10 and 15 respectively. Note that this is point *d* in Figure 6, the point where the capacity constraint lines for machines *A* and *B* intersect. This is an important observation that we shall use in the next chapter in understanding how the linear programming algorithm actually works.

Using the solution values of *CHEMX* and *CHEMY*, let us insert them in the objective function and compute Z,

$$Z = 60 \times 10 + 50 \times 15 = 1350 \,.$$

This result checks with the optimal value of Z given by the computer solution.

Checking one further bit of logic, if the solution to our problem is at the intersection of the two capacity constraint equations, then we should be able to solve the equations for the two lines simultaneously to determine the values of *CHEMX* and *CHEMY* that are common to the equations. First, let us use the equation for machine *A* and solve for *x*,

$$2x + 4y = 80 \,.$$

Therefore,

$$x = 80/2 - 4y/2 = 40 - 2y \,.$$

We then substitute this value of x in the constraint equation for machine B,

$$3(40 - 2y) + 2y = 60,$$
$$120 - 6y + 2y = 60,$$
$$4y = 60,$$
$$y = 15.$$

This value of y checks with our computer solution. Now, substitute $y = 15$ in the machine A constraint equation to determine the value of x,

$$2x + 4(15) = 80,$$
$$x = (80 - 60)/2 = 10.$$

Thus, we have verified that the solution to our problem is at point d of Figure 6 where the two constraint equations intersect. Another interpretation of this fact is that machines A and B, our two productive resources, are completely utilized in this solution—there is no residual slack capacity. This fact is important because any of the other feasible solutions in the polygon *abcdef* of Figure 6 would have involved some slack capacity in one or both of the two machines. If there had been slack capacity for either of the machines in the optimum solution, that fact would have been indicated in the computer output for the optimum solution. In some more complex problems, there might be slack capacity of a productive resource in an optimum solution.

Now, note that the computer output gave us the value of variables that we did not ask for explicitly, *SLK3* and *SLK4*. These are the slack values related to constraints [3] and [4], the market constraints. Constraint [003], *CHEMX* ≤ 16 was the market limit for that product. The solution simply points out to us that if we produce according to the optimum solution where *CHEMX* = 10, there will be unsatisfied demand (slack) of 6, and this fits in with the market constraint since, *CHEMX* + *SLK3* = 10 + 6 = 16. Similarly, the value of *SLK4* = 3 agrees with the market constraint, *CHEMY* ≤ 18, since *CHEMY* + *SLK4* = 15 + 3 = 18.

These interpretations of the optimum solution to the chemical production problem are rather simple. The important point is that equivalent interpretations of more complex problems are a straightforward extension of these ideas. The solution will state the combination of variables that optimizes the objective function. Some but not all of the constraints will be the controlling ones, and there will be slack in some of the resources; that is, they will not all be fully utilized. In our example, the slack was in the demands for the two products. Note, however, that if the demand for *CHEMY* dropped to only 14, that is ($y = 14$), it would have become one of the controlling ("tight") constraints as may be seen from Figure 6, and there would have been some slack capacity in machine A.

SENSITIVITY ANALYSIS AND INTERPRETATION OF RESULTS

If we wanted only the solution to the problem—the optimal combination of variables, the value of slack variables, and the optimum value of the objective function—we could stop at this point by answering "NO" to the next question typed out by the terminal, "*DO YOU WISH SENSITIVITY ANALYSIS?*" There is available to the decision maker, however, additional valuable information, and he can obtain it by simply answering the question, "*YES,*" as we have done in Figure 8 for the chemical production problem.

While the optimum solution states what to do now, given the objective function and the constraints, the sensitivity analysis raises questions about opportunities and perhaps about what could or should be done to improve the solution to the managerial problem.

Figure 8 presents the sensitivity analysis in tabular form, first for each constraint and then for the prices (contributions) for each product. For each constraint there is listed a "*SHADOW*" (shadow price), the "*LB*" (lower bound of the right-hand side of the constraint), "*CURRENT*" (current value of the right-hand side), and "*UB*" (upper bound of the right-hand side). At first this appears complex, but let us define what these terms mean in our chemical production example.

```
DO YOU WISH SENSITIVITY ANALYSIS? YES

                        SHADOW          LB          CURRENT          UB
CONSTRAINT      1      3.7500E0      5.6000E1      8.0000E1      8.8000E1
                2      1.7500E1      4.8000E1      6.0000E1      7.2000E1
                3      0.0000E0      1.0000E1      1.6000E1      7.2370E75
                4      0.0000E0      1.5000E1      1.8000E1      7.2370E75


PRICE        CHEMX                    2.5000E1      6.0000E1      7.5000E1
             CHEMY                    4.0000E1      5.0000E1      1.2000E2

 -<END>-
```

Figure 8. Sensitivity analysis for the chemical production problem

Shadow Prices   The shadow prices indicate the value of a marginal unit in the right-hand side of the constraint. For example, recall the meaning of the first constraint for machine A (2 $CHEMX$ + 4 $CHEMY$ ≤ 80). It states that the total available capacity for machine A is 80 hours. What would be the marginal value (in the objective function) of one additional unit of capacity? The answer is given in Figure 8 as $3.75. If the capacity of machine A were 81 hours, the extra hour would add $3.75 to the total contribution. Conversely, if only 79 hours were available, this amount would be subtracted from total contribution.

Now observe that the shadow price for machine B capacity is $17.50. The marginal value of capacity for machine B is $17.50/3.75 = 4.7$ times that for machine A. The shadow prices tell the manager that the opportunity provided by increasing machine B capacity is relatively large and allow him to appraise expansion proposals for both machines.

The shadow prices for constraints 3 and 4 (demands) are zero because these constraints do not limit us in the current situation. If demand for CHEMY dropped to 14, then it would become one of the controlling constraints, as we noted previously. The optimum solution would change, but in addition, the shadow price for constraint 4 would become some positive value, indicating a marginal value to increasing demand for CHEMY, perhaps providing the manager with information to appraise programs to stimulate demand.

Lower, Current, and Upper Bounds We just stated the meaning of the shadow prices, that is, the value of marginal units of resources. But, for what ranges are these marginal rates valid? Can we increase capacity for machine B to two or three times its present capacity and expect to obtain an additional $17.50 per unit in the objective function? No, there are limits, and the bounds tell us exactly what they are. Taking the capacity of machine B as an example, it is currently 60 hours as shown in Figure 8 under the "CURRENT" column, but we see that the shadow price is valid in the range of 48 to 72 hours.

If we could increase the capacity of machine B to 72 hours, we would obtain an additional $17.5 \times 12 = \$210$ in total contribution. We would be able to increase contribution by $210 \times 100/1350 = 15.6$ percent. On the down side, if we had a breakdown of machine B, for example, and available hours fell to the lower bound of 48, we would lose $210 in total contribution. The interpretation for the bounds on the capacity of machine A is similar.

Now let us examine the significance of the bounds on the demand for the two products. Take constraint [4], the demand for CHEMY, for example. Its lower bound is 15. A shadow price of zero applies if demand falls to 15, that is, the constraint is ineffective in that range. But, as we have already noted, if demand falls below 15 the constraint becomes one of those controlling the solution.

Now, the upper bound for constraint [4] is listed as 7.2370E75. This is the code for infinity in this particular linear programming computer program. There is no upper bound in effect.

Price Sensitivity The contribution rates in the objective function are termed generally "prices." Recall that the contribution of a unit of CHEMX was $60 and of CHEMY $50, and these are shown as the "CURRENT" values in Figure 8. But, what if "prices" change? Would the changes affect the solution? The lower and upper bounds for prices shown in Figure 8 indicate the range of prices (contribution rates) for which the optimum solution is valid. For example, the contribution rate for CHEMX could be anywhere in the range of $25 to $75 and the optimum amount of CHEMX and CHEMY would still be as indicated in the present solution: produce 10 units of *CHEMX* and 15 units of *CHEMY*. Of course, the total contribution would change because of the change in the contribution rate, but the optimal *decision* would remain the same.

There is a practical significance to the price sensitivity. For example, the manager might estimate contribution for *CHEMX* at $60, but these kinds of figures are seldom absolutely precise. Suppose that the contribution is somewhere in the $55 to $65 range. In this case, the same solution applies. The result is that the use of *rough* estimates for the contribution rate is adequate, and we should not spend additional time and money to refine the estimate. Thus, the bounds help indicate how we should allocate time and money to refine cost information — if the bounds are tight it may be worthwhile to be precise, but if they are loose we would gain nothing by attempting to improve the estimates.

Summary

Let us take a moment to summarize at this point. Given a linear optimization model stated in the format we have specified, we can use a computer program to provide the optimum combination of the decision variables, the optimum value of the objective function, and the values of slack capacity or other resources in the system. In interpreting the solution, however, we can also obtain the value of a marginal unit of each resource (shadow prices) and the range over which the shadow price is valid. In addition, we can obtain the range of prices (contribution rates in our example) in the objective function for which the printed solution is valid.

Understanding the significance of the optimum solution and the sensitivity analysis in the context of the real problem has great value. The decision maker is in a position to appraise various proposals for changing the optimum solution. He should not look on the optimum solution as necessarily the final decision, but as a basis for asking "what if" questions. The sensitivity analysis provides him with information regarding many possible "what if" questions, and may also suggest variations of the model that may require additional computer runs.

The examples we have used to this point are toy problems to illustrate the formulation and interpretation of linear optimization models. The crucial point is that the formulation and interpretation of real problems are straightforward extensions of what we have already discussed. They are larger and more complex, but they apply the same principles. Nevertheless, since the linear optimization models have been so significant as practical decision aids, each manager as a potential user of this methodology should have some exposure to the analysis of a real-world problem. Therefore, we shall now consider first a more complex two-product model, and then a real problem in which a linear optimization model was used in the post office to aid decision makers. We shall formulate the models, solve, and interpret the results.

A MORE COMPLEX TWO-PRODUCT MODEL

We shall now consider a more complex two-product model that may be viewed as a straightforward extension of the two-product example. This example introduces the important concept of the use of *ratios* or *proportions* in the formulation of constraints, and provides a bridge to the presentation of a real world problem.

Suppose a production process is used to manufacture two products. The daily demand for the first product is 50 units, while the demand for the second is 100 units. These products can be processed either manually or by a mechanized system during a two-shift day. However, the capacity of the mechanized system is restricted to less than or equal to 40 units of product 1 per shift, or less than or equal to 75 units of product 2 per shift. Similarly, the manual system is restricted to less than or equal to 30 units of product 1 per shift, or 50 units of product 2 per shift. Suppose that, according to our accounting records, the costs of producing the products vary depending on the system used (mechanized or manual), the type of product, and the shift as shown in Table 2. The obvious question to be answered is how many units should be processed on which system during each shift assuming that we must meet the demand.

Definition of Decision Variables

In order to define the decision variables, it is convenient to introduce some notation that may appear complex at first, but that actually simplifies the formulation of the model. We will let M_{ij} be the number of tens of units of product i (1 or 2) processed during shift j (1 or 2) on the manual system and let MCH_{ij} be the number of tens of units of product i processed during shift j on the mechanized system. Thus, if we determine that $M_{11} = 2$ and $MCH_{21} = 6$, this would indicate that 20 units of product 1 are to be processed by the manual system during shift 1, and 60 units of product 2 are to

TABLE 2. Production Costs for Products 1 and 2 on Manual and Mechanized Systems During Shifts 1 and 2

	Manual	Mechanized
Product 1 (cost/10 units)		
Shift 1	10	8
Shift 2	15	11
Product 2 (cost/10 units)		
Shift 1	5	4
Shift 2	6	6

be processed on the mechanized system during shift 1. Since there are two products that can be processed on two systems during two shifts, there are a total of $2 \times 2 \times 2 = 8$ decision variables.

Definition of the Objective Function

Now we wish to let the computer determine the values of M_{ij} and MCH_{ij} that minimize the cost of meeting our daily production demand. That is, we wish to let the computer minimize the expression

$$Z = 10M_{11} + 8MCH_{11} + 15M_{12} + 11MCH_{12} +$$
$$5M_{21} + 4MCH_{21} + 6M_{22} + 6MCH_{22} ,$$

where the cost coefficients are taken directly from Table 2. For example, the cost of processing 10 units of product 2 using the manual system during shift 1 is \$5, so $5M_{21}$ appears as the fifth term in this objective function.

Definition of Constraints

The constraints result from the demand requirements and the capacity restrictions. In order to meet the demand for product 1, we must have

$$M_{11} + MCH_{11} + M_{12} + MCH_{12} = 5 ,$$

which says that the total number of units of product 1 produced using manual labor and the mechanized system during both shifts must equal 50, or 5 tens of units. Similarly, for product 2,

$$M_{21} + MCH_{21} + M_{22} + MCH_{22} = 10 .$$

Finally, we have capacity restrictions on both the manual and the mechanized systems during each shift. Consider the problem on the manual system during the first shift. Clearly M_{11} must be less than or equal to 3, and M_{21} must be less than or equal to 5. The temptation is to jump to the conclusion that these capacity constraints are very simple; for example, for the manual system during the first shift, we would write

$$M_{11} \leq 3 ,$$
$$M_{21} \leq 5 ,$$

and so on for the other shift and for the mechanized system.

The problem with this approach becomes apparent when we note that on shift 1 we seem to be allowing the simultaneous use of the manual system in two different ways. For example, if we use the full capacity for product 1 ($M_{11} = 3$), then M_{21} must be zero. We cannot use the same capacity more than once, and that is the key to the proper construction of the capacity constraints.

During shift 1, the total available capacity of the manual system can be used up to 100 percent. Therefore, the sum of the *fractions* or *proportions* of this capacity used by each product must be less than or equal to *one*. The fraction of the capacity used for product 1 is the number of tens of units of product 1 processed on the manual system during shift 1, M_{11}, divided by the capacity for product 1, or $M_{11}/3$; for product 2, $M_{21}/5$. Thus, if $M_{11} = 1$, then we are using one third of the available capacity on the manual system during shift 1 to process product 1. The capacity constraint for the manual system during shift 1 is then,

$$M_{11}/3 + M_{21}/5 \leqslant 1 .$$

Now, let us simplify this constraint by multiplying through by 15, the common denominator, and we obtain

$$5M_{11} + 3M_{21} \leqslant 15 .$$

Following exactly the same process, we develop a similar constraint for the capacity of the manual system during the second shift. Test your understanding of this important point by writing down the capacity constraints for the mechanized system, using the same reasoning.

Figure 9 shows part of the computer output for the problem. The complete problem formulation is shown as the computer input in (a). According to the computer solution shown in (b), $MCH_{11} = 1.33$, $MCH_{12} = 3.67$, $M_{21} = 5.0$, and $MCH_{21} = 5.0$. The optimal values of the decision variables not listed in the computer solution are 0.0. This result indicates that we should produce 13.33 units of product 1 during the first shift and 36.67 during the second shift, all on the mechanized system. Further, we produce 50 units of product 2 on the manual system and 50 on the mechanized system, all during the first shift. Check to see that this result satisfies our constraints. The minimum total cost of this solution is 96. Finally the slack variables *SLK*4 and *SLK*6, corresponding to constraints [4] and [6] respectively, indicate that there is unused capacity on both the manual and mechanized systems during shift 2.

THE POST OFFICE—A MORE COMPLEX LINEAR OPTIMIZATION MODEL

In the break-even and two-product examples, our objective was to maximize profit. The post office, however, is a service organization, and its objectives are not measured by a profit function. Thus, the post office example we shall now discuss provides a new and different kind of environment, and it presents a quite realistic example of an actual problem where linear optimization models were used.

We shall consider the letter processing system phase of post office operations, a block diagram for which is shown in Figure 10. The block diagram describes the flow and processing for the three types of letters. The

```
      LPENTER

ENTER THE NAME OF THIS PROJECT    PRELIMINARY EXAMPLE
MAXIMIZE OR MINIMIZE: MINIMIZE
OBJECTIVE FUNCTION:Z=10M11+8MCH11+15M12+11MCH12+5M21+4MCH21+6M22+6MCH22
ENTER CONSTRAINT EQUATIONS, (STRIKE JUST A CARRIAGE RETURN TO STOP INPUT)
[1]  M11+MCH11+M12+MCH12=5
[2]  M21+MCH21+M22+MCH22=10
[3]  5M11+3M21≤15
[4]  5M12+3M22≤15
[5]  7.5MCH11+4MCH21≤30
[6]  7.5MCH12+4MCH22≤30
[7]
```

(A)

```
      LPRUN

                  PRELIMINARY EXAMPLE

THE OPTIMAL VALUE OF THE OBJECTIVE FUNCTION IS:      96.000

               THE VARIABLES IN THE SOLUTION ARE

VARIABLE   MCH11   AT LEVEL    1.3333E0
           MCH12               3.6667E0
           M21                 5.0000E0
           MCH21               5.0000E0
           SLK4                1.5000E1
           SLK6                2.5000E0
```

(B)

Figure 9. The more complex two-product example: (a) computer input and (b) computer solution

three types of letter mail are "collections and acceptance" (Type 1), which consists of mail collected from local mail boxes or brought to the post office by large mailers; "transit mail" (Type 2), which originates in and is destined for other post offices; and "incoming mail" (Type 3), which originates in another city and is destined for local delivery. In general, each type of letter mail is subjected to preparatory operations, then to a sequence of sorting operations before being dispatched. Most of these operations are manual except for the letter sorting machine (LSM).

The nature of the letter mail volume is highly variable. For example, studies of daily mail volume at Cincinnati varied from 400,000 to 4,000,000 pieces [Cohen et al., 1970, p. 89]. Also, as a result of day-end mailing practices of business establishments, 40 to 60 percent of the collections and acceptance mail (C&A) is received between 4:00 and 8:00 P.M. This highly variable demand pattern suggests that it may be difficult to obtain good utilization from letter sorting machines, each of which costs $130,000.

On the other hand, manual sorting is flexible in that labor from low priority (third and fourth class) mail can be allocated to work on first-class

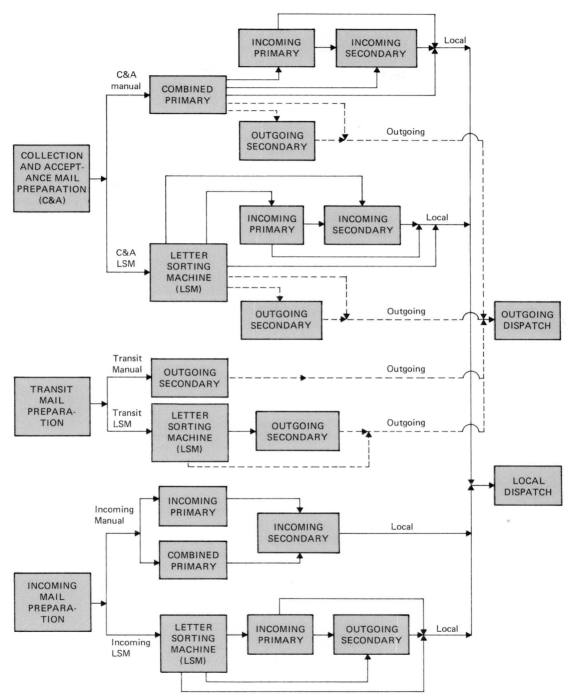

Figure 10. Letter mail processing system

Note: The above diagram is not a typical post office processing plan and the U.S. Postal Service neither approves nor sanctions it as official.

Adapted from R. Cohen, C. McBride, R. Thornton, and T. White, *Letter Mail System Reference Design: An Analytical Method for Evaluating Candidate Mechanization*, p. 9; and information used by permission. See also C. C. McBride, "Post Office Mail Operations," in *Analysis of Public Systems* [1972].

sorting during peak hours of the day and times of the year. Furthermore, sorting clerks work on an hourly basis and can be allocated to meet peak periods. Thus, we have three different kinds of mail that can be processed by either the manual or mechanized modes. The costs of processing are different, however, as shown in Table 3.

Specifically then, the problem is to determine the most efficient use of the LSM's and the manual resources to sort mail, all within the capacity limitations of the LSM's and the mail volume load patterns for the arrival of mail. Note the cost differences between the LSM and manual processing modes. We can save $6.30, $4.10, and $1.50 per thousand respectively using the LSM's on types 1, 2, and 3 mail. Place your bets now for what you think might be the best use of the limited capacity of the LSM's!

The capacity of the LSM's is different for the three types of mail and we have summarized these data for each tour (shift) in Table 4. The capacity of the manual system, however, is elastic. The post office could presumably hire enough people to sort all mail manually, and might do so if that were the most economical way of getting the job done.

Also, as input data, let us perform the analysis for a typical mail volume of 2,000,000 letters divided according to the percentages indicated in Table 3. The mail volume for each type of mail is also indicated in thousands of letters per day in Table 4.

TABLE 3. Comparative Costs for Sorting Letter Mail by Manual and Mechanized Modes

Type of Mail	Percentage of Volume	Cost (dollar per 1000 letters)	
		Letter Sorting Machine (LSM)	Manual
(1) Collection and Acceptance (C&A)	40	$11.90	$18.20
(2) Incoming	40	16.00	20.10
(3) Transit	20	8.50	10.00

TABLE 4. Capacity of the Letter Sorting Machine (LSM) per Tour and Daily Load for the Three Types of Mail

Type of Mail	LSM Capacity (thousands of letters/tour)	Mail Volume (thousands of letters/day)
(1) Collection and Acceptance (C&A)	100	800
(2) Incoming	200	800
(3) Transit	300	400
		2000

Given these data and the statement of the general problem, let us follow the procedure we have established to formulate a linear optimization model for the resource allocation problem in a post office.

Definition of Decision Variables

The decision variables are straightforward and follow from the verbal statement of the problem; that is, how should manual and LSM resources be allocated over the three tours for the three different types of mail? Notice the similarity among the decisions to be made here and those made in the more complex two-product example. Since each sorting mode is measured in terms of the number of letters processed (in thousands), and since we will allocate by tours because the load varies over the day, let M_{ij} be the thousands of letters of mail type i processed during tour j by the *manual* system. Similarly, let LSM_{ij} be the thousands of letters of mail type i processed during tour j by the LSM's. There are three mail types and three tours, so a decision that 4,000 letters of C&A mail on tour 2 should be sorted manually would be represented by $M_{12} = 4$. For each day then there are 18 decisions called for, allocating the number of letters to be sorted by each system, for each mail type, and for each of the three tours.

Definition of the Objective Function

Since we are dealing with a not-for-profit service organization, and we have explicit costs available for using the sorting resources, our objective will be to minimize costs of sorting for the system. We will have an objective function that will aggregate the costs of using each resource for each type of mail in each of the three tours. Since we have 18 decision variables the objective function will have 18 terms, each of which is made up of the appropriate cost factor multiplied by the decision variable. Let us develop the objective function in two components, the LSM and the manual costs.

Objective Function for the LSM System   The costs for each system vary according to the type of mail as indicated in Table 3. We can develop the cost equation systematically by mail type as follows:

$$\text{C\&A (type 1) costs} = 11.9LSM_{11} + 11.9LSM_{12} + 11.9LSM_{13}, \quad (1)$$
$$\text{Incoming (type 2) costs} = 16LSM_{21} + 16LSM_{22} + 16LSM_{23}, \quad (2)$$
$$\text{Transit (type 3) costs} = 8.5LSM_{31} + 8.5LSM_{32} + 8.5LSM_{33}. \quad (3)$$

Objective Function for the Manual System   The costs for the manual system are developed in an entirely parallel way, using the appropriate cost data from Table 3 as follows:

$$\text{C\&A (type 1) costs} \quad = 18.2M_{11} + 18.2M_{12} + 18.2M_{13}, \quad (4)$$
$$\text{Incoming (type 2) costs} = 20.1M_{21} + 20.1M_{22} + 20.1M_{23}, \quad (5)$$
$$\text{Transit (type 3) costs} \quad = 10M_{31} + 10M_{32} + 10M_{33}. \quad (6)$$

Objective Function for the Total System The objective function for the system as a whole is then simply to minimize Z, the aggregate of the costs for equations (1) through (6), or

$$\text{minimize } Z = (1) + (2) + (3) + (4) + (5) + (6).$$

The objective function appears complex only because it is made up of many terms. When constructed systematically, however, it is seen to be composed of simple cost terms.

Definition of Constraints

Our next task in order to complete the post office linear optimization model is to define the constraints. They too are made up of simple components. Basically, Table 4 summarizes some of the constraints in terms of capacities and demands on the system. In addition, we need to know something about the arrival pattern of mail in order to know when it will be available to be sorted—obviously we cannot sort mail until it arrives. Let us develop the constraints systematically.

Capacity Constraints The capacity of the LSM for each of the three types of mail is given in Table 4 and, again the temptation is to jump to the conclusion that these capacities are as simple as they appear; for example, for tour 1,

$$LSM_{11} \leq 100,$$
$$LSM_{21} \leq 200,$$
$$LSM_{31} \leq 300,$$

and so on for the other tours. However, as in the more complex two-product example, we cannot use the same capacity in three different ways simultaneously. We must again use the concept that the total *fraction*, or *proportion*, of the available capacity used by the different products (types of mail in this example) must be less than or equal to one.

The fraction of capacity used for type 1 mail is the amount of type 1 mail on tour 1, LSM_{11}, divided by the capacity for type 1 mail, or $LSM_{11}/100$; for type 2 mail $LSM_{21}/200$; and for type 3 mail $LSM_{31}/300$. The capacity constraint for tour 1 is then,

$$LSM_{11}/100 + LSM_{21}/200 + LSM_{31}/300 \leq 1.$$

Now, let us simplify the constraint by multiplying through by 600, the common denominator, and we have

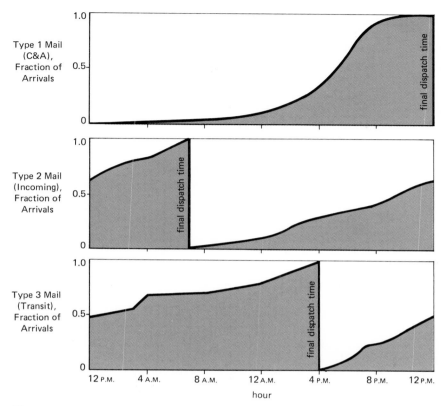

Figure 11. Mail arrivals for the Cincinnati Post Office

From R. Cohen, C. McBride, R. Thornton, and T. White, *Letter Mail System Reference Design: an Analytical Method for Evaluating Candidate Mechanization,* Institute for Defense Analyses, Report R–168, 1970, p. 87; used by permission.

$$(\text{tour } 1),\ 6LSM_{11} + 3LSM_{21} + 2LSM_{31} \leq 600 . \tag{7}$$

Following exactly the same process, we have similar capacity constraints on tours 2 and 3 as follows:

$$(\text{tour } 2),\ 6LSM_{12} + 3LSM_{22} + 2LSM_{32} \leq 600 , \tag{8}$$

$$(\text{tour } 3),\ 6LSM_{13} + 3LSM_{23} + 2LSM_{33} \leq 600 . \tag{9}$$

Mail Volume Constraints   Table 4 indicates the expected amount of each type of mail (in thousands of letters) received per day — 800, 800, and 400 for types 1, 2, and 3 respectively. In addition, however, we need more information about the patterns of mail arrival, which is given in Figure 11. In Figure 11 we see that type 1 mail is received for the most part during the third tour (4 P.M. to 12 P.M.) and has a processing deadline of midnight, at the end of the third tour (final dispatch time). For example, only about 5 percent of type 1 mail is available for sorting by the end of tour 1, 35 percent is available by the end of tour 2, but it must all be processed by the end of tour 3. Unless we take the variable pattern into account, we might propose processing mail in tour 1 that has not yet arrived.

Thus we need constraints to account for type 1 load patterns. Since 5 percent or $0.05 \times 800{,}000 = 40{,}000$ pieces of type 1 mail arrive for tour 1, we must constrain the total processing by both modes as follows,

$$\text{(type 1), } LSM_{11} + M_{11} \leqslant 40 . \tag{10}$$

Then, since 35 percent of type 1 mail has arrived by the end of tour 2, the sum of tour 1 and tour 2 sorting must be less than or equal to $0.35 \times 800 = 280$, or

$$\text{(type 1), } LSM_{11} + M_{11} + LSM_{12} + M_{12} \leqslant 280 . \tag{11}$$

Finally, for type 1 mail, everything must be processed by the end of tour 3, so we have

$$\text{(type 1), } LSM_{11} + M_{11} + LSM_{12} + M_{12} + LSM_{13} + M_{13} = 800 . \tag{12}$$

Now, the relationships of constraints (10), (11), and (12) cover the volume constraints for type 1 mail. Tour 1 volume is limited to 40, tours 1 plus 2 volume is limited to 280, and the total volume for all three tours must be *equal* to 800.

We must now follow a similar general pattern for types 2 and 3 mail. Note in Figure 11 that approximately 30 percent (240) of type 2 mail is received for sorting in *tour 2*, so that

$$\text{(type 2), } LSM_{22} + M_{22} \leqslant 240 . \tag{13}$$

Approximately 65 percent (520) is received by the end of tour 3; therefore,

$$\text{(type 2), } LSM_{22} + M_{22} + LSM_{23} + M_{23} \leqslant 520 . \tag{14}$$

All type 2 mail is received by the end of tour 1 of the following day, so that

$$\text{(type 2), } LSM_{22} + M_{22} + LSM_{23} + M_{23} + LSM_{21} + M_{21} = 800 . \tag{15}$$

Finally, to allow for the arrival pattern of 400,000 letters of type 3 mail, we note from Figure 11 that about 50 percent (200) arrives during tour 3, 70 percent (280) by the end of tour 1 of the following day, and 100 percent by the end of tour 2 that day. Therefore,

$$\text{(type 3), } LSM_{33} + M_{33} \leqslant 200 , \tag{16}$$
$$\text{(type 3), } LSM_{33} + M_{33} + LSM_{31} + M_{31} \leqslant 280 , \tag{17}$$
$$\text{(type 3), } LSM_{33} + M_{33} + LSM_{31} + M_{31} + LSM_{32} + M_{32} = 400 . \tag{18}$$

The formulation of the post office model is now complete. The linear optimization model is restated in standard form in Figure 12. In Figure 12 we have rearranged the sequence of some of the terms in constraints (10) through (18) so that they occur in numerical order of the subscripts, whereas in their development we followed the sequence of the tours in which mail was received.

Computer Solution and Interpretation

Using the interactive linear programming computer code, we follow the same procedure as before and enter the linear optimization model shown in Figure 12. We will not show this entry step but will proceed directly to the solution output shown in Figure 13.

$$
\begin{array}{lr}
\text{MINIMIZE } Z = \quad & 11.9 \ LSM_{11} + 11.9 \ LSM_{12} + 11.9 \ LSM_{13} & (1) \\
& + \ 16.0 \ LSM_{21} + 16.0 \ LSM_{22} + 16.0 \ LSM_{23} & (2) \\
& + \ \ 8.5 \ LSM_{31} + \ \ 8.5 \ LSM_{32} + \ \ 8.5 \ LSM_{33} & (3) \\
& + \ 18.2 \quad M_{11} + 18.2 \quad M_{12} + 18.2 \quad M_{13} & (4) \\
& + \ 20.1 \quad M_{21} + 20.1 \quad M_{22} + 20.1 \quad M_{23} & (5) \\
& + \ 10.0 \quad M_{31} + 10.0 \quad M_{32} + 10.0 \quad M_{33} & (6)
\end{array}
$$

SUBJECT TO:

Capacity constraints,

$$
\begin{array}{lr}
[1] \ 6 \ LSM_{11} + 3 \ LSM_{21} + 2 \ LSM_{31} \leqslant 600 & (7) \\
[2] \ 6 \ LSM_{12} + 3 \ LSM_{22} + 2 \ LSM_{32} \leqslant 600 & (8) \\
[3] \ 6 \ LSM_{13} + 3 \ LSM_{23} + 2 \ LSM_{33} \leqslant 600 & (9)
\end{array}
$$

Mail volume constraints,

$$
\begin{array}{lr}
[4] \ LSM_{11} + M_{11} \leqslant 40 & (10) \\
[5] \ LSM_{11} + M_{11} + LSM_{12} + M_{12} \leqslant 280 & (11) \\
[6] \ LSM_{11} + M_{11} + LSM_{12} + M_{12} + LSM_{13} + M_{13} = 800 & (12) \\
[7] \ LSM_{22} + M_{22} \leqslant 240 & (13) \\
[8] \ LSM_{22} + M_{22} + LSM_{23} + M_{23} \leqslant 520 & (14) \\
[9] \ LSM_{21} + M_{21} + LSM_{22} + M_{22} + LSM_{23} + M_{23} = 800 & (15) \\
[10] \ LSM_{33} + M_{33} \leqslant 200 & (16) \\
[11] \ LSM_{31} + M_{31} + LSM_{33} + M_{33} \leqslant 280 & (17) \\
[12] \ LSM_{31} + M_{31} + LSM_{32} + M_{32} + LSM_{33} + M_{33} = 400 & (18)
\end{array}
$$
$$
LSM_{ij} \geqslant 0, \quad M_{ij} \geqslant 0
$$

Figure 12. Linear optimization model for the post office problem. Numbers in parentheses in the right hand column refer to the corresponding equations and constraints in the text. The numbers in brackets to the left of the constraints are the constraint numbers as assigned in the computer solution

POST OFFICE

THE OPTIMAL VALUE OF THE OBJECTIVE FUNCTION IS: 32180.000

THE VARIABLES IN THE SOLUTION ARE

VARIABLE		
LSM21	AT LEVEL	2.0000E2
LSM22		2.0000E2
LSM23		2.0000E2
M11		4.0000E1
M12		2.4000E2
M13		5.2000E2
M21		2.0000E2
M31		2.8000E2
M32		1.2000E2
SLK7		4.0000E1
SLK8		1.2000E2
SLK10		2.0000E2

Figure 13. Computer solution for the post office problem

Computer Solution   We see in Figure 13 that the minimum possible cost for processing 2,000,000 pieces of mail per day is $32,180 and that the values for the decision variables are as listed. There are positive values for 9 of the decision variables and the program provides values for 3 slack variables.

Let us now look at the values of the decision variables in tabular form as shown in Table 5. There are some startling observations to be made about the minimum cost solution. First, the LSM's are allocated exclusively to type 2 mail, and the manual mode is used to process the excess of type 2 mail plus all of types 1 and 3. In view of the cost differences noted in Table 3, this solution may not have been expected.

Second, note that 9 of the decision variables are zero. This feature seems different from the solution to the chemical production problem in which both of the decision variables were given positive values in the solution. It is not different really, but we can reserve the explanation for the next chapter in which we look inside the black box. The important point to observe now is that a result of zero for many decision variables in optimal solutions to linear models is characteristic. This fact is of practical value because, even though there were 18 decision variables, only 9 of them take on significance in the solution. In other words, the solution is simpler to work with from a managerial point of view than we might have suspected from the statement of the objective function.

The optimal solution is not obvious. Why, for example, would the optimal solution not use the LSM for type 1 mail where it could save $6.30 per thousand letters? In general, the answer is that we can process many more pieces of type 2 mail because of the mail volume constraints, and although the savings per thousand are smaller, the larger volume of mail processed

TABLE 5. Optimal Solution
for the Post Office Linear Model

	Mail Processed* in Tour:		
	1	2	3
(1) Collection and Acceptance (C&A)			
Manual	40	240	520
LSM	---	---	---
(2) Incoming			
Manual	200	---	---
LSM	200	200	200
(3) Transit			
Manual	280	120	---
LSM	---	---	---

*Data in thousands.

produces a greater total saving. Also, looking at Figure 11 and Table 5, note that the pattern of arrivals for type 1 mail is such that the LSM would have very poor utilization during tour 1 where only 40,000 pieces of type 1 mail would be available. To fill out the LSM capacity it would have to be used for types 2 or 3 mail on that tour. Not only is the cost of such an allocation greater, but it entails a more complex schedule.

The computer solution has again provided us with values for variables for which we did not ask, the slack variables. $SLK7$ in Figure 13 states that we did not process all of the type 2 mail available on tour 2, but carried 40,000 letters into tour 3 (see constraint [7] in Figure 12). $SLK8$ in Figure 13 states a similar fact; that is, we did not process all of the type 2 mail available on tours 2 plus 3, but carried 120,000 letters over to be processed on tour 1 the following day in order to meet the final dispatch time. $SLK10$ in Figure 13 states a similar fact for type 3 mail on tour 3 — the mail available for processing was not sorted, but delayed until tour 1 the following day.

Sensitivity Analysis   Now let us turn to the sensitivity analysis shown in Figure 14. The general interpretations are similar to those given for the chemical production problem, but we must take into account the fact that for the post office problem we are minimizing costs rather than maximizing profits. This goal affects the interpretation of the shadow prices and we see for constraints [1], [2], and [3] that the shadow prices are −$1.36. That is, additional LSM capacity would *decrease* the objective function. The value of greater capacity is the same for each tour. The post office could use more LSM capacity to advantage.

		SHADOW	LB	CURRENT	UB
CONSTRAINT	1	-1.3667E0	0.0000E0	6.0000E2	1.2000E3
	2	-1.3667E0	0.0000E0	6.0000E2	7.2000E2
	3	-1.3667E0	0.0000E0	6.0000E2	9.6000E2
	4	0.0000E0	0.0000E0	4.0000E1	2.8000E2
	5	0.0000E0	4.0000E1	2.8000E2	8.0000E2
	6	1.8200E1	2.8000E2	8.0000E2	7.2370E75
	7	0.0000E0	2.0000E2	2.4000E2	7.2370E75
	8	0.0000E2	4.0000E0	5.2000E2	7.2370E75
	9	2.0100E1	6.0000E2	8.0000E2	7.2370E75
	10	0.0000E0	0.0000E0	2.0000E2	7.2370E75
	11	0.0000E0	0.0000E0	2.8000E2	4.0000E2
	12	1.0000E1	2.8000E2	4.0000E2	7.2370E75
PRICE	LSM11		1.0000E1	1.1900E1	7.2370E75
	LSM12		1.0000E1	1.1900E1	7.2370E75
	LSM13		1.0000E1	1.1900E1	7.2370E75
	LSM21		-7.2370E75	1.6000E1	1.6950E1
	LSM22		-7.2370E75	1.6000E1	1.6950E1
	LSM23		-7.2370E75	1.6000E1	1.6950E1
	LSM31		7.2667E0	8.5000E0	7.2370E75
	LSM32		7.2667E0	8.5000E0	7.2370E75
	LSM33		7.2667E0	8.5000E0	7.2370E75
	M11		-7.2370E75	1.8200E1	1.8200E1
	M12		1.8200E1	1.8200E1	1.8200E1
	M13		1.8200E1	1.8200E1	2.0100E1
	M21		1.9150E1	2.0100E1	2.0100E1
	M22		2.0100E1	2.0100E1	7.2370E75
	M23		2.0100E1	2.0100E1	7.2370E75
	M31		-7.2370E75	1.0000E1	1.0000E1
	M32		1.0000E1	1.0000E1	1.1233E1
	M33		1.0000E1	1.0000E1	7.2370E75

-< END >-

Figure 14. Sensitivity analysis for the post office problem. The numbers of the constraints correspond to the constraint numbers in brackets in Figure 12

The upper and lower bounds indicate that the shadow price is valid within certain limits, and these limits are different for the three tours. The upper bound for tour 1 is 1200, for tour 2 is 720, and for tour 3 is 960. Since there is an advantage in using the LSM's and the shadow price indicates that we could use more capacity, why not enlarge capacity? Now we must be careful, for we are using the full capacity of the present machines. To enlarge capacity means that we obtain another, resulting in a discrete increment to capacity.

Can we use the increased capacity within the limits of the present solution? It would be necessary to see if the increased capacity would take us above the upper bound, for under these conditions, the marginal values would not apply. If the new capacity were above the upper bound, we would need to alter the model, but only by altering the capacity constraints (1, 2, and 3). With the computer code available, this would not be a difficult task.

The shadow prices for constraints [4] through [12] are all positive (see Figure 14). This means, of course, that changing the right-hand side of these constraints would increase cost in the ranges shown by the bounds. This result is logical, since processing additional mail would increase all costs. If we examine the shadow prices for constraints [6], [9], and [12] we note positive values. These are the marginal costs to process an additional thousand units of types 1, 2, and 3 mail, or $18.20, $20.10, and $10.00 respectively.

The price sensitivity bounds indicate the range of costs (from Table 3) for which the optimal solution is valid. Note that the bounds depend largely on the type of mail, since the costs themselves are related to mail type. Notice that the bounds on prices for the manual mode are extremely tight: in several instances the lower bound and the current value are the same, and in the case of M_{12} the upper and lower bounds are identical, resulting in no flexibility whatever. The costs for the manual system are apparently very sensitive and any change in these costs might change the solution. Note also that if the processing cost for type 2 mail on the LSM were $17 rather than $16, the solution would change. Thus, the precision of these cost estimates is relatively important.

Use of the Post Office Model

The post office model is quite realistic, representing an actual application. (For full details of the post office example see R. Cohen et al. [1970].) The main difference between the model we have developed and the actual application is that we developed the mail volume constraints on the basis of tours, while in the actual application they were developed for an hourly schedule. The form of the constraints is exactly the same, but the hourly schedule results in 24 mail volume constraints for each type of mail rather than 3. Again, this is a straightforward extension that causes greater complexity of a type that is handled easily by computers.

How could a manager use the results of the linear optimization model? First, the obvious use is as a basis for scheduling the LSM's and sorting labor at minimum cost. In addition, however, the model forms the basis for evaluating mechanization programs.

Evaluation of Mechanization Programs   Our model assumed that we had a fixed LSM capacity and raised the question of its use for minimum cost operation. In order to evaluate the effectiveness of LSM's we need to estimate minimum mail sorting costs for the future. For this reason, we must take into account the growth of mail volume and real wages of postal employees over time. All of the future costs can then be discounted to present value by the appropriate interest rate.

This results in the present value of the minimum mail sorting cost for a given future year and comparable values must be computed for a series of years over equipment life, reflecting the growing mail volume and real wage costs. In addition, the total mail volume varies considerably throughout the year. To determine annual savings, the linear programming model must be run for various ranges of daily volume, reflecting variable demand. The optimum savings for each range of volumes can then be multiplied by the number of occurrences and accumulated to determine annual savings.

The initial capital investment must be added to the total sorting costs to produce the present value of all future costs. Different systems involving different machines and sizes can be evaluated by the same model to provide managers with the economic evaluation of a full range of alternatives.

Note that the linear optimization model provides the crucial input for the equipment justification study. A simplistic approach to the evaluation of mechanization would be to use directly the data given in Table 3, where we noted that the cost advantage of the LSM is $6.30, $4.10, and $1.50 per thousand letters for types 1, 2, and 3 mail respectively. If we multiply these differences by the corresponding average annual mail volume the resulting total is an estimate of the cost reduction due to LSM's. This method, however, overstates the cost reduction possible since it does not take into account mail volume constraints, and the linear optimization model savings are actually about 25 percent less.

WHAT SHOULD THE MANAGER KNOW?

Linear optimization models can become very complex, involving an enormous number of variables and constraints, and a manager's initial reaction could easily be one of rejection. However, the manager need not concern himself with the mathematical complexities. The real value for him lies in being aware of the characteristics of problems for which linear optimization models may be useful, so that he can both suggest applications and evaluate proposals for application. In addition, a knowledge of the nature of model formulation, information requirements, and particularly interpretation of results is important for the manager. If he so chooses, he need not know the mathematical methods of the linear programming solution technique. Given the existence of linear programming computer codes similar to the one used in this chapter, the manager can assume that if the problem can be put in standard form for input, the "black box" will perform its function and provide the solution output, complete with sensitivity analysis.

Problem Characteristics

What is the nature of problems for which linear optimization methods are applicable? First, linear optimization models are of value in problems that involve the allocation of limited resources to competing demands. The chemical production and post office problems both had these general characteristics. In the chemical production problem, the limited resources were the productive capacities and the limited market demands. In the post office problem, the LSM's had limited capacity and the mail volume patterns posed limitations on how the available resources could be used. In both examples the problem was to optimize the use of the resources with respect to a criterion—maximum profits in the first and minimum costs in the second case.

Now let us think more broadly about allocation problems to see the range of candidate problems that occur in all kinds of enterprises (profit and not for profit) and in various enterprise functions such as finance, production, and marketing. The reference list of applications in the literature at the end of this chapter serves as a source of applications, but in addition we will describe some of the general areas of application.

The general financing mix problem has been approached by linear optimization methods at various levels in organizations. At the overall enterprise level we can raise the question of the most profitable combination of financing sources, such as equity versus debt. Or, for the shorter term use of funds, what is the most profitable allocation of funds to accounts receivable, planned payments for purchases, cash needs for operation, and cash surplus from operations? Robichek, Teichroew, and Jones [1965] formulated linear optimization models in which the objective was to minimize net interest cost while meeting cash needs. The sources of short-term funds were pledges of accounts receivable at specific interest costs, extension of payments for purchases at a cost of loss of discounts, and short-term loans. There were constraints on the amounts of all sources. Through an extension of linear programming, Hughes and Lewellen [1974] have formulated the capital rationing problem in which limited capital funds are allocated to specific capital investment projects. The objective is to select from among the complete set of investment opportunities those projects that will provide the highest possible returns without exceeding the allowed budget.

The applications in production and distribution have been the most common, including the optimum distribution of products from a set of origin points to a number of destinations, multiple plant location problems, scheduling problems, blending of raw materials for minimum cost, and the optimum product mix problem. An extension of linear optimization models called goal programming has been used in a number of production-oriented applications. For example, Lee and Moore [1973] applied the methodology to distribution problems in which management had a hierarchy of goals such as guaranteed delivery to a specific customer, use of certain routes because of union agreements, fulfillment of a transportation cost budget, and so on. The constraints were the supplies available at origin points, the market demands, and the goals. The solution procedure using linear programming succesively seeks the achievement of goals in their order of priority, and higher priority goals are considered as constraints that cannot be violated. The results are that higher priority goals may be achieved at the expense of lower priority goals.

In marketing, a classical allocation problem is in media selection for a given limited promotion and advertising budget. Both Engle and Warshaw [1964] and Bass and Lonsdale [1966] have applied linear optimization models to media selection. The manager's objective may be to maximize the number of potential buyers exposed to his advertising, within a limited budget. The costs of the media exposures are known and different, and the manager has survey data concerning the consumers' use of the media. Also, depending on how an enterprise is organized, the problems of product distribution to limited markets may be regarded as a marketing application.

In addition to the preceding kinds of applications, linear programming has been applied to many managerial problems in the public and not-for-profit sectors. For example, in the health care field, Revelle, Feldmann, and Lynn [1969] have developed a mathematical model that predicts future states of the disease tuberculosis. Controls in the form of therapy, vaccinations, or prophylaxis may be superimposed on the actual processes, thus altering the future cause of the disease. Linear programming is used to select the forms of control that achieve specific reductions at minimum cost. Sensitivity analysis can then be used to determine the marginal cost of an even greater reduction in the future disease level.

Linear programming has also been applied to the problem of integrating public schools, as reported by Franklin and Koenigsberg [1973]. The objective function and constraints in their model can be modified so that the solution of each formulation provides a policy or point of view. The authors emphasize that, "School authorities, judges, and the public can see the logical implications of each point of view and select school assignment plans on a rational basis." Notice that there is not even a hint that the purpose of the linear programming models is to provide *the answer*. Rather its purpose is to generate the consequences in terms of costs and school assignments of different levels of desegregation and of different approaches. The selection of the best approach is still a matter for the school authorities, the judges, and the public to decide.

Problems of the environment have also been studied using linear programming. Glassey and Gupta [1974] have developed a linear model of the production, use, and recycling of various paper and related products. The linear programming analysis indicates that if 70 percent of the potentially recoverable paper had been recycled in 1970, the annual virgin pulp consumption could have been reduced from 45 million tons to 28 million tons (or by 38 percent). The reduction in the annual cost of collecting and disposing of solid waste would have been approximately $238 million, which presumably could be used to offset the cost of collecting and processing wastepaper. In a related study, Ignall, Kolesar, and Walker [1972] used a linear programming model to improve crew assignments for solid waste collection.

Model Formulation

The manager needs to know and understand something about formulating linear models in order to use the services of staff analysts appropriately and to interpret results. He needs to be able to think in terms of the criterion function and the constraints to his problem. If he can formulate the simpler kinds of problems we used as examples in this chapter, he can work effectively through analysts to help formulate more complex problems, for as we noted, the more complex problems are straightforward extensions of the concepts involved in the simple ones.

Interpretation of Results

The heart of the managerial function is focused in the interpretation of results and in decision making. While the solution output has obvious value for the manager, the power of the results is greatly enhanced by the sensitivity analysis. The manager can put himself in the interactive mode that we discussed in connection with predictive models. He can raise intelligent "what if" questions if he understands the meaning of shadow prices and the upper and lower bounds on solutions. These questions often result in additional computing runs to evaluate alternatives that are not automatically generated within the optimizing model, such as the mechanization alternatives of the post office example.

Check Your Understanding

1. Which of the following mathematical expressions are linear? Why?
   a. $x + y = 1$
   b. $x^2 + y^2 = 10$
   c. $1/x + 2x = 10$
   d. $x + xy + y = 1$
   e. $x_1 + x_2 + x_3 + x_4 = 1$

2. Graph each of the following constraints on a separate graph and shade or cross-hatch the areas of the graph that include admissible points.
   a. $x + y \leq 4$
   b. $x + y \geq 10$
   c. $2x + 3y = 15$
   d. $x \leq 10$

3. Outline the model-building process used for developing linear optimization models.

4. How are alternatives generated within the structure of the model-building process?

5. In the break-even analysis example, explain why we were able to simply drop the variable f (fixed cost) from the objective function.

6. In the break-even analysis example, there was a slack capacity of 100 units per month. Suppose that the demand constraint had been $x \leqslant 400$. How would the concept of slack apply?

7. In the chemical production example, the objective function that we developed was a statement of contribution to profit and overhead. Why maximize this function instead of an expression for profit? Isn't it really profit that we wish to maximize?

8. Suppose that in the chemical production problems, the availability of time on machine A is drastically reduced to only 40 hours because of a breakdown. How does this change the solution space shown in Figure 6? Is it likely to change the optimum number of units of each chemical to produce?

9. Explain the concept of shadow prices. How can a manager use his knowledge of shadow prices in decision making?

10. What is the interpretation of the upper and lower bounds on the shadow prices indicated in Figure 8? Of what value is this information to a manager?

11. What is the interpretation of the upper and lower bounds on the "prices" given in Figure 8? Of what value is this information to the manager?

12. What may be the practical value of knowing that the bounds on one or more prices may be "tight"?

13. Suppose we have a machine that is flexible and can be used to process various sizes of a product by a simple adjustment. The capacity of the machine is greater for small sizes. The capacity of the machine for three sizes is $x_1 = 500$ per month, $x_2 = 1000$ per month, and $x_3 = 2500$ per month. The monthly capacity of the machine for an average mix is stated to be 1500 per month. Write the constraint expression for the machine.

14. Interpret the significance of SLK10 in the computer solution of the post office problem in Figure 13. Check in Figure 12 to see the nature of constraint [10].

15. Explain why the computer solution of the post office problem summarized in Table 5 did not use the LSM at all for type 3 (transit) mail.

16. What is the significance of the shadow price of 10 with bounds 280 to infinity for constraint [12] of Figure 14? See equation (18) in Figure 12 in the text for the rationale behind the constraint.

CONSTRAINT		SHADOW	LB	CURRENT	UB
CONSTRAINT	1	1.1000E1	1.3333E0	5.0000E0	5.3333E0
	2	5.6000E0	5.0000E0	1.0000E1	1.0625E1
	3	-2.0000E-1	1.3125E1	1.5000E1	3.0000E1
	4	0.0000E0	0.0000E0	1.5000E1	7.2370E75
	5	-4.0000E-1	2.7500E1	3.0000E1	5.7500E1
	6	0.0000E0	2.7500E1	3.0000E1	7.2370E75
PRICE	M11		1.0000E1	1.0000E1	7.2370E75
	MCH11		7.2500E0	8.0000E0	8.0000E0
	M12		1.1000E1	1.5000E1	7.2370E75
	MCH12		9.8750E0	1.1000E1	1.1000E1
	M21		-7.2370E75	5.0000E0	5.0000E0
	MCH21		4.0000E0	4.0000E0	4.4000E0
	M22		5.6000E0	6.0000E0	7.2370E75
	MCH22		5.6000E0	6.0000E0	7.2370E75

-+ END >-

Figure 15. Sensitivity analysis for the more complex two-product example

17. The sensitivity analysis for the more complex two-product model (see Figure 9) is shown in Figure 15. Using this result and Figure 9, answer the following questions:

   a. The shadow prices for constraints [4] and [6] are 0.0. Why should you expect this result, considering the solution in Figure 9?

   b. Suppose the demand for product 1 increased from 50 units to 52 units. What would the total cost of production become?

   c. Suppose you can sell an additional 6 units of product 2 for a discounted price of $0.50 per unit. Should you make the sale?

   d. Your accountant announces that the costs of producing product 2 on the manual system during shift 2 have increased to $10 per 10 units. Would the optimal solution be affected? How do you know?

   e. What if the cost of producing product 2 on the manual system during shift 1 decreases? Would there by any effect on the solution? What if it increases slightly?

Problems

1. The Elmore Electronics Corporation is a manufacturer of two kinds of electronic test equipment: oscilloscopes (O) and vacuum tube voltmeters (V). The physical facilities are organized into three main departments: the circuit board department (CB), the chassis department (C) and final assembly (A). Monthly capacities for each of the two products in the three departments are given in Table 6, and financial data are given in Table 7.

TABLE 6. Monthly Capacities for the Elmore Electronic Corporation

	Time Requirements (hours/unit)		
	Oscilloscopes (O)	Voltmeters (V)	Hours Available Next Month
Chassis Department (C)	4.5	2.0	2000
Circuit Board Department (CB)	6.3	1.5	2500
Assembly Department (A)	7.0	3.0	3000

TABLE 7. Costs and Prices for the Elmore Electronics Corporation

Costs and Prices (per unit)	Oscilloscopes (O)	Voltmeters (V)
Sales prices	$170	$55
Costs		
Variable labor	20	5
Material	50	10
Overhead (at current volume)	40	10

Current market forecasts for the two products for the coming month are for 400 oscilloscopes and 600 voltmeters.

Formulate a linear optimization model for the manager of Elmore that can be used as a basis for scheduling production for next month.

2. Elmore is contemplating the addition of a third product for the coming month, which it thinks will have a broad appeal to TV repairmen. It is a portable circuit board tester that can quickly check a standard circuit board be setting dials and switches to standard settings. The product has been market tested and estimates of the market and production costs have been made.

The foremen in the chassis and circuit board departments state that they can absorb the small added load with present facilities and labor force. The assembly department foreman, however, states that he must enlarge his labor force to a total of 3500 available hours in order to absorb the new product load.

The new product is dubbed (P) for "portable" and alternate plans must be generated to include the item in next month's production schedule. The manager is delighted with the prospect that the new product may go into production, partly because overhead costs will be spread over a larger product base, making existing products more "profitable." He estimates that the per unit overhead costs will decline to $38 for oscilloscopes and $9 for voltmeters.

The portable circuit board testers (P) will sell for $400 each, and initial cost estimates indicate that variable labor will be $100, materials $125, and allocated overhead $60 per unit. Initial sales estimates are set at 50 for next month. Hours requirements in the three departments for P are estimated to be 9 per unit in the chassis department, 10 per unit in the circuit board department, and 15 per unit in assembly. Reformulate Elmore's problem as a linear optimization model.

3. The Goodwear Shoe Company has three plants, all of which can produce the full line of shoes: dress shoes (D), which yield a net contribution of $10 each; work shoes (W), which yield $8; and sport shoes (S), which yield $4.

A decline in the market has caused an excess capacity in all three plants amounting to 550, 650, and 300 units per day in plants 1, 2, and 3 respectively (regardless of shoe type). Even though there is excess capacity, there is an in-process inventory capacity limit because of physical layout limitations. These limitations, in turn, limit output rates. The three plants have available 1000, 850, and 400 square feet of storage space respectively. Shoe lines D, W, and S require 1.0, 1.5, and 0.8 equivalent square feet of storage respectively. Sales forecasts are 700, 850, and 750 respectively for shoe lines D, W, and S.

Formulate a linear optimization model that will provide management with a program of how many of each shoe type to produce in each plant. The model must meet the constraints and maximize contribution.

4. A Federal Home Loan Bank makes essentially four kinds of loans, which yield the following annual interest rates:

First mortgages	10%
Second mortgages	16%
Home improvement loans	18%
Loans against accounts	5%

The bank has a maximum lending capability of $2 million and must stay within the following limits and policies:
a. First mortgages must be at least 45 percent of all mortgages and at least 25 percent of loans outstanding.
b. Second mortgages cannot exceed 30 percent of loans.

Formulate the bank's loan problem as a linear optimization model designed to maximize interest income within the stated policy limits.

5. The Appliance Manufacturing Company produces airconditioners (A), refrigerators (R), and electric stoves (S). The manufacturing facility needs for the three product lines are common in certain respects, which accounts for the fact that manufacturing costs are generally low. The facilities are composed of a machine shop, which fabricates a variety of parts needed in all three products; a metal stamping department, which stamps out a variety of sheet metal parts for all three products; a unit department, which produces the refrigeration units used in A and R; and independent assembly lines for each of the three products.

Because some of the facilities are shared between the product lines, specifying their capacities posed a problem. The manufacturing manager finally resolved the difficulty by computing the limiting capacity of the machine shop if, for example, it were entirely devoted to each of the three products. He summarized these results in Table 8.

The contribution rates for the three products were $60, $50, and $40 per unit respectively for A, R, and S. Also, the maximums that the marketing department estimated could be sold in the coming planning period were 4000, 3000, and 2000 respectively, for A, R, and S.

Formulate a linear optimization model designed to maximize contribution within the constraints under which the company must operate.

TABLE 8. Capacities of Shop Facilities for Air Conditioners, Refrigerators, and Stoves

	Department Capacity for:		
	Air Conditioners	Refrigerators	Stoves
Machine shop	6000	7000	8000
Stamping department	9000	5000	4000
Unit department	7000	6000	---
A Assembly	5000	---	---
R Assembly	---	4000	---
S Assembly	---	---	3000

TABLE 9. Refinery and Market Data

Crude	Delivered Price per Gallon (cents)	Percentage of Optimal Throughput for Each Crude			
		Regular Gas	High-Test Gas	Diesel Fuel	Fuel Oil
Oklahoma	14	30	10	40	20
West Texas	12	20	10	60	10
Wyoming	10	10	---	30	60
Pennsylvania	18	30	50	20	---
Present market requirement (gallons per hour)	---	20,000	15,000	28,000	33,000

6. A refinery operating in Nebraska uses four crude oils: Oklahoma, West Texas, Wyoming, and Pennsylvania. These crudes have different delivered costs as indicated in Table 9. The refinery makes four basic end products: regular gas, high-test gas, diesel fuel, and fuel oil. The catalytic cracking and reforming characteristics of the refinery dictate a limited and different

input mix of the crude oils, as is also indicated in Table 9. For example, 30 percent of the Oklahoma crude must be used for regular gas, 10 percent for high-test gas, 40 percent for diesel fuel, and the remaining 20 percent for fuel oil.

The objective is to minimize crude oil costs, but meet market requirements. Let A, B, C, and D represent the number of gallons of crude oil from Oklahoma, West Texas, Wyoming, and Pennsylvania respectively that must be used per hour.

Formulate the refinery problem as a linear optimization model.

7. The Three Mines Company owns three different mines that produce an ore that, after being crushed, is graded into three classes: high, medium, and low grade. There is some demand for each grade of ore. The Three Mines Company has contracted to provide a smelting plant with 12 tons of high-grade, 8 tons of medium-grade, and 24 tons of low-grade ore per week. Operating costs are $180 per day for mine W, $200 per day for mine X, and $160 per day for mine Y.

The three mines have different capacities. Mine W produces 6, 3, and 4 tons per day of high-, medium-, and low-grade ores respectively. Mine X produces 3, 1, and 2 tons per day of the three ores, and Mine Y produces 1, 1, and 6 tons per day of the three ores.

How many days per week should each mine be operated to fill the orders and minimize operating costs? Let W, X, and Y represent the number of days per week each of the mines operates. Formulate the Three Mines Company's problem as a linear optimization model.

TABLE 10. Man-Hour Requirements and Capacities for the Two-Product Company

Department	Man-Hours per unit		Department Capacities (man-hours per month)
	A	B	
1	3	0	6000
2	0	2.9	8000
3	2.5	2	7500
4	1.3	1.5	5000

8. The Two-Product Company manufactures two products, A and B, and currently the product mix is 615 units of A and 2600 units of B per month. Current issues are whether or not the present mix is the most profitable, and whether the four manufacturing departments should be enlarged, in view of the possibility of introducing a new product. The man-hour requirements, and department capacities, are shown in Table 10. Contributions are $50 per unit for product A and $40 for B. Figure 16 is the computer input and output for a linear optimization model constructed for this situation. How do you interpret the results?

```
MAXIMIZE OR MINIMIZE: MAX
OBJECTIVE FUNCTION:Z=50A+40B
ENTER CONSTRAINT EQUATIONS.
[001]3A≤6000
[002]2.9B≤8000
[003]2.5A+2B≤7500
[004]1.3A+1.5B≤5000
[005]

        LPRUN

                          TWO-PRODUCT COMPANY

THE OPTIMAL VALUE OF THE OBJECTIVE FUNCTION IS: 150000.000

                    THE VARIABLES IN THE SOLUTION ARE

VARIABLE   A        AT LEVEL    2.0000E3
           B                    1.2500E3
           SLK2                 4.3750E3
           SLK4                 5.2500E2

DO YOU WISH SENSITIVITY ANALYSIS? Y

                         SHADOW         LB         CURRENT         UB
CONSTRAINT     1       0.0000E0     3.2609E3     6.0000E3     9.0000E3
               2       0.0000E0     3.6250E3     8.0000E3     7.2370E75
               3       2.0000E1     5.0000E3     7.5000E3     8.2000E3
               4       0.0000E0     4.4750E3     5.0000E3     7.2370E75

PRICE       A                      5.0000E1     5.0000E1     7.2370E75
            B                      0.0000E0     4.0000E1     4.0000E1

-< END >-
```

Figure 16. Computer input and output for the
Two-Product Company

9. The Two-Product Company now wishes to become the Three-Product
    Company by adding product *C*. Product *C* has uniqueness, and market
    tests indicate that it can command a contribution of $75 per unit. The
    manufacturing manager contends that existing capacities are adequate
    and that, indeed, the reason that product *C* "fits" so well is that it can use
    existing slack capacity. The man-hour requirements for product *C* are
    0.15, 2.5, 3.5, and 1.5 respectively for each of the four departments.
       Figure 17 is the computer input and output for the linear optimization
    model including product *C*. How do you interpret the results? What recom-
    mendations would you make?

10. The Two-Product Company felt that the result of the previous output was a
    little risky, since all capacity was turned over to product *C*, the new prod-
    uct. They realized that their bread and butter had been in products *A* and
    B, and that the market for the new product as an introduction was probably
    limited to 50 units. They also placed limits on the market for products *A*
    and *B* of 2200 and 1500 respectively.

```
MAXIMIZE OR MINIMIZE: MAX

OBJECTIVE FUNCTION: Z=50A+40B+75C
ENTER CONSTRAINT EQUATIONS, (STRIKE JUST A CARRIAGE RETURN TO STOP INPUT)
[001]3A+0.15C≤6000
[002]2.9B+2.5C≤8000
[003]2.5A+2B+3.5C≤7500
[004]1.3A+1.5B+1.5C≤5000
[005]
      LPRUN
                    THREE-PRODUCT COMPANY

THE OPTIMAL VALUE OF THE OBJECTIVE FUNCTION IS: 160714.286

                  THE VARIABLES IN THE SOLUTION ARE

VARIABLE  C        AT LEVEL    2.1429E3
          SLK1                 5.6786E3
          SLK2                 2.6429E3
          SLK4                 1.7857E3

DO YOU WISH SENSITIVITY ANALYSIS? Y

                     SHADOW       LB        CURRENT      UB
CONSTRAINT     1    0.0000E0    3.2143E2   6.0000E3   7.2370E75
               2    0.0000E0    5.3571E3   8.0000E3   7.2370E75
               3    2.1429E1    0.0000E0   7.5000E3   1.1200E4
               4    0.0000E0    3.2143E3   5.0000E3   7.2370E75

PRICE          A              -7.2370E75   5.0000E1   5.3571E1
               B              -7.2370E75   4.0000E1   4.2857E1
               C               7.0000E1    7.5000E1   7.2370E75

-< END >-
```

Figure 17. Computer input and output for the
potential Three-Product Company

The input and output for the market-limited model is shown in Figure
18. How do you interpret the results?

11. Mesa Plastics Company is a bulk producer of sheet plastic, that they sell
in three sizes (thicknesses). They have two plants located on the same site.
Plant B is of later design and was specifically built to produce sizes 1 and
2 economically since these two sizes had the largest demand. However,
plant B is less economical than A for size 3. Time requirements for the three
products in the two plants, and the variable hourly costs and time availability for plants A and B are shown in Table 11. Sales revenue and maximum demand for the three products are shown in Table 12. Management is
considering how production should be allocated to the two plants for the
upcoming period so as to maximize contribution.

A computer input and output for a linear optimization model is given
in Figure 19. How do you interpret the results?

12. Select three or four references from the applications reference list, and
read them in order to gain an understanding of the nature of the application (do not concern yourself with mathematical details.) Select one of

TABLE 11. Time Requirements, Costs, and Capacities for the Mesa Plastics Company

	Hours per 100 Pounds	
	Plant *A*	Plant *B*
Size 1	0.25	0.20
Size 2	0.40	0.25
Size 3	0.35	0.40
Variable costs per hour	$250	$300
Maximum available hours per week	100	100

TABLE 12. Sales Revenue and Maximum Demand for the Mesa Plastics Company

Size	Sales Revenue per 100 Pounds	Maximum Demand per Week (100 Pounds)
1	$100	310
2	$120	300
3	$150	125

these articles and summarize it. Include the following in the summary:

a. What was the nature of the problem that was analyzed?

b. What were the major decision variables in the model?

c. What was the objective function; that is, tell in words what was being optimized?

d. What was the nature of the important constraints?

e. How was the solution actually used?

f. If you were a manager faced with this problem, would you consider these results useful? What were the limitations of the model? Were there other considerations that should also influence the ultimate decision?

General References

Bierman, H., C. P. Bonini and W. H. Hausman, *Quantitative Analysis for Business Decisions,* fifth edition, Richard D. Irwin, Inc., Homewood, Ill., 1977.

Buckley, J. W., M. R. Nagarai, D. L. Sharp, and J. W. Schenck, *Management Problem-Solving with APL*, Melville Publishing Company, Los Angeles, 1974.

Charnes, A., and W. W. Cooper, *Management Models and Industrial Applications of Linear Programming*, Vols. 1 and 2, John Wiley & Sons, New York, 1961.

Daellenbach, H. G., and E. J. Bell, *User's Guide to Linear Programming*, Prentice-Hall, Englewood Cliffs, N.J., 1970.

```
                    THREE PRODUCT COMPANY

MAXIMIZE OR MINIMIZE: MAX
OBJECTIVE FUNCTION: Z=50A+40B+75C
ENTER CONSTRAINT EQUATIONS,
[001]  3A+0.15C≤6000
[002]  2.9B+2.5C≤8000
[003]  2.5A+2B+3.5C≤7500
[004]  1.3A+1.5B+1.5C≤5000
[005]  A≤2200
[006]  B≤1500
[007]  C≤50
[008]
       LPRUN

                    THREE PRODUCT COMPANY
                  (WITH MARKET RESTRICTION)

THE OPTIMAL VALUE OF THE OBJECTIVE FUNCTION IS: 150250.000

              THE VARIABLES IN THE SOLUTION ARE

VARIABLE   A      AT LEVEL   1.9975E3
           B                 1.1656E3
           C                 5.0000E1
           SLK2              4.4947E3
           SLK4              5.7981E2
           SLK5              2.0250E2
           SLK6              3.3438E2

DO YOU WISH SENSITIVITY ANALYSIS? YES

                      SHADOW         LB        CURRENT         UB
CONSTRAINT    1     0.0000E0     5.1975E3     6.0000E3     6.6075E3
              2     0.0000E0     3.5053E3     8.0000E3     7.2370E75
              3     2.0000E1     5.1688E3     7.5000E3     8.1687E3
              4     0.0000E0     4.4202F3     5.0000E3     7.2370E75
              5     0.0000E0     1.9975E3     2.2000E3     7.2370E75
              6     0.0000E0     1.1656E3     1.5000E3     7.2370E75
              7     5.0000E0     0.0000E0     5.0000E1     7.4074F2

PRICE         A                  5.0000E1     5.0000E1     1.5000F2
              B                  0.0000E0     4.0000E1     4.0000E1
              C                  7.0000E1     7.5000E1     7.2370E75

-< END >-
```

Figure 18. Computer input and output for the
market-limited model, potential Three-Product
Company

Dantzig, G. B., *Linear Programming and Extensions*, Princeton University Press, Princeton, N.J., 1963.

Hillier, F. S., and G. J. Lieberman, *Introduction to Operations Research*, second edition, Holden-Day, San Francisco, 1974.

```
                            MESA PLASTICS COMPANY
MAXIMIZE OR MINIMIZE:  MAX
OBJECTIVE FUNCTION:    Z=37.5A1+40B1+20A2+45B2+62.5A3+30B3
ENTER CONSTRAINT EQUATIONS,
[001]  0.25A1+0.4A2+0.35A3≤100
[002]  0.2B1+0.25B2+0.4B3≤100
[003]  A1+B1≤310
[004]  A2+B2≤300
[005]  A3+B3≤125
[006]
       LPRUN

                        MESA PLASTICS COMPANY

THE OPTIMAL VALUE OF THE OBJECTIVE FUNCTION IS:   33250.000

                    THE VARIABLES IN THE SOLUTION ARE

VARIABLE    A1       AT LEVEL      1.8500E2
            B1                     1.2500E2
            B2                     3.0000E2
            A3                     1.2500E2
            SLK1                   1.0000E1

DO YOU WISH SENSITIVITY ANALYSIS?   Y

                        SHADOW         LB          CURRENT         UB
CONSTRAINT      1    0.0000E0      9.0000E1      1.0000E2      7.2370E75
                2    1.2500E1      9.2000E1      1.0000E2      1.3700E2
                3    3.7500E1      1.2500E2      3.1000E2      3.5000E2
                4    4.1875E1      1.5200E2      3.0000E2      3.3200E2
                5    6.2500E1      0.0000E2      1.2500E2      1.5375E2

PRICE
            A1                     2.0000E1      3.7500E1      4.0000E1
            B1                     3.7500E1      4.0000E1      5.7500E1
            A2                    -7.2370E75     2.0000E1      4.1875E1
            B2                     2.3125E1      4.5000E1      7.2370E75
            A3                     2.5000E1      6.2500E1      7.2370E75
            B3                    -7.2370E75     3.0000E1      6.7500E1

->END<-
```

Figure 19. Computer input and output for the Mesa Plastics Company

Thierauf, R. J., and R. C. Klekamp, *Decision Making Through Operations Research,* second edition, John Wiley & Sons, New York, 1975.

Wagner, H. M., *Principles of Operations Research,* second edition, Prentice-Hall, Englewood Cliffs, N.J., 1975.

Applications References

Adelman, I., "A Linear Programming Model of Educational Planning: A Case Study of Argentina," in *The Theory of Design of Economic Development*, I. Adelman and E. Thorbecke, editors, The Johns-Hopkins Press, Baltimore, 1966.

Allman, W. P., "An Optimization Approach to Freight Car Allocation Under Fiscal-Mileage per Diem Rental Rates," *Management Science*, Vol. 18, No. 10, June 1972.

Anderson, D., "Models for Determining Least-Cost Investments in Electricity Supply," *The Bell Journal of Economics and Management Science*, Spring 1972.

Bass, F. M., and R. T. Lonsdale, "An Exploration of Linear Programming in Media Selection," *Journal of Marketing Research*, Vol. 3, 1966.

Bertoletti, M. E., J. Chapiro, and H. R. Rieznik, "Optimization of Investment— A Solution by Linear Programming," *Management Technology*, No. 1, January 1960, pp. 64–75.

Bruno, M., "A Programming Model for Israel," in *The Theory and Design of Economic Development*, I. Adelman, and E. Thorbecke, editors, The Johns-Hopkins Press, Baltimore, 1966.

———, "An Alternative to Uniform Expenditure Reductions in Multiple Resource State Finance Programs," *Management Science*, Vol. 17, No. 6, February 1971, pp. 386–98.

Carleton, W., "An Analytical Model for Long-Range Financial Planning," *Journal of Finance*, May 1970.

Charnes, A., W. W. Cooper, and R. Ferguson, "Blending Aviation Gasolines, A Study in Programming Interdependent Activities," *Econometrica*, Vol. 20, No. 2, April 1952, pp. 135–59.

———, "Optimal Estimation of Executive Compensation by Linear Programming," *Management Science*, Vol. 1, No. 2, January 1955, pp. 138–51.

Chenery, H. B., and A. MacEwan, "Optimal Patterns of Growth and Aid: The Case of Pakistan," in *The Theory and Design of Economic Development*, I. Adelman, and E. Thorbecke, editors, The Johns-Hopkins Press, Baltimore, 1966.

Cohen, K. J., and F. S. Hammer, "Linear Programming and Optimal Bank-Asset Management Decisions," *Journal of Finance*, Vol. 21, 1967.

Cohen, R., C. McBride, R. Thornton, and T. White, *Letter Mail System Reference Design: An Analytical Method for Evaluating Candidate Mechanization*, Institute for Defense Analyses, Report R-168, 1970.

Dickens, J. H., "Linear Programming in Corporate Simulation," in *Corporate Simulation Models*, A. H. Schrieber, editor, University of Washington, Seattle, 1970.

Drayer, W., and S. Seabury, "Facilities Expansion Model," *Interfaces: Practice of Management Science*, Vol. 5, No. 2, February 1975.

Eisemann, K., and W. N. Young, "Study of a Textile Mill with the Aid of Linear Programming," *Management Technology*, No. 1, January 1960, pp. 52–63.

Engle, J. F., and M. W. Warshaw, "Allocating Advertising Research," *Journal of Advertising Research*, Vol. 4, No. 3, 1964, pp. 42–48.

Fabian, T., "Blast Furnace Production Planning—A Linear Programming Example," *Management Science*, Vol. 14, No. 2, October 1967, pp. 1–27.

Fetter, R. B., "A Linear Programming Model for Long Range Capacity Planning," *Management Science*, Vol. 7, No. 4, 1961, pp. 372–78.

Franklin, A. D., and E. Koenigsberg, "Computed School Assignments in a Large District," *Operations Research*, Vol. 21, No. 2, March–April 1973, pp. 413–26.

Garvin, W. W., H. W. Crandall, J. B. John, and R. A. Spellman, "Applications of Linear Programming in the Oil Industry," *Management Science*, Vol. 3, No. 4, July 1957, pp. 407–30.

Gilmore, P. C., and R. E. Gomory, "A Linear Programming Approach to the Cutting Stock Problem," *Operations Research*, Vol. 9, 1961, pp. 849–59.

———, "A Linear Programming Approach to the Cutting Stock Problem — Part II," *Operations Research*, Vol. 11, No. 6, November–December 1963, pp. 863–88.

———, "Multistage Cutting Stock Problems of Two and More Dimensions," *Operations Research*, Vol. 13, No. 1, January–February 1965, pp. 94–120.

Glassey, C. R., and V. K. Gupta, "A Linear Programming Analysis of Paper Recycling," *Management Science*, Vol. 21, No. 4, December 1974, pp. 392–408.

Greene, J. H., K. Chatto, C. R. Hicks, and C. B. Cox, "Linear Programming in the Packing Industry," *Journal of Industrial Engineering*, Vol. 10, No. 5, 1959, pp. 364–72.

Hamilton, W. F., and M. A. Moses, "An Optimization Model for Corporate Financial Planning," *Operations Research*, Vol. 21, No. 3, May–June 1973, pp. 677–92.

Hanssmann, F., and S. W. Hess, "A Linear Programming Approach to Production and Employment Scheduling," *Management Technology*, No. 1, January 1960, pp. 46–52.

Heady, E. O., et al., "Programming Models for the Planning of the Agricultural Sector," in *The Theory and Design of Economic Development*, I. Adelman, and E. Thorbecke, editors, The Johns-Hopkins Press, Baltimore, 1966.

Heroux, R. L., and W. A. Wallace, "Linear Programming and Financial Analysis of the New Community Development Process," *Management Science*, Vol. 19, No. 8, April 1973, pp. 857–72.

Hughes, J. S., and W. G. Lewellen, "Programming Solutions to Capital Rationing Problems," *Journal of Business, Finance and Accounting*, Vol. 1, No. 1, Spring 1974.

Ignall, E., P. Kolesar, and W. Walker, "Linear Programming Models of Crew Assignments for Refuse Collection," P-4717, The Rand Corporation, Santa Monica, Calif., November 1972.

Ijiri, Y., F. K. Levy, and R. C. Lyon, "A Linear Programming Model for Budgeting and Financial Planning," *Journal of Accounting Research*, Autumn, 1968.

Jewell, W. S., "Warehousing and Distribution of a Seasonal Product," *Naval Research Logistics Quarterly*, Vol. 4, 1957.

Kohn, R. E., "Application of Linear Programming to a Controversy on Air Pollution Control," *Management Science*, Vol. 17, No. 10, June 1971, pp. 609–21.

Lee, S. M., and L. J. Moore, "Optimizing Transportation Problems with Multiple Objectives," *AIIE Transactions*, Vol. 5, No. 4, December 1973, pp. 333–38.

Loucks, D. P., C. S. ReVelle, and W. R. Lynn, "Linear Programming Models for Water Pollution Control," *Management Science*, Vol. 14, No. 4, December 1967, pp. 166–81.

Manne, A. S., "A Linear Programming Model for the U.S. Petroleum Refining Industry," *Econometrica*, January 1958.

———, "Key Sectors of the Mexican Economy, 1962–72," in *The Theory and Design of Economic Development*, I. Adelman, and E. Thorbecke, editors, The Johns-Hopkins Press, Baltimore, 1966.

Manne, A. S., and T. E. Weisskopf, "A Dynamic Multisectoral Model for India, 1967–75," in *Input-Output Techniques*, Vol. 2, A. P. Carter, and A. Brody, editors, North-Holland, Amsterdam, 1970.

Masse, P., and R. Gibrat, "Application of Linear Programming to Investments in the Electric Power Industry," *Management Science*, Vol. 3, No. 2, January 1957, pp. 149–66.

McBride, C. C., "Post Office Mail Operations," in *Analysis of Public Systems*, edited by A. W. Drake, R. L. Keeney, and P. M. Morse, MIT Press, Cambridge, Mass., 1972.

Metzger, R. W., and R. Schwarzbek, "A Linear Programming Application to Cupola Charging," *Journal of Industrial Engineering*, Vol. 12, No. 2, March–April 1961, pp. 87–93.

Meyer, M., "Applying Linear Programming to the Design of Ultimate Pit Limits," *Management Science*, Vol. 16, No. 2, October 1969, pp. 121–35.

Orgler, Y. E., "An Unequal-Period Model for Cash Management Decisions," *Management Science*, Vol. 16, No. 2, October 1969, pp. 77–92.

Revelle, C., F. Feldmann, and W. Lynn, "An Optimization Model for Tuberculosis Epidemiology," *Management Science*, Vol. 16, No. 4, December 1969, pp. 190–211.

Revelle, C., et al., "Linear Programming Applied to Water Quality Management," *Water Resources Research*, February 1968.

Robichek, A. A., D. Teichroew, and J. M. Jones, "Optimal Short Term Financing Decisions," *Management Science*, Vol. 12, No. 1, September 1965, pp. 1–36.

Kay, E., and E. Duckworth, "Linear Programming in Practice," *Applied Statistics*, March 1957.

Rutenburg, D. R., "Maneuvering Liquid Assets in a Multi-National Company: Formulation and Deterministic Solution Procedure," *Management Science*, Vol. 16, No. 10, June 1970, pp. 671–84.

Sharpe, W. F., "A Linear Programming Algorithm for Mutual Fund Portfolio Selection," *Management Science*, Vol. 13, No. 7, 1967, pp. 499–510.

Smith, S. B., "Planning Transistor Production by Linear Programming," *Operations Research*, Vol. 13, No. 1, January–February, 1965, pp. 132–39.

Thomas, J., "Linear Programming Models for Production-Advertising Decisions," *Management Science*, Vol. 17, No. 8, April 1971, pp. 474–84.

Tsao, C. S., and R. H. Day, "A Process Analysis Model for the U.S. Steel Industry," *Management Science*, Vol. 19, No. 10, June 1971, pp. 588–608.

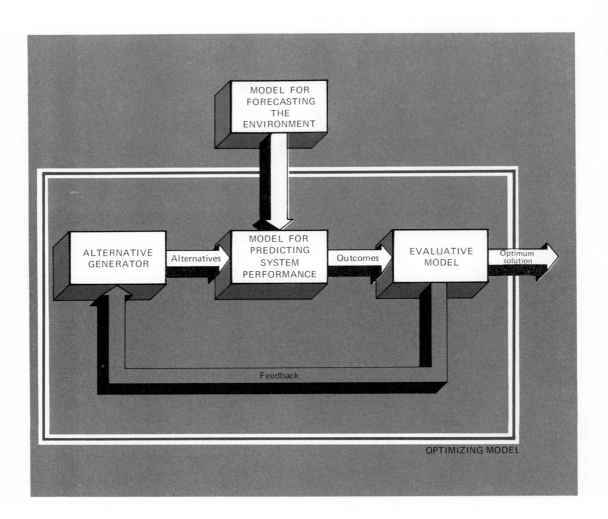

14

The Simplex Method

In the previous chapter we discussed the formulation and interpretation of linear optimization models, assuming that the solution was provided by a computer program. Now let us look inside the linear programming solution technique, the *simplex method*. An understanding of how the simplex algorithm functions will contribute to an understanding of the interpretation of results.

We first present an algebraic development of the solution strategy as an aid to understanding the solution process. Next the simplex algorithm is explained as a series of steps that can be formulated for computer solution. The discussion within the chapter presents the simplex algorithm as a special way of solving simultaneous linear equations. Also, an alternative self-contained description of the simplex algorithm is provided in the appendix to this chapter. The appendix reduces the algorithm to a series of mechanical steps, based on organizing the data into a tableau. The reader may wish to concentrate on one or the other of these presentations, or he may prefer to study both.

We shall use the chemical production problem as a vehicle for discussion. Since we can represent that problem in graphic form, and since we already know the answer, we can see readily what is happening at each stage of the solution. We shall simplify the problem slightly by eliminating the demand constraints. Recall that for the stated problem, these constraints were not effective in dictating the optimal solution anyway. Eliminating them provides a simpler, more direct explanation of the procedure.

Formulation

The statement of the problem was one of allocating time on machines A and B to the two products, x and y, in such a way that contribution to profit and overhead would be maximized. The time requirements on the two machines for each product were given and the total available time on the two machines was limited. (Rereading the Chapter 13 formulation may be of value, but all conditions for the problem are the same except that we will assume that we can sell all products produced within the limits of machine capacity.) Therefore, the resulting linear optimization model is

$$\text{maximize } Z = 60x + 50y,$$

subject to

$$2x + 4y \leqslant 80 \text{ (machine A)},$$
$$3x + 2y \leqslant 60 \text{ (machine B)},$$
$$x \geqslant 0 \text{ (minimum production for chemical } x),$$
$$y \geqslant 0 \text{ (minimum production for chemical } y).$$

Graphic Solution

Figure 1 shows the constraints plotted on a graph and identifies the feasible solution space, *abcd*, and the previously determined optimal allocation of machine time at point c; that is, produce $x = 10$ units and $y = 15$ units. Recall also that the contribution for the optimal solution was $1350.

We have plotted in Figure 1 the linear objective function for two values of total contribution, $Z = \$900$ and $Z = \$1200$. When we set $Z = \$900$, for example,

$$60x + 50y = 900.$$

Then, when $x = 0$, we must have $y = 18$, since $60(0) + 50(18) = 900$, and when $y = 0$, we have $x = 15$, since $60(15) + 50(0) = 900$. The resulting straight line is very simple to plot on Figure 1. The "$900 line" within the constraints defines all of the feasible solutions that would produce a contribution of $Z = \$900$. Since our objective is to maximize contribution, what happens if we increase Z to $1200? Since the slope of the objective function has not changed, the line for $Z = \$1200$ is parallel to the $900 line, and closer to point c, as we note in Figure 1. It is now rather obvious for the simple problem that if we substituted larger and larger values of Z in the objective function, lines parallel to the $900 and $1200 lines would result, and a line through point c would define a combination of x and y with the maximum possible contribution within the feasible solution space. Figure 1 then provides us with a clear picture of the problem and the relationships for various solutions evaluated by the objective function.

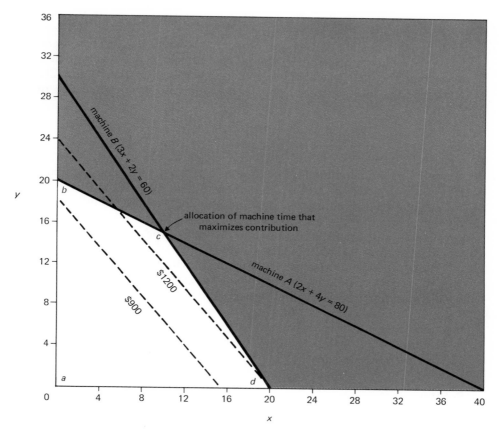

Figure 1. Graphic solution of example used for algebraic interpretation of the simplex method

ALGEBRAIC SOLUTION

Let us now proceed through the algebraic steps of the simplex solution to the chemical production problem.

Slack Variables

First, let us note the physical meaning of the constraints on available time for machines A and B. For machine A, since x requires 2 hours per unit and y requires 4 hours per unit, and we are limited to a total of 80 hours, we wrote the inequality constraint

$$2x + 4y \leq 80,\qquad(1)$$

and for machine B,

$$3x + 2y \leqslant 60 .\tag{2}$$

The inequalities state that the use of machines A and B is less than or equal to 80 and 60 hours respectively; that is, there *could* be idle machine time. If we take up the slack available, we could convert inequalities (1) and (2) into equations by defining *slack variables* to represent the possible idle time. Therefore,

$$2x + 4y + W_A = 80 ,\tag{3}$$

$$3x + 2y + W_B = 60 ,\tag{4}$$

where W_A is the idle time for machine A, and W_B the idle time for machine B. We also require W_A and W_B to be nonnegative (W_A, $W_B \geqslant 0$). The constraints plotted in Figure 1 are then lines that indicate the full use of the two machines when $W_A = W_B = 0$. Solutions that involve some idle time are permissible and would fall below one or both of the constraint lines, and would be within the solution space *abcd*.

Now, we have two equations, (3) and (4), with four unknown variables, plus the objective function that we shall use as an evaluative model. Now, recall from simple algebra that we can solve equations simultaneously if there are the same number of unknowns as equations. If we set any two of the four variables to zero, we can solve the two equations simultaneously to find the values of the other two. This is exactly what we will be doing in the following step-by-step procedure.

Solution Procedure

Step 1. *Establish an initial solution.* To start, let us develop a trivial solution whose implications we know and understand—the worst possible solution. We assume no production; that is, $x = y = 0$. We know then that all of the available time on the two machines will be idle, and using the objective function to evaluate the solution, we know that $Z = 0$, since we have produced nothing. Let us solve equations (3) and (4) for W_A and W_B as follows:

$$W_A = 80 - 2x - 4y ,\tag{5}$$

$$W_B = 60 - 3x - 2y ,\tag{6}$$

and our statement of the objective function is

$$Z = 60x + 50y .\tag{7}$$

If x and y are zero, the values of W_A and W_B are

$$W_A = 80 - 2(0) - 4(0) = 80 ,$$
$$W_B = 60 - 3(0) - 2(0) = 60 .$$

The evaluation of this solution by the objective function is

$$Z = 60(0) + 50(0) = 0 ,$$

which is the contribution expected when nothing is produced. Note that this is point a in Figure 1.

Step 2. *Can the initial solution be improved?* Now, we need a test for optimality in order to know whether to stop or to continue in search of a better solution. We look at the last statement of the objective function, equation (7), and note that both x and y have positive contributions. In other words, we can improve the initial solution by introducing either x or y into the solution with nonzero values.

This is the test: if we examine the last statement of the objective function and find variables in it that improve the objective function, then the solution can be improved. If at some point in the procedure we find only variables that offer no positive contribution to the objective function, then no improvement is possible and we have an optimal solution.

Step 3. *Selecting the incoming variable.* We can improve the solution by making either x or y nonzero. Let us choose the variable that provides the greatest improvement per unit. Since in equation (7), a unit of x earns $60 and a unit of y only $50, we select x as the variable to enter the solution with a nonzero value. We shall refer to x as the *incoming variable*. In doing so, we have determined the direction of change in our solution, since x will *increase* from its initial value of zero.

Step 4. *Determine the amount of change in x.* We know that allocating productive time to x will improve the objective function value. For each unit of x produced, we obtain a contribution of $60. Now, how many units of x should we produce? Since we have found an advantageous direction of change, we wish to press this advantage by producing the maximum possible amount of x, within the constraints of the problem. Suppose we solve equations (3) and (4) for x. From (3) we obtain

$$x = 40 - 2y - \frac{W_A}{2},\tag{8}$$

and from (4),

$$x = 20 - \frac{2y}{3} - \frac{W_B}{3}.\tag{9}$$

In the initial solution, $y = 0$. What if W_A were set equal to 0 along with y? From (8), x would equal 40. If W_B were set equal to zero along with y, x would equal 20 in (9).

The smaller of these two numbers, 20, determines how large x can become. From (9), there is no way that x can become larger than 20 without either y or W_B being a negative number, and this is not permitted. This can also be seen in Figure 1, since equation (8) refers to the constraint for machine A and equation (9) to the constraint for machine B. Note that $x = 40$ is not in the feasible solution region, but that 20 is the maximum value of x in the feasible region. Therefore, equation (4) determines how large we can make x.

In order to increase x to 20, we must reduce W_B to 0, as seen in equation (9). Thus, we will again have a solution with two nonzero values, x and W_A, and with two variables, y and W_B, set equal to zero. To determine the effect of setting x equal to 20 on W_A, we substitute $20 - 2y/3 - W_B/3$ from (9) into (5), and obtain

$$W_A = 80 - 2\left(20 - \frac{2y}{3} - \frac{W_B}{3}\right) - 4y,$$

which simplifies to

$$W_A = 40 - \frac{8y}{3} + \frac{2W_B}{3}. \tag{10}$$

Thus, with $y = W_B = 0$, we have $W_A = 40$.

Expressions (9) and (10) would be obtained if we simply solved equations (3) and (4) simultaneously for the common values of x and W_A, when y and W_B are assumed to be constants. To accomplish this, we would rewrite (5) and (6) as

$$2x + W_A = 80 - 4y, \tag{11}$$

$$3x = 60 - 2y - W_B. \tag{12}$$

To solve these equations, we simply divide (12) by 3, the coefficient of x, so it becomes

$$x = 20 - \frac{2y}{3} - \frac{W_B}{3}.$$

Notice that this is equation (9). Now, we multiply (9) by -2, the negative of the coefficient of x in (11), and add it to (11) as shown below:

$$\begin{array}{ll} 2x + W_A = 80 - 4y & (11) \\ -2x = -40 + \dfrac{4y}{3} + \dfrac{2W_B}{3} & [\,(9)\ \text{multiplied by} -2] \\ \hline W_A = 40 - \dfrac{8y}{3} + \dfrac{2W_B}{3} & (10) \end{array}$$

The result is equation (10). This solution strategy for linear equations is reviewed in Appendix C.

We also substitute (9) as the value of x into the last statement of the objective function, equation (7). The objective function then becomes

$$Z = 60\left(20 - \frac{2y}{3} - \frac{W_B}{3}\right) + 50y = 1200 + 10y - 20W_B. \tag{13}$$

With y and W_B set to zero, (13) gives the total contribution of the solution $x = 20$ and $W_A = 40$, which is 1200.

To summarize, by letting y and W_B be zero, we obtain the solution

$$x \;= 20, \text{ from (9)},$$
$$W_A = 40, \text{ from (10)},$$
$$y \;= 0,$$
$$W_B = 0,$$
$$Z \;= 1200, \text{ from (13)}.$$

This solution is an obvious improvement over the first solution, since the value of the objective function has now increased from zero to \$1200. We can see from Figure 1 that the second stage of our solution is represented by point d.

Now you may be asking yourself the following question: "If we are going to set y and W_B equal to zero anyway, why do we carry them along as excess baggage in equations (9), (10), and (13)?" The answer is that we obtain additional information from having them in (9), (10), and (13). For example, in (13) we now see that an additional unit of y will increase the value of the objective function Z by \$10 per unit. Why is the increase only \$10 per unit, since the contribution per unit from y as shown in the original formulation is \$50 per unit? To increase y from its current value of zero, we will have to decrease x, which has a per unit contribution of \$60. However, (13) tells us that the *net effect* of increasing y from the *current solution* will be worth \$10 per unit. We can now use the "excess baggage" in (9) and (10) to quickly determine how large to make y.

Step 5. *Repeat steps 2, 3, and 4.* Since y has a positive coefficient in (13), we would like to increase it from its current solution value of zero. Notice that W_B has a negative coefficient in (13). The value of the objective function would increase if we could *decrease* W_B. However, W_B is zero in the current solution, and so it cannot be reduced any further. Therefore, we select y as our entering variable.

Using the "excess baggage" in (9) and (10), we solve for y and obtain

$$y = 30 - \frac{3x}{2} - \frac{W_B}{2} \tag{14}$$

from (9) and

$$y = 15 - \frac{3W_A}{8} + \frac{W_B}{4} \tag{15}$$

from (10). W_B is equal to zero in the current solution; setting $x = 0$ gives $y = 30$ from (14), while setting $W_A = 0$ gives $y = 15$ from (15), with the latter being more restrictive. Therefore, we can make $y = 15$ in the revised solution.

Substituting the right hand side of (15) for y in (9) gives

$$x = 20 - \frac{2}{3}\left(15 - \frac{3W_A}{8} + \frac{W_B}{4}\right) - \frac{W_B}{3},$$

which simplifies to

$$x = 10 + \frac{W_A}{4} - \frac{W_B}{2}. \tag{16}$$

Again, we would obtain (15) and (16) by solving (3) and (4) simultaneously for x and y while treating W_A and W_B as constants (check this yourself).

We also substitute the value of y given by equation (15) in the last statement of the objective function (13), and we obtain

$$Z = 1350 - \frac{15W_A}{4} - \frac{35W_B}{2}. \tag{17}$$

When W_A and W_B are zero, the values of the variables and of the objective function are then as follows:

$$
\begin{aligned}
y &= 15, \text{ from (15)}, \\
x &= 10, \text{ from (16)}, \\
W_A &= 0, \\
W_B &= 0, \\
Z &= 1350, \text{ from (17)}.
\end{aligned}
$$

We see that this is point c in Figure 1, and we know that this is the optimal solution by inspection of Figure 1. According to our procedure, however, we know this is true by examining the last statement of the objective function, equation (17). We note that the only possible way that the contribution could be increased is by decreasing either W_A, W_B, or both, since their respective coefficients in (17) are negative. Since the solution at this stage already specifies that W_A and W_B are at their minimum values of zero, and since none of the variables can take on negative values, there is no way to increase contribution, and we have met the requirements for the test of optimality.

Shadow Prices

Recall that the sensitivity analysis provided by the computer program in Figure 8 of Chapter 13 indicated that the value for a marginal unit of capacity for machine A was $3.75 and for machine B, $17.50. Where do we find these values in the algebraic solution? They are contained in the last statement of the objective function, equation (17). The significance of the coefficients $-15/4$ and $-35/2$ for W_A and W_B respectively is that they are the shadow prices for marginal units of capacity. In other words, for every unit of W_A added in the solution at this point (idle time on machine A), contribution declines by $15/4 = \$3.75$. But conversely, if the original capacity of machine A had been 81 hours instead of 80, net contribution could have been increased by $3.75.

Thus, the coefficients of the slack variables in the objective function are the shadow prices and indeed, had this equivalent meaning at every stage of the solution. In the initial statement of the objective function (7), x and y had marginal contribution rates of 60 and 50 respectively and W_A and W_B had zero rates. In the second stage of solution the objective function was represented by equation (13), and y had a contribution rate of 10 and W_B a rate of -20.

Characteristics of the Simplex Solution

The optimizing model we have developed involved a trial solution of the constraint equations, an evaluation of that solution by the objective function, and a test for optimality. If the optimality test indicated that improvement was possible, we determined the direction of change of the solution (selection of the entering variable) and the amount of change (testing constraints to see how much the entering variable could be increased and selecting the most restrictive equation). This generated a new solution, which was subjected to the same procedure until the test for optimality indicated that no further improvement was possible. The general nature of the algorithmic solution is summarized by Figure 2. In Figure 2 the predictive model and the objective function are modified to reflect the values of the decision variables for each stage of the solution.

Note that, in fact, we did not consider all possible feasible solutions. Rather, we proceeded to the optimum solution by considering only three alternate solutions, points a, d, and finally c in Figure 1. There are an infinite number of combinations of the four variables that we did not bother with as we converged on the optimum solution. For example, proceeding from a to d, we considered none of the feasible solutions along the line ad, which would have yielded progressively larger values of contribution as x increased. Instead, we jumped from a to d. Similarly, we did not consider any of the feasible solutions along the line dc, although each one would have progressively yielded a larger contribution as we converged on the optimum. For example, the point $(x = 16, y = 6)$ results in $W_A = 24$, $W_B = 0$, and a contribution of $1260.

Also, we did not consider any of the feasible solutions that fell inside the solution space $abcd$. We should note that all of these other solutions that we did not consider, that lie inside the solution space but not on constraint lines, are feasible solutions that involve more than two of the four variables with positive values. By requiring that we deal only with solutions where two, and only two, variables could be positive, we jumped from corner to corner, rather than moving more slowly in a larger number of steps along the sides of the solution space or even within its interior. The solutions that involve only two of the four variables are called *basic solutions*. There are only four such basic solutions in our example, at points a, b, c, and d.

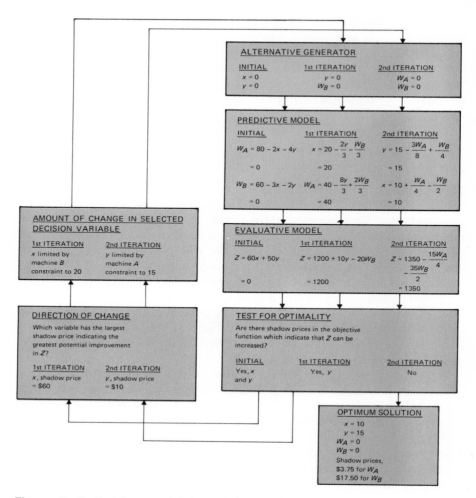

Figure 2. Optimizing model indicating initial solution and two iterations for the chemical production problem

In the larger scale problems, we are doing a similar thing; that is, moving from one basic solution to a better one, jumping over an entire set of other feasible solutions that are in between. These basic solutions are always at the corners of two- and three-dimensional problems, and conceptually at the equivalent of corners of multidimensional problems. This solution strategy is advantageous, since it can be shown that if a linear optimization model actually has an optimal solution, it will lie at a corner point. The proof of this important result is beyond our scope in this discussion, but it provides the rationale for the simplex algorithm.

THE SIMPLEX ALGORITHM

We used simple, even naive problems to explain linear optimization models and the simplex solution technique. The power of linear programming, however, is in the solution of large-scale problems, and the key to their solution has been the simplex algorithm. The simplex algorithm uses the algebraic logic we have just discussed, but reduces this logic to a very efficient set of arithmetic and logical operations so that computing effort is minimized. When the algorithm has been developed in a rigorous way, the computing effort can be further minimized by programming the algorithm for computers. Large-scale problems of resource allocation can then be formulated and solved at reasonable cost. Without the simplex algorithm and without computers, the solution of large-scale problems would be entirely out of reason.

We shall now present a more rigorous description of the simplex method, so that the logic can be programmed on a computer. This description is based on an approach for solving several simultaneous linear equations. An alternative description is presented in the appendix to this chapter, that follows even more closely a series of computational rules that can be programmed. The reader may choose either of these self-contained descriptions of the algorithm, or both.

In reducing the simplex algorithm to a set of rigorous rules, there is a risk that we may begin to think of it as a mechanical procedure, losing contact with what is being accomplished at each stage of solution. We shall try to maintain contact with the meaning of each step by using the chemical production problem as an example again, and relating our manipulations to the process of the preceding algebraic development and to the graphic solution shown in Figure 1.

Recall that after the addition of the slack variables to account for idle time, our two restricting equations for machines A and B were respectively

$$2x + 4y + W_A = 80 , \tag{18}$$

$$3x + 2y + W_B = 60 . \tag{19}$$

An initial solution to this set of equations is found by setting $x = y = 0$, which gives $W_A = 80$ and $W_B = 60$. This solution is easy to see, since W_A has a coefficient of $+1$ in (18) but does not appear in (19), and W_B has a coefficient of $+1$ in (19) but does not appear in (18).

The objective function for this problem can be written as

$$Z = 60x + 50y + (0)W_A + (0)W_B , \tag{20}$$

since idle time contributes nothing to profits or overhead. Substituting the initial solution of $W_A = 80$ and $W_B = 60$ into 20 gives

$$Z - 60x - 50y = (0)80 + (0)60 = 0 \tag{21}$$

as the corresponding value of the objective function.

Since (21) is also an equation, we can combine it with (18) and (19) and write

$$Z - 60x - 50y \qquad\qquad\quad = 0, \qquad \text{(row 0)}$$
$$2x + 4y + W_A \qquad = 80, \qquad \text{(row 1)}$$
$$3x + 2y \qquad + W_B = 60, \qquad \text{(row 2)}$$

where all of the variables must also be nonnegative. This is our set of *initial equations* that are associated with the initial solution $x = y = 0$, $W_A = 80$, and $W_B = 60$.

Improving the Initial Solution

To improve the initial solution, we use the test for optimality: "Are there shadow prices in the objective function that indicate that Z can be increased?" If there are, we know we can substitute a variable in the solution that has a higher contribution rate to the objective function than one of the variables now in the solution.

    Row 0 is the same as equation (7) developed during the algebraic solution, except that the terms involving x and y have been moved to the other side of the equality sign, changing their signs from plus to minus. Thus, variables with *negative* coefficients in row 0 will improve the objective function if they are brought into the solution.

Identifying the Entering Variable Any variable with a negative coefficient in row 0 will improve (increase) the objective function if its value is increased from 0. The following rule is useful in selecting the entering variable:

> **Rule I.** If there are variables with negative coefficients in row 0, choose the one with the most negative coefficient as the *entering variable*. If there are no variables with negative coefficients in row 0, the solution is optimal.

In this example, we chose x as the entering variable according to rule I. This choice determines the "direction of change" as indicated in the flow chart for this example in Figure 2.

Identifying the Limiting Row If x increases by 1 unit, W_A must decrease by 2 units (the coefficient of x in row 1) in order to maintain the equality in row 1, and W_B must decrease by 3 units (the coefficient of x in row 2) in order to maintain the equality in row 2. If W_A decreases from its initial value of 80 units to 0, x could increase to $80/2 = 40$; if W_B decreases from its initial value of 60, x could increase to $60/3 = 20$. The latter, 20, would be reached first as x increases. Therefore, the relationship between W_B and x in row 2 *limits* the size of x, so we designate row 2 as the *limiting row*.

Notice that this result was determined by dividing the right-hand side of each row (ignoring row 0) by the corresponding coefficient of the *entering variable*. If the coefficient of the entering variable in a row were negative or zero, the row would be ignored, since increasing the entering variable would not force another variable to zero. This idea can be implemented in the simplex algorithm with a second rule.

Rule II. Taking the ratios of the right-hand sides of the rows to the corresponding coefficients of the entering variable (ignoring zero or negative coefficients), choose the row with the smallest ratio as the *limiting row*.

In the algebraic solution, we solved each constraint equation for the entering variable, then set the remaining variables equal to zero. The constraint that gave the minimum value for the entering variable was identified as the limiting constraint. Rule II achieves exactly the same result and determines the "amount of change" in the solution.

Pivoting   We now know the entering variable x and the limiting row, row 2. The limiting row was determined by the first nonzero variable to be *decreased to zero* as the entering variable is *increased from zero*. From our rule II calculations, we know that the variable x will be increased to 20 and the variable W_B will be decreased to 0 in the new solution. The *pivoting operation* also determines the values of the other variables and of the objective function in the new solution.

Pivoting requires the following steps:

1. Divide each coefficient in the limiting row and its right-hand side by the coefficient of the entering variable.
2. For each row *except* the limiting row:
    a. Multiply each coefficient of the newly transformed limiting row (found in step 1 above) by the negative of the coefficient of the entering variable in the nonlimiting row.
    b. Add the result to the nonlimiting row.

In our example problem, we carry out these steps by dividing row 2 (the limiting row) by the coefficient of the entering variable x, which is 3. The result is

$$x + \frac{2y}{3} \qquad + \frac{W_B}{3} = 20 . \qquad (22)$$

Next, we modify rows 0 and 1 as indicated.

> Row 0: multiply (22) by 60 and add to row 0.
> Row 1: multiply (22) by −2 and add to row 1.

For row 0, the calculations would be

$$\begin{array}{llll} Z - 60x - 50y & = 0 & \text{(row 0)} \\ \underline{60x + 40y \qquad + 20W_B = 1200} & [\,(22)\text{ multiplied by }60\,] \\ Z \qquad\ - 10y \qquad + 20W_B = 1200 \end{array}$$

After carrying out similar calculations for row 1 (check them for yourself), the revised set of equations are

$$Z \qquad - 10y \qquad + 20W_B = 1200 \qquad \text{(row 0)}$$

$$\frac{8y}{3} + W_A - \frac{2W_B}{3} = 40 , \qquad \text{(row 1)}$$

$$x + \frac{2y}{3} \qquad + \frac{W_B}{3} = 20 . \qquad \text{(row 2)}$$

Notice that in each row there is one variable with a coefficient of 1 and with coefficients of 0 in the other rows (including row 0). This variable is "in the solution" with a value equal to the number on the right-hand side of the equal sign. In row 0, this variable is Z, which equals 1200; in row 1, $W_A = 40$; and in row 2, $x = 20$. The variables that are "in the solution" are called *basic variables*. The other variables, y and W_A in this case, are required to equal 0, and are called *nonbasic variables*.

This is the solution we obtained after solving for x using the limiting equation, and substituting back into the other equations in the algebraic development. We also demonstrated the same result using another solution technique for simultaneous equations [equations (11) through (13)]. When examined closely, pivoting is simply an approach for solving a system of simultaneous equations very similar to the approach presented in Appendix C. Although the arithmetic is a bit tedious, there is nothing at all that is particularly sophisticated or mathematically "advanced" about this basic solution strategy.

Accomplishing the pivoting operation completes one *iteration* of the simplex algorithm. Thus, an iteration corresponds to a movement from one corner point of the solution space to another corner point, or from one basic solution to another.

Improving the Solution

The variable y has the only negative coefficient in row 0, and so we know that it should enter the solution by rule I. We can determine the limiting row from the ratios shown in Table 1. The minimum ratio of 15 corresponds to row 1, which is designated as the limiting row according to rule II.

Performing the pivoting operation, we divide each coefficient in row 1 by the coefficient of the entering variable y, $8/3$, to obtain

$$y + \frac{3W_A}{8} - \frac{W_B}{4} = 15 . \qquad (23)$$

TABLE 1. Applying Rule II

Row	Current Right-Hand Side	Coefficient of y	Ratio
1	40	$\frac{8}{3}$	15
2	20	$\frac{2}{3}$	30

We modify rows 0 and 2 as indicated.

Row 0: multiply (23) by 10 and add to row 0 .

Row 2: multiply (23) by −2/3 and add to row 2 .

The resulting system of equations is

$$Z \qquad + \frac{15W_A}{4} + \frac{35W_B}{2} = 1350 , \qquad \text{(row 0)}$$

$$y + \frac{3W_A}{8} - \frac{W_B}{4} = 15 , \qquad \text{(row 1)}$$

$$x \qquad - \frac{W_A}{4} + \frac{W_B}{2} = 10 . \qquad \text{(row 2)}$$

By identifying the variable in each row with a coefficient of 1 and with coefficients of 0 in the other rows, we see that the solution is $Z = 1350$, $x = 10$, and $y = 15$, with $W_A = W_B = 0$. Now both x and y are basic variables, while W_A and W_B are nonbasic.

Since there are no variables in row 0 with negative coefficients, this solution is optimal. As we expected, these values coincide with our previous algebraic solution and with the graphic solution. Note also that the coefficients in row 0 yield the negative of the shadow prices obtained previously for W_A and W_B.

Summary of the Procedure

The steps of the simplex algorthim may be summarized as follows:

1. Formulate the constraints and the objective function.
2. Develop the set of *initial equations*, using the slack variables in the initial solution.
3. Identify the *entering variable*, the variable with the most negative coefficient in row 0.
4. Identify the *limiting row*, the row with the minimum ratio, determined by dividing the right-hand side of each row by the positive coefficient of the entering variable in that row (if the coefficient is zero or negative, the row is ignored).
5. Perform the *pivoting operation*.
   a. Divide the limiting row by the coefficient of the entering variable.

b. For each nonlimiting row:
  1) Multiply the newly transformed limiting row [found in (a) above] by the negative of the coefficient of the entering variable in the nonlimiting row.
  2) Add the result to the nonlimiting row.

6. Repeat steps 3 through 5 until all of the coefficients in row 0 are non-negative. An optimal solution then results.

7. The resulting optimal solution is interpreted in the following manner: in each row there is exactly one basic variable with a coefficient of 1 and with coefficients of 0 in the other rows. This variable is equal to the right-hand side of the row. The value of the objective function is given by the value of Z. All other nonbasic variables are zero. The shadow prices, which indicate the value of a marginal unit of each variable not in the solution, are the coefficients of the slack variables in row 0.

The output for the computer solution, including sensitivity analysis for the simplified chemical production problem, is shown in Figure 3. Note that the format is the same as the computer output illustrated in Chapter 13, showing the optimal value of the objective function, the optimal value of the decision variables, the shadow prices, and the upper and lower bounds on the right-hand values of the constraints and of the prices in the objective function.

SENSITIVITY ANALYSIS

The manager can use the sensitivty analysis shown in Figure 3 in the ways that we indicated in the previous chapter. To an alert manager, the optimum solution not only provides answers — given assumptions about resources, prices, and capacities — but should raise questions about what would happen *if* conditions should change. Some of these changes might be imposed by the environment, such as changes in resource costs and market constraints, or they might occur if resources were curtailed. Some, however, represent questions raised by the manager because they are changes that he can initiate, such as enlarging capacities or adding new activities. Obviously, it is possible to answer some of these questions by new computer runs, but why make the added runs if the information is already available in the present optimal solution? Sensitivity analysis is focused on the objective function and on the values for the right-hand sides of the constraints. Let us now consider how such analyses are developed.

Analysis of the Objective Function

We have already referred to the shadow prices and their significance. What happens if the unit prices (contributions or costs) in the objective function should change? Would the optimal solution remain, comprised of the same

```
        LPRUN

                  CHEMICAL PRODUCTION

THE OPTIMAL VALUE OF THE OBJECTIVE FUNCTION IS:    1350.000

                  THE VARIABLES IN THE SOLUTION ARE

VARIABLE X       AT LEVEL      1.0000E1
         Y                     1.5000E1

DO YOU WISH SENSITIVITY ANALYSIS? Y

                         SHADOW        LB        CURRENT       UB
CONSTRAINT       1      3.7500E0    4.0000E1    8.0000E1    1.2000E2
                 2      1.7500E1    4.0000E1    6.0000E1    1.2000E2

PRICE     X                        2.5000E1    6.0000E1    7.5000E1
          Y                        4.0000E1    5.0000E1    1.2000E2
```

Figure 3. Computer solution and sensitivity analysis for the simplified chemical production problem

combination of decision variables? (Of course, the *value* of the objective function would change if the prices changed.)

Changes in Nonbasic Variables For our example, let us first consider the prices for the nonbasic variables W_A and W_B, which are not in the optimal solution. If we could sufficiently increase the profitability of idle time, the solution could change. (This is seemingly ridiculous for the chemical production example, but consider other cases, where a value is placed on idle resources, for example, government agricultural subsidies. Of course, another company might be willing to pay rent on available idle capacity.) If the W_A unit contribution were increased by Δ, then the initial row 0 becomes

$$Z - 60x - 50y - (0 + \Delta)W_A - (0)W_B = 0 .$$

If we perform the simplex arithmetic transformations at each iteration, the final row 0 becomes

$$Z + \left(\frac{15}{4} - \Delta\right)W_A + \frac{35W_B}{2} = 1350 .$$

Therefore, if $\Delta > 15/4$, the coefficient of W_A becomes negative, and by rule I would enter the solution in exchange for x or y. Thus, the final row 0 coefficients of the *nonbasic* variables represent the largest positive increments to the original objective function coefficients for those variables that would not alter the current optimal solution.

Now, what is the effect of changing the contribution of basic variables in the final solution, such as x and y? For example, within what range is the coefficient for x valid for the current solution? If we add an increment Δ_x to the contribution for x in the initial row 0, we have

$$Z - (60 + \Delta_x)x - 50y - (0)W_A - (0)W_B = 0 .$$

Again, if we perform the simplex arithmetic transformations at each iteration, the final row 0 equation is

$$Z - \Delta_x x + \frac{15W_A}{4} + \frac{35W_B}{2} = 1350 . \tag{24}$$

However, since x is a basic variable, its coefficient must equal 0 in every row, including row 0, except for the row in which its coefficient is 1 (row 2 in this example). Applying our rules for pivoting to (24) with respect to x as the entering variable and row 2 as the limiting row, we multiply row 2 by Δ_x and add the result to (24). The computations are as follows:

$$Z - \Delta_x x \qquad + \frac{15W_A}{4} + \qquad \frac{35W_B}{2} = 1350 \tag{24}$$

$$\Delta_x x \qquad - \frac{\Delta_x W_A}{4} + \qquad \frac{\Delta_x W_B}{2} = 10\Delta_x \qquad \text{(row 2 multiplied by } \Delta_x)$$

$$\overline{Z \qquad + \left(\frac{15}{4} - \frac{\Delta_x}{4}\right)W_A + \left(\frac{35}{2} + \frac{\Delta_x}{2}\right)W_B = 1350 + 10\Delta_x}$$

Now, for the current solution to remain optimal, the coefficients of W_A and W_B must remain nonnegative. Therefore, we require

$$\frac{15}{4} - \frac{\Delta_x}{4} \geq 0$$

for W_A. Simplifying, we obtain $\Delta_x \leq 15$. Similarly we have

$$\frac{35}{2} + \frac{\Delta_x}{2} \geq 0$$

for W_B, so $\Delta_x \geq -35$. Thus, the *change* to the original contribution of x, 60, must be between -35 and 15 units. This means that the same solution will be optimal if the contribution of x is any number as small as $60 - 35 = 25$ or as large as $60 + 15 = 75$, as long as the other data in the problem remain unchanged. A similar analysis for chemical y indicates its range to be 40 to 120. Check these bounds on x and y with the computer sensitivity analysis in Figure 3.

Sensitivity of Right-Hand Side Constants

Now if the resources were to change, under what conditions would the solution change? These resources for our problem were the available hours on machines A and B of 80 and 60 hours respectively. First, let us consider the machine A constraint. If we added an increment of hours, Δ_A, to the 80-hour limit, the set of initial equations becomes

$$Z - 60x - 50y \qquad\qquad = 0, \qquad\qquad \text{(row 0)}$$
$$2x + 4y + W_A \qquad = 80 + \Delta_A, \qquad \text{(row 1)}$$
$$3x + 2y \qquad + W_B = 60. \qquad\qquad \text{(row 2)}$$

Notice that we have added a new variable to this problem on the right-hand side of the equations. The coefficients of this new variable are 1 in row 1 and 0 in rows 0 and 2. These are the same coefficients as for the variable W_A, the slack variable for row 1. In applying the simplex method, we divide every coefficient in the same row by the same constant, or we multiply every coefficient in a row by the same constant. The result is that if the coefficients of two different variables are identical in every row in the set of initial equations, they will be identical after every iteration, including the final one. Therefore, it is not necessary to re-solve the set of initial equations with Δ_A added to the right-hand side. We know that the solution would be

$$Z \qquad + \frac{15W_A}{4} + \frac{35W_B}{2} = 1350 + \frac{15\Delta_A}{4}, \qquad \text{(row 0)}$$

$$y + \frac{3W_A}{8} - \frac{W_B}{4} = 15 + \frac{3\Delta_A}{8}, \qquad \text{(row 1)}$$

$$x \qquad - \frac{W_A}{4} + \frac{W_B}{2} = 10 - \frac{\Delta_A}{4}, \qquad \text{(row 2)}$$

where the coefficients of Δ_A are identical to those of W_A.

For the optimal solution to be feasible, the optimal values of the basic variables must be nonnegative. Therefore, we have the relation

$$15 + \frac{3}{8}\Delta_A \geq 0$$

from row 1, which simplifies to $\Delta_A \geq -40$. From row 2,

$$10 - \frac{1}{4}\Delta_A \geq 0$$

or $\Delta_A \leq 40$. The same basic variables will be "in the solution" as long as $-40 \leq \Delta_A \leq 40$, or as long as the available hours on machine A are between $80 - 40 = 40$ and $80 + 40 = 120$. However, in this case the *values* of these basic variables would change.

Note in row 0 the value of the objective function, Z, is $1350 + (15/4)\Delta_A$. This value emphasizes that 15/4 is the shadow price, or marginal value, of an additional hour on Machine A. This shadow price is valid for any number of machine hours within the range of 40 to 120.

For example, suppose we can obtain 10 additional hours of time on machine A by changing our maintenance techniques. Thus, $\Delta_A = 10$, which is within the range −40 to +40. The new values of the basic variables are given by

$$y = 15 + \frac{3\Delta_A}{8}$$

$$x = 10 - \frac{\Delta_A}{4}$$

Substituting $\Delta_A = 10$, we obtain

$$y = 15 + \frac{3(10)}{8} = 18.75\,,$$

$$x = 10 - \frac{10}{4} = 7.50\,,$$

and the new value of the objective function is

$$Z = 1350 + \frac{15(10)}{4} = 1387.5\,.$$

We can apply the same type of analysis for the machine B constraint. Suppose we add an increment of Δ_B to the 60-hour limit on machine B in the initial set of equations. Then the coefficients for Δ_B in the final set of equations will be the same as the coefficients for W_B in the final set of equations. Therefore, the right-hand sides of the final set of equations, and the associated values of Δ_B will be

$$15 - \frac{\Delta_B}{4} \geqslant 0\,,$$

which gives $\Delta_B \leqslant 60$ from row 1, and

$$10 + \frac{\Delta_B}{2} \geqslant 0\,,$$

which gives $\Delta_B \geqslant -20$ from row 2. The range for the right-hand side constant for machine B is then $60 - 20 = 40$, and $60 + 60 = 120$, or 40 to 120. Check these ranges with the computer sensitivity analysis in Figure 3. (Note that these ranges are not the same as those given in Figure 8 of Chapter 13, because the constraint set included market limitations in that problem.)

These bounds apply when each right-hand side constant is varied independently. A similar, but more complex analysis is called for when several changes are made simultaneously [see Wagner, 1975].

EXTENSIONS OF THE SIMPLEX ALGORITHM

The simplex algorithm may be extended to deal with alternative optimal solutions and with degenerate solutions, as well as with other forms of the constraints (as described later in this section). These extensions are of definite interest to the manager.

Alternate Optimal Solutions   The identification of alternate optimal solutions is important, since they provide flexibility for the manager in his decisions. What if one of the coefficients of a nonbasic variable is 0 in row 0 of an iteration, and the other coefficients are all positive? Recall that the coefficients of the nonbasic variables indicate how much the objective function will change with a unit increase in the associated variable. If the coefficient in row 0 is 0, then the corresponding variable can enter the solution without changing the value of the objective function. If this occurs when there are no negative coefficients in row 0, the existing solution is optimal, but the solution that would be found by "bringing in" the variable with the 0 coefficient would also be optimal. It would have the same objective function value since the change per unit is 0.

Degeneracy   When one or more of the basic variables are actually "in the solution" with a value of 0, the solution is said to be degenerate. This condition was the cause for some alarm in the early days of linear programming, since theoretically the simplex algorithm can fail if degeneracy occurs. However, this failure has never been reported in a practical problem, so the issue now seems of concern only to analysts.

Minimizing an Objective Function   The procedure with which we have been dealing is a maximizing one, but it can also be applied to minimize an objective function. Suppose that we had wished to maximize the time that the equipment was in use. Using the chemical production problem as an example, the objective function would have been

$$\text{minimize } Z = W_A + W_B$$

since W_A and W_B represent the slack or idle time on machines A and B respectively. To convert the minimizing objective function for use in the maximizing algorithm that we developed, we simply multiply the foregoing statement by -1 and obtain

$$\text{maximize } Z = -W_A - W_B .$$

This procedure does not alter the objective function, but makes it possible to use the maximizing procedure. We may also alter the procedure to minimize an objective function by changing one simple rule in the algorithm. When selecting the entering variable, the one with the largest positive number in row 0 is selected, rather than the one with the most negative number. All other steps remain exactly the same.

Requirements   The constraints in the example problem were both restrictions that the values of the left-hand sides be less than or equal to the maximum amounts of time available on machines A and B. There may be situations, however, in which we are given a requirement that some combination of the variables must be greater than or equal to a given number. For example, the inequality

$$3x + 2y \geqslant 12$$

has a requirement of at least 12. To convert this statement to an equation, we must *subtract* a slack variable, and the result is

$$3x + 2y - W_1 = 12 .$$

A slack variable that is subtracted in a requirement is sometimes called a *surplus variable* because it indicates an excess supply relative to the right-hand side constant.

As it stands, this equation cannot be used in the simplex method because the coefficient for W_1 is -1. The simplex method requires that each row must have exactly one variable with a coefficient of $+1$, which appears in no other row. When all of the constraints are restrictions, this requirement is achieved for the initial set of equations by adding the slack variables. We can accomplish the same objective in this case by addition of an *artificial variable U*, so that the equation becomes

$$3x + 2y - W_1 + U = 12 .$$

The artificial variable is included simply as a computational device that permits us to stay within the rules of the algorithm. Consequently, an artificial variable is not wanted in the optimum solution. To be sure that the artificial variable will always be zero in the optimum solution, we may assign an arbitrarily large negative contribution to it in the objective function, which we shall call $-M$. The $-M$ is in reality an overwhelming cost in relation to the positive contributions in the objective function, so that as the objective function is maximized through the usual procedure, the artificial variable is driven to zero.

Equations   A problem may state that a certain combination of variables must total some exact quantity, as in the mail arrival constraints in the post office example of Chapter 13. To fit into the requirements of the simplex format we must have a variable in the equation with a coefficient of $+1$, that appears in no other constraint. For example, the equation

$$2x + 3y = 90$$

can be modified to fit into the simplex format by adding an artificial variable U. The equation then becomes

$$2x + 3y + U = 90 .$$

As with the approach for requirements, a $-M$ price is assigned to the artificial variable U in the objective function so that the artificial variable is always zero in the optimum solution.

Goal Programming In some cases, the objective of an organization may be expressed in terms of "goals" rather than in terms of maximizing or minimizing a single criterion. This situation is especially true in the public sector where obtaining "goals" is often considered more appropriate than maximizing profits or minimizing costs.

A linear optimization model can easily be formulated to minimize deviations from goals, using an approach known as goal programming. In the chemical production problem, suppose there are only 80 hours of time available on machine A. However, the amount of time available on machine B is flexible. The "goals" of the production planning problem are given as:

1. Use as close to 60 hours of time on machine B as possible.
2. Produce as close to a total of 30 units of chemical x and chemical y as possible.

Thus, our objective is to find values of x and y that satisfy

$$
\begin{aligned}
2x + 4y &\leqslant 80, &&\text{(machine A constraint)} \\
3x + 2y &\cong 60, &&\text{(machine B "goal")} \\
x + y &\cong 30, &&\text{(total production "goal")}
\end{aligned}
$$

as well as the usual nonnegativity restrictions. (The symbol $\cong$ means "is approximately equal to.")

Let us take the machine B goal statement and rewrite it as an equation,

$$3x + 2y + z_B^+ - z_B^- = 60,$$

by introducing the nonnegative variables z_B^+ and z_B^-. Similarly, we can rewrite the total production goal statement as

$$x + y + z_T^+ - z_T^- = 30$$

by introducing z_T^+ and z_T^-. We can then find values of x and y that minimize the sum of the deviations from our two goals by solving the linear optimization model

minimize $$Z = z_B^+ - z_B^- + z_T^+ - z_T^-,$$

subject to

$$
\begin{aligned}
2x + 4y &&&\leqslant 80, \\
3x + 2y + z_B^+ - z_B^- &&&= 60, \\
x + y &+ z_T^+ - z_T^- &&= 30, \\
x, y, z_B^+, z_B^-, z_T^+, z_T^- &&&\geqslant 0.
\end{aligned}
$$

There are various extensions of this idea that are also relevant for problems involving multiple criteria.

Nonlinear Expressions   The simplex algorithm can only be applied to problems that can be transformed into systems of linear equations. If nonlinear relationships exist, in some cases it may be possible to approximate them with linear relationships. If this can be accomplished, then the powerful simplex algorithm can still be used. The use of linear approximations to nonlinear relationships is a topic of importance for the analyst, but clearly beyond our scope here. However, the manager should be willing to work with the analyst in evaluating whether or not such approximations can be used. When linear approximations cannot be used and the analyst must work with the nonlinear relationships, the algorithms become much more complex, and problem solution becomes much more costly.

WHAT SHOULD THE MANAGER KNOW?

In Chapter 13 we argued that the manager need not concern himself with the mathematical complexities of the linear programming solution technique. Yet, in this chapter, we have presented that technique in some detail. The relevant question at this point is, "What should the manager know about the simplex algorithm?"

The Simplex Algorithm   It is most unlikely that a manager would ever consider solving a practical linear programming problem by hand. The computational effort would not be justified, since standard computer codes are available that can efficiently handle problems involving more than 1000 constraints. Therefore, the rationale for studying the algorithm must be based on other considerations.

   A manager should not be intimidated by the techniques of management science. Understanding the basic strategy of the simplex algorithm may be helpful in appreciating what linear programming can and cannot do. After all, when reduced to simplest terms, the nature of the simplex technique is to solve simultaneous equations successively in a sequence controlled by a test for optimality. The logic of the method is straightforward and relatively simple to comprehend. This knowledge may make the manager more comfortable in dealing with technical analysts and more confident in using the results of computerized solutions to linear optimization models.

Sensitivity Analysis   An understanding of the simplex algorithm is necessary to truly understand how the results of a sensitivity analysis are generated. Since these results are extremely important for a manager, he should have confidence in his ability to interpret them properly.

Shadow prices indicate the value of a marginal unit of a resource, and the sensitivity analysis of the right-hand side of the constraints can determine the ranges over which these shadow prices are valid. The analysis of the objective function can be important in identifying coefficients to which the solution is especially sensitive. This identification may help focus effort on refining estimates of those coefficients to which the solution is extremely sensitive.

Extensions   The manager should be sufficiently familiar with linear programming to be able to exploit certain simple extensions in problem formulation. For example, if the solution indicates that an alternative optimal solution exists, it should be welcomed as providing additional flexibility and a further opportunity to exercise judgment. Flexibility in the form of the objective function and the constraints is also important in increasing the number of real-world problems that can be formulated as linear optimization models.

The objective function is usually an evaluative model involving a single criterion. However, the concept of "coming as close as possible" to certain managerial goals can also be expressed in a linear optimization model. This approach, known as goal programming, may be especially important in public and not-for-profit organizations.

APPENDIX TO CHAPTER 14
THE SIMPLEX TABLEAU

The simplex algorithm can be reduced to a set of rigorous rules or a mechanical procedure. We shall try to maintain contact with the meaning of each step by using the chemical production problem as an example again, relating our manipulations to the graphic solution shown in Figure 1.

Recall that after the addition of the slack variables to account for idle time, our two restricting equations for machines A and B were respectively

$$2x + 4y + W_A + (0)W_B = 80 \,,$$
$$3x + 2y + (0)W_A + W_B = 60 \,,$$

and the objective function was

$$\text{maximize } 60x + 50y + (0)W_A + (0)W_B = Z \,.$$

To minimize the recopying of x, y, W_A and W_B, let us rearrange the two restricting equations with the variables at the heads of columns and the coefficients of these variables in rows to represent the equations. The equal signs have also been dropped.

x	y	W_A	W_B	
2	4	1	0	80
3	2	0	1	60

This format for a linear optimization model is called the simplex tableau.

Next we place the coefficients from the objective function above the variables, and to the right we place beside the constants 80 and 60, two columns that identify the variables in the solution and their contribution rates in the objective function, as shown in Table 2. Table 2 shows the condition of the tableau for the initial solution. Recall that in the algebraic interpretation we started with an initial trivial solution where all of the available machine time was idle. The stub of the tableau identifies the variables in the solution that are nonzero and shows their values. Also shown in the far right column of the stub is the contribution to the objective function made by each of these variables.

TABLE 2. Initial Simplex Tableau

60	50	0	0	←	Coefficients of objective function added		
x	y	W_A	W_B				
2	4	1	0		80	W_A	0
3	2	0	1		60	W_B	0

Answer shown here; variables not shown in this stub are zero

These numbers show the contribution rates of the variables W_A and W_B in the objective function

Before proceeding, let us name the various parts of the tableau as shown in Figure 4. The objective row contains the coefficients that show the contribution rates for each of the variables in the objective function. For example, the contribution of each unit of x is $60 per unit, y is $50 per unit, W_A is 0, etc. The variable row simply identifies the variable associated with each of the coefficients in the various columns.

The solution stub will always contain three columns. The variable column shows the variables that have positive values (basic variables) at a given stage of solution, *and the variables not shown in the variable column have a value of zero.* The constant column shows the value of each of the variables in the solution. The objective column shows the contribution rates of the variables in the solution, and these coefficients come from the objective row. For example, in the initial solution, the coefficients above W_A and W_B are zeros.

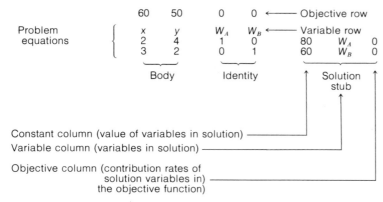

FIGURE 4. Nomenclature of the simplex tableau

The body and identity will vary in size, depending on the particular problem. The initial identity will be that portion of the tableau showing the coefficients for slack variables.

We must not lose sight of the fact that the coefficients in the body and the identity are the coefficients of the variables in the variable row, and that the numbers in the constant column are the numerical values of the right-hand side of the constraint equations. They are equations at every stage of solution.

Improving the Initial Solution

To improve the initial solution, we use the test for optimality: "Are there coefficients in the objective function that indicate that Z can be increased?" If there are, we know that we can substitute a variable in the solution that has a higher contribution rate to the objective function than one of the variables now in the solution. In order to establish a systematic index of potential improvement we develop an *index row* of coefficients, that will be placed just below the present initial tableau. The index numbers will appear under the body, the identity, and the constant column and are calculated from the following formula:

index number = (number in objective row at head of column)

$$- \sum \text{(numbers in column)} \times \text{(corresponding} \qquad (25)$$

number in objective column).

Recall that the numbers in the objective column represent the contribution rates of the variables that are in the solution to the two constraint equations in the initial tableau. The numbers in the column, such as the coefficient 2 under column x, are the coefficients of the variables for which the index row is being computed. What we have then is a modification of the objective function to reflect the marginal contribution rates of variables not now in the solution. If the coefficient for any of the variables is positive, they are candidates for changes in allocation.

For our problem, the index row numbers are as follows:

1. index number for first column of body
   $= 60 - (2 \times 0 + 3 \times 0) = 60$

2. index number for second column of body
   $= 50 - (4 \times 0 + 2 \times 0) = 50$

3. index number for first column of identity
   $= 0 - (1 \times 0 + 0 \times 0) = 0$

4. index number for second column of identity
   $= 0 - (0 \times 0 + 1 \times 0) = 0$

5. index number for constant column
   $= 0 - (80 \times 0 + 60 \times 0) = 0$

We now place the index numbers in the initial simplex tableau as indicated in Table 3. We see that this was a trivial step in that we have merely copied the objective row coefficients and inserted the value of the objective function, 0, as the left-hand side of the objective function equation. Note, however, that this trivial transformation occurs only when the objective column contains all zeros, that is, when the variables in the solution all have the value of zero.

TABLE 3. Initial Simplex Tableau with Index Row Included

	60	50	0	0			
	x	y	W_A	W_B			
	2	4	1	0	80	W_A	0
	3	2	0	1	60	W_B	0
Index row →	60	50	0	0	0		

Selecting the Key Column and Key Row We can see from Table 3 that the column headed by the variable x has the greatest improvement potential, since its contribution rate is \$60, so we select it as the *key column*. This selection means that the variable x will be introduced into the solution in favor of W_A or W_B. The selection of the key column then determines the "direction of change" as indicated in the flow chart for this example in Figure 2.

To determine whether x will replace W_A or W_B, we must select a key row. To do this, we *divide each number in the constant column by the corresponding positive nonzero number in the key column*. The resulting quotients are compared, and the key row is selected as the row yielding the smallest nonnegative quotient. For our problem, the quotients are:

$$\text{first row, } \frac{80}{2} = 40,$$

$$\text{second row, } \frac{60}{3} = 20 \text{ (key row)}.$$

Through the selection of the key row, we are determining which of the two constraint equations will be the more restrictive on the value of x. See equations (8) and (9) to verify that we have performed exactly the same computation as we did at that point in the algebraic development. The essence of this step is related easily to Figure 1. If y is 0, we can see from Figure 1 that the maximum value for x in the machine A constraint equation is 40. Similarly, the maximum value for x in the machine B constraint equation is 20 when y is set to 0. Note that the latter is point d in Figure 1. The second row is selected as the key row, then, because the point d is in the feasible solution set, whereas, the value of $x = 40$ is not feasible.

Since the second row limits the value of x, it is designated the key row, and the number at the intersection of the key row and the key column is designated the *key number*. Table 4 shows the initial tableau with the key column, key row, and key number identified.

TABLE 4. Initial Simplex Tableau
with Key Column, Row, and Number Identified

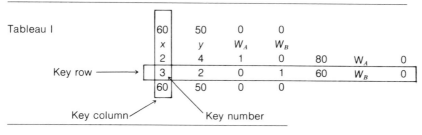

Developing an Improved Solution

With the key column and key row selected, we can now prepare a new table representing an improved solution. The first step in developing the new table is to calculate the coefficients for the *main row*. This main row appears in the relative position in the new table as the key row in the preceding table. It is computed by dividing the coefficients of the key row by the key number. Table 5 shows this development. The variable and its objective number from the head of the key column; that is, x and 60, are placed in the stub of the main row replacing W_B and 0 from the previous table. The balance of the objective and variable columns in the stub is copied from the previous table and the new tableau developed to this point now appears in Table 6.

TABLE 5. Simplex Tableau with Main Row of New Table

Tableau I

60	50	0	0			
x	y	W_A	W_B			
2	4	1	0	80	W_A	0
3	2	0	1	60	W_B	0
60	50	0	0			

Tableau II

1	$\frac{2}{3}$	0	$\frac{1}{3}$	20	Main row

TABLE 6. Simplex Tableau
with Variable and Objective Columns Completed

Tableau I

60	50	0	0			
x	y	W_A	W_B			
2	4	1	0	80	W_A	0
3	2	0	1	60	W_B	0
60	50	0	0			

Tableau II

					W_A	0
1	$\frac{2}{3}$	0	$\frac{1}{3}$	20	x	60

Now all of the remaining coefficients in the new tableau, including the constant column, the body, identity, and index row can be calculated by the following formula:

$$\text{new number} = \text{old number} - \frac{\left(\begin{array}{c}\text{corresponding}\\ \text{number of}\\ \text{key row}\end{array}\right) \times \left(\begin{array}{c}\text{corresponding}\\ \text{number of}\\ \text{key column}\end{array}\right)}{\text{key number}} \tag{26}$$

1. first row, constant column,
    new number $= 80 - (60 \times 2)/3 = 40$

2. first row, constant column of body,
    new number $= 2 - (3 \times 2)/3 = 0$

3. index row, first column of body,
    new number $= 60 - (3 \times 60)/3 = 0$

The remaining coefficients can be calculated in the same way and the completed improved solution is shown in Table 7.

Note that the solution at this stage is $x = 20$, $W_A = 40$, $y = 0$, $W_B = 0$, and that the value of the objective function is 1,200, as shown in the solu-

TABLE 7. Simplex Tableau with First Iteration Completed

Tableau I

60	50	0	0			
x	y	W_A	W_B			
2	4	1	0	80	W_A	0
3	2	0	1	60	W_B	0
60	50	0	0			

Tableau II

0	$2\frac{2}{3}$	1	$-\frac{2}{3}$	40	W_A	0
1	$\frac{2}{3}$	0	$\frac{1}{3}$	20	x	60
0	10	0	-20	-1200		

tion stub. (While the right-hand side of the index row in Table 7 is -1200, when transposed and solved for Z, as in equation (13), the value is, $Z = 1200 + 10y - 20W_B = 1200$, a positive contribution.)

Next, examining the index row of Tableau II in Table 7, we see that potential improvement still exists since the coefficient 10 appears under the variable y. Since the index row has only one positive number, y is selected as the key column for the next iteration. The key row is selected in the same way as previously and the two quotients are:

first row, $40/(8/3) = 15$ (key row),

second row, $20/(2/3) = 30$.

The first row has the smallest nonnegative quotient, so it is selected as the key row. A new main row is calculated as before, by dividing the coefficients in the main row by the key number. The new variable y and its objective number are entered in the stub, and the new numbers in the body, identity, and index row are computed as before. The remaining variable and its objective number are copied from the preceding iteration table, and Table 8 shows the new solution in Tableau III.

The new solution in Table 8 is optimal, since no further improvement is indicated in the index row; that is, the shadow prices are either zero or negative. The values of the variables in the solution for maximum contribution are given in the solution stub. The values of the variables for the optimal solution are: $x = 10$, $y = 15$, $W_A = 0$, $W_B = 0$, and the value of the objective function is $1350. Of course, all these values check with our previous algebraic solution, with the graphic solution, and with the solution determined by the approach for solving several simultaneous linear equations. Note also that the final index row yields the shadow prices obtained previously for W_A and W_B.

TABLE 8. Simplex Tableau
Second and Final Iterations Completed

Tableau I

60	50	0	0			
x	y	W_A	W_B			
2	4	1	0	80	W_A	0
3	2	0	1	60	W_B	0
60	50	0	0			

Tableau II

0	$2\frac{2}{3}$	1	$-\frac{2}{3}$	40	W_A	0
1	$\frac{2}{3}$	0	$\frac{1}{3}$	20	x	60
0	10	0	-20	-1200		

Tableau III

0	1	$\frac{3}{8}$	$-\frac{1}{4}$	15	y	50
1	0	$-\frac{1}{4}$	$\frac{1}{2}$	10	x	60
0	0	$-3\frac{3}{4}$	$-17\frac{1}{2}$	-1350		

Summary of the Procedure

The simplex tableau approach can be summarized by the following steps:

1. Formulate the problem and the objective function.
2. Develop the initial simplex tableau, including the initial trivial solution and the index row numbers. The index row numbers in the initial tableau are calculated by the formula:

$$\text{index number} = \left(\begin{array}{c}\text{number in}\\\text{objective}\\\text{row at head}\\\text{of column}\end{array}\right) - \sum \left(\begin{array}{c}\text{numbers}\\\text{in}\\\text{column}\end{array}\right) \times \left(\begin{array}{c}\text{corresponding}\\\text{number in}\\\text{objective}\\\text{column}\end{array}\right).$$

3. *Select the key column,* the column with the largest positive number in the index row of the body or the identity.
4. *Select the key row,* the row with the smallest nonnegative quotient obtained by dividing each number of the constant column by the corresponding positive number in the key column.
5. *The key number* is at the intersection of the key row and key column.
6. *Develop the main row of the new tableau.*

$$\text{Main row} = \frac{\text{numbers in key row of preceding tableau}}{\text{key number}}.$$

The main row appears in the new tableau in the same relative position as the key row of the preceding tableau.

7. *Develop the balance of the new tableau.*
   a. The variable and its objective number at the head of the key column are entered in the stub of the new tableau to the left of the main row. These new numbers replace the variable and objective number from the key row of the preceding tableau.
   b. The remainder of the variable and objective columns are reproduced in the new tableau exactly as they were in the preceding tableau.
   c. The balance of the coefficients for the new tableau are calculated by the formula:

$$\text{new number} = \text{old number} - \frac{\left(\begin{array}{c}\text{corresponding}\\\text{number of}\\\text{key row}\end{array}\right) \times \left(\begin{array}{c}\text{corresponding}\\\text{number of}\\\text{key column}\end{array}\right)}{\text{key number}}$$

8. Repeat steps 3 through 7c until all the index numbers (not including the constant column) are negative. An optimal solution then results.

9. The resulting optimum solution is interpreted in the following manner: the solution appears in the stub. The variables shown in the variable column have the values shown in the corresponding rows of the constant column. The value of the objective function is shown in the constant column, index row. All variables not shown in the stub are zero. The shadow prices that indicate the value of a marginal unit of each variable not in the solution are shown in the index row of the final solution.

Check Your Understanding

1. The Elmore Electronics Corporation was presented as problem 1 in Chapter 13. Continue your study of that problem by creating a graphic means of solution.
   a. Plot the constraints on a graph, using the number of oscilloscopes (O) for the horizontal axes, and the number of voltmeters (V) for the vertical axes.
   b. Plot the objective function on the same graph for the value of $Z = \$36,000$. Which two constraints appear to limit the size of the contribution?
   c. Solve simultaneously for values of O and V the two equations that limit the size of total contribution.
   d. Look at your graph of constraints. Are there any constraints that can be ignored completely since they have no possible effect, that is, they are redundant?

2. What is the function of slack variables in the simplex method of solution?

3. What is the physical meaning of slack variables in the following types of constraints?
   a. constraint on the capacity of a machine
   b. constraint on the size of the market
   c. constraint on the total expenditure on advertising in various media
   d. constraint on mail volume as indicated in the post office problem in the previous chapter

4. Explain the rationale of step 1, "establish an initial solution," in the algebraic solution. Why start with the worst possible solution?

5. In the algebraic solution procedure, what is the test for determining whether or not an initial or other solution can be improved?

6. Suppose in attempting to improve a solution, we have several variables with positive contributions in the objective function. How do we select the incoming variable?

7. Given that we have selected the incoming variable, which indicates the variable that will increase from its initial value of zero, how do we determine how much to increase the value of that variable? What limits the size of the incoming variable?

8. When we have decided on the limiting size of the incoming variable by testing to determine the maximum value it can have in either of the constraints, how do we modify the objective function in order to determine whether or not we now have an optimum solution?

   In the text example, the original contribution y in the objective function was $50 per unit. Why is the contribution of y only $10 at the end of the first cycle of steps?

9. What is the test for optimality in the algebraic procedure?

10. Following is a linear optimization model for a simplified version of the Elmore Electronics Corporation problem that you solved graphically in problem 1. Now solve it using the algebraic procedure we have outlined:

    maximize $\quad\quad\quad\quad Z = 100\ O + 40\ V$,

    subject to $\quad\quad\quad\quad 6.3\ O + 1.5\ V \leqslant 2500$
    $\quad\quad\quad\quad\quad\quad\quad\quad\quad 7\ O + \quad 3\ V \leqslant 3000$
    $\quad\quad\quad\quad\quad\quad\quad\quad\quad\quad\quad O, V \geqslant 0$

11. Place the preceding problem solved by the algebraic method into the optimization model framework of Figure 2. As is done in Figure 2, divide the steps into alternative generator, predictive model, evaluative model, test for optimality, direction of change, amount of change,

and optimum solution. For your example problem, indicate each iteration for each block equivalent to Figure 2.

12. What is a feasible solution? A basic solution? Identify both kinds of solutions in Figure 1. Can a feasible solution be basic? Must a feasible solution be basic?

Problems

1. The Two-Product Company was formulated as a linear optimization model in problem 8 of Chapter 13, with computer input and output given. With that formulation, solve the problem by the simplex methods of this chapter.

2. Consider the following linear optimization model:

maximize $Z = 3x_1 + x_2 + 4x_3$,

subject to $6x_1 + 3x_2 + 5x_3 \leq 25$,

$3x_1 + 4x_2 + 5x_3 \leq 20$,

$x_1, x_2, x_3 \geq 0$.

After adding slack variables and performing one simplex iteration, we have

$$Z - \frac{3x_1}{5} + \frac{11x_2}{5} \qquad\qquad + \frac{4x_5}{5} = 16,$$

$$3x_1 - \quad x_2 \qquad + x_4 - \quad x_5 = 5,$$

$$\frac{3x_1}{5} + \frac{4x_2}{5} + x_3 \qquad + \frac{1x_5}{5} = 4.$$

If the above result is not optimal, perform the next iteration. Indicate the resulting values of the variables and the objective function.

3. Consider the following linear optimization model:

maximize $Z = 3x_1 + 6x_2 + 2x_3$,

subject to $3x_1 + 4x_2 + \quad x_3 \leq 2$, \qquad (resource A)

$x_1 + 3x_2 + 2x_3 \leq 1$, \qquad (resource B)

$x_1, x_2, x_3 \geq 0$.

If you add x_4 and x_5 as slack variables, you have at the final iteration of the simplex method

$$Z \qquad\qquad + x_3 + \frac{3x_4}{5} + \frac{6x_5}{5} = 2\frac{2}{5},$$

$$x_1 \qquad - x_3 + \frac{3x_4}{5} - \frac{4x_5}{5} = \frac{2}{5},$$

$$x_2 + x_3 - \frac{1x_4}{5} + \frac{3x_5}{5} = \frac{1}{5}.$$

a. State the optimal values for each x_j and the value of the objective function.

b. Suppose the number of units of resource A is increased to 3. What are the optimal values for each x_j and the value of the objective function? (Note: Do not rework the problem. Use the techniques of sensitivity analysis.)

c. Suppose that the company can only guarantee that the price of x_3 is between 1.5 and 2.5. Should additional study be undertaken to determine the exact figure, or will the solution remain unchanged if the price of x_3 falls within this range? Show why.

d. Suppose that the company can purchase additional units of resource A at a cost of $0.75 per unit. Would this be a wise investment? Why or why not?

4. A manufacturer has two products, both of which are made in two steps by machines A and B. The process times for the two products on the two machines are as follows:

Product	Machine A (hr)	Machine B (hr)
1	4	5
2	5	2

For the coming period, machine A has available 100 hours and B has available 80 hours. The contribution for product 1 is $10 per 100 units and for product 2, $5 per 100 units. Using the methods of the simplex tableau in the appendix to this chapter, formulate and solve the problem for maximum contribution.

5. Mesa Plastics Company was formulated as problem 11 in Chapter 13 with computer input and output given. Using the simplex methods of the appendix to this chapter, we obtained the simplex tableau shown in Table 9.

TABLE 9. Simplex Tableau for Mesa Plastics

37.5	40	20	45	62.5	30	0	0	0	0	0			
X_{1A}	X_{1B}	X_{2A}	X_{2B}	X_{3A}	X_{3B}	W_A	W_B	W_1	W_2	W_3			
0	0	0.0875	0	0	0.15	1	1.25	−0.25	−0.3125	−0.35	10	W_A	0
0	1	−1.25	0	0	2	0	5	0	−1.25	0	125	X_{1B}	40
1	0	1.25	0	0	−2	0	−5	1	1.25	0	185	X_{1A}	37.5
0	0	1	1	0	0	0	0	0	1	0	300	X_{2B}	45
0	0	0	0	1	1	0	0	0	0	1	125	X_{3A}	62.5
0	0	−21.875	0	0	−37.5	0	−12.5	−37.5	−41.875	−62.5	−33,250		

a. Identify the optimal solution.
b. What are the shadow prices?
c. What would be the value of increasing the capacity of machine A? Of machine B? Show by the methods of sensitivity analysis discussed in this chapter what the limits or bounds are on capacity changes. Check your answers with the sensitivity analysis given in the computer output.

d. Using the methods of sensitivity analysis discussed in this chapter, determine the upper and lower bounds on the contributions of each of the three sizes in each of the two plants. Check your answers with the sensitivity analysis given in the computer output of Chapter 13.

References

Bierman, H., C. P. Bonini, and W. H. Hausman, *Quantitative Analysis for Business Decisions,* fifth edition, Richard D. Irwin, Inc., Homewood, Ill., 1977.

Charnes, A., and W. W. Cooper, *Management Models and Industrial Applications of Linear Programming*, Vols. 1 and 2, John Wiley & Sons, New York, 1961.

Daellenbach, H. G., and E. J. Bell, *User's Guide to Linear Programming,* Prentice-Hall, Englewood Cliffs, N.J., 1970.

Dantzig, G. B., *Linear Programming and Extensions,* Princeton University Press, Princeton, N.J., 1963.

Hillier, F. S., and G. J. Lieberman, *Introduction to Operations Research,* second edition, Holden-Day, San Francisco, 1974.

Machol, R. E., *Elementary Systems Mathematics: Linear Programming for Business and the Social Sciences,* McGraw-Hill, New York, 1976.

Thierauf, R. J., and R. C. Klekamp, *Decision Making Through Operations Research,* second edition, John Wiley & Sons, New York, 1975.

Wagner, H. M., *Principles of Operations Research,* second edition, Prentice-Hall, Englewood Cliffs, N.J., 1975.

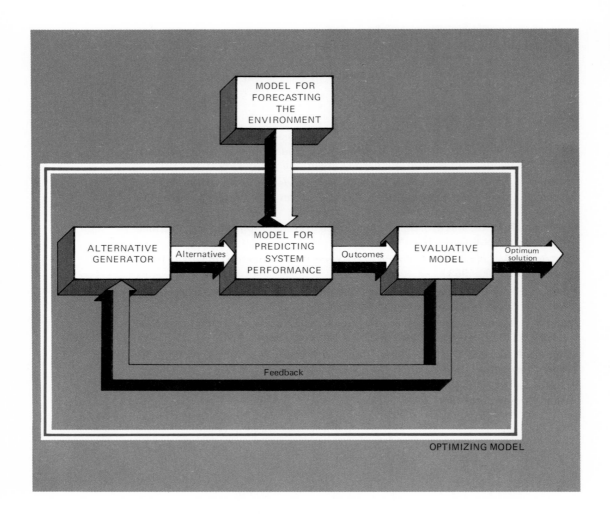

15

Network Models — Transportation and Transshipment

Network models are an important special case of linear optimization models for three reasons. First, many real-world problems can be modeled by using networks. Problems related to the determination of transportation and distribution systems are routinely solved in many organizations by this method. A special form of a network, known as the *transportation model*, takes its name from this use. A generalization of the transportation model is the *transshipment model*, that allows greater flexibility in the nature of the distribution system being analyzed. These models can also be used as aids in assigning workers to jobs. Other network models can be used to determine the longest or *shortest path* through a network. These models can be applied to determining equipment replacement policies and in scheduling activities in large-scale projects. The latter models include the network scheduling techniques PERT and CPM.

This chapter presents the transportation and transshipment network models. The shortest path models are discussed in Chapter 16.

A second important feature of the network is that the model has a visual interpretation in addition to the mathematical formulation. The ability to visualize a network, much like a decision tree, significantly reduces problems of communication between managers and technical analysts and among managers. Since one of the most important factors limiting the use of management science models by managers is their confidence in the model, this feature cannot be overemphasized.

Finally, the third advantage of the network is that the corresponding mathematical formulation has a special structure that allows extremely large problems to be solved very quickly by using specialized versions of the simplex algorithm for solving linear programming problems. The resulting low cost encourages the user to run the model many times to gain full advantage of it. An additional bonus is that integer-valued optimal solutions are obtained automatically. When a problem cannot be formulated as a network problem and an interger-valued solution is required, the additional computational effort can become quite burdensome, as we explain in Chapter 17.

These three advantages of network models—the large number of potential real-world applications, the visual interpretation, and an efficient solution strategy—are so important that the modern manager should be familiar with problems that can be analyzed with networks. Therefore, we shall present several examples of these models and concentrate on how they are formulated.

THE TRANSPORTATION MODEL

The transportation model is a special form of network optimization model that is routinely applied to problems of allocating the production from several factories to different warehouses or other distribution centers. The purpose of the model is to aid in selecting the most economical transportation routes for the required shipments. Such decisions must be made regularly in many large organizations. This same model can also be used to analyze other problems with a similar mathematical structure that do not involve the selection of transportation routes.

An Introductory Example

Suppose we have three different factories that can ship our product to three different retail outlets, as shown in Figure 1. The weekly capacity in terms of units produced varies among the factories as follows:

Factory	Supply (units/week)
(Chicago) 1	50
(New York) 2	70
(Dallas) 3	20

The average weekly shipment required by each retail outlet is

Outlet	Demand (units/week)
(Kansas City) 1	50
(Atlanta) 2	60
(Detroit) 3	30

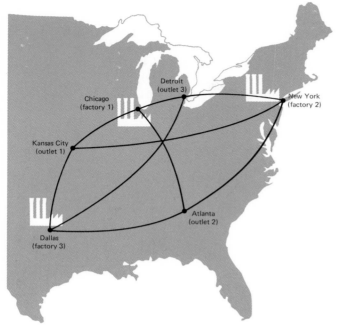

Figure 1. Geographical locations of factories and retail outlets

However, the costs of shipping depend on which factories ship to which outlets, as the shipping distances vary. These costs are as follows:

From Factory	Per-Unit Costs to Outlet:		
	1	2	3
1	$ 3	$2	$ 3
2	10	5	8
3	1	3	10

As the table shows, factory 1 can ship one unit to outlet 2 for $2. Our problem is to determine how much should be shipped to where by whom.

Let us first consider whether this problem might be formulated as a linear optimization model. It is a *resource allocation problem*, since we are trying to allocate shipments of the product among nine different alternative routes. Further, there are constraints on our decisions. We assume that we must meet the demand at each retail outlet, and we cannot ship more than the available supply from each factory. The appropriate evaluative model will involve a single criterion under certainty, cost.

What are the decision variables? We are trying to determine how much to ship from each factory i ($i = 1, 2, 3$) to each retail outlet j ($j = 1, 2, 3$).

Thus, it is convenient to use double subscripts and to denote our decision variables as x_{ij}, that equal the amount shipped from factory i to outlet j. If we discover that the optimum solution indicates $x_{31} = 20$, then 20 units should be shipped from factory 3 to outlet 1.

We can now write down our objective function. Using the data in the cost table, we wish to minimize

the total cost of
shipping from factory $1 = 3x_{11} + 2x_{12} + 3x_{13}$,

plus the total cost of
shipping from factory $2 = 10x_{21} + 5x_{22} + 8x_{23}$,

plus the total cost of
shipping from factory $3 = x_{31} + 3x_{32} + 10x_{33}$.

Given specific values for the decision variables, this expression predicts the costs.

Next, we need the constraints on the decision variables to serve as the alternative generator. For factory 1, we must have $x_{11} + x_{12} + x_{13} \leq 50$, which says that the total amount shipped from factory 1 per week cannot exceed the weekly capacity of that factory. We have similar expressions corresponding to factories 2 and 3. Finally, for each retail outlet, we need a logical relationship which states that the total number of units shipped to the outlet each week is equal to the weekly demand. For outlet 2, we have $x_{12} + x_{22} + x_{32} = 60$. Two similar constraints can be determined for outlets 1 and 3. The six constraints, three for the factories and three for the retail outlets, along with the requirements that the decision variables cannot take on negative values, determine the set of feasible alternatives for our problem.

Thus, the linear optimization model appropriate for solving this problem is

minimize
$$3x_{11} + 2x_{12} + 3x_{13} + 10x_{21} + 5x_{22} + 8x_{23} + x_{31} + 3x_{32} + 10x_{33},$$
subject to
$$
\begin{aligned}
x_{11} + x_{12} + x_{13} & & & \leq 50, \\
x_{21} + x_{22} + x_{23} & & & \leq 70, \\
x_{31} + x_{32} + x_{33} & & & \leq 20, \\
x_{11} \quad + \quad x_{21} \quad + \quad x_{31} & & & = 50, \\
x_{12} \quad + \quad x_{22} \quad + \quad x_{32} & & & = 60, \\
x_{13} \quad + \quad x_{23} \quad + \quad x_{33} & & & = 30, \\
x_{ij} \geq 0, \quad i = 1, 2, 3; \quad j = 1, 2, 3.
\end{aligned}
$$

Notice, however, that this model has a special form. The coefficients in the constraints of all of the decision variables are equal to 1. Also, each decision variable appears in only two constraints. These characteristics suggest that a special version of the simplex method for solving linear optimization models may be applied to this problem—a version that is extremely efficient for solving models such as this one. Further, these same characteristics also indicate that the linear optimization model may be given a visual interpretation as a network.

The Network   Now let us see how this same problem may be modeled as a network. Suppose we take the map in Figure 1 and rearrange it by placing all of the factories on the left and all of the outlets on the right. Rather than using pictures of the factories and outlets, we will use circles to represent each one. The routes between the factories and the outlets will be represented by arrows. This is illustrated in Figure 2.

Now we can write the number of units available at each factory with a plus sign in front of it, and the number of units required at each warehouse with a minus sign in front of it. The plus sign indicates that units are placed into the system at the corresponding circle, while the minus sign indicates that units are removed. Finally, we can write the cost per unit of shipping on each of the corresponding arrows. For example, the cost of shipping from factory 1 to outlet 3 is $3 per unit, which is written on the arrow from the factory circle 1 to the outlet circle 3 (see Figure 2).

Now look carefully at both the linear optimization formulation of this problem, and the diagram in Figure 2. Which do you understand more easily? Unless you are an extremely sophisticated mathematician, Figure 2 probably conveys more easily understood information than the mathemati-

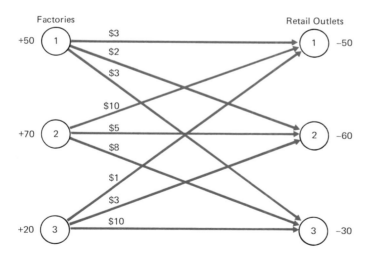

Figure 2. Network formulation of the transportation problem

TABLE 1. The Transportation Table

To Outlet / From Factory	1 (Kansas City)	2 (Atlanta)	3 (Detroit)	Available at Factories
1 (Chicago)	3*	2	3	50
2 (New York)	10	5	8	70
3 (Dallas)	1	3	10	20
Required at Outlets	50	60	30	140

*Per-unit cost ($) of shipping from factory to outlet.

cal relationships. This ability to portray the logic of the model graphically is one of the important advantages of network models. Thus, the problem of communication between a manager and an analyst is greatly simplified when network models are used.

More formally, the circles in Figure 2 are called *nodes*, and the arrows are called *arcs*. We shall use these terms in the following discussion.

The Transportation Table   The information in Figure 2 can also be entered in a table especially suited for analyzing transportation problems, as shown in Table 1. There is one row for each factory, and one column for each outlet. The number of units available from the factory is written to the right of each row, and the number of units required at each outlet is written at the bottom of each column. Further, the costs are written in the small boxes; for example, the cost of shipping one unit from factory 2 to outlet 1 is $10.

We can now begin our analysis of this problem by writing down an initial solution as shown in Table 2. This alternative must satisfy the restrictions on capacity at each factory and the demand at each retail outlet. Further, since we are trying to minimize costs, we might start with factory 1. The cheapest means of shipping from factory 1 is to send units to outlet 2.

TABLE 2. An Initial Solution

From Factory \ To Outlet	1 (Kansas City)		2 (Atlanta)		3 (Detroit)		Available at Factories
1 (Chicago)	(+1)	3	(−1) 50	2		3	50
2 (New York)	(−1) 30	10	(+1) 10	5	30	8	70
3 (Dallas)	20	1		3		10	20
Required at Outlets	50		60		30		140

Since we have 50 units available at factory 1, and outlet 2 requires 60, we can ship all 50 units from factory 1 to outlet 2. To fill the demand at outlet 2, we can ship an additional 10 units from factory 2. As luck would have it, this is also the cheapest route for shipping from factory 2 to any of the outlets.

So far so good. Now let us consider the remaining supply of units at factory 2 ($70 − 10 = 60$). Since the demand at outlet 2 is satisfied, the next cheapest route for factory 2 is to ship to outlet 3, which requires 30 units. We can ship 30 units to outlet 3 and still have an additional 30 units of supply to ship to outlet 1.

Finally, consider factory 3. We are shipping 30 units from factory 2 to outlet 1, which has a demand of 50. The remaining demand ($50 − 30 = 20$) is the supply at factory 3. Notice that shipping from factory 3 to outlet 1 is also the cheapest route, so this seems attractive.

As our initial solution in Table 2 shows, we began by shipping from factory 1 on the cheapest route and ended by shipping from factory 3 on the cheapest route. The latter was a matter of luck, but it suggests that we may have found a good solution by using our intuition. Notice also that this solution satisfies the original set of constraints. We can easily check the solution by summing the entries in each row and in each column.

Using our evaluative cost model, we find the total cost of this alternative to be:

Units		Cost per Unit		
50	×	$ 2	=	$100
30	×	10	=	300
10	×	5	=	50
30	×	8	=	240
20	×	1	=	20
				$710

Now we consider whether or not the initial solution can be improved.

Improving the Solution   To investigate the possibility of improving the solution, let us suppose we ship along the route from factory 1 to outlet 1. Just for the moment, suppose we ship only 1 unit along this route. We can indicate this shipment by placing a small +1 in the upper right-hand corner of the cell in the transportation table corresponding to factory 1 and outlet 1, as shown in Table 2. What does this additional unit do to our supply and demand constraints?

The supply at factory 1 is only 50 units, but this additional unit plus the 50 shipped from factory 1 to outlet 2 sum to 51. In order to observe this supply restriction of 50 units, let us reduce the number of units shipped from factory 1 to outlet 2 by 1 unit, and denote this by placing a −1 in the corresponding cell of the transportation table (Table 2).

However, when we remove 1 unit from the demand at outlet 2, we need to compensate. Notice that if we add 1 unit in row 2, column 2 of the transportation table and subtract 1 unit from row 2, column 1, all of our original constraints on supplies and demands will be met. Thus, we again have a feasible solution, as shown in Table 2.

Now, in the cells with the +1s, we will incur additional costs of $3 + $5 = $8. However, the cells with −1s indicate savings since 1 less unit will be shipped in each. The savings from this trial solution are $2 + $10 = $12. Thus, we would incur an additional cost of $8 but a savings of $12, resulting in a *net* savings of $4 for each additional unit we ship from factory 1 to outlet 1. This fact suggests that a desirable *direction of change* in the initial solution would be to increase the number of units shipped from factory 1 to outlet 1 from its initial value of 0 units.

We clearly want to ship as many units as possible on this route by shifting them away from the routes between factory 1 and outlet 2, and between factory 2 and outlet 1. How many units can we shift around? In the cells in Table 2 with the minus signs, we are removing units. Clearly, we cannot remove more than 50 units from the route from factory 1 to outlet 2, or more than 30 units from the route from factory 2 to outlet 1. The smaller of these

TABLE 3. A Revised Solution

From Factory \ To Outlet	1 (Kansas City)	2 (Atlanta)	3 (Detroit)	Available at Factories
1 (Chicago)	3 / 30	2 / 20	3 /	50
2 (New York)	10 /	5 / 40	8 / 30	70
3 (Dallas)	1 / 20	3 /	10 /	20
Required at Outlets	50	60	30	140

numbers is 30, so the most we can shift around is 30 units. This 30 units is the appropriate *amount of change* in the desirable direction. The results of a shift of 30 units are shown in Table 3. Notice that there are 30 additional units in each of the cells that have +1s in Table 2, and 30 fewer units in each cell with a −1. The net savings for this change is $4 (net savings/unit shifted) × 30 (units shifted) = $120.

What about other changes in the solution? Suppose one unit is shipped from factory 1 to outlet 3. You should verify, using the approach described above, that the net savings will be $2 per unit shifted. This time, the maximum number of units that can be shifted among transportation routes is 20. The new solution is shown in Table 4.

The result shown in Table 4 is actually the optimal solution to the problem, since no further improvements can be made by shifting units (check this yourself). The search for further improvements corresponds to the "test for optimality" in the simplex method of solving linear optimization models. Notice also that all of the shipments are integer-valued, although we did not specify this as a restriction.

TABLE 4. The Final Solution

From Factory \ To Outlet	1 (Kansas City)	2 (Atlanta)	3 (Detroit)	Available at Factories
1 (Chicago)	3 (30)	2	3 (20)	50
2 (New York)	10	5 (60)	8 (10)	70
3 (Dallas)	1 (20)	3	10	20
Required at Outlets	50	60	30	140

The total cost of shipping according to this solution is as follows:

Units		Cost per Unit		
30	×	$3	=	$ 90
20	×	3	=	60
60	×	5	=	300
10	×	8	=	80
20	×	1	=	20
				$550

Thus, through a simple analysis, we have reduced the cost by $710 − $550 = $160. This cost savings is 29 percent of the actual optimal solution. Furthermore, our original solution was determined by using an apparently reasonable strategy, and the problem was relatively simple with only three factories and three outlets. The strategy we employed to improve the initial solution can be formalized as an algorithm. This algorithm and another example problem are presented in the appendix to this chapter.

In a much more realistic problem in terms of size, determining a good solution by hand would be much more difficult; however, the potential cost

TABLE 5. A Transportation Table With a Dummy Outlet to Adjust for Unequal Total Supplies and Demands

From Factory \ To Outlet	1 (Kansas City)		2 (Atlanta)		3 (Detroit)		4 (Dummy)		Available at Factories
1 (Chicago)		3		2		3		0	60
2 (New York)		10		5		8		0	80
3 (Dallas)		1		3		10		0	30
Required at Outlets	50		60		30		30		170

savings are even greater than in this example. These much larger problems can be solved efficiently using a modified version of the simplex method for linear programming.

Unequal Supply and Demand Suppose that the capacities at the three factories in this example had been 60, 80, and 30 respectively. Then the total potential supply of $60 + 80 + 30 = 170$ units is 30 more than the total demand of $50 + 60 + 30 = 140$ units. How do we adjust for the unequal supply and demand totals? We can define a "dummy" outlet with a demand equal to the difference between the total supply and the total demand; that is, with a demand of $170 - 140 = 30$ units. The cost of shipping from each factory to this "dummy" outlet will be zero. Naturally, any units assigned by our solution strategy to this nonexistent outlet would not actually be produced and shipped, which justifies the use of the zero costs. This process will help us in determining the appropriate production schedule in each factory. The resulting initial table, corresponding to Table 1, is shown in Table 5.

If the demand in a problem exceeds the supply, a similar strategy could be adopted by adding a "dummy" row with zero costs of shipping. These "dummy" shipping routes correspond to slack variables in the equivalent linear programming formulation of the problem.

The Practical Use of the Transportation Model

The transportation model is routinely used in determining transportation and distribution policies for many large organizations. When production capacity exceeds the demand for a product, this same model can also be used to determine the production schedule at each of the factories. This use of the model is illustrated in the example problem in the chapter appendix. In actual practice, organizations may use such models on an annual or semiannual basis to revise their transportation and distribution policies.

One obvious limitation of the transportation model is that it assumes the units to be shipped from each source to each destination are identical and interchangeable. However, many organizations have multiple products with different demands in the different market areas. It may not be appropriate to solve the distribution problem for each product independently of the others because it is cheaper per unit when large quantities are shipped on the same routes. The transportation problem with multiple products (the multicommodity problem) can be formulated mathematically, and algorithms for its solution have been proposed. However, the multicommodity problems cannot be represented by a network. Consequently, they are much harder to solve computationally and require much more computer time. For these reasons their practical usefulness is limited.

An alternative is to define a *standard commodity bundle* for the organization, that represents a combination of the multiple products proportional to their respective market demands. This strategy works well when the relative market demands for the products do not differ significantly in each market area. For example, suppose a firm manufactures two products. The total demand for product 1 is 1500 units, while the total demand for product 2 is 500 units. Thus, product 1 outsells product 2 at a ratio of 3 to 1. Further, this sales proportion is relatively constant in each of the different market areas. Then the organization can solve its transportation and distribution problems by assuming a standard commodity bundle with a total demand of $1500 + 500 = 2000$ units. Suppose the cost of shipping product 1 from a particular factory to a specific outlet is $2 per unit, while the cost of shipping product 2 from the same factory to the same outlet is $1 per unit. Then, the cost of shipping each unit of the standard commodity bundle from this factory to this outlet would be $(\$2)(0.75) + (\$1)(0.25) = \$1.75$. The transportation model could then be applied to analyze this problem.

It is also possible to add lower and upper bounds on the number of units to be shipped along each route (or arc). For example, we might require that the number of units shipped from factory 1 to outlet 2 be at least 30 but no more than 40. We could write these lower and upper bounds as the pair (30, 40), and place them next to the appropriate arc in the network. Mathematically, this corresponds to adding the constraints

$$x_{12} \geq 30 \,,$$
$$x_{12} \leq 40 \,,$$

to the linear programming formulation of the problem. The simple form of these constraints means that they can be satisfied with little additional computational burden. When lower and upper bounds are placed on the routes, the resulting model is often called a *capacitated* transportation problem.

It is also important to recognize that an optimizing model, such as the transportation model, may be used to answer "what if" questions and to provide data for a more extensive analysis of a broader problem. For example, suppose a firm is currently producing a product at three different factories, each of which is operating at near capacity. Further, a market analysis shows that the demand for the product is expected to grow even higher over the next ten years before leveling off. The company may be trying to decide 1) whether or not to build a new factory, and 2) if so, in which of several alternative locations.

In order to analyze this problem, the company could estimate the total production and distribution costs associated with manufacturing the product in the three existing factories over the expected market life of the product. This estimate could be made by solving the transportation problem with the new market forecasts for each year in the estimated market life of the product and discounting the results to determine the equivalent present values of the costs. Next, the assumption could be made that a factory was built at one of the locations under consideration and the transportation problem could be re-solved for each of the years in the market life of the product, given this new factory. The estimated costs of producing and distributing with this new factory, plus the cost of constructing it, could then be compared with the cost of operating the existing factories, perhaps using overtime.

By repeating the analysis for the alternative sites under consideration, the cost implications of the various choices could be estimated. These results would play an important role in the determination of the new plant site, if a plant is to be built. This process is similar to the analysis suggested for determining whether or not it is appropriate to purchase a new LSM for the post office as described in Chapter 13. Naturally, we recognize that the president of the company may still choose to construct a new plant in Columbus, Ohio, because his wife has relatives there, but at least the opportunity costs of such a decision would be clear.

THE TRANSSHIPMENT PROBLEM

The use of the transportation model was based on the assumption that direct routes existed from each factory (or supply point) to each outlet (or demand point). Again, in the real world, things are not always so simple. Major transportation routes actually pass through major distribution centers before going to smaller market areas. For example, a passenger flying into a city in the South will generally be routed through Atlanta. However, if the city is in the Middle Atlantic states, and he is flying in from the West Coast, he

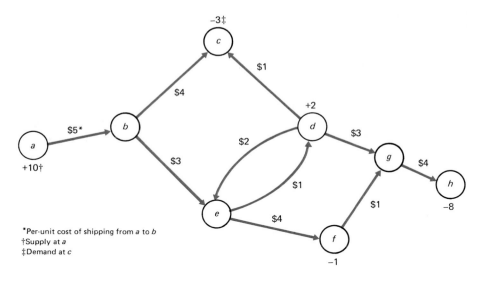

*Per-unit cost of shipping from *a* to *b*
†Supply at *a*
‡Demand at *c*

Figure 3. An example of a transshipment problem

may have the option of being routed through Atlanta, New York, Washington, D.C., or even Chicago. For an airline passenger the fare will be the same no matter which of these alternatives he chooses. However, the same is not generally true with the transportation and distribution costs of products.

Suppose we wish to redistribute goods among eight cities (the circled letters) as shown in Figure 3. The arrows, or arcs, indicate possible shipping routes. The arcs point in a specific direction indicating that goods can only be shipped along the route in that direction. In some cases, as for example between cities *d* and *e*, there are arcs pointing in two different directions indicating that goods can be shipped from *e* to *d*, or from *d* to *e*. The number written above each arc is the cost per unit of shipping on that arc. The number associated with each city is the supply (plus) or demand (minus) at that location. For example, city *a* has a supply of 10, city *c* has a demand of −3, and city *e* has neither a supply nor a demand.

Notice that some cities may have goods shipped *through* them. These cities, such as *b*, have arrows pointing into and out of them, and are called *transshipment points*. Others, called *sources*, only supply goods, while still others, called *sinks*, only demand goods. In our example, city *a* is a source, cities *c* and *h* are sinks, and all others are transshipment points. Even though a supply of +2 is available at *d*, it is still a transshipment point, since goods may be shipped through it. For a similar reason, *f* is also a transshipment point.

The total supply in the system is 12 units (10 at *a* plus 2 at *d*), and the total demand is 12 units (3 at *c* plus 1 at *f* plus 8 at *h*). If the supplies and demands were not equally balanced, we could compensate by defining a "dummy" supply or demand point.

A network such as this one, that includes transshipment points, is called a transshipment problem. As in the case of the transportation problem, the fact that the model can be represented as a network means that extremely efficient computer codes exist for its solution.

Furthermore, there is a strong relationship between the mathematical structures of the transshipment and the transportation models. This relationship makes it possible to treat the transshipment problem as a transportation problem, and develop a transportation table for it. The network shown in Figure 3 is presented in tabular form in Table 6.

TABLE 6. Transportation Table for the Transshipment Problem

From City \ To City	b	c (sink)	d	e	f	g	h (sink)	Supply
a (source)	5*	500	500	500	500	500	500	10
b	0	4	500	3	500	500	500	12
d	500	1	0	2	500	3	500	14
e	500	500	1	0	4	500	500	12
f	500	500	500	500	0	1	500	11
g	500	500	500	500	500	0	4	12
Demand	12	3	12	12	12	12	8	71

*Per-unit cost of shipment.

In order to construct such a table, we use the following simple rules:

1. Designate a row for each source. Its *supply* is the number of units available at that source. In our example, only a is a source, since d is a transshipment point.

2. Designate a column for each sink. Its *demand* is the number of units required at that sink. In our example, only c and h are sinks, since f is a transshipment point.

3. Designate a row *and* a column for each *transshipment point*. The demand for the column of a transshipment point is equal to the sum of the number of units available at *all* points. The supply for the row is the sum of the number of units available at *all* points (including the point in question) *plus* any supply or *minus* any demand at that point. For example, the demand for the column associated with city d (as for all transshipment points) is 12 units (10 at a plus 2 at d). The supply for the row associated with d is the total number of units available at all points, 12, plus the supply at d, 2, for a total of $12 + 2 = 14$.

4. Finally, we complete the table formed by the designated rows and columns by entering the costs associated with shipping units from a row supply point to a column destination point. At the intersection of a row and column that corresponds to the same point (a transshipment point), we fill in a zero, since there is no cost for shipping from a location to itself. At the intersection of the rows and columns representing feasible routes (i.e., identified by arcs on the diagram in Figure 3), we enter the number associated with each arc. The remaining intersections of rows and columns represent routes that are not feasible. Infeasible routes have no direct arc connection in the network diagram. We enter a "large number" (e.g., 500) for those costs. This large number will ensure that no goods are assigned to a nonexistent (nonfeasible) route. We may use any number that is very large relative to the actual costs.

Notice that there are rows in Table 6 for the source a and the transshipment points, but not for the sinks c and h. Similarly, there are columns for the sinks c and h, and for the transshipment points, but not for the source a. The supply for the row for the source a is simply 10, the number of units available at a, while the demands at the sinks c and h are 3 and 8 respectively, the amounts required there.

Now let us consider the supply and demand at the transshipment points. Take e for example. Since e is a transshipment point, units can be shipped through it. Potentially, *all* of the units in the network might pass through e. Since there are a total of 10 units (at a) plus 2 units (at d), the total number of units which might pass through e is 12 units. Therefore, we say the demand at e is 12 units. What if 12 units actually do not pass through e in the optimal solution? Then in the box in the table corresponding to a shipment from e to e, the difference between what is actually shipped into e and the demand of 12 will appear, at a cost of 0 per unit since the units are not actually shipped. Thus, the cells in the transportation table representing shipments from a particular transshipment point to itself correspond to slack variables in a linear programming formulation of the problem. Since the demand at e is 12 units and no units are removed or added there, the supply, or number of units shipped out of e must also equal 12.

Now consider the transshipment point d. Without looking at the network, we again say that the demand at a transshipment point is equal to the total number of units in the system, 12. It would seem that as many as 12 units could be shipped into d. However, upon looking at the network, you can see that 2 units are *added* to the network at d, so only the 10 units from a could actually be shipped *into* d. This is true, but before we clear up this point, we shall add some further confusion. The supply at d is equal to the 12 unit potential demand *plus* the number of units added to the system at d, 2, for a total of $12 + 2 = 14$. How can this be? There are only a total of 12 units in the system, and yet we show a supply of 14 at d.

What we are doing is providing self-correcting rules that eliminate the problem of studying the network. It is true that fewer than 12 units will actually be shipped into d in the optimal solution. However, the difference between the number actually shipped into d and the demand of 12 will simply appear in the cell in the transportation table corresponding to a shipment from d to d. In addition, 2 more units will actually be shipped out of d than are shipped into d. This is the purpose of adding 2 units to the supply at d, relative to the demand.

A similar explanation holds for the situation at the transshipment point b. Even though the network clearly indicates that only 10 units can actually be shipped into b, we have followed the rules and recorded a demand of 12 units. The difference of 2 units between this demand of 12 and the 10 units that will actually be shipped into b will appear in the b to b cell in the transportation table.

It will be helpful to look at the solution to this problem to increase your understanding of this point. We could solve the problem by hand, using the algorithm described in the appendix. However, Figure 4 shows the results of using a special-purpose computer program to solve this problem. The solution is shown at the bottom as a transportation table of shipments. For example, the 10 in the row for a and the column for b indicates that 10 units should be shipped from a to b. Looking at the network in Figure 3, this should come as no surprise, since it is the only route from a. However, it is comforting to note that the computer understands this limitation also.

Of the 10 units going into b, 3 are shipped to c and 7 to e. Notice the 2 in the b to b box. This is simply the difference between the demand at b of 12 that we wrote down using our rules, and the 10 units that were actually shipped there, as we expected. Now consider e. Only 7 units were shipped in from b, and 6 were then shipped to d, while 1 unit goes to f. Again, the 5 in the e to e box is the difference between the demand of 12 units and the 7

ENTER NUMBER OF ORIGIN POINTS
□:
   6
NUMBER OF DESTINATION POINTS
□:
   7
ENTER UNIT COSTS OF SHIPPING TO EVERY DESTINATION FROM: ORIGIN 1
□:
   5 500 500 500 500 500 500
ORIGIN 2
□:
   0 4 500 3 500 500 500
ORIGIN 3
□:
   500 1 0 2 500 3 500
ORIGIN 4
□:
   500 500 1 0 4 500 500
ORIGIN 5
□:
   500 500 500 500 0 1 500
ORIGIN 6
□:
   500 500 500 500 500 0 4
ENTER AMOUNT AVAILABLE AT THE 6 ORIGINS
□:
   10 12 14 12 11 12
ENTER AMOUNT REQUIRED AT THE 7 DESTINATIONS
□:
   12 3 12 12 12 12 8
THE MINIMUM COST IS 149
THE OPTIMUM SHIPMENTS ARE FROM ORIGINS (ROWS) TO DESTINATIONS (COLUMNS)

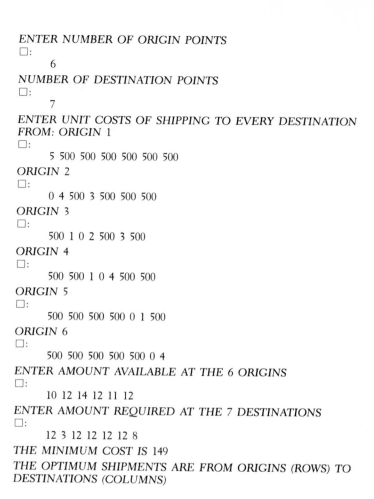

	b	c	d	e	f	g	h
a	10	0	0	0	0	0	0
b	2	3	0	7	0	0	0
d	0	0	6	0	0	8	0
e	0	0	6	5	1	0	0
f	0	0	0	0	11	0	0
g	0	0	0	0	0	4	8

Figure 4. Computer solution to the transshipment problem

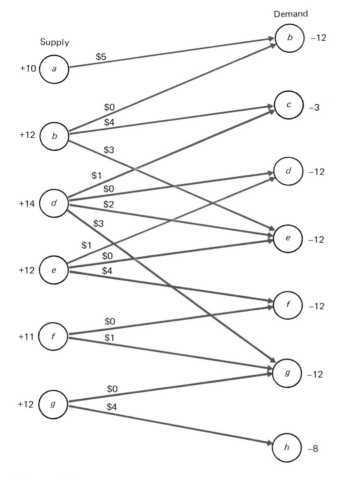

Figure 5. The equivalent transportation network
(arcs with high costs [500] omitted)

actually shipped into *e*. Carefully study this solution to be sure you understand its interpretation.

Another way of appreciating what we have done with these rules for converting a transshipment problem into a transportation problem is to consider the equivalent transportation network shown in Figure 5. This network has the same solution as the transshipment problem in Figure 3, and yet obviously has the same form as the transportation problem shown in Figure 2. Notice that the circles or nodes corresponding to the transshipment points appear as both supply and demand points in this revised network.

AN EXAMPLE OF THE USE OF A NETWORK MODEL

We shall now present an example of the actual use of a network model to aid in solving a real-world problem. This example illustrates the following points:

1. A network model may be used for problems other than those related to transportation and distribution issues.
2. Optimizing management science models can be successfully applied to problems in the public and not-for-profit sectors.
3. The visual interpretation of a network model is an important advantage in communicating its logic to individuals who have not been formally exposed to management science techniques.
4. The computational advantage of a particular model formulation can significantly enhance its practical usefulness.
5. An optimizing model does not always "solve" the problem, but it can be a helpful aid to the decision maker.

The problem is the assignment of faculty members to courses during the three quarters of an academic year. The particular implementation we describe took place in the Graduate School of Management (GSM) at UCLA (for further details, see Dyer and Mulvey [1976]).

The faculty/course scheduling problem is complicated by the lack of a clearly defined objective to serve as the evaluative model that guides a solution process. The preferences of the faculty members must be balanced against the needs and desires of the students, while administrative policies and resource constraints must also be considered. Even these constraints are "loose," and some may be recognized only as the solution evolves.

How can one go about formulating an optimizing model for aiding a decision maker in analyzing a complex problem such as this one? First, the model builder may look for analogies with more familiar models. For example, he might note that each faculty member teaches a specific number of courses per academic year (usually five quarter courses per year at GSM). Thus, he might view a typical faculty member as "supplying" five "course section equivalents," one unit of which is defined as the time and effort equal to the actual teaching of one course section. Further, each course "demands" one "course section equivalent" for each section that is to be offered. Thus, if three sections of course MGT 240 are to be offered during the year, the annual "demand" is three course section equivalents. This analogy suggests that the problem might be modeled as a transportation problem, with each faculty member being represented as a supply point that supplies course section equivalents into the system, and with each course viewed as a demand point that takes course section equivalents out of the system. An arc from a particular faculty member to a particular course

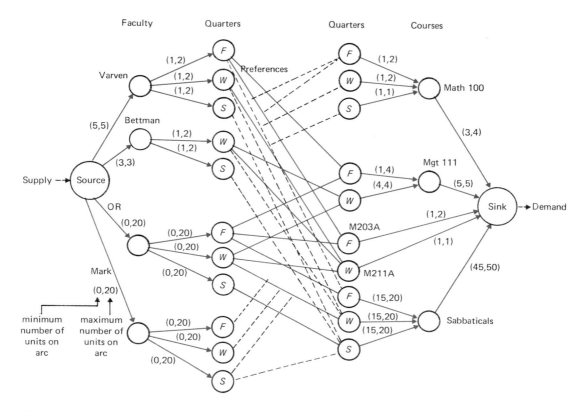

Figure 6. Network representation of the faculty/
course scheduling problem

would indicate that he could teach that course. Otherwise, the arc would
be omitted.

In addition, the courses are taught over three quarters, and the schedule
must be determined by quarters. Thus, the analogy went further. The quarters could be viewed as transshipment points, with the course section equivalents of the faculty "shipped" through particular quarters to corresponding
quarter transshipment points for the courses. The network model that resulted from this analogy is shown in Figure 6.

The flow on the arcs of the network is in course section equivalents.
The nodes in the network are either faculty or course related. For each
faculty member, there are up to four nodes corresponding to the annual,
fall, winter, and spring schedules respectively. However, if a faculty member
is not teaching during a particular quarter, the corresponding node is deleted. There are similar sets of nodes for the courses. Figure 7 portrays
several examples of how lower and upper bounds of the flows on the arcs
can be useful in achieving various objectives. As illustrated in Figure 7(a),

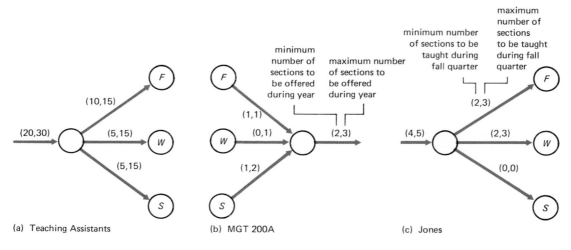

Figure 7. Individual faculty/course nodes and associated arcs (examples)

(a) Teaching Assistants

(b) MGT 200A

(c) Jones

the total number of course sections to be offered by teaching assistants during the year is restricted to between 20 and 30. However, any one quarter cannot have more than 15 course sections offered by teaching assistants because of the capacity restrictions of the other arcs.

Similar restrictions determine the number of offerings of the courses. For example, MGT 200A will be offered either two or three times during the academic year as shown in Figure 7(b). One section will be offered during the fall as indicated by the corresponding minimum and maximum flow restrictions of one. At least one section will be offered during the spring quarter, and a third section *may* be offered during either the winter or the spring. The determination of whether this third section will actually be offered, and during which of the two quarters, will be made by the model, based on the availability of faculty resources. Thus, the user is able to incorporate many options within the context of a simple network model. Further, this visual interpretation makes it easy to convey the logic of the model to actual users.

The desires of the faculty members receive consideration in the model in two ways. Subject to administrative policies, a faculty member may determine the number of courses he will teach each quarter by manipulating the lower and upper bounds of the flow restrictions as illustrated in Figure 7(c). Jones will be assigned all five of his courses in the fall and winter and be free from formal teaching duties in the spring. In addition, the optimization in the model is carried out with respect to the "preference weights" of the faculty members for teaching the various courses. These preference weights range from −2 to +2, and are assigned by the faculty members.

Thus, it would appear that the evaluative model for this formulation is "maximize faculty happiness." However, it was assumed that the objective of maximizing faculty "happiness" and student "satisfaction" are complementary. Faculty members generally prefer teaching courses that are consistent with their professional abilities and teaching styles. Likewise, students generally prefer instructors who are enthusiastic about a course and its contents. While there may be some exceptional cases, it was not felt that these occurrences justify the burden of collecting additional information beyond simple expressions of faculty preference. In addition, information concerning the needs and desires of the students can be used to determine the lower and upper bounds on the number of sections of each course offered per academic year, and by quarter.

This network formulation is extremely attractive from a computational standpoint. The current costs for solving this model for GSM (with approximately 1000 nodes and 4500 arcs*) is in the range of $0.50 to $1 for the optimization, and $4 to $7 for a complete run, including input and output charges. Prior to recent developments in the field of network optimization, the cost of solving the same model would have been approximately $50 per run, which would have greatly inhibited its usefulness. The advantage of this low cost encourages the scheduler to make use of the model much more freely.

Although a number of considerations relevant to the faculty/course scheduling problem can be incorporated into this network model, and it has an obvious computational advantage, this formulation is only a crude approximation to the "ideal" model that would actually solve the scheduling problem in a single run. Therefore, the actual solution strategy for the problem is iterative, with the model providing a "first cut," an approximate solution that must be modified by the decision maker to include more subtle issues not considered in the model.

The scheduler must determine first if a solution is feasible, given the faculty resources and the projected demand for courses. If not, he must consider whether to obtain additional resources, if possible, or to reduce the number of offerings of courses. Once the appropriate balance is achieved between faculty resources and course demands, he must decide whether a solution is "acceptable." In making this decision, he must consider all of the criteria relevant for evaluating this schedule, as well as his implicit estimate of the probability that he could improve the schedule, and of the time and trouble such an attempt would require. If he does not accept the schedule, he must attempt to modify it.

The user may wish to attempt to improve the solution by modifying it by hand. If he feels that the solution determined by the approximate model is "close" to an acceptable schedule, he may persist with these hand assignments until an acceptable solution is obtained, or until he wishes to be aided by the approximate model.

---

*   Note that each arc in a network corresponds to a variable in the equivalent linear programming formulation.

The user may wish to modify the network formulation by defining new arcs from some faculty members to certain courses and by deleting other arcs. He may also change preference weights to influence the assignments and modify the lower and upper bounds on the faculty/quarter arcs that determine the number of courses a faculty member teaches each quarter. In such a manner, he can generate new candidate schedules for his evaluation.

The general solution strategy is summarized in Figure 8, and described step by step as follows:

Step 1. Generate the data required for the approximate model. These data include faculty information and course information, both modified to reflect the administrative policies.

Step 2. (Approximation) Generate the network model, and solve.

Step 3. (Evaluation) Determine whether the schedule is a feasible alternative. If not, return to step 1.

Step 4. (Evaluation) Determine whether the schedule is acceptable. If not, go to step 6.

Step 5. Print the schedule.

Step 6. Decide whether to persist in attempting to improve the schedule by hand. If not, go to step 8.

Step 7. (Modification) Make manual changes in the schedule. Go to step 3.

Step 8. (Modification) Make changes in the network formulation. Go to step 3.

The purpose of this presentation of the solution strategy is to emphasize again that a model need not be sufficiently detailed to "solve" a problem in a single computer run in order to be useful. Rather, the manager should view it as a decision-making aid that efficiently does much of the required

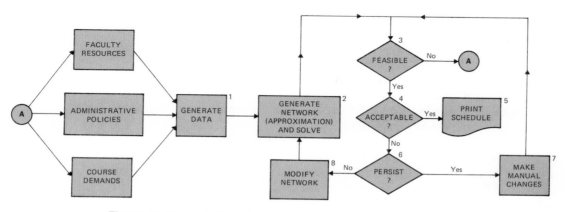

Figure 8. The solution strategy for the faculty/ course scheduling model

computational work for him, but that must be used intelligently in order to actually provide some benefit.

WHAT SHOULD THE MANAGER KNOW?

Network models are among the most practical and useful management science models because they have many advantageous characteristics.

1. Many real-world problems can be formulated with network models.
2. The visual interpretation of the network reduces the problem of communication between the manager and the analyst.
3. Efficient computer codes are available to analyze the networks, and integer valued solutions are obtained automatically.

These advantages enhance the practical usefulness of the transportation and transshipment models.

Problem Characteristics   The transportation and transshipment models may be applied to problems that require the allocation of units from sources of "supply" to sources of "demand." The most obvious examples of such problems are the product distribution problems of large organizations. Certainly these models have been used to advantage for analyzing such problems in many instances. In addition, by solving transportation or transshipment problems several times for new facilities located on alternative sites, the problem of locating new facilities can also be analyzed.

It is also possible to use this model to assign "workers" to "tasks," as illustrated in the description of the actual application of this methodology to the problem of faculty/course scheduling. This methodology is the basis for assigning military manpower to different jobs, as described by Charnes, Cooper, Niehaus and Sholtz [1970], and assigning workers to shifts as described by Segal [1974].

Thus, if the manager is studying any problem and recognizes that the task is to allocate units of a resource from sources of "supply" to sources of "demand," he should consider formulating the problem with a transportation or transshipment model.

Formulation and Information Requirements   The formulation of large-scale transportation and transshipment problems will probably be the responsibility of an analyst with specialized skills in management science. However, the visual interpretation of these models makes it easy for the manager to get involved in this task and to satisfy himself that the logic of the model is correct. This involvement on the part of the manager significantly reduces the problem of validating the model.

The information requirements are the shipping costs per unit on each route, the supply capacities at the supply points, and the demands. The latter may be market demands, which are based on market surveys or other marketing estimates. Sensitivity analysis can be used to determine if the solution is particularly sensitive to changes in any one of these estimates. Then, when changes occur in the estimates, the sensitivity analysis can be used to determine whether or not a new solution needs to be calculated, or what the potential costs of *not* changing an existing distribution policy actually are.

Computational Considerations   The computational advantage of the network formulation is significant. Table 7 shows the time required to solve several transshipment problems on a CDC 6600 computer and gives an estimate of the costs of solving these problems based on computer charges of $0.04 per second [Mulvey, 1975]. A transportation problem with 8000 nodes would require a transportation table with a total of 8000 rows and columns. Yet it is possible to solve such a problem in approximately 80.5 seconds on a large computer at an estimated cost of $3.22. This result is not only of interest to technical analysts. The important practical implication is that the manager can use such a model freely once it has been formulated. Making 50 different runs to explore "what if" questions under various scenarios would cost only $161. The potential savings from such analyses can run into millions of dollars (for examples see Geoffrion [1976]).

TABLE 7. Solution Times and Costs for Large Transshipment Problems

Problem	No. of Nodes	No. of Arcs	Solution Time* (seconds)	Solution Cost†
1	8000	15,000	80.5	$3.22
2	5000	23,000	80	3.20
3	3000	35,000	63	2.52
4	5000	15,000	51	2.04
5	3000	23,000	37.5	1.50

*On a CDC 6600.
†Assuming $0.04 per second.

One of the problems in Table 7 includes 35,000 arcs. Recall that an arc corresponds to a variable in a linear programming formulation. Can you imagine keypunching in the data for this problem! Naturally, special computer programs have been written to develop the input data for problems of this size.

In order to emphasize again the power of these solution methods, we suggest that when you are solving a transportation problem by hand with a total of 8 or 10 rows *and* columns and perhaps 16 variables, you should take a second look at the solution times and costs in Table 7.

Advantages and Disadvantages of the Model   The advantages of the transportation and transshipment models have been discussed. The only disadvantage is that they are somewhat restricted in the amount of problem detail that can be incorporated. Some important logic in a problem may not be amenable to formulation in the network format. This situation occurred in the faculty/course scheduling problem, but the computational advantage of the network formulation suggested that a man-machine solution strategy would be successful. The network model could be used to provide an "approximate" solution, that could then be adjusted by hand to determine the final solution. This same strategy might be of value in other practical situations.

APPENDIX TO CHAPTER 15
THE TRANSPORTATION ALGORITHM

In this appendix, we shall provide one algorithm for solving transportation problems by hand. This algorithm is presented to emphasize that the special structure of the transportation problem makes its solution much easier than ordinary linear programming problems. While other more efficient algorithms for solving transportation problems by hand are available, they are more complex conceptually. Since the chances that you will ever have to solve a real-world transportation problem by hand are remote, we have selected this particular algorithm because of its intuitive appeal. For reasons that will become apparent as you study the algorithm, it is called the "stepping-stone method" for solving transportation problems. Details regarding alternative solution strategies are provided in Dantzig [1963] and Wagner [1975].

The Problem   A company with factories at cities A and B supplies warehouses at cities C, D, E, and F. Monthly factory capacities are 150 at A and 200 at B. If overtime production is utilized, the capacities can be increased to 250 at A and 300 at B. Incremental unit overtime costs are $5 at A and $3 at B. Contributions to profit and overhead per unit excluding shipping costs are $14 at A and $16 at B for regular production. The current monthly warehouse requirements are 110 at C, 70 at D, 160 at E, and 130 at F. Unit shipping costs are as follows:

	To:			
From	C	D	E	F
A	$3	$4	$5	$7
B	5	8	3	4

Notice that the total monthly capacity with overtime is $250 + 300 = 550$, while the total demand is only $110 + 70 + 160 + 130 = 470$. Thus, the questions are: How much should be produced during regular production? How much should be produced during overtime at each factory? To which warehouses should the units be shipped?

Unequal Supply and Demand Each factory is a source of supply with a regular capacity at one contribution to profit per unit and an overtime capacity at another contribution to profit per unit. Thus, we can define two rows in a transportation table for each factory, corresponding to regular and overtime capacity respectively. For example, the "supply" for factory A operating at regular production capacity is 150 units, while the overtime "supply" of factory A is $250 - 150 = 100$ units. We label the row in the transportation table corresponding to regular production as AR, and the row corresponding to overtime production as AO. Similarly we define two rows for factory B.

We have a column in the transportation table corresponding to each warehouse. However, how do we adjust for the fact that the total supply capacity of 550 units does not equal the total demand of 470 units? To account for this fact, we define a "dummy" warehouse with a demand equal to the difference between the total supply and the total demand; that is, with a demand of $550 - 470 = 80$ units. The cost of shipping from each factory to this "dummy" warehouse will be zero.

TABLE 8. The Transportation Table With a Dummy Warehouse

To Warehouse From Factory	C		D		E		F		Dummy (Dum)		Available at Factories
AR (regular)	AR,C	11*	AR,D	10	AR,E	9	AR,F	7	AR, Dum	0	150
AO (overtime)	AO,C	6	AO,D	5	AO,E	4	AO,F	2	AO, Dum	0	100
BR (regular)	BR,C	11	BR,D	8	BR,E	13	BR,F	12	BR, Dum	0	200
BO (overtime)	BO,C	8	BO,D	5	BO,E	10	BO,F	9	BO, Dum	0	100
Required at Outlets	110		70		160		130		80		550

*Net contribution to profit and overhead.

To complete the information for the transportation table, we need the costs of shipping. However, in this example, we actually have the contribution to profit and overhead per unit at each factory, and these values should be taken into account. For example, units produced at factory A and shipped to warehouse C will bring a net contribution of $\$14 - \$3 = \$11$ if produced during regular hours, and $\$11 - \$5 = \$6$ if produced during overtime. The transportation table for this problem is shown in Table 8.

In order to facilitate the discussion of the algorithm, we have labeled the cells in the transportation table in the upper left-hand corner, as shown in Table 8. For example, the cell AO, D corresponds to a shipment of units made during overtime in plant A to warehouse D.

The Algorithm

We now present an algorithm for solving this problem. This algorithm is simply a formal presentation of the logic used in solving the example problem presented earlier in the chapter. In order to be effective, the algorithm must determine the following:

1. an initial solution
2. a test for improvement
3. a means of improving the solution

We shall now consider each of these requirements.

An Initial Solution   The simplest approach to obtaining an initial solution is to ignore the distribution costs (or contributions to profit and overhead as in this example). This initial solution is obtained by the following step-by-step procedure, sometimes called the northwest corner rule.

Step 1.   Start allocating supply to demand in the upper left-hand corner (the northwest corner) of the transportation table.

Step 2.   Allocate as many units as possible while observing the restrictions on total supply for the row and on total demand for the column.

Step 3.   If the demand in the column is met, move to the right to the cell in the next column. Go to step 2.

Step 4.   If the supply for the row is exhausted, move down to the cell in the next row. Go to step 2.

Applying these rules to Table 9, we begin with cell AR, C (step 1), and we see that factory A operating at regular capacity has 150 units available, while warehouse C requires 110. We assign 110 units from AR to C, and circle this number, completing step 2. We have met the demand at C, so we move to the right under column D (step 3), and assign the balance of the supply from AR, 40 units, to D (step 2). Now that the supply has been exhausted,

TABLE 9. Initial Solution by the Northwest Corner Rule

To Warehouse / From Factory	C	D	E	F	Dummy (Dum)	Available at Factories
AR (regular)	AR,C 11 — (110)	AR,D 10 — (40)	AR,E 9	AR,F 7	AR, Dum 0	150
AO (overtime)	AO,C 6	AO,D 5 — (30)	AO,E 4 — (70)	AO,F 2	AO, Dum 0	100
BR (regular)	BR,C 11	BR,D 8	BR,E 13 — (90)	BR,F 12 — (110)	BR, Dum 0	200
BO (overtime)	BO,C 8	BO,D 5	BO,E 10	BO,F 9 — (20)	BO, Dum 0 — (80)	100
Required at Outlets	110	70	160	130	80	550

AR,C : 11 x 110 = 1210	BR,E : 13 x 90 = 1170
AR,D : 10 x 40 = 400	BR,F : 12 x 110 = 1320
AO,D : 5 x 30 = 150	BO,F : 9 x 20 = 180
AO,E : 4 x 70 = 280	BO,Dum: 0 x 80 = 0
	4710

we drop down to row *AO* (step 4), and assign the balance of *D*'s requirement, 30 units, from the overtime capacity at factory A (step 2). We continue in this fashion, stair-stepping down the table until all of the assignments have been made, as shown in Table 9. The total contribution associated with this solution, $4710, is also calculated in Table 9 by multiplying the number of units shipped to each warehouse from each factory using regular or over-time production, by the appropriate net contribution per unit.

Notice that the application of the northwest corner rule determines a solution that satisfies the restrictions on supply and demand at each factory and at each warehouse. Thus, the solution is feasible. Also, there are four rows and five columns in Table 9. The number of cells in the table with assignments is $4 + 5 - 1 = 8$. In general, if n is the number of rows in a transportation table, and m is the number of columns, we want $n + m - 1$ assignments in the table. Otherwise, we call the solution *degenerate*, and we discuss special procedures for dealing with degenerate solutions later in this appendix.

According to this initial solution, the regular and overtime capacities of factory A will be utilized completely. However, the 80 units in cell BO, Dum indicates that the overtime capacity of factory B is not completely utilized. The 20 units actually produced during overtime at factory B are shipped to warehouse F (cell BO, F).

A Test for Improvement   Is the initial northwest corner solution in Table 9 the best possible solution? We can answer this question by examining each of the open cells in the transportation table to determine whether it would be better to move some of the units into it. In doing so, we want to be sure that any new solution satisfies the supply and demand restrictions shown in the right column and in the bottom row in the transportation table.

In evaluating each open cell, the following steps are used:

Step 1.   Determine a closed path, starting at the open cell being evaluated, and "stepping" from cells with assignments back to the original cell. Right angle turns in this path are permitted only at cells with assignments and at the original open cell. Since only the cells at the turning points are considered to be on the closed path, both open and assigned cells may be skipped over.

Step 2.   Beginning at the cell being evaluated, assign a plus, then alternate minus and plus signs at the assigned cells on the corner points of the path.

Step 3.   Add the unit costs in the squares with plus signs, and subtract the unit costs in the squares with minus signs. If we are minimizing costs (maximizing profits), the result is the net change in the cost (profit) per unit from the changes made in the assignments.

Step 4.   Repeat this procedure for each unused cell in the transportation table.

Steps 1 and 2 correspond to the intuitively appealing strategy of assigning a single unit to the unused square, then adjusting the shipments in the squares with assignments until all of the row supply and column demand constraints are satisfied. Step 3 simply calculates the cost (or contribution to profit) that would result from such a modification in the assignments.

If the net changes are all greater than or equal to 0, and if we are minimizing costs, or if they are all less than or equal to 0, and we are maximizing profits, we have found an optimal solution.

The application of these steps to the open square AR, E is shown in Table 10. Notice that the closed path forms a simple rectangle. The net change associated with a single unit being shipped from factory A using regular capacity to factory E is

$$9 - 4 + 5 - 10 = 0 .$$

This value is written in the bottom lefthand corner of cell AR, E in Table

TABLE 10. Closed Path for *AR,E* and Cell Evaluations

To Warehouse / From Factory	C		D		E		F		Dummy (Dum)		Available at Factories
AR (regular)	AR,C	11	AR,D	10	AR,E	9	AR,F	7	AR, Dum	0	150
	110		40 (−)		(+) 0		−1		+1		
AO (overtime)	AO,C	6	AO,D	5	AO,E	4	AO,F	2	AO, Dum	0	100
	0		30 (+)		70 (−)		−1		+6		
BR (regular)	BR,C	11	BR,D	8	BR,E	13	BR,F	12	BR, Dum	0	200
	−4		−6		90		110		−3		
BO (overtime)	BO,C	8	BO,D	5	BO,E	10	BO,F	9	BO, Dum	0	100
	−4		−6		0		20		80		
Required at Outlets	110		70		160		130		80		550

TABLE 11. Closed Path for Cell *BO,C*

To Warehouse / From Factory	C		D		E		F		Dummy (Dum)		Available at Factories
AR (regular)	AR,C	11	AR,D	10	AR,E	9	AR,F	7	AR, Dum	0	150
	110 (−)		40 (+)								
AO (overtime)	AO,C	6	AO,D	5	AO,E	4	AO,F	2	AO, Dum	0	100
			30 (−)		70 (+)						
BR (regular)	BR,C	11	BR,D	8	BR,E	13	BR,F	12	BR, Dum	0	200
					90 (−)		110 (+)				
BO (overtime)	BO,C	8	BO,D	5	BO,E	10	BO,F	9	BO, Dum	0	100
	(+) −4						20 (−)		80		
Required at Outlets	110		70		160		130		80		550

10. The net changes in profit for all of the unused cells are also shown in Table 10.

The evaluation of all open squares is not so easy. For example, the closed path for evaluating cell BO,C is shown in Table 11, and the net change is

$$8 - 9 + 12 - 13 + 4 - 5 + 10 - 11 = -4 .$$

Since we are trying to maximize profits in this example, this would not be a desirable cell in which to switch some units.

Improving the Solution   Each negative net change indicates the amount by which the total solution will be reduced if one unit were shipped in the corresponding cell, while each positive net change indicates the amount by which it will be increased.

Notice that in Table 10, two open cells, AR to the dummy warehouse and AO to the dummy warehouse, have positive net changes. Which one shall we choose in determining the new solution? One reasonable rule for small problems and hand solutions is always to select the one with the most negative (if minimizing costs) or the most positive net change (if maximizing profits). Therefore, we choose the cell AO, Dum.

To improve the solution, carry out the following steps:

Step 1.   Identify again the closed path for the chosen open cell, and assign the plus and minus signs as before. Determine the minimum number of units assigned to a cell on this path that is marked with a minus sign.

Step 2.   Add this number to the open cell and to all other cells on the path marked with a plus sign. Subtract this number from cells on the path marked with a minus sign.

The closed path for AO, Dum is $+ AO, Dum - BO, Dum + BO, F - BR, F + BR, E - AO, E$. The minimum number of units in a cell with a minus sign is the 70 in AO, E. Thus, we add 70 units to cells AO, Dum; BO, F; and BR, E, and subtract 70 units from cells BO, Dum; BR, F; and AO, E. This reassignment of units determines a new alternative, as shown in Table 12. This new solution corresponds to switching 70 units from overtime production in factory A to overtime production in factory B.

Now we repeat the process for the evaluation of each unused cell. The results are also shown in Table 12. The cells with the largest net change are BR, C and BO, C. Since these net changes are equal, suppose we arbitrarily choose cell BR, C, and improve the solution again. The result, shown in Table 13, again corresponds to switching some additional units from overtime production at factory A to overtime production in factory B.

The evaluation of the open cells in Table 13 reveals that there are no positive net changes, so there are no switches in shipments that will lead to a further improvement in the solution. Therefore, this is an *optimal*

TABLE 12. New Solution (First Iteration)

From Factory \ To Warehouse	C		D		E		F		Dummy (Dum)		Available at Factories
AR (regular)	AR,C	11	AR,D	10	AR,E	9	AR,F	7	AR,Dum	0	150
	(110)		(40)		-6		-7		-5		
AO (overtime)	AO,C	6	AO,D	5	AO,E	4	AO,F	2	AO,Dum	0	100
	0		(30)		-6		-7		(70)		
BR (regular)	BR,C	11	BR,D	8	BR,E	13	BR,F	12	BR,Dum	0	200
	+2		0		(160)		(40)		-3		
BO (overtime)	BO,C	8	BO,D	5	BO,E	10	BO,F	9	BO,Dum	0	100
	+2		0		0		(90)		(10)		
Required at Outlets	110		70		160		130		80		550

solution to the problem. The total incremental contribution to profit and overhead associated with this solution is $5150, as calculated in Table 13. This compares with the total incremental contribution of $4710 associated with the initial solution, for an increase of $440, or approximately 9 percent.

Alternative Optimal Solutions

The fact that open cells *AO, C; BO, C;* and *BO, E* have zero evaluations in Table 13 is important, and gives us flexibility in determining the final plan of action. These zero evaluations allow us to generate other solutions that have the same total net contribution as the optimal solution shown in Table 13. For example, since open cell *AO, C* has a zero evaluation, we may make the shifts in assignments as indicated by its closed path and generate the alternative optimal solution shown in Table 14. The managerial implication of this result is that in the optimal solution, a total of 150 units should be produced using regular capacity at factory *A*, while an additional 20 units should be produced on overtime at factory *A*. Of this total of 170 units, 100 should be shipped to warehouse *C*, and 70 units should be shipped to warehouse *D*. As the alternative optimal solution indicates, it makes no difference in the total contribution of the solution whether the 20 units produced on overtime are shipped to *C* or *D*. Give your own interpretation of the

TABLE 13. An Optimal Solution

To Warehouse / From Factory	C		D		E		F		Dummy (Dum)		Available at Factories
AR (regular)	AR,C	11	AR,D	10	AR,E	9	AR,F	7	AR, Dum	0	150
	(100)		(50)		−4		−5		−5		
AO (overtime)	AO,C	6	AO,D	5	AO,E	4	AO,F	2	AO, Dum	0	100
	0		(20)		−4		−5		(80)		
BR (regular)	BR,C	11	BR,D	8	BR,E	13	BR,F	12	BR, Dum	0	200
	(10)		−2		(160)		(30)		−5		
BO (overtime)	BO,C	8	BO,D	5	BO,E	10	BO,F	9	BO, Dum	0	100
	0		−2		0		(100)		−2		
Required at Outlets	110		70		160		130		80		550

```
AR,C    : 11 x 100 = 1100
AR,D    : 10 x  50 =  500
AO,D    :  5 x  20 =  100
AO,Dum  :  0 x  80 =    0
BR,C    : 10 x  11 =  110
BR,E    : 13 x 160 = 2080
BR,F    : 12 x  30 =  360
BO,F    :  9 x 100 =  900
                     5150
```

managerial implications of the alternative optimal solutions afforded by the zero evaluations in open cells BO, C and BO, E.

Degeneracy

If n is the number of rows, and m is the number of columns in a transportation table, we want $n + m - 1$ assignments in the table. A solution with fewer than $n + m - 1$ assignments is called a *degenerate solution*. Such a solution may arise when the rules for improving the solution are applied, or even in determining an initial solution by the northwest corner rule.

An example in Table 15 shows that a degenerate solution will arise if the rule for improving the solution is followed by shifting the minimum number of units in a cell marked with a minus sign. This minimum number, 80, occurs in two cells, AO, E and BO, Dum.

TABLE 14. An Alternative Optimal Solution

To Warehouse / From Factory	C	D	E	F	Dummy (Dum)	Available at Factories
AR (regular)	AR,C 11 (80)	AR,D 10 (70)	AR,E 9	AR,F 7	AR,Dum 0	150
AO (overtime)	AO,C 6 (20)	AO,D 5	AO,E 4	AO,F 2	AO,Dum 0 (80)	100
BR (regular)	BR,C 11 (10)	BR,D 8	BR,E 13 (160)	BR,F 12 (30)	BR,Dum 0	200
BO (overtime)	BO,C 8	BO,D 5	BO,E 10	BO,F 9 (100)	BO,Dum 0	100
Required at Outlets	110	70	160	130	80	550

TABLE 15. Transportation Table Where Degeneracy Will Occur

To Warehouse / From Factory	C	D	E	F	Dummy (Dum)	Available at Factories
AR (regular)	AR,C 11 (110)	AR,D 10 (40)	AR,E 9	AR,F 7	AR,Dum 0	150
AO (overtime)	AO,C 6	AO,D 5 (30)	AO,E 4 (80) (−)	AO,F 2	AO,Dum 0 (+) +6	110
BR (regular)	BR,C 11	BR,D 8	BR,E 13 (90) (+)	BR,F 12 (110) (−)	BR,Dum 0	200
BO (overtime)	BO,C 8	BO,D 5	BO,E 10	BO,F 9 (20) (+)	BO,Dum 0 (80) (−)	100
Required at Outlets	110	70	170	130	80	560

TABLE 16. A Degenerate Solution

To Warehouse / From Factory	C		D		E		F		Dummy (Dum)		Available at Factories
AR (regular)	AR,C	11	AR,D	10	AR,E	9	AR,F	7	AR, Dum	0	150
	(110)		(40)								
AO (overtime)	AO,C	6	AO,D	5	AO,E	4	AO,F	2	AO, Dum	0	110
			(30)						(80)		
BR (regular)	BR,C	11	BR,D	8	BR,E	13	BR,F	12	BR, Dum	0	200
					(170)		(30)				
BO (overtime)	BO,C	8	BO,D	5	BO,E	10	BO,F	9	BO, Dum	0	100
							(100)				
Required at Outlets	110		70		170		130		80		560

Note that the problem in Table 15 is only a slight modification of the problem we have been using. The overtime capacity of factory A and the demand at warehouse E have each been increased by 10 units. Otherwise, the northwest corner rule was applied to determine the initial solution as before.

When the shift of 80 units occurs, the assignments in cells AO, E and BO, Dum both go to 0, as shown in Table 16. We have only 7 assignments in Table 16 rather than the $4 + 5 - 1 = 8$ assignments we obtain in a nondegenerate solution. The practical effect is that several of the open cells in Table 16 cannot be evaluated in the usual way since a closed path cannot be established for them. For example, try to devise a closed path for evaluating cell AR, E.

The degeneracy can be resolved, however, by regarding one of the two cells where assignments have disappeared as an assigned cell with an extremely small allocation, that we shall call an ϵ (epsilon) allocation. This is illustrated in Table 17, where the ϵ is placed in cell BO, Dum. Table 17 also shows the closed path for cell AR, E. Conceptually, we shall regard the ϵ allocation as being infinitesimally small, so that it does not affect the supply and demand totals. The ϵ allocation, however, does make it possible to meet the $n + m - 1$ restriction on the number of assignments so that evaluation paths may be established for all open cells. The ϵ allocation is then

TABLE 17. The ϵ Allocation and the Closed Path for Cell AR,E

To Warehouse / From Factory	C		D		E		F		Dummy (Dum)		Available at Factories
AR (regular)	AR,C	11	AR,D	10	AR,E	9	AR,F	7	AR, Dum	0	150
	110		40 (−) ←		(+)						
AO (overtime)	AO,C	6	AO,D	5	AO,E	4	AO,F	2	AO, Dum	0	110
			30 (+)						80 (−)		
BR (regular)	BR,C	11	BR,D	8	BR,E	13	BR,F	12	BR, Dum	0	200
					170 (−) ←		30 (+)				
BO (overtime)	BO,C	8	BO,D	5	BO,E	10	BO,F	9	BO, Dum	0	100
							100 (−) ←		ϵ (+)		
Required at Outlets	110		70		170		130		80		560

manipulated as though it were no different from any other allocation. If in subsequent manipulations, the ϵ cell is the one that limits shifts of units, the ϵ is simply shifted to the cell being evaluated, and the usual procedure is then continued.

Summary

The application of the stepping-stone method to the transportation model is equivalent to the use of the simplex method. However, the special structure of the transportation model provides certain computational advantages that are exploited in the stepping-stone algorithm. For example, in a transportation problem, it is very easy to find an initial starting solution involving only decision variables, rather than the starting solution with all slack variables or with some artificial variables as in the general simplex algorithm.

The evaluation of the open cells in the transportation table is equivalent to the calculation of shadow prices for the corresponding variables in the linear programming formulation. Again, the special structure of the transportation model simplifies the calculations so much that they can easily be accomplished by hand. Likewise, the shift of units to improve a solution is equivalent to a pivot in the simplex algorithm.

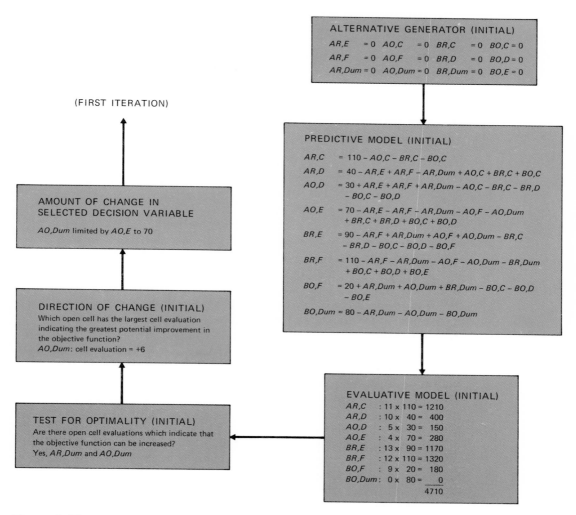

(FIRST ITERATION)

ALTERNATIVE GENERATOR (INITIAL)

$AR,E = 0$	$AO,C = 0$	$BR,C = 0$	$BO,C = 0$
$AR,F = 0$	$AO,F = 0$	$BR,D = 0$	$BO,D = 0$
$AR,Dum = 0$	$AO,Dum = 0$	$BR,Dum = 0$	$BO,E = 0$

PREDICTIVE MODEL (INITIAL)

$AR,C = 110 - AO,C - BR,C - BO,C$

$AR,D = 40 - AR,E + AR,F - AR,Dum + AO,C + BR,C + BO,C$

$AO,D = 30 + AR,E + AR,F + AR,Dum - AO,C - BR,C - BR,D - BO,C - BO,D$

$AO,E = 70 - AR,E - AR,F - AR,Dum - AO,F - AO,Dum + BR,C + BR,D + BO,C + BO,D$

$BR,E = 90 - AR,F + AR,Dum + AO,F + AO,Dum - BR,C - BR,D - BO,C - BO,D - BO,F$

$BR,F = 110 - AR,F - AR,Dum - AO,F - AO,Dum - BR,Dum + BO,C + BO,D + BO,E$

$BO,F = 20 + AR,Dum + AO,Dum + BR,Dum - BO,C - BO,D - BO,E$

$BO,Dum = 80 - AR,Dum - AO,Dum - BO,Dum$

AMOUNT OF CHANGE IN SELECTED DECISION VARIABLE

AO,Dum limited by AO,E to 70

DIRECTION OF CHANGE (INITIAL)

Which open cell has the largest cell evaluation indicating the greatest potential improvement in the objective function?

AO,Dum: cell evaluation = +6

EVALUATIVE MODEL (INITIAL)

AR,C	: 11 x 110 =	1210
AR,D	: 10 x 40 =	400
AO,D	: 5 x 30 =	150
AO,E	: 4 x 70 =	280
BR,E	: 13 x 90 =	1170
BR,F	: 12 x 110 =	1320
BO,F	: 9 x 20 =	180
BO,Dum	: 0 x 80 =	0
		4710

TEST FOR OPTIMALITY (INITIAL)

Are there open cell evaluations which indicate that the objective function can be increased?

Yes, AR,Dum and AO,Dum

Figure 9. The stepping-stone algorithm for the transportation problem

To emphasize this point, Figure 9 illustrates the first iteration of the stepping-stone algorithm for this example problem in exactly the same format used to illustrate the solution to the linear programming problem in Figure 2 in Chapter 14. The alternative generator specifies the unused cells in Table 9. The predictive model for calculating the value of each assigned cell is determined in the following way: first write down the "closed path" for each empty cell in Table 9 as shown in Table 18. Now, since cell AR, C is on the closed path for cell AO, C with a minus sign, if units are added to the unused cell, AO, C, the number of units assigned to cell AR, C

TABLE 18. Cells on Closed Path of Open Cells in Table 9.

Open Cells	Cells on Closed Paths							
	AR,C	AR,D	AO,D	AO,E	BR,E	BR,F	BO,F	BO,Dum
AR,E		(−)	(+)	(−)				
AR,F		(−)	(+)	(−)	(+)	(−)		
AR,Dum		(−)	(+)	(−)	(+)	(−)	(+)	(−)
AO,C	(−)	(+)	(−)					
AO,F					(−)	(+)	(−)	
AO,Dum					(−)	(+)	(−)	(+)	(−)
BR,C	(−)	(+)	(−)	(+)	(−)			
BR,D			(−)	(+)	(−)			
BR,Dum						(−)	(+)	(−)
BO,C	(−)	(+)	(−)	(+)	(−)	(+)	(−)	
BO,D			(−)	(+)	(−)	(+)	(−)	
BO,E					(−)	(+)	(−)	

will be reduced by a corresponding amount. This is indicated in the predictive model for cell AR, C shown in Figure 9, where AO, C appears preceded by a minus sign. Likewise, AR, C appears on the closed paths for the open cells BR, C and BO, C as shown in Table 18, so they also appear in the predictive model for cell AR, C, as illustrated in Figure 9. Notice that it is not necessary to write down these relationships when solving the transportation problem, but they are implicit in its structure.

Continuing the example, the evaluative model is simply the net contribution to profit and overhead of the current solution plus the net changes per unit associated with each open cell times the number of units (0) placed in that cell. The rest of the operations shown in Figure 9 parallel those in Figure 2 of Chapter 14.

As we have argued, it is most unlikely that you will ever be involved in solving a practical transportation problem by hand. Therefore, the motivation for your learning how to apply the stepping-stone algorithm must lie elsewhere. Learning to solve these simple problems emphasizes how the special structure of the network simplifies the computations of linear programming, and may provide some additional insights regarding the economic interpretation and logic of linear programming. This awareness should make you even more sensitive to possible applications of network models.

Check Your Understanding*

1. Explain the significance of the visual interpretation of a network.
2. Comment on the following statement: "A manager does not need to

* Questions that require an understanding of the materials in the appendix are introduced with the notation (Appendix).

TABLE 19. An Alternative Initial Solution

To Outlet / From Factory	1 (Kansas City)	2 (Atlanta)	3 (Detroit)	Available at Factories
1 (Chicago)	3	2 ⟨20⟩	3 ⟨30⟩	50
2 (New York)	10 ⟨30⟩	5 ⟨40⟩	8	70
3 (Dallas)	1 ⟨20⟩	3	10	20
Required at Outlets	50	60	30	140

worry about how efficient a computer program is for solving a problem. The machine can run all night so long as it finally gets *the* answer."

3. Compute the net savings (costs) associated with shipping one additional unit in each open cell in Table 4. That is, compute the net savings (costs) associated with shipping from factory 1 to outlet 2, from factory 2 to outlet 1, and from factory 3 to outlets 2 and 3. Why do we say that the solution in Table 4 is optimal?

4. Suppose we begin the introductory example problem with the initial solution shown in Table 19.
   a. Compute the total shipping costs associated with this initial solution.
   b. Suppose we ship one unit from factory 1 to outlet 1. Compute the *net savings* that result. Have you found a desirable *direction of change*?
   c. How many units can be shifted around to the route from factory 1 to outlet 1. In other words, what is the appropriate *amount of change* in the desirable direction?
   d. Revise the solution by shifting the necessary units. Check to see that the supply and demand restrictions are satisfied.
   e. Now compute the *net savings* from shipping one unit from factory 2 to outlet 3 while observing the supply and demand restrictions. If this is a desirable direction of change, compute the appropriate amount of change and shift the necessary units. Compare your result with the optimal solution in Table 4.

5. What is the significance of the notion of a "standard commodity bundle"? When can it be used?

6. In Figure 3, why is f a transshipment point and c a sink since they both have a demand for goods?

7. In Table 6, the "demand" at f is 12 units and the "supply" is only 11. What does this signify?

8. Using the computer solution shown in Figure 4, how many units should be shipped on each of these routes:

From	To	From	To
a	b	d	g
b	c	e	d
b	e	e	f
d	c	f	g
d	e	g	h

What is the significance of the remaining nonzero entries in the solution table?

9. What is the effect of placing a large cost (e.g., 500) on nonexistent routes in a transportation table for a transshipment problem?

10. In the solution strategy for the faculty/course scheduling problem shown in Figure 8, why is the solution of an optimizing model only an "approximating" step (step 2)?

11. Compare the solution strategy shown in Figure 8 to the diagram of the "models of management science" first illustrated in Figure 4 of Chapter 1 that serve as a basis for the organization of this book.
    a. In which boxes in Figure 8 is the decision maker "forecasting" the environment?
    b. Which box(es) correspond to an "alternative generator"?
    c. Which box(es) correspond to the use of a "predictive model"?
    d. Which box(es) correspond to the use of an "evaluative model"?
    e. Where is the "feedback" from the evaluative model to the alternative generator?

12. (Appendix) Modify steps 1 through 4 of the northwest corner rule for finding an initial solution so that it becomes the "northeast" corner rule. That is, modify the steps so that you begin in the upper right-hand corner (the northeast corner) of the transportation table. Apply this new northeast corner rule to the introductory example shown in Table 1. Verify that you obtain the initial solution shown in Table 19.

13. (Appendix) Apply the *northwest* corner rule to the introductory example shown in Table 1. What happens? The supply in row 1 and the demand in column 1 are met simultaneously by an allocation of 50 units. If no entry appears in row 1, column 2 or in row 2, column 1, the so-

lution will be *degenerate*. Place an ϵ in row 1, column 2 (the shipment from factory 1 to outlet 2), and continue to allocate the remainder of the units to the cells using the northwest corner rule.

a. Evaluate the open cell in row 1, column 3.

b. How many units can be shifted into the cell in row 1, column 3 (hint: not zero, but a "very small" number)?

c. Make this shift, and continue to apply the stepping-stone algorithm until the optimal solution is obtained.

Problems*

1. Factories 1 and 2 distribute an identical product through two regional warehouses. Normal production costs are $2 per unit at factory 1, and $4 per unit at factory 2. Normal capacity is 100 units at each plant. Shipping costs are given below:

	Warehouse	
Factory	1	2
1	$2	$4
2	3	1

The demand at warehouse 1 is 75 units, and demand at warehouse 2 is 125 units.

a. Set up the transportation table that you would use to determine the optimal production-shipping schedule. Do *not* work the problem.

b. Now assume that the demand at warehouse 2 has increased to 150 units. Suppose that additional overtime capacity of 20 units is available at each plant. Overtime production costs are $3 per unit at plant 1, and $5 per unit at plant 2. Set up the new transportation table that you would use to determine the optimal production-shipping schedule, utilizing both regular and overtime capacity. Do *not* work the problem.

c. (Appendix) Use the northwest corner rule to obtain an initial solution and solve for the optimal production-shipping schedules for (a) and (b) above.

2. Temple-Stark, Inc., produces a cleaning fluid at its plants in Albuquerque and Boston. Cleaning fluid sells for $0.50 a can in the Midwest and Southwest (serviced by warehouses located in Omaha and Houston respectively) and for $0.55 a can in the Rocky Mountains, which are served by a warehouse in Salt Lake City. Transportation costs per can are as follows:

---

* Questions that require an understanding of the materials in the appendix are introduced with the notation (Appendix).

	Transportation Cost to:		
From	Salt Lake City	Omaha	Houston
Albuquerque	$0.07	$0.08	$0.05
Boston	0.10	0.05	0.09

Production information is as follows:

Plant	Monthly Capacity	Unit Production Cost
Albuquerque	1700	$0.35
Boston	1800	0.29

a. Suppose the monthly demand is for 1300 cans in Salt Lake City, 1200 cans in Omaha, and 1000 cans in Houston. Set up a transportation table that could be used to determine the optimum production-shipping schedule. Do *not* work the problem.

b. Suppose the monthly demand is for 1200 cans in Salt Lake City, 1000 cans in Omaha, and 1000 cans in Houston. Set up a transportation table that could be used to determine the optimum production-shipping schedule. Do *not* work the problem.

c. (Appendix) Use the northwest corner rule to obtain an initial solution and solve for the optimal production-shipping schedules for cleaning fluid for (a) and (b) above.

3. Factories A, B, and C distribute an identical product through three regional warehouses, X, Y, and Z. Monthly factory capacities are 160, 190, and 150 units respectively. Monthly warehouse requirements average 150, 160, and 90 units, respectively. The unit distribution costs differ and are shown below:

	To:		
From	X	Y	Z
A	$ 3	$5	$ 8
B	5	6	15
C	12	7	4

The current shipping schedule is as follows:

From	To	No. of Units
A	X	150
A	Y	10
B	Y	150
B	Z	40
C	Z	50

a. Set up a transportation table that could be used to determine the optimum shipping plan.
b. Use the current shipping schedule as the initial solution. Evaluate the net savings (cost) associated with shipping one additional unit on each of the following routes while observing the supply and demand restrictions:

From	To
A	Z
A	dummy warehouse
B	X
B	dummy warehouse
C	X
C	Y

c. If one or more of the evaluations in (b) reveals a net savings, shift the units in the transportation table. Interpret the results.
d. Evaluate the net savings (cost) associated with shipping one additional unit on each of the unused routes in the revised table. Is the solution optimal? How do you know?

4. Four workers are available, each of whom may be assigned to only one of four jobs. The number of minutes required to perform each job by each worker is shown in the table below:

	Job			
Worker	1	2	3	4
1	2	4	5	---
2	7	3	2	3
3	9	---	8	6
4	---	6	2	3

The empty cells indicate that the worker does not have the necessary skills to do the particular job.
a. Set up a transportation problem that can be used to assign one worker to each job so that the *sum* of the minutes required for the jobs is minimized. What is the appropriate interpretation of the supply and the demand in this case?
b. Draw the network corresponding to this problem.
c. (Appendix) Use an initial solution of 1s in row 1, column 1; row 2, column 2; row 3, column 3; and row 4, column 4. This solution is degenerate. Place ϵ's in row 1, column 2; row 2, column 3; and row 3, column 4. Solve by the stepping-stone method.
d. (Appendix) If, after a little practice, worker number four can perform job two in two minutes instead of six, should the solution be changed? If so, what should it become?

5. Texas Electronics, Inc., has just received a large government contract to deliver radar units to three different locations over a three-year period. The radar units are currently manufactured in plants in Atlanta (A) and Boston (B). Each plant has a normal capacity of 100 units per year. However, an extra shift could be added in either or in both plants that could boost the annual capacity by an additional 75 units in each plant. Any units produced on an extra shift would cost an additional $2 per unit (these costs are "scaled" so they are simple numbers).

   The units must be shipped to Rhode Island (R), South Dakota (S), and Tennessee (T). The annual demands vary over the three year period of the contract as shown in the following table:

	Location		
Demand in Year:	R	S	T
1	50	60	100
2	75	70	120
3	100	80	150

The per-unit costs of shipping also vary as follows:

	To:		
From	R	S	T
A	$3	$1	$5
B	8	2	4

On the basis of these data, a management science analyst has determined the optimum production-shipping schedule for each of the three years by using the transportation model and a special-purpose computer program. The results are shown in Table 20.

   As an alternative, Texas Electronics, Inc., can purchase a new plant in Chicago (C), operate it for three years, and sell it at an estimated total net loss of $1,000. This new plant has a normal capacity of 130 units per year, and an extra shift could produce an additional 100 units per year, although there would be an estimated incremental cost of $2 per unit manufactured on the second shift. It costs $2 per unit to ship from Chicago to Rhode Island, $6 to ship to South Dakota, and $3 to ship to Tennessee.

   The management science analyst has also performed a "what if" analysis of the optimum production-shipping schedule, based on the assumption that the plant in Chicago has been purchased. His results are shown in Table 21. Should Texas Electronics, Inc., purchase this new plant? Based on the monetary criterion alone, what is the appropriate decision? What other factors might alter this decision?

6. (Appendix) The Stellar Steel Company makes automotive parts that are used in the assembly of automobiles. At present, the company has three plants,

TABLE 20. Production-Shipping Schedule for Texas Electronics

From	To: R	S	T
Year 1			
A (normal)	50	50	0
A (extra shift)	0	10	0
B (normal)	0	0	100
B (extra shift)	0	0	0
Year 2			
A (normal)	75	25	0
A (extra shift)	0	45	0
B (normal)	0	0	100
B (extra shift)	0	0	20
Year 3			
A (normal)	100	0	0
A (extra shift)	0	75	0
B (normal)	0	0	100
B (extra shift)	0	5	50

TABLE 21. Production-Shipping Schedule for Texas Electronics with Chicago Plant

From	To: R	S	T
Year 1			
A (normal)	0	60	0
A (extra shift)	0	0	0
B (normal)	0	0	20
B (extra shift)	0	0	0
C (normal)	50	0	80
C (extra shift)	0	0	0
Year 2			
A (normal)	0	70	0
A (extra shift)	0	0	0
B (normal)	0	0	65
B (extra shift)	0	0	0
C (normal)	75	0	55
C (extra shift)	0	0	0
Year 3			
A (normal)	20	80	0
A (extra shift)	0	0	0
B (normal)	0	0	100
B (extra shift)	0	0	0
C (normal)	80	0	50
C (extra shift)	0	0	0

one in Cleveland, one in Denver, and one in Philadelphia. These plants supply four automobile assembly plants in Oakland, Gary, Houston, and Newark. Of late, the output from the company's plants has not been able to keep pace with its orders. As a result, the company has decided to build a new plant to expand its productive capacity. It is considering San Francisco and Atlanta as possible sites; both appear to be excellent choices in terms of subjective, noncost factors.

The production and output requirements for each of the existing plants, together with the estimated production costs of the two locations are shown in Table 22. Transportation costs from all these plants to the assembly plants are also given. Which of the two new locations should be selected on the basis of the cost criterion?

7. Suppose a firm must redistribute goods over the network of shipping routes shown in Figure 10. The number associated with each city is the supply (plus) or demand (minus) at that location. The number on each arrow is the cost per unit of shipping on that route.

TABLE 22. Production-Distribution Data for the Stellar Steel Company

Demand		Production		
	Assembly Plant Requirements (units per month)		Normal Production Load (units per month)	Production Costs (per unit)
Oakland	9,000	Denver	6,000	$0.48
Gary	10,000	Philadelphia	14,000	0.50
Houston	12,000	Cleveland	15,000	0.52
Newark	15,000	Atlanta (estimate)	---	0.49
	46,000	San Francisco (estimate)	---	0.53
			35,000	

Transportation Costs ($ per unit)

	To:			
From	Gary	Houston	Newark	Oakland
Cleveland	$0.25	$0.55	$0.40	$0.60
Denver	0.35	0.30	0.50	0.40
Philadelphia	0.36	0.45	0.26	0.66
Atlanta	0.35	0.30	0.41	0.50
San Francisco	0.60	0.38	0.65	0.27

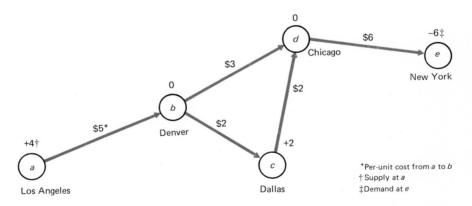

Figure 10. A network of shipping routes

a. Set up the appropriate transportation table for solving this transshipment problem.
b. Draw the equivalent transportation network similar to Figure 5.
c. Use the following initial solution in the transportation table:

From	To	No. of Units
Los Angeles (a)	Denver (b)	4
Denver (b)	Denver (b)	2
Denver (b)	Dallas (c)	4
Dallas (c)	Dallas (c)	2
Dallas (c)	Chicago (d)	6
Chicago (d)	Chicago (d)	ε (a very small number)
Chicago (d)	New York (e)	6

Evaluate the effect of shipping one unit from Denver to Chicago while observing the restrictions on supply and demand. If this represents a net savings, shift the appropriate units. Interpret the results.

8. A furniture manufacturer must ship units from its main plant in San Francisco and a small plant in Phoenix to other demand areas. The supplies and demands at each location and the cost per unit of shipping are shown on the network in Figure 11.

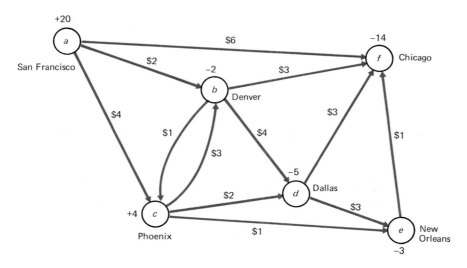

Figure 11. Shipping routes of furniture manufacturer

a. Set up the transportation table appropriate for solving this problem.
b. Draw the equivalent transportation network similar to Figure 5.

c. A management science analyst has used a special purpose computer program to obtain the following results:

	b	c	d	e	f
a	20	0	0	0	0
b	4	5	0	0	13
c	0	19	5	4	0
d	0	0	19	0	0
e	0	0	0	20	1

Interpret these results. How many units are shipped from city to city? What is the total cost of shipping associated with this solution?

9. A firm is attempting to manage its cash balance so that it obtains the maximum return on its assets.* It has forecasted the cash payments it can expect from its accounts receivables, and the accounts payable from its own commitments in each of the next four months as shown:

Month	Forecasted Cash Inflow (in $ thousands)	Forecasted Accounts Payable (in $ thousands)
1 (Jan.)	10	40
2 (Feb.)	20	60
3 (Mar.)	40	50
4 (Apr.)	30	40
	100	190

The firm can delay payment of an account by one month and pay a penalty of 2 percent. However, it cannot delay payment by more than one month.

The firm also has two marketable securities. Security A matures on April 1 with a face value of $50,000, while security B matures on February 1 with a face value of $25,000. These securities could be sold early, if necessary, to provide cash for the accounts receivable. The penalties are as follows:

Number of Months Before Maturity	Penalty (percent)
1	0.5
2	1.5
3	3.0

* Based on V. Srinivasan, "A Transshipment Model for Cash Decisions," *Management Science*, Vol. 20, No. 10, June 1974.

In addition, the firm has a line of credit with a bank. The interest charges for borrowing are as follows:

Borrow in Month	Interest Charge (percent)
1 (Jan.)	4.0
2 (Feb.)	3.0
3 (Mar.)	2.0
4 (Apr.)	1.0

This credit can be used to cover the excess cash demands over the total cash availabilities during this four-month period.

Finally, any excess cash available during one month may be invested in short-term securities which mature in 30 days, 60 days, or 90 days. The returns from these securities are as follows:

Maturity (days)	Return (percent)
30	0.75
60	1.60
90	2.5

a. Formulate the cash management problem as a transshipment problem. Assume that all of the accounts payable, including those for April, must be paid before May 1. (Hint: Define nodes representing "cash" in each month that are the transshipment nodes, as are nodes representing the short term securities. The other nodes will be either "sources" or "sinks.")
b. Set up the corresponding transportation table as a means of summarizing the relevant data.

References

Charnes, A., W. Cooper, R. Niehaus, and D. Sholtz, "A Model for Civilian Manpower Management in the U.S. Navy," in *Models of Manpower Systems*, edited by A. Smith, English Universities Press, 1970.

Dantzig, G., *Linear Programming and Extensions*, Princeton University Press, Princeton, 1963.

Dyer, J., and J. Mulvey, "An Integrated Optimization/Information System for Academic Planning," *Management Science*, Vol. 22, No. 12, August 1976.

Geoffrion, A., "Better Distribution Planning with Computer Models," *Harvard Business Review*, Vol. 54, No. 4, July–August 1976.

Klingman, A., A. Napier, and J. Stutz, "Netgen: A Program for Generating Large Scale Capacitated Assignment, Transportation, and Minimum Cost Flow Network Problems," *Management Science,* Vol. 20, No. 5, January 1974.

Mulvey, J., "Special Structures in Network Models and Associated Applications," Ph.D. dissertation, The Graduate School of Management, The University of California, Los Angeles, 1975.

Segal, M., "The Operator Scheduling Problem: A Network Flow Approach," *Operations Research*, Vol. 22, No. 4, July–August 1974, pp. 808–823.

Srinivasan, V., "A Transshipment Model for Cash Decisions," *Management Science*, Vol. 20, No. 10, June 1974.

Wagner, H., *Principals of Management Science*, Prentice-Hall, Englewood Cliffs, N.J., 1975.

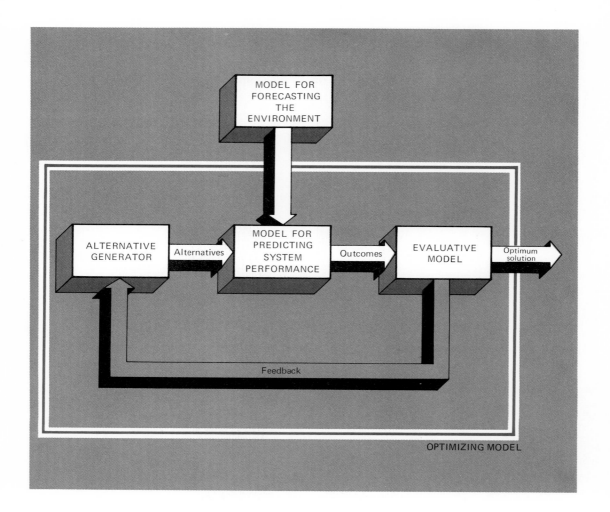

16

Network Models — Shortest Path and Network Scheduling

Another important class of network models involves the determination of the longest or the shortest path through a network. In most real-world applications, the length of the path is not actually a measure of distance, but rather a measure of money or of time. If the measure is money, the shortest path algorithm can be applied to determine the least cost route through a network. This strategy is often employed in developing a policy for replacing equipment. If the measure is time, the "longest path" through the network may be of interest as an estimate of the duration of a large-scale project. This latter concept is the basis for the well-known network scheduling techniques PERT and CPM. Examples of these applications will be provided.

These network models also share the following important characteristics:

1. Many real-world problems can be formulated with shortest path or network scheduling models.
2. The visual interpretation of the network reduces the problems of communication.
3. Efficient computer codes are available to analyze the networks, and integer valued solutions are obtained automatically.

Therefore, a manager should be able to recognize opportunities for using these models.

THE SHORTEST PATH MODEL

The problem of finding the shortest path from the beginning to the end of a large network may be viewed as a special case of the transshipment problem.

All of the nodes in the network are viewed as transshipment points except for the starting and ending nodes. A supply of one unit is assumed at the start, and a demand of one is assumed at the end, or terminal node. The problem can be solved as a normal transshipment problem, which means it can also be restructured into an equivalent transportation problem. The path over which the single unit is shipped is actually the "shortest path" when the costs are interpreted as distances. This model can be used to analyze several commonly occurring real-world problems.

The Shortest Path Algorithm

As we have said, the shortest path problem can be formulated as a transshipment problem, which can be formulated as a transportation problem. The problem can then be solved efficiently by using a specially modified computer program for linear programming problems. Perhaps this is beginning to sound like the old song, "the foot bone is connected to the ankle bone, etc." However, the special nature of the shortest path problem makes it possible to develop an especially simple algorithm for its solution. This is particularly true when the network is *acyclic*.

A network is *acyclic* if it contains no cycles. A cycle is a path from a node that eventually returns to the same node. For example, the network in Figure 1(a) contains a cycle, since it is possible to travel from node 2 to node 3, from node 3 to node 5, from node 5 to node 4, and from node 4 back to node 2. However, the network shown in Figure 1(b) contains no such cycles, and is therefore acyclic.

To find the shortest path in an acyclic network, we can take the following steps:

Step 1. Begin at the terminal node in the network (node 8 in Figure 1(b)). Label it with a zero.

Step 2. Consider a node whose outward pointing arcs all go into labeled nodes. Add the distance on each outward arc to the label value on the node it goes into. Label this new node with the minimum of these sums.

Step 3. Repeat step 2 until the beginning node is labeled. This label is the length of the shortest path.

Step 4. To identify the shortest path, trace forward through the network from the beginning node, selecting at each node the outgoing arc with the minimum sum in step 2. If a tie occurs, there are alternate paths.

Let us apply this algorithm to the acyclic network shown in Figure 1(b). At step 1, we first label node 8 with a 0, placing the label in a box below the node. Next, for step 2, we choose a node whose outgoing arcs all go into labeled nodes. Since node 8 is labeled, nodes 5, 6, and 7 are eligible. Suppose

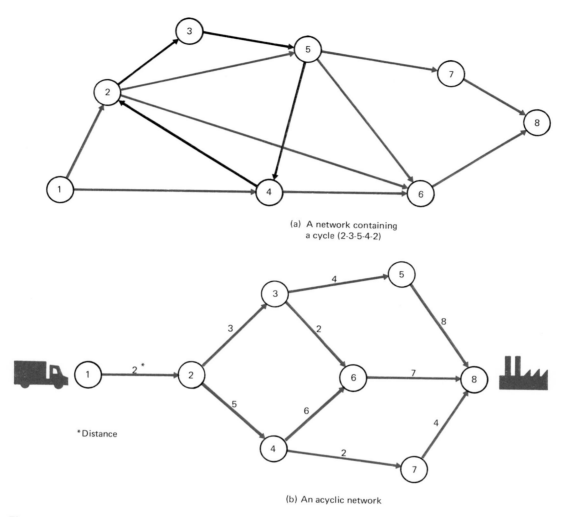

(a) A network containing
a cycle (2-3-5-4-2)

*Distance

(b) An acyclic network

Figure 1. Examples of cyclic and acyclic networks

we choose node 6. The distance on the arc from node 6 to node 8 is 7, plus the label value of 0, equals 7. This is the label we place on node 6 in Figure 2.

Now we repeat step 2. Nodes 5 and 7 are still eligible to be labeled. What about node 3, since an outgoing arc goes from node 3 to the now labeled node 6? No, it is *not* eligible, because another outgoing arc goes from node 3 to node 5, and node 5 has not been labeled yet. So, let us label node 5 with the value $8 + 0 = 8$, and we now obtain the labelings shown in Figure 2.

Since both nodes 5 and 6 have been labeled, node 3 is eligible, as is node 7. Choosing node 3, we add the distance on the arc from node 3 to node 5, 4,

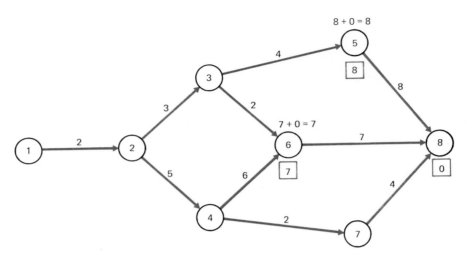

Figure 2. Partially labeled network

plus the label on node 5, 8, and obtain $4 + 8 = 12$. Similarly, for the arc from node 3 to node 6, we obtain $2 + 7 = 9$. Now, we take the minimum of these two numbers, 9, as the label for node 3, since the minimum of the lengths on the alternative paths identifies the shortest path.

Continuing this process, we eventually label the beginning node 1, as shown in Figure 3. Thus, the length of the shortest path is given by the label on node 1, 13. To find the path, we trace forward through the network. Obviously, it includes the arc from node 1 to node 2. At node 2, we note that the minimum sum in step 2 was for the arc from node 2 to node 4 (the distance of 5 plus the label value on node 4 gives the label value on node 2). Thus, the arc from node 2 to node 4 is on the path. Tracing forward to the terminal node, we determine that the shortest path is from node 1 to node 2, node 2 to node 4, node 4 to node 7, and node 7 to node 8. In this simple network, you could have discovered this solution without the aid of the algorithm. However, the algorithm can be computerized and applied to much more complicated networks.

The Equipment Replacement Problem

In the most common applications of the shortest path algorithm, the "distances" are actually either costs or measures of time. The problem of determining when to replace a piece of equipment can often be analyzed through use of this model by allowing the distances to be costs.

Suppose a company has just received a contract for producing a new product for five years. The production of this new product requires the purchase of a new piece of machinery, that can only be used for this product. The cost of this machinery is $200 now. However, the company estimates

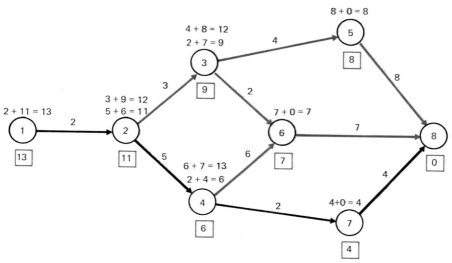

Figure 3. The shortest path (1–2–4–7–8)

that after two more years, the price will increase to $250 for the same piece of equipment. The salvage value of the equipment depends on the number of years it has been used, as shown in Table 1. Similarly, the operating costs depend on its age, since maintenance increases as the machine becomes older. These costs are also shown in Table 1.

TABLE 1. Salvage Value and Annual Operating Costs

Number of Years Used	Salvage Value at End of Year	Annual Operating Costs
1	$100	$ 10
2	75	50
3	50	100
4	25	120
5	0	130

How can we best analyze this problem? One way might be to assume that we purchase the machine at the start of the first year (which we must do) and compute the cost of keeping it for each of one, two, three, four, or five years. These calculations are shown in Table 2. Next, we might suppose we purchase a new machine at the beginning of the second year and keep it for one, two, three, or four years. We can calculate these costs in a similar manner, as shown in Table 3. We can do the same for the assumption that we purchase a new machine at the beginning of the third year, using the new purchase price of $250, and for years four and five also, as shown in Table 4. Notice that if we purchase a machine at the beginning of the fifth

TABLE 2. Costs of Purchasing a
Machine at the Beginning of Year 1

	Keep Machine Until End of Year:				
	1	2	3	4	5
Purchase price	$200	$200	$200	$200	$200
Operating cost:					
Year 1	10	10	10	10	10
Year 2	---	50	50	50	50
Year 3	---	---	100	100	100
Year 4	---	---	---	120	120
Year 5	---	---	---	---	130
Total cost	210	260	360	480	610
Less salvage value	100	75	50	25	0
Net cost	110	185	310	455	610

TABLE 3. Costs of Purchasing a
Machine at the Beginning of Year 2

	Keep Machine Until End of Year:			
	2	3	4	5
Purchase price	$200	$200	$200	$200
Operating cost				
Year 2	10	10	10	10
Year 3	---	50	50	50
Year 4	---	---	100	100
Year 5	---	---	---	120
Total cost	210	260	360	480
Less salvage value	100	75	50	25
Net cost	110	185	310	455

year, the total cost will be $250 for the purchase plus $10 for operating expenses and minus the $100 salvage value, since we must sell it at the end of the fifth year. This gives $250 + $10 − $100 = $160.

Now, the problem is to determine a strategy that takes us from the beginning of year 1 to the end of year 5 as cheaply as possible. We know the cost of purchasing a new machine at the beginning of any year and holding it until the beginning of any other year. If we look at the problem closely, we can see an analogy with the shortest route problem.

TABLE 4. Costs of Purchasing a
Machine at the Beginnings of Years 3, 4, and 5

	Purchased Year 3			Purchased Year 4		Purchased Year 5
	Keep Machine Until End of Year:					
	3	4	5	4	5	5
Purchase price	$250	$250	$250	$250	$250	$250
Operating cost						
Year 3	10	10	10	---	---	---
Year 4	---	50	50	10	10	---
Year 5	---	---	100	---	50	10
Total cost	260	310	410	260	310	260
Less salvage value	100	75	50	100	75	100
Net cost	160	235	360	160	235	160

Suppose we construct a network by defining nodes as the beginnings of each of the five years in the time horizon of this study, plus one additional node to mark the beginning of the sixth year (or the end of the fifth year). We can draw arcs from the beginning of each year to the beginning of each of the subsequent years, as shown in Figure 4. For example, the arc from node 1 to node 4 represents the decision to purchase a machine at the beginning of year 1 and keep it three years, until the beginning of year 4. The cost of this strategy from Table 2 is $310, which appears on the arc from node 1 to node 4. Notice how the other costs on the arcs in Figure 4 correspond to the costs in Tables 2, 3, and 4.

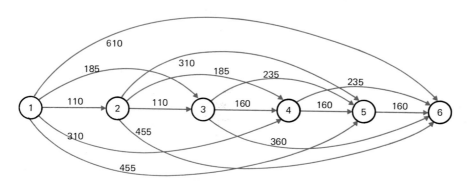

Figure 4. Shortest path network for analyzing the equipment replacement problem

The network in Figure 4 is acyclic, so it can be solved using the shortest path algorithm for minimizing total costs. Using the four-step manual procedure, verify that the minimum total cost of the optimal equipment replacement strategy is $530, and the strategy is to sell the machine purchased at the beginning of year 1 at the end of year 1; then purchase a second machine to be held for two years, and finally, purchase a third machine also to be held for two years. Notice that it is not obvious that such a strategy would be optimal.

Since these costs are incurred over several years, it might be appropriate to discount them by the proper rate for the firm. The length of the shortest path would then correspond to the present value of the optimal equipment replacement policy. An example of this approach is given as an exercise at the end of the chapter.

NETWORK SCHEDULING MODELS

One of the most practical and important uses of the concept of the length of the path through a network is found in network scheduling models. Network scheduling models are used to plan, schedule, control, and evaluate complex projects and tasks. The basic idea is to analyze a complex project—for example, the development of a new weapons system, the construction of a large building, or the production of a motion picture—by identifying the specific tasks that must be accomplished to complete the project and interrelating them in a network.

The network planning techniques known as the critical path method (CPM) and the Program Evaluation and Review Technique (PERT) were originally developed in the 1950s. PERT was first used to help manage the successful Polaris project, and since that time, some form of network scheduling model has been required for every government defense contract.

The nodes in the network scheduling models represent "events" in the project.* An event generally corresponds to the beginning or end of a specific task, or "activity," that must be performed as part of the project. The activities are represented by the arcs in the network.

The rules of logic in the network are relatively simple. Suppose an activity D can be started only after activities A, B, and C have been completed. This situation would be diagramed as shown in Figure 5. Thus, all activities represented by arcs into an event node must be completed before an activity represented by an arc out of an event node can begin.

In addition, because of restrictions imposed by most computer routines that analyze network schedules, two activities cannot have the same beginning and ending event nodes. Thus, if activities B and C can begin after activity A, and activity D can begin after activities B and C have been com-

---

* We are presenting the "activity on the arcs" approach to network scheduling, although it is also possible to develop "activities on the nodes" models.

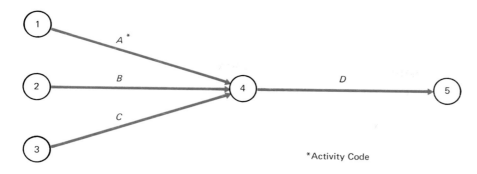

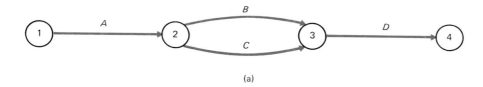

Figure 5. Activity *D* can begin only after activities *A*, *B*, and *C* have been completed

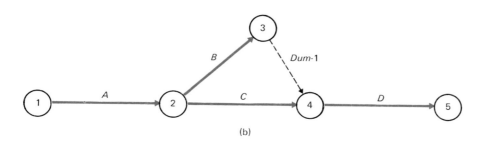

Figure 6. Network diagraming rules

pleted, we might be tempted to diagram this relationship as shown in Figure 6(a). However, since computer codes identify activities by their beginning and ending nodes, they could not distinguish between activity *B* and activity *C*, which both begin with event 2 and end with event 3. Therefore, a "dummy" activity is used as shown in Figure 6(b). The dummy activity has a time duration of zero and is used for logical purposes in the network.

Now, consider a simple example of a project that might be analyzed by using network scheduling. Suppose we wish to conduct a market survey. Our first activity, A, will be to study the purpose of the survey. After completing this task, we can hire data collection personnel (B) and design the questionnaire (C). After both B and C are completed, we can train the personnel (D). However, after completing only the design of the questionnaire (C), we can begin selecting households for our survey (E), even before the personnel have been hired (B). Finally, after completing tasks (D) and (E) we can take the survey (F). These tasks and the precedence relationships are shown in Table 5. Try to construct your own network for analyzing this problem before looking at the solution in Figure 7. Notice that one dummy activity was required to indicate that activity D cannot start until *both* activities B and C have been completed, but activity E depends only on activity C.

TABLE 5. Activities Required and Immediate Predecessors for the Market Survey

Activity Code	Description	Immediate Predecessors
A	Study purpose	---
B	Hire personnel	A
C	Design questionnaire	A
D	Train personnel	B, C
E	Select households	C
F	Survey	D, E

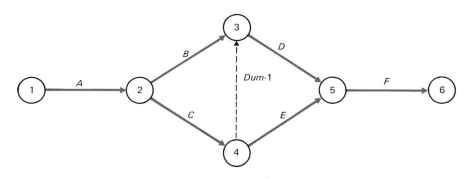

Figure 7. Network diagram for the market survey

Just the construction of such a network could be a significant managerial aid in dealing with a complex problem. In preparing Table 5, it was necessary to do an *activity analysis*; that is, the activities required to complete the project had to be identified and the technical precedence relationships among the activities had to be determined. These precedence relationships are the statements of which activities must immediately precede an activity. The value from the network can be enhanced if the activity analysis also uses estimates of the time required to complete each activity, and these are included in the network. In order to determine these time estimates, decisions must be made regarding the methods and tools to be used in completing each activity. Again, this forces the manager to break down the project into its individual tasks, and to plan each of these in detail before beginning the project. Suppose that the time estimates for the activities in the market survey are 2 weeks for A, 4 weeks for B, 2 weeks for C, 1 week for D, 2 weeks for E, and 3 weeks for F. These time estimates are shown in parentheses on the network in Figure 8.

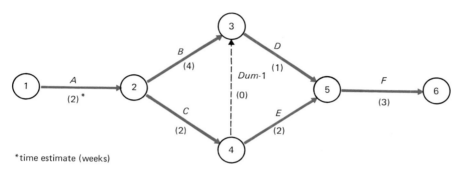

*time estimate (weeks)

Figure 8. Time estimates for the activities in the network diagram

Given these time estimates, the network may be analyzed to provide additional information of importance to managers. The most obvious information of interest is the total length of time required for the project. This time is computed by applying a modified version of the shortest path algorithm. However since we are interested in completing each of the activities, the total time for the project will be equal to the *longest path* through the network. Thus, we apply a suitably modified algorithm to obtain this estimate.

This algorithm computes the "earliest" and "latest" start and finish times for each of the activities. The early start and finish times are simply the earliest that each activity can be started and finished respectively, given the technical precedence relationships in the network. The latest start and finish times are the latest that an activity can be started and finished respectively, *without delaying the total time to complete the project*. The difference between the early and late start (finish) time is the "slack" associated with an activity. This slack is the amount of time that a particular activity could be delayed without delaying the completion of the project. This information can be very useful to managers in scheduling work and the use of equipment. The activities with zero slack cannot be delayed without delaying the entire project. These activities are on the longest path through the network, which is called the *critical path*.

Earliest Start and Finish Times   We can begin with zero as the starting time for the project, which becomes the earliest start time (ES) for the first activity. Given ES for an activity, the earliest finish time (EF) is simply ES + activity time. The procedure for computing ES and EF, which is similar to the shortest path algorithm, is as follows:

Step 1.   Place the value of the project start time to the left of the beginning activity in the position shown for the early start time in Figure 9. In Figure 9 we see a zero for the ES of activity A. The early finish time is then ES + activity time, or 2 weeks for activity A. This *labels* activity A.

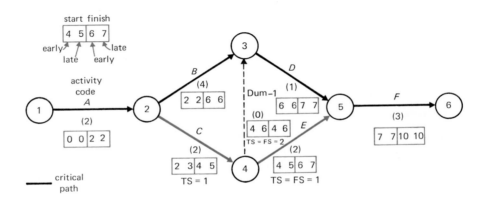

Figure 9. Network diagram for the market survey showing early and late start and finish times, and critical path. *TS* = total slack; *FS* = free slack

Step 2.   Consider any activity not yet labeled, all of whose predecessors have been labeled with their ES's and EF's. The ES for this activity is the *largest number* in the EF position of its immediate predecessors. That is to say, the earliest an activity can begin is the earliest that *all* of its predecessor activities are finished. The ES for activity B in Figure 9 is 2 weeks.

Step 3.   The EF for this activity is ES + activity time. For activity B, EF = 2 + 4 = 6 weeks.

Step 4.   Repeat steps 2 and 3 until the last activity is labeled. This label

NETWORK MODELS – SHORTEST PATH AND NETWORK SCHEDULING

is the *length* of the critical (longest) path in the network, and the total duration for the project.

In our simple example, the length of the critical path is 10 weeks, which is the minimum amount of time required to complete the market survey.

Latest Start and Finish Times   If we assume that the target for completing the market survey is the EF time of 10 weeks, then we have defined the latest finish time (LF) of 10 weeks, allowing no slack in the project as a whole. Therefore, the latest start time (LS) for the final activity is $LF -$ activity time. The procedure for computing LS and LF for the remaining activities is as follows:

Step 1.   Label the LF and LS values for the terminal activities as shown in Figure 9. For the market survey, $LF = 10$, and $LS = 7$ for activity F.

Step 2.   Consider any activity not yet labeled, all of whose successors have been labeled with these LS's and LF's. The LF for this activity is the *smallest number* in the LS position of its immediate successors. That is to say, the latest that an activity can be finished is the latest that *any* of its successors can start. The LF for activity E in Figure 9 is 7 weeks.

Step 3.   The LS for this activity is $LF -$ activity time. For activity E, $LS = 7 - 2 = 5$ weeks.

Step 4.   Repeat steps 2 and 3 until the initial activity is labeled.

Slack and Critical Path   Total slack (TS) for an activity is the maximum time that the activity can be delayed beyond its ES without delaying the project completion time. The critical activities are those that are in the sequence of the longest time path through the network, and therefore the activities on this path all have minimum possible TS. Since for our example the target date and the EF for activity F (the finish activity) are the same, all critical activities will have zero TS. The project target date may of course be later than the EF of the finish activity, in which case all activities on the critical path would have the same TS equal to the difference. Then all non-critical activities will have greater TS than critical activities.

Free slack (FS) is the amount of time that an activity can be delayed without delaying the ES of any other activity. Free slack for an activity never exceeds its TS. Free slack is computed as the difference between the EF for that activity and the earliest of the ES times of all of its immediate successors. For example, activity E has $FS = 1$, since the ES of its successor is 7 and its own EF is 6.

An Example   Network scheduling techniques are often applied to large-scale projects, such as the development of the Polaris missile or the construction of the Mexico City subway. However, they can also be used to analyze relatively simple operations, such as rebuilding a device known as a tool cutter-grinder. This latter example is realistic, yet simple enough to present in its entirety.

The first step is the activity analysis, which generates the activities required, the activity time requirements in days, and the technical precedence requirements to build a tool cutter-grinder, as shown in Table 6. The network corresponding to this activity analysis is then generated, and the critical path analysis is performed, as illustrated in Figure 10. For practical problems, these computations are actually performed by computer codes. The output from a computer code that has analyzed the tool cutter-grinder network is shown in Figure 10.

Extensions and Managerial Uses of Network Scheduling Techniques

There are numerous extensions of the network scheduling techniques that enhance their practical usefulness to managers. One important extension is the use of probabilistic time estimates. The time estimate for completing a particular activity may be uncertain, especially in research and development activities where there is no previous experience to use as a guide. Therefore, instead of a single time estimate for an activity, *three* time estimates are obtained. The three different time estimates are:

1. The *optimistic time, a,* is the shortest possible time in which the activity may be accomplished if all goes well. The estimate is based on the assumption that the activity would have no more than one chance in 100 of being completed in less than this time.

2. The *pessimistic time, b,* is the longest time that an activity could take under adverse conditions, barring acts of nature. This time estimate is based on the assumption that the activity would have no more than one chance in 100 of being completed in a time larger than b.

3. The *most likely time, m.*

These three time estimates are reduced to a single time estimate t_e, the *mean* of the implied probability distribution for the activity time. In addition, the *variance* of this distribution, σ^2, can also be estimated. The formulas are:

$$t_e = \frac{1}{6} (a + 4m + b), \tag{1}$$

$$\sigma^2 = \left[\frac{1}{6} (b - a) \right]^2. \tag{2}$$

The t_e estimates are then used in the computation of the critical path for a project exactly as before. However, the total time for the critical path is now interpreted as the *mean* estimate.

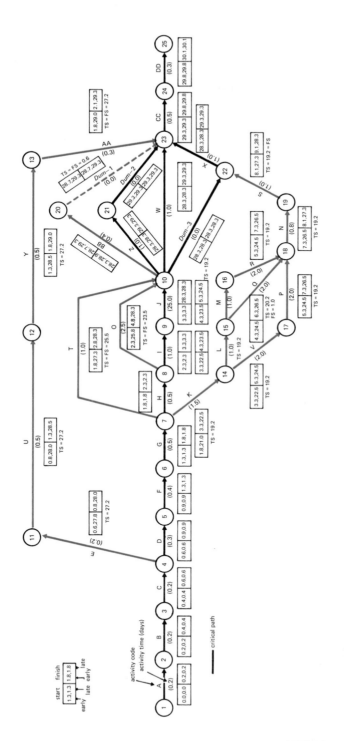

Figure 10. Arrow diagram for rebuilding Cincinnati No. 2 cutter-grinder showing early and late start and finish times, and critical path. TS = total slack; FS = free slack.

Adapted from R. D. Archibald and R. L. Villoria, *Network Based Management Systems*, John Wiley & Sons, New York, 1967.

TABLE 6. Rebuilding a Tool Cutter-Grinder

Activity Code	Description	Days Required	Immediate Predecessors
A	Disconnect and move	0.2	---
B	Connect power and pretest	0.2	A
C	Remove electrical units	0.2	B
D	Clean machine	0.3	C
E	Remove and disassemble mechanical units	0.2	C
F	Clean machine parts	0.4	D
G	List mechanical parts	0.5	F
H	Order machine parts	0.5	G
I	Receive machine parts	1.0	H
J	Paint cross slides	25.0	I
K	Machine parts	1.5	G
L	Inspect and list electrical parts	1.0	K
M	Paint motor	1.0	L
N	Assemble motor	0.8	P, Q, R
O	Machine saddle	2.5	H
P	Machine slides	2.0	V
Q	Machine table	2.0	L
R	Paint machine	2.0	M
S	Scrape slides	1.0	N
T	Scrape table	1.0	G
U	Scrape saddles	0.5	E
V	Machine gibs	2.0	K
W	Install spindle	1.0	J, O, T
X	Assemble parts	1.0	J, O, S, T
Y	Scrape gibs	0.5	U
Z	Assemble head	1.0	J, O, T
AA	Install motor and electrical parts	0.3	Y
BB	Assemble cross slides	0.4	J, O, T
CC	Connect power and test	0.5	AA, BB, Z, W, X
DD	Touch up, move, reinstall	0.3	CC

Source: data from R. D. Archibald and R. L. Villoria, *Network-Based Management Systems*, John Wiley & Sons, New York, 1967; used by permission.

When we add several random variables, the sum is also a random variable with a normal probability distribution, even if the random variables that are added are not normally distributed. The mean of this normal distribution is equal to the sum of the means of the individual random variables, and the variance is equal to the sum of the variances of the random variables. Therefore, the length of the critical path is the mean of a normal probability distribution whose variance is equal to the sum of the variances of the individual activites on the critical path.

Operation Code	i	j	Days Req'd.	Earliest Start	Earliest Finish	Latest Start	Latest Finish	Days Slack	Free Slack
A	1	2	.2	.0	.2	.0	.2	.0	**
B	2	3	.2	.2	.4	.2	.4	.0	**
C	3	4	.2	.4	.6	.4	.6	.0	**
D	4	5	.3	.6	.9	.6	.9	.0	**
E	4	11	.2	.6	.8	27.8	28.0	27.2	.0
F	5	6	.4	.9	1.3	.9	1.3	.0	**
G	6	7	.5	1.3	1.8	1.3	1.8	.0	**
H	7	8	.5	1.8	2.3	1.8	2.3	.0	**
I	8	9	1.0	2.3	3.3	2.3	3.3	.0	**
J	9	10	25.0	3.3	28.3	3.3	28.3	.0	**
K	7	14	1.5	1.8	3.3	21.0	22.5	19.2	.0
L	4	15	1.0	3.3	4.3	22.5	23.5	19.2	.0
M	15	16	1.0	4.3	5.3	23.5	24.5	19.2	.0
N	18	19	.8	7.3	8.1	26.5	27.3	19.2	.0
O	8	10	2.5	2.3	4.8	25.8	28.3	23.5	23.5
P	17	18	2.0	5.3	7.3	24.5	26.5	19.2	.0
Q	15	18	2.0	4.3	6.3	24.5	26.5	20.2	1.0
R	16	18	2.0	5.3	7.3	24.5	26.5	19.2	.0
S	19	22	1.0	8.1	9.1	27.3	28.3	19.2	19.2
T	7	10	1.0	1.8	2.8	27.3	28.3	25.5	25.5
U	11	12	.5	.8	1.3	28.0	28.5	27.2	.0
V	14	17	2.0	3.3	5.3	22.5	24.5	19.2	.0
W	10	23	1.0	28.3	29.3	28.3	29.3	.0	**
X	22	23	1.0	28.3	29.3	28.3	29.3	.0	**
Y	12	13	.5	1.3	1.8	28.5	29.0	27.2	.0
Z	10	21	1.0	28.3	29.3	28.3	29.3	.0	**
AA	13	23	.3	1.8	2.1	29.0	29.3	27.2	27.2
BB	10	20	.4	28.3	28.7	28.9	29.3	.6	.0
CC	23	24	.5	29.3	29.8	29.3	29.8	.0	**
DD	24	25	.3	29.8	30.1	29.8	30.1	.0	**
Dum-1	20	23	.0	28.7	28.7	29.3	29.3	.6	.6
Dum-2	21	23	.0	29.3	29.3	29.3	29.3	.0	**
Dum-3	10	22	.0	28.3	28.3	28.3	28.3	.0	**

**Critical Operations

Figure 11. Sample output of network analysis program for the tool cutter-grinder

Management can then compute the *probability* of completing the project in any specified length of time. For example, since the length of the critical path is only the mean of a normal probability distribution for the total project time, there is only a 50 percent chance that the project will actually be completed by this time. Management can plan, reschedule, or even renegotiate contracts on the basis of the expected outcomes and risk levels. Obviously, however, the output is no better than the input data, and there is a danger that the very existence of such precise probability statements will give an aura of accuracy that may not be justified.

The network schedule can also be used to study questions of time/cost trade-offs. In order to estimate the time required to complete an activity, assumptions regarding the level of manpower and the resources to be used must be made. In some cases, it may be advantageous to develop multiple time estimates for multiple levels of resource input. The critical path analysis could be performed with each activity by using a maximum of its resources. Then, for activities with slack, resources could be reduced, extending the time for the activity but not increasing the time for the network, as long as the time extension does not exceed the slack on the activity's path.

In some cases, even activities on the critical path may be extended when the cost savings exceed the costs of delaying the project completion. Computer algorithms are also available to perform such analyses. Managers may also wish to use the early start-late start information for activities not on the critical path to schedule their start in such a way as to smooth the manpower requirements over the total life of the project, or to make the most efficient use of other limited resources, such as special-purpose machinery.

Finally, the network schedule can be used for project control. Cost estimates can be developed for the activities and these data can be entered into computer programs along with the time estimates. As work on a project progresses, the actual cost and time figures can be compared with the estimates. Areas in which significant cost or time overruns are occurring can be identified easily, and managerial actions can be considered to overcome them. For example, if a time overrun is occurring on a network path that has a relatively large slack value, the manager may choose to do nothing. However, if the time overrun is on the critical path or on one with little slack, he may wish to take immediate action. These topics are treated in further detail at a managerial level in Weist and Levy [1969], while more technical issues are examined in Moder and Phillips [1970] and in Archibald and Villoria [1967].

WHAT SHOULD THE MANAGER KNOW?

The shortest path model may be viewed as a special case of the transshipment problem. In pure form, the most obvious application of the shortest path problem is to capital budgeting and equipment replacement problems. However, a modification of the shortest path algorithm may be applied to network representations of large-scale projects to determine the critical path in the network and other information of managerial significance. Therefore, we shall confine this discussion to the network scheduling techniques.

Problem Characteristics Network scheduling methods are advantageously applied to complex, large-scale projects. Generally, these are one-of-a-kind projects, so that previous plans and experience for completing this type of effort are not available. Among the successful applications that have been reported are the following cases:

1. construction of new homes, shopping centers, subways, etc. [Glasser and Young, 1961; O'Brian, 1965]
2. introduction of new products [Wong, 1964]
3. major maintenance efforts [Reeves, 1960]
4. pilot production runs [Odom and Blystone, 1964]
5. development of new weapon systems [Fazar, 1961]

Thus, any time the manager confronts a problem that is complex in that it requires the completion of several interrelated activities, is relatively large in terms of the resource requirements, and is nonroutine (no one in the organization has had significant experience in dealing with this type of problem previously), a network scheduling technique should be considered as a managerial aid.

Formulation The manager and all persons who will be responsible for some of the activities to be performed should be involved in formulating the initial network. Some experts claim that 90 percent of the benefits of the technique are obtained from this exercise. The activities must be identified and the interrelationships must be clarified. Responsibility for accomplishing each activity must be assigned to individuals, and the person responsible should be involved in determining how to conduct the activity and in estimating the time required for its completion. This involvement provides the participants with an overview of the entire project and an understanding of how their activities relate to others.

Computational Considerations Once the initial network has been formulated, it can be entered into the computer for analysis. Rather than providing the answer, the result of this analysis should be the basis for another round of planning with the managers involved in the project. Issues of trading off costs versus time and of manpower smoothing can be raised. Alternative solutions can be generated by moving activities from their early start to their late start times. Several computer runs would doubtless be required before the final plan is determined.

When the project is under way, the actual time and cost performances can be entered into the computer to compare against the initial estimates. Potentially, areas of cost or time overruns can be identified early, and managerial action can be taken.

Interpretation   The manager must be careful not to put too much reliance on the network. Just because the network terminates before the project due date does not mean that the actual project will. Thus, the manager must ensure that the data used in the analysis are an accurate portrayal of what is actually occurring in the project.

Disadvantages of the Network Scheduling Models   Network scheduling, especially for the control of a project, can be relatively costly. The costs of obtaining information and updating the network may not justify the benefits of the method in relatively small projects. As a rough rule of thumb, O'Brian [1965] suggests that computer network scheduling techniques are probably not justified on projects involving costs of $100,000 or less and should be questioned on projects even up to $500,000 in costs. However, the hand calculations for these networks are so straightforward that smaller projects can be organized with a simple analysis and "back of the envelope" calculations.

Even if computer network scheduling and control techniques are not used, the manager should always consider an initial planning session devoted to the construction of a network. Again, much of the value of a management science model is not in the solution it provides, but in the knowledge gained in the process of its formulation.

Check Your Understanding

1. Distinguish between an acyclic and a cyclic network. Give a real-world example of a problem in which each might be encountered.

2. In applying the steps to find the shortest path in an acyclic network, why do we begin at the *terminal* node rather than the *beginning* node?

3. At node 3 in Figure 3, what is the length of the shortest path from node 3 to node 8? How does this length relate to the label value on node 3? Answer the same question for node 2. See if you can use this insight to summarize the logic of the solution strategy in one or two sentences.

4. Apply the four-step procedure for solving shortest path problems to the network shown in Figure 4, labeling the nodes. Interpret the results.

5. What is an "event" in a project? How does it relate to an "activity"?

6. What is the function of a "dummy" activity?

7. What is the managerial significance of information regarding the "slack" associated with an activity? How might this information be used?

8. What is the "critical path"? What is its managerial significance?

9. What is the difference between "free slack" and "total slack" for an activity? What is its managerial significance?

10. Suppose that the target for completing the market survey shown in Figure 9 is twelve weeks, so that the late finish time (LF) for the terminal activity F is 12. Compute the revised late start and late finish times for the activities. Also compute the revised total slack and free slack for each activity.

11. The following comment was heard in industry: "Every time the PERT chart is revised, the management sends a bunch of supervisors to check on the activities on the critical path. When they ask us for time estimates for our activity, we always revise our actual estimates to ensure that our activity won't be on the critical path. We don't want a bunch of supervisors hanging around!" What are the implications of this comment for the proper use of network scheduling techniques in real-world situations?

12. Suppose the critical path of a project was determined by using probabilistic time estimates. The mean length of the critical path is 12 days, and the variance (determined by summing the variance of each activity on the critical path) is 4 days. Thus, the standard deviation associated with the critical path is $\sqrt{4} = 2$ days. Using the area under the standardized normal curve in Table 1 of Appendix E, compute the probability that the project will actually be completed in 10 days, 12 days, 14 days, 16 days.

13. Describe how the network schedule may be used to accomplish each of the following:
    a. a time/cost trade-off analysis
    b. a resource scheduling and allocation analysis
    c. cost control

Problems

1. Find the shortest path in the acyclic network shown in Figure 12 by labeling all of the nodes in the manner illustrated in Figures 2 and 3.

2. Suppose the company considering the purchase of a new piece of equipment applies a 15 percent discount factor to the costs shown in Tables 2, 3, and 4.

   The results for purchasing at the beginning of the year 1 are as follows:

	Keep Until End of Year:				
	1	2	3	4	5
Net discounted cost	$121.79	$189.78	$279.37	$366.56	$445.48

For purchasing at the beginning of year 2:

	Keep Until End of Year:			
	2	3	4	5
Net discounted cost	$105.86	$165.03	$242.92	$318.74

For purchasing at the beginning of years 3, 4, and 5:

	Purchase at Beginning of Year:					
	Year 3			Year 4		Year 5
	Keep Until End of Year:					
	3	4	5	4	5	5
Net discounted cost	$129.85	$181.31	$249.05	$112.92	$157.66	$98.19

Using the four-step strategy for finding the shortest path in an acyclic network, find the optimum equipment replacement policy for this company, using these discounted costs. Does the solution change when the costs are discounted? Is this surprising? Why or why not?

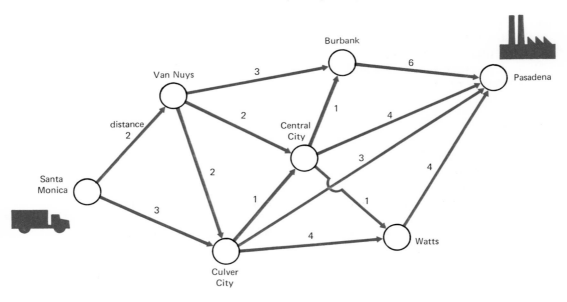

Figure 12. Alternative paths in an acyclic network (problem 1)

3. The South Bay Company must purchase a new truck to haul heavy rocks from a large construction site. The truck will only be used for four years. The cost of the truck is $20,000 now, but it is estimated that the cost will jump to $22,000 after two more years. The operating costs and salvage values are shown below:

Number of Years Used	Salvage Value at End of Year	Annual Operating Costs
1	$15,000	$1,000
2	10,000	2,000
3	8,000	4,000
4	7,000	8,000

a. Set up tables similar to Tables 2, 3 and 4 to estimate the net cost of purchasing a truck at the beginning of each year.
b. Using the shortest path approach, determine the optimum purchasing plan for this truck.

4. A small maintenance project consists of ten jobs, whose precedence relationships are identified by their node numbers as shown in Table 7.
a. Draw an arrow diagram representing the project.

TABLE 7. Jobs for a Small Maintenance Project

Job	Network Description (initial node, final node)	Estimated Duration (days)
a	(1, 2)	2
b	(2, 3)	3
c	(2, 4)	5
d	(3, 5)	4
e	(3, 6)	1
f	(4, 6)	6
g	(4, 7)	2
h	(5, 8)	8
i	(6, 8)	7
j	(7, 8)	4

b. Calculate early and late start and finish times for each job.
c. How much total slack does job d have? Job f? Job j?
d. Which jobs are critical?
e. If job b were to take six days instead of three, how would the project finish date be affected?

5. An architect has been awarded a contract to prepare plans and specifications for an urban renewal project. The job consists of the following
activities and their estimated times.

Activity	Description	Immediate Predecessors	Time (days)
a	Preliminary sketches	---	2
b	Outline of specifications	---	1
c	Prepare drawings	a	3
d	Write specifications	a, b	2
e	Run off prints	c, d	1
f	Have specifications printed	c, d	3
g	Assemble bid packages	e, f	1

a. Draw an arrow diagram for this job, indicate the critical path and calculate the total slack and free slack for each activity.
b. During the first day of work it is learned that activity c (Prepare draw-
ings) will take 4 days instead of 3. What effect does this delay have on
the project completion date and project management?

6. The following tasks are required for the production of a play:

Activity	Description	Immediate Predecessors	Time (weeks)
a	Play selection	---	3
b	Casting	a	4
c	Costume design	a	3
d	Set design	a	2
e	Set construction	d	4
f	Rehearsals	b	3
g	Dress rehearsals	c, e, f	2
h	Printing tickets and programs	b	6

a. Draw the arrow diagram for this play.
b. Calculate the early and late start and finish times for each activity, and
the total slack and free slack for each activity.
c. Indicate the critical path.

7. Consider the project network shown in Figure 13.
a. Supply the information indicated in the following table:

Activity	Network Description (initial node, terminal node)	Time (weeks)	ES	EF	LS	LF	TS	FS
a	(1, 2)	2						
b	(1, 3)	3						
c	(2, 4)	4						
d	(3, 4)	1						
e	(4, 5)	3						
f	(4, 6)	2						
g	(5, 6)	0						
h	(5, 7)	3						
i	(6, 7)	1						
j	(7, 8)	2						

b. If activities *e* and *f* both require the use of a special piece of equipment (i.e., cannot be performed at the same time), what adjustment would you make? In particular, how would the project duration be affected?

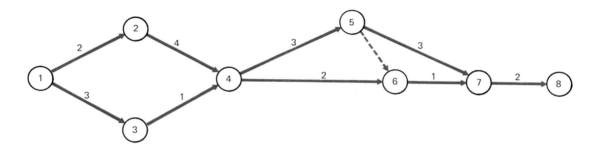

Figure 13. Project network (problem 7)

8. An established company has decided to add a new product to its line. It will buy the product from a manufacturing concern, package it, and sell it to a number of distributors selected on a geographical basis. Market research has indicated the volume expected and size of sales force required. The steps shown in Table 8 are to be planned. The precedence relationships among these activities are shown in Figure 14. As the figure shows, the company can begin to organize the sales office, design the package, and order the stock immediately. Also, the stock must be ordered and the packaging facility must be set up before the initial stocks are packaged.
   a. Draw the arrow diagram for this project.
   b. Calculate the early and late start and finish times for each activity, and the total and free slack for each activity.
   c. Indicate the critical path.

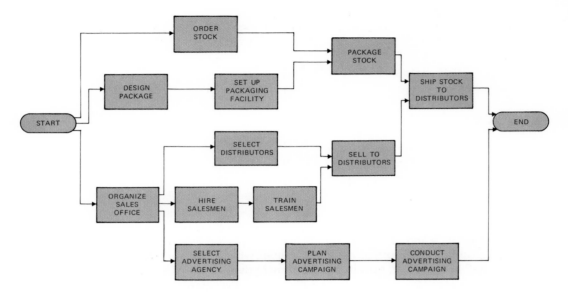

Figure 14. New product introduction—precedence diagram

TABLE 8. Planning Activities for New Product Introduction

Activity	Description	Time (weeks)
a	Organize Sales Office	6
b	Hire Salesmen	4
c	Train Salesmen	7
d	Select Advertising Agency	2
e	Plan Advertising Campaign	4
f	Conduct Advertising Campaign	10
g	Design Package	2
h	Set Up Packaging Facilities	10
i	Package Initial Stocks	6
j	Order Stock from Manufacturer	13
k	Select Distributors	9
l	Sell to Distributors	3
m	Ship Stock	5

9. Probabilistic time estimates have been obtained for the activities in the simple project network shown in Figure 15.

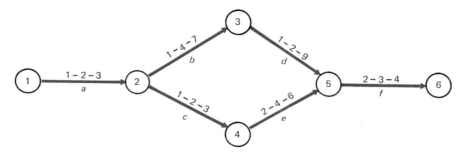

Figure 15. Project network (problem 9)

For example, the estimate of the "optimistic time," a, for job a is 1; the estimate of the "most likely time," m, for job a is 2; and the estimate of the "pessimistic time," b, for job a is 3. Using the formulas (1) and (2), calculate the mean and variance for each activity time.

b. Using the mean values, determine the critical path and its mean duration.

c. Sum the variances of the times of the activities on the critical path to obtain the variance associated with the mean duration of the project.

d. Using the area under the standardized normal curve in Table 1 of Appendix E, compute the probability that the project will actually be completed in 10 days, 12 days, 14 days, 16 days.

e. A penalty cost of $50,000 must be paid if the project is not completed in 12 days. For an additional cost of $20,000, the management can guarantee that activity d can be completed in exactly 1 day. Should they pay the $20,000 for sure, or accept the risk regarding the penalty cost? Use the expected monetary value evaluative model as a guide to your recommendation.

10. For the network shown in Figure 16, determine the critical path and the probability of finishing the project in less than 32 time periods. The optimistic, most likely, and pessimistic time estimates are shown above each activity.

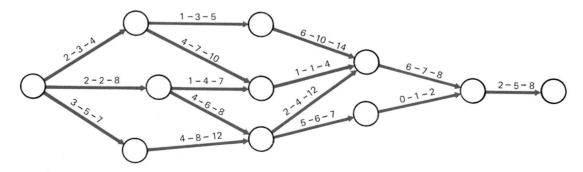

Figure 16. Project network (problem 10)

11. Miller Manufacturing Company is engaged in the small project shown in Figure 17.

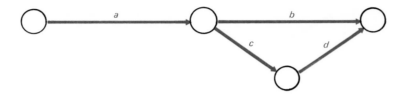

Figure 17. Project network (problem 11)

The times required to accomplish each activity depend on the level of resources allocated to it. For example, activity a can be accomplished in 3 days with a normal allocation of resources. However, for an additional $400 worth of resources, the time can be reduced to 2 days, and for another allocation of $400 worth of resources, it can be cut to 1 day. No further reductions are possible. Similar reductions in time are possible for the other activities. The data for each activity are as follows:

Activity	Minimum Time (days)	Normal Time (days)	Cost to Reduce Time by 1 Day
a	1	3	$400
b	3	7	100
c	2	4	400
d	2	5	200

a. What is the normal project duration and the minimum project duration?
b. Overhead costs of $450 per day are incurred for every day the project is not completed. What is the optimum duration of the project considering both overhead costs and the costs to reduce the time on each activity?

12. A small maintenance project consists of the jobs in the following table. With each job is listed its normal time and a minimum time (in days). The cost in dollars per day of reducing the time for each job is also given.

Job	Network Description (initial node, terminal node)	Minimum Time (days)	Normal Time (days)	Cost to Reduce Time by 1 Day
a	(1, 2)	6	9	$20
b	(1, 3)	5	8	25
c	(1, 4)	10	15	30
d	(2, 4)	3	5	10
e	(3, 4)	6	9	15
f	(4, 5)	1	2	40

a. What is the normal project duration and the minimum project duration?

b. Overhead costs are $50 per day. What is the optimum length schedule in terms of both time reduction and overhead costs? List the scheduled durations for each job for your solution.

References

Archibald, R., and R. Villoria, *Network-Based Management Systems*, John Wiley & Sons, New York, 1967.

Fazar, W., "Navy's PERT System," *Federal Accountant*, Vol. 11, December 1961.

Glasser, L., and R. Young, "Critical Path Planning and Scheduling: Application to Engineering and Construction," *Chemical Engineering Progress*, Vol. 57, November 1961.

Levy, F., G. Thompson, and J. Wiest, "The ABC's of the Critical Path Method," *Harvard Business Review*, Vol. 41, No. 5, October 1963.

Moder, J., and C. Phillips, *Project Management with CPM and PERT*, second edition, Reinhold Corporation, New York, 1970.

O'Brian, J., *CPM in Construction Management*, McGraw-Hill, New York, 1965.

Odom, R., and E. Blystone, "A Case Study of CPM in a Manufacturing Situation," *Journal of Industrial Engineering*, Vol. 15, No. 6, November–December 1964.

Paige, H. W., "How PERT-Cost Helps the General Manager," *Harvard Business Review*, Vol. 40, No. 2, March–April 1962.

Reeves, E., "Critical Path Speeds Refinery Revamp," *Canadian Chemical Processing*, Vol. 44, October 1960.

Weist, J., and F. Levy, *A Management Guide to PERT/CPM*, Prentice-Hall, Englewood Cliffs, N.J., 1969.

Wong, Y., "Critical Path Analysis for New Product Planning," *Journal of Marketing*, Vol. 28, No. 4, October 1964.

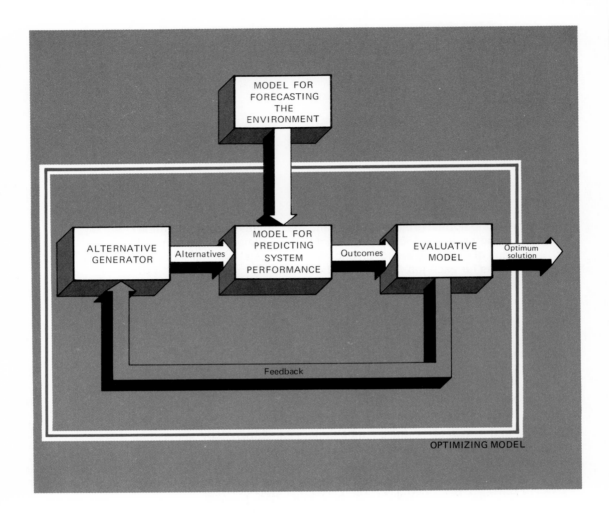

17

Optimizing Models With Integer Variables

The solution to the two-product linear optimization model in Chapter 13 indicated that 10 units of chemical x and 15 units of chemical y should be produced. This is an integer solution; that is, the solution values have no fractional components. In our formulation of this two-product linear optimization model, we did not require that the solution should be in integer values; it happened by chance. In this example, obtaining an integer-valued solution may not have been particularly important. It might be possible to produce 10.5 units of chemical x during each time period, so that a total of 21 units would be produced over two time periods. However, in some real-world problems, it will be desirable, perhaps even necessary, to obtain integer-valued solutions.

Solutions obtained from linear programming are not always integer valued, and the strategy of "rounding off" the linear programming solution may not provide the optimal integer solution. Glover and Sommers [1975] describe examples of real-world problems for which the strategy of rounding the linear programming solution cannot even be used to find a *feasible* integer solution.

The network models of the previous chapters have natural integer solutions that are obtained automatically by the solution techniques. If the supplies and demands and the upper and lower bounds on the flows in the network are originally stated as integers, an integer solution will result. However, it is not possible to use network models for all analyses, so special modeling strategies and solution algorithms have been developed.

This chapter discusses optimizing models with integer values. These models are generally formulated in the same format as linear optimization models, with the additional constraint that some or all of the decision variables must be integer valued in the final solution. Several examples of such models will be presented first, then a solution strategy for these models will be discussed. The section on solution strategies may be omitted by readers primarily interested in model formulation and interpretation.

EXAMPLES OF MODELS WITH INTEGER VARIABLES

There are two important types of integer variables that appear in optimizing models. The first, integer decision variables, simply represents the number of units of a product, a machine, or of some other resource that should be produced or allocated, much like the ordinary decision variables in linear optimization models. The second type of integer variable is a *logical* variable that allows the optimizing model to evaluate mutually exclusive alternative decisions and to analyze various combinatorial problems. An example of a combinatorial problem is the selection of three of ten alternative sites for new warehouses.

Integer Decision Variables

Integer decision variables may simply be the number of units of a particular product that are produced or the number of pieces of equipment that are purchased. The problem formulations would be identical to linear optimization models with one exception; instead of nonnegativity requirements for the variables in the form $x \geq 0$, integer requirements would be written in the form $x = 1, 2, 3, \ldots$.

If all of the variables in the model are required to have integer values, the formulation is called an *integer programming* model. If some of the variables are required to be integer while others can have any nonnegative values as in an ordinary linear optimization model, the problem is termed a *mixed integer programming* model.

Variables that are required to have integer values often represent expensive resources. For example, a company planning a product distribution system will not consider a solution requiring them to build 3.5 warehouses to be particularly meaningful. Similarly, an oil company may wish to purchase either 4 or 5 supertankers, but not 4.3 supertankers. In some cases, a linear programming problem can be solved by ignoring the integer restrictions, and the variables that are required to have integer values can be "rounded off" to the nearest integer solution. This procedure may or may not give the best integer solution that can actually be obtained. When significant costs or other resources are involved, the additional computational burden generally associated with integer programming models may be justified in order to find the best integer solution.

Example of an Integer Programming Formulation The objective of the two-product model of Chapter 13 was to determine the number of units of chemical x and of chemical y to be produced over a two-week period. Suppose that, at the end of the two-week period, new products must be produced. Any unfinished units of chemical x or chemical y cannot be completed and must be destroyed since there are no adequate storage facilities. Therefore, the problem is to determine the number of *integer valued* units of chemical x and chemical y to be produced.

Using the data from Chapter 13, the problem would be formulated as

maximize $Z = 60x + 50y$,

subject to

$2x + 4y \leq 80$,	(machine A)
$3x + 2y \leq 60$,	(machine B)
$x \quad\quad \leq 16$,	(demand for chemical x)
$\quad\quad y \leq 18$,	(demand for chemical y)
$x \quad\quad = 0, 1, 2, \ldots,$	(integer value for chemical x)
$\quad\quad y = 0, 1, 2, \ldots$	(integer value for chemical y)

This integer programming problem formulation is identical to the linear programming problem formulation of Chapter 13 except that the integer valued restrictions $x = 0, 1, 2, \ldots$ and $y = 0, 1, 2, \ldots$ have replaced the nonnegativity constraints $x \geq 0$ and $y \geq 0$.

Notice that the integer requirements are more *restrictive* than the nonnegativity requirements, since the nonnegativity requirements allow the decision variables to assume both integer and noninteger values. Thus, this integer programming formulation is called a *restriction* of the linear programming formulation. Likewise, the linear programming formulation is called a *relaxation* of the integer programming formulation since its constraint set includes all of the feasible solutions to the integer programming problem and other solutions as well. These concepts will be important in understanding the solution strategy for integer programming problems.

Example of a Mixed Integer Programming Formulation The machines that provide radiology services in a hospital are expensive to purchase and operate. Suppose a hospital is attempting to determine the number of machines of each type to purchase for a radiology department. The department provides two services, X-rays and radiation therapy.

There are four different machines that the hospital could use. Two of these machines can be used for normal X-rays only, one for radiation therapy only, and the other for either X-rays or radiation therapy. The average daily costs for each machine, that include both depreciation and operating costs, are shown in Table 1. Also shown in Table 1 are the estimates of the average time required to provide each service on each machine. The hospital estimates that each machine is available for only 5 hours of productive work each day because of maintenance requirements and other interruptions.

TABLE 1. Costs and Times for the Machines

	Machines			
	X-ray Only (1)	X-ray Only (2)	X-ray and Radiation (3)	Radiation Only (4)
Cost per day ($)	200	300	350	250
Time per X-ray (hr)	0.50	0.25	0.50	---
Time per radiation (hr)	---	---	0.75	0.50

The average daily demand for the services is relatively constant at 30 for normal X-rays and at 20 for radiation therapy treatments. If these services are not provided in the hospital, they can be purchased externally at a cost to the hospital of $20 for each X-ray and $40 for each radiation therapy treatment.

The problem is to minimize the total cost to the hospital of operating the machines plus any charges for outside services. Suppose we define *MACH1*, *MACH2*, *MACH3*, and *MACH4* as the number of machines of type 1, type 2, type 3, and type 4 respectively that are purchased. Then the daily cost of operating the machines will be given by

$$200 \; MACH1 + 300 \; MACH2 + 350 \; MACH3 + 250 \; MACH4 \, .$$

Letting *XEXT* be the number of X-rays performed externally, and *REXT* be the number of radiation therapy treatments purchased externally, the cost of these external purchases will be

$$20 \; XEXT + 40 \; REXT \, .$$

Therefore, the objective function for the optimizing model for this problem would be

$$\begin{aligned} \text{minimize } Z = {} & 200 \; MACH1 + 300 \; MACH2 + 350 \; MACH3 + \\ & 250 \; MACH4 + 20 \; XEXT + 40 \; REXT \, . \end{aligned} \tag{1}$$

The constraints require that we define some additional decision variables. Let *XMACH1*, *XMACH2*, *XMACH3* be the number of X-rays performed on machines of type 1, type 2, and type 3 respectively. Likewise, *RMACH3* and *RMACH4* are the number of radiation therapy treatments performed on the type 3 and type 4 machines. Now, since each X-ray on a machine of type 1 takes 0.5 hours, and each machine of type 1 is productive for only 5 hours per day, we must have

$$0.5 \; XMACH1 \leq 5 \; MACH1 \, , \qquad \qquad \text{(type 1)} \quad (2)$$

since *MACH1* is the number of machines of type 1 that are available. Similarly, we have for the other three machines,

$$0.25 \; XMACH2 \leq 5 \; MACH2 \,, \qquad\qquad \text{(type 2)} \quad (3)$$

$$0.5 \; XMACH3 + 0.75 \; RMACH3 \leq 5 \; MACH3 \,, \qquad \text{(type 3)} \quad (4)$$

$$0.5 \; RMACH4 \leq 5 \; MACH4 \qquad\qquad\qquad \text{(type 4)} \quad (5)$$

In order to meet the daily demand of 30 X-rays, we require

$$XMACH1 + XMACH2 + XMACH3 + XEXT = 30 \,, \qquad (6)$$

and for the radiation therapy treatment demand,

$$RMACH3 + RMACH4 + REXT = 20 \,. \qquad (7)$$

Finally, suppose that space availabilities limit the total number of machines that can be used to a maximum of 7, and the number of machines of type 1 (which is especially cumbersome) to 2. Then we would need the constraints

$$MACH1 + MACH2 + MACH3 + MACH4 \leq 7 \qquad (8)$$

and

$$MACH1 \leq 2 \,. \qquad (9)$$

Using these relationships, we could now write down a formulation of a linear optimization model to solve this problem *if* noninteger values for the decision variables are acceptable solutions. In this problem, that seems unlikely. We need to know how many machines of each type to purchase, and a solution with $MACH1 = 1.5$ would be of limited usefulness. Thus, it seems clear that we should restrict the variables $MACH1$, $MACH2$, $MACH3$, and $MACH4$ to integer values.

What about the other variables? Again, we cannot perform half of an X-ray or provide a fractional radiation treatment during a day. Therefore, it would seem that the variables corresponding to the number of treatments provided on each machine should be integer valued also. But, is this really necessary?

The answer to this question is a matter of judgment. This example shows why we argue that the manager should be involved in model formulation. What is the true purpose of this model? If it is to provide guidance regarding the number of machines of each type to purchase, then it may not be necessary to require the treatment variables to be integer valued. After all, each X-ray treatment *averages* 0.5 hours on machine 1, and machine 1 is available approximately 5 hours per day. Thus, if the model sets $XMACH1 = 8.5$, we could interpret this to mean that *about* 8.5 X-rays will be performed on machine 1 each day, with more on some days and less on others. The issue of integer values for these variables does not seem to be critical for the assumed purpose of the model. On the other hand, if we were developing a model to assist in actually *scheduling* treatments, then we would require the treatment variables to be integer valued.

It is important *not* to require integer values for variables unless it is critical for the use of the model, because such a requirement introduces additional computational difficulties in the solution algorithm. If problems have a large number of integer variables, it may be impractical to actually solve them even with the most sophisticated computers and algorithms.

In the standard format for the constraints to a linear or integer programming model, all of the decision variables are written to the left of the equality or inequality sign, so that only a constant appears to the right. Therefore, we transpose a decision variable in each of constraints (2)–(5), and state the *mixed integer* programming problem as follows:

minimize $Z = 200\ MACH1 + 300\ MACH2 + 350\ MACH3 +$
$\qquad\qquad 250\ MACH4 + 20\ XEXT + 40\ REXT$

subject to

$0.5\ XMACH1 - 5\ MACH1 \le 0,$
$0.25\ XMACH2 - 5\ MACH2 \le 0,$
$0.5\ XMACH3 + 0.75\ RMACH3 - 5\ MACH3 \le 0,$ (capacity restrictions)
$0.5\ RMACH4 - 5\ MACH4 \le 0,$

$XMACH1 + XMACH2 + XMACH3 + XEXT = 30,$ (demand
$RMACH3 + RMACH4 + REXT = 20,$ restrictions)

$MACH1 + MACH2 + MACH3 + MACH4 \le 7,$ (space
$MACH1 \le 2,$ restrictions)

$XMACH1, XMACH2, XMACH3, XEXT \ge 0,$ (nonnegativity
$RMACH3, RMACH4, REXT \ge 0,$ restrictions)

$MACH1, MACH2, MACH3, MACH4 = 0, 1, 2, \ldots$ (integer-value restrictions)

This model is a simple version of a more complex mixed integer model developed by Vora [1974] to actually plan the facilities for a diagnostic radiology department of a short-term general hospital in upstate New York.

Logical Integer Variables

Perhaps the most important use of integer variables in optimizing models is as logical variables. As such, the integer variables generally indicate "yes" or "no" decisions rather than the number of units used or produced.

Capital Budgeting   The simplest example is a capital budgeting problem in which we have several alternative investments. We can define integer variables restricted to 0 or 1 (simply called 0–1 variables) and corresponding to each alternative. If the optimal value for the variable corresponding to an alternative is 0, the investment is not accepted; if the value is 1, it is accepted.

For example, suppose we have the investment opportunities shown in Table 2 and a total available budget of 22 units. We can let x_1, x_2, and x_3 be defined as 0–1 variables corresponding to investment opportunities 1, 2, and 3 respectively. With the expected return values from Table 2, the objective function for the optimizing model for this problem would be

$$\text{maximize } Z = 20x_1 + 30x_2 + 15x_3 . \tag{10}$$

If the proposed solution values of the variables are $x_1 = x_2 = 1$ and $x_3 = 0$, then investments 1 and 2 should be accepted and investment 3 should be rejected. The value of the objective function (10) would be $(20)(1) + (30)(1) + (15)(0) = 50$, the total expected return from accepting opportunities 1 and 2.

TABLE 2.
Investment Opportunities

Investment Opportunity	Expected Return	Cost
1	20	10
2	30	20
3	15	12

The constraint on the budget is incorporated into the model by using the cost data from Table 2,

$$10x_1 + 20x_2 + 12x_3 \leq 22 . \tag{11}$$

Also required is the integer-value restriction on the variables,

$$x_1, x_2, x_3 = 0, 1 . \tag{12}$$

Notice that the solution $x_1 = x_2 = 1$ and $x_3 = 0$ does not satisfy the budget constraint (11), so it is not a feasible solution. Similarly, the integer solution $x_1 = 0$, $x_2 = x_3 = 1$ does not satisfy (11). However, the solution $x_1 = x_3 = 1$, $x_2 = 0$ is feasible, and the corresponding value of the objective function (10) is larger than for any other feasible integer solution. (Convince yourself of this.) Therefore, the optimal feasible solution is to accept investment opportunities 1 and 3 and to reject opportunity 2. Although this solution is obvious from a careful analysis of the data in Table 2, much more complex problems that do not have obvious solutions can be formulated in a similar manner.

Additional logical complexity can be introduced into this problem through the use of the appropriate constraints. *Either/or* decisions can be enforced very simply. For example, suppose investment opportunities 2 and 3 in Table 2 are mutually exclusive. That is, we could invest in *either* opportunity 2 *or* opportunity 3, but not in both. This logic could be incorporated into our formulation of the problem [(10), (11), (12)] by adding the constraint

$$x_2 + x_3 \leq 1 . \tag{13}$$

Notice, if $x_2 = 1$, then x_3 must equal 0 to satisfy this inequality, and vice versa. Of course, both x_2 and x_3 could equal 0. We could *require* that one or the other of the opportunities be accepted by changing the inequality sign in (13) to an equality.

A slightly more complex example of logic that can be imposed through constraints on 0–1 variables is the *if-then* requirement. Suppose we require that investment opportunity 1 be accepted *if* opportunity 3 is accepted; that is, if we accept opportunity 3, *then* we must accept opportunity 1. We can impose this restriction through the constraint

$$x_3 - x_1 \leq 0 .$$

If $x_3 = 0$, then x_1 can be either 0 or 1; however, *if* $x_3 = 1$, signifying that x_3 is accepted, *then* x_1 must equal 1 in order to satisfy this constraint.

Using similar reasoning, many other logical interdependencies can be represented by constraints on 0–1 variables.

The Fixed-Charge Problem Several real-world problems require that certain continuous variables either be set equal to 0 or that they be greater than some number N. For example, a variable x may represent the capacity of a warehouse, and we may require that either the warehouse not be built at all (in which case $x = 0$), or that the capacity be larger than some minimum value ($x \geq N$). Similarly, if x represents the number of units of a product produced during a particular time period, we may require either $x = 0$ or $x \geq N$ to ensure a minimum "lot size" for production.

This type of restriction can be imposed by introducing a 0–1 variable, y, and an arbitrarily large number M, and writing the constraints

$$x - My \leq 0 \tag{14}$$

and

$$x - Ny \geq 0 , \tag{15}$$

where $N \leq M$, and M is selected so that x will be less than M for any feasible solution to the original problem. If $y = 0$ in the optimal solution, (14) constrains $x \leq 0$, but if $y = 1$, then (15) requires $x \geq N$, as we have stipulated. Notice that the only purpose of introducing the 0–1 variable y into this problem is to enforce this restriction; y has no other meaning in the problem.

To illustrate this concept, suppose x is defined as the capacity of a proposed warehouse. Because of company policy and other considerations, we require that either $x = 0$ or $x \geq 200$ units. From an analysis of other information, including the product demand, it is clear that the largest feasible value of x will be less than 1000 units. We impose this minimum capacity restriction by introducing the 0–1 variable y, and the constraints

$$x - 1000y \leq 0$$

and

$$x - 200y \geq 0 .$$

Facility Location   An important example of a real-world problem common to many organizations is the facility location problem. We can illustrate this problem by modifying the data for the transportation problem (introductory example) of Chapter 15. Suppose we currently have two facilities in operation and are trying to decide where to locate a third facility. The weekly capacities for the existing and proposed facilities are as follows:

Factory	Supply (units/week)
1	50
2	70
3 (proposed)	20
4 (proposed)	20

Factories 1 and 2 are currently in operation, while factories 3 and 4 represent new facilities at different locations, only one of which will actually be constructed. The projected weekly demand at each retail outlet is given below.

Outlet	Demand (units/week)
1	50
2	60
3	30

The costs for shipping follow, with estimates for the proposed factories 3 and 4.

| | Outlet | | |
Factory	1	2	3
1	3	2	3
2	10	5	8
3 (proposed)	1	3	10
4 (proposed)	4	5	3

Further, the estimated weekly cost of operating the proposed factory 3, including depreciation, is 100, while the estimated operating cost of factory 4 is 120. Which of the two proposed plants should be constructed?

In this simple example, the most obvious and efficient solution strategy would be to solve the problem by using the specialized network code for the distribution problem, assuming factory 3 had been built (ignoring factory 4), then solve again, assuming factory 4 had been built (ignoring factory 3). The transportation costs in each case should be compared to the operating costs of the new facility, and the better alternative could be identified.

In real-world problems, the number of feasible alternatives often increases to the point that it is impractical to solve individual problems for each alternative. In such cases, integer programming is the appropriate solution strategy, so it will be worthwhile to study the integer programming formulation of this problem.

We must introduce two logical, 0-1 variables, y_3 and y_4, such that $y_3 = 1$ indicates factory 3 should be built, while $y_3 = 0$ indicates that it should not be built. A similar interpretation holds for y_4.

Thus, the objective function for this problem would be (refer to Chapter 15 for additional details):

minimize $Z =$

$$
\begin{array}{ll}
3x_{11} + \quad 2x_{12} + \quad 3x_{13} & \text{(total cost of shipping from factory 1)} \\
+ \quad 10x_{21} + \quad 5x_{22} + \quad 8x_{23} & \text{(total cost of shipping from factory 2)} \\
+ \quad x_{31} + \quad 3x_{32} + 10x_{33} & \text{(total cost of shipping from factory 3)} \\
+ \quad 4x_{41} + \quad 5x_{42} + \quad 3x_{43} & \text{(total cost of shipping from factory 4)} \\
+ 100y_3 + 120y_4 . & \text{(operating costs of factories 3 and 4)} \quad (16)
\end{array}
$$

The operating costs for factory 3 or factory 4 will be incurred if $y_3 = 1$ or $y_4 = 1$.

The supply constraints for factories 1 and 2 will be identical to the original formulation of this problem; that is,

$$x_{11} + x_{12} + x_{13} \leq 50 , \tag{17}$$

$$x_{21} + x_{22} + x_{23} \leq 70 . \tag{18}$$

The demand constraints will be modified by the addition of variables representing potential supply from factories 3 and 4, so we have

$$x_{11} + x_{21} + x_{31} + x_{41} = 50 , \tag{19}$$

$$x_{12} + x_{22} + x_{32} + x_{42} = 60 , \tag{20}$$

$$x_{13} + x_{23} + x_{33} + x_{43} = 30 . \tag{21}$$

The only significant change is in the supply constraints for the proposed facilities, 3 and 4.

If facility 3 is built, it can supply 20 units, and $y_3 = 1$; otherwise, if $y_3 = 0$, its supply must equal 0 also. This restriction can be incorporated easily by writing

$$x_{31} + x_{32} + x_{33} \leq 20y_3 . \tag{22}$$

If $y_3 = 1$, the right hand side of this inequality is 20; otherwise, it is 0 as desired. Similarly, we would write

$$x_{41} + x_{42} + x_{43} \leq 20y_4 \tag{23}$$

for factory 4.

We might wish to ensure that only factory 3 or factory 4 will be included in the final solution. This restriction could be imposed by the additional constraint

$$y_3 + y_4 \leq 1 . \tag{24}$$

The solution to this *mixed integer* programming model, (16) through (24), nonnegativity restrictions on the x_{ij} variables, and 0–1 integer restrictions on y_3 and y_4, would yield the optimum solution in terms of the best distribution policy *and* the appropriate new factory to open.

THE DESIGN OF A DISTRIBUTION SYSTEM WITH A MIXED INTEGER OPTIMIZATION MODEL

Geoffrion [1976] presents a case study of an application of a mixed integer optimization model to the analysis and design of the distribution system for Hunt-Wesson Foods. We shall briefly summarize this study; however, the article is written for managers and is highly recommended as supplemental reading.

At the beginning of the study, Hunt-Wesson Foods produced several hundred products at 14 locations and distributed nationally through 12 distribution centers. Annual sales were in the neighborhood of $450 million. Transportation was by rail and by truck carriers. The firm's policy was to service each customer from a single distribution center for all products. This policy was intended to simplify operations for the firm and to be convenient for the customer.

The questions to be answered by the study included the following:

- How many distribution centers should there be?
- In which cities should they be located?
- What size should each distribution center be, and which products should it carry?
- Which distribution center(s) or plant(s) should service each customer?
- How should each plant's output of each product be allocated among distribution centers or customers?
- What should the annual transportation flows be throughout the system?
- For a given level of customer service, what is the breakdown of total annual cost for the best distribution system as compared with a projection of the current system to the target period?

Obviously, there were numerous restrictions and constraints that had to be imposed on the problem. Examples include:

- No plant can produce above its stipulated production capacity for each product.
- The size of each open distribution center must be within a prescribed range.
- Each customer must be served by a single distribution center for all products.
- A distribution center can be assigned to serve a customer only if it is sufficiently close to permit the desired standard of customer service.
- There must be between 10 and 15 distribution centers.
- There are certain subsets of distribution centers among which no more than one may be open, exactly one must be open, etc.

Notice that several of these constraints imply the need for logical integer variables, as discussed in the presentation of the simple facility location problem and in the capital budgeting example.

A mixed integer optimization model was formulated to analyze this problem. The model was run many times to check solution sensitivity to the various assumptions, to balance total costs against service levels, to answer "what if" questions regarding possible future events, and to develop a priority ranking for the implementation of the various recommendations. As a result of this analysis, five changes were recommended in the locations of the firm's distribution centers, and at least three of these changes were made. Improvements in the assignment of customers to distribution centers were also implemented. Annual cost savings directly attributable to this study were estimated to be *several million dollars.*

A SOLUTION STRATEGY

There are many different strategies for solving integer programming problems, only one of which we shall present. Some of these strategies are most appropriate for all integer programming problems, while others are designed for mixed integer programming problems. Some strategies allow the integer variables to take on any nonnegative integer values, while others treat only 0–1 integer variables.

The choice of a solution strategy for a particular integer or mixed integer programming problem is best left to an expert in the field of management science. However, we shall present the solution strategy known as "branch and bound" to illustrate some basic concepts and some of the difficulties associated with solving integer programming problems.

Branch and Bound

The branch and bound solution strategy can be used for integer or mixed integer programming problems. As an example, we shall consider the integer programming formulation of the chemical production problem

$$\text{maximize } Z = 60x + 50y, \tag{25}$$

subject to

$$2x + 4y \leq 80, \tag{26}$$

$$3x + 2y \leq 60, \tag{27}$$

$$x \qquad \leq 16, \tag{28}$$

$$y \leq 18, \tag{29}$$

$$x, y = 0, 1, 2, \ldots, \tag{30}$$

which we shall call $\overline{IP}$. The only difference between this formulation and the original linear programming formulation is constraint (30), which replaces the nonnegativity constraints $x, y \geq 0$.

The solution set for this problem is shown in Figure 1. This set consists of all pairs of integer values, denoted by the dots in Figure 1, that satisfy the constraints of the problem. If you count these dots, you will find 260 alternative feasible solutions. In this example it would be possible, but time consuming, to evaluate each of these alternative solutions with the objective function of the model and choose the one that maximizes this evaluative model. In practical problems, such a strategy would be most inefficient.

The logic of branch and bound is really quite simple, and is based on

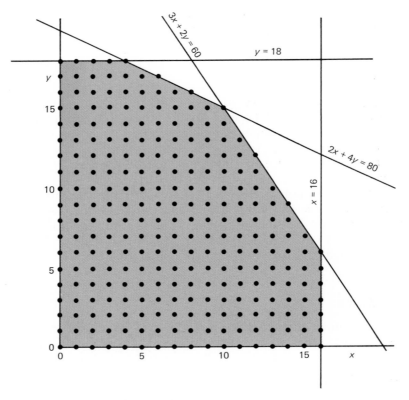

Figure 1. Solutions to the integer programming problem

the general concepts of *relaxation* and *separation* [Geoffrion and Marsten, 1972].

Relaxation We begin with the initial integer programming problem formulation $\overline{IP}$, as shown in expressions (25) through (30). First, we note that this problem is identical to a linear programming problem except for the integer value restrictions (30). We can relax $\overline{IP}$ by replacing the integer constraints (30) by the less restrictive nonnegativity constraints

$$x, y \geqslant 0 . \tag{31}$$

By less restrictive, we mean that all values of the variables feasible in the original problem will also be feasible in the relaxed problem, as well as additional values of these variables.

The set of feasible solutions for the relaxed $\overline{IP}$ with (31) replacing (30) is the shaded portion of Figure 1, that contains all of the feasible solutions to the original $\overline{IP}$ as well as noninteger solutions. Thus, the optimal solution to the relaxed problem will be at least as good as the optimal solution to the original problem. Further, it follows that if the optimal solution to the relaxed problem is feasible in the original problem, i.e., integer valued, it is also the optimal solution in the original problem. (Think about this for a moment.)

Now we can solve the relaxed $\overline{IP}$ with (31) replacing (30), using the simplex algorithm. If we happen to obtain an all integer solution, we know we have also found the optimal integer solution to $\overline{IP}$ since the optimal solution in the relaxed problem is feasible in the original problem.

What if we do not obtain an integer solution when we solve the relaxed $\overline{IP}$ using the simplex method? Then we must use the concept of *separation*.

Separation   When using the branch and bound solution strategy, we *separate* a problem by creating two new problems with the following characteristics:

1.   Every feasible integer solution to the original problem is a feasible integer solution to exactly *one* of the subproblems.

2.   Any feasible integer solution to one of the subproblems is a feasible integer solution to the original problem.

3.   Some of the feasible noninteger solutions to the relaxed version of the original problem are no longer feasible noninteger solutions of the relaxed version of either subproblem.

In other words, we divide up the feasible set of solutions to the relaxed (linear programming) version of the original (integer) problem so that all of the feasible integer solutions are retained in one or the other of the subproblems, but some of the noninteger solutions have been eliminated. When we eliminate enough of the noninteger solutions, we will obtain an integer solution.

The two subproblems are called *descendants* of the original problem. The descendants are placed in a *candidate* list of new problems to be solved. Eventually, the solution to the relaxed version of one of the problems from this candidate list will be the optimal solution to the original integer programming problem.

Separation is implemented by adding additional constraints to the orginal problem. For example, suppose we separate $\overline{IP}$ by adding the constraint $x \leqslant 10$ to the original constraint set, expressions (25) through (30), to create descendant 1, and $x \geqslant 11$ to expressions (25) through (30) to create descendant 2. The feasible regions for these two descendants of $\overline{IP}$ are shown in Figure 2. The feasible solutions to descendant 1 are the dots in the lightly shaded area, while the feasible solutions to descendant 2 are the dots in the heavily shaded area. Notice that characteristics 1, 2, and 3 above are satisfied by this problem separation; that is, every feasible solution to $\overline{IP}$ is a feasible solution to either descendant 1 or descendant 2 but not to both, any feasible solution to descendant 1 or descendant 2 is a feasible solution to $\overline{IP}$, and a

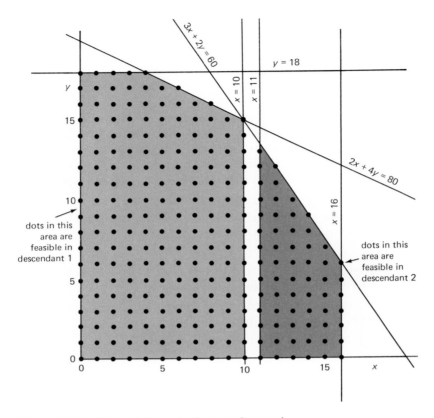

Figure 2. Feasible solutions to the two descendants of $\overline{IP}$

portion of the feasible region for the linear programming solution of the relaxed version of $\overline{IP}$ is excluded from consideration by this restriction. Notice also that no integer solutions are excluded.

The Steps   The branch and bound algorithm searches the set of all possible integer solutions in such a way that all of the possibilities do not have to be considered explicitly. It creates a list of candidate problems by separating the original integer programming problem into descendants. The candidate problems are solved by relaxing the integer constraints. The best solution for each candidate problem is compared, and the overall optimal integer solution is identified.

When we speak in general of an integer or mixed integer programming model, we shall refer to it simply as *IP*, omitting the "bar" used in referring to the specific problem of expressions (25) through (30). The steps for the branch and bound as suggested by Dakin [1965] for maximizing *IP* are as follows:

Step 1. The original candidate list consists of *IP* only, and the best feasible integer solution obtained so far (Z^*) is set at an arbitrarily small number (if we are minimizing *IP*, Z^* is set at an arbitrarily large number).

Step 2. Stop if the candidate list is empty. The best feasible integer solution previously discovered is the optimal solution.

Step 3. The last problem placed into the candidate list is selected (last in, first out, or LIFO).

Step 4. Relax all integer requirements.

Step 5. Solve by the simplex method.

Step 6. If there is no feasible solution to the relaxed problem, go to step 2.

Step 7. If step 5 reveals that the problem selected from the candidate list has no feasible solution better than the best solution obtained so far (Z^*), go to step 2.

Step 8. If step 5 reveals an optimal integer solution to the problem selected from the candidate list, go to step 10.

Step 9. Separate the problem from the candidate list by selecting a fractional valued variable $\bar{x}_j$ in the solution determined in step 5. Let $[\bar{x}_j]$ denote the largest integer smaller than $\bar{x}_j$ (e.g., if $\bar{x}_j = 3.6$, $[\bar{x}_j] = 3$). Create the first descendant by adding the constraint $x_j \leq [\bar{x}_j]$, and create the second descendant by adding the constraint $x_j \geq [\bar{x}_j] + 1$. Add these descendants to the candidate list and go to step 2.

Step 10. A new feasible solution to *IP* has been found. If the value of the objective function is greater than the best solution obtained so far, set Z^* equal to this value and go to step 2.

The result of applying step 9 is the creation of two descendants, as illustrated in Figure 2. In actual implementations of the branch and bound algorithm, a particular rule for choosing the fractional valued variable is included. For our purposes, we shall assume that this selection is arbitrary.

A flow chart portraying these ten steps is shown in Figure 3. In order to understand the logic of these steps, it may be helpful to refer to the general framework of an optimizing model, which introduces each chapter in Part Four. According to this general framework, an optimizing model consists of an alternative generator, a predictive model, and an evaluative model, with feedback flowing from the evaluative model to the alternative generator. As indicated in Figure 3, steps 1 through 4 may be viewed as the alternative generator, since the candidate list contains the alternative problems to be analyzed.

In step 5, the simplex algorithm is applied to a relaxed version of a problem from the candidate list in order to *predict* its objective function value. If the application of this algorithm to the relaxed problem leads to an integer-

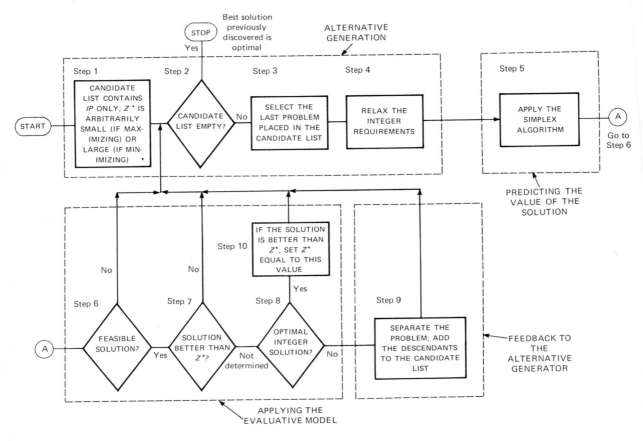

Figure 3. The general framework for solving integer programming problems

valued solution, this prediction is exact. Otherwise, it is only a *bound* on the actual optimal integer solution to the problem from the candidate list.

Steps 6, 7, 8, and 10 *evaluate* the solution obtained from the prediction of step 5. Finally, step 9 provides *feedback* to the alternative generating steps by producing new descendants for the candidate list.

Now let us see how our particular example $\overline{IP}$ [expressions (25) through (30)] might be solved using this framework. We would perform the following steps:

Step 1. The candidate list consists of $\overline{IP}$, and let $Z^* = 0$.

Step 2. Continue to step 3.

Step 3. Select $\overline{IP}$ from the candidate list.

Step 4. Relax $\overline{IP}$ by substituting (31) for (30), thus relaxing the integer restrictions.

Step 5. Apply the simplex algorithm to the resulting linear optimization model. From Chapter 13, the solution is $x = 10$, $y = 15$, and $Z = 1350$. Since this is an integer solution, it is also a feasible solution to $\overline{IP}$.

Step 6. Continue to step 7.

Step 7. Continue to step 8.

Step 8. Since we have an optimal solution to the problem selected from the candidate list, we go to step 10.

Step 10. Since 1350 is greater than the current value of $Z^* = 0$, we set $Z^* = 1350$, and go to step 2.

Step 2. Stop, since the candidate list is empty. The best feasible solution previously discovered, $Z^* = 1350$ is the optimal solution.

Notice that this procedure was particularly simple since the application of the simplex algorithm to the relaxed version of $\overline{IP}$ resulted in an integer solution. We will not always be so fortunate.

Now suppose the total available time on machine B for the chemical production problem is 55 rather than 60. We will have the following revised integer programming problem, which we designate as IP':

maximize $Z = 60x + 50y$, $\qquad\qquad$ (25)

subject to

$$2x + 4y \leqslant 80, \qquad\qquad (26)$$
$$3x + 2y \leqslant 55, \qquad\qquad (27')$$
$$x \qquad\quad \leqslant 16, \qquad\qquad (28)$$
$$y \leqslant 18, \qquad\qquad (29)$$
$$x, y = 0, 1, 2, \ldots . \qquad\qquad (30)$$

As we shall see, the solution to the linear optimization model obtained by relaxing (30) is not integer valued for this revised problem.

Applying the branch and bound algorithm, we perform the following steps:

Step 1. The candidate list contains IP' only, and $Z^* = 0$.

Step 2. Continue.

Step 3. Select IP'.

Step 4. Relax IP' by substituting (31) for (30). Thus, the nonnegativity restrictions are substituted for the integer-value restrictions.

Step 5. Apply the simplex algorithm to the resulting linear optimization model. The solution is $x = 7.5$, $y = 16.25$, $Z = 1262.5$.

Steps 6, 7, 8. Continue.

Step 9. Separate IP'. We choose $\bar{x} = 7.5$ as the fractional valued variable

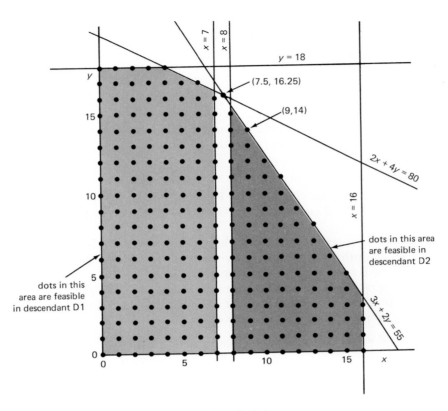

Figure 4. Feasible solutions to the first two descendants of IP′

on which to separate, and $[7.5] = 7$. Descendant $D1$ is created by adding $x \leq 7$ to the constraints, and descendant $D2$ is created by adding $x \geq 8$. The feasible solutions to these descendants are shown in Figure 4. These problems are added to the candidate list.

Step 2. Continue.

Step 3. The candidate list contains $D1$ and $D2$. Select $D2$ (LIFO) from the candidate list.

Step 4. Relax the integer requirements in $D2$.

Step 5. Applying the simplex algorithm gives $x = 8$, $y = 15.5$, $Z = 1255$.

Steps 6, 7, 8. Continue.

Step 9. Separate $D2$ by adding $y \leq 15$ to the constraints of $D2$ to create $D3$, and by adding $y \geq 16$ to the constraints of $D2$ to create $D4$. These two problems are added to the candidate list.

Step 2. Continue the process.

Rather than continuing this step-by-step description of the application of branch and bound, we have summarized the process in Figure 5. Each square in Figure 5 corresponds to a problem, with the initial integer programming problem IP' at the top and the various descendants labeled below it. We can see from this diagram the origin of the term "branch" in the name of this approach, since the creation of the descendants can be visualized as creating branches of alternative solutions. The problem number in the squares indicates the order in which the problems on the candidate list were solved using the simplex algorithm, since we are using the LIFO strategy in step 3. The value of Z^* is the value of the best feasible integer solution found prior to the solution of the associated problem from the candidate list.

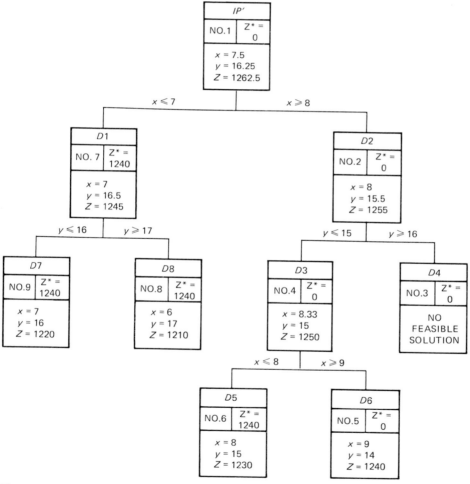

Figure 5. Summary of the branch and bound solution of IP'

In our verbal discussion, the descendants $D3$ and $D4$ had been created from $D2$ and added to the candidate list. The candidate list at this point contains $D1$, which was added to the list "first"; $D3$, which was added next; and $D4$, which was added "last." The next problem selected from the candidate list is $D4$, again using the "last in, first out" LIFO rule. As we can see from Figure 5, there is no feasible solution to the linear programming relaxation corresponding to $D4$ (study Figure 4 carefully to see why). We return immediately to the candidate list (step 6) and select $D3$ (LIFO). Again, the solution to the linear programming relaxation is noninteger, so we create the two descendants $D5$ and $D6$. The solution to the linear programming relaxation corresponding to $D6$ gives the first all integer solution, $x = 9$, $y = 14$, $Z = 1240$. Thus, Z^* is set equal to 1240 prior to selecting $D5$ from the candidate list. The solution to $D5$ is also integer valued, but since $Z = 1230$ is less than Z^*, it is ignored as a inferior solution.

What if the solution to $D5$ had *not* been integer valued? We would *not* have created descendants of $D5$ because the objective function value of 1230 is less than Z^*. Notice that the objective function values of descendants are always less than or equal to the objective function values of the problem that was separated to produce them. Thus, any descendants of $D5$ would have had objective function values of less than or equal to 1230. These values would be less than the objective function value of a previously discovered integer solution. This branch is therefore *bounded*, and would not be pursued further. Thus, the term "branch and bound" is descriptive of the solution strategy.

After $D5$ was eliminated, only $D1$ remained in the candidate list, so it was selected. The solution was noninteger, but the objective function value $Z = 1245$ is greater than $Z^* = 1240$. Therefore, we cannot bound this branch, and we must create two more descendants, $D7$ and $D8$. The objective function values for $D7$ and $D8$ are both less than Z^*, so we can eliminate them from further consideration. Notice that both $D7$ and $D8$ have all integer solutions. Since there are no more problems in the candidate list, the procedure stops (Step 2), and the solution corresponding to $Z^* = 1240$ is $x = 9$, $y = 14$, the optimal integer solution.

There are several points worth noting regarding this solution strategy. First, the solution of an integer optimization model is considerably more work than the solution of the corresponding linear optimization model created by relaxing the integer constraints. To solve this integer programming problem, we were required to solve *nine* linear programming problems, as well as do the bookkeeping regarding the candidate list and the value of Z^*. However, a careful count of the feasible solutions to this integer optimization model (the "dots" in Figure 4) reveals 240 alternatives. We only evaluated four of these ($x = 6$ and $y = 17$, $x = 7$ and $y = 16$, $x = 8$ and $y = 15$, and $x = 9$ and $y = 14$), or 1.7 percent, using the branch and bound strategy.

Also, consider the results of the "common sense" strategy: find the best solution to the relaxed linear optimization model, and round off to the nearest feasible integer value. The optimal solution to the relaxed linear optimization model corresponding to IP' is $x = 7.5$, $y = 16.25$, and the "closest" feasible integer solution is $x = 7$, $y = 16$. Notice that this is *not* the optimal integer solution determined by branch and bound, although it was the solution for a descendant problem D7 (see Figure 5), and has an objective function value of 1220. This value compares with the optimal objective function value of 1240. In this case, the difference might not be considered significant, although in many real-world problems, the difference between this "common sense" solution and the actual optimal integer solution can be dramatic.

WHAT SHOULD THE MANAGER KNOW?

Optimizing models with integer variables provide powerful tools of analysis for managers. However, the computational burden associated with these problems has inhibited their widespread use until recently. Extremely large linear optimization models can be solved on the computer by efficiently programmed versions of the simplex algorithm, but there is no single algorithm that is equally general when applied to integer or mixed integer optimization models. The branch and bound strategy described in this chapter may perform satisfactorily for some problems, but not so well for others.

The choice of a particular integer programming algorithm is an issue for the technical analyst. However, it is important that the manager work closely with the analyst so that the formulation of the model with integer variables can be as efficient as possible.

Problem Formulation   As we noted in the example of the selection of machines for the radiology department of a hospital, it is important that as few variables as are actually necessary to analyze the problem be required to have integer values. Only variables that are associated with significant costs, like the number of expensive machines to be purchased or the number of warehouses to be built, should be forced to achieve an integer value in a model. Logical variables also must be integer valued, but they should be used sparingly. By working with the technical analyst, the manager can help to ensure that the formulation of the model is efficient in the sense that extraneous integer variables or logical variables are not included. This efficiency will increase the usefulness of the model, since it can be used more often.

Problem Characteristics   Problems that are obviously candidates for analysis with integer models are those involving expensive items such as capital budgeting projects, machines, or facilities. Logical variables also occur in many facility design problems and can be used to advantage.

Scheduling problems can also be analyzed by using integer optimization models. Since many scheduling problems can also be formulated as network models, such as the example of scheduling faculty members to teach courses, this alternative should be explored first, because the network solution algorithms are much more efficient. However, if there is additional complexity that cannot be captured in a network, an integer model may be appropriate and useful.

Computational Algorithms The specific algorithms for solving integer optimization models are relatively complex and of little interest to the practicing manager (for further details, see Salkin [1975]). However, it should be helpful for the manager to understand the specific example of the branch and bound approach. This understanding should provide some appreciation of the logic of the solution strategy and should emphasize the need for cooperation with the technical analyst in the task of problem formulation.

Check Your Understanding

1. Comment on the following statement: "To find the optimal integer solution, simply ignore the integer restrictions and solve the equivalent linear programming problem. Then round off this solution to the closest set of integer values."
   a. Give an example of a problem in which this might be a reasonable solution strategy.
   b. Give an example of a problem in which this might *not* be a reasonable solution strategy.

2. Distinguish between integer "decision variables" and integer "logical" variables. Give an example of each.

3. What is meant by the terms "restriction" and "relaxation" when applied to mathematical programming problems?

4. What is the basis for determining whether a particular variable should be required to have integer values in an optimizing model?

5. Refer to the capital budgeting problem [expressions (10) through (12)] with three logical 0–1 variables. Write the constraints that impose the following restrictions:
   a. We cannot invest in more than two of the opportunities.
   b. Opportunity 1 can be accepted only *if* opportunity 3 is accepted; that is, if opportunity 3 is not accepted, neither is opportunity 1, but if opportunity 3 is accepted, then we have the option of accepting opportunity 1.
   c. Opportunity 1 can be accepted only if *either* opportunity 2 or opportunity 3 is accepted.

d. Opportunity 1 can be accepted only if *both* opportunities 2 and 3 are accepted. (Hint: This restriction may require two constraints).

6. Suppose we define x as the number of units of a product that are to be produced during the next month. The maximum capacity of the plant for this product is 2500 units. However, we require that a minimum production run of at least 500 units must be produced, if any are produced at all, to avoid scheduling production for a large number of different products during the month. Write the appropriate constraints to impose these restrictions, defining any new variable(s) that you introduce.

7. We can "relax" an integer programming problem by ignoring the integer value restrictions on the variables, but the concept of *relaxation* is a general one. Describe at least one other way that a mathematical programming problem (not necessarily an integer programming problem) could be "relaxed."

8. Justify the following statement: "If the optimal solution to the relaxed problem is feasible in the original problem, it is also the optimal solution in the original problem."

9. Suppose we attempt to *separate* $\overline{IP}$ [expressions (25) through (30)] by adding the constraint $x \leq 9$ to create one subproblem, and the constraint $x \geq 11$ to create another subproblem. Does this procedure satisfy the characteristics of a legitimate problem separation? (Graph the problem and these new constraints.)

10. Suppose we attempt to *separate* $\overline{IP}$ by adding the constraints $x + y \leq 3$ to create one subproblem and $x + y \geq 4$ to create another subproblem. Does this procedure satisfy the characteristics of a legitimate problem separation? (Graph the problem and these new constraints.)

11. The branch and bound algorithm described in steps 1 through 10 used the LIFO (last in, first out) strategy to select problems from the candidate list. Redraw Figure 5 assuming that a FIFO (first in, first out) strategy is used to select the problems. This change will affect the order in which the various candidate problems are solved.

12. Justify the following statement: "If the solution to D5 had *not* been integer valued, we would not have created its descendants, because the objective function value of 1230 is less than Z^*." How would we know that one of the descendants of D5 does not contain an *integer solution* with an objective function value greater than Z^*? Use the properties of the techniques of separation and relaxation in your argument.

Problems

1. Hypol Industries makes large industrial machines that are used to manufacture other products. The existing Hypol plant is cramped and outdated. It

must either be modernized or a new plant must be purchased. If a new facility is purchased, management must decide whether to install a fully automated production line or to stay with the cheaper, more conventional methods.

The completed products are initially shipped on a company-owned barge to a major shipping area. Another investment alternative would be a new, more efficient barge. If a new barge were purchased *and* the old facility were modernized, a new shipping dock would have to be built.

Finally, the company could also invest in modernizing the sales offices in the cities where the sales representatives are based.

The alternative projects are shown in Table 3 along with the net present values of their associated future income streams. All of the projects are desirable in the sense that they have positive net present values. However, they also consume man hours and cash. Hypol must observe the following limitations, which were estimated by the accounting department:

$$\text{Man hours:} \quad 15,000$$
$$\text{Expenditures: Year 1} \quad \$600,000$$
$$\text{Year 2} \quad \$300,000$$

TABLE 3. Project List for Hypol Industries

Project Number	Description	Net Present Value of Future Income	Manpower Hours	Expenditures	
				Year 1	Year 2
1	Modernize existing facility	$100,000	7,000	$200,000	$100,000
2	Purchase new facility	200,000	6,000	500,000	0
3	Add fully automated assembly line to new facility	40,000	1,000	50,000	0
4	Modernize sales offices	200,000	2,000	100,000	100,000
5	Purchase a new shipping barge	75,000	1,000	0	200,000
6	Add new shipping dock to existing facility	50,000	3,000	50,000	25,000

a. Formulate the appropriate optimizing model for analyzing this problem.
b. Other than being computationally more efficient, why might a simple linear programming formulation be useful in analyzing this problem? (Hint: What if the constraints in expenditures are not absolutely fixed, but they could vary a bit. What information would you like to have to determine the appropriate expenditure level?)

2. Consider problem 1 in Chapter 15. Suppose we decide that we should not use overtime at either of the existing plants. Therefore, we consider a second

alternative for meeting the increase in demand to 150 units at warehouse 2. This alternative is the construction of a third plant (plant 3) with a capacity of 200 units. Being modern, the normal production costs would be only $1 per unit, and the cost per unit of shipping to warehouse 1 would be $2, and the cost to warehouse 2, $3. *If* we construct this new plant, we incur a fixed operating cost of $100. However, because of the third plants' capacity, we have the option of closing plants 1 and 2. Closing plant 1 would *save* the fixed operating cost of $75, while closing plant 2 would *save* the fixed operating cost of $50. Assume that we must meet the demand requirements at the warehouses using normal production capacities only. Formulate the problem. (Hint: The formulation would be similar to one for considering three potential plant locations.)

3. A manufacturer has two products, x and y, both of which are made in two steps by machines A and B. Process times per 100 are:

	x (hr)	y (hr)
Machine A	4	5
Machine B	5	2

For the coming period machine A has 100 hours available and machine B 80 hours. The sales prices and variable cost components per 100 units for the two products are:

	x	y
Price	$20	$10
Variable cost	10	5

The organization can sell all it can make in the current market and wishes to know the quantities of each product to make in order to maximize some function that approximates profit.

a. Write the constraints and objective function to describe the situation as a linear programming problem.

b. Suppose that the total "set-up" costs to produce x are $100 and the "set-up" costs for y are $75. This means that these costs are incurred *in full* if any of x or y respectively are produced. Write the constraints and objective function to describe this modified situation. Be sure to define any variables you introduce.

4. (Requires the use of the simplex algorithm) In the analysis preceding the launch of astronauts for the first space shuttle mission, the following problem was discussed: The spacecraft was limited to 8 cubic feet of storage for the added supplies to be used in case of an emergency. To deal with the problem of allocating these supplies, "packages" of supplies were created and valued using approaches similar to those described in Part Two.

Package Description	Cubic Feet Required per Package	Value
Medical supplies	2	3
Repair devices	3	6
Safety devices	3	4

Each additional package of each type was considered to have the same value as the first one placed on board. The problem was to determine how many of each type of package to take so as to maximize the total value obtained.

a. Formulate the appropriate integer programming problem.

b. Solve this formulation for the optimal integer solution using the branch and bound algorithm.

5. Suppose we have a metropolitan area where we are trying to locate several Health Maintenance Organizations (HMO's) that provide prepaid health care. There are 3 potential site locations and 5 census tracts to be served by these sites. If we open an HMO at a particular site, we can estimate the number of subscribers from each tract who would go to that site *if* the persons in the tract were *assigned* to go to the HMO at that site. These numbers will vary from site to site depending on how close it is to a census tract and how close it is to major public transportation routes. The tracts are to be assigned to *only one* of the HMO's that is actually built. The estimated number of subscribers are shown below:

Site	Census Tract				
	1	2	3	4	5
1	50,000	10,000	25,000	12,000	20,000
2	20,000	15,000	20,000	20,000	40,000
3	25,000	20,000	10,000	20,000	25,000

In addition, we know that it will cost $5 million to construct an HMO at site 1, $3 million to construct one at site 2, and $2 million to construct one at site 3. The total available budget for construction is $7 million. Finally, each new HMO requires a minimum enrollment of 70,000 subscribers or it should not be built.

Formulate a model to maximize the total number of subscribers in the metropolitan area subject to the constraints described above.

6. Study the network formulation of the faculty/course scheduling problem described in Chapter 15 and illustrated in Figures 6 and 7 of Chapter 15. In the network formulation, we can place upper and lower bounds on the following:

1) the total number of courses taught by a faculty member each academic year

2) the number of courses taught by a faculty member each quarter

3) the total number of sections of a particular course offered each academic year
4) the number of sections of a particular course offered each quarter

However, there are some types of constraints that *cannot* be included in the network formulation.

Suppose we consider a scheduling problem with only the following courses and four faculty members:

Course Number	Name of Course	Faculty Member Number	Name
1	Introduction to Management Science	1	Janes
2	Advanced Management Science	2	Gillespie
3	Basic Mathematical Concepts	3	Mitoff
4	Elective	4	Pulliam

All four faculty members can teach courses 1 and 4, Introduction to Management Science and the elective. However, only Janes and Pulliam can teach course 3, Basic Mathematical Concepts, and Mitoff does not have the background to offer course 2, Advanced Management Science.

Let x_{ij}, y_{ij}, and z_{ij} be the number of sections of course $i(i = 1, 2, 3,$ or $4)$ offered by faculty member $j(j = 1, 2, 3,$ or $4)$ in the fall, winter, and spring respectively. For example, $y_{24} = 2$ would signify that two sections of course 2, Advanced Management Science, should be offered by faculty member 4, Pulliam, in the winter.

a. Formulate constraints to impose the following restrictions:
   1) Course 2 should be offered in the winter *only* if course 1 is offered in the fall.
   2) Pulliam is willing to teach as many as two sections of either course 1 or course 3 in the winter, but not one or more sections of both courses.
   3) If Janes teaches course 1 in the fall, he must offer course 4 in the spring.
   4) No sections of course 4 should be offered unless at least one section of each of courses 1, 2, and 3 is offered.

b. None of the above constraints can be introduced explicitly in the network formulation, which is why the iterative solution strategy shown in Figure 8 in Chapter 15 was emphasized.
   1) In what ways does an integer programming formulation of the faculty / course scheduling problem have an advantage over the network formulation?
   2) In what ways does the network formulation have an advantage?
   3) What is the appropriate basis for preferring one formulation over the other?

References

Atkins, R., and R. Shriver, "New Approach to Facilities Location," *Harvard Business Review*, May–June 1968.

Dakin, R., "A Tree Search Algorithm for Mixed Integer Programming Problems," *Computer Journal,* Vol. 8, No. 3, 1965.

Garfinkel, R., and G. Nemhauser, *Integer Programming,* John Wiley & Sons, New York, 1972.

Geoffrion, A., "Better Distribution Planning with Computer Models," *Harvard Business Review,* Vol. 54, No. 4, July–August 1976.

Geoffrion, A., and R. Marsten, "Integer Programming Algorithms: A Framework and State-of-the-Art Survey," *Management Science,* Vol. 18, No. 7, March 1972.

Glover, F., "Management Decisions and Integer Programming," *The Accounting Review,* January 1972.

Glover, F., and D. Sommers, "Pitfalls of Rounding in Discrete Management Decision Problems," *Decision Sciences,* Vol. 6, May–June 1975.

Salkin, H., *Integer Programming,* Addison-Wesley Publishing Co., Reading, Mass., 1975.

Vora, J., "Heuristics and Optimizing Techniques Applied to Long Range Facility Planning for Hospital Ancillary Departments," *Management Science,* Vol. 21, No. 4, December 1974.

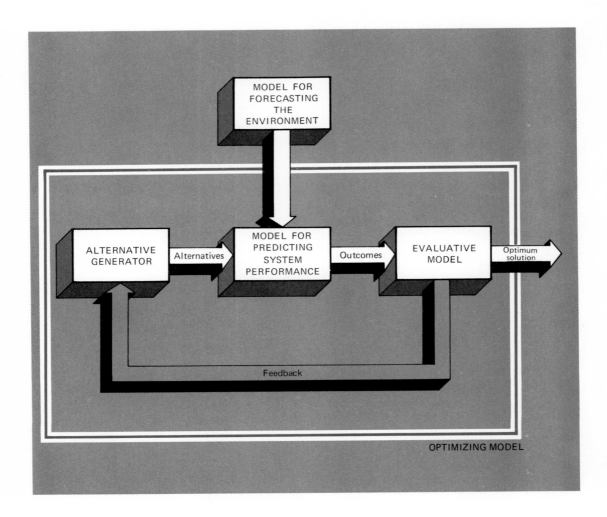

18

Optimizing Models for Sequential Decisions — Dynamic Programming

An important special class of optimizing models requires a series of sequential decisions. Most often, these decisions must be made sequentially over discrete periods of time. For example, we may have to decide how many units of a particular product to produce each month. If we produce more units of our product than the actual demand for a particular month and place the excess production in inventory, the production decision for the following month will be affected. Thus, when it is possible to place items in inventory, the production level decision for one month is not independent of the production level decision for the preceding month.

The production level decision is only one example of a problem involving sequential, interrelated decisions that must be made over time. This problem and others with similar characteristics can be solved using a solution strategy known as *dynamic programming*. The term "dynamic" emphasizes the sequential nature of the decisions and problems to which it is applied.

In previous chapters, especially in Part Three, we presented examples of models that analyzed dynamic system behavior. The dynamic structural models of Chapter 8, the Markov chain models of Chapter 9, and the queuing and Monte Carlo simulation models of Chapters 10 and 11 immediately come to mind. If the structure of the underlying system is sufficiently simple, it may be possible to couple such a predictive model with an evaluative model and solve for an optimal sequence of decisions by using dynamic programming.

Dynamic programming is not really an algorithm in the sense of the simplex method; it is more a solution strategy. We can define a set of terms and a series of steps to be carried out in solving a dynamic programming problem, but the details of these steps are dependent on the particular problem being solved and, to some extent, the discretion of the analyst.

It may be helpful to point out that we have previously presented examples of problems involving sequential decisions that were solved by dynamic programming. The strategy of "rolling back" a decision tree described in Chapter 2 provides one example, while the shortest path algorithm of Chapter 16 is another. We shall first review the solution strategy for these two problems and introduce some important concepts and terminology. We will then present a general formulation of a dynamic programming problem. This general formulation will be applied to the problem of scheduling production over a series of adjacent time periods, known as a *planning horizon*.

EXAMPLES OF SEQUENTIAL DECISION PROBLEMS

There are many examples of sequential decision problems that can be analyzed by using the concepts of dynamic programming. Two examples, previously presented, are problems solved by using the decision tree and the shortest path method. As we shall see, these two problems are conceptually very similar.

The Decision Tree

Figure 1 is the decision tree for the analysis of the oil shale development problem of the Pacific Oil Company (POCO), which was originally presented as Figure 7 in Chapter 2. The squares represent decision points and the circles represent probability branch points. If the initial decision is to follow either a research-only strategy or a combined research and development effort *and* a breakthrough in technology occurs, there is a secondary decision point. This secondary decision may be viewed as a *sequential* decision following the initial decision.

We analyzed this tree in Chapter 2 using the expected value evaluative model. That is, we agreed to make the initial decision based on its expected monetary value. The analysis involved starting at the right of the tree and "rolling back" by replacing each probability branch point by its expected value. Accomplishing this step for the first set of probability branch points in the decision tree in Figure 1 led to the simplified tree shown in Figure 2. This tree is identical to the one presented as Figure 8 in Chapter 2 with one exception. We have added three additional decision points shown in dotted lines to correspond to the two secondary decision points originally in the tree.

For example, if we choose an initial development strategy of research only and a breakthrough occurs, we reach a decision point with two options, either change to a research and development strategy or change to a crash development strategy. If no breakthrough occurs, we now reach a decision point (shown with dotted lines in Figure 2) with only one option, continue

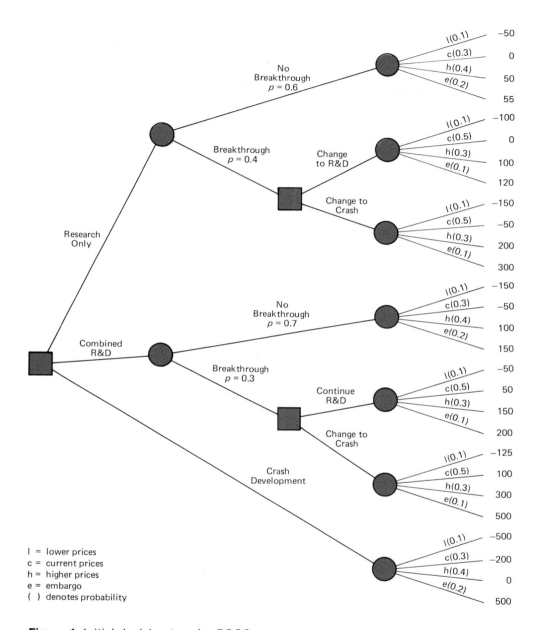

l = lower prices
c = current prices
h = higher prices
e = embargo
( ) denotes probability

Figure 1. Initial decision tree for POCO

the research-only strategy. Similarly, if the initial strategy is a crash development effort and no technological breakthrough occurs (an event that will occur with certainty) our only decision option is to continue the crash development.

The advantage of adding these "dummy" decision points is that we can now visualize the problem of analyzing the simple decision tree in Figure 2 as a two *stage* decision problem. The two *stages* correspond to the two decisions that must be made sequentially. At the initial stage, we choose the initial oil shale development strategy; at the second stage, we automatically

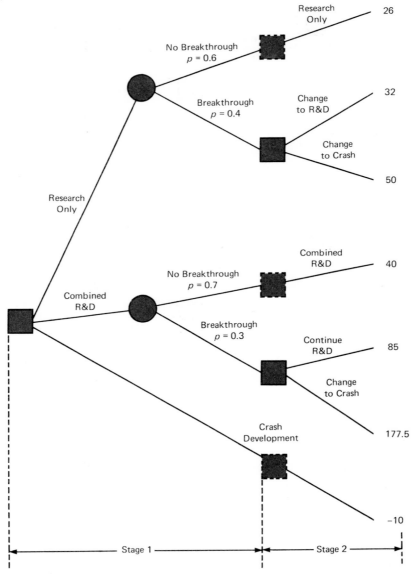

Figure 2. Simplification of the POCO decision tree

decide to continue the initial strategy if no technological breakthrough occurs, or we may select a new strategy if a technological breakthrough does occur. Since these interdependent decisions are made sequentially over time, it seems that the appropriate solution technique may be *dynamic programming*.

Let us consider the problem at the secondary stage first. Both the decisions that can be made and the returns (or payoffs) depend on the *state* of the system when the secondary stage is reached. The *state* of the system is described in terms of the *initial decision* and the *occurrence* or the *non-occurrence* of a breakthrough. Thus, there are five possible *states* of the system at the secondary stage. They are

NBR   = no breakthrough from an initial research only strategy,

BR   = breakthrough from an initial research only strategy,

NBRD = no breakthrough from an initial research and development strategy,

BRD   = breakthrough from an initial research and development strategy,

NBC   = no breakthrough from an initial crash development strategy.

The available decisions at the secondary stage, some of which are not feasible given a particular state of the system, are the following:

R   = research only,

RD = combined research and development,

C   = crash development.

Denoting the state of the system by s and the decision by j, we can summarize the options in the secondary stage as shown in Table 1, which has a row for each possible state of the secondary stage, and a column for each possible decision. The combination of states and decisions that are not feasible are identified by the shaded cells in the table, while the returns corresponding to the feasible state and decision combinations are shown in the remaining cells. Study carefully the definitions of the states and the decisions and Figure 2 to ensure that you understand how Table 1 was constructed before continuing.

We do not yet know what state s the system will be in at the secondary stage. However, for any given state s, we will wish to maximize the return expressed here in terms of the expected monetary value evaluative model. Therefore, we wish to maximize some function f of the state of the system s where

$$f(s) = \underset{j(s)}{\text{maximum}} \ [r(s, j(s))] .$$

This notation may appear confusing (it is, unfortunately), but it is neces-

TABLE 1. A Summary of
the States, Decisions, and
Returns at the
Secondary Stage

s	j		
	R	RD	C
NBR	26		
BR		32	50
NBRD		40	
BRD		85	177.5
NBC			-10

sary to convey the concepts, so let us analyze it carefully. The notation $f(s)$ indicates that f is a function of the state of the system s. This function is defined as the maximum over the feasible decisions given s, $j(s)$, of the returns r. As indicated by the notation $r(s, j(s))$, the return depends on both the state of the system s and the feasible decision $j(s)$.

To illustrate, for the state $s = NBR$; that is, no breakthrough given an initial research only strategy there is only one feasible decision, $j(NBR) = R$, continue the research only strategy. Therefore, we have

$$f(NBR) = \underset{j(NBR) = R}{\text{maximum}} \quad [r(NBR, R)] = 26.$$

Similarly,

$$f(BR) = \underset{j(BR) = RD, C}{\text{maximum}} \quad [r(BR, RD), r(BR, C)],$$

$$= \text{maximum } (32, 50) = 50.$$

since the maximum of the two numbers 32 and 50 is 50. The function $f(s)$ may be calculated from Table 1 simply by circling the maximum entry in each row. These calculations are shown in Table 2, where the additional columns correspond to $f(s)$ and the decision that produces $f(s)$, denoted as $j(s)$.

Now, all that we need to know about this secondary decision stage is summarized in the two right-hand columns of Table 2. That is, we need to know the maximum return f and the decision that produces that return for each possible state of the system at this stage, s. The other information, such as the return of 32 associated with the decision to adopt a research and development strategy (RD) if a breakthrough occurs from an initial research-

TABLE 2. The Computation of $f(s)$

s	j			$j(s)$	$f(s)$
	R	RD	C		
NBR	(26)			R	26
BR		32	(50)	C	50
NBRD		(40)		RD	40
BRD		85	(177.5)	C	177.5
NBC			(−10)	C	−10

only strategy (BR), can be ignored. This is based on the intuitively appealing *Principle of Optimality*, which states the following:

> *An optimal sequence of decisions must have the property that regardless of the decisions which lead to a particular stage in a particular state, the remaining series of sequential decisions must be optimal for leaving that stage and state.*

In other words, *if* we arrive at the secondary stage in a particular state, it does not matter how we got there. Our objective is to find an optimal decision for leaving that state (i.e., moving to the end of the decision tree in this example).

Notice that the information required for the analysis of the secondary stage can be summarized very compactly as shown in Figure 3. Although this representation is not as intuitive as the expanded decision tree with five decision branch points at the secondary stage, the same notation could be applied to a tree with thousands of decision branch points at a particular stage. In the latter case, it would be a convenient means of summarizing this complexity.

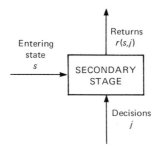

Figure 3. A summary of the information in the secondary stage of the decision tree

At the initial stage in the decision tree, there is only one state of the system (the beginning state). To analyze each decision, we simply take the expected values of the probability branch points associated with each initial decision R, RD, or C. We can use the notation g to represent the function to be maximized at the initial stage, and let $k = R$, RD, or C represent the initial decision. Again using the expected monetary value evaluative model, we wish to determine

$$g = \underset{k = R, RD, C}{\text{maximum}} \left[\sum_{\text{all } s} p(s|k) \cdot f(s) \right]$$

where $p(s|k)$ is the probability of state s ($= $ NBR, BR, NBRD, BRD, or NBC) in the secondary stage given the decision k in the primary stage, and $f(s)$ is shown in Table 2.

From the decision tree in Figure 2, we see that

$$
\begin{aligned}
p(NBR|R) &= 0.6, \\
p(BR|R) &= 0.4, \\
p(NBRD|RD) &= 0.7, \\
p(BRD|RD) &= 0.3, \\
p(NBC|C) &= 1.0,
\end{aligned}
$$

and $p(s|k) = 0.0$ for all other s and k. Therefore,

$$g = \text{maximum} \left[\sum_{\text{all } s} p(s|R) \cdot f(s), \sum_{\text{all } s} p(s|RD) \cdot f(s), \sum_{\text{all } s} p(s|C) \cdot f(s) \right],$$

which gives

$$
\begin{aligned}
g &= \text{maximum} \left[(0.6 \cdot 26 + 0.4 \cdot 50), (0.7 \cdot 40 + 0.3 \cdot 177.5), (1.0 \cdot -10) \right], \\
&= \text{maximum} [35.6, 81.25, -10], \\
&= 81.25,
\end{aligned}
$$

which is associated with the decision $k = RD$.

Thus, the expected monetary value of this dynamic programming analysis of the decision tree is identical to the one determined in Chapter 2. The best initial decision is a combined research and development strategy, changing to a crash development effort if a technological breakthrough is determined. This sequence of decisions is known as the *optimal policy* for this dynamic programming problem.

In terms of a solution strategy, we performed the following steps:

Step 1.   Identify the stages where the decisions must be made.

Step 2.   Identify the possible states of the system at each stage.

Step 3. Identify the decisions that are feasible, given each state of the system at each stage.

Step 4. Identify the returns associated with each feasible combination of a decision and a state.

Step 5. Beginning with the last stage, determine the maximum return (or minimum cost) associated with leaving that stage for each state (applying the Principle of Optimality). Continue to the next stage until the initial stage and state have been evaluated.

These five steps are a summary of the dynamic programming solution strategy for optimizing models involving sequential decisions.

The Shortest Path Problem

Let us now apply this solution strategy to the shortest path problem shown in Figure 4. This problem is identical to the one illustrated in Figure 1(b) of Chapter 16, except that the node numbers have been changed to letters to avoid potential confusion with stage numbers.

The shortest path problem may be viewed as a series of sequential decisions in which the number of nodes between the start node and the terminal node is reduced by one at each stage. Thus, the stages to be used in analyzing the shortest path network in Figure 4 do *not* correspond to the

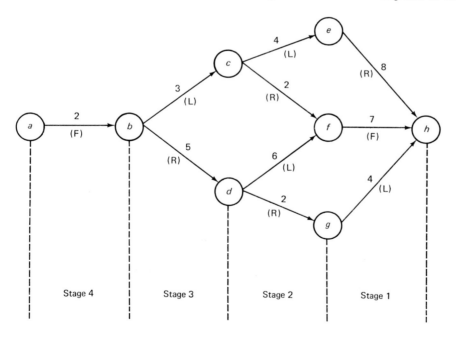

Figure 4. The shortest path problem network

nodes or even to sets of nodes. Rather they correspond to decisions regarding ets of arcs that link the nodes. In this particular example problem, each stage represents the decision to move from n to $n - 1$ nodes from the terminal node, where $n = 1, \ldots, 4$. For example, at stage 2 we move from node c or node d, each two nodes away from the terminal node h, to node e, f, or g, each only one node away from the terminal node. The particular arcs that will be relevant at each stage for this example problem are indicated in Figure 4. The identification of the stages accomplishes step 1.

Since there are four stages in this problem and the analysis will progress from the last stage *backward* to the initial stage, we will number the stages beginning with the last stage and ending with the initial stage. This numbering system is *backward* with respect to the order of the sequential decisions, but follows the order of the analysis itself.

The state at each stage corresponds to the name of the node on the path entering the stage. At stage 1, the state will be either e, f, or g for the network shown in Figure 4 since any path will enter stage 1 through one of these three nodes. Identifying the states for each stage completes step 2.

The decision at each stage is the choice of an arc, given an entering state. We could identify these arcs by name. However, it is instructive in this example to take the perspective of a traveler moving through the network who must decide whether to move to the left (L), forward (F), or to the right (R) when in any particular stage and state. For example, a traveler at stage 2 in state c would have the option of moving to the left (L) or to the right (R), but not of moving directly forward. Similarly, a traveler at stage 1 in state F can *only* move forward (F). Thus, the available decisions may be summarized as L, F, and R, completing step 3. The returns (costs) and the directions of movement are indicated in Figure 4 on each arc, completing step 4.

Finally, for step 5 we must perform the analysis on a stage-by-stage basis, beginning with the last stage before the terminal node, which we identified as stage 1. As before, we identify a function f_1, a set of states, $s_1 = e$, f, and g, and a set of decisions $j_1 = L$, F, or R, where the subscript refers to the stage number. We define

$$f_1(s_1) = \operatorname*{minimum}_{j_1 = L, F, R} [r(s_1, j_1)]$$

for each s_1 where $r(s_1, j_1)$ is the cost of the decision j_1, given the state s_1. For example, if the decision j_1 is R and the state s_1 is e, then $r(e, R) = 8$, as can be seen in Figure 4. Since for each value of s_1 there is only one feasible decision j_1, the computation of $f_1(s_1)$ is particularly easy. The results are shown in Table 3.

Next, we must perform a similar analysis for stage 2. The states at stage 2 are $s_2 = c$ or d, and the decisions are $j_2 = L$ or R, since it is impossible to move forward (F) from either state c or state d. Now we must write down

TABLE 3. Computation of $f_1(s_1)$

s_1	j_1			$f_1(s_1)$	$j_1(s_1)$
	L	F	R		
e			(8)	8	R
f		(7)		7	F
g	(4)			4	L

$f_2(s_2)$. Recall that this function should represent the minimum cost associated with leaving this stage, but since we must move from stage 2 to stage 1, it must also include the costs of stage 1. Thus, we write

$$f_2(s_2) = \underset{j_2 = L, R}{\text{minimum}} \quad [r(s_2, j_2) + f_1(s_1)] . \qquad (1)$$

Since $f_1(s_1)$ is the minimum cost of stage 1, the last stage, $f_2(s_2)$ is the minimum cost of leaving stage 2 *and* passing through stage 1. The only difficulty is the determination of s_1 in this expression.

Now we emphasize an extremely important point. In this problem, the state s_2 and the decision j_2 *determine* the state of the system at stage 1, s_1. Therefore, (1) can be rewritten as

$$f_2(s_2) = \underset{j_2 = L, R}{\text{minimum}} \quad [r(s_2, j_2) + f_1(s_1(s_2, j_2))] \qquad (2)$$

to indicate that s_1 is a function of j_2 and s_2. To illustrate, notice in Figure 4 that if $s_2 = c$ (node c) and j_2 is R, then we enter stage 1 with $s_1 = f$ (node f). Thus, we can solve (2) for $s_2 = c$ as follows:

$$f_2(c) = \text{minimum} \quad [r(c, L) + f_1(s_1(c, L)), r(c, R) + f_1(s_1(c, R))] .$$

Since $s_1(c, L) = e$ and $s_1(c, R) = f$,

$$f_2(c) = \text{minimum} \quad [r(c, L) + f_1(e), r(c, R) + f_1(f)] .$$

Using $r(c, L) = 4$ and $r(c, R) = 2$ from Figure 4, and $f_1(e) = 8$ and $f_1(f) = 7$ from Table 3, we obtain

$$f_2(c) = \text{minimum} [4 + 8, 2 + 7]$$

$$= \text{minimum} [12, 9] = 9 .$$

In a similar manner, we solve for $f_2(d)$. The results for stage 2 are summarized in Table 4.

Stage 3 is now analyzed in the same way. We wish to evaluate

$$f_3(s_3) = \underset{j_3 = L, R}{\text{minimum}} \quad [r(s_3, j_3) + f_2(s_2(s_3, j_3))] .$$

TABLE 4. Computation of $f_2(s_2)$

s_2	j_2		$f_2(s_2)$	$j_2(s_2)$
	L	R		
c	12	(9)	9	R
d	13	(6)	6	R

The only state in stage 3 is $s_3 = b$, which simplifies the calculation. Since $s_2(b, L) = c$ and $s_2(b, R) = d$, we have

$$f_3(b) = \text{minimum} \quad [r(b, L) + f_2(c), \ r(b, R) + f_2(d)]$$
$$= \text{minimum} \quad [3 + 9, \ 5 + 6] = 11 .$$

The simple tabular summary is shown in Table 5.

TABLE 5. Computation of $f_3(s_3)$

s_3	j_3		$f_3(s_3)$	$j_3(s_3)$
	L	R		
b	12	(11)	11	R

Finally, we come to stage 4, which, in this problem, allows only one state $s_4 = a$ and one decision $j_4 = F$. We minimize

$$f_4(s_4) = \underset{j_4 = F}{\text{minimum}} \quad [r(s_4, j_4) + f_3(s_3(s_4, j_4))]$$

by substituting $r(a, F) = 2$, $s_3(a, F) = b$, and $f_3(b) = 11$ to obtain

$$f_4(a) = 2 + 11 = 13 ,$$

the minimum cost of moving from state a in stage 4 (the initial node in the network) through the other stages (to the terminal node in the network).

Thus, 13 is the *cost* of the shortest path, but what is the shortest path itself? To discover this, we must pass back through the network from stage 4 to stage 1. The obvious decision at stage 4 for state a was F, which means that we enter stage 3 in state b and travel from a to b on the shortest path. From Table 5, the decision $j_3(b)$ corresponding to entering stage 3 in state b is R, which takes us to state d upon entering stage 2 (see Figure 4). From Table 4, $j_2(d) = R$, which leads to state g in stage 1 (again see Figure 4). Finally, since $j_1(g) = L$, we terminate at state h. Thus, the shortest path is reconstructed as a series of states, from a to b, b to d, d to g, and g to h.

Naturally, this is the same path we discovered in Chapter 16 using the "labelling" procedure.

A GENERAL FORMULATION

We have seen that the decision tree and the shortest path problem can be analyzed using dynamic programming. However, the computations appeared much more cumbersome than those used in the original "roll-back" approach for the decision tree and the "labelling" procedure for the shortest path problem. A natural question at this point would be, "If dynamic programming has anything to offer, why didn't we use it in the first place in analyzing the decision tree and the shortest path problem?" The answer, of course, is that we did. The roll-back procedure and the labelling algorithm are actually special, simplified versions of dynamic programming that were developed especially for the decision tree and the shortest path problem, respectively. However, the framework as suggested by steps 1 through 5 and expressions such as (2) are much more general in their applicability.

The most important task in formulating a dynamic programming problem is the definition of the function $f_n(s_n)$ which is the maximum return (or minimum cost) when in state s_n at stage n (with n more stages to pass through). In general, we write

$$f_n(s_n) = \underset{j_n}{\text{maximum}} \quad [r(s_n, j_n) + f_{n-1}(s_{n-1}(s_n, j_n))]. \tag{3}$$

This expression indicates the solution strategy. We start by calculating all of the values for f_1, and then use these values to compute all of the values of f_2. The values of f_2 are used to compute f_3, and so on until the stage corresponding to the initial decision is reached. This solution process is called a *recursive* algorithm, while expression (3) is known as a *recursion*.

Expression (3) is appropriate for problems in which the state at stage s_{n-1} is determined exactly by the decision j_n and state s_n at stage n. In the case of the decision tree, j_n and s_n only determine the *probability* $p(s_{n-1}| s_n, j_n)$ of being in state s_{n-1} given j_n and s_n. The straightforward modification of (3) to incorporate this extension (assuming the use of the expected value evaluative model) is

$$f_n(s_n) = \underset{j_n}{\text{maximum}} \left[r(s_n, j_n) + \sum_{\text{all } s_n} p(s_{n-1}|s_n, j_n) \cdot f_{n-1}(s_{n-1}) \right] \tag{4}$$

It may be helpful to view the logic of dynamic programming in terms of our general description of an optimizing model, which includes an alternative generator, a model for predicting system performance, an evaluative model, and a feedback of information to the alternative generator. Figure 5 shows an extension of Figure 3, a summary of information flows in a stage of a dynamic programming formulation.

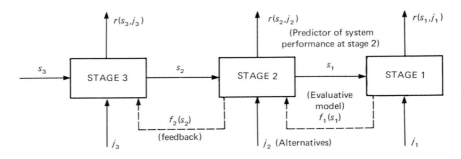

Figure 5. Information flows in dynamic programming

At each stage in a dynamic programming formulation, a feasible set of alternative decisions is determined from an alternative generator (generally a simple set of inequalities or a predetermined list of values) for each possible state of the system. The model for predicting system performance at stage n is simply $r(s_n, j_n)$, while the evaluative model is $f_n(s_n)$. Since the analysis proceeds from stage to stage, the important feedback in this optimizing model is in terms of the values of $f_n(s_n)$, which are passed to stage $n + 1$.

PRODUCTION-INVENTORY SCHEDULING

The scheduling of production and inventory is a problem common to many organizations. The importance of inventories and efficient inventory management was stressed in Chapter 12, and several elementary inventory models were presented. However, these models were based on the assumption of either a constant demand for a product or a random demand fluctuating about a constant mean value. Further, these models did *not* consider the costs that might be associated with different production levels for a product.

When costs of production vary on a per unit basis with the number of units actually produced, the results provided by the elementary inventory models of Chapter 12 may not be appropriate. Further, if future demand can be forecasted with a high degree of accuracy and if it varies from time period to time period, this information should be taken into account in simultaneously determining the optimal production rate and inventory level for the firm.

Since the determination of a production schedule over a planning horizon of several time periods involves a series of sequential decisions, this problem can often be analyzed with dynamic programming. This application is perhaps the most common one for dynamic programming, and numerous companies have successfully exploited this approach in actual practice. Therefore, we shall present the formulation and solution of a simple production-inventory scheduling problem for the dual purposes of illustrating the technique of dynamic programming and of presenting a solution strategy that can be applied to many similar, real-world problems.

The Problem The West Coast Manufacturing Company produces large electrical transformers for use by major power companies. These transformers are ordered several months in advance by the power companies, so it is possible to predict the demand for four to six months into the future with a high degree of certainty. This demand must be met each month, so backlogging of orders is not permitted.

The company wishes to develop a production schedule for the first four months of the new year. The projected demands are shown in Table 6.

TABLE 6.
Projected Demand
for the West Coast
Manufacturing Company

Month	Demand
January	3
February	4
March	2
April	3

The production costs vary according to the number of transformers produced each month. Since the company can produce other products as well, there is a relatively large "set up" cost associated with producing even one transformer. This set up cost is 5 (the costs have been scaled). In addition to the set up cost, the first 2 units produced each month cost 2 each, while the incremental cost of the next 2 units is 1 each. The maximum production capacity for the transformers during any one month is 4 because of the demand for the firm's other products. These costs are summarized in Table 7.

TABLE 7. Cost of Production

Number of Units Produced	Total Cost
0	0
1	7
2	9
3	10
4	11

Finally, there is a holding cost of 1 for each transformer held in inventory from one month to the next. The maximum capacity of the inventory storage area is 3 transformers.

The company wishes to determine a production schedule that will minimize the total cost of production and the inventory holding costs over the four-month planning horizon. The inventory at the beginning of the planning horizon (on January 1), contains 2 transformers. The company also requires that the inventory at the end of the planning horizon (April 30) should be equal to zero.

The Formulation   We must carry out steps 1 through 4 presented earlier in this chapter in order to identify the components of the recursion (3). In this problem, a production level decision must be made each month, so there will be four stages corresponding to the four months in the planning horizon. Since we begin our analysis with the last stage (numbered 1), stage 1 corresponds to April, stage 2 to March, stage 3 to February, and stage 4 to January.

What are the states of the system at each month? Let us think carefully about this. A state is determined by the relationship among the stages. How does a production decision in January affect the production decision in February? What information regarding the operations in January is needed? To schedule production in February, it would seem that we would only require information regarding the inventory level on February 1 (or January 31, if you prefer). This information would be important for the production level decision in February; however, the manner in which it was produced (e.g., all in January or a carry-over of excess inventory from December) is irrelevant. Therefore, the inventory level at the beginning of a production period is the appropriate descriptor of the state of the system. We define

$$s_n = \text{the beginning inventory level in stage } n.$$

Since the maximum capacity of the inventory storage area for transformers is 3 units, we will have $s_n = 0, 1, 2,$ or 3.

The decision that must be made at each stage is the determination of the production level. For this production-inventory scheduling problem, we have

$$j_n = \text{the production level in stage } n.$$

Since we wish the ending inventory in April to be zero, and the demand in April is 3 units, the value of j_1 is determined by the state s_1. We must have

$$s_1 + j_1 - 3 = 0$$

in order to achieve the ending inventory level; that is, the beginning inventory level at stage 1, s_1, plus the number of units produced in stage 1, j_1, must equal the demand in stage 1, 3 units. If $s_1 = 1$, then j_1 must equal 2 units, since $j_1 = 3 - s_1$.

At stage 2, j_2 must be greater than or equal to the demand, 2, minus the beginning inventory s_2. In order to achieve the limitation of a zero ending inventory level for stage 1 (April), j_2 must be less than or equal to the sum of the demands in stages 1 and 2, $3 + 2 = 5$, minus the beginning inventory s_2. It must also be less than or equal to the maximum production capacity for a month, 4 units. Therefore, we must have

$$2 - s_2 \leqslant j_2 \leqslant \text{minimum } (5 - s_2, 4) .$$

In general, if d_n is the demand in stage n and j_{max} is the maximum production capacity, we have

$$d_n - s_n \leqslant j_n \leqslant \text{minimum} \left(\left(\sum_{i=1}^{n} d_i \right) - s_n, j_{max} \right)$$

at each stage n.

The Analysis   The costs at stage 1 are simply the production costs associated with $j_1 = 3 - s_1$ units. The return function $r(s_n, j_n)$ can be divided into two parts,

$$r(s_n, j_n) = c(j_n) + h(s_n, j_n) ,$$

where $c(j_n)$ is the cost of production as shown in Table 7, and h is the holding cost. The holding costs are simply 1 times the ending inventory for a particular strategy.

From our relationship among j_n, s_n, and d_n, we know that the ending inventory in stage n will be equal to $s_n + j_n - d_n$. That is, the ending inventory for a stage (month) is simply the beginning inventory, s_n, plus the production level for the month, j_n, minus the demand in that month, d_n. Since the ending inventory for stage n is the beginning inventory in stage $n - 1$, we also have the important relation

$$s_{n-1} = s_n + j_n - d_n .$$

For stage 1, we have required $s_1 + j_1 - d_1 = 0$, so the holding costs are 0. The production costs $c(j_n)$ can be read from Table 7 for $j_1 = 0$, 1, 2, or 3 units. Therefore, we can write the recursive relation

$$f_1(s_1) = c(3 - s_1) + 1(0)$$

for stage 1. The values of f_1 are tabulated in Table 8 for each feasible value of s_1.

At stage 2, the recursion takes the more general form of expression (3). The return function $r(s_2, j_2)$ is given by

$$c_2(j_2) + 1 \cdot (s_2 + j_2 - d_2) ,$$

and since $s_1 = s_2 + j_2 - d_2$, we have

$$f_2(s_2) = \underset{2 - s_2 \leqslant j_2 \leqslant \text{minimum } (4, 5 - s_2)}{\text{minimum}} [c(j_2) + 1 \cdot (s_2 + j_2 - 2) + f_1(s_2 + j_2 - 2)]$$

for the demand $d_2 = 2$.

TABLE 8. Computation of $f_1(s_1)$

s_1	j_1				$f_1(s_1)$	$j_1(s_1)$
	0	1	2	3		
0				(10)	10	3
1			(9)		9	2
2		(7)			7	1
3	(0)				0	0

If the beginning inventory for stage 2, s_2, is equal to 1 unit and the production decision j_2 is 2 units, then $s_2 + j_2 - 2 = 1 + 2 - 2 = 1$, so that the production cost $c(2)$ would equal 9 (from Table 7). The holding cost for the 1 unit of ending inventory would equal $1 \cdot 1 = 1$, and $f_1(1)$ would equal 9 (from Table 8). The total cost associated with this state and decision is $9 + 1 + 9 = 19$. This result, along with similar results for the other feasible combinations of s_2 and j_2, are shown in Table 9. Notice that the optimal production level for stage 2 (March) will be either 0, 2, or 4 units, depending on the entering inventory level s_2.

TABLE 9. Computation of $f_2(s_2)$

s_2	j_2					$f_2(s_2)$	$j_2(s_2)$
	0	1	2	3	4		
0			(9 + 0 + 10)	10 + 1 + 9	11 + 2 + 7	19	2
1		7 + 0 + 10	9 + 1 + 9	10 + 2 + 7	(11 + 3 + 0)	14	4
2	(0 + 0 + 10)	7 + 1 + 9	9 + 2 + 7	10 + 3 + 0		10	0
3	(0 + 1 + 9)	7 + 2 + 7	9 + 3 + 0			10	0

The analysis at stage 3 is virtually identical to the analysis at stage 2. The recursion is

$$f_3(s_3) = \underset{4 - s_3 \leq j_3 \leq \text{minimum } (4,\, 9 - s_2)}{\text{minimum}} [c(j_3) + 1 \cdot (s_3 + j_3 - 4) + f_2(s_3 + j_3 - 4)]$$

for the demand $d_3 = 4$, and the results are shown in Table 10.

Finally, we come to stage 4. The beginning inventory for stage 4, s_4, is known to be 2 units, and the demand, d_4, is 3 units. Therefore, we simply evaluate

$$f_4(s_4) = \operatorname*{minimum}_{1 \leqslant j_4 \leqslant 4} \quad [c(j_4) + 1 \cdot (2 + j_4 - 3) + f_3(2 + j_4 - 3)]$$

for each feasible value of j_4. The result, shown in Table 11, indicates that the minimum total cost for the four-month planning horizon is 35. The decision in state 4 is $j_4 = 3$ units. This results in an ending inventory of 2 units in stage 4, which is the state variable s_3 of stage 3. From Table 10, $j_3(2) = 4$ units, and the ending inventory in stage 3 is 2 units. From Table 9, $j_2(2) = 0$, so no units are produced at stage 2. The ending inventory of stage 2, corresponding to $j_2(2)$, is 0, and $j_1(0) = 3$ units. Therefore, the optimal policy, corresponding to the minimum cost of 35, is to produce 3 transformers in January (stage 4), 4 transformers in February (stage 3), 0 transformers in March (stage 2), and 3 transformers in April (stage 1). Notice that the total produced for the four months of $3 + 4 + 0 + 3 = 10$ transformers is 2 less than the total demand. The difference is accounted for by the 2 transformers in beginning inventory at the start of the planning horizon.

TABLE 10. Computation of $f_3(s_3)$

s_3	j_3					$f_3(s_3)$	$j_3(s_3)$
	0	1	2	3	4		
0					11 + 0 + 19	30	4
1				10 + 0 + 19	11 + 1 + 14	26	4
2			9 + 0 + 19	10 + 1 + 14	11 + 2 + 10	23	4
3		7 + 0 + 19	9 + 1 + 14	10 + 2 + 10	11 + 3 + 10	22	3

TABLE 11. Computation of $f_4(s_4)$

s_4	j_4					$f_4(s_4)$	$j_4(s_4)$
	0	1	2	3	4		
2		7 + 0 + 30	9 + 1 + 26	10 + 2 + 23	11 + 3 + 22	35	3

Managerial Use   We have presented an extremely simple, artificial example of a production-inventory scheduling problem in order to emphasize concepts. As we shall see, however, this basic formulation can be extended to a highly realistic situation and solved by a computer search methodology.

One important issue in the actual use of this approach is the choice of the planning horizon and the value of the state variable at the end of the last time period (stage 1). The latter choice is known as the terminal condition. The solution is sensitive to these choices and will often change as these parameters are changed. One strategy is to use an estimate of the "average" inventory level for the product as the terminal condition, rather than arbitrarily setting the ending inventory for stage 1 equal to zero. It is easy, and often instructive, to perform a sensitivity analysis with different planning horizon lengths and different terminal conditions, once the problem has been formulated.

A related issue is the assumption of a perfect forecast for demand over the planning horizon. Again, sensitivity analysis can be used to study the effects of errors in forecasts. As an alternative, one strategy often used with actual applications is the creation of a "rolling" production-inventory schedule. The idea is to create the production schedule over a planning horizon of arbitrary length, such as four months, as we have just done. Only the production plan for the first month (January in our example) will actually be implemented. At the end of the first month, the demand forecasts for the remaining months in the original planning horizon are updated, and a forecast is made for one additional month into the future, which is added to create a new planning horizon of the same total length as the original one. Again, the production schedule for the revised planning horizon is determined, but implemented only for the first month. This process is repeated each month. The rationale for this strategy is that the decisions that are most sensitive to the choice of the planning horizon and the terminal condition, as well as to correct forecasts of demand, occur toward the end of the planning horizon. The optimal decision for the first month is often stable under reasonable variations in other parameters.

Another strategy for dealing with probabilistic estimates of demand would be to employ the recursion (4). The details of such an application are primarily of interest to analysts rather than managers, so we omit them here. (Wagner [1975] presents a discussion of this approach.)

This same model can also be applied to the problem of ordering units for inventory rather than manufacturing them. The actual price of the units plus the reorder costs would correspond to the manufacturing costs in this example. Otherwise, the formulation would be unchanged.

In our example, the production costs and inventory holding costs were assumed to be identical for each time period. This assumption could easily be relaxed by defining a different production cost function c_n and holding cost function h_n for each stage n. Similarly, the option of backlogging items could be allowed with only a simple modification of the basic formulation. Thus, this formulation of the production-inventory scheduling problem has sufficient flexibility to handle many of the important considerations associated with the development of a production schedule in practical situations.

Limitations and Advantages As we have noted, problems that can be analyzed using dynamic programming must have a very special structure.

They must involve a series of sequential decisions, usually occurring over time. At each stage in the formulation, only one decision is made and only one state description can be used to convey information from stage to stage regarding the interdependencies among the decisions. In theory, it is possible to overcome these limitations, but the computational burden of the analysis increases dramatically when more than one decision is made at each stage, or when the state is described by two or more descriptors. The number of feasible values for the decision at each stage and for the state descriptor must be limited in order to avoid huge tables at each stage of the type shown in Tables 9 and 10. When this cannot be done, the large size of these tables may make it impossible to solve the dynamic programming problem. This phenomenon is called the "curse of dimensionality." Another serious disadvantage is that no one standard computer code can handle all dynamic programming problems, although codes for particular problems are not difficult to write.

However, when a problem can be formulated as a recursion, dynamic programming does have certain advantages. As illustrated in the production-inventory example, "fixed charges," integer decision variables, and nonlinear objective functions pose no difficulty for dynamic programming. They can be handled routinely in the solution process. If the objective function has certain special mathematical forms, the solution procedure can be streamlined considerably so that it is possible to handle much larger problems efficiently. These issues are of primary interest to the analyst, but they should be exploited whenever possible. (Wagner [1975] presents a discussion of these issues.)

Finally, if the relationships among the stages remain constant, it is possible to solve *infinite horizon* dynamic programming problems. This capability allows us to ignore the problem of arbitrarily determining a planning horizon for the period. Infinite horizon formulations can be used to study long-range industrial expansion problems. For example, Erlenkotter [1969] has used an infinite horizon dynamic programming formulation to determine an optimal policy for the expansion of the fertilizer industry in India. Similar models are used to determine the optimal age at which forests should be cut and replanted.

Direct Search Formulation and Solution of the Production-Inventory Problem

Now let us consider a more realistic representation of the production-inventory problem. The decision required in our previous formulation was to determine the *number* of transformers to produce that would minimize cost over the planning horizon.

Decision Variables   Implicitly, we know that different production schedules may involve an expansion or contraction in short-term capacity, which may be achieved by changes in the size of the work force. Now we have two related decision variables for each stage, production rate P and work force size W, with production rate depending in some way on the work force size. But, the work force can be divided into both direct (WD) and indirect (WI), and while both contribute to production, the indirect work force acts in a supporting role. If we were to expand the work force size, we need to make separate but related decisions with respect to each type of labor, so we now have three decision variables WD, WI, and P.

Now let us expand our thinking about the transformer company. Suppose that it makes an entire line of transformers and the large power transformers represent only one department or division. In addition, there is a department that makes audio transformers for the radio, hi-fi, and television market. First, note that we must make two aggregate production rate decisions, one for the power department P_p and one for the audio department P_a. Of course, these are quite different markets subject to rather different causal factors in demand. If we aggregate demand, the aggregate direct work force size WD may need to increase, but masked in the increase may be a relatively large increase for power transformers and a decrease for audio transformers, resulting in a net increase. The ratios of labor requirements per unit will be quite different for the two product lines, so we need to make separate decisions on at least direct work force size. Now we have five decision variables WD_p, WD_a, WI, P_p, and P_a. Perhaps we could also justify dividing the indirect work force by department, but we have made our point; in a more realistic situation, there are likely to be several related decision variables. The state of the system from one stage to another is now specified by ending inventories, work force sizes, and production rates.

Cost Model   Now let us consider the costs affected by decisions. In the simplified production-inventory example, we considered total cost and its variation with the number of units produced in making the scheduling decision. With our expanded set of decision variables, however, we must develop a relevant cost model. First, the expansion or contraction of the work force in itself involves incremental hiring and layoff costs. Then, there are regular payroll costs that vary with the work force size in each category. In addition, there is the possibility of overtime cost, which depends on both production rates and work force sizes. The intriguing aspect of overtime adds another important dimension, however, because overtime is also a component of short-term capacity, and reflects back on the fundamental decision variable of work force size. Because both work force size and overtime involve costs, the most economical decision will involve not only the size of the work force but the related decision of the manner in which the work force is used.

Then, there are costs of holding inventory as well as the costs associated with shortages, back ordering, or possible loss of sales. Finally, there

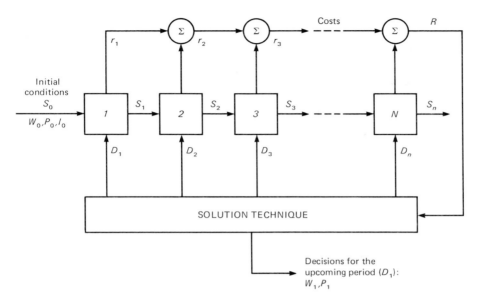

Figure 6. Multistage sequential decision system for the production-inventory problem

From E. S. Buffa and W. H. Taubert, *Production-Inventory Systems: Planning and Control*, Richard D. Irwin, Homewood, Ill., (Rev. ed.) 1972, used by permission.

may be costs associated with increasing or decreasing the production rate and start-up or shutdown one-time costs associated with a second shift.

The cost model is, then, the sum of the regular payroll costs, hiring and layoff costs, and overtime costs for each work-force decision variable; inventory and shortage costs, which are partially dependent on production rates; and production rate change and second shift costs. These costs are aggregated over the entire planning horizon, as indicated in Figure 6. Through some solution technique, that set of decision variables for the various stages which minimizes the aggregate stage costs is identified. Of course, only the decisions for the first period are implemented, but we have projected decisions for each of the decision variables over the entire planning horizon. The entire procedure must be repeated with updated forecasts and possibly changed costs one month hence, thus creating a "rolling" production-inventory schedule.

Solution Technique   The general formulation involves five decision variables, several states passed from stage to stage, and a complex cost model involving linear, nonlinear, and one-time costs. As we noted, the curse of dimensionality makes it impossible to solve our more complex problem using dynamic programming. How then can we solve this sequential decision problem?

Recall Figure 4 in the Introduction to Part Four. That figure represents a complex profit surface for two decision variables, so that it could be represented graphically. A direct search computer code can be used to search the surface to find the optimum combination of variables. Our problem is much more complex, but we can use the same kind of solution technique. If we assume a six-month planning horizon and five basic decision variables, we have a $5 \times 6 = 30$ dimensional cost surface over which we must search to find the optimum combination of decision variables for each stage in the planning horizon. As noted previously, decisions for the first stage would be considered firm, while those for subsequent stages are projections of decisions that will be revised in subsequent decision cycles.

This approach to solving sequential decision problems has been termed the Search Decision Rule and has been applied to scheduling in a large research laboratory involving 10 decision variables over a six-month planning horizon [Buffa and Taubert, 1972], to a steel mill involving 21 variables over a six-month planning horizon [Buffa, 1972], and to cost minimization in a network scheduling program [Buffa and Taubert, 1972]. This direct search solution strategy does not provide an integer-valued solution, which can be a drawback in some situations.

The basic formulation of the sequential decision problem comes from dynamic programming. We have here an excellent example in which formulation has followed the general structure of a format that was expressive of unique decision characteristics, but that must be coupled with a practical solution technique for larger scale realistic problems.

WHAT SHOULD THE MANAGER KNOW?

Certain optimizing models involving sequential decisions can be formulated effectively by using recursion relations and can be analyzed with dynamic programming. These problems must have a special structure in order to be amenable to this modeling strategy. However, in cases where this structure does exist, dynamic programming is a powerful, practical tool for the manager. When the structure of the system is too complex, the dynamic predictive models of Chapters 8, 9, 10, and 11 may provide alternative methods of analysis.

As we noted, there are currently limitations on the number of decision variables and state descriptions used to convey information from stage to stage because the computational requirements increase rapidly as the number of decision variables and state descriptors increase. Under these conditions, however, computer search methods may provide a solution.

Problem Recognition   It is particularly important for a manager to be able to recognize problems that can be analyzed effectively using dynamic programming or the direct search methods. Problems that have been successfully studied include the following:

1. production-inventory scheduling
2. determination of optimal inventory reordering policies
3. capital budgeting (For example, the shortest path formulation of the equipment replacement problem can also be represented as a dynamic programming problem.)
4. scheduling of maintenance for equipment
5. choice of advertising media for a product
6. long-run replacement and expansion of depreciating capital equipment

These problems can all be viewed as involving a series of sequential, interrelated decisions.

Problem Formulation   The formulation of a dynamic programming problem is both more difficult and simpler than the formulation of other optimizing models, such as a linear optimization model. It is simpler because there are generally fewer variables and constraints to consider. However, the strategy of dividing the larger problems into a series of smaller problems represented by the recursion (3) is perhaps not as intuitively appealing as the formulation of other optimizing models. One must get used to the concepts of stages and system states.

However, it is important that the manager be aware of the concepts of dynamic programming. The notion of a series of sequential decisions linked by a descriptor of the state of the system may be a helpful conceptual tool in problem solving even when formal analysis is not used. If the manager works with an analyst in actually formulating a dynamic programming problem, his awareness of the important considerations may be invaluable in restricting the number of decisions to be made at each stage to one, in determining a single state descriptor, in limiting the number of values that the decisions and state descriptors can have, and in limiting the number of stages that must be analyzed. Such insights are extremely important in developing a formulation of a practical problem that is both á useful representation of the problem and amenable to an efficient solution method.

Check Your Understanding

1. What is a "stage" in dynamic programming? Does it necessarily correspond to a time period?
2. What is meant by the "state" of the system in dynamic programming?
3. Study carefully the four steps in the procedure for finding the shortest path in an acyclic network presented in Chapter 16. Explain how these four steps implement the Principle of Optimality.

4. Why are the stages numbered *backward* with respect to the order of the sequential decisions?

5. What is the significance of the statement that the state and the decision at stage n determines the state at stage $n - 1$?

6. Write out the expressions required to solve for $f_2(d)$ in the shortest path example and compute the results. Check your solution against Table 4.

7. What is the unique feature of a *recursive* algorithm?

8. Explain the meaning of the notation and the implied solution strategy in the general expression for the recursion (3).

9. Suppose the West Coast Manufacturing Company wishes to have 2 transformers in inventory at the end of the four-month planning horizon. This means that $s_1 + j_1 - 3 = 2$. Compute the revised production plan for the four months. Does the production decision for January change?

10. Suppose the West Coast Manufacturing Company wishes to develop the production schedule for only the first *three* months of the new year. They ignore the demand in April of 3 units and require that the ending inventory on March 30 should be equal to zero. Does this affect the production decision in January?

11. What approaches can be used to compensate for the sensitivity of the solution to the choice of the terminal conditions and the planning horizon?

12. What is the "curse of dimensionality"? How can it be overcome?

13. When should a direct search computer code be used to solve a sequential decision problem, rather than the dynamic programming solution strategy?

14. Discuss the pros and cons of the following statement: "The choice of a solution strategy is irrelevant. The important thing is the problem formulation."

Problems

1. Draw the decision tree for the capacity expansion problem described in problem 6 of Chapter 2. Add "dummy" decision points as necessary to those appearing naturally in the tree so that it can be visualized as a two-stage decision problem. Define the states and the decisions at each stage. Solve by using the dynamic programming optimization strategy.

2. Find the shortest path in the acyclic network described in problem 1 of Chapter 16 by using dynamic programming. Redraw the network and label it in a manner similar to Figure 4. (This process may also require "dummy" nodes.) Create tables similar to Tables 3, 4, and 5.

3. Solve the equipment replacement problem shown in Figure 4 of Chapter 16 by using dynamic programming. What are the appropriate definitions of the state variables and the decision variables?

4. Solve the spacecraft loading problem presented as problem 4 in Chapter 17 by using dynamic programming. (Hint: A "stage" concerns the "decision" of how many packages of a particular type to take. A "state" is the number of cubic feet that are left to be allocated at each stage.)

5. Solve the capital budgeting problem defined by expressions (10), (11), and (12) in Chapter 17 by using dynamic programming. When can an integer programming problem be solved by using the dynamic programming solution strategy?

6. Suppose a company is trying to schedule production over a planning horizon of 3 months. The problem is complicated by the fact that the production costs vary from month to month because of seasonal fluctuations in the prices of raw materials. The relevant production cost and demand data are shown in Table 12.

TABLE 12. Production Cost and Demand Data (Problem 6)

	MONTH 1	MONTH 2	MONTH 3
	Variable Production Cost of Unit k (per unit)		
Production of unit k			
$k = 1, 2$	6	4	5
$k = 3, 4$	5	3	2
$k = 5$	2	1	1
	Demand		
	4	2	3

As Table 12 shows, the cost of producing the first 2 units in month 1 is 6 per unit, the cost of the next 2 units is 5 per unit, and the cost of the fifth unit is 2. There is also a holding cost of 1 for each unit held in inventory from one month to the next.

a. Suppose that the maximum ending inventory capacity is 3 units, and the maximum production capacity is 5 units. Also, assume that the beginning inventory (in month 1) is 0, and that we require the ending inventory (in month 3) to be 0. What is the optimal production schedule?

b. Suppose there is a "set up" cost of 2 in months 1 and 2, and of 3 in month 3 that is incurred if any units are produced in that month. If $k = 0$ in a month, this set up cost is not incurred. Does the solution change?

7. Suppose a company is trying to plan production for next month only. The company is using a forecast of demand for four months and determining an optimal production schedule for all four months, but only implementing the result for the first month (a "rolling" schedule). Assume that there is a holding cost of 1.5 for each unit held in inventory from one month to the

next, that the maximum ending inventory capacity is 3 units, and that the beginning (month 1) and ending (month 4) inventory levels are equal to 0. Further, suppose we have the data shown in Table 13.

TABLE 13. Production Cost and Demand Data (Problem 7)

	MONTH 1	MONTH 2	MONTH 3	MONTH 4
Production of unit k				
$1 \leqslant k \leqslant 5$	1	2	3	3
$6 \leqslant k \leqslant 10$	3	5	4	7
$11 \leqslant k \leqslant 15$	9	8	7	10
Demand				
Optimistic	10	12	5	14
Pessimistic	10	10	3	8

As indicated in Table 13, the first 5 units produced in month 1 cost 1 per unit, the next 5 units cost 3 per unit, and the last 5 cost 9 per unit (the production capacity is 15 units per month). Notice that we have an "optimistic" and a "pessimistic" demand forecast. What should the production level be in month 1?

8. A company must determine the best pricing policy over the next four years for a new product. Six different price levels seem reasonable: $20, $21, $22, $23, $24, and $25. At a price lower than $20, the company could not cover the costs of production. At more than $25, the competition would take the market. After evaluating the potential demand and the likely strategies of the competition, a table has been constructed that relates the price in a given year to the estimated present value of profits in that year (the values in the table have been scaled):

Price	Year 1	2	3	4
$20	2	1	2	4
21	3	2	3	3
22	5	6	5	2
23	5	4	2	5
24	6	3	2	6
25	8	5	3	1

   a. Suppose the company wishes to avoid price changes of more than a one dollar increase or decrease each year. What would be the optimal pricing strategy? (Hint: The "decision" each year is how much to *change* the price, not the price itself.)

b. Suppose the company wishes to avoid *reducing* the price, but it will consider increases of one or two dollars from year to year, as well as keeping the price unchanged. What would be the optimal pricing policy?

References

Bellman, R., *Dynamic Programming,* Princeton University Press, 1957.

Buffa, E., *Operations Management: Problems and Models,* third edition, John Wiley & Sons, New York, 1972.

Buffa, E., and W. Taubert, *Production and Inventory Systems: Planning and Control,* revised edition, Richard D. Irwin, Inc., Homewood, Ill., 1972.

Erlenkotter, D., "Preinvestment Planning for Capacity Expansion: A Multi-Location Model," Ph.D. Dissertation, Graduate School of Business, Stanford University, Palo Alto, California, 1969. (Published by the United States of America Agency for International Development, New Delhi, India, 1970.)

Nemhauser, G., *Introduction to Dynamic Programming,* John Wiley & Sons, New York, 1966.

Wagner, H. M., *Principles of Operations Research,* Prentice-Hall, second edition, Englewood Cliffs, N.J., 1975.

Part Five

SYNTHESIS

Synthesis

In Chapter 1, we argued that a model simplifies a problem solver's view of a problem by leaving out much information and by creating categories. In a similar manner, an introductory textbook simplifies a complex body of knowledge by leaving out much information (recall our numerous comments that such details were primarily of interest to analysts) and by creating categories (called chapters). A useful model contains not only the important categories, but also the essential interrelationships among these categories. Continuing the analogy, the material in a textbook will be of significant value only if the reader understands the interrelationships among the materials within different chapters, as well as the more specific details in each chapter.

As you have read each chapter, the title and the introduction have identified the nature of the problems and of the associated mathematical models and solution techniques to be discussed. In the real world there are no titles or introductory statements to tell you that a particular problem can best be modeled and analyzed using linear programming or any other technique of management science. An ability to recognize key problem characteristics that aid in identifying the appropriate form of the model must be developed. This ability can be of significant value in enhancing the problem-solving skills of a manager, even if a formal, mathematical analysis is not performed.

The latter statement raises another important question: When should a formal, mathematical analysis of a problem be performed? There are no firm rules for selecting a particular model or for deciding whether to perform an analysis, but we shall attempt to provide some guidance in Chapter 19.

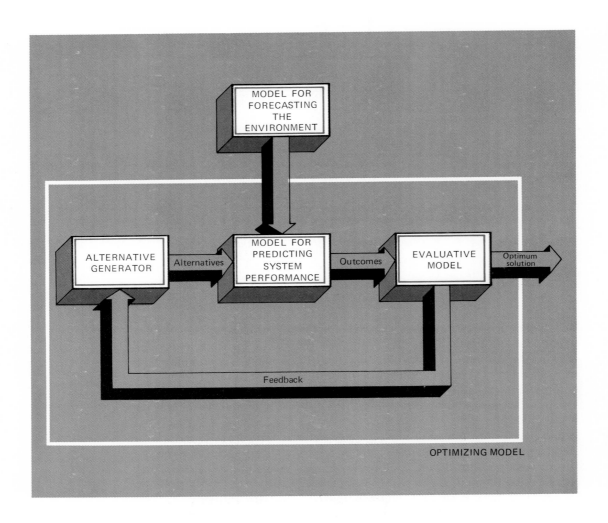

19

What Should The Manager Know?

What should the manager know about the tools, techniques, and concepts of management science/operations research? At the end of each chapter, we have addressed this important question in terms of the specific materials included within the chapter. Now it is time to address this question by looking across the chapters in order to gain an appreciation for the total body of knowledge associated with the hybrid term "management science/operations research." In doing so, we shall first address the question of whether a formal, mathematical analysis should be used to deal with a particular, real-world problem. Next, we shall provide some summary guidelines for matching problems with models and solution techniques. These guidelines also serve as a means of summarizing and synthesizing the topics we have covered.

WHEN SHOULD MANAGEMENT SCIENCE/ OPERATIONS RESEARCH BE USED?

We have presented numerous examples of "successful" applications of the models and tools of management science/operations research to real-world problems, but it is clear that every real-world problem should not be dealt with by formally applying these models and tools. How can an intelligent decision be made with regard to the use of these approaches? Perhaps some insights can be gained by considering what is meant by the term "successful application."

Benefits Versus Costs

The use of a formal, mathematical model in the analysis of a problem is "successful" if the benefits exceed the costs. The costs include the time for model formulation, the time and cost of data collection, the time and cost of the development of necessary computer programs, and the cost of any computer runs required for the formal analysis.

These costs can be substantial and can easily exceed subjective estimates of the benefits that might result from an analysis. However, the continuing research and development in the fields of computer hardware design and information systems, and the development of efficient computer programs for performing the analyses guarantee that these costs will continue to decrease, so that in the future the potential benefits of applying formal mathematical models will exceed the costs in a growing number of problem areas.

This relationship between the benefits and costs of analysis can be illustrated diagrammatically as shown in Figure 1. The gross benefits of applying formal mathematical models to problems within an organization increase rapidly as the problems with the highest payoff are analyzed first, and continue to increase, but at a decreasing rate. The costs of applying the models are initially small, but increase at an increasing rate. However, the costs associated with 1965 technology, in terms of computers, information systems, and computer programs, increase much faster than the costs associated with 1975 technology. Therefore, the number of problems to which the formal analysis should be applied in order to maximize *net benefits* has increased from point A in 1965 to point B in 1975 (see Figure 1). It is likely that this increase will continue, making it even more important for the modern manager to have model-building skills in the future.

In any particular situation, a rough estimate of the potential benefits and costs will have to be made. For example, the expenses from the product transportation and distribution system of a large organization may run into the millions of dollars annually. A large-scale formal analysis of the system could easily be justified, even if the costs of the analysis were several hundred thousand dollars.

In other situations, computer programs may be available that can analyze a problem by using readily accessible data. The costs of the analysis may be only a few hundred dollars, and these costs can easily be justified, even in small organizations dealing with relatively small problems.

Conceptual Value

Suppose that you estimate that a formal mathematical model-building effort is not justified in a particular situation — perhaps because adequate data or the appropriate computer programs are not available, and the cost or time

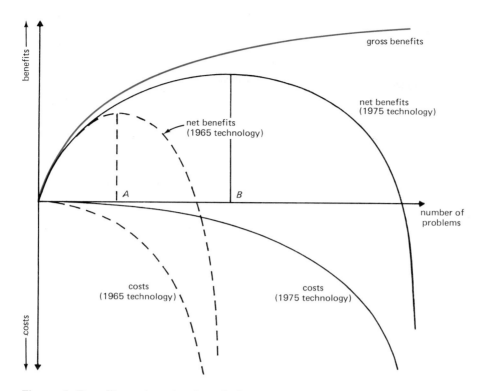

Figure 1. Benefits and costs of analysis

required to develop them is prohibitive. Are the concepts of model building still of use in the problem-solving effort?

What you have learned may seem at first to be some detailed knowledge about linear optimization models, corporate planning models, network models, waiting-line models, decision trees, and so on. But it should have been more than that. Formal models should also teach us something about the basic structure of certain kinds of important problems.

For example, in studying linear optimization models we learn not only the structure and application of this important model but also something fundamental about allocation problems in general. We learn to handle the effects of interacting and competing demands for limited resources and, perhaps more important, we learn the general nature of optimum solutions. Understanding these general concepts is important, because they should carry over into situations for which the formal model is not applicable. In the practical operating situation, allocations of limited resources must often be made on an intuitive basis, either because there is not time for formal analysis or because the most important variables are not quantifiable. We believe that a manager can exercise intuitive judgment most effectively if he understands the basic nature of a formal problem and the probable nature of good solutions.

Another excellent example is the general waiting-line model. The individual who understands formal waiting-line models should be able to make a good snap judgment about the level of service to provide in a practical situation because he realizes the great value of idle time of the server. The value of idle time, of course, is a concept that runs contrary to our fundamental training to conserve time, yet in the design of many systems, provision of apparent overcapacity is the key to success.

Thus, one benefit of an understanding of formal mathematical model building is that it provides alternative ways of thinking about a problem—as a linear optimization model, a network model, or a waiting-line model. In each case, thinking about a model in these terms can also help determine the information that should be collected and the probable nature of the best solution. These benefits should occur to a manager with model-building skills even if no formal analysis is undertaken.

CHOOSING A MODEL

Which model should be used in analyzing a specific problem, either formally or simply as a way of thinking about the problem? Perhaps this issue is not critical, since there is often no *one correct way* of modeling a problem. Additional insights may be obtained by trying to conceptualize a problem in terms of different mathematical forms—as a linear optimization model or a network model, for example. However, some models do "match" better with a particular problem than others, and thus offer greater insights into the problem. Therefore, it is important to be able to recognize key characteristics of a problem that have implications for model selection.

One strategy is to look for the problem characteristics that can be related to the categories of models shown in the now familiar Figure 2. In thinking about a problem, we may ask ourselves about the nature of the problem environment. Can it be *forecasted* with relative certainty, or is risk a major factor to be considered in the decision? Some of the models we have studied are appropriate for problems in which important elements can only be described in terms of probability statements. Examples are the waiting-line models and the Monte Carlo simulation models. Other models assume that the environment is relatively certain. These include the important optimizing models described in Part Four and the computer-based corporate simulation models discussed in Chapter 7.

A second question relates to the nature of the relationships among the important elements in the problem. In effect, we are trying to identify the nature of the mathematical expressions that may exist in the *predictive* model. The corporate simulation models and the elementary inventory models use simple, algebraic relationships. The relationships are required to be linear expressions in order to use the linear optimization models, and linear

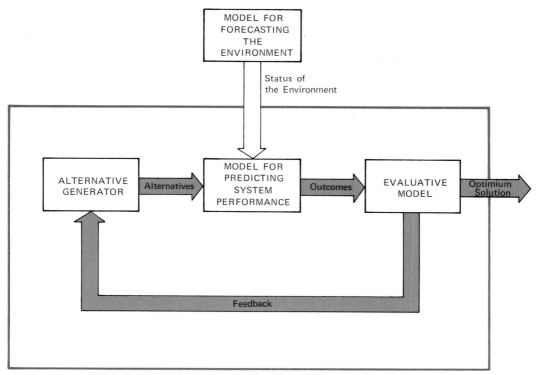

Figure 2. Models of management science

expressions with some integer-valued variables were considered in Chapter 17. If the relationships can be described with a network of arrows and circles, then one of the models in Chapter 15 or 16 might be appropriate. An important issue in a problem might be how the relationships among the problem elements change over time. If so, the dynamic structural models of Chapter 8 might be appropriate, if the future can be forecasted with relative certainty; otherwise, the Markov chain models might be helpful in analyzing the transition of problem elements from one state to another. If the important problem relationships are those among a series of sequential decisions, the dynamic programming models might provide the most useful formulation.

Finally, a third question relates to the purpose of the analysis. If we are seeking the *best* solution to a problem according to some clearly defined, quantifiable function of the decision variables *(evaluative model)*, then we should look to the optimizing models of Part Four. If we only wish to predict the outcomes of selecting an alternative, or the impact of changing one element of the problem on the other elements, then one of the predictive models of Part Three would be appropriate.

Table 1 provides a summary of the topics we have covered and a description of the assumptions regarding the nature of the environment, the predictive model, and the evaluative model for each topic. Like any other model, Table 1 omits some information in simplifying and summarizing these assumptions. As you gain experience with the techniques and tools of management science, you may recognize exceptions or quibble with some of the categorizations in Table 1. However, we hope that this summary will be helpful to the beginner in relating the materials.

Matching Problem Characteristics and Models

Let us now illustrate how the summary in Table 1 might be used. Suppose we ask questions about the environment, the nature of the relationships among elements, and the purpose of the analysis of a specific problem. We identify the following problem characteristics:

1. a relatively certain environment
2. simple algebraic relationships among the elements of the problem
3. no clearly defined quantifiable objective

Then from Table 1 the predictive models described in Chapters 6 and 7 seem most likely to provide a useful analysis.

As a second example suppose we ask similar questions about a second problem and obtain the following conclusions:

1. a relatively certain environment
2. the logical relationships and/or the parameters change as a function of time
3. no clearly defined, quantifiable objective

Again from Table 1 the dynamic structural models provide the appropriate "match."

Finally, this questioning procedure might lead to the following set of problem characteristics in another study:

1. a relatively certain environment
2. linear relationships among the elements of the problem
3. a clearly defined, quantifiable function of the decision variables to be maximized (minimized)

This time, a linear optimization model would be selected from Table 1.

Turn back through the book to any problem description, either in the text or in the problem section. Read it carefully, and then ask the following questions:

TABLE 1. Assumptions Regarding the Nature of the
Environment, the Predictive Model, and the Evaluative Model

Chapter	Title	Environment	Relationships Among Elements	Objective
2	An Introduction to Evaluative Models and Decision Trees	Risky	Outcomes from predictive models, optimizing models, or subjective estimates	Maximize expected value
3	Utility Theory and Subjective Probability	Risky	Outcomes from predictive models, optimizing models, or subjective estimates	Maximize expected utility
4	Evaluative Models for Multiple Criteria	Certain or risky	Outcomes from predictive models, optimizing models, or subjective estimates	Maximize (expected) utility
5	Forecasting the Environment	Risky	Statistical	Minimize forecast error
6	Building Mathematical Models to Predict System Performance	Certain	Simple, algebraic	Complex and/or not defined quantitatively
7	Computer-Based Corporate Simulation Models	Certain	Simple, algebraic	Complex and/or not defined quantitatively
8	Dynamic Structural Models	Certain	Change as a function of time	Complex and/or not defined quantitatively
9	Predicting the Effects of Risk—Markov Chains	Risky	Probability of transition from state to state over time	Complex and/or not defined quantitatively
10	Predicting the Effects of Risk—Queuing Models	Risky	Waiting lines and service facilities	Complex and/or not defined quantitatively
11	Predicting the Effects of Risk—Monte Carlo Simulation	Risky	May involve several waiting lines and service facilities	Complex and/or not defined quantitatively
12	Elementary Optimizing Models for Inventory Management	Certain	Simple, algebraic	Minimize costs
13	Linear Optimization Models	Certain	Linear expressions	Maximize (minimize) a quantifiable function of the decision variables
14	The Simplex Method	Certain	Linear expressions	Maximize (minimize) a quantifiable function of the decision variables
15	Network Models— Transportation and Transshipment	Certain	Network	Maximize (minimize) a quantifiable function of the decision variables
16	Network Models—Shortest Path and Network Scheduling	Certain	Network	Maximize (minimize) a quantifiable function of the decision variables
17	Optimizing Models with Integer Variables	Certain	Linear expressions with some variables restricted to integer values	Maximize (minimize) a quantifiable function of the decision variables
18	Optimizing Models for Sequential Decisions— Dynamic Programming	Certain or risky	Recursive (interrelated sequential decisions)	Maximize (minimize) a quantifiable function of the decision variables
Appendix D	Assessing Risks in Inventory Models	Risky	Algebraic and statistical	Minimize expected costs

1. What is the nature of the environment (certain or risky)?
2. What is the nature of the relationships among the problem elements?
3. Is there a clearly defined, quantifiable function of the decision variables to be maximized (minimized)?

See if your answers to these questions for a problem in a particular chapter are consistent with the summary for that chapter shown in Table 1. If not, try to reconcile the differences.

Example: The Cash Management Problem   The cash balance of a firm normally fluctuates because of a lack of synchronization between cash inflows from accounts receivable, cash sales, and so forth, and cash outflows from payments on accounts and notes payable. The cash management problem is concerned with optimally financing these outflows with cash-on-hand, lines of credit, or sales of marketable securities, while investing net inflows in the appropriate marketable securities.

Suppose you were presented with the cash management problem of a large organization. How would you make your analysis? Are any of the models of management science appropriate for aiding this analysis? What questions should you ask, and what additional information would you require?

First of all, let us take stock of what we know from this brief problem description. What is the nature of the environment? Can a firm accurately forecast its inflows and outflows of cash over a time horizon of several months? The answer depends on the nature of the organization and the stability of its market. It may also depend on the degree of detail that is required in the analysis. Very few firms can forecast cash inflows and outflows with *complete* certainty, but the assumption that they can may be a reasonable abstraction from reality for the purposes of analysis.

We shall consider the following three different conditions of the environment:

1. The outflow of cash is relatively constant over time.
2. The inflows and outflows of cash can be described only by probability statements.
3. Cash inflows and outflows vary, but these variations can be forecasted with certainty.

Each of these conditions has implications for the choice of the appropriate model.

Skipping to the last question in our list of three, is there a clearly defined function of the decision variables to be maximized (minimized)? At first glance, the objective seems clear: maximize the returns (minimize the costs) from the cash management decisions. The returns are from the interest paid on marketable securities and from discounts commonly offered by creditors for early payments. The costs are from interest charges from the lines of credit, from losses on the sales of marketable securities that must be sold before maturity, and from the costs of the transactions.

But is the problem really this simple? Excess cash deposits improve a firm's credit rating and the banker's goodwill at the cost of earnings foregone from investments in securities. The determination of an appropriate "minimum" cash balance will require the consideration of issues other than short-term profits. However, it may still be appropriate to adopt the assumption of a single quantifiable objective function for the purpose of analysis, realizing that we are abstracting from and simplifying reality in order to gain the advantage of alternative ways of viewing this problem.

Now let us couple our assumption of a quantifiable objective function with each of the three different conditions of the environment. It is generally necessary to know the nature of the environment before we can identify the relationships among the problem elements. Suppose the outflow of cash is relatively constant over time. Given this condition in the environment, would it be possible to express the relationships among the problem elements in terms of simple, algebraic statements? Perhaps so. We might view the cash management problem in the following manner. All cash outflows are to be made from a cash account. There is a cost associated with *holding* cash in this account, since it could be earning interest in marketable securities. There is also a cost of adding cash to this account, since marketable securities must be sold or lines of credit must be used. These latter *transaction* costs are similar to *reordering* costs in inventory management models. Thus, we have an analogy. We have a constant demand for cash, a holding cost, and a reordering (transaction) cost. The relationships among these elements can be expressed as simple, algebraic statements. The simple economic order quantity model of Chapter 12 could be employed to determine the maximum size of the cash account and frequency with which it should be replenished. Such an approach to cash management was suggested by Baumol [1952] in one of the first formal analyses of this problem.

Suppose the outflows of cash are not constant and can be described only by probability statements. It would be natural to adopt one of the inventory models described in Appendix D, which account for risk. An example of such an extension is provided by Miller and Orr [1966].

The inventory models may be a useful guide to cash management in some firms, but they do not provide much detail. For example, they assume that the decision on when to transfer a specified amount of money to the cash account can be made independently of information regarding the inflows of cash. However, if we complicate the problem by relating information on cash inflows and outflows, it is no longer possible to express these relationships in simple, algebraic statements. Consequently, the simple inventory models will no longer be appropriate.

What other optimizing models that allow additional detail might be used to analyze the cash management problem? Cash management decisions are sequential and interrelated. From Table 1, we see that the dynamic programming models of Chapter 18 are a natural choice. This choice is also to be expected, since one of the most common applications of dynamic programming is to inventory management problems that are too complex for the simple inventory models. We have already established the analogy between inventory and cash management problems. Furthermore, dynamic programming models can deal with all three of our alternative descriptions of the environment, since models involving risk or certainty can be formulated. Dynamic programming models of the cash management problem have been formulated by Eppen and Fama [1969], Neave [1970], and White and Norman [1965].

The simple inventory and dynamic programming models have been criticized on the grounds that they do not take into account all of the information that is actually available regarding cash inflows and outflows. The argument is that our third condition, that variations in cash inflows and outflows can be forecasted with certainty, is actually correct. With these detailed forecasts, more complex models involving more detailed decision variables can be formulated.

Many firms *can* provide reasonable sales forecasts, from forecasting models such as those described in Chapter 5, and historical data can be used to relate sales to payments on accounts receivable. This information provides a reasonably certain forecast of cash inflows from sales. In addition, the firm may hold securities that can be sold before maturity to generate additional cash inflows if necessary, but these inflows result from controllable decisions by the cash manager.

Likewise, production (or service activity) level forecasts can be used as the basis for estimating cash outflow requirements, and it may be possible to obtain reasonably certain estimates of these. Cash outflows for the purchase of securities also result from controllable decisions.

Given these certain forecasts, it is a straightforward task to formulate a linear programming model of the cash management problem. The relationships among the problem elements can be written as linear expressions involving the following decision variables:

1. payment schedules for the predicted purchases in periods 1, 2, . . .
2. transactions to be made on the securities held by the firm at the beginning of the planning period
3. the new investments to be made in securities in periods 1, 2, . . .
4. the use of the available lines of credit in periods 1, 2, . . .

An example of such a formulation is presented by Orgler [1969, 1970]. This model provides a detailed guide to cash management decisions. The only criticism of Orgler's model is that the level of detail may actually be too high.

The complexity of the model may hinder its acceptance and use by managers.

Srinivasan [1974] took advantage of another analogy in constructing a different model of the cash management problem. Cash inflows and marketable securities are *sources* of funds, while accounts payable and the purchases of securities are *uses*. "Sources and uses" sounds like "supplies and demands." Recall the transportation and transshipment models of Chapter 15. Given the certain forecasts of cash inflows and outflows, Srinivasan realized that it would be possible to develop a *network model* of the cash management problem (see problem 9 in Chapter 15).

The resulting transshipment formulation is shown in Figure 3. Suppose there are only three time periods. The three nodes labeled C1, C2, and C3 denote cash availabilities in periods 1, 2, and 3 respectively. Notice that it is possible to "ship" excess cash from period 1 to periods 2 and 3, and from period 2 to period 3. Since this could be accomplished by investing in short-term securities that mature in periods 2 and 3, there would be a negative cost (a contribution) on each of these arcs. The positive number by each cash node represents the forecast of the cash inflow in that period from payments on accounts receivable.

The nodes labeled A1, A2, and A3 represent the accounts payable by the firm in periods 1, 2, and 3 respectively. The forecasts of the amounts are shown as negative numbers written by the nodes. Cash available in period 1

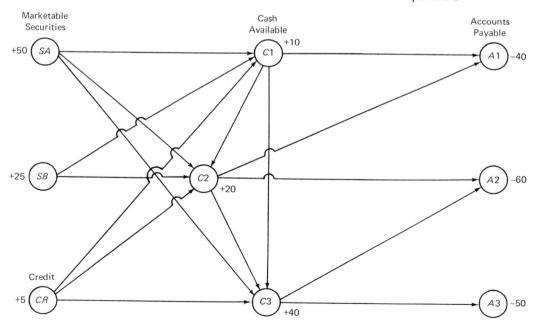

Figure 3. A transshipment model formulation of the cash management problem

may be used to pay accounts in period 1, as indicated by the arc from node C1 to node A1. Cash available in period 2 may be used to pay accounts in period 1 with an interest penalty (a cost on the arc from node C2 to node A1) or to pay accounts in period 2 (A2) at no charge. All accounts must be paid after a delay of no more than one period, so there is no arc from node C3 to node A1.

Nodes SA and SB represent marketable securities held by the firm. SA matures in period 3 at a face value of 50, so there is no cost on the arc from node SA to node C3. However, SA could be sold at a penalty to provide cash in periods 1 or 2. These penalty costs would be on the arcs from SA to C1 and to C2. Similarly, security SB matures in period 2, so there is no arc from SB to C3.

Node CR represents the line of credit of the firm, which could be used in any of the three periods to obtain additional cash. The costs on the arcs from CR would represent interest payments.

The advantages of this model are that is has the visual interpretation of Figure 3, and the relevant information can be summarized in a transportation table in a convenient, easy to understand format. Srinivasan [1974] estimates that the computer run time would be about 3 percent of that required for a linear programming model of the same cash management problem in a large organization. Since it is proposed that this model should be run each day, such considerations can become important.

The transshipment formulation does have some disadvantages, since some details included in Orgler's linear optimization model must be omitted. (Srinivasan [1974] presents a more complete discussion).

In summary, this example illustrates several important points. First, there is no one model that is "best" for analyzing a particular problem. We have seen that the cash management problem may be analyzed using a simple inventory model, an inventory model that allows probabilistic demand statements, a dynamic programming model, a linear optimization model, or a network model. The choice of the appropriate model is dependent on the nature of the environment, the desired level of detail in the model, and the costs of computation. Such decisions should not be left entirely to a staff analyst, but should involve the individual who will actually be using the model.

Second, the appropriate model can be identified by determining the nature of the environment, the nature of the relationships among the problem elements, and the objective of the analysis. This process is not automatic and requires judgment, but the manager can play an important and valuable role in it.

Adding Complexity

Unfortunately, real-world problems are not always categorized as neatly as those we have presented here. It may actually be necessary to combine ideas from several types of models in order to analyze a complex problem. Moses [1975] describes the implementation of a corporate simulation model with an embedded linear optimization model that simply provides additional information to the simulation model.

Another example in which substantially different kinds of models have been coupled together is reported by Buffa [1972, pp. 690–704] concerning the firm of Van Den Berghs & Jurgens, a subsidiary of Unilever. In general, a number of planning models of the type discussed in Chapter 7 are coupled together in a complex planning system. There are a raw material model, a distribution model, a packaging model, marketing models, brand models, a fixed expenses model, a cash flow model, an expense extraction model, a cost type model, and a divisional model. The company is a major producer of margarine and other fat products, and crude oil costs are of significance. Therefore, the formulation for each of the product groups is chosen on the basis of refined oil costs. The formulations themselves are generated by an off-line linear programming model, and entered into the system as necessary by way of the formulations model. Thus, we have an optimizing model coupled with a set of predictive models.

Finally, an excellent example of the coupling of different kinds of models was developed by Hax and Meal [1975] and applied as a planning system in a process manufacturing firm described as being analogous to a chemical plant or steel mill. The example firm is a multiplant, multiproduct operation with three distinct seasonal patterns. There is a strong incentive to maintain a nearly level manufacturing rate for the following reasons:

1. The capital cost of equipment is very high compared with the cost of shift premium for labor, and the plants normally operate three shifts five days a week with occasional weekend work.
2. The labor union is very strong and exerts pressure to maintain constant production levels throughout the year for employment stabilization.

System Structure   In structuring the system, levels of aggregation for the various items produced were developed first. The extent to which sets of decisions regarding production were interdependent was examined. If two sets of decisions were found to be independent, they were totally separated in the hierarchy of decisions. Beginning at the most detailed level, items sharing a major "set up" cost were grouped into "families." Thus, scheduling decisions for items in a family were very dependent, while the opposite was true for items in different families. It was also found that decisions for a family in one time period were strongly tied to decisions for the same family in other time periods. This time dependence resulted from the need to accumulate seasonal inventories in both product families. Product families were aggregated into "types" if they shared a common seasonal pattern and production rate. This process facilitated seasonal planning, since only the aggregate for all families in the type needed to be considered in developing the plan.

The next step in the process was the development of a hierarchy of decisions based on the relationships developed in the aggregation process. The following steps were developed:

1. assignment of families to plants
2. seasonal planning
3. scheduling of families
4. scheduling of items

In addition to the preceding steps, basic inventory models were used to establish minimum production run lengths and overstock limits. The complete decision sequence is shown in Figure 4. A brief description of the several submodels and the nature of their interaction follows.

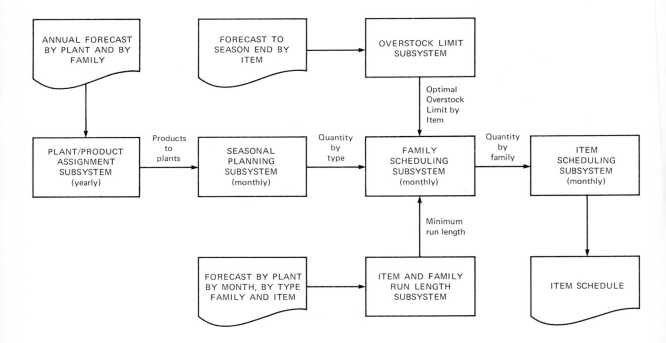

Figure 4. Decision sequence in planning and scheduling

From A. C. Haz and H. C. Meal, "Hierarchical Integration of Production Planning and Scheduling," in *Studies in the Management Science*, Vol. 1, "Logistics," edited by M. A. Geisler, North Holland-American Elsevier, 1975; used by permission.

Plant Product Assignment Subsystem (PAS) The PAS system determines the plant locations at which each family should be manufactured. The model balances the cost of interterritory transportation against the incremental capital investment cost required to manufacture the product family in question. The model is run annually to take account of new products and changes in variable manufacturing cost and demand patterns.

Seasonal Planning Subsystem (SPS) SPS, the aggregate planning subsystem, determines the production requirements and seasonal stock accumulations by product type for each plant. The objective is to minimize total regular and overtime production costs plus inventory holding costs, subject to constraints on available regular and overtime labor. Demand and safety stock requirements must also be met. Linear programming was used as the solution technique.

Family Scheduling Subsystem (FSS) The FSS subsystem is used to schedule enough production for the families in a product type to use the time allocated to the type by the SPS. This production includes the accumulation of the necessary seasonal stock.

Item Scheduling Subsystem (ISS) The ISS subsystem determines the production quantities for each item within the constraints of the family schedules determined by the FSS. As in FSS, overstock limits are observed and an attempt is made to maximize customer service. In order to carry out this task, Hax and Meal developed approaches that equalized the expected run out times for the items in the family.

Hax and Meal report a total development cost in the range of $150,000 to $200,000. While exact benefits were not reported, cost reductions from smoother production, fewer emergency interruptions, and reduced inventory carrying cost were expected to be more than $200,000 per year in each plant.

Most of these more complex models generally result from a bootstrapping approach to model building as described in Chapter 6. A manager who has the basic knowledge of the models and solution techniques that we have studied should have no difficulty in participating in the development of more complex models such as these and in using their results.

WHAT SHOULD THE MANAGER KNOW?

We have come full circle. In the introduction, we argued that the modern manager should have the following skills:

1. The ability to recognize situations in which management science might be used effectively.

2. The ability to conduct two-way communication with a technical specialist; that is, he must be able to
    a. explain the nature of his problem to a specialist in a meaningful way
    b. understand the specialist's product sufficiently well to verify its appropriateness and potential usefulness.

3. The ability to understand the results of management science studies so that he can obtain full value from the information available to him.

4. The ability to conceptualize a problem in terms of a particular model of management science, even if no formal analysis is performed.

5. The ability to formulate models appropriate for analyzing small, straightforward problems, utilize standard computer programs written by others to obtain the solutions, and interpret the results.

If you have mastered these skills, you have added an important dimension to your managerial growth and abilities.

References

Baumol, W. J., "The Transactions Demand for Cash: An Inventory Theoretic Approach," *Quarterly Journal of Economics,* Vol. 66, 1952, pp. 454–56.

Buffa, E. S., *Operations Management: Problems and Models,* third edition, John Wiley & Sons, New York, 1972.

Eppen, G. D., and E. F. Fama, "Cash Balance and Simple Dynamic Portfolio Problems with Proportional Costs," *International Economic Review,* Vol. 10, 1969, pp. 119–33.

Hax, A. C., and H. C. Meal, "Hierarchical Integration of Production Planning and Scheduling," in *Studies in the Management Science, Vol. I, Logistics,* edited by M. A. Geisler, North Holland-American Elsevier, 1975.

Miller, M. H., and D. J. Orr, "A Model of the Demand for Money by Firms," *Quarterly Journal of Economics,* Vol. 80, 1966, pp. 413–35.

Moses, M. A., "Implementation of Analytical Planning Systems," *Management Science,* Vol. 21, 1975, pp. 1133–43.

Neave, E. H., "The Stochastic Cash Balance Problem with Fixed Costs for Increases and Decreases," *Management Science,* Vol. 16, 1970, pp. 472–90.

Orgler, Y. E., "An Unequal-Period Model for Cash Management Decisions," *Management Science,* Vol. 16, 1969, pp. B77–B92.

———, *Cash Management: Methods and Models,* Wadsworth Publishing Company, Belmont, Calif., 1970.

Srinivasan, V., "A Transshipment Model for Cash Management Decisions," *Management Science,* Vol. 20, June, 1974, pp. 1350–1363.

White, D. J., and J. M. Norman, "Control of Cash Reserves," *Operational Research Quarterly,* Vol. 16, 1965, pp. 309–28.

APPENDIXES

Appendix A
Review of Some Mathematical Concepts

The following review of mathematical concepts is intended as a "prompter" or reminder to those who have been exposed to comparable materials elsewhere. As with the other review materials in these appendixes, it is not intended as a substitute for rigorous mathematics courses.

SETS

Set theory is part of the language of modern mathematics and is often used in the analysis of managerial problems, particularly those associated with with probability analysis.

Definitions

Set   A set is a *well-defined collection of objects*. All of the letters in the alphabet define a set. The last five letters in the alphabet define a set. The letters in the word "number" define a set. The English language is full of words often used as synonyms for the term "set," such as a *swarm* of bees, a *team* of horses, a *clutch* of eggs, a *bed* of oysters, a *tyranny* of deans, a *covey* of quail, and a *group* of students.

   If the definition is vague, we do not have a set. For example, it would be difficult to think in terms of lovers, hippies, or analysts as sets because the definitions of these terms may not be crystal clear to everyone.

Element   Each object of a set is called an *element*. For example, the set of all of the odd integer numbers between 1 and 99 contains the number 25 as an element.

Notation

It is common to denote a set by a capital letter and to define it by enclosing the elements with braces, for example,

$A = \{a, b, c\}$,

$B = \{\text{the six odd numbers between 6 and 18}\}$,

$C = \{\text{colors of the American flag}\}$,

$D = \{\text{the months of the year}\}$.

Empty Set   A set with no elements in it is called an empty set, usually denoted by the symbol ϕ or by $\{\ \}$.

Element in a Set   If c is an element in the set A, then in notational form $c \in A$. On the other hand, if c is *not* an element of the set A, then $c \notin A$.

Equal Set   Two sets are identical or *equal* if and only if each and every element of set A is also an element of set B, and if each and every element of set B is also an element of set A. For example, $A = B$ if

$$A = \{a, b, c\} ,$$
$$B = \{c, b, a\} .$$

The order in which the elements are listed is irrelevant. If $C = \{1, 2\}$, and $D = \{1, 2, 3\}$, then the two sets are not equal and the standard notation is $C \neq D$.

Subset   If each element of set C is also an element of set D, then set C is a subset of D. To denote this relationship, we use the inclusion sign ($\subset$), for example, $C \subset D$ when $C = \{1, 2\}$ and $D = \{1, 2, 3\}$.

Universal Set   The set that includes all of the elements is called the *universal set*, commonly denoted by $\mathcal{U}$.

Venn Diagram

Graphic representations of sets in the form of Venn diagrams are often useful. The universal set $\mathcal{U}$ is usually denoted graphically as a rectangle. A circle within the rectangle then denotes a set, as shown in Figure 1. Therefore, Figure 1 shows that the set A is a subset of the universal set $\mathcal{U}$, or symbolically, $A \subset \mathcal{U}$.

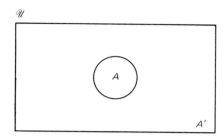

Figure 1. Venn diagram showing the set *A* as a subset of the universal set $\mathcal{U}$. The complement of set *A* contains all elements not in *A*, that is, *A'*

Complement   Note in Figure 1 that all of the elements of the universal set $\mathcal{U}$ which are *not* in set A are denoted by the *complement* set A', read A prime.

Intersections   When there are common elements in two sets, we describe them as having an intersection as shown in Figure 2. In Figure 2, the universal set is all of the letters of the alphabet, and $R = \{a, b, c, d\}$, and $S = \{c, d, e, f\}$. Thus, we have a new set defined by the intersection of R and S comprised of the elements c and d, and this new set is denoted as $R \cap S$, where $\cap$ is read as the "intersection" of R and S. In common usage, $\cap$ is pronounced "cap." Thus, we might speak of R cap S.

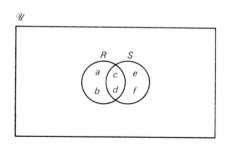

Figure 2. Venn diagram showing the intersection of sets *R* and *S*, since both sets contain *c* and *d*. The new set is denoted $R \cap S$

Union   The union of two sets is defined as a new set consisting of those elements belonging to either or both. For example, in Figure 2, $R = \{a, b, c, d\}$ and $S = \{c, d, e, f\}$. However, the *union* of R and S is a set that is denoted symbolically as $R \cup S = \{a, b, c, d, e, f\}$ and is pronounced R cup S.

Disjoint or Mutually Exclusive Sets If two sets have no common elements, they are said to be *disjoint* or *mutually exclusive*. They can, nevertheless, be a part of the same universal set, as shown in Figure 3. For example, the universal set might be comprised of all of the college football teams. The set F = {all of the teams in the Pacific Eight Conference} and G = {all of the teams in the Big Ten Conference}. There are no teams common to the two defined sets; they are mutually exclusive, or disjoint.

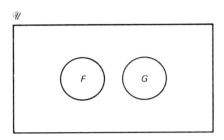

Figure 3. Venn diagram of disjoint or mutually exclusive sets F and G

FUNCTIONS

A function is a particular kind of relationship where for each element x of set X, a single value y can be determined in set Y. For example, suppose that the number of items held in inventory is the set X = {1, 2, 3}, and the corresponding cost of holding items in inventory is the set Y = {30, 40, 50}.

Domain The set X of the number of items held in inventory is defined as the domain.

Range The set Y is defined as the range.

Thus, when we have one set defining a domain and a corresponding set defining a range for the domain, the association between the two sets is called a function. When a functional relationship exists we can express the relationship in terms of an equation. For our example, we note that each additional unit of inventory adds \$10 to the cost, so there must be a fixed cost of \$20. The equation is then

$$y = 20 + 10x. \tag{1}$$

Independent and Dependent Variables The inventory cost y is dependent on the number of units in inventory x. Therefore, the number of units x defines the domain and is designated the *independent* variable, and since y *depends* on x, we designate y as the dependent variable.

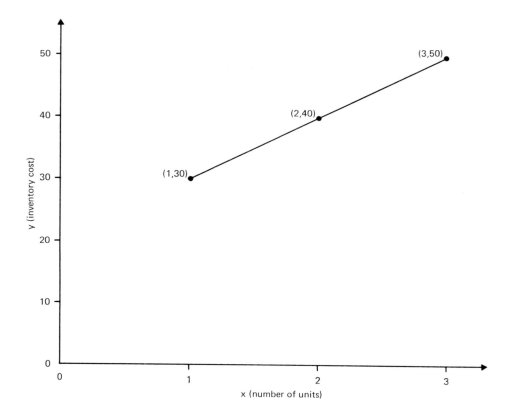

Figure 4. Graph of the equation $y = 20 + 10x$ for the domain $X = \{1, 2, 3\}$ and the range $Y = \{30, 40, 50\}$

The Graph of a Function

The graphic representation of a function is another way of showing that for a given element x of set X, one and only one value of y is determined in the set Y. Standard graphic representation of a function designates the horizontal axis for the independent variable x and the vertical axis for the dependent variable y, as shown in Figure 4. Then to plot equation (1) we determine points on the graph by paired values (x, y), by substituting values of x in equation (1) and computing corresponding values of y. For example, three paired values from equation (1) are (1, 30), (2, 40), and (3, 50). These values are plotted in Figure 4 and connected by a line that defines the relationship within the stated domain and range.

Functional Notation

It is common to state the dependent side of an equation y in terms of its functional dependency by substituting $f(x)$ for y so that equation (1) would read

$$f(x) = 20 + 10x. \tag{2}$$

The functional notation $f(x)$ is read, "the value of the function at x," or usually condensed to read simply "f of x."

The dependent variable might be a function of several independent variables and the functional notation is shorthand for stating this fact. For example, overall production cost y might be dependent on several variables, such as the number of units produced x_1, wage rates x_2, overtime used x_3, materials used x_4, and inventory costs x_5. In functional notation we could state the dependency relationship as

$$y = f(x_1, x_2, x_3, x_4, x_5). \tag{3}$$

Linear Functions

In the previous section we used a relationship between the number of items held in inventory to inventory cost as an example to discuss the nature of a function. The result was equation (1), $y = 20 + 10x$, which is a linear function because there are no squared or higher powers of variables, nor were there cross product terms of variables, such as xy. Graphically, linear functions plot as straight lines.

The Slope-Intercept Form   A linear equation with one independent variable can be placed in the slope-intercept form by solving for the dependent variable y, as follows:

$$y = a + bx,$$

where a is the constant or y intercept term (the value of y when $x = 0$), and b is the slope of the line, as shown in Figure 5. The slope b is simply the amount y increases for a *unit* increase in the independent variable x. The slope can be either negative, or positive as it is in Figure 5. Since only two points need be established to plot the equation for a straight line, one point is established by the y intercept, and one additional point can be established by substituting a value of x in the equation and computing the corresponding value of y.

The Standard Form   The standard form for a linear equation is

$$Ax + By = C, \tag{2}$$

where A, B, and C are coefficients. To convert to the slope-intercept form, we simply solve for y and obtain

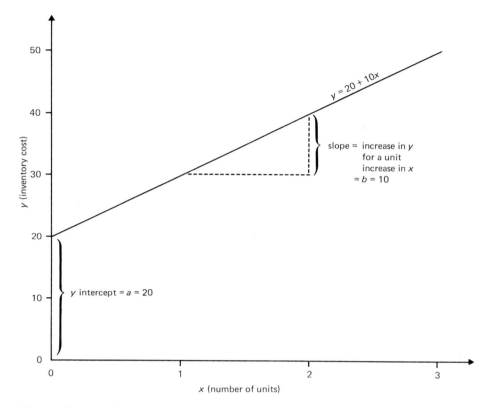

Figure 5. Graphic relationships for a linear equation of the form $y = a + bx$

$$y = \frac{C}{B} - \frac{Ax}{B}.$$

Equation (1) can be placed in standard form by rearranging as follows:

$$-10x + y = 20 ,$$

and the coefficients of the standard form for equation (1) are $A = -10$, $B = 1$, and $C = 20$.

Solving Simultaneous Linear Equations

Suppose we own two machines, both of which can perform the same operation; however, the fixed and variable costs of using the two processes are different. The costs are a function of the number of units produced and are therefore expressed in general terms as $f(x) = a + bx$, where a represents the fixed costs and b the variable costs.

For machine A, the fixed costs are $10 to set up the machine, and the variable costs are $3 per unit produced. The cost equation is then, $y = 10 + 3x$.

For machine B, the fixed costs are $20 to set up the machine, and the variable costs are only $2 per unit produced. The machine B cost equation is then, $y = 20 + 2x$.

The two cost equations are plotted in Figure 6. We wish to determine the volume at which the costs are equal for the two machines. This volume can be seen to be the value of x common to the two equations, that is, where the two lines cross in Figure 6, yielding the same cost and number of units produced.

Analytically, we determine this point by solving the two equations simultaneously. Recall from basic algebra that if we have two independent equations and two unknowns, we can solve simultaneously to determine

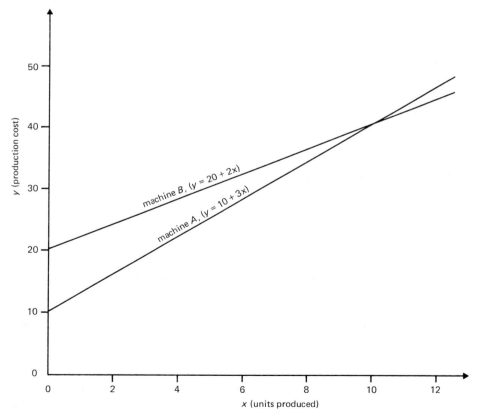

Figure 6. Simultaneous solution of equations A and B occurs where the graphs of the two equations intersect—the point at which the two equations have common values of x and y

the values of the two unknowns, in our case x (number of units) and y (cost for x units). More generally, if we have n independent equations and n variables, we can solve simultaneously to determine the values of the n variables.

We can take two approaches to solution, substitution and Gaussian elimination.

Substitution   For our simple example, the easiest procedure is to solve for one variable, using one of the equations, and insert that expression in the other equation. This process produces an equation that has eliminated one of the variables, and we can then determine a numerical value for the remaining variable. Then we substitute this numerical value back into the first equation and solve for the value of the second variable.

Using our example, the value of y for machine A is, $y = 10 + 3x$. Substituting this value of y in the machine B equation, we have

$$10 + 3x = 20 + 2x \,,$$
$$x = 10 \text{ units} \,.$$

Now, inserting $x = 10$ in the machine A equation we have, $y = 10 + 3\,(10) = \$40$. Therefore, the volume is $x = 10$ units, and the cost is $y = \$40$ for either machine. Below 10 units machine A is more economical, and above 10 units machine B is more economical. Compare this result with the point where the graphs of the two equations cross in Figure 6.

Gaussian Elimination   Though it is not necessary to do so, let us rearrange the equations for machines A and B in standard form,

$$A, \; -3x + \; y = \; 10 \,,$$
$$B, \; -2x + \; y = \; 20 \,.$$

Suppose we wish to eliminate the variable x from one of the two equations by Gaussian elimination. First, we divide equation A by its x coefficient (-3) to obtain

$$A, \quad x - \frac{1y}{3} = \frac{-10}{3} \,,$$
$$B, \; -2x + \; y = \; 20 \,.$$

Then, we multiply A by the negative of the x coefficient in equation B, $-(-2) = 2$, and add the resulting equation A to equation B.
This process results in the revised equations

$$A, \; x - \frac{1y}{3} = \frac{-10}{3} \,,$$
$$B, \quad \frac{1y}{3} = \frac{40}{3} \,.$$

To see how B was obtained, the calculations are shown below:

$$2x - \frac{2y}{3} = \frac{-20}{3} \qquad \text{(from multiplying A by 2)}$$

$$\frac{-2x + \ y = \ 20}{\frac{1y}{3} = \ \frac{40}{3}} \qquad \begin{array}{l} \text{(from B)} \\[1mm] \text{(adding equals)} \end{array}$$

Next, divide B by the y coefficient (1/3), which gives

$$A, \ x - \frac{1y}{3} = \frac{-10}{3} \ ,$$

$$B, \qquad y = \ 40 \ .$$

The solution for y, 40, is the same as the one obtained previously by substitution. Finally, multiply B by the negative of the y coefficient in equation A, $-(-1/3) = 1/3$, and add the resulting equation B to equation A:

$$A, \ x = 10 \ ,$$

$$B, \ y = 40 \ ,$$

which gives the solution of 10 units for x. Again, the calculations for this step are shown below:

$$x - \frac{1y}{3} = \frac{-10}{3} \qquad \text{(from A)}$$

$$\frac{\frac{1y}{3} = -\frac{40}{3}}{x \qquad = \ \frac{30}{3}} \qquad \begin{array}{l} \text{(from multiplying B by 1/3)} \\[1mm] \text{(adding equals)} \end{array}$$

Note that this process is like that of a linear programming pivot.

Appendix B
Review of Some Probability Concepts

The following review of probability concepts is intended as a "prompter" or reminder to those who have been exposed to comparable materials elsewhere. As with the other review materials in these appendixes, it is not intended as a substitute for a rigorous exposure to probability theory.

Probability concepts are important in many problems in management. These concepts enter the models associated with decisions under risk and uncertainty.

Objective Probability   When we have considerable data concerning the probability of an event, we say that the estimate of probability is *objective*. The usual examples of objective probability are experiments in tossing coins or dice, and other activities that are easily repeated for a large number of trials. In managerial problems, however, the best examples are situations where we have data on *frequency distributions* of events from which probabilities can be computed, such as frequency distributions of demand.

Subjective Probability   In many managerial problems, there is little past experience available, and we may be forced to use an estimate of the probability of an event based on our personal belief in what the chances are that the event will occur. Such estimates of probabilities are called *subjective* or personal. The term, subjective probability, arises from an attempt to discriminate between probabilities whose values depend on the subject who assigns those values and objective probabilities whose values are determined only by the object and the experiment in which it is involved.

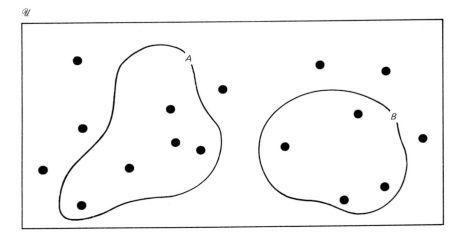

Figure 1. Sample space with two mutually exclusive events

MUTUALLY EXCLUSIVE EVENTS

Definition: The probability that a composite event A will occur is the sum of the probabilities of the simple events of which it is composed. Note from this simple definition that the probability of the composite event A, written $P(A)$, in Figure 1 is simply the ratio of the number of simple events falling within the enclosure A, $n(A)$, divided by the total number n in the universal set $\mathcal{U}$,

$$P(A) = \frac{n(A)}{n}. \tag{1}$$

If two events A and B possess the property that the occurrence of one prevents the occurrence of the other, they are called *mutually exclusive* events; that is, there is no overlap in their sets as shown in Figure 1. Using equation (1) then, the probability that *either* A or B will occur, $P(A \text{ or } B)$, is seen to be

$$P(A \text{ or } B) = \frac{n(A) + n(B)}{n}$$

$$= \frac{n(A)}{n} + \frac{n(B)}{n}.$$

Since the last statement is composed of two fractions which define $P(A)$ and $P(B)$, the result yields the addition rule, which is expressed as follows:

Addition rule. When A and B are mutually exclusive events,

$$P(A \text{ or } B) = P(A) + P(B). \tag{2}$$

INDEPENDENT EVENTS

It is possible that events may be independent of each other, or one may be dependent on the other. When events are independent, the occurrence of one has no effect on the probability of the occurrence of the other.

For example, if the composite events A and B diagrammed in Figure 1 are independent of each other, the probability that both will occur, $P(AB)$, is equal to the product of the probabilities of the individual events. Thus, the rule for their joint occurrence is:

$$Joint\ probability:\ P(AB) = P(A) \cdot P(B) . \tag{3}$$

DEPENDENT EVENTS

We may also have events A and B, which have overlap in their sets. The overlap provides information that makes it possible to estimate the probability of B if we know that event A has occurred.

Figure 2 provides a specific example. The universal set $\mathcal{U}$ contains 36 simple events or points. The composite event A is defined by the set A, which contains 16 points. The probability of A is $P(A) = 16/36 = 4/9$. The probability of B is, $P(B) = 6/36 = 1/6$. Note, however, that there is overlap between the two sets since 2 points in B are also contained in A. Now suppose that we already know that A has occurred, and we wish now to estimate the probability that B has also occurred. Since A contains the 2 points also in B, we can compute from the subset A the probability of B, given that A has occurred, written as the conditional probability $P(B|A)$,

$$P(B|A) = 2/16 = 1/8 .$$

Now in general terms, $P(A) = n(A)/n$, and the joint probability of A and B is, $P(AB) = n(AB)/n$. If we divide the second of these two statements by the first and cancel n, we have

$$\frac{P(AB)}{P(A)} = \frac{n(AB)}{n(A)} = P(B|A) .$$

This expression defines the *conditional* probability of B, given the occurrence of A, and when rearranged gives:

$$Multiplication\ rule:\ P(AB) = P(A) \cdot P(B|A) . \tag{4}$$

Therefore, with the multiplication rule we can compute the joint probability $P(AB)$ if we know the probability of one event and the conditional probability of the other. For the example of Figure 2 we have

$$P(AB) = (4/9)\ (1/8) = 1/18 .$$

Equation (4) is for dependent events as we have noted. As a check of the logic, let us assume independence. Recall from equation (3) that the

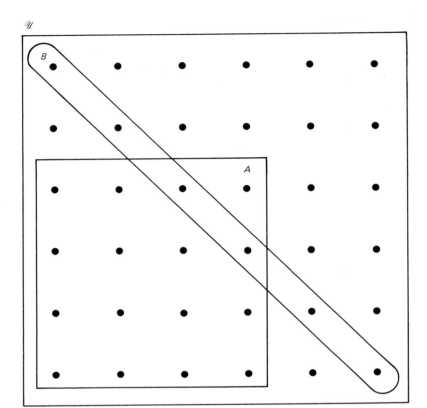

Figure 2. Sample space for a conditional probability problem where the universal set $\mathscr{U}$ has 36 simple events, and the set *A* contains 16 events, two of which are also in the set *B*, which contains six simple events

probability for joint independent events is the product of the probabilities of the two independent events. Therefore, if we substitute the value of $P(AB)$ from equation (3) in equation (4) and solve for the conditional probability $P(B|A)$ we have

$$P(B|A) = \frac{P(A) \cdot P(B)}{P(A)} = P(B) .$$

Marginal or Unconditional Probabilities Previously we discussed the conditional probability, given the occurrence of an event. When we have such compound and dependent events, what is the final probability of an event without prior conditions? Consider the following simple drawing process: we have two boxes, and box 1 contains three balls (two red and one white). Box 2 contains four balls (two red and two white). The process is to select one of the boxes at random and then select one ball from that box.

Figure 3 shows a tree diagram of the sequential process indicating all of the possible outcomes. Taking the upper branch, $P(\text{box } 1) = 1/2$. Given that box 1 has been selected, the conditional probability of drawing a red ball is $P(R|1) = 2/3$, since there are two red balls in the box of three. Similarly, the probability of drawing a white ball, given that box 1 was selected, is $P(W|1) = 1/3$. Now, the joint probability of drawing box 1 *and* a red ball is $P(R1) = (1/2)(2/3) = 1/3$, and of drawing box 1 and a white ball is $P(W1)$

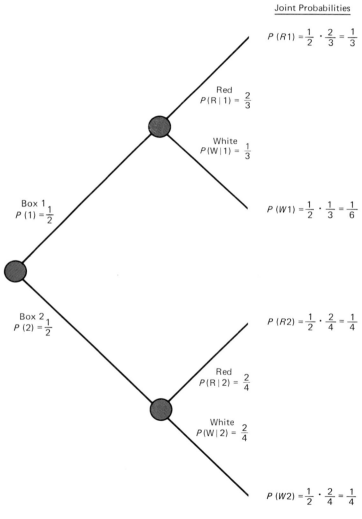

Joint Probabilities

$P(R1) = \frac{1}{2} \cdot \frac{2}{3} = \frac{1}{3}$

Red
$P(R|1) = \frac{2}{3}$

White
$P(W|1) = \frac{1}{3}$

Box 1
$P(1) = \frac{1}{2}$

$P(W1) = \frac{1}{2} \cdot \frac{1}{3} = \frac{1}{6}$

Box 2
$P(2) = \frac{1}{2}$

$P(R2) = \frac{1}{2} \cdot \frac{2}{4} = \frac{1}{4}$

Red
$P(R|2) = \frac{2}{4}$

White
$P(W|2) = \frac{2}{4}$

$P(W2) = \frac{1}{2} \cdot \frac{2}{4} = \frac{1}{4}$

Figure 3. Tree diagram of the box-ball drawing process

$= (1/2) (1/3) = 1/6$. The other main branch probabilities are calculated in a similar way. Note that the joint probabilities at the right-hand side of the tree enumerate all of the outcomes and must therefore total to 1.

Let us now assemble the joint probability data from Figure 3 in the form of Table 1. The *unconditional* probabilities associated with selecting box 1 or 2 are the sums of the two joint probabilities of $P(R1)$ and $P(W1)$ for box 1 and $P(R2)$ and $P(W2)$ for box 2, and are 1/2 each, shown as the marginal probabilities in the right-hand column. Similarly, the unconditional probabilities associated with selecting red or white balls are the sums of the two joint probabilities in the bottom row. These probabilities are called *marginal* simply because they occur in the margins of the table as shown. Their significance is that they are the probabilities of the ending events without stated conditions; that is, they are unconditional.

TABLE 1. Joint and Marginal Probabilities for the Box-Ball Drawing Process

Second Draw: Which Ball? / First Draw: Which Box?	Joint Probabilities		Marginal (Unconditional) Probabilities of Outcomes on First Draw
	Red Ball	White Ball	
Box 1	$P(R1) = \frac{1}{3}$	$P(W1) = \frac{1}{6}$	$\frac{1}{3} + \frac{1}{6} = \frac{1}{2}$
Box 2	$P(R2) = \frac{1}{4}$	$P(W2) = \frac{1}{4}$	$\frac{1}{4} + \frac{1}{4} = \frac{1}{2}$
Marginal (Unconditional) Probabilities of Outcomes on Second Draw	$\frac{1}{3} + \frac{1}{4} = \frac{7}{12}$	$\frac{1}{6} + \frac{1}{4} = \frac{5}{12}$	1.00

Bayes Theorem

In many managerial problems, we may start with probabilities of occurrence but be in a position to revise (improve) them as we obtain new information. For example, suppose we have a process which, when set up properly, has been shown to produce products that are 95 percent good. On the other hand, when it is improperly set up, only 20 percent of the products are acceptable. Previous data also indicate that 90 percent of the process settings have been correct in the past. Suppose we set the process and the first output of the process is *good*. What is the probability that the process has been properly set up?

Bayes formula provides the mechanism for using the new information to refine probability estimates. The initial probability estimates are called the *prior* probabilities. If subsequent new information becomes available, the newly computed probabilities become *revised prior* probabilities in an iterative set of computations.

We can compute the probability that the setup is correct, given the new information, through the use of Bayes formula

$$P(A_i|B) = \frac{P(A_iB)}{P(B)},$$

which you may recognize as the formula for the *conditional probability* of A_i, given the occurrence of B.

Suppose we define the event A_1 as "a correct setup," the event A_2 as "an incorrect setup," and the event B as "a good product." From previous data, we know that $P(A_1) = 0.9$ *prior* to observing the first output of the process. This value is called the *prior probability* of the event A_1. Likewise, the prior probability of a bad setup, $P(A_2)$, is 0.1.

We know the conditional probability of a good product given a good setup, $P(B|A_1)$, is 0.95, while the conditional probability of a good product given a bad setup, $P(B|A_2)$ is 0.20. From the *multiplication rule*, we can compute

$$P(A_1B) = P(A_1) \cdot P(B|A_1)$$
$$= (0.9)(0.95) = 0.855,$$

the *joint probability* of A_1 and B. Similarly, we obtain the *joint probability* of A_2 and B from

$$P(A_2B) = P(A_2) \cdot P(B|A_2)$$
$$= (0.1) \cdot (0.2) = 0.02.$$

The *unconditional* or *marginal* probability of a good product, event B, is obtained from the sum of these two joint probabilities, so that

$$P(B) = P(A_1B) + P(A_2B)$$
$$= 0.855 + 0.02 = 0.875.$$

We can now compute the probability that the process has a correct setup, given the *additional information* that the first output of the process is good.

Using Bayes formula, we obtain

$$P(A_1|B) = \frac{P(A_1 B)}{P(B)}$$

$$= \frac{0.855}{0.875} = 0.977 \,,$$

which is the *revised prior* or *posterior* probability of A_1. Additional information regarding the output of the process could be used in an iterative fashion to continue to revise the probability of A_1.

Appendix C
Review of Some Concepts of Statistics

The following review of statistical concepts is intended as a "prompter" or reminder to those who have been exposed to comparable materials elsewhere. As with the other review materials in these appendixes, it is not intended as a substitute for a rigorous course in statistics.

UNIVERSE AND SAMPLE

A sample is drawn from a *universe* or *population* and is therefore a subset of a universe or population.

A *finite universe* might be a lot of 1,000 parts produced on a lathe. Any of the dimensions produced might in themselves be considered a finite universe.

An *infinite universe* might be represented by the time required for a worker to perform the lathe operation.

If we selected 100 parts from the 1,000 and measured their diameters, we would have a sample distribution of diameters. If we let the selection of the sample of 100 parts be based strictly on chance, we would have a *random sample*.

It is often true that the entire universe data are difficult and expensive to obtain, or impossible in the case of an infinite universe. Therefore, one of the important objectives of statistics is to infer from a sample distribution the characteristics of the universe distribution.

Parameters are designated as the characteristics of the universe, such as the average, variance, and range (these terms will be defined later).

Statistics are designated as characteristics of a sample drawn from a universe and are intended to infer the characteristics of the universe.

Notation

It is of some importance to retain the distinction between *parameters* and *statistics*, and we shall attempt to do this through a system of notation. In general, when we are referring to the parameters of a universe, we shall use one set of symbols, and when we are referring to the statistics of a sample, we shall use another set. In most instances, we shall be dealing with statistics rather than parameters. The notation is as follows:

μ = the population mean (parameter),

$\bar{x}$ = the mean of a sample drawn from the population (statistic),

σ^2 = the population variance (parameter),

s^2 = the variance of a sample drawn from the population (statistic).

DESCRIPTIVE STATISTICS

One major area of the study of statistics has to do with the precise and efficient ways of describing what otherwise would be a mass of data that would communicate very little worthwhile information. Table 1 illustrates this point. It lists measurements of the diameters of a sample of 50 shafts from a production lot of 10,000. By scanning the table we can pick out the maximum reading, 1.0043 inches, and the minimum reading, 0.9954 inches, but any generalization about the diameters of the 50 shafts is difficult. Similarly, inferences about the entire lot of 10,000 shafts are difficult.

TABLE 1. Diameters of 50 Shafts

1.0039	0.9956	1.0026	1.0004	1.0005
1.0014	0.9996	0.9994	0.9977	1.0023
0.9980	1.0025	1.0043	1.0004	0.9989
1.0000	1.0028	0.9954	0.9974	0.9992
0.9973	0.9994	1.0009	1.0033	1.0005
0.9996	0.9998	1.0026	1.0031	1.0034
1.0010	0.9995	0.9976	1.0009	0.9991
0.9999	0.9979	0.9983	0.9972	0.9998
1.0003	0.9968	1.0013	1.0007	1.0041
1.0037	1.0012	0.9985	1.0018	0.9987

Frequency Distributions

The situation is improved by grouping the data into a frequency distribution. This process involves tabulating the number of shaft measurements that fall into certain class intervals, as in Table 2. Immediately we observe some characteristics of the data that were difficult to see before. For example, we see that the high and low readings represent a small minority of the cases,

TABLE 2. Frequency Distribution of the Data in Table 1

Class limits (in.)	Frequency (no. of shafts)
0.9946–0.9955	1
0.9956–0.9965	1
0.9966–0.9975	4
0.9976–0.9985	6
0.9986–0.9995	7
0.9996–1.0005	11
1.0006–1.0015	7
1.0016–1.0025	3
1.0026–1.0035	6
1.0036–1.0045	4
	50

and that a large percentage of the shafts measured somewhere between 0.9982 inch and 1.0018 inch, with the largest number occurring around 1.0000 inch. When the data are plotted in a histogram (see Figure 1) the general relationships show up clearly. We see that we have a fairly symmetrical bell-shaped distribution of the measurements, centering on 1.0000 inch.

The Normal Distribution   The smooth bell-shaped curve that has been superimposed on the histogram of Figure 1 is called the normal or Gaussian distribution. We see that the distribution of diameter measurements fairly well approximates the normal distribution. The term *normal distribution* does not imply that distributions which do not approximate it are abnormal. The curve for the normal distribution has a specific mathematical function, so that for a distribution to approximate normality, the occurrence frequencies must follow closely the general pattern indicated in Figure 1. There are statistical tests that can be used to determine how closely a distribution approximates normality. If there is anything "normal" about the normal distribution, it may be that a great number of actual distributions in industry, science, and nature can be closely approximated by it. Thus a large part of statistical method is based on the normal distribution. Table 1 in Appendix E gives areas under a standardized normal curve.

Other Distributions   There are a number of other important distributions that are useful in management science. For example, the Poisson and the negative exponential distributions are used in waiting line theory and are useful in determining buffer inventory levels. Their distributions are given in Tables 2 and 3 in Appendix E.

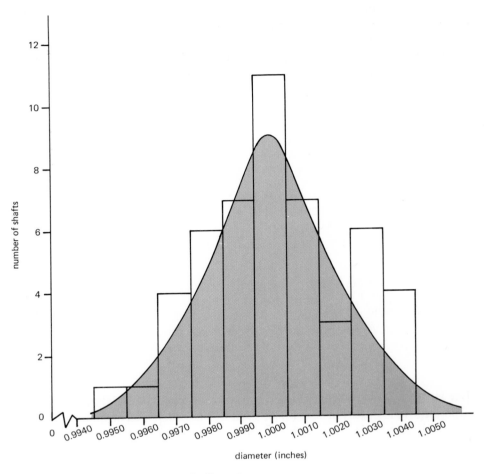

Figure 1. Histogram of 50 shaft diameter measurements

Techniques parallel to those discussed here for the normal distribution have been developed for these other distributions as well as for situations in which no specific distribution is implied. We will review general statistical methods for the normal distribution and will not attempt to review the details of analysis for the other distributions.

Measures of a Distribution

Several characteristics of distributions can be used to describe or specify them. In Figure 1 we note that, first, the measurements tend to group around some central value; second, there is variability, that is, no one value represents the whole; third, the distribution is symmetric; and fourth, there is one peak or mode. To describe a distribution we need measures of central value, variability, and symmetry and an observation of the number of modes. Note that if a distribution can be assumed to be normal, only the first two measures will specify it, since a normal distribution is unimodal and symmetric. Therefore, we shall discuss measures of central value and of variability.

Measures of Central Value   A measure of central value in the population is often made from a random sample drawn from the population. Suppose that the values for n individual items in a random sample are represented by $x_1, x_2, x_3, \ldots, x_i, \ldots, x_n$. Then the arithmetic mean $\bar{x}$ of the sample can be computed by

$$\bar{x} = \frac{\sum\limits_{i=1}^{n} x_i}{n} = \frac{x_1 + x_2 + x_3 + \cdots + x_{n-1} + x_n}{n}.$$

The Greek letter Σ means "sum of," and the x_i are the individual observations, which are numbered from 1 to n, where n is the total number of observations.[*] Therefore, for our shaft diameter example, we calculate $\bar{x}$ from Table 1 as follows:

$$\bar{x} = \frac{1.0039 + 1.0014 + 0.9980 + \cdots + 0.9987}{50} = 1.0002.$$

The result, $\bar{x}$, is the estimate of the population mean of the parent distribution. There are two other measures of the center of a distribution, the median and the mode. The *median* is that point on the horizontal scale which divides the area under the histogram into two equal parts.

The *mode* is the most frequently occurring value. On a histogram it is the midpoint of the class interval that has the largest frequency of occurrence. For the data of Table 2, represented by the histogram of Figure 1, the mode is 1.0000. Note then, that for a symmetrical distribution, the mean, the median, and the mode will all be equal.

Measures of Variability or Dispersion   The *range*, which is the simplest and most easily determined measure of variability, is the difference between the highest and lowest values in the distribution. For the data of Table 1, the range is $1.0043 - 0.9954 = 0.0089$ inch. It is not as stable a measure as the variance, since it is based on only two values instead of the entire set of data.

The *variance* is the most commonly used measure of variability in

---

[*]   There is, of course, a short-cut method for calculating the mean based on the grouped data of Table 2.

statistics because of its stability as a measure and because of other valuable properties that we shall discuss. The sample variance is defined by

$$s^2 = \frac{\sum\limits_{i=1}^{n} (x_i - \bar{x})^2}{n - 1}.$$

It is simply the sum of the squares of the differences between the individual observations and the mean of a distribution, divided by $n - 1$. For the data of Table 1, where we have already computed $\bar{x} = 1.0002$, the variance 0.00000494 is calculated as follows:

$$s^2 = \frac{(1.0039 - 1.0002)^2 + (1.0014 - 1.0002)^2 + (0.9980 - 1.0002)^2 + \cdots + (0.9987 - 1.0002)^2}{49}$$

$$= 0.00000494;$$

$$s = \sqrt{s^2} = 0.00222$$

It is the estimate of the actual population variance of the parent distribution.

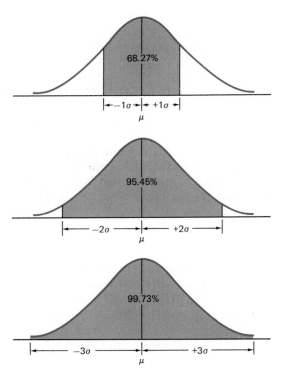

Figure 2. Areas under the normal curve for different σ limits

The *standard deviation* is the square root of the variance and is commonly denoted by s. For the data of Table 1,

$$s = \sqrt{s^2} = \sqrt{0.00000494} = 0.00222 \,.$$

The standard deviation has special properties that are useful to us. If we consider a normal distribution with mean, μ, and standard deviation, σ, it is true that 68.27 percent of the area under the curve (equivalent to the frequency of occurrence in the histogram) is included within the limits of $\mu \pm \sigma$; 95.45 percent is included within the limits $\mu \pm 2\sigma$; and 99.73 percent is included within the limits $\mu \pm 3\sigma$ (see Figure 2).

The significance of Figure 2 is that we can now make a probability statement about values that we presume come from the universe or population from which the sample distribution is drawn. Using the shaft diameter example, which had an $\bar{x} = 1.0002$ inch and $s = 0.00222$ inch, we can say that there is a 0.9545 probability that shafts coming from the lot or universe from which the sample was drawn will have outside diameters measuring between 0.99546 and 1.00464 inches, and that there is only a 0.0455 probability that shafts will measure outside these limits. Similarly, virtually all shafts will measure between 0.99354 and 1.00686 inches, and there is only a 0.0027 probability that any shafts will measure outside these limits.

REGRESSION AND CORRELATION

The statistical methods known as regression and correlation can help answer such questions as the following: What is the relationship between product demand and gross national product? How good is the relationship? Is it good enough to help predict product demand?

The regression line that best represents a set of points, (x_1, y_1), (x_2, y_2), ..., (x_i, y_i), ..., (x_n, y_n), is often needed as a basis for an estimating function. Take the data represented by the scatter diagram of Figure 3. An estimate of job difficulty has been developed by a system of points that varies with the degree that jobs require certain factors of skill, education, experience, physical fitness, etc. In Figure 3, estimates of job difficulty have been plotted versus existing wages on the job. The line that best fits the points is commonly the linear regression line, that is, the line that minimizes the squares of the wage deviations from it, as well as setting the simple deviations to zero. This least squares line is the linear function

$$y = a + bx \,,$$

$$\text{where } b = \frac{\sum\limits_{i=1}^{n} x_i y_i - \bar{x} \sum\limits_{i=1}^{n} y_i}{\sum\limits_{i=1}^{n} x_i^2 - \bar{x} \sum\limits_{i=1}^{n} x_i} \,,$$

$$a = \bar{y} - b\bar{x} \,,$$

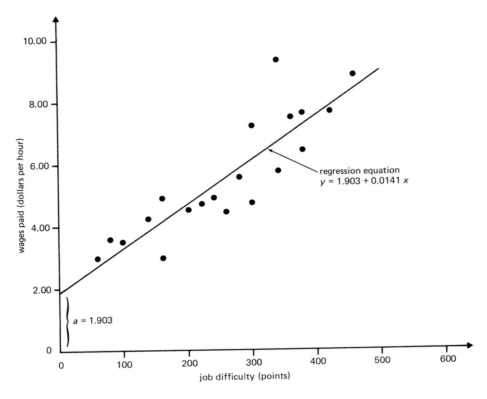

Figure 3. Scatter diagram showing difficulty points versus wages paid, with regression line

$$y's = \text{wages},$$
$$x's = \text{point ratings}.$$

The line can be computed easily with the aid of a calculator and plotted on the scatter diagram as the line of best fit for the given points. Table 3 shows this computation for the data of Figure 3. Since the resulting equation, $y = x + bx$, is a straight line, the value computed for a is the point where the line intersects the vertical axis, and the computed value for b is the slope of the line. For the data of Figure 3, the equation of the line is $y = 1.903 + 0.0141\ x$. The line intersects the wages axis at $1.903, and for each point of job difficulty we add $0.0141. The regression line is superimposed on the scatter diagram in Figure 3.

Let us note further the assumed structure with which we are dealing in the regression equation. For each level of job difficulty there is a distribution of wages. The reasons for variation might be related to the people on the jobs, their skills, seniority, etc., and to errors made in appraising

REVIEW OF SOME CONCEPTS OF STATISTICS

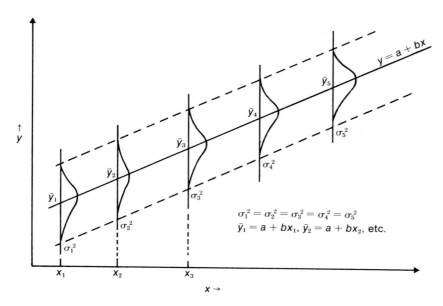

The equations within the figure:

$$\sigma_1^2 = \sigma_2^2 = \sigma_3^2 = \sigma_4^2 = \sigma_5^2$$
$$\bar{y}_1 = a + bx_1,\ \bar{y}_2 = a + bx_2,\ \text{etc.}$$

Figure 4. Diagram of assumptions in regression analysis

both jobs and people. The distributions are assumed to be normal. They each have a mean that falls on the regression line and they have equal variances. These assumptions are diagramed in Figure 4.

The regression equation is often used to estimate y within certain probability limits, given a value of x, since the value of x specifies a normal distribution with a mean and a variance. The probability that y will be beyond certain values is specified by the standard deviation limits.

There are other regression techniques that are appropriate when a straight line does not represent the data. Also, there are appropriate techniques for multiple regression, where there are more than two variables to be related.

Correlation is a measure of the degree of relationship between two variables. Although many times we suspect that a relationship exists because of the appearance of a scatter diagram, a correlation coefficient tells us how close that relationship is.

Correlation coefficients vary from -1.00 to $+1.00$. Figure 5 illustrates this general picture. Thus a correlation coefficient, r, of 0.85 indicates a higher degree of relationship than 0.50, and similarly an r of -0.85 indicates a higher degree of relationship than -0.50. It is important to note, however, that $r = 0.90$ does not imply twice as close a relationship as $r = 0.45$, since our ability to forecast y, given x, is better indicated by r^2, the square of the correlation coefficient. Loosely speaking, $r = 0.90$ ($r^2 = 0.81$) is about twice as good as $r = 0.636$ ($r^2 = 0.405$).

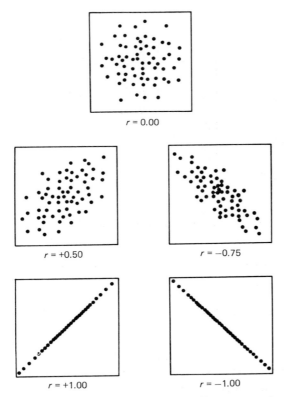

$r = 0.00$

$r = +0.50$ $r = -0.75$

$r = +1.00$ $r = -1.00$

Figure 5. Scatter diagrams for different correlation coefficients

Calculation of Correlation Coefficients   The correlation coefficient may be calculated by the following formula:

$$r = \frac{\displaystyle\sum_{i=1}^{n} (x_i - \bar{x})(y_i - \bar{y})}{n s_x s_y}.$$

The deviations from the means from each pair of observations are multiplied. There are as many such multiplications as there are observations. The entire set is summed and divided by $n s_x s_y$. It is actually simpler computationally to use

$$r = \frac{n \displaystyle\sum_{i=1}^{n} x_i y_i - \displaystyle\sum_{i=1}^{n} x_i \displaystyle\sum_{i=1}^{n} y_i}{\sqrt{\left[n \displaystyle\sum_{i=1}^{n} x_i^2 - \left(\displaystyle\sum_{i=1}^{n} x_i \right)^2 \right]\left[n \displaystyle\sum_{i=1}^{n} y_i^2 - \left(\displaystyle\sum_{i=1}^{n} y_i \right)^2 \right]}}.$$

TABLE 3. Computation of Regression Line
Coefficients *a* and *b* for the Data from Figure 3

x (points)	y (wages)	xy	x²
60	3.00	180	3600
80	3.60	288	6400
100	3.50	350	10,000
140	4.20	588	19,600
160	2.96	---	---
160	4.90	---	---
200	4.50	---	---
220	4.70	---	---
240	4.90	---	---
260	4.40	---	---
280	5.60	---	---
300	4.70	---	---
300	7.20	---	---
340	5.70	---	---
340	9.30	---	---
360	7.50	---	---
380	6.40	---	---
380	7.60	---	---
420	7.65	---	---
460	8.80	---	---
$\Sigma x = 5180.0$	$\Sigma y = 111.11$	$\Sigma xy = 32,436.6$	$\Sigma x^2 = 1,600,400.0$

Computation of regression coefficients:

$N = 20$, $\bar{x} = \dfrac{\Sigma x}{N} = \dfrac{5180}{20} = 259.0$, $\bar{y} = \dfrac{\Sigma y}{N} = \dfrac{111.11}{20} = 5.555$,

$b = \dfrac{\Sigma xy - \bar{x}\Sigma y}{\Sigma x^2 - \bar{x}\Sigma x} = \dfrac{32,436.6 - 259 \times 111.11}{1,600,400 - 259 \times 5180} = 0.0141$,

$a = \bar{y} - b\bar{x} = 5.555 - 0.0141 \times 259 = 1.903$,

$\Sigma y^2 = 685.5341$.

Equation of regression line, $y = 1.903 + 0.0141\,x$.

All of the necessary components to compute *r* from the preceding formula are included at the bottom of Table 3, and the result is $r = 0.87$.

Reliability of Correlation Coefficients   Too often correlation coefficients are quoted without any indication of how much confidence we are justified in placing in them. There are statistical tests that allow us to make a probability statement about observed *r*'s. By adopting a significance level we may be able to say, for example, that we are 95 percent sure that an $r = 0.80$ observed for a sample will not be less than 0.75 for the parent population.

One easy check is to compare the observed value of *r* with the values given in Table 4. This table gives the critical values of *r* that must be ex-

TABLE 4. Critical Values of r for
95 Percent and 99 Percent Confidence

n	95%	99%	n	95%	99%	n	95%	99%
10	.632	.765	30	.361	.463	50	.279	.361
12	.576	.708	32	.349	.449	60	.254	.330
14	.532	.661	34	.339	.436	70	.235	.306
16	.497	.623	36	.329	.424	80	.220	.287
18	.468	.590	38	.320	.413	100	.197	.256
20	.444	.561	40	.312	.403	150	.161	.210
22	.423	.537	42	.304	.393	200	.139	.182
24	.404	.515	44	.297	.384	400	.098	.128
26	.388	.496	46	.291	.376	1000	.062	.081
28	.374	.479	48	.284	.368			

Note: These values must be exceeded for a given sample size n to be sure that the value of r is not really zero for the parent population.
Source: from W. J. Dixon and F. J. Massey, *Introduction to Statistical Analysis*, second edition, © 1957 by the McGraw-Hill Book Company; used by permission.

ceeded for various numbers of observations n, to be confident that r is not really zero for the parent population. The critical values are given for both the 95- and 99-percent confidence levels. This test assumes that both the variables, x and y, are normally distributed.

Appendix D
Assessing Risks In Inventory Models

In the basic EOQ model and in the simple extensions that we developed in Chapter 12, we assumed that both demand and supply lead time were constant; that is, we assumed a deterministic model. Yet, variability of demand and supply lead time are elements of reality that can be of great importance because they impose risks, and the risks are commonly two-sided.

We can cushion the effects of demand and supply lead time variation, absorbing risks by carrying larger inventories, called buffer or safety stocks. The larger we make these buffer stocks, the greater the risk associated with the funds tied up in inventories, the possibility of obsolescence, and so on. But large buffer stocks minimize the risk of running out of stock. On the other hand, the inventory risk can be minimized by reducing buffer inventories, but the risks associated with poor inventory service increase, including the costs of back ordering, lost sales, disruptions of production, and so on. Our objective then will be to find a rational model for balancing these risks.

Service Levels and Buffer Stocks with Constant Lead Time

In order to examine service levels and buffer stocks, let us begin by dealing with the effects of demand variability, assuming that supply lead time is known and constant. Figure 1 shows the general structure of inventory balance with a reordering system similar to the one we developed previously in Chapter 12. When inventory falls to a preset reorder point P, an order for the quantity Q is placed. The reorder point P is set to take account of the supply lead time L, so that if we experience normal usage rates during L,

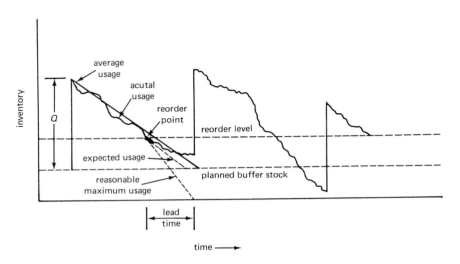

Figure 1. Structure of inventory balance for a fixed order quantity system, with safety stocks to absorb fluctuations in demand and in supply time. The buffer stock level is set so that a reasonable figure for maximum usage would draw down the inventory to zero during the lead time. Q is a fixed quantity ordered each cycle

inventory would be reduced to minimum levels when the order for Q units is received.

Note, however, that demand may not be at a constant rate. Inventories may decline to the reorder point P earlier or later than expected. But, what is more important, if demand during lead time is greater than expected values, inventory levels may decline below the minimum or planned buffer stock level. In the limiting situation, if we experienced maximum demand during lead time as shown in Figure 1, inventory levels would decline to zero by the time the order for Q units was received. The size of the needed buffer stock is then the difference between the expected or average demand $\bar{D}$ and D_{max}, the maximum demand during the supply lead time, or $B = D_{max} - \bar{D}$. The issue then must focus on how we define D_{max}.

Defining Maximum Demand   Maximum demand, D_{max}, is not a fixed number that we can simply abstract from a distribution of demand, but depends on an analysis of the risks. Let us take as an example the record for the distribution of demand for an item shown in Figure 2. Figure 2 represents just the random variations, and if there were other effects such as trend and seasonals, they have been removed by standard statistical techniques. We note that for the sample of $N = 113$, average biweekly demand was $\bar{D} = 1,214$ units and the standard deviation was $s = 313.6$ units. The

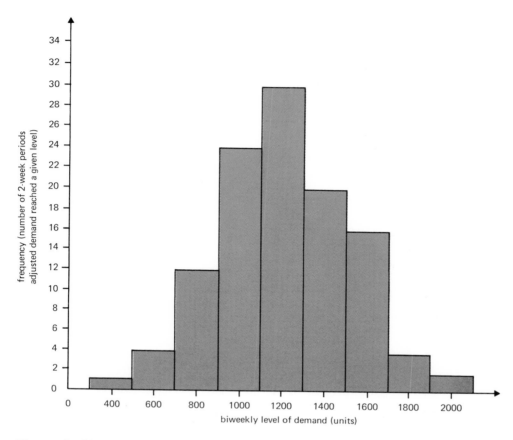

Figure 2. Distribution representing expected random variation in weekly sales, exclusive of seasonal and trend variations. $\overline{D} = 1214$ units per two weeks, $s = 313.6$ units, $N = 113$

maximum *recorded* demand in the sample was 2,000 units, which occurred twice in the distribution.

Let us convert Figure 2 to the form shown in Figure 3, so we can conveniently estimate the probability of various demand rates. Figure 3 was constructed from Figure 2 by plotting the number of periods in which demand exceeded a given level. We then established a percentage scale to estimate the probability of various levels of demand. Since the average two-week usage rate is 1,214 units, if we assume a normal lead time of $L = 2$ weeks, we could be 90 percent sure of not running out of stock by having 1,520 units on hand when the replenishment order is placed (see Figure 3 for the demand rate for 10 percent). The buffer stock required for this 90 percent service level is then $B = 1,520 - 1,214 = 306$ units. Similarly, if we wish to be 95 percent sure of not running out of stock, then $B = 1,640 -$

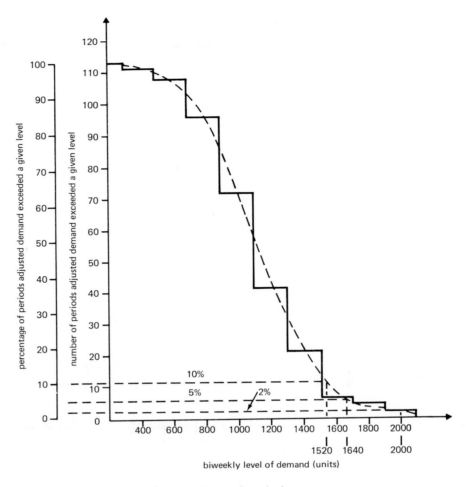

Figure 3. Distribution of percentage of periods that demand exceeded a given level, developed from Figure 2. $\bar{D} = 1214$ units per two weeks, $s = 313.6$ units, $N = 113$

1,214 = 426 units. For a 98 percent service level (2 percent risk of stockout) the buffer stock level must be increased to 786 units.

From the shape of the demand curve, it is clear that required buffer stock goes up rapidly as we increase service level, and therefore the cost of providing this assurance goes up. These effects are shown by the calculations in Table 1 where we have assumed the demand curve of Figure 3, assigning a value of $50 to the item and inventory holding costs of 20 percent of inventory value. The average inventory required to cover expected maximum usage rates during the two-week lead time is calculated for the three service levels shown. To offer service at the 95 percent level instead of the

90 percent level requires an incremental $1,200 per year, but to move to the 98 percent level of service from the 95 percent level requires an additional $3,600 in inventory cost.

Management could define any of the three levels of demand as D_{max} by setting a service level policy. Given the service level policy, the buffer stock required to implement that policy is simply $B = D_{max} - \overline{D}$.

TABLE 1. Cost of Providing Three Levels of Service (from Figure 3) When the Item is Valued at $50 Each and Inventory Holding Costs Are 20 Percent

	Service Level (percent)		
	90	95	98
Expected maximum usage for 2-week replenishment time	1520	1640	2000
Buffer stock required ($B = D_{max} - 1214$)	306	426	786
Value of buffer stock (50 B)	$15,300	$21,300	$39,300
Inventory holding cost at 20 percent	$3060	$4260	$7860

Practical Methods for Determining Buffer Stocks

The general methodology for setting buffer stocks that we have discussed here is too cumbersome for practical use in systems where large numbers of items may be involved. Computations are simplified considerably if we can justify the assumption that the demand distribution follows some particular mathematical function, such as the normal, Poisson, or negative exponential distributions.

First let us recall the general statement for buffer stocks,

$$B = D_{max} - \overline{D} . \tag{1}$$

Note, however, that $D_{max} = \overline{D} + n\sigma_D$, that is, the defined reasonable maximum demand is the average demand $\overline{D}$ plus some number of standard deviation units n that is associated with the probability of occurrence of that demand (n is now defined as the safety factor). Substituting this statement of D_{max} in our general definition of B, equation (1), we have

$$B = D_{max} - \overline{D} = (\overline{D} + n\sigma_D) - \overline{D} ,$$

or

$$B = n\sigma_D . \tag{2}$$

This simple statement allows us to determine easily buffer stocks that meet risk requirements when we know the mathematical form of the demand distribution. The procedure is as follows:

1. Determine whether the normal, Poisson, or negative exponential distribution approximately describes demand during lead time for the case under consideration. This determination is critically important, involving well-known statistical methodology.

2. Set a service level based on managerial policy, an assessment of the balance of incremental inventory and stockout costs, or an assessment of the manager's trade-off between service level and inventory cost when stockout costs are not known.

3. Using the service level, define D_{max} during lead time in terms of the appropriate distribution.

4. Compute the required buffer stock from equation (2) where n is termed the safety factor and σ_D is the standard deviation for the demand distribution during lead time.

Buffer Stocks for the Normal Distribution   The normal distribution has been found to describe many demand functions adequately, particularly at the factory level of the supply-production-distribution system [Buchan and Koenigsberg, 1963]. Given the assumption of normality and a service level of perhaps 95 percent, we can determine B by reference to the normal distribution tables. A small part of these tables has been reproduced as Table 2.

The normal distribution is a two parameter distribution that is completely described by its mean value $\overline{D}$ and the standard deviation σ_D. To implement a service level of 95 percent means that we are willing to accept a 5 percent risk of running out of stock. From Table 2, demand exceeds $\overline{D} + n\sigma_D$ with a probability of 0.05, or 5 percent of the time when $n = 1.645$; therefore, this policy is implemented when $B = 1.645\sigma_D$. Using Figure 2 as an example, and assuming that it is drawn from a normal distribution, we find that a buffer stock to implement a 95 percent service level would be $B = 1.645 \times 313.6 = 516$ units. Such a policy would protect against the occurrence of demands up to $D_{max} = 1{,}214 + 516 = 1{,}730$ units per two weeks. Obviously any other service level policy could be implemented in a similar way.

Buffer Stocks for the Poisson Distribution   The Poisson distribution has been found to be applicable to retail sales in many situations [Buchan and Koenigsberg, 1963]. Buffer stock determination for the Poisson distribution is very simple because it is a single parameter distribution, since $\sigma_D = \sqrt{\overline{D}}$. Thus, a knowledge of the average demand, $\overline{D}$, is sufficient to completely

TABLE 2. Portion of a Normal Distribution Table Showing the Probability of Demand Exceeding $\bar{D} + n\sigma_D$ for Selected Values of n

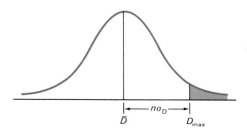

D_{max}	Probability
$\bar{D} + 3.090\sigma_D$	0.001
$\bar{D} + 2.576\sigma_D$	0.005
$\bar{D} + 2.326\sigma_D$	0.010
$\bar{D} + 1.960\sigma_D$	0.025
$\bar{D} + 1.645\sigma_D$	0.050
$\bar{D} + 1.282\sigma_D$	0.100
$\bar{D} + 1.036\sigma_D$	0.150
$\bar{D} + 0.842\sigma_D$	0.200
$\bar{D} + 0.674\sigma_D$	0.250
$\bar{D} + 0.524\sigma_D$	0.300
$\bar{D} + 0.385\sigma_D$	0.350
$\bar{D} + 0.253\sigma_D$	0.400
$\bar{D} + 0.126\sigma_D$	0.450
$\bar{D}$	0.500

Note: The figure shows the area under the right tail of the normal distribution.

describe the demand distribution. Using equation (2) then, $B = n\sigma_D = n\sqrt{\bar{D}}$.

Table 3 shows a small portion of the right tail of the Poisson distribution for selected values of $\bar{D}$ between 12 and 20. The Poisson distribution is not commonly applicable to distributions with mean values above 20. Since the risk values vary slightly for a given multiple of σ_D for different values of $\bar{D}$ in the Poisson distribution, the most satisfactory way of maintaining a preset risk level is by reference to the tables. For example, if average demand is $\bar{D} = 14$ per week, and we wish to hold the risk of stockout to about 5 percent, then from Table 3, $D_{max} = 20$ per week and $B = 20 - 14 = 6$ units,

TABLE 3. Portion of a Poisson Distribution Table Showing the Probability of Demand Exceeding a Given Value D_{max} for Selected Values of Average Demand, $\bar{D}$

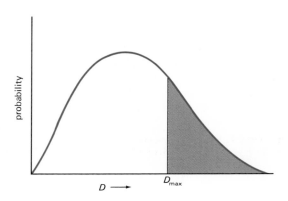

D_{max} Demand Greater Than	Average Demand ($\bar{D}$)				
	12	14	16	18	20
14	0.228				
15	0.156				
16	0.101	0.244			
17	0.063	0.173			
18	0.037	0.118	0.258		
19	0.021	0.077	0.188		
20	0.012	0.048	0.123	0.269	
21	0.006	0.029	0.089	0.201	
22	0.003	0.017	0.058	0.145	0.279
23	0.001	0.009	0.037	0.101	0.213
24		0.005	0.022	0.068	0.157
25		0.003	0.012	0.045	0.113
26		0.001	0.007	0.028	0.078
27			0.004	0.017	0.052
28			0.002	0.010	0.034
29			0.001	0.006	0.022
30				0.003	0.013
31				0.002	0.008
32				0.001	0.005
33					0.003
34					0.001

if L is one week. (From Table 3, the probability of D being greater than 20 is 0.048, or approximately 5 percent.)

Buffer Stocks for the Negative Exponential Distribution The negative exponential distribution has been found to describe demand in some retail and wholesale situations [Buchan and Koenigsberg, 1963]. As with the Poisson distribution, the negative exponential distribution is a single parameter distribution described completely by its mean value ($\sigma_D = \overline{D}$). Therefore, $D_{max} = \overline{D} + n\sigma_D = \overline{D} + n\overline{D} = (n+1)\overline{D}$.

Table 4 shows data on the unitized negative exponential distribution that is useful in implementing a given risk level. The ratio $D_{max}/\overline{D}$ is used to determine the probability that the stated D_{max} will be exceeded. For example, if $\overline{D} = 5$ units per week and we wished to hold the risk of stockout to 5 percent, then from Table 4 for a probability of 0.050, $D_{max}/\overline{D} = 3$. Therefore, $D_{max} = 3 \times 5 = 15$ units per week, and $B = 15 - 5 = 10$ units.

TABLE 4. Unit Negative Exponential Distribution Showing the Probability of Given Demands Being Exceeded

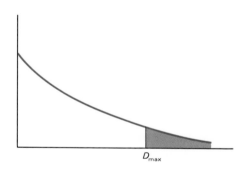

Unitized Demand ($D_{max}/\overline{D}$)	Probability That Demand Exceeds D_{max}	Unitized Demand ($D_{max}/\overline{D}$)	Probability That Demand Exceeds D_{max}
0.00	1.000	1.50	0.223
0.05	0.951	2.00	0.135
0.10	0.905	2.50	0.082
0.15	0.861	3.00	0.050
0.20	0.819	3.50	0.030
0.25	0.779	4.00	0.018
0.50	0.607	4.50	0.011
0.75	0.472	5.00	0.007
1.00	0.368	6.00	0.002

Note: Demand, $\overline{D} = 1$; $\sigma_D = 1$.

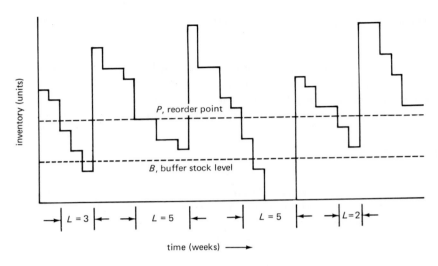

Figure 4. Inventory balance when both demand and lead time vary. When inventory falls to the reorder point *P*, the quantity *Q* is ordered. Inventory falls below the buffer stock level *B* twice, and a stockout occurs during the third cycle

Buffer Stocks with Variable Demand and Lead Time   The problem of determining buffer stocks when both demand and lead time vary is somewhat more complex. When lead times also vary, we are faced with an interaction between the fluctuating demand and the fluctuating lead times similar to the situation shown in Figure 4.

In such situations, buffer stocks may be determined by a Monte Carlo simulation through a straightforward application of the methods presented in Chapter 11. To carry out the simulation, we need data describing both the demand and lead time distributions. With these distribution data, we can simulate demand during lead time and finally develop buffer stock requirements for the various risk levels of stockout. We can then implement whatever risk level we choose by selecting the corresponding buffer stock. The methodology and computed examples are developed in Buffa and Taubert, [1972].

DETERMINING SERVICE LEVELS

The service level states the probability that all orders can be filled directly from inventory during a reorder cycle and, as we have stated, the buffer inventory designed to provide for the risk of stockout is $B = n\sigma_{D_L}$. Assuming a normal distribution and a safety factor of $n = 1.645$, then the chance of a stockout is 0.05 from Table 2, and the service level is 95 percent.

Now let us examine more closely the meaning of a service level statement of policy. It means that there is one chance in twenty that demand during lead time will exceed the buffer stock *when there is exposure to risk*. It does not mean that 5 percent of the demand is unsatisfied. It means that demand during lead time can be expected to exceed buffer stock for 5 percent of the replenishment orders, or that the chance that demand will exceed the buffer stock for any given replenishment order is 5 percent.

Effect of Order Size

With this interpretation of service level, we see immediately that the expected quantity short over a period of time is proportional to the number of times we order, for we are exposed to shortages only once for each reordering cycle. For our example, if we ordered Q units twenty times per year we would expect shortages to occur an average of only once per year. If we ordered in quantities of $2Q$ only ten times per year, we would expect stockouts to occur only once every other year on the average. Larger orders provide exposure to risk less often and will result in lower annual expected quantities short for the same service level.

Expected Quantities Short

For a given safety factor and distribution of demand during lead time, we can compute the expected quantity short. Assuming a normal distribution of $\overline{D} = 50$ units during lead time, and $\sigma_D = 10$ units, let us determine the expected quantity short for service levels of 80, 90, 95, and 99 percent. From Table 2, the safety factors and computed buffer stocks are

$$B_1 = 0.842 \times 10 = 8.4, \text{ or } 9 \text{ units,}$$
$$B_2 = 1.282 \times 10 = 12.8, \text{ or } 13 \text{ units,}$$
$$B_3 = 1.645 \times 10 = 16.45, \text{ or } 17 \text{ units,}$$
$$B_4 = 2.326 \times 10 = 23.26, \text{ or } 24 \text{ units,}$$

The values of B approximate the stated service levels, giving slightly better service because of rounding upwards to integer units.

Brown [1963] has shown that the expected quantity short per order is the product of σ_D and $E(k)$, where $E(k)$ is the partial expectation for a distribution with unit standard deviation. The partial expectation is the expected value of demands beyond some specified level. Brown [1967, 1959] developed tables of partial expectations for the normal distribution in 1967 and provided a graph of the function in 1959, which is reproduced in Figure 5. Estimates of the expected quantity short per order can be obtained from Figure 5 for a given safety factor, which in turn is associated with a given service level. From Figure 5, the expected quantities short per order for our example and the four service levels are as follows:

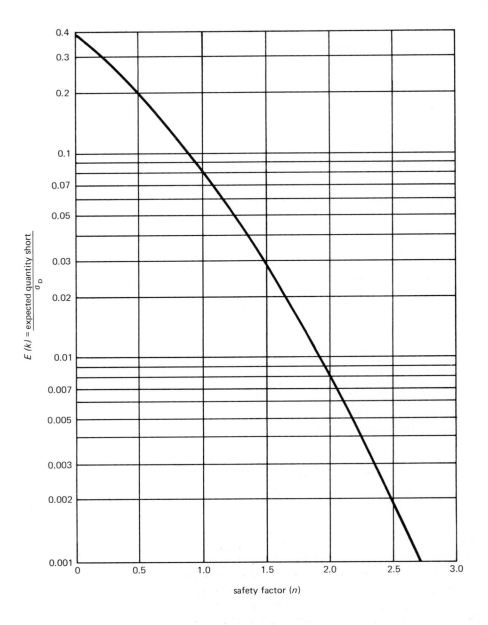

Figure 5. Graph for estimating the expected quantity short per order for a given safety factor *n*

From R. G. Brown, *Statistical Forecasting for Inventory Control*, Figure 4.1, p. 109, McGraw-Hill Book Company, New York, 1959; used by permission.

ASSESSING RISKS IN INVENTORY MODELS

Service Level (percent)	Expected Quantity Short per Order (units)
80	$0.10 \times 10 = 1.00$
90	$0.04 \times 10 = 0.40$
95	$0.02 \times 10 = 0.20$
99	$0.003 \times 10 = 0.03$

For each of the service levels indicated, the expected quantity short for each order is as given, and these expected shortages are rather startlingly small. Thus, the effect of a given service policy may be misleading unless it is translated into its equivalent expected quantity short per order. While a 90-percent service policy may seem relatively loose, it holds fairly tight control in terms of the expected shortages on each ordering cycle.

Optimal Service Levels with Shortage Costs Known

Now that we have methods for estimating the expected quantity short per order, we can determine the optimal service level if we know the relevant costs. Let us amplify slightly the example we have been using. Suppose that annual requirements for the example item are $R = 3,000$ units per year, inventory holding costs are $c_H = \$20$ per unit per year, ordering costs are $c_P = \$25$ per order, and shortage costs are $c_S = \$100$ per unit short. If the order quantity were $Q = 500$ units, six orders per year would be required.

Let us examine the annual buffer inventory and shortage costs for the four different service levels. We computed the buffer inventory and expected quantities short per order previously. Since there are six orders per year, the *annual* expected quantity short is $6\sigma_D E(k)$. These values and the relevant costs are summarized in Table 5. The service policy that minimizes relevant costs for these data is the 95 percent policy that involves maintaining a buffer of $B = 17$ units and results in an annual expected quantity short of $6 \times 0.20 = 1.2$ units and a minimum total relevant cost of $\$460$ per year. What would be the optimal service policy if the cost of shortages was only $c_S = \$40$?

Previously, we alluded to the fact that the annual expected quantity short depended on the quantity ordered at one time. Of course, this fact could affect the decision on service policy. You should now compare costs for order sizes of $Q = 500$ and $1,000$ for the different service levels. What are the relevant costs?

TABLE 5. Annual Buffer Inventory and
Shortage Costs for Four Service Levels

	Approximate Service Level (%)			
	80	90	95	99
Buffer inventory,* $B = n\sigma_D = 10 \times n$	9	13	17	24
Expected quantity short per order,† $\sigma_D E(k) = 10 \times E(k)$	1.0	0.4	0.20	0.03
Buffer inventory cost, $c_H B = 20 \times B$	$180	$260	$340	$480
Shortage cost, $c_S (R/Q) \times$ (expected quantity short per order) $= 100 \times 6 \times$ (expected quantity short per order)	$600	$240	$120	$ 18
Total incremental costs	$780	$500	$460	$498

Note: $\bar{D} = 50$ units during lead time, $\sigma_D = 10$ units, $c_H = \$20$ per unit per year, $c_S = \$100$ per unit short, $R = 3000$ units per year, and $Q = 500$ units per order.
*Values of n from Table 2 for given service level. Values of B rounded to next highest integer.
†$E(k)$ estimated from Figure 5.

Optimal Service Levels with Shortage Costs Unknown

It is perhaps most often true that we do not know the value of shortage costs, c_S, with any degree of confidence. There are many factors in a given situation that may affect the true cost of shortages. Some of these factors may be reasonably objective, but difficult to measure. For example, we know that part shortages in assembly processes cause disruptions and delays that are costly, but measuring these costs is quite complex. When shortages occur, it may be necessary to place the parts on back order, or they may be expedited with special handling and extra costs. These incremental costs are real, but they are not segregated in cost records, so making realistic estimates of their value would in itself be costly, and these costs could exceed the value of the information. If a shortage definitely causes a lost sale, we could impute a shortage cost equal to the lost contribution to profit and overhead. But is the sale lost with certainty or must we estimate the probability of a lost sale? Furthermore, the loss may be intangible, such as the loss of goodwill of a valued customer who receives poor service.

For all of the preceding reasons, we may not be able to estimate values of c_S with sufficient precision to justify an analysis similar to that given in Table 5 as a basis for selecting an optimum service level policy.

Nevertheless, in the absence of known shortage costs, we still have valuable data from Table 5. We have objective annual buffer inventory costs

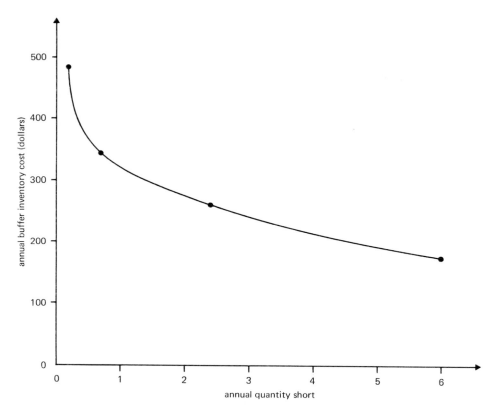

Figure 6. Annual buffer inventory costs versus annual quantity short for a system where $\overline{D} =$ 50 units during lead time, $\sigma_D = 10$ units, $c_H =$ \$20 per unit per year, $R = 3000$ units per year, and $Q = 500$ units per order

for various service level policies, and we have the expected annual quantities short that would result from each service level policy. The graphic relationship between buffer inventory cost and quantities short is shown in Figure 6. These data provide the manager with the basis for a trade-off analysis in which we can apply the methods of Chapter 4.

Thus, the problem of determining the optimal service level may be viewed as a problem involving multiple criteria under certainty (where the uncertain demand fluctuations are taken into account by the certain quantity, the expected annual quantity of units short). The alternatives are the service levels. Although there are actually an infinite number of possible service levels, we can simplify the problem by considering service level policies of 80 percent (alternative A_1), 90 percent (A_2), 95 percent (A_3), and 99 percent (A_4). The criteria are simply the annual cost of the buffer inventory and the annual quantity of units short. From Table 5 we see that the outcome O_1 associated with the 80 percent service level policy (A_1) is ($180,6.0), since we expected to be short 1.0 units per order, and to order six times per year ($6 \times 1.0 = 6.0$). Table 6 summarizes these outcomes for the four alternatives.

We now ask the manager to use the notion of trade-offs to determine his preferred service level. We might say: "For an annual cost of $180, you expect to be short of inventory a total of 6.0 units during one or more of the six reorder periods. Suppose you could reduce this total annual shortage to 2.4 units. How much more would you be willing to pay? Consider both tangible and intangible costs in determining your answer."

The manager might estimate that the tangible costs of back ordering and expediting special orders are approximately $20 per unit. Therefore, he would be willing to pay at least $20 \times 3.6 = \$72$ for this reduction, but how much more? To aid him with this question, we might say the following: "You would pay at least $72 more to reduce the annual shortage from 6.0 to 2.4 units. Would eliminating the uncertain costs of lost sales and the intangible costs of lost goodwill associated with the extra 3.6 units of inventory shortage be worth *at least* $8?" Suppose he answers "Yes" to this question.

TABLE 6. Annual Buffer Inventory Costs and Expected Annual Shortages for Four Service Levels

	Service Level (percent)			
	80 (A_1)	90 (A_2)	95 (A_3)	99 (A_4)
Annual buffer cost	$180	$260	$340	$480
Expected annual shortages (units)	6.0	2.4	1.2	0.18

Since the savings of tangible costs of $72 plus the uncertain and intangible costs of at least $8 are greater than $80, then the 90 percent service level (A_2) is preferred to the 80 percent service level (A_1). The $80 target comes from the difference between the annual buffer inventory costs for the two service levels, that is, $260 - \$180 = \$80$.

Continuing in the same manner, we might ask if the manager would be willing to pay an additional $80 (difference in annual buffer inventory costs between the 95 and 90 percent service levels) to reduce the annual shortages from 2.4 units to approximately 1.2 units (2.4 units $- 1.2$ units $= 1.2$ unit reduction). This time, the savings in tangible costs would be $20 \times 1.2 = \$24$. Would the uncertain and intangible costs be worth an additional $56? Suppose this time that the manager says "No." The optimal service level would then be approximately 90 percent.

MANAGERIAL CONTROL SYSTEMS

Let us now summarize the results of optimizing inventory models for managerial use. What are the variables under managerial control and how can they be incorporated in useful control systems? The basic control variables are the quantity ordered at one time, the service level, and the particular way these elements are combined in a control system.

The elements of inventory models that are normally outside of managerial control are the costs c_H, c_P, c_S, and the supply lead time. These are parameters that the manager cannot change at will, though he may try to reduce or control them in the longer term. The annual requirement, R, is dependent on external market factors, and again, the manager can try to influence R through marketing techniques, but he cannot decide what it will be.

We shall summarize two basic kinds of control systems that are widely used, recognizing that there are many variations in practice.

The Fixed Reorder Quantity System

The fixed reorder quantity system is the one we have used for illustrative purposes in developing optimizing inventory models. Its structure is best illustrated by Figure 1, in which a reorder level has been set by the point P, which allows the inventory level to be drawn down to the buffer stock level within the lead time if average usage rates are experienced. Replenishment orders are placed in a fixed predetermined amount (in practice, not necessarily the minimum cost quantity, Q_0) timed to be received at the end of the supply lead time. The maximum inventory level becomes the order quantity Q plus the buffer stock B. The average inventory is then $B + Q/2$.

Usage rates are reviewed periodically in an attempt to react to seasonal or long-term trends in requirements. At the time of the periodic reviews, the order quantities and buffer stock levels may be changed to reflect the new conditions. Buffer stock levels are set, based on determinations of the appropriate service level policy, which in turn reflects the balancing of buffer inventory costs and shortage costs, or the manager's trade-off between buffer inventory cost and the expected quantity short.

Fixed reorder quantity systems are common where a perpetual inventory record is kept, or where the inventory level is under rather continuous surveillance so that notice can be given when the reorder point has been reached.

One of the simplest methods for maintaining this close watch on inventory level is the use of the "two bin" system. In this system, the inventory is physically (or conceptually) separated into two bins, one of which contains an amount equal to the reorder inventory level. The balance of the stock is placed in the other bin, and day-to-day needs are drawn from it until it is empty. At that point it is obvious that the reorder level has been reached and a stock requisition is issued. From that point on, stock is drawn from the second bin, which contains an amount equal to the average use over the lead time plus a buffer stock. When the stock is replenished by the receipt of the order, the physical segregation into two bins is made again and the cycle is repeated. Fixed reorder quantity systems are common with low-valued valued items such as nuts and bolts.

Fixed Reorder Cycle Systems

In fixed cycle systems, control is maintained by ordering regularly on some fixed cycle, perhaps each week or each month. In its simplest form, the amount ordered is the quantity needed to replenish inventory to I_{max}, a pre-set level. This reorder quantity Q is variable and is equal to the amount used during the current period plus the expected usage during the supply lead time, as shown in Figure 7. The service level policies and resulting buffer stock requirements are based on the same general concepts and methods as before.

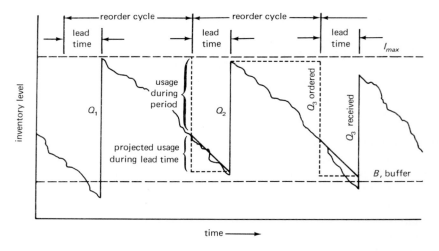

Figure 7. Fixed reorder cycle system of control. An order is placed at regular intervals. Stock is replenished by an order of variable size Q, which is the sum of usage during the immediate past period plus projected usage during the supply lead time

The managerial control variable is now the length of the reorder cycle, commonly called the review period, since inventory status is reviewed in order to determine replenishment orders during the period. Optimal review periods can be derived with this system—periods that are equivalent to the optimum order quantity Q_0 in the fixed order quantity system. The optimal review period can be approximated by Q_0/R, where Q_0 is computed from equation (4) in Chapter 12. As we shall note, however, the optimal review period is seldom used, because other criteria tend to dominate in reorder cycle selection.

Fixed reorder cycle systems are prominent with higher valued items and with a large number of items that are regularly ordered from the same vendor. Thus, one of the significant advantages of the fixed cycle system is that freight cost advantages can often be gained by grouping these orders together for shipment. Also, the regular review of all items for replenishment ordering on the same basic cycle has procedural advantages and provides close surveillance over inventory levels for all items. Thus, while it is possible to determine optimal review periods for each item — periods that depend on the cost parameters of the optimizing model — review periods are actually set on the basis of all the considerations discussed, including individual optimal review periods.

Combination systems exist in which stock levels are reviewed periodically but orders are placed only when inventories have fallen to a predetermined reorder point. When an order is placed, its size is sufficient to replenish inventories, as in the fixed cycle system. Periodic reviews of current usage rates may result in changes in I_{max}, P, and B. The combination systems have the advantages of close control associated with the fixed cycle system, but since replenishment orders are placed only when the reorder point has been reached, fewer orders are placed on the average, so that annual ordering costs are comparable to those associated with the fixed quantity systems.

Check Your Understanding

1. Define the following terms:
   a. buffer stock
   b. maximum demand
   c. safety factor
   d. expected quantity short
   e. optimal service level

2. If average demand is $\overline{D} = 52$ units during the supply lead time, and management designed a system where the buffer stock is set at $B = 23$ units, what is management's definition of maximum demand for this situation?

3. Using the demand distribution described by Figure 2 and 3 as an example, if service levels are set at 15 percent, estimate D_{max} and B.

4. Suppose on statistical analysis of the demand for an item we isolate trend, seasonal, and random components of demand variation. Can we construct a meaningful buffer inventory for the item? How?

5. Explain why the cost of providing service goes up rapidly as the service level increases.

6. Give the mathematical statement defining buffer stock if the distribution of demand during lead time is:
   a. normal
   b. Poisson
   c. negative exponential

7. For the normal distribution, if the service level is set at 10 percent and the standard deviation is estimated to be $s = 50.3$ units, compute the buffer stock B. What is the value of the safety factor n?

8. For the Poisson distribution with an average demand of $\bar{D} = 18$ units during lead time, and a service level of 99 percent, what is the value of D_{max}? B? What is the implied safety factor n?

9. For the negative exponential distribution, if the service level is 97 percent and the standard deviation is estimated to be $s = 9$ units, compute the values of D_{max} and B. What is the implied value of n?

10. Explain the importance of "exposure to risk" in the concept of service levels. What is the effect of order size on actual service levels?

11. If average demand is $\bar{D} = 100$ units during lead time, the standard deviation is $s = 24.3$ units (normal distribution), and the service level is set at 99 percent, what is the expected quantity short per order?

12. Assume a situation in which annual requirements are $R = 10,000$ units, $c_P = \$20$ per order, and $c_H = \$10$ per unit per year. Average demand during the supply lead time is $\bar{D} = 385$ units with a standard deviation of $s = 75$ units (normal distribution). Which of the following service levels is most economical if the organization uses an EOQ ordering policy and shortages cost $100 per unit: 90, 95, or 99 percent?

13. Given the data generated in producing your answer to question 12, suppose you had no reasonable estimate of an objective shortage cost. Outline how you could develop a service level policy. Plot a curve similar to Figure 6 as a basis for a manager's trade-off analysis.

References

Brown, R. G., *Statistical Forecasting and Inventory Control*, McGraw-Hill, New York, 1959.

———, *Smoothing, Forecasting and Prediction*, Prentice-Hall, Englewood Cliffs, N.J., 1963.

———, *Decision Rules for Inventory Management*, Holt, Rinehart and Winston, New York, 1967.

Buchan, J., and E. Koenigsberg, *Scientific Inventory Management*, Prentice-Hall, Englewood Cliffs, N.J., 1963.

Buffa, E. S., and W. H. Taubert, *Production-Inventory Systems: Planning and Control,* revised edition, Richard D. Irwin, Inc., Homewood, Illinois, 1972.

Magee, J. F., and D. M. Boodman, *Production Planning and Inventory Control,* second edition, McGraw-Hill, New York, 1967.

Starr, N. K., and D. W. Miller, *Inventory Control: Theory and Practice,* Prentice-Hall, Englewood Cliffs, N.J., 1962.

Appendix E
Tables

TABLE 1. Areas Under the Normal Curve

Areas under the normal curve to the left of x for decimal units
of σ' from the mean, $\bar{x}'$

x	Area	x	Area	x	Area	x	Area
$\bar{x}' - 3.0\sigma'$	0.0013	$\bar{x}' - 1.5\sigma'$	0.0668	$\bar{x}' + 0.1\sigma'$	0.5398	$\bar{x}' + 1.6\sigma'$	0.9452
$\bar{x}' - 2.9\sigma'$	0.0019	$\bar{x}' - 1.4\sigma'$	0.0808	$\bar{x}' + 0.2\sigma'$	0.5793	$\bar{x}' + 1.7\sigma'$	0.9554
$\bar{x}' - 2.8\sigma'$	0.0026	$\bar{x}' - 1.3\sigma'$	0.0968	$\bar{x}' + 0.3\sigma'$	0.6179	$\bar{x}' + 1.8\sigma'$	0.9641
$\bar{x}' - 2.7\sigma'$	0.0035	$\bar{x}' - 1.2\sigma'$	0.1151	$\bar{x}' + 0.4\sigma'$	0.6554	$\bar{x}' + 1.9\sigma'$	0.9713
$\bar{x}' - 2.6\sigma'$	0.0047	$\bar{x}' - 1.1\sigma'$	0.1357	$\bar{x}' + 0.5\sigma'$	0.6915	$\bar{x}' + 2.0\sigma'$	0.9772
$\bar{x}' - 2.5\sigma'$	0.0062	$\bar{x}' - 1.0\sigma'$	0.1587	$\bar{x}' + 0.6\sigma'$	0.7257	$\bar{x}' + 2.1\sigma'$	0.9821
$\bar{x}' - 2.4\sigma'$	0.0082	$\bar{x}' - 0.9\sigma'$	0.1841	$\bar{x}' + 0.7\sigma'$	0.7580	$\bar{x}' + 2.2\sigma'$	0.9861
$\bar{x}' - 2.3\sigma'$	0.0107	$\bar{x}' - 0.8\sigma'$	0.2119	$\bar{x}' + 0.8\sigma'$	0.7881	$\bar{x}' + 2.3\sigma'$	0.9893
$\bar{x}' - 2.2\sigma'$	0.0139	$\bar{x}' - 0.7\sigma'$	0.2420	$\bar{x}' + 0.9\sigma'$	0.8159	$\bar{x}' + 2.4\sigma'$	0.9918
$\bar{x}' - 2.1\sigma'$	0.0179	$\bar{x}' - 0.6\sigma'$	0.2741	$\bar{x}' + 1.0\sigma'$	0.8413	$\bar{x}' + 2.5\sigma'$	0.9938
$\bar{x}' - 2.0\sigma'$	0.0228	$\bar{x}' - 0.5\sigma'$	0.3085	$\bar{x}' + 1.1\sigma'$	0.8643	$\bar{x}' + 2.6\sigma'$	0.9953
$\bar{x}' - 1.9\sigma'$	0.0287	$\bar{x}' - 0.4\sigma'$	0.3446	$\bar{x}' + 1.2\sigma'$	0.8849	$\bar{x}' + 2.7\sigma'$	0.9965
$\bar{x}' - 1.8\sigma'$	0.0359	$\bar{x}' - 0.3\sigma'$	0.3821	$\bar{x}' + 1.3\sigma'$	0.9032	$\bar{x}' + 2.8\sigma'$	0.9974
$\bar{x}' - 1.7\sigma'$	0.0446	$\bar{x}' - 0.2\sigma'$	0.4207	$\bar{x}' + 1.4\sigma'$	0.9192	$\bar{x}' + 2.9\sigma'$	0.9981
$\bar{x}' - 1.6\sigma'$	0.0548	$\bar{x}' - 0.1\sigma'$	0.4602	$\bar{x}' + 1.5\sigma'$	0.9332	$\bar{x}' + 3.0\sigma'$	0.9987
		$\bar{x}'$	0.5000				

σ' units from the mean, $\bar{x}'$, associated with
given values of the area under the
normal curve to the left of x

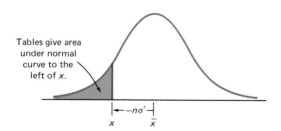

Tables give area
under normal
curve to the
left of x.

x	Area	x	Area
$\bar{x}' - 3.090\sigma'$	0.001	$\bar{x}' + 3.090\sigma'$	0.999
$\bar{x}' - 2.576\sigma'$	0.005	$\bar{x}' + 2.576\sigma'$	0.995
$\bar{x}' - 2.326\sigma'$	0.010	$\bar{x}' + 2.326\sigma'$	0.990
$\bar{x}' - 1.960\sigma'$	0.025	$\bar{x}' + 1.960\sigma'$	0.975
$\bar{x}' - 1.645\sigma'$	0.050	$\bar{x}' + 1.645\sigma'$	0.950
$\bar{x}' - 1.282\sigma'$	0.100	$\bar{x}' + 1.282\sigma'$	0.900
$\bar{x}' - 1.036\sigma'$	0.150	$\bar{x}' + 1.036\sigma'$	0.850
$\bar{x}' - 0.842\sigma'$	0.200	$\bar{x}' + 0.842\sigma'$	0.800
$\bar{x}' - 0.674\sigma'$	0.250	$\bar{x}' + 0.674\sigma'$	0.750
$\bar{x}' - 0.524\sigma'$	0.300	$\bar{x}' + 0.524\sigma'$	0.700
$\bar{x}' - 0.385\sigma'$	0.350	$\bar{x}' + 0.385\sigma'$	0.650
$\bar{x}' - 0.253\sigma'$	0.400	$\bar{x}' + 0.253\sigma'$	0.600
$\bar{x}' - 0.126\sigma'$	0.450	$\bar{x}' + 0.126\sigma'$	0.550
$\bar{x}'$	0.500		

TABLE 1   697

TABLE 2. Cumulative Poisson Distribution for Selected Values of the Mean, m

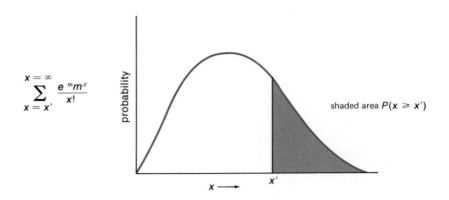

$$\sum_{x=x'}^{x=\infty} \frac{e^{-m}m^x}{x!}$$

shaded area $P(x \geq x')$

x	$m = .001$	$m = .005$	$m = .010$	$m = .05$	$m = .10$
0	1.0000000	1.0000000	1.0000000	1.0000000	1.0000000
1	0.0009995	0.0049875	0.0099502	0.0487706	0.0951626
2	0.0000005	0.0000125	0.0000497	0.0012091	0.0046788
3			0.0000002	0.0000201	0.0001547
4				0.0000003	0.0000038

x	$m = .5$	$m = 1.0$	$m = 1.5$	$m = 2.0$	$m = 2.5$
0	1.000000	1.000000	1.000000	1.000000	1.000000
1	0.393469	0.632121	0.776870	0.864665	0.917915
2	0.090204	0.264241	0.442175	0.593994	0.712703
3	0.014388	0.080301	0.191153	0.323324	0.456187
4	0.001752	0.018988	0.065642	0.142877	0.242424
5	0.000172	0.003660	0.018576	0.052653	0.108822
6	0.000014	0.000594	0.004456	0.016564	0.042021
7	0.000001	0.000083	0.000926	0.004534	0.014187
8		0.000010	0.000170	0.001097	0.004247
9		0.000001	0.000028	0.000237	0.001140
10			0.000004	0.000046	0.000277
11			0.000001	0.000008	0.000062
12				0.000001	0.000013
13					0.000002

Source: From E. C. Molina, *Poisson's Exponential Binomial Limit.* © 1942 by Litton Educational Publishing, Inc.; reprinted by permission of Van Nostrand Reinhold Company. Published by Krieger Publishing Company.

TABLE 2. Cumulative Poisson Distribution for
Selected Values of the Mean, *m* (Continued)

x	m = 3.0	m = 3.5	m = 4.0	m = 4.5	m = 5.0
0	1.000000	1.000000	1.000000	1.000000	1.000000
1	0.950213	0.969803	0.981684	0.988891	0.993262
2	0.800852	0.864112	0.908422	0.938901	0.959572
3	0.576810	0.679153	0.761897	0.826422	0.875348
4	0.352768	0.463367	0.566530	0.657704	0.734974
5	0.184737	0.274555	0.371163	0.467896	0.559507
6	0.083918	0.142386	0.214870	0.297070	0.384039
7	0.033509	0.065288	0.110674	0.168949	0.237817
8	0.011905	0.026739	0.051134	0.086586	0.133372
9	0.003803	0.009874	0.021363	0.040257	0.068094
10	0.001102	0.003315	0.008132	0.017093	0.031828
11	0.000292	0.001019	0.002840	0.006669	0.013695
12	0.000071	0.000289	0.000915	0.002404	0.005453
13	0.000016	0.000076	0.000274	0.000805	0.002019
14	0.000003	0.000019	0.000076	0.000252	0.000698
15	0.000001	0.000004	0.000020	0.000074	0.000226
16		0.000001	0.000005	0.000020	0.000069
17			0.000001	0.000005	0.000020
18				0.000001	0.000005
19					0.000001

x	m = 5.5	m = 6.0	m = 6.5	m = 7.0	m = 7.5
0	1.000000	1.000000	1.000000	1.000000	1.000000
1	0.995913	0.997521	0.998497	0.999088	0.999447
2	0.973436	0.982649	0.988724	0.992705	0.995299
3	0.911624	0.938031	0.956964	0.970364	0.979743
4	0.798301	0.848796	0.888150	0.918235	0.940855
5	0.642482	0.714943	0.776328	0.827008	0.867938
6	0.471081	0.554320	0.630959	0.699292	0.758564
7	0.313964	0.393697	0.473476	0.550289	0.621845
8	0.190515	0.256020	0.327242	0.401286	0.475361
9	0.105643	0.152763	0.208427	0.270909	0.338033
10	0.053777	0.083924	0.122616	0.169504	0.223592
11	0.025251	0.042621	0.066839	0.098521	0.137762
12	0.010988	0.020092	0.033880	0.053350	0.079241
13	0.004451	0.008827	0.016027	0.027000	0.042666
14	0.001685	0.003628	0.007100	0.012811	0.021565
15	0.000599	0.001400	0.002956	0.005717	0.010260
16	0.000200	0.000509	0.001160	0.002407	0.004608
17	0.000063	0.000175	0.000430	0.000958	0.001959
18	0.000019	0.000057	0.000151	0.000362	0.000790
19	0.000005	0.000018	0.000051	0.000130	0.000303

TABLE 2   **699**

TABLE 2. Cumulative Poisson Distribution for Selected Values of the Mean, m (Continued)

x	$m = 5.5$	$m = 6$	$m = 6.5$	$m = 7$	$m = 7.5$
20	0.000001	0.000005	0.000016	0.000044	0.000111
21		0.000001	0.000005	0.000014	0.000039
22			0.000001	0.000005	0.000013
23				0.000001	0.000004
24					0.000001

x	$m = 8$	$m = 9$	$m = 10$	$m = 11$	$m = 12$
0	1.000000	1.000000	1.000000	1.000000	1.000000
1	0.999665	0.999877	0.999955	0.999983	0.999994
2	0.996981	0.998766	0.999501	0.999800	0.999920
3	0.986246	0.993768	0.997231	0.998789	0.999478
4	0.957620	0.978774	0.989664	0.995084	0.997708
5	0.900368	0.945036	0.970747	0.984895	0.992400
6	0.808764	0.884309	0.932914	0.962480	0.979659
7	0.686626	0.793819	0.869859	0.921386	0.954178
8	0.547039	0.676103	0.779779	0.856808	0.910496
9	0.407453	0.544347	0.667180	0.768015	0.844972
10	0.283376	0.412592	0.542070	0.659489	0.757608
11	0.184114	0.294012	0.416960	0.540111	0.652771
12	0.111924	0.196992	0.303224	0.420733	0.538403
13	0.063797	0.124227	0.208444	0.311303	0.424035
14	0.034181	0.073851	0.135536	0.218709	0.318464
15	0.017257	0.041466	0.083458	0.145956	0.227975
16	0.008231	0.022036	0.048740	0.092604	0.155584
17	0.003718	0.011106	0.027042	0.055924	0.101291
18	0.001594	0.005320	0.014278	0.032191	0.062966
19	0.000650	0.002426	0.007187	0.017687	0.037417
20	0.000253	0.001056	0.003454	0.009289	0.021280
21	0.000094	0.000439	0.001588	0.004671	0.011598
22	0.000033	0.000175	0.000700	0.002252	0.006065
23	0.000011	0.000067	0.000296	0.001042	0.003047
24	0.000004	0.000025	0.000120	0.000464	0.001473
25	0.000001	0.000009	0.000047	0.000199	0.000686
26		0.000003	0.000018	0.000082	0.000308
27		0.000001	0.000006	0.000033	0.000133
28			0.000002	0.000013	0.000056
29			0.000001	0.000005	0.000023
30				0.000002	0.000009
21				0.000001	0.000003
32					0.000001

TABLE 2. Cumulative Poisson Distribution for
Selected Values of the Mean, m (Continued)

x	$m = 13$	$m = 14$	$m = 15$	$m = 16$	$m = 17$
0	1.000000	1.000000	---	---	---
1	0.999998	0.999999	1.000000	1.000000	1.000000
2	0.999968	0.999988	0.999995	0.999998	0.999999
3	0.999777	0.999906	0.999961	0.999984	0.999993
4	0.998950	0.999526	0.999789	0.999907	0.999959
5	0.996260	0.998195	0.999143	0.999600	0.999815
6	0.989266	0.994468	0.997208	0.998616	0.999325
7	0.974113	0.985772	0.992368	0.995994	0.997938
8	0.945972	0.968380	0.981998	0.990000	0.994567
9	0.900242	0.937945	0.962554	0.978013	0.987404
10	0.834188	0.890601	0.930146	0.956702	0.973875
11	0.748318	0.824319	0.881536	0.922604	0.950876
12	0.646835	0.739960	0.815248	0.873007	0.915331
13	0.536895	0.641542	0.732389	0.806878	0.864976
14	0.426955	0.535552	0.636782	0.725489	0.799127
15	0.324868	0.429563	0.534346	0.632473	0.719167
16	0.236393	0.330640	0.431910	0.533255	0.628546
17	0.164507	0.244082	0.335877	0.434038	0.532262
18	0.109535	0.172799	0.251141	0.340656	0.435977
19	0.069833	0.117357	0.180528	0.257651	0.345042
20	0.042669	0.076505	0.124781	0.187751	0.263678
21	0.025012	0.047908	0.082971	0.131832	0.194519
22	0.014081	0.028844	0.053106	0.089227	0.138534
23	0.007622	0.016712	0.032744	0.058241	0.095272
24	0.003972	0.009328	0.019465	0.036686	0.063296
25	0.001994	0.005020	0.011165	0.022315	0.040646
26	0.000966	0.002608	0.006185	0.013119	0.025245
27	0.000452	0.001309	0.003312	0.007459	0.015174
28	0.000204	0.000635	0.001716	0.004105	0.008834
29	0.000089	0.000298	0.000861	0.002189	0.004984
30	0.000038	0.000136	0.000418	0.001131	0.002727
31	0.000016	0.000060	0.000197	0.000567	0.001448
32	0.000006	0.000026	0.000090	0.000276	0.000747
33	0.000002	0.000011	0.000040	0.000131	0.000375
34	0.000001	0.000004	0.000017	0.000060	0.000183
35		0.000002	0.000007	0.000027	0.000087
36		0.000001	0.000003	0.000012	0.000040
37			0.000001	0.000005	0.000018
38				0.000002	0.000008
39				0.000001	0.000003
40					0.000001
41					0.000001

TABLE 2   701

TABLE 2. Cumulative Poisson Distribution for
Selected Values of the Mean, *m* (Continued)

x	m = 18	m = 19	m = 20	m = 21	m = 22
2	1.000000	1.000000	---	---	---
3	0.999997	0.999999	1.000000	1.000000	1.000000
4	0.999982	0.999992	0.999997	0.999999	0.999999
5	0.999916	0.999962	0.999983	0.999993	0.999997
6	0.999676	0.999846	0.999928	0.999967	0.999985
7	0.998957	0.999480	0.999745	0.999876	0.999941
8	0.997107	0.998487	0.999221	0.999605	0.999803
9	0.992944	0.996127	0.997913	0.998894	0.999423
10	0.984619	0.991144	0.995005	0.997234	0.998495
11	0.969634	0.981678	0.989188	0.993749	0.996453
12	0.945113	0.965327	0.978613	0.987095	0.992370
13	0.908331	0.939439	0.960988	0.975451	0.984884
14	0.857402	0.901601	0.933872	0.956641	0.972215
15	0.791923	0.850250	0.895136	0.928426	0.952307
16	0.713347	0.785206	0.843487	0.888925	0.923108
17	0.624950	0.707966	0.778926	0.837081	0.882960
18	0.531352	0.621639	0.702972	0.773037	0.831004
19	0.437755	0.530516	0.618578	0.698320	0.767502
20	0.349084	0.439393	0.529743	0.615737	0.693973
21	0.269280	0.352826	0.440907	0.529026	0.613091
22	0.200876	0.274503	0.356302	0.442314	0.528358
23	0.144910	0.206861	0.279389	0.359544	0.443625
24	0.101110	0.150983	0.212507	0.283971	0.362576
25	0.068260	0.106746	0.156773	0.217845	0.288281
26	0.044608	0.073126	0.112185	0.162299	0.222901
27	0.028234	0.048557	0.077887	0.117435	0.167580
28	0.017318	0.031268	0.052481	0.082541	0.122503
29	0.010300	0.019536	0.034334	0.056370	0.087086
30	0.005944	0.011850	0.021818	0.037419	0.060217
31	0.003331	0.006982	0.013475	0.024153	0.040514
32	0.001813	0.003998	0.008092	0.015166	0.026531
33	0.000960	0.002227	0.004727	0.009269	0.016918
34	0.000494	0.001207	0.002688	0.005516	0.010509
35	0.000248	0.000637	0.001489	0.003198	0.006362
36	0.000121	0.000327	0.000804	0.001807	0.003755
37	0.000058	0.000164	0.000423	0.000996	0.002162
38	0.000027	0.000080	0.000217	0.000536	0.001215
39	0.000012	0.000038	0.000109	0.000281	0.000667
40	0.000005	0.000018	0.000053	0.000144	0.000357
41	0.000002	0.000008	0.000025	0.000072	0.000187
42	0.000001	0.000004	0.000012	0.000035	0.000096
43		0.000002	0.000005	0.000017	0.000048

TABLE 2. Cumulative Poisson Distribution for Selected Values of the Mean, m (Continued.

x	m = 18	m = 19	m = 20	m = 21	m = 22
44		0.000001	0.000002	0.000008	0.000024
45			0.000001	0.000004	0.000011
46				0.000002	0.000005
47				0.000001	0.000002
48					0.000001

TABLE 3. The Negative Exponential Distribution

Unitized negative exponential distribution where the mean and standard deviation are equal to one ($\mu = \sigma = 1$). Table values indicate the probability that a given value of x, x', will be exceeded.

x'/μ	Value of e^{-x}	x'/μ	Value of e^{-x}	x'/μ	Value of e^{-x}	x'/μ	Value of e^{-x}
0.00	1.000	0.20	0.819	0.80	0.449	2.30	0.100
0.01	0.990	0.21	0.811	0.85	0.427	2.40	0.091
0.02	0.980	0.22	0.803	0.90	0.407	2.50	0.082
0.03	0.970	0.23	0.795	0.95	0.387	2.60	0.074
0.04	0.961	0.24	0.787	1.00	0.368	2.70	0.067
0.05	0.951	0.25	0.779	1.05	0.350	2.80	0.061
0.06	0.942	0.26	0.771	1.10	0.333	2.90	0.055
0.07	0.932	0.27	0.763	1.15	0.317	3.00	0.050
0.08	0.923	0.28	0.756	1.20	0.301	3.10	0.045
0.09	0.914	0.29	0.748	1.25	0.287	3.20	0.041
0.10	0.905	0.30	0.741	1.30	0.273	3.40	0.033
0.11	0.896	0.35	0.705	1.40	0.247	3.60	0.027
0.12	0.887	0.40	0.670	1.50	0.223	3.80	0.022
0.13	0.878	0.45	0.638	1.60	0.202	4.00	0.018
0.14	0.869	0.50	0.607	1.70	0.183	4.20	0.015
0.15	0.861	0.55	0.577	1.80	0.165	4.40	0.012
0.16	0.852	0.60	0.549	1.90	0.150	4.60	0.010
0.17	0.844	0.65	0.522	2.00	0.135	4.80	0.008
0.18	0.835	0.70	0.497	2.10	0.122	5.00	0.007
0.19	0.827	0.75	0.472	2.20	0.111	5.50	0.004
						6.00	0.002

TABLE 3　703

TABLE 4. Values of L_q for $M = 1 - 15$, and Various Values
of $r = \lambda/\mu$. Poisson Arrivals, Negative Exponential Service Times

	Number of Service Channels (M)														
r	1	2	3	4	5	6	7	8	9	10	11	12	13	14	15
0.10	0.0111														
0.15	0.0264	0.0008													
0.20	0.0500	0.0020													
0.25	0.0833	0.0039													
0.30	0.1285	0.0069													
0.35	0.1884	0.0110													
0.40	0.2666	0.0166													
0.45	0.3681	0.0239	0.0019												
0.50	0.5000	0.0333	0.0030												
0.55	0.6722	0.0449	0.0043												
0.60	0.9000	0.0593	0.0061												
0.65	1.2071	0.0767	0.0084												
0.70	1.6333	0.0976	0.0112												
0.75	2.2500	0.1227	0.0147												
0.80	3.2000	0.1523	0.0189												
0.85	4.8166	0.1873	0.0239	0.0031											
0.90	8.1000	0.2285	0.0300	0.0041											
0.95	18.0500	0.2767	0.0371	0.0053											
1.0		0.3333	0.0454	0.0067											
1.2		0.6748	0.0904	0.0158											
1.4		1.3449	0.1778	0.0324	0.0059										
1.6		2.8444	0.3128	0.0604	0.0121										
1.8		7.6734	0.5320	0.1051	0.0227	0.0047									
2.0			0.8888	0.1739	0.0398	0.0090									
2.2			1.4907	0.2770	0.0659	0.0158									
2.4			2.1261	0.4305	0.1047	0.0266	0.0065								
2.6			4.9322	0.6581	0.1609	0.0426	0.0110								
2.8			12.2724	1.0000	0.2411	0.0659	0.0180								

x												
3.0	1.5282	0.3541	0.0991	0.0282	0.0077							
3.2	2.3856	0.5128	0.1452	0.0427	0.0122							
3.4	3.9060	0.7365	0.2085	0.0631	0.0189							
3.6	7.0893	1.0550	0.2947	0.0912	0.0283							
3.8	16.9366	1.5184	0.4114	0.1292	0.0412							
4.0		2.2164	0.5694	0.1801	0.0590							
4.2		3.3269	0.7837	0.2475	0.0827							
4.4		5.2675	1.0777	0.3364	0.1142							
4.6		9.2885	1.4867	0.4532	0.1555							
4.8		21.6384	2.0708	0.6071	0.2092							
5.0			2.9375	0.8102	0.2786	0.1006	0.0361	0.0125				
5.2			4.3004	1.0804	0.3680	0.1345	0.0492	0.0175				
5.4			6.6609	1.4441	0.5871	0.1779	0.0663	0.0243	0.0085			
5.6			11.5178	1.9436	0.6313	0.2330	0.0883	0.0330	0.0119			
5.8			26.3726	2.6481	0.8225	0.3032	0.1164	0.0443	0.0164			
6.0				3.6828	1.0707	0.3918	0.1518	0.0590	0.0224			
6.2				5.2979	1.3967	0.5037	0.1964	0.0775	0.0300	0.0113		
6.4				8.0768	1.8040	0.6454	0.2524	0.1008	0.0398	0.0153		
6.6				13.7692	2.4198	0.8247	0.3222	0.1302	0.0523	0.0205		
6.8				31.1270	3.2441	1.0533	0.4090	0.1666	0.0679	0.0271	0.0105	
7.0					4.4471	1.3471	0.5172	0.2119	0.0876	0.0357	0.0141	
7.2					6.3135	1.7288	0.6521	0.2677	0.1119	0.0463	0.0187	
7.4					9.5102	2.2324	0.8202	0.3364	0.1420	0.0595	0.0245	0.0097
7.6					16.0379	2.9113	1.0310	0.4211	0.1789	0.0761	0.0318	0.0129
7.8					35.8956	3.8558	1.2972	0.5250	0.2243	0.0966	0.0410	0.0168
8.0						5.2264	1.6364	0.6530	0.2796	0.1214	0.0522	0.0220
8.2						7.3441	2.0736	0.8109	0.3469	0.1520	0.0663	0.0283
8.4						10.9592	2.6470	1.0060	0.4288	0.1891	0.0834	0.0361
8.6						18.3223	3.4160	1.2484	0.5286	0.2341	0.1043	0.0459
8.8						40.6824	4.4806	1.5524	0.6501	0.2885	0.1298	0.0577
9.0							6.0183	1.9368	0.7980	0.3543	0.1603	0.0723
9.2							8.3869	2.4298	0.9788	0.4333	0.1974	0.0899
9.4							12.4189	3.0732	1.2010	0.5287	0.2419	0.1111
9.6							20.6160	3.9318	1.4752	0.6437	0.2952	0.1367
9.8							45.4769	5.1156	1.8165	0.7827	0.3588	0.1673
10.0								6.8210	2.2465	0.9506	0.4352	0.2040

TABLE 4   705

TABLE 5. Finite Queuing Tables (Continued)

X	M	D	F	L_q	X	M	D	F	L_q	X	M	D	F	L_q
					1	0.404	0.945	0.275		1	0.713	0.783	1.085
POPULATION 5					0.110	2	0.065	0.996	0.020	0.220	3	0.036	0.997	0.015
					1	0.421	0.939	0.305		2	0.229	0.969	0.155
0.012	1	0.048	0.999	0.005	0.115	2	0.071	0.995	0.025		1	0.735	0.765	1.175
0.019	1	0.076	0.998	0.010		1	0.439	0.933	0.335	0.230	3	0.041	0.997	0.015
0.025	1	0.100	0.997	0.015	0.120	2	0.076	0.995	0.025		2	0.247	0.965	0.175
0.030	1	0.120	0.996	0.020		1	0.456	0.927	0.365		1	0.756	0.747	1.265
0.034	1	0.135	0.995	0.025	0.125	2	0.082	0.994	0.030	0.240	3	0.046	0.996	0.020
0.036	1	0.143	0.994	0.030		1	0.473	0.920	0.400		2	0.265	0.960	0.200
0.040	1	0.159	0.993	0.035	0.130	2	0.089	0.993	0.035		1	0.775	0.730	1.350
0.042	1	0.167	0.992	0.045		1	0.489	0.914	0.430	0.250	3	0.052	0.995	0.025
0.044	1	0.175	0.991	0.045	0.135	2	0.095	0.993	0.035		2	0.284	0.955	0.225
0.046	1	0.183	0.990	0.050		1	0.505	0.907	0.465		1	0.794	0.712	1.440
0.050	1	0.198	0.989	0.055	0.140	2	0.102	0.992	0.040	0.260	3	0.058	0.994	0.030
0.052	1	0.206	0.988	0.060		1	0.521	0.900	0.500		2	0.303	0.950	0.250
0.054	1	0.214	0.987	0.065	0.145	3	0.011	0.999	0.005		1	0.811	0.695	1.525
0.056	2	0.018	0.999	0.005		2	0.109	0.991	0.045	0.270	3	0.064	0.994	0.030
	1	0.222	0.985	0.075		1	0.537	0.892	0.540		2	0.323	0.944	0.280
0.058	2	0.019	0.999	0.005	0.150	3	0.012	0.999	0.005		1	0.827	0.677	1.615
	1	0.229	0.984	0.080		2	0.115	0.990	0.050	0.280	3	0.071	0.993	0.035
0.060	2	0.020	0.999	0.005		1	0.553	0.885	0.575		2	0.342	0.938	0.310
	1	0.237	0.983	0.085	0.155	3	0.013	0.999	0.005		1	0.842	0.661	1.695
0.062	2	0.022	0.999	0.005		2	0.123	0.989	0.055	0.290	4	0.007	0.999	0.005
	1	0.245	0.982	0.090		1	0.568	0.877	0.615		3	0.079	0.992	0.040
0.064	2	0.023	0.999	0.005	0.160	3	0.015	0.999	0.005		2	0.362	0.932	0.340
	1	0.253	0.981	0.095		2	0.130	0.988	0.060		1	0.856	0.644	1.780
0.066	2	0.024	0.999	0.005		1	0.582	0.869	0.655	0.300	4	0.008	0.999	0.005
	1	0.260	0.979	0.105	0.165	3	0.016	0.999	0.005		3	0.086	0.990	0.050
0.068	2	0.026	0.999	0.005		2	0.137	0.987	0.065		2	0.382	0.926	0.370
	1	0.268	0.978	0.110		1	0.597	0.861	0.695		1	0.869	0.628	1.860
0.070	2	0.027	0.999	0.005	0.170	3	0.017	0.999	0.005	0.310	4	0.009	0.999	0.005
	1	0.275	0.977	0.115		2	0.145	0.985	0.075		3	0.094	0.989	0.055
0.075	2	0.031	0.999	0.005		1	0.611	0.853	0.735		2	0.402	0.919	0.405
	1	0.294	0.973	0.135	0.180	3	0.021	0.999	0.005		1	0.881	0.613	1.935
0.080	2	0.035	0.998	0.010		2	0.161	0.983	0.085	0.320	4	0.010	0.999	0.005
	1	0.313	0.969	0.155		1	0.638	0.836	0.820		3	0.103	0.988	0.060
0.085	2	0.040	0.998	0.010	0.190	3	0.024	0.998	0.010		2	0.422	0.912	0.440
	1	0.332	0.965	0.175		2	0.177	0.980	0.100		1	0.892	0.597	2.015
0.090	2	0.044	0.998	0.010		1	0.665	0.819	0.905	0.330	4	0.012	0.999	0.005
	1	0.350	0.960	0.200	0.200	3	0.028	0.998	0.010		3	0.112	0.986	0.070
0.095	2	0.049	0.997	0.015		2	0.194	0.976	0.120		2	0.442	0.904	0.480
	1	0.368	0.955	0.255		1	0.689	0.801	0.995		1	0.902	0.583	2.085
0.100	2	0.054	0.997	0.015	0.210	3	0.032	0.998	0.010	0.340	4	0.013	0.999	0.005
	1	0.386	0.950	0.250		2	0.211	0.973	0.135		3	0.121	0.985	0.075
0.105	2	0.059	0.997	0.015										

TABLE 5. Finite Queuing Tables (Continued)

POPULATION 5, Cont.

X	M	D	F	L_q	X	M	D	F	L_q	X	M	D	F	L_q
	2	0.462	0.896	0.520		2	0.831	0.689	1.555		1	0.285	0.988	0.12
	1	0.911	0.569	2.155		1	0.993	0.357	3.215	0.034	2	0.037	0.999	0.01
0.360	4	0.017	0.998	0.010	0.580	4	0.113	0.984	0.080		1	0.302	0.986	0.14
	3	0.141	0.981	0.060		3	0.461	0.895	0.525	0.036	2	0.041	0.999	0.01
	2	0.501	0.880	0.600		2	0.854	0.670	1.650		1	0.320	0.984	0.16
	1	0.927	0.542	2.290		1	0.994	0.345	3.275	0.038	2	0.046	0.999	0.01
0.380	4	0.021	0.998	0.010	0.600	4	0.130	0.981	0.095		1	0.337	0.982	0.18
	3	0.163	0.976	0.120		3	0.497	0.883	0.585	0.040	2	0.050	0.999	0.01
	2	0.540	0.863	0.685		2	0.875	0.652	1.740		1	0.354	0.980	0.20
	1	0.941	0.516	2.420		1	0.996	0.333	3.335	0.042	2	0.055	0.999	0.01
0.400	4	0.026	0.997	0.015	0.650	4	0.179	0.972	0.140		1	0.371	0.978	0.22
	3	0.186	0.972	0.140		3	0.588	0.850	0.750	0.044	2	0.060	0.998	0.02
	2	0.579	0.845	0.775		2	0.918	0.608	1.960		1	0.388	0.975	0.25
	1	0.952	0.493	2.535		1	0.998	0.308	3.460	0.046	2	0.065	0.998	0.02
0.420	4	0.031	0.997	0.015	0.700	4	0.240	0.960	0.200		1	0.404	0.973	0.27
	3	0.211	0.966	0.170		3	0.678	0.815	0.925	0.048	2	0.071	0.998	0.02
	2	0.616	0.826	0.870		2	0.950	0.568	2.160		1	0.421	0.970	0.30
	1	0.961	0.471	2.645		1	0.999	0.286	3.570	0.050	2	0.076	0.998	0.02
0.440	4	0.037	0.996	0.020	0.750	4	0.316	0.944	0.280		1	0.437	0.967	0.33
	3	0.238	0.960	0.200		3	0.763	0.777	1.115	0.052	2	0.082	0.997	0.03
	2	0.652	0.807	0.965		2	0.972	0.532	2.340		1	0.454	0.963	0.37
	1	0.969	0.451	2.745	0.800	4	0.410	0.924	0.380	0.054	2	0.088	0.997	0.03
0.460	4	0.045	0.995	0.025		3	0.841	0.739	1.305		1	0.470	0.960	0.40
	3	0.266	0.953	0.235		2	0.987	0.500	2.500	0.056	2	0.094	0.997	0.03
	2	0.686	0.787	1.065	0.850	4	0.522	0.900	0.500		1	0.486	0.956	0.44
	1	0.975	0.432	2.840		3	0.907	0.702	1.490	0.058	2	0.100	0.996	0.04
0.480	4	0.053	0.994	0.030		2	0.995	0.470	2.650		1	0.501	0.953	0.47
	3	0.296	0.945	0.275	0.900	4	0.656	0.871	0.645	0.060	2	0.106	0.996	0.04
	2	0.719	0.767	1.165		3	0.957	0.666	1.670		1	0.517	0.949	0.51
	1	0.980	0.415	2.925		2	0.998	0.444	2.780	0.062	2	0.113	0.996	0.04
0.500	4	0.063	0.992	0.040	0.950	4	0.815	0.838	0.810		1	0.532	0.945	0.55
	3	0.327	0.936	0.320		3	0.989	0.631	1.845	0.064	2	0.119	0.995	0.05
	2	0.750	0.748	1.260							1	0.547	0.940	0.60
	1	0.985	0.399	3.005	POPULATION 10					0.066	2	0.126	0.995	0.05
0.520	4	0.073	0.991	0.045							1	0.562	0.936	0.64
	3	0.359	0.927	0.365	0.016	1	0.144	0.997	0.03	0.068	3	0.020	0.999	0.01
	2	0.779	0.728	1.360	0.019	1	0.170	0.996	0.04		2	0.133	0.994	0.06
	1	0.988	0.384	3.080	0.021	1	0.188	0.995	0.05		1	0.577	0.931	0.69
0.540	4	0.085	0.989	0.055	0.023	1	0.206	0.994	0.06	0.070	3	0.022	0.999	0.01
	3	0.392	0.917	0.415	0.025	1	0.224	0.993	0.07		2	0.140	0.994	0.06
	2	0.806	0.708	1.460	0.026	1	0.232	0.992	0.08		1	0.591	0.926	0.74
	1	0.991	0.370	3.150	0.028	1	0.250	0.991	0.09	0.075	3	0.026	0.999	0.01
0.560	4	0.098	0.986	0.070	0.030	1	0.268	0.990	0.10		2	0.158	0.992	0.08
	3	0.426	0.906	0.470	0.032	2	0.033	0.999	0.01		1	0.627	0.913	0.87

TABLE 5   707

TABLE 5. Finite Queuing Tables (Continued)

X	M	D	F	L_q	X	M	D	F	L_q	X	M	D	F	L_q
POPULATION 10, Cont.														
0.080	3	0.031	0.999	0.01	0.145	4	0.032	0.999	0.01	0.220	5	0.030	0.998	0.02
	2	0.177	0.990	0.10		3	0.144	0.990	0.10		4	0.124	0.990	0.10
	1	0.660	0.899	1.01		2	0.460	0.941	0.59		3	0.366	0.954	0.46
0.085	3	0.037	0.999	0.01		1	0.929	0.662	3.38		2	0.761	0.815	1.85
	2	0.196	0.988	0.12	0.150	4	0.036	0.998	0.02		1	0.993	0.453	5.47
	1	0.692	0.883	1.17		3	0.156	0.989	0.11	0.230	5	0.037	0.998	0.02
0.090	3	0.043	0.998	0.02		2	0.483	0.935	0.65		4	0.142	0.988	0.12
	2	0.216	0.986	0.14		1	0.939	0.644	3.56		3	0.400	0.947	0.53
	1	0.722	0.867	1.33	0.155	4	0.040	0.998	0.02		2	0.791	0.794	2.06
0.095	3	0.049	0.998	0.02		3	0.169	0.987	0.13		1	0.995	0.434	5.66
	2	0.237	0.984	0.16		2	0.505	0.928	0.72	0.240	5	0.044	0.997	0.03
	1	0.750	0.850	1.50		1	0.947	0.627	3.73		4	0.162	0.986	0.14
0.100	3	0.056	0.998	0.02	0.160	4	0.044	0.998	0.02		3	0.434	0.938	0.62
	2	0.258	0.981	0.19		3	0.182	0.986	0.14		2	0.819	0.774	2.26
	1	0.776	0.832	1.68		2	0.528	0.921	0.79		1	0.996	0.416	5.84
0.105	3	0.064	0.997	0.03		1	0.954	0.610	3.90	0.250	6	0.010	0.999	0.01
	2	0.279	0.978	0.22	0.165	4	0.049	0.997	0.03		5	0.052	0.997	0.03
	1	0.800	0.814	1.86		3	0.195	0.984	0.16		4	0.183	0.983	0.17
0.110	3	0.072	0.997	0.03		2	0.550	0.914	0.86		3	0.469	0.929	0.71
	2	0.301	0.974	0.26		1	0.961	0.594	4.06		2	0.844	0.753	2.47
	1	0.822	0.795	2.05	0.170	4	0.054	0.997	0.03		1	0.997	0.400	6.00
0.115	3	0.081	0.996	0.04		3	0.209	0.982	0.18	0.260	6	0.013	0.999	0.01
	2	0.324	0.971	0.29		2	0.571	0.906	0.94		5	0.060	0.996	0.04
	1	0.843	0.776	2.24		1	0.966	0.579	4.21		4	0.205	0.980	0.20
0.120	4	0.016	0.999	0.01	0.180	5	0.013	0.999	0.01		3	0.503	0.919	0.81
	3	0.090	0.995	0.05		4	0.066	0.996	0.04		2	0.866	0.732	2.68
	2	0.346	0.967	0.33		3	0.238	0.978	0.22		1	0.998	0.384	6.16
	1	0.861	0.756	2.44		2	0.614	0.890	1.10	0.270	6	0.015	0.999	0.01
0.125	4	0.019	0.999	0.01		1	0.975	0.549	4.51		5	0.070	0.995	0.05
	3	0.100	0.994	0.06	0.190	5	0.016	0.999	0.01		4	0.228	0.976	0.24
	2	0.369	0.962	0.38		4	0.078	0.995	0.05		3	0.537	0.908	0.92
	1	0.878	0.737	2.63		3	0.269	0.973	0.27		2	0.886	0.712	2.88
0.130	4	0.022	0.999	0.01		2	0.654	0.873	1.27		1	0.999	0.370	6.30
	3	0.110	0.994	0.06		1	0.982	0.522	4.78	0.280	6	0.018	0.999	0.01
	2	0.392	0.958	0.42	0.200	5	0.020	0.999	0.01		5	0.081	0.994	0.06
	1	0.893	0.718	2.82		4	0.092	0.994	0.06		4	0.252	0.972	0.28
0.135	4	0.025	0.999	0.01		3	0.300	0.968	0.32		3	0.571	0.896	1.04
	3	0.121	0.993	0.07		2	0.692	0.854	1.46		2	0.903	0.692	3.08
	2	0.415	0.952	0.48		1	0.987	0.497	5.03		1	0.999	0.357	6.43
	1	0.907	0.699	3.01	0.210	5	0.025	0.999	0.01	0.290	6	0.022	0.999	0.01
0.140	4	0.028	0.999	0.01		4	0.108	0.992	0.08		5	0.093	0.993	0.07
	3	0.132	0.991	0.09		3	0.333	0.961	0.39		4	0.278	0.968	0.32
	2	0.437	0.947	0.53		2	0.728	0.835	1.65		3	0.603	0.884	1.16
	1	0.919	0.680	3.20		1	0.990	0.474	5.26		2	0.918	0.672	3.28

TABLE 5. Finite Queuing Tables (Continued)

X	M	D	F	L_q	X	M	D	F	L_q	X	M	D	F	L_q
POPULATION 10, Cont.														
0.300	1	0.999	0.345	6.55		3	0.875	0.728	2.72		6	0.363	0.949	0.51
	6	0.026	0.998	0.02		2	0.991	0.499	5.01		5	0.658	0.867	1.33
	5	0.106	0.991	0.09	0.420	7	0.034	0.993	0.07		4	0.893	0.729	2.71
	4	0.304	0.963	0.37		6	0.130	0.987	0.13		3	0.986	0.555	4.45
	3	0.635	0.872	1.28		5	0.341	0.954	0.46	0.560	8	0.044	0.996	0.04
	2	0.932	0.653	3.47		4	0.646	0.866	1.34		7	0.171	0.982	0.18
0.310	1	0.999	0.333	6.67		3	0.905	0.700	3.00		6	0.413	0.939	0.61
	6	0.031	0.998	0.02		2	0.994	0.476	5.24		5	0.707	0.848	1.52
	5	0.120	0.990	0.10	0.440	7	0.045	0.997	0.03		4	0.917	0.706	2.94
	4	0.331	0.957	0.43		6	0.160	0.984	0.16		3	0.991	0.535	4.65
	3	0.666	0.858	1.42		5	0.392	0.943	0.57	0.580	8	0.057	0.995	0.05
	2	0.943	0.635	3.65		4	0.698	0.845	1.55		7	0.204	0.977	0.23
0.320	6	0.036	0.998	0.02		3	0.928	0.672	3.28		6	0.465	0.927	0.73
	5	0.135	0.988	0.12		2	0.996	0.454	5.46		5	0.753	0.829	1.71
	4	0.359	0.952	0.48	0.460	8	0.011	0.999	0.01		4	0.937	0.684	3.16
	3	0.695	0.845	1.55		7	0.058	0.995	0.05		3	0.994	0.517	4.83
	2	0.952	0.617	3.83		6	0.193	0.979	0.21		9	0.010	0.999	0.01
0.330	6	0.042	0.997	0.03		5	0.445	0.930	0.70		8	0.072	0.994	0.06
	5	0.151	0.986	0.14		4	0.747	0.822	1.78		7	0.242	0.972	0.28
	4	0.387	0.945	0.55		3	0.947	0.646	3.54	0.600	6	0.518	0.915	0.85
	3	0.723	0.831	1.69		2	0.998	0.435	5.65		5	0.795	0.809	1.91
	2	0.961	0.600	4.00	0.480	8	0.015	0.999	0.01		4	0.953	0.663	3.37
0.340	7	0.010	0.999	0.01		7	0.074	0.994	0.06		3	0.996	0.500	5.00
	6	0.049	0.997	0.03		6	0.230	0.973	0.27	0.650	9	0.021	0.999	0.01
	5	0.168	0.983	0.17		5	0.499	0.916	0.84		8	0.123	0.988	0.12
	4	0.416	0.938	0.62		4	0.791	0.799	2.01		7	0.353	0.954	0.46
	3	0.750	0.816	1.84		3	0.961	0.621	3.79		6	0.651	0.878	1.22
	2	0.968	0.584	4.16		2	0.998	0.417	5.83		5	0.882	0.759	2.41
0.360	7	0.014	0.999	0.01	0.500	8	0.020	0.999	0.01		4	0.980	0.614	3.86
	6	0.064	0.995	0.05		7	0.093	0.992	0.08		3	0.999	0.461	5.39
	5	0.205	0.978	0.22		6	0.271	0.966	0.34	0.700	9	0.040	0.997	0.03
	4	0.474	0.923	0.77		5	0.553	0.901	0.99		8	0.200	0.979	0.21
	3	0.798	0.787	2.13		4	0.830	0.775	2.25		7	0.484	0.929	0.71
	2	0.978	0.553	4.47		3	0.972	0.598	4.02		6	0.772	0.836	1.64
0.380	7	0.019	0.999	0.01		2	0.999	0.400	6.00		5	0.940	0.711	2.89
	6	0.083	0.993	0.07	0.520	8	0.026	0.998	0.02		4	0.992	0.571	4.29
	5	0.247	0.971	0.29		7	0.115	0.989	0.11	0.750	9	0.075	0.994	0.06
	4	0.533	0.906	0.94		6	0.316	0.958	0.42		8	0.307	0.965	0.35
	3	0.840	0.758	2.42		5	0.606	0.884	1.16		7	0.626	0.897	1.03
	2	0.986	0.525	4.75		4	0.864	0.752	2.48		6	0.870	0.792	2.08
0.400	7	0.026	0.998	0.02		3	0.980	0.575	4.25		5	0.975	0.666	3.34
	6	0.105	0.991	0.09		2	0.999	0.385	6.15		4	0.998	0.533	4.67
	5	0.292	0.963	0.37	0.540	8	0.034	0.997	0.03	0.800	9	0.134	0.988	0.12
	4	0.591	0.887	1.13		7	0.141	0.986	0.14		8	0.446	0.944	0.56

TABLE 5   709

TABLE 5. Finite Queuing Tables (Continued)

POPULATION 10, Cont.

X	M	D	F	L_q
	7	0.763	0.859	1.41
	6	0.939	0.747	2.53
	5	0.991	0.625	3.75
	4	0.999	0.500	5.00
0.850	9	0.232	0.979	0.21
	8	0.611	0.916	0.84
	7	0.879	0.818	1.82
	6	0.978	0.705	2.95
	5	0.998	0.588	4.12
0.900	9	0.387	0.963	0.37
	8	0.785	0.881	1.19
	7	0.957	0.777	2.23
	6	0.995	0.667	3.33
0.950	9	0.630	0.938	0.62
	8	0.934	0.841	1.59
	7	0.994	0.737	2.63

POPULATION 20

X	M	D	F	L_q
0.005	1	0.095	0.999	0.02
0.009	1	0.171	0.998	0.04
0.011	1	0.208	0.997	0.06
0.013	1	0.246	0.996	0.08
0.014	1	0.265	0.995	0.10
0.015	1	0.283	0.994	0.12
0.016	1	0.302	0.993	0.14
0.017	1	0.321	0.992	0.16
0.018	2	0.048	0.999	0.02
	1	0.339	0.991	0.18
0.019	2	0.053	0.999	0.02
	1	0.358	0.990	0.20
0.020	2	0.058	0.999	0.02
	1	0.376	0.989	0.22
0.021	2	0.064	0.999	0.02
	1	0.394	0.987	0.26
0.022	2	0.070	0.999	0.02
	1	0.412	0.986	0.28
0.023	2	0.075	0.999	0.02
	1	0.431	0.984	0.32
0.024	2	0.082	0.999	0.02
	1	0.449	0.982	0.36
0.025	2	0.088	0.999	0.02
	1	0.466	0.980	0.40
0.026	2	0.094	0.998	0.04

X	M	D	F	L_q
	1	0.484	0.978	0.44
0.028	2	0.108	0.998	0.04
	1	0.519	0.973	0.54
0.030	2	0.122	0.998	0.04
	1	0.553	0.968	0.64
0.032	2	0.137	0.997	0.06
	1	0.587	0.962	0.76
0.034	2	0.152	0.996	0.08
	1	0.620	0.955	0.90
0.036	2	0.168	0.996	0.08
	1	0.651	0.947	1.06
0.038	3	0.036	0.999	0.02
	2	0.185	0.995	0.10
	1	0.682	0.938	1.24
0.040	3	0.041	0.999	0.02
	2	0.202	0.994	0.12
	1	0.712	0.929	1.42
0.042	3	0.047	0.999	0.02
	2	0.219	0.993	0.14
	1	0.740	0.918	1.64
0.044	3	0.053	0.999	0.02
	2	0.237	0.992	0.16
	1	0.767	0.906	1.88
0.046	3	0.059	0.999	0.02
	2	0.255	0.991	0.18
	1	0.792	0.894	2.12
0.048	3	0.066	0.999	0.02
	2	0.274	0.989	0.22
	1	0.815	0.881	2.38
0.050	3	0.073	0.998	0.04
	2	0.293	0.988	0.24
	1	0.837	0.866	2.68
0.052	3	0.080	0.998	0.04
	2	0.312	0.986	0.28
	1	0.858	0.851	2.98
0.054	3	0.088	0.998	0.04
	2	0.332	0.984	0.32
	1	0.876	0.835	3.30
0.056	3	0.097	0.997	0.06
	2	0.352	0.982	0.36
	1	0.893	0.819	3.62
0.058	3	0.105	0.997	0.06
	2	0.372	0.980	0.40
	1	0.908	0.802	3.96

X	M	D	F	L_q
0.060	4	0.026	0.999	0.02
	3	0.115	0.997	0.06
	2	0.392	0.978	0.44
	1	0.922	0.785	4.30
0.062	4	0.029	0.999	0.02
	3	0.124	0.996	0.08
	2	0.413	0.975	0.50
	1	0.934	0.768	4.64
0.064	4	0.032	0.999	0.02
	3	0.134	0.996	0.08
	2	0.433	0.972	0.56
	1	0.944	0.751	4.98
0.066	4	0.036	0.999	0.02
	3	0.144	0.995	0.10
	2	0.454	0.969	0.62
	1	0.953	0.733	5.34
0.068	4	0.039	0.999	0.02
	3	0.155	0.995	0.10
	2	0.474	0.966	0.68
	1	0.961	0.716	5.68
0.070	4	0.043	0.999	0.02
	3	0.165	0.994	0.12
	2	0.495	0.962	0.76
	1	0.967	0.699	6.02
0.075	4	0.054	0.999	0.02
	3	0.194	0.992	0.16
	2	0.545	0.953	0.94
	1	0.980	0.659	6.82
0.080	4	0.066	0.998	0.04
	3	0.225	0.990	0.20
	2	0.595	0.941	1.18
	1	0.988	0.621	7.58
0.085	4	0.080	0.997	0.06
	3	0.257	0.987	0.26
	2	0.643	0.928	1.44
	1	0.993	0.586	8.28
0.090	5	0.025	0.999	0.02
	4	0.095	0.997	0.06
	3	0.291	0.984	0.32
	2	0.689	0.913	1.74
	1	0.996	0.554	8.92
0.095	5	0.031	0.999	0.02
	4	0.112	0.996	0.08
	3	0.326	0.980	0.40

TABLE 5. Finite Queuing Tables (Continued)

POPULATION 20, Cont.

X	M	D	F	L_q	X	M	D	F	L_q	X	M	D	F	L_q
	2	0.733	0.896	2.08		2	0.960	0.703	5.94		6	0.154	0.991	0.18
	1	0.998	0.526	9.48	0.145	6	0.051	0.998	0.04		5	0.345	0.971	0.58
0.100	5	0.038	0.999	0.02		5	0.148	0.993	0.14		4	0.636	0.914	1.72
	4	0.131	0.995	0.10		4	0.358	0.972	0.56		3	0.913	0.768	4.64
	3	0.363	0.975	0.50		3	0.695	0.900	2.00		2	0.998	0.526	9.48
	2	0.773	0.878	2.44		2	0.969	0.682	6.36	0.200	8	0.025	0.999	0.02
0.105	1	0.999	0.500	10.00	0.150	7	0.017	0.999	0.02		7	0.074	0.997	0.06
	5	0.046	0.999	0.02		6	0.059	0.998	0.04		6	0.187	0.988	0.24
	4	0.151	0.993	0.14		5	0.166	0.991	0.18		5	0.397	0.963	0.74
	3	0.400	0.970	0.60		4	0.388	0.968	0.64		4	0.693	0.895	2.10
	2	0.809	0.858	2.84		3	0.728	0.887	2.26		3	0.938	0.736	5.28
0.110	1	0.999	0.476	10.48		2	0.976	0.661	6.78		2	0.999	0.500	10.00
	5	0.055	0.998	0.04	0.155	7	0.021	0.999	0.02	0.210	8	0.033	0.999	0.02
	4	0.172	0.992	0.16		6	0.068	0.997	0.06		7	0.093	0.995	0.10
	3	0.438	0.964	0.72		5	0.185	0.990	0.20		6	0.223	0.985	0.30
	2	0.842	0.837	3.26		4	0.419	0.963	0.74		5	0.451	0.954	0.92
0.115	5	0.065	0.998	0.04		3	0.758	0.874	2.52		4	0.745	0.874	2.52
	4	0.195	0.990	0.20		2	0.982	0.641	7.18		3	0.958	0.706	5.88
	3	0.476	0.958	0.84	0.160	7	0.024	0.999	0.02		2	0.999	0.476	10.48
	2	0.870	0.816	3.68		6	0.077	0.997	0.06	0.220	8	0.043	0.998	0.04
0.120	6	0.022	0.999	0.02		5	0.205	0.988	0.24		7	0.115	0.994	0.12
	5	0.076	0.997	0.06		4	0.450	0.957	0.86		6	0.263	0.980	0.40
	4	0.219	0.988	0.24		3	0.787	0.860	2.80		5	0.505	0.943	1.14
	3	0.514	0.950	1.00		2	0.987	0.622	7.56		4	0.793	0.852	2.96
	2	0.895	0.793	4.14	0.165	7	0.029	0.999	0.02		3	0.971	0.677	6.46
0.125	6	0.026	0.999	0.02		6	0.088	0.996	0.08	0.230	9	0.018	0.999	0.02
	5	0.088	0.997	0.06		5	0.226	0.986	0.28		8	0.054	0.998	0.04
	4	0.245	0.986	0.28		4	0.482	0.951	0.98		7	0.140	0.992	0.16
	3	0.552	0.942	1.16		3	0.813	0.845	3.10		6	0.306	0.975	0.50
	2	0.916	0.770	4.60		2	0.990	0.604	7.92		5	0.560	0.931	1.38
0.130	6	0.031	0.999	0.02	0.170	7	0.033	0.999	0.02		4	0.834	0.828	3.44
	5	0.101	0.996	0.08		6	0.099	0.995	0.10		3	0.981	0.649	7.02
	4	0.271	0.983	0.34		5	0.248	0.983	0.34	0.240	9	0.024	0.999	0.02
	3	0.589	0.933	1.34		4	0.513	0.945	1.10		8	0.068	0.997	0.06
	2	0.934	0.748	5.04		3	0.838	0.830	3.40		7	0.168	0.989	0.22
0.135	6	0.037	0.999	0.02		2	0.993	0.587	8.26		6	0.351	0.969	0.62
	5	0.116	0.995	0.10	0.180	7	0.044	0.998	0.04		5	0.613	0.917	1.66
	4	0.299	0.980	0.40		6	0.125	0.994	0.12		4	0.870	0.804	3.92
	3	0.626	0.923	1.54		5	0.295	0.978	0.44		3	0.988	0.623	7.54
	2	0.948	0.725	5.50		4	0.575	0.930	1.40	0.250	9	0.031	0.999	0.02
0.140	6	0.043	0.998	0.04		3	0.879	0.799	4.02		8	0.085	0.996	0.08
	5	0.131	0.994	0.12		2	0.996	0.555	8.90		7	0.199	0.986	0.28
	4	0.328	0.976	0.48	0.190	8	0.018	0.999	0.02		6	0.398	0.961	0.78
	3	0.661	0.912	1.76		7	0.058	0.998	0.04		5	0.664	0.901	1.98

TABLE 5   711

TABLE 5. Finite Queuing Tables (Continued)

X	M	D	F	L_q	X	M	D	F	L_q	X	M	D	F	L_q
POPULATION 20, Cont.														
	4	0.900	0.780	4.40		8	0.237	0.981	0.38		6	0.909	0.777	4.46
	3	0.992	0.599	8.02		7	0.438	0.953	0.94		5	0.984	0.656	6.88
0.260	9	0.039	0.998	0.04		6	0.684	0.893	2.14		4	0.999	0.526	9.48
	8	0.104	0.994	0.12		5	0.892	0.788	4.24	0.400	13	0.012	0.999	0.02
	7	0.233	0.983	0.34		4	0.985	0.643	7.14		12	0.037	0.998	0.04
	6	0.446	0.953	0.94	0.320	11	0.018	0.999	0.02		11	0.095	0.994	0.12
	5	0.712	0.884	2.32		10	0.053	0.997	0.06		10	0.205	0.984	0.32
	4	0.924	0.755	4.90		9	0.130	0.992	0.16		9	0.379	0.962	0.76
	3	0.995	0.576	8.48		8	0.272	0.977	0.46		8	0.598	0.918	1.64
0.270	10	0.016	0.999	0.02		7	0.483	0.944	1.12		7	0.807	0.845	3.10
	9	0.049	0.998	0.04		6	0.727	0.878	2.44		6	0.942	0.744	5.12
	8	0.125	0.992	0.16		5	0.915	0.768	4.64		5	0.992	0.624	7.52
	7	0.270	0.978	0.44		4	0.989	0.624	7.52	0.420	13	0.019	0.999	0.02
	6	0.495	0.943	1.14	0.330	11	0.023	0.999	0.02		12	0.055	0.997	0.06
	5	0.757	0.867	2.66		10	0.065	0.997	0.06		11	0.131	0.991	0.18
	4	0.943	0.731	5.38		9	0.154	0.990	0.20		10	0.265	0.977	0.46
	3	0.997	0.555	8.90		8	0.309	0.973	0.54		9	0.458	0.949	1.02
0.280	10	0.021	0.999	0.02		7	0.529	0.935	1.30		8	0.678	0.896	2.08
	9	0.061	0.997	0.06		6	0.766	0.862	2.76		7	0.863	0.815	3.70
	8	0.149	0.990	0.20		5	0.933	0.748	5.04		6	0.965	0.711	5.78
	7	0.309	0.973	0.54		4	0.993	0.605	7.90		5	0.996	0.595	8.10
	6	0.544	0.932	1.36	0.340	11	0.029	0.999	0.02	0.440	13	0.029	0.999	0.02
	5	0.797	0.848	3.04		10	0.079	0.996	0.08		12	0.078	0.995	0.10
	4	0.958	0.708	5.84		9	0.179	0.987	0.26		11	0.175	0.987	0.26
	3	0.998	0.536	9.28		8	0.347	0.967	0.66		10	0.333	0.969	0.62
0.290	10	0.027	0.999	0.02		7	0.573	0.924	1.52		9	0.540	0.933	1.34
	9	0.075	0.996	0.08		6	0.802	0.846	3.08		8	0.751	0.872	2.56
	8	0.176	0.988	0.24		5	0.949	0.729	5.42		7	0.907	0.785	4.30
	7	0.351	0.967	0.66		4	0.995	0.588	8.24		6	0.980	0.680	6.40
	6	0.592	0.920	1.60	0.360	12	0.015	0.999	0.02		5	0.998	0.568	8.64
	5	0.833	0.828	3.44		11	0.045	0.998	0.04	0.460	14	0.014	0.999	0.02
	4	0.970	0.685	6.30		10	0.112	0.993	0.14		13	0.043	0.998	0.04
	3	0.999	0.517	9.66		9	0.237	0.981	0.38		12	0.109	0.993	0.14
0.300	10	0.034	0.998	0.04		8	0.429	0.954	0.92		11	0.228	0.982	0.36
	9	0.091	0.995	0.10		7	0.660	0.901	1.98		10	0.407	0.958	0.84
	8	0.205	0.985	0.30		6	0.863	0.812	3.76		9	0.620	0.914	1.72
	7	0.394	0.961	0.78		5	0.971	0.691	6.18		8	0.815	0.846	3.08
	6	0.639	0.907	1.86		4	0.998	0.555	8.90		7	0.939	0.755	4.90
	5	0.865	0.808	3.84	0.380	12	0.024	0.999	0.02		6	0.989	0.651	6.98
	4	0.978	0.664	6.72		11	0.067	0.996	0.08		5	0.999	0.543	9.14
	3	0.999	0.500	10.00		10	0.154	0.989	0.22	0.480	14	0.022	0.999	0.02
0.310	11	0.014	0.999	0.02		9	0.305	0.973	0.54		13	0.063	0.996	0.08
	10	0.043	0.998	0.04		8	0.513	0.938	1.24		12	0.147	0.990	0.20
	9	0.110	0.993	0.14		7	0.739	0.874	2.52		11	0.289	0.974	0.52

TABLE 5. Finite Queuing Tables (Continued)

X	M	D	F	L_q	X	M	D	F	L_q	X	M	D	F	L_q
POPULATION 20, Cont.														
	10	0.484	0.944	1.12		15	0.051	0.997	0.06		12	0.952	0.798	4.04
	9	0.695	0.893	2.14		14	0.129	0.991	0.18		11	0.988	0.733	5.34
	8	0.867	0.819	3.62		13	0.266	0.978	0.44		10	0.998	0.667	6.66
	7	0.962	0.726	5.48		12	0.455	0.952	0.96	0.800	19	0.014	0.999	0.02
	6	0.994	0.625	7.50		11	0.662	0.908	1.84		18	0.084	0.996	0.08
0.500	14	0.033	0.998	0.04		10	0.835	0.847	3.06		17	0.242	0.984	0.32
	13	0.088	0.995	0.10		9	0.941	0.772	4.56		16	0.470	0.959	0.82
	12	0.194	0.985	0.30		8	0.986	0.689	6.22		15	0.700	0.920	1.60
	11	0.358	0.965	0.70		7	0.998	0.603	7.94		14	0.867	0.869	2.62
	10	0.563	0.929	1.42	0.600	16	0.023	0.999	0.02		13	0.955	0.811	3.78
	9	0.764	0.870	2.60		15	0.072	0.996	0.08		12	0.989	0.750	5.00
	8	0.908	0.791	4.18		14	0.171	0.988	0.24		11	0.998	0.687	6.26
	7	0.977	0.698	6.04		13	0.331	0.970	0.60	0.850	19	0.046	0.998	0.04
	6	0.997	0.600	8.00		12	0.532	0.938	1.24		18	0.201	0.988	0.24
0.520	15	0.015	0.999	0.02		11	0.732	0.889	2.22		17	0.451	0.965	0.70
	14	0.048	0.997	0.06		10	0.882	0.824	3.52		16	0.703	0.927	1.46
	13	0.120	0.992	0.16		9	0.962	0.748	5.04		15	0.877	0.878	2.44
	12	0.248	0.979	0.42		8	0.992	0.666	6.68		14	0.962	0.823	3.54
	11	0.432	0.954	0.92		7	0.999	0.583	8.34		13	0.991	0.765	4.70
	10	0.641	0.911	1.78	0.650	17	0.017	0.999	0.02		12	0.998	0.706	5.88
	9	0.824	0.846	3.08		16	0.061	0.997	0.06	0.900	19	0.135	0.994	0.12
	8	0.939	0.764	4.72		15	0.156	0.989	0.22		18	0.425	0.972	0.56
	7	0.987	0.672	6.56		14	0.314	0.973	0.54		17	0.717	0.935	1.30
	6	0.998	0.577	8.46		13	0.518	0.943	1.14		16	0.898	0.886	2.28
0.540	15	0.023	0.999	0.02		12	0.720	0.898	2.04		15	0.973	0.833	3.34
	14	0.069	0.996	0.08		11	0.872	0.837	3.26		14	0.995	0.778	4.44
	13	0.161	0.988	0.24		10	0.957	0.767	4.66		13	0.999	0.722	5.56
	12	0.311	0.972	0.56		9	0.990	0.692	6.16	0.950	19	0.377	0.981	0.38
	11	0.509	0.941	1.18		8	0.998	0.615	7.70		18	0.760	0.943	1.14
	10	0.713	0.891	2.18	0.700	17	0.047	0.998	0.04		17	0.939	0.894	2.12
	9	0.873	0.821	3.58		16	0.137	0.991	0.18		16	0.989	0.842	3.16
	8	0.961	0.738	5.24		15	0.295	0.976	0.48		15	0.999	0.789	4.22
	7	0.993	0.648	7.04		14	0.503	0.948	1.04					
	6	0.999	0.556	8.88		13	0.710	0.905	1.90	POPULATION 30				
0.560	15	0.035	0.998	0.04		12	0.866	0.849	3.02	0.004	1	0.116	0.999	0.03
	14	0.095	0.994	0.12		11	0.953	0.783	4.34	0.007	1	0.203	0.998	0.06
	13	0.209	0.984	0.32		10	0.988	0.714	5.72	0.009	1	0.260	0.997	0.09
	12	0.381	0.963	0.74		9	0.998	0.643	7.14	0.010	1	0.289	0.996	0.12
	11	0.586	0.926	1.48	0.750	18	0.031	0.999	0.02	0.011	1	0.317	0.995	0.15
	10	0.778	0.869	2.62		17	0.113	0.993	0.14	0.012	1	0.346	0.994	0.18
	9	0.912	0.796	4.08		16	0.272	0.980	0.40	0.013	1	0.374	0.993	0.21
	8	0.976	0.713	5.74		15	0.487	0.954	0.92	0.014	2	0.067	0.999	0.03
	7	0.996	0.625	7.50		14	0.703	0.913	1.74		1	0.403	0.991	0.27
0.580	16	0.015	0.999	0.02		13	0.864	0.859	2.82	0.015	2	0.076	0.999	0.03

TABLE 5   713

TABLE 5. Finite Queuing Tables (Continued)

POPULATION 30, Cont.

X	M	D	F	L_q
	1	0.431	0.989	0.33
0.016	2	0.085	0.999	0.03
	1	0.458	0.987	0.39
0.017	2	0.095	0.999	0.03
	1	0.486	0.985	0.45
0.018	2	0.105	0.999	0.03
	1	0.513	0.983	0.51
0.019	2	0.116	0.999	0.03
	1	0.541	0.980	0.60
0.020	2	0.127	0.998	0.06
	1	0.567	0.976	0.72
0.021	2	0.139	0.998	0.06
	1	0.594	0.973	0.81
0.022	2	0.151	0.998	0.06
	1	0.620	0.969	0.93
0.023	2	0.163	0.997	0.09
	1	0.645	0.965	1.05
0.024	2	0.175	0.997	0.09
	1	0.670	0.960	1.20
0.025	2	0.188	0.996	0.12
	1	0.694	0.954	1.38
0.026	2	0.201	0.996	0.12
	1	0.718	0.948	1.56
0.028	3	0.051	0.999	0.03
	2	0.229	0.995	0.15
	1	0.763	0.935	1.95
0.030	3	0.060	0.999	0.03
	2	0.257	0.994	0.18
	1	0.805	0.918	2.46
0.032	3	0.071	0.999	0.03
	2	0.286	0.992	0.24
	1	0.843	0.899	3.03
0.034	3	0.083	0.999	0.03
	2	0.316	0.990	0.30
	1	0.876	0.877	3.69
0.036	3	0.095	0.998	0.06
	2	0.347	0.988	0.36
	1	0.905	0.853	4.41
0.038	3	0.109	0.998	0.06
	2	0.378	0.986	0.42
	1	0.929	0.827	5.19
0.040	3	0.123	0.997	0.09
	2	0.410	0.983	0.51
	1	0.948	0.800	6.00

X	M	D	F	L_q
0.042	3	0.138	0.997	0.09
	2	0.442	0.980	0.60
	1	0.963	0.772	6.84
0.044	4	0.040	0.999	0.03
	3	0.154	0.996	0.12
	2	0.474	0.977	0.69
	1	0.974	0.744	7.68
0.046	4	0.046	0.999	0.03
	3	0.171	0.996	0.12
	2	0.506	0.972	0.84
	1	0.982	0.716	8.52
0.048	4	0.053	0.999	0.03
	3	0.189	0.995	0.15
	2	0.539	0.968	0.96
	1	0.988	0.689	9.33
0.050	4	0.060	0.999	0.03
	3	0.208	0.994	0.18
	2	0.571	0.963	1.11
	1	0.992	0.663	10.11
0.052	4	0.068	0.999	0.03
	3	0.227	0.993	0.21
	2	0.603	0.957	1.29
	1	0.995	0.639	10.83
0.054	4	0.077	0.998	0.06
	3	0.247	0.992	0.24
	2	0.634	0.951	1.47
	1	0.997	0.616	11.52
0.056	4	0.086	0.998	0.06
	3	0.267	0.991	0.27
	2	0.665	0.944	1.68
	1	0.998	0.595	12.15
0.058	4	0.096	0.998	0.06
	3	0.288	0.989	0.33
	2	0.695	0.936	1.92
	1	0.999	0.574	12.78
0.060	5	0.030	0.999	0.03
	4	0.106	0.997	0.09
	3	0.310	0.987	0.39
	2	0.723	0.927	2.19
	1	0.999	0.555	13.35
0.062	5	0.034	0.999	0.03
	4	0.117	0.997	0.09
	3	0.332	0.986	0.42
	2	0.751	0.918	2.46

X	M	D	F	L_q
0.064	5	0.038	0.999	0.03
	4	0.128	0.997	0.09
	3	0.355	0.984	0.48
	2	0.777	0.908	2.76
0.066	5	0.043	0.999	0.03
	4	0.140	0.996	0.12
	3	0.378	0.982	0.54
	2	0.802	0.897	3.09
0.068	5	0.048	0.999	0.03
	4	0.153	0.995	0.15
	3	0.402	0.979	0.63
	2	0.825	0.885	3.45
0.070	5	0.054	0.999	0.03
	4	0.166	0.995	0.15
	3	0.426	0.976	0.72
	2	0.847	0.873	3.81
0.075	5	0.069	0.998	0.06
	4	0.201	0.993	0.21
	3	0.486	0.969	0.93
	2	0.893	0.840	4.80
0.080	6	0.027	0.999	0.03
	5	0.088	0.998	0.06
	4	0.240	0.990	0.30
	3	0.547	0.959	1.23
	2	0.929	0.805	5.85
0.085	6	0.036	0.999	0.03
	5	0.108	0.997	0.09
	4	0.282	0.987	0.39
	3	0.607	0.948	1.56
	2	0.955	0.768	6.96
0.090	6	0.046	0.999	0.03
	5	0.132	0.996	0.12
	4	0.326	0.984	0.48
	3	0.665	0.934	1.98
	2	0.972	0.732	8.04
0.095	6	0.057	0.999	0.03
	5	0.158	0.994	0.18
	4	0.372	0.979	0.63
	3	0.720	0.918	2.46
	2	0.984	0.697	9.09
0.100	6	0.071	0.998	0.06
	5	0.187	0.993	0.21
	4	0.421	0.973	0.81
	3	0.771	0.899	3.03

TABLE 5. Finite Queuing Tables (Continued)

POPULATION 30, Cont.

X	M	D	F	L_q	X	M	D	F	L_q	X	M	D	F	L_q
	2	0.991	0.664	10.08		7	0.115	0.996	0.12		5	0.739	0.901	2.97
0.105	7	0.030	0.999	0.03		6	0.256	0.987	0.39		4	0.946	0.773	6.81
	6	0.087	0.997	0.09		5	0.494	0.960	1.20		3	0.998	0.588	12.36
	5	0.219	0.991	0.27		4	0.793	0.884	3.48	0.180	10	0.028	0.999	0.03
	4	0.470	0.967	0.99		3	0.979	0.710	8.70		9	0.070	0.997	0.09
	3	0.816	0.879	3.63	0.145	8	0.055	0.998	0.06		8	0.158	0.993	0.21
	2	0.995	0.634	10.98		7	0.134	0.995	0.15		7	0.313	0.980	0.60
0.110	7	0.038	0.999	0.03		6	0.288	0.984	0.48		6	0.546	0.948	1.56
	6	0.105	0.997	0.09		5	0.537	0.952	1.44		5	0.806	0.874	3.78
	5	0.253	0.988	0.36		4	0.828	0.867	3.99		4	0.969	0.735	7.95
	4	0.520	0.959	1.23		3	0.986	0.687	9.39		3	0.999	0.555	13.35
	3	0.856	0.857	4.29	0.150	9	0.024	0.999	0.03	0.190	10	0.039	0.999	0.03
	2	0.997	0.605	11.85		8	0.065	0.998	0.06		9	0.094	0.996	0.12
0.115	7	0.047	0.999	0.03		7	0.155	0.993	0.21		8	0.200	0.990	0.30
	6	0.125	0.996	0.12		6	0.322	0.980	0.60		7	0.378	0.973	0.81
	5	0.289	0.985	0.45		5	0.580	0.944	1.68		6	0.621	0.932	2.04
	4	0.570	0.950	1.50		4	0.860	0.849	4.53		5	0.862	0.845	4.65
	3	0.890	0.833	5.01		3	0.991	0.665	10.05		4	0.983	0.699	9.03
	2	0.998	0.579	12.63	0.155	9	0.029	0.999	0.03	0.200	11	0.021	0.999	0.03
0.120	7	0.057	0.998	0.06		8	0.077	0.997	0.09		10	0.054	0.998	0.06
	6	0.147	0.994	0.18		7	0.177	0.992	0.24		9	0.123	0.995	0.15
	5	0.327	0.981	0.57		6	0.357	0.976	0.72		8	0.249	0.985	0.45
	4	0.619	0.939	1.83		5	0.622	0.935	1.95		7	0.446	0.963	1.11
	3	0.918	0.808	5.76		4	0.887	0.830	5.10		6	0.693	0.913	2.61
	2	0.999	0.555	13.35		3	0.994	0.644	10.68		5	0.905	0.814	5.58
0.125	8	0.024	0.999	0.03	0.160	9	0.036	0.999	0.03		4	0.991	0.665	10.05
	7	0.069	0.998	0.06		8	0.090	0.997	0.09	0.210	11	0.030	0.999	0.03
	6	0.171	0.993	0.21		7	0.201	0.990	0.30		10	0.073	0.997	0.09
	5	0.367	0.977	0.69		6	0.394	0.972	0.84		9	0.157	0.992	0.24
	4	0.666	0.927	2.19		5	0.663	0.924	2.28		8	0.303	0.980	0.60
	3	0.940	0.783	6.51		4	0.910	0.811	5.67		7	0.515	0.952	1.44
0.130	8	0.030	0.999	0.03		3	0.996	0.624	11.28		6	0.758	0.892	3.24
	7	0.083	0.997	0.09	0.165	9	0.043	0.999	0.03		5	0.938	0.782	6.54
	6	0.197	0.991	0.27		8	0.105	0.996	0.12		4	0.995	0.634	10.98
	5	0.409	0.972	0.84		7	0.227	0.988	0.36	0.220	11	0.041	0.999	0.03
	4	0.712	0.914	2.58		6	0.431	0.967	0.99		10	0.095	0.996	0.12
	3	0.957	0.758	7.26		5	0.702	0.913	2.61		9	0.197	0.989	0.33
0.135	8	0.037	0.999	0.03		4	0.930	0.792	6.24		8	0.361	0.974	0.78
	7	0.098	0.997	0.09		3	0.997	0.606	11.82		7	0.585	0.938	1.86
	6	0.226	0.989	0.33	0.170	10	0.019	0.999	0.03		6	0.816	0.868	3.96
	5	0.451	0.966	1.02		9	0.051	0.998	0.06		5	0.961	0.751	7.47
	4	0.754	0.899	3.03		8	0.121	0.995	0.15		4	0.998	0.606	11.82
	3	0.970	0.734	7.98		7	0.254	0.986	0.42	0.230	12	0.023	0.999	0.03
0.140	8	0.045	0.999	0.03		6	0.469	0.961	1.17		11	0.056	0.998	0.06

TABLE 5   715

TABLE 5. Finite Queuing Tables (Continued)

X	M	D	F	L_q	X	M	D	F	L_q	X	M	D	F	L_q
POPULATION 30, Cont.														
	10	0.123	0.994	0.18		13	0.042	0.998	0.06		9	0.748	0.893	3.21
	9	0.242	0.985	0.45		12	0.093	0.996	0.12		8	0.901	0.820	5.40
	8	0.423	0.965	1.05		11	0.185	0.989	0.33		7	0.977	0.727	8.19
	7	0.652	0.923	2.31		10	0.329	0.976	0.72		6	0.997	0.625	11.25
	6	0.864	0.842	4.74		9	0.522	0.949	1.53	0.330	15	0.030	0.999	0.03
	5	0.976	0.721	8.37		8	0.733	0.898	3.06		14	0.068	0.997	0.09
	4	0.999	0.580	12.60		7	0.901	0.818	5.46		13	0.139	0.993	0.21
0.240	12	0.031	0.999	0.03		6	0.981	0.712	8.64		12	0.253	0.983	0.51
	11	0.074	0.997	0.09		5	0.999	0.595	12.15		11	0.414	0.965	1.05
	10	0.155	0.992	0.24	0.290	14	0.023	0.999	0.03		10	0.608	0.931	2.07
	9	0.291	0.981	0.57		13	0.055	0.998	0.06		9	0.795	0.876	3.72
	8	0.487	0.955	1.35		12	0.117	0.994	0.18		8	0.927	0.799	6.03
	7	0.715	0.905	2.85		11	0.223	0.986	0.42		7	0.985	0.706	8.82
	6	0.902	0.816	5.52		10	0.382	0.969	0.93		6	0.999	0.606	11.82
	5	0.986	0.693	9.21		9	0.582	0.937	1.89	0.340	16	0.016	0.999	0.03
	4	0.999	0.556	13.32		8	0.785	0.880	3.60		15	0.040	0.998	0.06
0.250	13	0.017	0.999	0.03		7	0.929	0.795	6.15		14	0.086	0.996	0.12
	12	0.042	0.998	0.06		6	0.988	0.688	9.36		13	0.169	0.990	0.30
	11	0.095	0.996	0.12		5	0.999	0.575	12.75		12	0.296	0.979	0.63
	10	0.192	0.989	0.33	0.300	14	0.031	0.999	0.03		11	0.468	0.957	1.29
	9	0.345	0.975	0.75		13	0.071	0.997	0.09		10	0.663	0.918	2.46
	8	0.552	0.944	1.68		12	0.145	0.992	0.24		9	0.836	0.858	4.26
	7	0.773	0.885	3.45		11	0.266	0.982	0.54		8	0.947	0.778	6.66
	6	0.932	0.789	6.33		10	0.437	0.962	1.14		7	0.990	0.685	9.45
	5	0.992	0.666	10.02		9	0.641	0.924	2.28		6	0.999	0.588	12.36
0.260	13	0.023	0.999	0.03		8	0.830	0.861	4.17	0.360	16	0.029	0.999	0.03
	12	0.056	0.998	0.06		7	0.950	0.771	6.87		15	0.065	0.997	0.09
	11	0.121	0.994	0.18		6	0.993	0.666	10.02		14	0.132	0.993	0.21
	10	0.233	0.986	0.42	0.310	15	0.017	0.999	0.03		13	0.240	0.984	0.48
	9	0.402	0.967	0.99		14	0.041	0.998	0.06		12	0.392	0.967	0.99
	8	0.616	0.930	2.10		13	0.090	0.996	0.12		11	0.578	0.937	1.89
	7	0.823	0.864	4.08		12	0.177	0.990	0.30		10	0.762	0.889	3.33
	6	0.954	0.763	7.11		11	0.312	0.977	0.69		9	0.902	0.821	5.37
	5	0.995	0.641	10.77		10	0.494	0.953	1.41		8	0.974	0.738	7.86
0.270	13	0.032	0.999	0.03		9	0.697	0.909	2.73		7	0.996	0.648	10.56
	12	0.073	0.997	0.09		8	0.869	0.840	4.80	0.380	17	0.020	0.999	0.03
	11	0.151	0.992	0.24		7	0.966	0.749	7.53		16	0.048	0.998	0.06
	10	0.279	0.981	0.57		6	0.996	0.645	10.65		15	0.101	0.995	0.15
	9	0.462	0.959	1.23	0.320	15	0.023	0.999	0.03		14	0.191	0.988	0.36
	8	0.676	0.915	2.55		14	0.054	0.998	0.06		13	0.324	0.975	0.75
	7	0.866	0.841	4.77		13	0.113	0.994	0.18		12	0.496	0.952	1.44
	6	0.970	0.737	7.89		12	0.213	0.987	0.39		11	0.682	0.914	2.58
	5	0.997	0.617	11.49		11	0.362	0.971	0.87		10	0.843	0.857	4.29
0.280	14	0.017	0.999	0.03		10	0.552	0.943	1.71		9	0.945	0.784	6.48

TABLE 5. Finite Queuing Tables (Continued)

POPULATION 30, Cont.

X	M	D	F	L_q	X	M	D	F	L_q	X	M	D	F	L_q
	8	0.988	0.701	8.97		10	0.985	0.724	8.28		14	0.874	0.854	4.38
	7	0.999	0.614	11.58		9	0.997	0.652	10.44		13	0.949	0.799	6.03
0.400	17	0.035	0.999	0.03	0.480	20	0.019	0.999	0.03		12	0.985	0.740	7.80
	16	0.076	0.996	0.12		19	0.046	0.998	0.06		11	0.997	0.679	9.63
	15	0.150	0.992	0.24		18	0.098	0.995	0.15		10	0.999	0.617	11.49
	14	0.264	0.982	0.54		17	0.184	0.989	0.33	0.560	22	0.023	0.999	0.03
	13	0.420	0.964	1.08		16	0.310	0.977	0.69		21	0.056	0.997	0.09
	12	0.601	0.933	2.01		15	0.470	0.957	1.29		20	0.117	0.994	0.18
	11	0.775	0.886	3.42		14	0.643	0.926	2.22		19	0.215	0.986	0.42
	10	0.903	0.823	5.31		13	0.799	0.881	3.57		18	0.352	0.973	0.81
	9	0.972	0.748	7.56		12	0.910	0.826	5.22		17	0.516	0.952	1.44
	8	0.995	0.666	10.02		11	0.970	0.762	7.14		16	0.683	0.920	2.40
0.420	18	0.024	0.999	0.03		10	0.993	0.694	9.18		15	0.824	0.878	3.66
	17	0.056	0.997	0.09		9	0.999	0.625	11.25		14	0.920	0.828	5.16
	16	0.116	0.994	0.18	0.500	20	0.032	0.999	0.03		13	0.972	0.772	6.84
	15	0.212	0.986	0.42		19	0.072	0.997	0.09		12	0.993	0.714	8.58
	14	0.350	0.972	0.84		18	0.143	0.992	0.24		11	0.999	0.655	10.35
	13	0.521	0.948	1.56		17	0.252	0.983	0.51	0.580	23	0.014	0.999	0.03
	12	0.700	0.910	2.70		16	0.398	0.967	0.99		22	0.038	0.998	0.06
	11	0.850	0.856	4.32		15	0.568	0.941	1.77		21	0.085	0.996	0.12
	10	0.945	0.789	6.33		14	0.733	0.904	2.88		20	0.167	0.990	0.30
	9	0.986	0.713	8.61		13	0.865	0.854	4.38		19	0.288	0.980	0.60
	8	0.998	0.635	10.95		12	0.947	0.796	6.12		18	0.443	0.963	1.11
0.440	19	0.017	0.999	0.03		11	0.985	0.732	8.04		17	0.612	0.936	1.92
	18	0.041	0.998	0.06		10	0.997	0.667	9.99		16	0.766	0.899	3.03
	17	0.087	0.996	0.12	0.520	21	0.021	0.999	0.03		15	0.883	0.854	4.38
	16	0.167	0.990	0.30		20	0.051	0.998	0.06		14	0.953	0.802	5.94
	15	0.288	0.979	0.63		19	0.108	0.994	0.18		13	0.985	0.746	7.62
	14	0.446	0.960	1.20		18	0.200	0.988	0.36		12	0.997	0.690	9.30
	13	0.623	0.929	2.13		17	0.331	0.975	0.75		11	0.999	0.632	11.04
	12	0.787	0.883	3.51		16	0.493	0.954	1.38	0.600	23	0.024	0.999	0.03
	11	0.906	0.824	5.28		15	0.633	0.923	2.31		22	0.059	0.997	0.09
	10	0.970	0.755	7.35		14	0.811	0.880	3.60		21	0.125	0.993	0.21
	9	0.994	0.681	9.57		13	0.915	0.827	5.19		20	0.230	0.986	0.42
	8	0.999	0.606	11.82		12	0.971	0.767	6.99		19	0.372	0.972	0.84
0.460	19	0.028	0.999	0.03		11	0.993	0.705	8.85		18	0.538	0.949	1.53
	18	0.064	0.997	0.09		10	0.999	0.641	10.77		17	0.702	0.918	2.46
	17	0.129	0.993	0.21	0.540	21	0.035	0.999	0.03		16	0.837	0.877	3.69
	16	0.232	0.985	0.45		20	0.079	0.996	0.12		15	0.927	0.829	5.13
	15	0.375	0.970	0.90		19	0.155	0.991	0.27		14	0.974	0.776	6.72
	14	0.545	0.944	1.68		18	0.270	0.981	0.57		13	0.993	0.722	8.34
	13	0.717	0.906	2.82		17	0.421	0.965	1.05		12	0.999	0.667	9.99
	12	0.857	0.855	4.35		16	0.590	0.938	1.86	0.650	24	0.031	0.999	0.03
	11	0.945	0.793	6.21		15	0.750	0.901	2.97		23	0.076	0.996	0.12

TABLE 5 717

TABLE 5. Finite Queuing Tables (Continued)

POPULATION 30, Cont.

X	M	D	F	L_q	X	M	D	F	L_q	X	M	D	F	L_q
	22	0.158	0.991	0.27		24	0.240	0.986	0.42		24	0.760	0.932	2.04
	21	0.281	0.982	0.54		23	0.405	0.972	0.84		23	0.888	0.889	3.03
	20	0.439	0.965	1.05		22	0.587	0.950	1.50		22	0.957	0.862	4.14
	19	0.610	0.940	1.80		21	0.752	0.920	2.40		21	0.987	0.823	5.31
	18	0.764	0.906	2.82		20	0.873	0.883	3.51		20	0.997	0.784	6.48
	17	0.879	0.865	4.05		19	0.946	0.842	4.74		19	0.999	0.745	7.65
	16	0.949	0.818	5.46		18	0.981	0.799	6.03	0.900	29	0.047	0.999	0.03
	15	0.983	0.769	6.93		17	0.995	0.755	7.35		28	0.200	0.992	0.24
	14	0.996	0.718	8.46		16	0.999	0.711	8.67		27	0.441	0.977	0.69
	13	0.999	0.667	9.99	0.800	27	0.053	0.998	0.06		26	0.683	0.953	1.41
0.700	25	0.039	0.998	0.06		26	0.143	0.993	0.21		25	0.856	0.923	2.31
	24	0.096	0.995	0.15		25	0.292	0.984	0.48		24	0.947	0.888	3.36
	23	0.196	0.989	0.33		24	0.481	0.966	1.02		23	0.985	0.852	4.44
	22	0.339	0.977	0.69		23	0.670	0.941	1.77		22	0.996	0.815	5.55
	21	0.511	0.958	1.26		22	0.822	0.909	2.73		21	0.999	0.778	6.66
	20	0.681	0.930	2.10		21	0.919	0.872	3.84	0.950	29	0.226	0.993	0.21
	19	0.821	0.894	3.18		20	0.970	0.832	5.04		28	0.574	0.973	0.81
	18	0.916	0.853	4.41		19	0.991	0.791	6.27		27	0.831	0.945	1.65
	17	0.967	0.808	5.76		18	0.998	0.750	7.50		26	0.951	0.912	2.64
	16	0.990	0.762	7.14	0.850	28	0.055	0.998	0.06		25	0.989	0.877	3.69
	15	0.997	0.714	8.58		27	0.171	0.993	0.21		24	0.998	0.842	4.74
0.750	26	0.046	0.998	0.06		26	0.356	0.981	0.57					
	25	0.118	0.994	0.18		25	0.571	0.960	1.20					

TABLE 6. Table of Random Digits

03689	33090	43465	96789	56688	32389	77206	06534	10558	14478
43367	46409	44751	73410	35138	24910	70748	57336	56043	68550
45357	52080	62670	73877	20604	40408	98060	96733	65094	80335
62683	03171	77109	92515	78041	27590	42651	00254	73179	10159
04841	40918	69047	68986	08150	87984	08887	76083	37702	28523
85963	06992	65321	43521	46393	40491	06028	43865	58190	28142
03720	78942	61990	90812	98452	74098	69738	83272	39212	42817
10159	85560	35619	58248	65498	77977	02896	45198	10655	13973
80162	35686	57877	19552	63931	44171	40879	94532	17828	31848
74388	92906	65829	24572	79417	38460	96294	79201	47755	90980
12660	09571	29743	45447	64063	46295	44191	53957	62393	42229
81852	60620	87757	72165	23875	87844	84038	04994	93466	27418
03068	61317	65305	64944	27319	55263	84514	38374	11657	67723
29623	58530	17274	16908	39253	37595	57497	74780	88624	93333
30520	50588	51231	83816	01075	33098	81308	59036	49152	86262
93694	02984	91350	33929	41724	32403	42566	14232	55085	65628
86736	40641	37958	25415	19922	65966	98044	39583	26828	50919
28141	15630	37675	52545	24813	22075	05142	15374	84533	12933
79804	05165	21620	98400	55290	71877	60052	46320	79055	45913
63763	49985	88853	70681	52762	17670	62337	12199	44123	37993
49618	47068	63331	62675	51788	58283	04295	72904	05378	98085
26502	68980	26545	14204	34304	50284	47730	57299	73966	02566
13549	86048	27912	56733	14987	09850	72817	85168	09538	92347
89221	78076	40306	34045	52557	52383	67796	41382	50490	30117
97809	34056	76778	60417	05153	83827	67369	08602	56163	28793
65668	44694	34151	51741	11484	13226	49516	17391	39956	34839
53653	59804	59051	95074	38307	99546	32962	26962	86252	50704
34922	95041	17398	32789	26860	55536	82415	82911	42208	62725
74880	65198	61357	90209	71543	71114	94868	05645	44154	72254
66036	48794	30021	92601	21615	16952	18433	44903	51322	90379
39044	99503	11442	81344	57068	74662	90382	59433	48440	38146
87756	71151	68543	08358	10183	06432	97482	90301	76114	83778
47117	45575	29524	02522	08041	70698	80260	73588	86415	72523
71572	02109	96722	21684	64331	71644	18933	32801	11644	12364
35609	58072	63209	48429	53108	59173	55337	22445	85940	43707
73703	70069	74981	12197	48426	77365	26769	65078	27849	41311
42979	88161	56531	46443	47148	42773	18601	38532	22594	12395
12279	42308	00380	17181	38757	09071	89804	15232	99007	39495

TABLE 6   **719**

Index

SOCIAL SCIENCE LIBRARY

Manor Road Building
Manor Road
Oxford OX1 3UQ
Tel: (2)71093 (enquiries and renewals)
http://www.ssl.ox.ac.uk

This is a NORMAL LOAN item. **WITHDRAWN**

We will email you a reminder before this item is due.

Please see http://www.ssl.ox.ac.uk/lending.html
for details on:

- loan policies; these are also displayed on the notice boards and in our library guide.

- how to check when your books are due back.

- how to renew your books, including information on the maximum number of renewals. Items may be renewed if not reserved by another reader. Items must be renewed before the library closes on the due date.

- level of fines; fines are charged on overdue books.

Please note that this item may be recalled during Term.